PENGUIN BOOKS
INDIA SINCE INDEPENDENCE

Bipan Chandra, recipient of the Padma Bhushan, was born in Kangra, Himachal Pradesh. He was educated at Forman Christian College, Lahore, and at Stanford University, California. He was Professor of Modern History at Jawaharlal Nehru University (JNU), New Delhi, where he was Professor Emeritus. He was honoured as National Professor and was also the Chairperson of the National Book Trust. Professor Chandra has authored several books on nationalism, colonialism and communalism in modern India.

Mridula Mukherjee was educated at Lady Shri Ram College, New Delhi, and at JNU. She was Professor of Modern Indian History at the Centre for Historical Studies, JNU, and Director, Nehru Memorial Museum and Library. Her areas of special interest are agrarian history, peasant movements and the national movement, particularly the Gandhian phase.

Aditya Mukherjee was educated at St Stephen's College, Delhi, and at JNU. He is Professor of Contemporary Indian History at the Centre for Historical Studies, JNU, and was Director, Jawaharlal Nehru Institute of Advanced Studies at JNU. His research interests are in modern business history and capitalist development, and contemporary economy and politics.

T0190532

PRAISE FOR THE BOOK

'As an introduction to the history of post-Independence India, it is non-pareil'—M.V. Kamath

'The book fills a major gap in the literature on contemporary history and is a must-read for the general public, especially students of history, sociology, economics and politics'—*Tribune*

'A comprehensive volume . . . These scholars have succeeded in presenting the story of an extremely difficult and challenging journey'—C.P. Bhambri, former Professor of Political Science and Distinguished Scholar, Jawaharlal Nehru University

'Rewarding reading for students of Indian politics and economy'— *Business Standard*

INDIA SINCE INDEPENDENCE

Revised and Updated

Bipan Chandra

Mridula Mukherjee

Aditya Mukherjee

PENGUIN BOOKS

An imprint of Penguin Random House

PENGUIN BOOKS

USA | Canada | UK | Ireland | Australia
New Zealand | India | South Africa | China

Penguin Books is part of the Penguin Random House group of companies
whose addresses can be found at global.penguinrandomhouse.com

Published by Penguin Random House India Pvt. Ltd
7th Floor, Infinity Tower C, DLF Cyber City,
Gurgaon 122 002, Haryana, India

Penguin
Random House
India

First published as *India After Independence, 1947–2000* in Viking by Penguin
Books India 1999
Published in Penguin Books 2000
This revised edition published as *India Since Independence* by Penguin Books
India 2008

37 36 35

ISBN 9780143104094

Typeset in Sabon by InoSoft Systems, Noida

www.penguin.co.in

To
Late Professor V.D. Mahajan

Contents

Preface to the Revised Edition

This book was conceived as a sequel to our *Struggle for India's Independence*, (1857-1947) which was very well received, selling over 100,000 copies in English and many more in translations into Hindi and several other Indian languages. We were persuaded by David Davidar of Penguin, who had published this book, to write a companion volume covering the period from Indian independence to the end of the millennium. We did manage to finish the manuscript by end of 1999 so that it could come out in beginning of the new millennium as the first edition of this book titled *India After Independence: 1947-2000*.

We were persuaded to work on a second edition of this book for a number of reasons. The response the book got from the general public and especially students of history, sociology, economics, politics and contemporary affairs was very encouraging. It appeared to fill a major gap in the literature on contemporary history with several universities and management institutes adopting this work as a recommended text. This volume too was translated into Hindi and several other Indian languages. In recent years we received repeated requests from both our readers and publishers to bring out a revised edition bringing the book up to date.

Indeed, many significant developments did take place since the book was written in 1999 and needed to be incorporated in the book. The economy in the new millennium was at the verge of a breakthrough registering unprecedented rates of growth. A paradigm change in India's relationship with the outside world was being shaped not only by the major economic strides India was taking but also by the prolonged negotiations on a changed nuclear status for India among the nuclear powers. On the other hand Indian politics saw some unprecedented dips. The gravest threat to Indian democracy since independence was witnessed during the Gujarat killings following the Godhra tragedy in 2002. The state government, police and bureaucracy connived or remained silent spectators while thousands of Muslims were murdered or hounded and made homeless. But then other segments of India's civil society and state institutions stood up and fought. The period also saw a brazen attempt to communalize our education system at the school textbook-level with the Central government's active participation. This too was followed by nationwide protest. A change of government in 2004 put a stop to this most dangerous trend. On the whole, though the period was characterized by spectacular economic growth it also was a period when the fruits of this growth did not spread very widely (with India's ranking in the Human Development Index actually falling) and the country faced a resurgence of the communal and caste divide.

It therefore was a very agreeable push from Ravi Singh of Penguin which got us to work on revising the book. We have added three substantive chapters trying to include some of the major events from 1999-2000 till 2007. There is a new chapter on *The Indian Economy in the New Millennium* which highlights the multiple dimensions of the economic breakthrough that occurred in the period while emphasizing the critical challenges that still remain to be adequately addressed. Another new chapter called *Communalism and the Use of State Power* analyses the Gujarat events and the issue of communalization of education in the context of state power being available to the communal forces to further their agenda. The third new chapter, *Land Reforms: Colonial Impact and the Legacy of the National and Peasant Movements* precedes three substantive chapters discussing land reforms in India since independence. This chapter shows the critical link between the colonial impact on Indian agriculture and the position taken by the Indian national and peasant movements on the agrarian question for over half a century and the nature of land reforms post independence. A thoroughly revised and considerably expanded chapter titled *Run up to the New Millennium and After* analyses the main political events and the major foreign policy issues that emerged during the tumultuous years following Rajiv Gandhi's assassination which saw numerous governments representing virtually the entire mainstream political spectrum of India right up to 2007. Additions and alterations have been made to a number of other chapters such as in the chapter called *The Dawn of the New Millennium Achievements, Problems and Prospects*, bringing them up to date.

This work of contemporary history takes a holistic view of the political economy of Indian development since independence evaluating it in the context of the nearly two hundred years of colonial rule and a prolonged and powerful anti-imperialist mass movement which gave birth to the independent Indian Republic. We are particularly happy to be able bring this work to our readers on the sixtieth anniversary of India's independence.

November 2007   Bipan Chandra
                                         Mridula Mukherjee
                                          Aditya Mukherjee

Acknowledgements

In the making of this book, we have benefited immensely from our long-term interaction with and support of our colleagues at the Centre for Historical Studies at the Jawaharlal Nehru University, New Delhi. Many friends—Mohit Sen, Kewal Varma, V.P. Dutt, Barun De, Girish Mathur, Girish Mishra, Gopi Arora, S. Gopal, Romila Thapar, Irfan Habib, V.N. Datta, Ravinder Kumar, C.P. Bhambri, Darshan and Shiela Bhalla, Amit Bhaduri, Arjun Sengupta, Shireen Moosvi, Arun Kumar, Arjun Dev, K.P. Jain, G.M. Telang, Swadesh Mahajan, Madhu Kishwar, Shekhar Singh, Shantha Sinha, Narinder Bedi Amrita Patel and Bodh Prakash—have over the years helped us grapple with the contemporary world, often through a great deal of polemics and many heated discussions and disagreements.

A large number of colleagues and students—D.N. Gupta, Mohinder Singh, Sucheta Mahajan, Visalakshi Menon, Antony Thomas, Sudhir Mathur, Neerja Singh, Salil Mishra, Rakesh Batabyal, Bikash Chandra, Vikram Menon, Gyanesh Kudaisya, John Zavos, Amit Mishra, Tulika Sharan, Dipa Sinha, Himangshu, Bhuvan Jha, Kalyani and Amman Madan—have contributed to evolving our ideas and have also been of assistance in several other ways, and have helped us keep our optimism alive.

The Japan Foundation enabled us (Aditya Mukherjee and Mridula Mukherjee) to be at the Institute of Oriental Culture, University of Tokyo, for a year since March 1999. A considerable part of the drafting and research for the book was done in Japan. Professor Asis Datta, Vice Chancellor, JNU, very kindly made it possible for us to avail of this opportunity to complete our book. A large number of friends and colleagues made our visit in Japan extremely fruitful intellectually and otherwise. They include Professors Nariaki Nakazato, Haruka Yanagisawa, Tsukasa Mizushima, Shingo Einoo, Toru Matsui, Nobuko Nagasaki, Takako Hirose, Hiroko Hara, Shigeru Akita, Fumiko Oshikawa, Mr Takashi Oishi, Dr Shuji Uchikawa, Mr Shusaku Matsumoto, Professor and Mrs Hisashi Nakamura, Mrs Emiko Kothari, Dr Kyoko Inoue, Umesh and Ruby Pawankar, Dr Malavika Karlekar, Chieko Mizushima, Dr Jaishankar and Professor B.R. Tomlinson, Mr Shin'ichiro Horie of the Japan Foundation, Tokyo, enabled us to take time off from Japan and present many aspects of this book in several universities in the US. Manuela Albuquerque, Catherine Harned, Abha and Anil Pandya, Mohan Sood, Tom Metcalfe, Vasudha Dalmia, Blair Kling, Arjun Appadurai, Bernard Cohn and Carol Breckenridge were critical in making the US visit very rewarding.

We would like to thank the staff of the Nehru Memorial Museum and Library, Jawaharlal Nehru University Library and the India International Centre Library in New Delhi and the Institute of Oriental Culture Library and Institute of Developing Economies Library in Tokyo.

Luxmi and Om Prakash shared a great deal of the burden of typing a large part of the manuscript. Colleagues at the Academic Staff College, JNU, particularly Savitri Bisht, Ajay Sharma and S.C. Sharma, went beyond the call of duty to help the authors write the book situated thousands of miles from each other, using information te chnology.

As usual Usha Chandra has contributed in multiple ways to the making of this book.

We are very thankful to Raj Kamini Mahadevan of Penguin India for undertaking the arduous task of editing the manuscript and thus vastly improving it and also for seeing to it that we didn't fall too far behind schedule. We are also very thankful to David Davidar for encouraging us to undertake the writing of this work and then giving us great deal of latitude in terms of time.

For the revised edition we are particularly grateful to Ravi Singh and Avanija Sundaramurti for persuading us to work on the revisions and additions and then patiently egging us on till we completed the project.

Introduction

India's independence represented for its people the start of an epoch that was imbued with a new vision. In 1947, the country commenced its long march to overcome the colonial legacy of economic underdevelopment, gross poverty, near total illiteracy, wide prevalence of disease and stark social inequality and injustice. 15 August 1947 was only the first stop, the first break—the end of colonial political control: centuries of backwardness were now to be overcome, the promises of the freedom struggle to be fulfilled, and people's hopes to be met.

The tasks of nation-building were taken up by the Indian people and their leaders with a certain elan and determination and with confidence in their capacity to succeed. Jawaharlal Nehru's famous 'Tryst with Destiny' speech on the eve of independence, on 14 August, reflected this buoyant mood.

Starting off with a broad social consensus on the basic contours of the India that was to be built—on the values of nationalism, secularism and democracy and the goals of rapid economic development and radical social change—was a great advantage. These values and goals, and the road to their achievement, had been mapped over more than seventy years by the national movement. Yet, there was a realization that this consensus had to be continuously widened and built upon. Crucial in this respect was the role played by Nehru and the ideas he developed and propounded.

The Basic Goals

The first and the most important task was to preserve, consolidate and strengthen India's unity, to push forward the process of the making of the Indian nation, and to build up and protect the national state as an instrument of development and social transformation. Indian unity, it was realized, was not to be taken for granted. It had to be strengthened by recognizing and accepting India's immense regional, linguistic, ethnic and religious diversity. Indianness was to be further developed by acknowledging and accommodating the Indians' multiple identities and by giving different parts of the country and various sections of the people adequate space in the Indian Union. The project was, moreover, rightly seen to be a long-term and continuing process with the concept of Indianness being constantly redefined.

Basic, in this respect, was also the secular vision. The nation's leaders set out to build a secular society and state, undaunted by the Partition of India and the ensuing riots.

It was also clear that India's revolution had to be taken beyond the merely political to include economic and social transformation. Independent India had to begin its upward economic climb from an abysmally low level. The technological and productivity levels of Indian agriculture and industry were to be constantly and rapidly raised. Moreover, the Indian economy, even while being an integral part of the world economy, was to be based on self-reliance, free of subordination to the metropolitan interests or domination by foreign capital. This could not be accomplished through the unhampered working of market forces and private enterprise. It would require planning and a large public sector. India, therefore, set out to achieve, especially after 1955, an integrated/national economy based on an indigenous industry, catering primarily to its domestic market. While socialism was also set out as an objective, the essence of India's effort was towards the structural transformation of her economy, leading to its becoming an independent, national economy.

The social scene also called for rapid transformation. Despite lower-caste movements in several parts of the country and Gandhiji's campaign against untouchability, the caste system still dominated rural society and untouchability was the prevailing mode—the lower castes had still not 'stood-up'. Male domination was still nearly total, and women suffered immense social oppression in the family. Polygamy prevailed among both Hindus and Muslims. Women had no right of inheritance, nor the right of divorce, and were still by and large denied access to education. For Indians, illiteracy and ignorance were the norm in 1951; only 25 per cent of males and 7.9 per cent of females were literate. The founders of the Indian Republic had the farsightedness and the courage to commit themselves to two major innovations of historical significance in nation-building and social engineering: first, to build a democratic and civil libertarian society among an illiterate people and, second, to undertake economic development within a democratic political structure. Hitherto, in all societies in which an economic take-off or an early industrial and agricultural breakthrough had occurred, effective democracy, especially for the working people, had been extremely limited. On the other hand, from the beginning, India was committed to a democratic and civil libertarian political order and a representative system of government based on free and fair elections to be conducted on the basis of universal adult franchise. Moreover, the state was to encroach as little as possible on rival civil sources of power such as universities, the Press, trade unions, peasant organizations and professional associations. The many social, economic and political challenges that the country was to face were to be dealt with in a democratic manner, under democratic conditions.

One of the major political tasks facing the leadership was to further develop the democratic consciousness among the people initiated during the period of the freedom struggle. The leadership completely rejected the different versions of the 'rice-bowl theory', that the poor in an underdeveloped country were more interested in a bowl of rice than in democracy, and that, in any case, democracy was useless to them if it could not guarantee them adequate food, clothing and shelter.

Further, it was realized that given India's diversity, a democratic political structure was necessary for promoting national integration. Democracy was also considered essential for bringing about social change. Jawaharlal Nehru, in particular, upheld perhaps the Utopian notion that the poor would sooner or later assert their power through their vote and bring into being a social order responsive to their needs.

Economic development and a democratic political order were to be accompanied by rapid social transformation so that existing gross economic, caste and gender inequalities were rapidly eliminated, poverty was removed and the levels of living raised. The structure of Indian society was to be rapidly transformed in a broadly socialist direction, but not necessarily to resemble Soviet-style communism. It was also realized that these objectives required the broadest unity of the Indian people. Therefore, a large social consensus had to be evolved around the vision of the freedom struggle and the democratic forms through which the objectives would be achieved.

The national movement had aroused expectations of a rapid rise in personal and societal prosperity, of social and economic equity and equality, of the good life. Indira Gandhi's slogan of 'Garibi Hatao' in 1971 further fuelled these expectations as did the process of continuous politicization since 1950. The constantly rising aspirations and expectations had to be fulfilled as rapidly as possible, and without letting too wide a gap develop between expectations and fulfilment. In short, the Indian people and their leaders hoped to achieve in a few decades what others had achieved in a century or more. And this was to be on the basis of democracy, avoiding bloodshed and authoritarianism, and through a process of accommodating diverse social, economic and regional interests. Agrarian reforms, state planning and a strong public sector were to serve as the major instruments for the purpose.

At the same time, political stability had to be ensured for the accomplishment of all these tasks. The political system had to combine stability with growth, social transformation and deepening of the political process. The Indian revolution had to be gradual, non-violent and based on political stability, but it had to be a revolution all the same.

A Troubled Democracy

Since 1947, many Indians and foreigners, critics and admirers, have expressed doubts about India's ability to develop or continue its advance, or even sustain its societal and developmental design. From the beginning there have existed vocal prophets of doom and gloom who have been predicting that neither freedom, nor democracy, nor socialism would survive in India for long, that the Indian political system would collapse sooner or later, that the Indian Union would not survive and the nation state would disintegrate into linguistic and ethnic fragments. They have repeatedly argued that India's numerous religious, caste, linguistic and tribal diversities, besides its poverty, social misery and inequity, growing disparities of wealth, rigid and hierarchical social structure, massive unemployment and multiple socio-economic problems were bound to undermine its national unity, its democratic institutions and its developmental efforts. India would, therefore, either break up or alternatively be held together by a civilian or military authoritarian, dictatorial regime.

Ever since regional parties started emerging in the 1960s and much more during the 1980s and 1990s, many commentators have been speculating—some with enthusiasm—as to when the disintegration of India would take place. Even the success in holding together and working a secular and democratic political system over the years has not deterred the prophets of doom. At every instance of turmoil or perceived political crisis, as for example the *wars with China and Pakistan, the death of the towering* Nehru, the assassination of Indira Gandhi, communal, linguistic or caste violence, Naxalite uprisings, secessionist movements in Kashmir, the Northeast, Punjab and earlier in Tamil Nadu, these critics articulated and renewed their foreboding.

As early as 1960, the American scholar-journalist Selig S. Harrison predicted: 'The odds are almost wholly against the survival of freedom and . . . the issue is, in fact, whether any Indian state can survive at all.'[1] In 1967, Neville Maxwell, a *Times* correspondent, in a series of articles entitled 'India's Disintegrating Democracy' declared, 'The great experiment of developing India within a democratic framework has failed.' He predicted that the fourth general elections which were then forthcoming would be surely the last elections to be held in India.[2]

Many of the Cassandras felt justified when the Emergency was imposed. Many argued that it provided a signpost to India's political future. Some went further and said that the democratic system in India was finally and permanently in eclipse, or at least that it would never be the same again. Another set of doom-wallas stressed the incapacity of India to achieve economic development. India's political institutional structure, according to them, did not coincide with the developmental goals that had been set as these required a degree of coercion if not dictatorship to be achieved.

Then there were left-wing sceptics who held that no social, economic or political development was possible without a violent revolution and that nation-building, political democracy, economic development, national unity and nationalism were mere shams meant to delude the oppressed and the exploited. They, therefore, argued for or anticipated a peasant-based revolution as in China during 1925–49 or a worker-peasant-based revolution as in Russia in 1917. According to them, poverty, inequality, class domination and social oppression would sooner or later lead the vast majority of the people on the path of revolution, putting an end not only to capitalism and feudalism but also to 'bourgeois democracy' and the 'multi-nation state'. In the early 1970s, many observers, including the writer of a note prepared by the Home Ministry, predicted that the Green Revolution would turn Red since it would benefit only rich farmers and displace small peasants from the land and create further unemployment among agricultural labourers. Some of the left-wing prophets of doom even denied the possibility of independent economic development in India and continued to maintain over the years that India was entering a phase of dependency and neo-colonialism, if it had not already done so.

It is also interesting that those who did not share this scepticism of the left or the non-left were usually portrayed by them as apologists of the Establishment. As W.H. Morris-Jones, perhaps the most perceptive of the political scientists studying India, put it as early as 1966: 'It has become customary to adopt highly sceptical views on Indian developments . . . The position is now reached where failure to share such attitudes is taken as the mark, in an Indian, of some kind of government public relations man and, in an outsider, of a misguided sentimentalist.'[3]

Another set of observers of the Indian scene, who were less pessimistic about the democratic political system, were puzzled by India's success in sustaining itself in the face of its failure on so many fronts—inadequacy of land reforms and the existence of large-scale landlessness in the rural areas, the slow rate of growth in industry and the national income, the failure to check the high rate of population growth, persistence of gross inequalities, caste oppression, discrimination against women, a dysfunctional education system, environmental degradation, growing pollution in the cities, human rights abuses, factionalism in politics, chaotic party situation, growing political unrest, seccessionist demands and movements, administrative decline and even chaos, police inefficiency, high levels of corruption and brutality, and criminalization of politics. The perplexity of many of these 'puzzled' observers was also fuelled by the truism that democratic institutions cannot be transferred by the fiat of the framers of a constitution. But what they failed to appreciate is that democracy had already been indigenized and rooted in the Indian soil by the freedom struggle and the modern Indian intelligentsia during the previous hundred years or so.

In our view the prophets of doom were basically wrong in their prophesies, but they were quite often right on the target as critics. Many other analysts of Indian developments, who have not shared their scepticism and predictions, have pondered over the problems of democracy and development in an extremely diverse society having an underdeveloped economy and facing economic scarcity. They, too, have been worried by the fragility of India's political stability. They do not believe that there is a situation for administrative or political breakdown but many of them would argue that India is beginning to face 'a crisis of governability'. Over the years they have continuously emphasized that basic structural and institutional changes were necessary for desirable social development and the deepening and effective functioning of democracy. Even while arguing against the supporters of authoritarianism, the feasibility or desirability of a violent revolution, and predictions of the break up of the country, they have advocated and worked for the implementation of a programme of radical reforms, more or less around the Gandhian and Nehruvian agenda and its further development.

Political Leadership

India's survival and growth as a nation and a democratic polity, as also the achievement of the national objectives set by the freedom struggle depended on the configuration and development of long-term socio-economic and political forces. But the quality, skills and approach of the political leaders would inevitably play a significant role.

An asset for India's early efforts at progress, starting in 1947, was the personal calibre of her leaders. They were dedicated, imaginative and idealistic. They enjoyed tremendous popular support among the people and had the capacity to communicate with them, to enthuse them around a national programme and national goals, to reflect their urges and aspirations, and to provide them strong leadership. The leaders had tremendous confidence and faith in the people and therefore in democratic institutions and depended for their power and legitimacy on them. During the national movement the leaders had also acquired the vast capacity to negotiate and accommodate diverse interests and approaches and to work within a consensual framework. They could take a long-term and all-India view and work through state and local leaders.

This high quality of leadership was not confined only to the Congress party. The conservative Swatantra Party was headed by C. Rajagopalachari, the dissident Congressmen by J.B. Kripalani, the Hindu communalists by Syama Prasad Mookerjee, the non-Congress dalits by B.R. Ambedkar, the Socialists by Acharya Narendra Dev and Jayaprakash Narayan, and the Communists by P.C. Joshi, Ajoy Ghosh and E.M.S. Namboodiripad.

In contrast, it can be asserted that a serious problem in the past few decades has been the paucity of political leaders with the qualities and skills of the founders of the Republic. Indira Gandhi did possess some of their qualities. But after her and even during the period that she dominated—and perhaps to some extent because of it—a gradual decline occurred in the stature of leadership, with few having wide appeal or acceptability or the larger vision. Most political leaders increasingly appealed to a region or a religion or a caste, or a conglomerate of castes. The outcome of this has been that while many Indians have looked for wider, all-India leadership to the descendants of Nehru and Indira Gandhi, others have given allegiance to leaders and parties following populist or opportunist or communal and casteist politics.

Our Approach

This work is the story of a people on the move, of a 'gradual revolution', of the efforts of the Indian people to realize the vision of the freedom struggle. For us writers it has also been a journey into our personal past, involving an effort at cool and dispassionate analysis though, perhaps, failing at times to avoid the passion which informs all those who are deeply involved in the effort to raise the social conditions of their people, and the biases acquired when living through the events. As readers will see, we have adopted a critical approach to our recent past and contemporary events but within a broadly optimistic framework.

The year 1947 ushered in a period of change and development. Inevitably, new problems, often engendered by the change itself, were added to the old ones, requiring fresh solutions. The questions needing to be addressed were of the nature of the problems and how, when and with what consequences they were tackled. After all, had not Gandhiji predicted on the eve of independence that 'with the end of slavery and the dawn of freedom, all the weaknesses of society are bound to come to the surface'. He, however, also saw 'no reason to be unnecessarily upset about it. If we keep our balance at such a time, every tangle will be solved.'[4] Historians will have to evaluate in the coming years, how far the aspirations aroused by the freedom struggle's legacy, in terms of national unity, democracy, secularism, independent economic development, equality, and removal of poverty, have been fulfilled in a substantive manner.

In the early years, during much of the Nehru era, there was an air of optimism and a sense of achievement. This was reflected in Nehru's letter to the chief ministers, written with self-confidence and satisfaction just after watching the Republic Day parade at Delhi in 1955: 'My heart was filled with pride and joy at this sight of our nation on the march realising its goals one by one. There was a sense of fulfilment in the air and of confidence in our future destiny.'[5] And he repeated a few months later: 'There is the breath of the dawn, the feeling of the beginning of a new era in the long and chequered history of India. I feel so and in this matter at least I think I represent innumerable others in our country.'[6] And what made Nehru so optimistic? To quote Nehru's biographer, S. Gopal: 'Individual freedom, social justice, popular participation, planned development, national self-reliance, a posture of self-respect in international affairs—all high and noble goals, yet all being steadily achieved under the guidance of the prime minister . . .'[7]

It is true that Nehru and the generation that witnessed the coming of independence had hoped for far more progress than the country was able to make. Still, the people and the intelligentsia remained optimistic, not only during the Nehru era but even under Indira Gandhi, at least till 1973–1974. But gradually the euphoria and the self-confidence, the enthusiasm and the pride in achievement began to disappear and give way to frustration, cynicism and a sense of despair.

Yet, as this work will bring out, while much more was needed and could have been achieved, but was not, especially in terms of the quality of life of the people (and which would justify a great deal of criticism and even despair), there was considerable gain. Our hopes and confidence in the future of the country and its people is justified by this achievement.

We believe what Verrier Elwin, the British scholar-missionary who made India his home and took up its citizenship, wrote in 1963 largely expresses our views and sentiments: 'All the same I am incurably optimistic about India. Her angry young men and disillusioned old men are full of criticism and resentment. It is true that there is some corruption and a good deal of inefficiency; there is hypocrisy, too much of it. But how much there is on the credit side! It is a thrilling experience to be part of a nation that is trying, against enormous odds, to reshape itself.'[8]

Perhaps the attitude for us to take towards our many failures is the one adopted by Gopal Krishna Gokhale towards those of the Moderate nationalists:

Let us not forget that we are at a stage of the country's progress when our achievements are bound to be small, and our disappointments frequent and trying. That is the place which it has pleased Providence to assign to us in this struggle, and our responsibility is ended when we have done the work which belongs to that place. It will, no doubt, be given to our countrymen of future generations to serve India by their successes; we, of the present generation, must be content to serve her mainly by our failures. For, hard though it be, out of those failures the strength will come which in the end will accomplish great tasks.[9]

The Colonial Legacy

India's colonial past has weighed heavily on her development since 1947. In the economic sphere, as in others, British rule drastically transformed India. But the changes that took place led only to what has been aptly described by A. Gunder Frank as the 'development of underdevelopment'. These changes—in agriculture, industry, transport and communication, finance, administration, education, and so on—were in themselves often positive, as for example the development of the railways. But operating within and as part of the colonial framework, they became inseparable from the process of underdevelopment. Further, they led to the crystallization of the colonial economic structure which generated poverty and dependence on and subordination to Britain.

Basic Features

There were four basic features of the colonial structure in India. First, colonialism led to the complete but complex integration of India's economy with the world capitalist system but in a subservient position. Since the 1750s, India's economic interests were wholly subordinated to those of Britain. This is a crucial aspect, for integration with the world economy was inevitable and was a characteristic also of independent economies.

Second, to suit British industry, a peculiar structure of production and international division of labour was forced upon India. It produced and exported foodstuffs and raw materials—cotton, jute, oilseeds, minerals—and imported manufactured products of British industry from biscuits and shoes to machinery, cars and railway engines.

This feature of colonialism continued even when India developed a few labour-intensive industries such as jute and cotton textiles. This was because of the existing peculiar pattern of international division of labour by which Britain produced high technology, high productivity and capital-intensive goods while India did the opposite. The pattern of India's foreign trade was an indication of the economy's colonial character. As late as 1935–39, food, drink, tobacco and raw materials constituted 68.5 per cent of India's exports while manufactured goods were 64.4 per cent of her imports.

Third, basic to the process of economic development is the size and utilization of the economic surplus or savings generated in the economy for investment and therefore expansion of the economy. The net savings in the Indian economy from 1914 to 1946 was only 2.75 per cent of Gross National Product (GNP) (i.e., national income). The small size may be contrasted with the net savings in 1971–75 when they constituted 12 per cent of GNP. The paltry total capital formation, 6.75 per cent of GNP during 1914–46 as against 20.14 per cent of GNP during 1971–75, reflects this jump. Moreover, the share of industry in this low level of capital formation was abysmally low, machinery forming only 1.78 per cent of GNP during 1914–46. (This figure was 6.53 for 1971–75.)

Furthermore, a large part of India's social surplus or savings was appropriated by the colonial state and misspent. Another large part was appropriated by the indigenous landlords and moneylenders. It has been calculated that by the end of the colonial period, the rent and interest paid by the peasantry amounted to Rs 1,400 million per year. By 1937, the total rural debt amounted to Rs 18,000 million. According to another estimate, princes, landlords and other intermediaries appropriated nearly 20 per cent of the national income. Only a very small part of this large surplus was invested in the development of agriculture and industry. Most of it was squandered on conspicuous consumption or used for further intensifying landlordism and usury.

Then there was the 'Drain', that is, the unilateral transfer to Britain of social surplus and potential investable capital by the colonial state and its officials and foreign merchants through excess of exports over imports. India got back no equivalent economic, commercial or material returns for it in any form. It has been estimated that 5 to 10 per cent of the total national income of

India was thus unilaterally exported out of the country. How could any country develop while undergoing such a drain of its financial resources and potential capital?

The fourth feature of colonialism in India was the crucial role played by the state in constructing, determining and maintaining other aspects of the colonial structure. India's policies were determined in Britain and in the interests of the British economy and the British capitalist class. An important aspect of the underdevelopment of India was the denial of state support to industry and agriculture. This was contrary to what happened in nearly all the capitalist countries, including Britain, which enjoyed active state support in the early stages of development. The colonial state imposed free trade in India and refused to give tariff protection to Indian industries as Britain, western Europe and the United States had done.

After 1918, under the pressure of the national movement, the Government of India was forced to grant some tariff protection to a few industries. But this was inadequate and ineffective. Moreover, since the 1880s, the currency policy was manipulated by the government to favour British industry and which was to the detriment of Indian industry.

As pointed out earlier, a very large part of India's social surplus was appropriated by the colonial state, but a very small part of it was spent by it on the development of agriculture or industry or on social infrastructure or nation-building activities such education, sanitation and health services.

The colonial state devoted almost its entire income to meeting the needs of British Indian administration, making payments of direct and indirect tribute to Britain and in serving the needs of British trade and industry. The bulk of public revenue was absorbed by military expenditure and civil administration which was geared to maintenance of law and order and tax collection. After 1890, military expenditure absorbed nearly 50 per cent of the central government's income. In 1947–48, this figure stood at nearly 47 per cent.

Besides, the Indian tax structure was highly inequitable. While the peasants were burdened with paying a heavy land revenue for most of the colonial period and the poor with the salt tax etc., the upper-income groups—highly paid bureaucrats, landlords, merchants and traders—paid hardly any taxes. The level of direct taxes was quite low. The number of income-tax payers was 360,000 in 1946–47. It was under the pressure from the national and peasant movements that the land revenue and salt tax started coming down in the twentieth century. As late as 1900–01 land revenue and salt tax formed 53 per cent and 16 per cent of the total tax revenue of the government.

Economic Backwardness

Colonialism became a fetter on India's agricultural and industrial development. Agriculture stagnated in most parts of the country and even deteriorated over the years, resulting in extremely low yields per acre, and sometimes even reaching zero. There was a decline in per capita agricultural production which fell by 14 per cent between 1901 and 1941. The fall in per capita foodgrains was even greater, being over 24 per cent.

Over the years, an agrarian structure evolved which was dominated by landlords, moneylenders, merchants and the colonial state. Subinfeudation, tenancy and sharecropping increasingly dominated both the zamindari and ryotwari areas. By the 1940s, the landlords controlled over 70 per cent of the land and along with the moneylenders and the colonial state appropriated more than half of the total agricultural production.

The colonial state's interest in agriculture was primarily confined to collecting land revenue and it spent very little on improving agriculture. Similarly, landlords and moneylenders found rack-renting of tenants and sharecroppers and usury far more profitable and safe than making productive investment in the land they owned or controlled. All this was hardly conducive to agricultural development.

In many areas, a class of rich peasants developed as a result of commercialization and tenancy legislation, but most of them too preferred to buy land and become landlords or to turn to moneylending. As a result capitalist farming was slow to develop except in a few pockets. On the other hand, impoverished cultivators, most of them small peasants, tenants-at-will and sharecroppers, had no resources or incentive to invest in the improvement of agriculture by using better cattle and seeds, more manure and fertilizers and improved techniques of production. For most of the colonial period, landlessness had been rising, so that the number of landless agricultural labourers grew from 13 per cent of the agricultural population in 1871 to 28 per cent in 1951. The increase in tenant farming and sharecropping and overcrowding of agriculture was followed by an extreme subdivision of land into small holdings and fragmentation. Further, these holdings were scattered into non-contiguous parcels which led to cultivation becoming uneconomic and incapable of maintaining the cultivator even at a subsistence level.

Of course, the linkage with the world market and development of roads and railways did lead to a large part of rural produce entering the urban and world markets and to the production of commercial crops. However, commercialization of agriculture did not lead to capitalist farming or improved technology. Its chief result was that better soil, available water and other resources were diverted from food crops to commercial crops.

At a time when agriculture in the developed countries was being modernized and revolutionized, there was a near absence of change in the technological and production base of Indian agriculture. Indian peasants continued to use the primitive implements they had used for centuries. For example, in 1951, there were only 930,000 iron ploughs in use while wooden ploughs numbered 31.3 million. The use of inorganic fertilizers was virtually unknown, while a large part of animal manure—cow dung, night soil and cattle bones—was wasted. In 1938–39, only 11 per cent of all cropped land was under improved seeds, their use being largely confined to non-food cash crops.

Agricultural education was completely neglected. In 1946, there were only nine agricultural colleges with 3,110 students. There was hardly any investment in terracing, flood-control, drainage, or desalination of soil. Irrigation was the only field in which some progress was made so that by the 1940s nearly 27 per cent of the total cultivated area was irrigated. But, then, India had always been quite advanced in irrigation cultivation.

Another central aspect of India's economic backwardness was the state of its industry. During the nineteenth century, there was a quick collapse of Indian handicraft and artisanal industries largely because of the competition from the cheaper imported manufactures from Britain together with the policy of free trade imposed on India. The ruined artisans failed to find alternative employment. The only choice open to them was to crowd into agriculture as tenants, sharecroppers and agricultural labourers.

Modern industries did develop in India from the second half of the nineteenth century. But, both in terms of production and employment, the level of industrial development was stunted and paltry compared with that of the developed countries. It did not compensate even for the handicraft industries it displaced. Industrial development was mainly confined to cotton, jute and tea in the nineteenth century and to sugar, cement and paper in the 1930s. There had been some development of the iron and steel industry after 1907, but as late as 1946, cotton and jute textiles accounted for nearly 30 per cent of all workers employed in factories and more than 55 per cent of the total value added by manufacturing. The share of modern industries in national income at the end of British rule was only 7.5 per cent. India also lagged in the development of electric power. Similarly, modern banking and insurance were grossly underdeveloped.

An important index of India's industrial backwardness and economic dependence on the metropolis was the virtual absence of capital goods and machine industries. In 1950, India met about 90 per cent of its needs of machine tools through imports. The underdeveloped character of this modern part of the economy can be seen by comparing certain economic statistics for 1950 and 1984 (the figures for 1984 are given within brackets). In 1950 India produced 1.04 million tons of steel (6.9 million tons), 32.8 million tons of coal (155.2 million tons), 2.7 million tons of cement (29.9 million tons), Rs. 3 million worth of machine tools and portable tools (Rs. 3.28 million), 7 locomotives (200), 99,000 bicycles (5,944,000), 14 million electrical lamps (317.8 million), 33,000 sewing machines (338,000), and generated 14 kWh electricity per capita (160 kWh). In 1950, the number of bank offices and branches was 5,072; in 1983 the figure had risen to 33,055. In 1950, out of a population of 357 million only 2.3 million were employed in modern industries.

Another index of economic backwardness was the high rural–urban ratio of India's population because of growing dependence on agriculture. In 1951, nearly 82.3 per cent of the population was rural. While in 1901, 63.7 per cent of Indians had depended on agriculture, by 1941 this figure had gone up to 70. On the other hand the number of persons engaged in processing and manufacturing fell from 10.3 million in 1901 to 8.8 million in 1951 even though the population increased by nearly 40 per cent.

Till the late 1930s, foreign capital dominated the industrial and financial fields and controlled foreign trade as also part of the internal trade that fed into exports. British firms dominated coal mining, the jute industry, shipping, banking and insurance, and tea and coffee plantations. Moreover, through their managing agencies, the British capitalists controlled many of the Indian-owned companies. It may be added that many of the negative effects of foreign capital arose out of state power being under alien control.

Lopsided industrial development was yet another striking feature. Industries were concentrated only in a few regions and cities of the country. This not only led to wide regional disparities in income but also affected the level of regional integration.

But there were some major changes that occurred in the Indian economy, especially during the 1930s and 1940s that did impart a certain strength to it and provided a base for post-independence economic development.

One positive feature was the growth of the means of transport and communication. In the 1940s, India had 65,000 miles of paved roads and nearly 42,000 miles of railway track. Roads and railways unified the country and made rapid transit of goods and persons possible. However, in the absence of a simultaneous industrial revolution, only a commercial revolution was produced which further colonialized the Indian economy. Also, railway lines were laid primarily with a view to link India's inland raw material-producing areas with the ports of export and to promote the spread of imported manufactures from the ports to the interior. The needs of Indian industries with regard to their markets and sources of raw materials were neglected as no steps were taken to encourage traffic between inland centres. The railway freight rates were also so fixed as to favour imports and exports and to discriminate against internal movement of goods. Moreover, unlike in Britain and the United States, railways did not initiate steel and machine industries in India. Instead, it was the British steel and machine industries which were the beneficiaries of railway development in India. The Government of India also established an efficient and modern postal and telegraph system, though the telephone system remained underdeveloped.

Another important feature was the development of the small but Indian-owned industrial base. It consisted of several consumer industries such as cotton and jute textiles, sugar, soap, paper and matches. Some intermediate capital goods industries such as iron and steel, cement, basic chemicals, metallurgy and engineering had also begun to come up, but on a paltry scale. By 1947, India already possessed a core of scientific and technical manpower, even though facilities for technical education were grossly inadequate, there being only seven engineering colleges with 2,217 students in the country in 1939. Also, most of the managerial and technical personnel in industry were non-Indian.

There was also, after 1914, the rise of a strong indigenous capitalist class with an independent economic and financial base. The Indian capitalists were, in the main, independent of foreign capital. Unlike in many other colonial countries, they were not intermediaries or middlemen between foreign capital and the Indian market, or junior partners in foreign-controlled enterprises. They were also perhaps more enterprising than the foreign capitalists in India, with the result that investment under Indian capital grew considerably faster than British and other foreign investment. By the end of the Second World War, Indian capital controlled 60 per cent of the large industrial units. The small-scale industrial sector, which generated more national income than the large-scale sector, was almost wholly based on Indian capital.

By 1947, Indian capital had also made a great deal of headway in banking and life insurance. Indian joint-stock banks held 64 cent of all bank deposits, and Indian-owned life insurance companies controlled nearly 75 per cent of life insurance business in the country. The bulk of internal trade and part of foreign trade was also in Indian hands.

These positive features of the Indian economy have, however, to be seen in a wider historical context. First, the development of Indian industry and capitalism was still relatively stunted and severely limited. Then, occurring within the framework of a colonial economy, this industrialization took place without India undergoing an industrial revolution as Britain did. The economy did not take off. Whatever development occurred was not because of, but in spite of colonialism and often in opposition to colonial policies. It was the result of intense economic and political struggle against colonialism in the context of Britain's declining position in the world economy and the two world wars and the Great Depression of the 1930s. Lastly, fuller, unfettered or autonomous economic development or take-off could not have taken place without break with and destructuring of colonialism.

The end result of colonial underdevelopment was the pauperization of the people, especially the peasantry and the artisans. Extreme and visible poverty, disease and hunger and starvation were the lot of the ordinary people. This found culmination in a series of major famines which ravaged all parts of India in the second half of the nineteenth century; there were regular scarcities and minor famines in one or the other part of the country throughout British rule. The last of the major famines in 1943 carried away nearly 3 million people in Bengal.

There were many other indications of India's economic backwardness and impoverishment. Throughout the twentieth century, per capita income had stagnated if not declined. During 1941–50, the annual death rate was 25 per 1,000 persons while the infant mortality rate was between 175 and 190 per 1,000 live births. An average Indian born between 1940 and 1951 could expect to live for barely thirty-two years. Epidemics of smallpox, plague and cholera and diseases like dysentery, diarrhoea, malaria and other fevers carried away millions every year. Malaria alone affected one-fourth of the population.

Health services were dismal. In 1943, there were only 10 medical colleges turning out 700 graduates every year and 27 medical schools turning out nearly 7,000 licentiates. In 1951, there were only about 18,000 graduate doctors, most of them to be found in cities. The number of hospitals was 1,915 with 116,731 beds and of dispensaries 6,589, with 7,072 beds. The vast majority of towns had no modern sanitation and large parts of even those cities which did, were kept out of the system, modern sanitation being confined to areas where the Europeans and rich Indians lived. A modern water supply system was unknown in villages and absent in a large number of towns. The vast majority of towns were without electricity, and electricity in the rural areas was unthinkable.

Already by the end of the nineteenth century it was fully recognized that education was a crucial input in economic development, but the vast majority of Indians had almost no access to any kind of education and, in 1951, nearly 84 per cent were illiterate, the rate of illiteracy being 92 per cent among women. There were only 13,590 middle schools and 7,288 high schools. These figures do not adequately reflect the state of the vast majority of Indians, for they ignore the prevalence of the extreme inequality of income, resources and opportunities. A vast human potential was thereby left untapped in societal development for very few from the poorer sections of society were able to rise to its middle and upper levels.

It is also to be noted that a high rate of population growth was not responsible for the poverty and impoverishment, for it had been only about 0.6 per cent per year between 1871 and 1941.

Thus, a stagnating per capita income, abysmal standards of living, stunted industrial development and low-productivity and semi-feudal agriculture marked the economic legacy of colonialism as it neared the end.

The Colonial State

The British evolved a general educational system, based on English as the common language of higher education, for the entire country. This system in time produced an India-wide intelligentsia which tended to have a similar approach to society and common ways of looking at it and which was, at its best, capable of developing a critique of colonialism—and this it did during the second half of the nineteenth century and after. But English-based education had two extremely negative consequences. One, it created a wide gulf between the educated and the masses. Though this gulf was bridged to some extent by the national movement which drew its leaders as well as its cadres from the intelligentsia, it still persisted to haunt independent India. Second, the emphasis on English prevented the fuller development of Indian languages as also the spread of education to the masses.

The colonial educational system, otherwise, also suffered from many weaknesses which still pervade India's schools and colleges. It encouraged learning by rote, memorization of texts, and proof by authority. The rational, logical, analytical and critical faculties of the students remained underdeveloped; in most cases the students could reproduce others' opinions but had difficulty in formulating their own. A major weakness of the colonial educational system was the neglect of mass education as also of scientific and technical education. There was also the almost total lack of concern for the education of girls, so that in 1951 only eight out of 100 women in India were literate.

The character of the colonial state was quite paradoxical. While it was basically authoritarian and autocratic, it also featured certain liberal elements, like the rule of law and a relatively independent judiciary. Administration was normally carried out in obedience to laws interpreted by the courts. This acted as a partial check on the autocratic and arbitrary administration and to a certain extent protected the rights and liberties of a citizen against the arbitrary actions of the bureaucracy. The laws were, however, often repressive. Not being framed by Indians, or through a democratic process, they left a great deal of arbitrary power in the hands of civil servants and the police. There was also no separation of powers between administrative and judicial functions. The same civil servant administered a district as collector and dispensed *justice as a district magistrate*.

The colonial legal system was based on the concept of equality of all before the law irrespective of a person's caste, religion, class or status, but here too it fell short of its promise. The court acted in a biased manner whenever effort was made to bring an European to justice. Besides, as court procedures were quite costly, the rich had better access to legal means than the poor.

Colonial rulers also extended a certain amount of civil liberties in the form of the freedoms of the Press, speech and association in normal times, but curtailed them drastically in periods of mass struggle. But, after 1897, these freedoms were increasingly tampered with and attacked even in normal times.

Another paradox of the colonial state was that after 1858 it regularly offered constitutional and economic concessions while throughout retaining the reins of state power. At first, British statesmen and administrators strongly and consistently resisted the idea of establishing a representative regime in India, arguing that democracy was not suited to India. They said only a system of 'benevolent despotism' was advisable because of India's culture and historical heritage. But under Indian pressure, elections and legislatures were introduced both at the Centre and in the provinces. Nevertheless, the franchise, or the right to vote, was extremely narrow. Only about 3 per cent Indians could vote after 1919, and about 15 per cent after 1935. The government thus hoped to co-opt and thereby weaken the national movement and use the constitutional structure to maintain its political domination. The legislatures, however, did not enjoy much power till 1935 and even then supreme power resided with the British. The government could take any action without the approval of the legislatures and, in fact, could do what it liked, when it liked. But legislators did have the possibility to expose the basic authoritarian character of the government and the hollowness of colonial constitutional reforms.

The legislatures did, however, provide some Indians with the experience of participating in elections at various levels and working in elected organs. This experience was useful after 1947 when Indians acquired representative institutions. Meanwhile, the nationalists used the constitutional space in conjunction with mass struggles and intense political, ideological campaigns to overthrow colonial rule.

The colonial legacy with regard to the unity of India was marked by a strange paradox. The colonial state brought about a greater political and administrative unification of India than ever achieved before. Building on the Mughal administrative system, it established a uniform system which penetrated the country's remotest areas and created a single administrative entity. The British also evolved a common educational structure which in time produced an India-wide intelligentsia which shared a common outlook on society and polity, and thought in national terms. Combined with the formation of a unified economy and the development of modern means of communication, colonialism helped lay the basis for the making of the Indian nation.

But having unified India, the British set into motion contrary forces. Fearing the unity of the Indian people to which their own rule had contributed, they followed the classic imperial policy of divide and rule. The diverse and divisive features of Indian society and polity were heightened to promote cleavages among the people and to turn province against province, caste against caste, class against class, Hindus against Muslims, and princes and landlords against the national movement. They succeeded in their endeavours to a varying extent, which culminated in India's Partition.

The British ruled India through a modern bureaucracy headed by the highly paid Indian Civil Service (ICS) whose members were recruited through merit based on open competition. The bureaucracy was rule-bound, efficient and, at the top, honest. Following Indian pressure the different services were gradually Indianized after 1918—by 1947, nearly 48 per cent of the members of the ICS were Indian—but positions of control and authority were up to the end retained by the British. Indians in these services too functioned as agents of British rule.

Though their senior echelons developed certain traditions of independence, integrity, hard work, and subordination to higher political direction they also came to form a rigid and exclusive caste, often having a conservative and narrow social, economic and political outlook. When massive social change and economic development was sought after 1947, the rigidity and the outlook of the bureaucracy became a major obstacle.

While the ICS was more or less free of corruption, corruption flourished at the lower levels of administration, especially in departments where there was scope for it, such as public works and irrigation, the Royal Army Supply Corps, and the police. During the Second World War, because of government regulation and controls, corruption and black marketing spread on a much wider scale in the administration as also did tax evasion, once rates of income tax and excise were revised to very high levels. There was also the rise of the parallel black economy.

The British left behind a strong but costly armed forces which had acted as an important pillar of the British regime in India. The British had made every effort to keep the armed forces apart from the life and thinking of the rest of the population, especially the national movement. Nationalist newspapers, journals and other publications were prevented from reaching the soldiers' and officers' messes. The other side of the medal, of course, was the tradition of the army being 'apolitical' and therefore also being subordinated, as was the civil service, to the political authorities. This would be a blessing in the long run to independent India, in contrast to the newly created Pakistan.

Referring reproachfully to the legacy bequeathed by colonialism, Rabindranath Tagore wrote just three months before his death in 1941:

> The wheels of fate will some day compel the English to give up their Indian Empire. But what kind of India will they leave behind, what stark misery? When the stream of their centuries' administration runs dry at last, what a waste of mud and filth will they leave behind them.

The National Movement and its Legacy

An appreciation of the hundred-year-old freedom struggle is integral to an analysis of developments in post-1947 India. While India inherited its economic and administrative structures from the precolonial and colonial period, the values and ideals— the vision—and the well-defined and comprehensive ideology that were to inspire it in nation-building were derived from the national movement. Representing the Indian people, it incorporated various political trends from the right and the left which were committed to its ideological goals; it excluded only communalists and those loyal to the colonial rulers.

These goals and values were, moreover, not confined to the intellectuals and the middle classes. During the era of mass politics, tens of thousands of the most humble cadres disseminated them among the common people in urban as well as rural areas. Consequently, these ideals were to play a critical role in integrating and keeping together Indian society and polity. They served to link the national liberation movement with the efforts to develop India, in what Jawaharlal Nehru characterized as 'a continuing revolution'. It is, in fact, these ideals by which people and parties are still evaluated and judged.

Character of the National Movement

The Indian freedom struggle was perhaps the greatest mass movement in world history. After 1919, it was built around the basic notion that the people had to and could play an active role in politics and in their own liberation, and it succeeded in politicizing, and drawing into political action a large part of the Indian people. Gandhiji, the leader who moved and mobilized millions into politics, all his life propagated the view that the people and not leaders created a mass movement, whether for the overthrow of the colonial regime or for social transformation. He added, though, that the success or failure of a movement depended a great deal on the quality of its leadership.

Satyagraha, as a form of struggle, was based on the active participation of the people and on the sympathy and support of the non-participating millions. In fact, unlike a violent revolution, which could be waged by a minority of committed cadres and fighters, a non-violent revolution needed the political mobilization of millions and the passive support of the vast majority.

It may be pointed out, parenthetically, that it was because of the long experience of this kind of political participation by common people that the founders of the Indian republic, who also led the freedom struggle in its last phase, could repose full faith in their political capacity. The leaders unhesitatingly introduced adult franchise despite widespread poverty and illiteracy.

The Indian national movement was fully committed to a polity based on representative democracy and the full range of civil liberties for the individual. It provided the experience through which these two could become an integral part of Indian political thinking.

From the very beginning the movement popularized democratic ideas and institutions among the people and struggled for the introduction of parliamentary institutions on the basis of popular elections. Starting from the turn of the twentieth century, the nationalists demanded the introduction of adult franchise. Much attention was also paid to the defence of the freedom of the Press and speech against attacks by the colonial authorities besides the promotion of other political and economic policies. Throughout, the movement struggled to expand the semi-democratic political arena and prevent the rulers fron limiting the existing space within which legal political activities and peaceful political agitations and mass struggle could be organized.

Congress ministries, formed in 1937, visibly extended civil liberties to the resurgent peasants', workers' and students' movements as also to radical groups and parties such as the Congress Socialist party and Communist Party.

From its foundation in 1885, the Indian National Congress, the main political organ of the national movement, was organized on democratic lines. It relied upon discussion at all levels as the chief mode for the formation of its policies and arriving at political decisions. Its policies and resolutions were publicly discussed and debated and then voted upon. Some of the most important decisions in its history were taken after rich and heated debates and on the basis of open voting. For example, the decision in 1920 to start the Non-Cooperation Movement was taken with 1,336 voting for and 884 voting against Gandhiji's resolution. Similarly, at the Lahore Congress in 1929, where Gandhiji was asked to take charge of the coming Civil Disobedience movement, a resolution sponsored by him condemning the bomb attack on the Viceroy's train by the revolutionary nationalists was passed by a narrow majority of 942 to 794. During the Second World War, Gandhiji's stand on cooperation with the war effort was rejected by Congress in January 1942.

Congress did not insist on uniformity of viewpoints or policy approach within its ranks. It allowed dissent and not only tolerated but encouraged different and minority opinions to be openly held and freely expressed. In fact, dissent became a part of its style. At independence, Congress, thus, had the experience of democratic functioning and struggle for civil liberties for over sixty years. Furthermore, the democratic style of functioning was not peculiar to Congress. Most other political organizations such as the Congress Socialist Party, trade unions and Kisan Sabhas, students', writers' and women's organizations, and professional associations functioned in the manner of political democracies.

The major leaders of the movement were committed wholeheartedly to civil liberties. It is worth quoting them. For example, Lokamanya Tilak proclaimed that 'liberty of the Press and liberty of speech give birth to a nation and nourish it'.[1] Gandhiji wrote in 1922: 'We must first make good the right of free speech and free association . . . We must defend these elementary rights with our lives.' And again in 1939: 'Civil liberty consistent with the observance of non-violence is the first step towards *Swaraj*. It is the breath of political and social life. It is the foundation of freedom. There is no room there for dilution or compromise. It is the water of life. I have never heard of water being diluted.'[2] It thus becomes clear that Gandhiji was fully committed to liberal, democratic values—only he also saw their deficiencies and believed that the existing liberal democratic structure, as prevailing in the West, was not adequate in enabling the people to control the wielders of political power. Jawaharlal Nehru wrote in 1936: 'If civil liberties are suppressed a nation loses all vitality and becomes impotent for anything substantial.'[3] Further, the resolution on Fundamental Rights, passed by the Karachi Congress in 1931, guaranteed the rights of free expression of opinion through speech or the Press, and freedom of association.

The consensus on the practice of non-violence during the national movement also contributed to the creation of a temper of democracy in the country. Discussion, debate and persuasion, backed by public opinion, was emphasized for bringing about political and social change as opposed to glorification of violence which lies at the heart of authoritarianism.

The defence of civil liberties was also not narrowly conceived in terms of a single group or viewpoint. Political trends and groups otherwise critical of each other and often at opposite ends of the political or ideological spectrum vigorously defended each other's civil rights. The Early Nationalists (then called Moderates)—Gopal Krishna Gokhale, Surendranath Banerjea and others—defended the Radical Nationalist (then called Extremist) leader Tilak's right to speak and write what he liked. And Congressmen, votaries of non-violence, defended Bhagat Singh and other revolutionary nationalists being tried in the Lahore and other conspiracy cases as also the Communists being tried in the Meerut Conspiracy Case. In 1928, the Public Safety Bill and the Trade Disputes Bill, aimed at suppressing trade unions, the left wing and the Communists, were opposed in the Central Legislative Assembly not only by Motilal Nehru but also by Conservatives such as Madan Mohan Malaviya and M.R. Jayakar, besides political spokespersons of Indian capitalists such as Ghanshyam Das Birla and Purshottamdas Thakurdas.

The basic notions of popular sovereignty, representative government and civil liberties to be exercised even against the rulers were not part of India's tradition nor were they, as some wrongly hold, 'the lasting contribution of colonialism'. It was the national movement and not the bureaucratic, authoritarian colonial state that indigenized, popularized and rooted them in India. As pointed out earlier, the colonial administration and ideologies not only tampered with civil liberties and resisted the nationalist demand for the introduction of a parliamentary system based on popular elections but, from the middle of the nineteenth century, promoted the view that for geographical, historical and socio-cultural reasons India was unfit for democracy. It was in opposition to this colonial ideology and practice that the national movement, influenced deeply by democratic thought and traditions of the Enlightenment, succeeded in making democracy and civil liberty basic elements of the Indian political ethos. If free India could start and persist with a democratic polity, it was because the national movement had already firmly established the civil libertarian and democratic tradition among the Indian people. It was this tradition which was reflected in the Indian constitution and which proved wrong the Cassandras who had repeatedly predicted that democracy and civil liberties would not survive in a society so divided by language, religion, caste and culture and in the absence of a minimum of prosperity or economic development and literacy as was the case in western Europe and the United States. It is this tradition which explains why multi-party democracy and civil liberties have met different fates in India and Pakistan, though both equally constituted colonial India. The political party that brought about Pakistan was not known for its defence of civil liberties, or its functioning on democratic lines, or its tolerance towards its political opponents. Democracy was not a significant part of its political culture. Besides, the national movement and its political culture were weak precisely in the areas which came to constitute Pakistan.

To conclude, over the years, the nationalist movement successfully created an alternative to colonial and precolonial political culture based on authoritarianism, bureaucratism, obedience and paternalism. Its ideology and culture of democracy and civil liberties were based on respect for dissent, freedom of expression, the majority principle, and the right of minority opinion to exist and develop.

Economic Underpinnings of the National Movement

The Indian national movement developed a complex and sophisticated critique of the basic features of India's colonial economy, especially of its subordination to the needs of the British economy. On the basis of this critique, the movement evolved a broad economic strategy to overcome India's economic backwardness and underdevelopment. This was to form the basis of India's economic thinking after independence. The vision of a self-reliant independent economy was developed and popularized. Self-reliance was defined not as autarchy but as avoidance of a subordinate position in the world economy. As Jawaharlal Nehru put it in 1946, self-reliance 'does not exclude international trade, which should be encouraged, but with a view to avoid economic imperialism'.[4] At the same time, the nationalists accepted from the beginning and with near unanimity the objective of economic development towards modern agriculture and industry on the basis of modern science and technology—India, they held, had to industrialize or go under. They also emphasized the close link between industry and agriculture. Industrial development was seen as essential for rural development, for it alone could reduce population pressure on land and rural unemployment. Within industrialization, the emphasis was on the creation of an indigenous heavy capital goods or machine-making sector whose absence was seen as a cause both of economic dependence and underdevelopment. Simultaneously, for essential consumer goods, the nationalists advocated reliance on medium, small-scale and cottage industries. Small-scale and cottage industries were to be encouraged and protected as a part of the development strategy of increasing employment.

Indian nationalists were opposed to the unrestricted entry of foreign capital because it replaced and suppressed Indian capital, especially under conditions of foreign political domination. According to them, real and self-reliant development could occur only through indigenous capital. On the other hand, the nationalists averred that if India was politically independent and free to evolve its own economic policies, it might use foreign capital to supplement indigenous efforts, because of India's vast capital requirements and need to import machinery and advanced technology from other countries.

During the 1930s and 1940s a basic restructuring of agrarian relations also became one of the objectives of the national movement. All intermediary rent receivers such as the zamindars and other landlords were to be abolished and agriculture based on peasant proprietors.

An active and central role was envisaged for the state in economic development by the nationalists. Rapid industrialization, in particular, needed a comprehensive policy of direct and systematic state intervention. Economic planning by the government and the massive development of the public sector were widely accepted in the 1930s. The state was to develop large-scale and key industries apart from infrastructure, such as power, irrigation, roads and water supply, where large resources were needed, and which were beyond the capacity of Indian capital. As early as 1931, the Resolution on Fundamental Rights and Economic Programme, adopted at the Karachi session of the Indian National Congress, declared that in independent India 'the State shall own or control key industries and services, mineral resources, railways, waterways, shipping and other means of public transport'.[5] Interestingly, the session was presided over by Sardar Patel, the Resolution drafted by Jawaharlal Nehru and moved in the open session by Gandhiji. To promote planning as an instrument of integrated and comprehensive development Congress sponsored in 1938 the National Planning Committee while the Indian capitalists formulated the Bombay Plan in 1943.

Gandhiji was the only major nationalist leader who disagreed with the emphasis on modern industry. But, in time, even he met the dominant view halfway. In the 1930s, he repeatedly asserted that he was not opposed to all machine industries but only to those which displaced human labour. He added that he would 'prize every invention of science made for the benefit of all'. But this was subject to one condition: all large-scale industries should be owned and controlled by the state and not by private capitalists. Nevertheless, Gandhiji did not insist that the national movement should accept his economic approach or agenda, as he did in the case of non-violence, Hindu–Muslim unity and opposition to untouchability. He also did not counterpose his views to those of the other nationalists as witnessed by his moving the resolution at the Karachi session of the Congress in 1931 which favoured development of large-scale industry under state ownership or control. It is also significant that in 1942 he made Jawaharlal Nehru his heir despite the latter's total commitment to the development of industry and agriculture on the basis of modern science and technology. At the same time, the nationalist movement accepted the Gandhian perspective on cottage and small-scale industries. This perspective was to find full reflection in the Nehruvian Second Five Year Plan.

The Indian national movement was quite radical by contemporary standards. From the beginning it had a pro-poor orientation. For example, the poverty of the masses and the role of colonialism as its source was the starting point of Dadabhai Naoroji's economic critique of colonialism. With Gandhiji and the rise of a socialist current this orientation was further strengthened. The removal of poverty became the most important objective next to the overthrow of colonialism.

From the late 1920s, Jawaharlal Nehru, Subhas Chandra Bose, the Congress socialists, the Communists, the Revolutionary Nationalists and various other socialist groups strove to give the national movement a socialist orientation and to popularize the vision of a socialist India after independence. Socialist ideas assumed prominence within the movement, attracting the younger nationalist cadre and large sections of the nationalist intelligentsia, but they did not become the dominant current. Jawaharlal Nehru, the major ideologue of socialism in pre-1947 India, readily conceded that Congress had not in any way accepted socialism as its ideal. Rather the goal it sought was the creation of an egalitarian society in which all citizens would have equal opportunities and 'a civilised standard of life . . . so as to make the attainment of this equal opportunity a reality'.[6]

Nevertheless, even while the question of the basic economic structure of free India remained open and undecided, the Socialists did succeed in giving the national movement a leftist tilt. It was committed to carrying out basic changes in society, economy and polity. It went on defining itself in more and more radical terms, based on equity and social justice and greater social and economic equality. It accepted and propagated a programme of reforms that was quite radical by contemporary standards: compulsory and free primary education, lowering of taxes on the poor and lower middle classes, reduction of the salt tax, land revenue and rent, debt relief and provision of cheap credit to agriculturists, protection of tenants' rights and ultimately the abolition of landlordism and 'land to the tiller', workers' right to a living wage and a shorter working day, workers' and peasants' rights to organize themselves, and reform of the machinery of law and order. A dramatic moment in the evolution of this radical orientation of the national movement was the Karachi Resolution of the 1931 Congress session which declared that 'in order to end the exploitation of the masses, political freedom must include real economic freedom of the starving millions'.[7]

And to crown this growing radicalism was that of Gandhiji who declared in 1942 that 'the land belongs to those who work on it and to no one else'.[8]

An aspect of its commitment to the creation of an egalitarian society was the national movement's opposition to all forms of inequality, discrimination and oppression based on gender and caste. It allied itself with and often subsumed movements and organizations for the social liberation of women and the lower castes. The national movement brought millions of women out of the home into the political arena. Its reform agenda included the improvement of their social position including the right to work and education and to equal political rights. As part of its struggle against caste inequality and caste oppression, abolition of untouchability became one of its major political priorities after 1920. The movement, however, failed to form and propagate a strong anti-caste ideology, though Gandhiji did advocate the total abolition of the caste system itself in the 1940s. It was because of the atmosphere and sentiments generated by the national movement that no voices of protest were raised in the Constituent Assembly when reservations for the Scheduled Castes and Scheduled Tribes were mooted. Similarly, the passage of the Hindu Code Bills in the 1950s was facilitated by the national movement's efforts in favour of the social liberation of women.

Secularism

From its early days, the national movement was committed to secularism. Secularism was defined in a comprehensive manner which meant the separation of religion from politics and the state, the treatment of religion as a private matter for the individual, state neutrality towards or equal respect for all religions, absence of discrimination between followers of different religions, and active opposition to communalism. For example, to counter communalism and give expression to its secular commitment, Congress in its Karachi Resolution of 1931 declared that in free India 'every citizen shall enjoy freedom of conscience and the right freely to profess and practise his religion', that all citizens would be 'equal before the law, irrespective of caste, creed or sex', that no disability would attach to any citizen because of caste, creed or gender 'in regard to public employment, office of power or honour, and in the exercise of any trade or calling', and that 'the State shall observe neutrality in regard to all religions'.[9]

It is true that in his early years, Gandhi, a deeply religious person, emphasized the close connection between religion and politics. This was because he believed that politics had to be based on morality, and to him all religions were the source of morality. Religion was, in fact, he believed, itself morality in the Indian sense of dharma. But he not only moved the Karachi Resolution in 1931, but when he saw that communalists were using religion as a sectarian belief system to divide the people, he overtly began to preach the separation of religion from politics. Thus he said in 1942: 'Religion is a personal matter which should have no place in politics.'[10] And again in 1947: 'Religion is the personal affair of each individual. It must not be mixed up with politics or national affairs.'[11] Jawaharlal Nehru wrote and spoke passionately and with deep understanding on communalism. He was perhaps the first Indian to see communalism as the Indian form of fascism. Interestingly, the leaders of the national movement never appealed to the people on religious grounds or that the British rulers' religion was Christianity. Their critique of British rule was invariably economic, political, social or cultural.

It is true that the national movement was not able to counter forces of communalism adequately or evolve an effective strategy against them. This contributed to the Partition and the communal carnage of 1946–47. But it was because of the strong secular commitment of the national movement that, despite these traumatic events, independent India made secularism a basic pillar of its constitution, as also of its state and society.

Nation-in-the-making

The national movement recognized early on that the process of nation-formation in India was a recent one. In other words, India was a nation-in-the-making. Promoting this process through the common struggle against colonialism became a basic objective. In this respect, the leadership of the movement acknowledged the role of colonialism in unifying India economically and administratively even while it criticized its furthering all kinds of politically divisive tendencies.

From the outset the movement emphasized its all-Indianness. For example, the Indian National Congress was founded in 1885 not as a federation of the existing provincial political organizations but as a new nationwide organization committed to nationwide political mobilization on the basis of all-India demands. Its cadres and its appeal, its audience and above all its leadership were drawn from all over India. And from the beginning it emphasized the unity and integrity of the country. In fact, it was the alliance of the states' peoples' movements, as part of the all-India national movement, that enabled easy integration of the princely states with the rest of India after independence.

This all-Indianness was not a feature peculiar to the Indian National Congress. Other political parties and popular mass organizations too followed suit.

To the nationalist leaders, the notion of a structured nation did not contradict its unity. They not only acknowledged but also appreciated India's rich cultural, linguistic, religious, ethnic and regional diversity. The emergence of a strong national identity and the flowering of other narrower identities were seen as mutually reinforcing processes. The diversity and multiple identities were not seen as obstacles to be overcome but as positive features that were sources of strength to Indian culture, civilization and the nation, and were integral to the emerging nationhood. These regional-cultural identities, in particular, developed not in opposition to but as part of the national movement and the all-India identity.

Indian society was also divided by class. But while not letting class divisions to segment it, the movement did not stand in the way of class organizations and class struggles.

Over time, the national movement evolved the dual concepts and objectives of unity in diversity and national integration. The former was to be based on cultural diversity and cultural interaction, leading to a federal polity. National integration was to lead to a strong political centre and the weaving of the different cultural strands into an evolving composite Indian culture.

Foreign Policy

Independent India's foreign policy was also rooted in the principles and policies evolved by the nationalists since the 1870s. Over time, Indian leaders had developed a broad international outlook based on opposition to colonialism and sympathy and support for the peoples fighting for their independence. In the 1930s and 1940s, the national movement took a strong anti-fascist stand. This was put forward in a most expressive manner by Gandhi. Condemning Hitler for the genocide of the Jews, and condoning violence, perhaps for the first time, he wrote in 1938: 'If there ever could be a justifiable war in the name of and for humanity, a war against Germany, to prevent the wanton persecution of a whole race, would be completely justified.'[12] The nationalist approach to world problems during the 1930s was clearly enunciated by Jawaharlal Nehru in his presidential address at the Lucknow session of the Congress in 1936:

> We see the world divided up into two vast groups today— the imperialist and fascist on one side, the socialist and nationalist on the other . . . Inevitably, we take our stand with the progressive forces of the world which are ranged against fascism and imperialism.[13]

It is of great significance that Indian nationalism was not chauvinist or jingoist. It did not take recourse to reverse racism even when actively opposing racism practised by the British in India. Opposing and hating British imperialism, it trained its cadre to eschew hatred or bitterness towards the British people.

Political Norms

In a mass-based struggle, ideology and its influence plays a critical role. Yet, a mass movement has also to incorporate and accommodate diverse political and ideological currents in order to mobilize millions. Besides, it has to be disciplined and organizationally strong and united; yet it cannot afford to be monolithic or authoritarian.

Recognizing this duality, Congress, under whose leadership and hegemony the anti-imperialist struggle was waged, was highly ideological and disciplined while also being ideologically and organizationally open-ended and accommodative. Representing the Indian people and not any one class or stratum, Congress could not be and was not ideologically homogeneous. Widely differing ideological and political streams coexisted within it. It is significant that at no stage did Gandhiji claim to have an ideological monopoly over it. Congress, therefore, succeeded in uniting persons of different ideological bents, different levels of commitment and of vastly different capacities to struggle together for some broad common objectives and principles.

Congress was able to achieve this task by functioning democratically. There was a constant public debate and contention between individuals and groups who subscribed to divergent political-ideological tendencies or paradigms, even though they shared many elements of a common vision and were united in struggle. The majority view regarding the strategic and tactical framework of the movement prevailed but the minority was not decimated. It remained part of the movement, hoping one day to have its approach accepted. Even groups and movements which were outside the Congress stream evolved a complex and friendly relationship with it. The communal, casteist and loyalist parties and groups were the only ones to adopt an adversarial approach towards the Congress.

The national movement thus bequeathed to independent India the political tradition of compromise, accommodation and reconciliation of different interests and points of view. Nehru worked within this tradition in evolving national policies after independence. This approach is, however, now running rather thin. It was, of course, never easy to transfer this tradition of a mass movement to a party of governance or to parties of opposition for that matter. But it was an invaluable experience and legacy for all those who wanted to build a strong and prosperous India and a just and egalitarian society.

The highest norms of politics and political behaviour were set by the movement. Its major leaders, for example, Dadabhai Naoroji, Gopal Krishna Gokhale, Lokamanya Tilak, Gandhiji, Bhagat Singh, Jawaharlal Nehru, Subhas Bose, Sardar Patel, Rajendra Prasad, C. Rajagopalachari, Acharya Narendra Dev, Jayaprakash Narayan, possessed moral integrity of the highest order. It was because of this moral authority and high moral standards of the leadership that the movement could mobilize millions. This was also true of the cadres, most of whom gave up their careers, their studies and their jobs, abandoned family life and devoted their entire lives to the movement. Also, judged in its totality, the movement was able to maintain harmony between means and ends. The movement was able to develop the capacity to evolve, renovate and change with the times. Its programme and policies underwent continuous change and moved in a radical direction in response to the urges of the masses as they were awakened to political activity and to the changing policies of the colonial rulers. The movement was, therefore, in many ways highly original and innovative, keeping abreast with contemporary world thought, processes and movements.

The legacy of the national movement could be summarized as: *a commitment to political and economic independence,* modern economic development, the ending of inequality, oppression and domination in all forms, representative democracy and civil liberties, internationalism and independent foreign policy, promotion of the process of nation-in-the-makmg on the basis of the joyous acceptance of the diversity, and achievement of all these objectives through accommodative politics and with the support of a large majority of the people.

Independent India has as a whole remained loyal to the basics of the legacy of the national movement, a large part of which is enshrined in the constitution and incorporated in the programmes and manifestos of most of the political parties. The Indian people have tended to use this legacy as the yardstick to judge the performance of governments, political parties and institutions.

A legacy, especially of a prolonged movement, tends to endure for a long time. But no legacy, however strong and sound, can last forever. It tends to erode and become irrelevant unless it is constantly reinforced and developed and sometimes transcended in a creative manner to suit the changing circumstances.

4

The Evolution of the Constitution and Main Provisions

The constitution of India came into force on 26 January 1950. Since then the day is celebrated as Republic Day. But before 1950, 26 January was called Independence Day. Since 26 January 1930, it was the day on which thousands of people, in villages, in mohallas, in towns, in small and big groups would take the independence pledge, committing themselves to the complete independence of India from British rule. It was only fitting that the new republic should come into being on that day, marking from its very inception the continuity between the struggle for independence and the adoption of the constitution that made India a republic.

The process of the evolution of the constitution began many decades before 26 January 1950 and has continued unabated since. Its origins lie deeply embedded in the struggle for independence from Britain and in the movements for responsible and constitutional government in the princely states.

More than passing resolutions on the need for, or framing proposals for constitutional reform, the heart of the national movement's contribution lay in its concrete political practice. This popularized among the people the notions of parliamentary democracy, republicanism, civil liberties, social and economic justice, which were among the essential principles of the constitution. For example, the idea of a parliamentary form of government was introduced into the Indian political consciousness by the inclusion of the term 'Congress' (the Lower House in the US), in the name of the Indian National Congress. The actual functioning of the

Congress organization, especially from 1920 onwards, after Gandhiji modified the Congress constitution, was based on the elective principle. All office-bearers were chosen through election, be it the president of the All India Congress Committee (AICC) or the secretary of the village-level Congress Committee. The AICC, which consisted of delegates elected by the Provincial Congress Committees (PCCs), was the equivalent of the Lok Sabha or parliament, and the Working Committee was the equivalent of the cabinet. The Congress president was the counterpart of the prime minister. Thus, when the constitution in 1950 adopted a parliamentary form of government, with a cabinet led by a prime minister, it was not, as is commonly supposed, the British parliament that it was emulating. It was formalizing nationalist practices, which the people were already familiar with.

Even more than the form, it was the spirit of democracy, on which in the last and first resort the foundations of the constitution rest, that was inculcated among the people by the national movement. This found expression in widespread mass participation. It ensured a place for adult franchise after independence. Could women have been denied the vote in 1950 after Gandhiji as early as 1930 had entrusted crucial parts of the Civil Disobedience movement to their care? Could a property or income qualification coexist with the concepts of *daridranarayan* and *antodya*? Could the literacy or educational qualification be smuggled into the constitution once Gandhiji had based his entire struggle on the 'dumb millions'?

The struggle for the freedom of the Press under British rule was vigorously fought by many leaders, and especially by Lokamanya Tilak who paid a very heavy price for the combative tone of his newspapers. Many other newspapers too like the *Leader, Amrita Bazar Patrika, Bombay Chronicle, The Hindustan Times, The Hindu,* the *Tribune, Searchlight, Andhra Patrika, Aaj, Ananda Bazar Patrika,* among others, functioned as unpaid organs of the national movement. This history ensured that freedom of expression became a fundamental right in the constitution.

Steps to the Constitution

Swaraj . . . will not be a free gift of the British Parliament.
It will be a declaration of India's full self-expression. That it

will be expressed through an Act of Parliament is true. But it will be merely a courteous ratification of the declared wish of the people of India even as it was in the case of the Union of South Africa . . . The British Parliament, when the settlement comes, will ratify the wishes of the people of India as expressed not through the bureaucracy but through her freely chosen representatives. Swaraj can never be a free gift by one nation to another. It is a treasure to be purchased with a nation's best blood. It will cease to be a gift when we have paid dearly for it.

This statement, made by Gandhiji in 1922,[1] makes clear that the British did not introduce any constitutional reforms or organs on their own initiative but always in belated and grudging response to sustained Indian nationalist pressure. There is a myth which has been carefully and often successfully purveyed by British administrators and later neo-imperialist scholars that the British initiated modern, responsible and constitutional government in India and that the constitution was merely the culmination of the series of constitutional initiatives made by them in 1861, 1892, 1909, 1919 and 1935. This can be disproved given the fact that their concessions, at every stage, fell far short of what Indians were demanding.

For example, the elective principle was first introduced by the British in the Indian Councils Act of 1892. The Congress and its nationalist precursors, and the Indian Press, had been demanding elections to the councils, elected majorities in them, and greater powers to the non-official members of councils for many years before that. Nationalist demands had already far exceeded what was granted in 1892.

It is also necessary to realize that nationalist demands were not just a little more advanced than British practice: they were far ahead. When the Congress demanded that at least half the members of the councils be elected, and that there should be male adult franchise, vote by ballot, power to the legislative councils to vote on the finance bills, etc., the actual British practice in India was that the Imperial or Central Legislative Council was a totally nominated body of a maximum of seventeen members with an official majority and a few token Indian members. The 1892 Act introduced elected members but they were still in a minority, and had very few powers. On the other hand, the nationalists' conception of the nature of India's constitutional framework was advancing rapidly. In 1895, there appeared the Constitution of India Bill, also known as the Home Rule Bill, about whose authorship there is no conclusive evidence, but which 'Annie Besant . . . thought . . . was probably issued under Lokamanya Bal Gangadhar Tilak's inspiration',[2] which conceived of basic human rights such as freedom of expression, equality before the law, right to the inviolability of one's home, right to property, etc., for all citizens of India. Even the Government of India Act, 1935, the last British enactment, failed to satisfy the repeated Indian demand, first made in 1895, for a declaration of the rights of the people of India.

The Indian leaders felt no necessity to abandon the constitutional legacy of the pre-independence period at the time of the writing of the constitution and start on a clean slate—this was their own legacy for which they had fought hard and made many sacrifices. The constitution could thus borrow heavily from the Government of India Act of 1935 because those who drafted the constitution had no need to prove their independent credentials. They also believed that the advantages of familiarity which existing institutions had should not be rejected. Since they also freely rejected what was unsuitable in the old and added much that was new, they did not hesitate to retain what was of value.

Constitutional Development

Beginning in the 1880s and 1890s with the notion that Britain must grant responsible government to India, the national movement, by the end of the second decade of the twentieth century had begun to espouse the doctrine of self-determination or the right of Indians to frame their own constitution. Tilak and Annie Besant, during the First World War, had launched a Home Rule agitation (the name being inspired by the Irish Home Rule Movement). The Congress–Muslim League Scheme for constitutional reforms which emerged out of the Congress–League Pact of 1916 demanded that four-fifths of the members of the provincial legislatures be elected 'by the people on as broad a franchise as possible'.[3] In 1918, the Congress session at Delhi resolved that: 'In view of the pronouncement of President Wilson, Mr Lloyd George, and other British statesmen, that to ensure the future peace of the world, the principle of Self-determination should be applied to all progressive nations, . . . this Congress claims recognition of India . . . as one of the progressive nations to whom the principle of Self-determination should be applied.'[4] The arguments did not impress the British rulers, and the new instalment of reforms in 1919 was introduced with the assertion that the 'timing and pace' of constitutional reform would be decided by the British alone. The Indian answer to this was the Non-Cooperation movement led by Gandhiji. After this movement ended in 1922, and sections of Congressmen now constituted as the Swaraj Party fought elections to the legislative councils, the constitutional battle was joined with a renewed vigour.

One initiative in which Annie Besant, Tej Bahadur Sapru, V.S. Srinivasa Sastri played a leading role, was the Commonwealth of India Bill which was drafted in India, revised by Labour party leaders, accepted unanimously by the executive committee of the Parliamentary Labour Party, and had its first reading in the House of Commons in December 1925. It could not, however, survive the defeat of the Labour government. It is significant that the Bill, which had the support of very wide sections of Indian opinion, specified in clear terms that 'India shall be placed on an equal footing with the Self-Governing Dominions'.[5] The Memorandum accompanying the Bill reminded the British of their history:[6]

> We seek an honourable agreement, such as Britain refused to her American Colonies and created a Republic, but made with her other Colonies and created peace and amity.

At this juncture, a very prominent role was also played by Motilal Nehru, who introduced a resolution on 8 February 1924 in the Central Legislative Assembly which asked the government 'to summon, at an early date, a representative Round Table Conference to recommend, with due regard to the protection of the rights and interests of important minorities, the scheme of a constitution for India'.[7] This scheme would be ratified by a newly elected Indian legislature and then sent to the British parliament to be embodied in a statute. This was the first time that the demand for a constitution and the procedure for its adoption were spelt out in such clear terms. This resolution, which came to be known as the 'National Demand', was passed by a large majority in the Central Legislative Assembly—76 for and 48 against.

The British, showing their contempt for the 'National Demand', appointed the all-white Simon Commission in November 1927 to recommend further constitutional changes. The move was roundly condemned by all sections of political opinion in India. Lord Birkenhead, the Secretary of State, while announcing the commission in the House of Lords on 24 November 1927, also repeated his challenge to Indians, first delivered on 7 July 1925: 'Let them produce a constitution which carries behind it a fair measure of general agreement among the great peoples of India'.[8]

The challenge was accepted and, at the initiative of the Congress, an All Parties Conference was called in May 1928 which appointed a committee chaired by Motilal Nehru 'to determine the principles of the Constitution for India'.[9] The Nehru Report, submitted on 10 August 1928, was in effect an outline of a draft constitution for India. Most of its features were later included in the Constitution of India. It visualized a parliamentary system with full responsible government and joint electorates with time-bound reservation of seats for minorities. The Nehru Report laid special emphasis on securing fundamental human rights for the people of India. These included the right to 'the freedom of conscience and the free profession and practise of religion', 'the right of free expression of opinion, as well as the right to assemble peaceably and without arms, and to form associations or unions', equal rights for men and women, and the right to free elementary education. Interestingly, the secular character of the state was listed as a fundamental right. Of the nineteen rights listed in the Nehru Report, ten were incorporated into the constitution. The Nehru Report also recommended that 'the redistribution of provinces should take place on a linguistic basis'.[10]

The Nehru Report was followed by a boycott of the Simon Commission and mass demonstrations wherever its members went. In December 1929, the Congress declared complete independence as its goal and followed this up with the launching of the mass Civil Disobedience movement in April 1930 which brought hundreds of thousands into the streets and saw around 100, 000 jail. It was becoming increasingly clear that Indians were unlikely to be satisfied with anything less than the right to frame their own constitution. The idea that this should be done not through the conference method, as was the case with the Nehru Report, but via a Constituent Assembly elected for this specific purpose, on the basis of the widest possible franchise, began to gain ground. Jawaharlal Nehru was the first national leader to articulate the idea in 1933 though M.N. Roy, the Marxist leader, had made the suggestion earlier. In June 1934, the Congress Working Committee (CWC), while rejecting the white paper presented by the British government on further constitutional reform, resolved that the 'only satisfactory alternative to the White Paper is a constitution drawn up by a Constituent Assembly elected on the basis of adult suffrage or as near it as possible'.[11]

The demand for a Constituent Assembly was repeated frequently after 1934 and included in the Congress manifesto for the 1936–37 elections. The Congress won majorities in seven out of eleven provinces and decided to form ministries. However, it made sure that this was not construed as acceptance of the existing constitutional framework. The meeting of the CWC at Wardha on 27–28 February 1937 which decided in favour of accepting office also reminded the legislators that a resolution of the Faizpur Congress had bound them to articulate the demand for a Constituent Assembly as soon as possible in the new legislatures.

From 19 to 20 March, the promised convention of Congress legislators and AICC members was held at Delhi, with Jawaharlal Nehru in the chair. Nehru told the delegates that they had to work for a *'panchayati raj,* fashioned by a Constituent Assembly, a grand *panchayat* of the nation, elected by all our people'. In unequivocal terms, he said 'this constitution must therefore go, lock, stock and barrel, and leave the field clear for our Constituent Assembly'.[12]

In July 1937, Nehru again, this time a trifle impatiently, pressed the legislators to introduce resolutions in the assemblies rejecting the present constitution and demanding a Constituent Assembly. In August, the Congress Working Committee accepted a draft resolution prepared by Acharya Kripalani, which was sent to Congressmen in the provincial assemblies. Between August and October 1937, all the Congress provinces—Bombay, Madras, United Provinces, Bihar, Orissa, Central Provinces, North West Frontier Province (NWFP)—as well as Sind passed this resolution which demanded that 'the Government of India Act, 1935 . . . be repealed and replaced by a constitution for a free India framed by a Constituent Assembly elected on the basis of adult franchise'.[13] On 17 September 1937, a resolution recommending replacement of the Government of India Act 1935 by a constitution framed by a Constituent Assembly was introduced in the Central Legislative Assembly. S. Satyamurti, the Congress leader who introduced it, urged the British government to grasp the hand of friendship extended by Mahatma Gandhi because 'once a great people make up their mind to obtain their freedom, there is no power on earth, not even Great Britain, which can stand in their way'.[14] The Haripura session of the Congress in February 1938 repeated the same demand.

Following the outbreak of the Second World War, Congress ministries resigned in protest against their being made a party to the war without eliciting their opinion or consent. At this juncture the ministries passed resolutions in the legislative assemblies which asserted that 'India should be regarded as an independent nation entitled to frame her own constitution'. Soon after, Gandhiji added his voice to that of Nehru and the Congress. In an article titled 'The Only Way', he declared that he was now even more enthusiastic about the Constituent Assembly than Nehru himself. 'Look at the question from any standpoint you like, it will be found that the way to democratic *Swaraj* lies only through a properly constituted Assembly, call it by whatever name you like.' He also thought that a body based on unadulterated suffrage including both men and women would do full justice to rival claims. 'I seem to see in it a remedy . . . for our communal and other distempers, besides being a vehicle for mass political and other education . . .'[15]

A discussion between Gandhiji and Jawaharlal Nehru at a meeting of the CWC held at Wardha from 15 to 19 April 1940 brought out Gandhiji's outstanding qualities of foresight and pragmatism. While Jawaharlal Nehru maintained that the British government must first declare India independent and then call a Constituent Assembly, Gandhiji felt that the Assembly could be called first and be left free to decide on the issue of independence. As it happened, and not for the first time, Gandhiji's view was closer to the actual turn of events.[16]

The 'August Offer' made by Viceroy Linlithgow in 1940 in an attempt to secure Indian cooperation in the war effort for the first time conceded that the framing of the new constitution should be primarily (though not solely) the responsibility of Indians themselves. It also offered to set up, after the conclusion of the war, 'a body representative of the principal elements in India's national life in order to devise the framework of the new Constitution'. How this body was to be constituted—by direct or indirect elections based on adult or restricted franchise, or by nomination—was not spelt out.[17]

The August Offer was spurned by all the major political parties in India. Congress proceeded in December 1940 to launch the individual Civil Disobedience campaign to register its protest against being made a party to the war without its consent. The party refrained from active obstruction of the war effort since it sympathized with the aims of the war. What it denied was the right to Britain to presume cooperation on India's behalf. The door was still left open for negotiations.

In March 1942, in the wake of the British collapse in Southeast Asia and three days after the fall of Rangoon, Winston Churchill, the prime minister of Britain, announced the dispatch to India of Sir Stafford Cripps, a prominent Labour Party member of the War Cabinet and a friend of Nehru. The Cripps proposals, as these constitutional concessions came to be called, for the first time clearly spelt out the procedure for the setting up of the Constituent Assembly. To quote:[18]

> Immediately upon the results being known of Provincial Elections which will be necessary at the end of hostilities, the entire membership of the Lower Houses of Provincial Legislatures shall as a single electoral college proceed to the election of the constitution-making body by the system of proportional representation . . . Indian States shall be invited to appoint representatives in the same proportion to their total population as in the case of representatives of British India as a whole and with the same powers as British Indian members.

The Cripps proposals were a major advance in the position of the British government. For the first time, it was clearly accepted that the constitution would be the sole responsibility of Indians alone. The idea of a Constituent Assembly was also unambiguously accepted and its modalities spelt out. However, other aspects of the Cripps proposals, which had divisive potential, stood in the way of the scheme being accepted by the Congress.

The failure of the Cripps' Mission led to another round of confrontation between the national movement and the British. The famous AICC resolution of 8 August 1942 which asked the British to 'Quit India' and exhorted the Indians to 'Do or Die', also said that the provisional government of free India would evolve a scheme for a Constituent Assembly. The mass upsurge that followed left the British in no doubt that the time for the final negotiations had arrived. Therefore, soon after the war ended in Europe in May 1945, a white paper on India was issued. This was followed by the abortive Simla Conference in June–July 1945.

The victory of the Labour Party in the British elections in July 1945 provided the opportunity for a fresh initiative. The Viceroy, Lord Wavell, announcing the India policy of the new government on 19 September 1945, promised to convene a constitution-making body as soon as possible. On 19 February 1946, the British government declared that they were sending a Cabinet Mission to India to resolve the whole issue of freedom and constitution-making.

The Cabinet Mission, which arrived in India on 24 March 1946, held prolonged discussions with Indian leaders. On 16 May 1946, having failed to secure an agreement, it announced a scheme of its own. It recognized that the best way of setting up a constitution-making machinery would 'be by election based on adult franchise; but any attempt to introduce such a step now would lead to a wholly unacceptable delay in the formulation of the new constitution'.[19] Therefore, it was decided that the newlyelected legislative assemblies of the provinces were to elect the members of the Constituent Assembly on the basis of one representative for roughly one million of the population. Sikh and Muslim legislators were to elect their quota on the basis of their population. There were numerous other details about procedures and suggestions about the powers of the Union and the provinces. Particularly important were the provisions relating to grouping of provinces into sections A, B and C. Section A consisted of Madras, Bombay, U.P., Bihar, the Central Provinces and Orissa—the 'Hindu-majority' provinces. Sections B and C similarly consisted of the 'Muslim-majority' provinces of Punjab, NWFP and Sind in the west and Assam and Bengal in the east. The Cabinet Mission scheme proposed that the Constituent Assembly, after meeting to elect the chairman and complete other formalities, should divide into sections. The provincial representatives meeting in their respective sections should first decide the constitutions of the constituent provinces and also whether they wanted to adopt any group constitution. It was only after this process had been completed that the representatives of all the provinces and those of the princely states were to meet again to settle the constitution of the Union. The Union of India was to deal with foreign affairs, defence and communications.

The Congress responded to the Cabinet Mission scheme by pointing out that in its view the Constituent Assembly, once it came into being, would be sovereign. It would have the right to accept or reject the Cabinet Mission's proposals on specifics. Though an assurance on those lines was not forthcoming from the British, the Congress nevertheless decided after a great deal of debate to accept the scheme, and try to work it, as there was a feeling that outright rejection would again delay the process of transfer of power. This is what the Muslim League hoped to achieve by its intransigence. The League continued to oppose the Constituent Assembly at every stage, before as well as after it was constituted.

The Constituent Assembly

The first task of this Assembly is to free India through a new constitution, to feed the starving people, and to clothe the naked masses, and to give every Indian the fullest opportunity to develop himself according to his capacity.

These were the hopes expressed by Jawaharlal Nehru before the Constituent Assembly.[20]

The Constituent Assembly was to have 389 members. Of these, 296 were to be from British India and 93 from the princely Indian states. Initially, however, the Constituent Assembly comprised only members from British India. Election of these were held in July–August 1946. Of the 210 seats in the general category, Congress won 199. It also won 3 out of the 4 Sikh seats from Punjab. The Congress also won 3 of the 78 Muslim seats and the 3 seats from Coorg, Ajmer-Merwara and Delhi. The total Congress tally was 208. The Muslim League won 73 out of the 78 Muslim seats.

Especially since the Constituent Assembly was not elected on the basis of universal adult franchise and was thus not as truly representative in character as the Congress had wished and demanded, and also because only Muslims and Sikhs were recognized as 'minorities' deserving special representation, a special effort was made to see that the Assembly did indeed reflect the diversity of perspectives present in the country. The Congress Working Committee in early July 1946 specifically instructed the Provincial Congress Committees to include representatives of Scheduled Castes, Parsis, Indian Christians, Anglo-Indians, tribals and women in the Congress list for the general category.

The other important consideration in choosing names for election to the Assembly was that the very best talent available in the country must be involved in the task of the making of the constitution. The lead was given by Gandhiji himself who suggested the names of sixteen eminent persons for inclusion in the Congress list. Altogether thirty people who were not members of the Congress were thus elected on the Congress ticket. Further, 'the ideological spectrum of the Assembly was broadened by . . . the *diverse nature of the Congress membership itself*'.[21]

Having failed to prevent the election of the Constituent Assembly, the Muslim League now concentrated its energies on refusing to join its deliberations. The Congress and Jawaharlal Nehru as vice president of the interim government continued to make conciliatory gestures, but to no avail. Accordingly, on 20 November 1946, the decision to convene the first session of the Constituent Assembly on 9 December 1946 was announced.

The Viceroy, Lord Wavell, in fact, had seemed reluctant to call the Assembly and it was Congress, which insisted that now that the Assembly had been elected, it was necessary that it begin to function, regardless of the wishes of those who chose to stay away. Nehru had also to firmly quash the Viceroy's desire to appoint the provisional president of the Assembly and issue invitations to the members to attend the first session in his own name. At Nehru's insistence, the oldest member of the Assembly, Dr Sachchidanand Sinha, became the provisional president and invitations were issued in the name of the secretary of the Constituent Assembly. In doing this Nehru was establishing, for all to see, the independence of the Assembly from British control. It would hardly be fair if the Constituent Assembly, which from conception to fulfilment was an achievement of the Congress and particularly of Nehru, should be finally presented to the world as a child of the British government. Besides, its credibility as a legitimate constitution-making body for independent India depended not only on its being autonomous but on its being seen as autonomous.

At 11 a.m. on 9 December 1946, the Constituent Assembly of India began its first session. For all practical purposes, the chronicle of independent India began on that historic day. Independence was now a matter of dates. The real responsibility of deciding the constitutional framework within which the government and people of India were to function had been transferred and assumed by the Indian people with the convening of the Constituent Assembly. Only a coup d'état could now reverse this constitutional logic.

The first session was attended by 207 members. The Muslim League, having failed to prevent the convening of the Assembly, now refused to join its deliberations. Consequently, the seventy-six Muslim members of the League stayed away and the four Congress Muslim members attended the session. On 11 December, Dr Rajendra Prasad was elected the permanent chairman, an office later designated as President of the Assembly. On 13 December, Jawaharlal Nehru moved the famous Objectives Resolution, which was debated till 19 December but its adoption was postponed to enable the representatives of the Muslim League and the princely states to join. At the next session, which took place from 20–22 January 1947, it was decided to not wait any longer for the League, and the Objectives Resolution was passed.

The third session was held from 28 April to 2 May 1947 and the League still did not join. On 3 June, the Mountbatten Plan was announced which made it clear that India was to be partitioned. This completely altered the perspective of the Constituent Assembly, as the Cabinet Mission Plan, the essence of which was a compromise with the League, was no longer relevant.

With India becoming independent on 15 August 1947, the Constituent Assembly became a sovereign body, and also doubled as the legislature for the new state. It was responsible for framing the constitution as well as making ordinary laws. That its function as a legislature as well as its large size did not come in the way of its effectively performing its duties as a constitution-making body is due to the enormous preparatory work as well as organizational skills and hard work of its leading members. The work was organized into five stages: first, committees were asked to present reports on basic issues; second, B.N. Rau, the constitutional adviser, prepared an initial draft on the basis of the reports of these committees and his own research into the constitutions of other countries; third, the drafting committee, chaired by Dr Ambedkar, presented a detailed draft constitution which was published for public discussion and comments; fourth, the draft constitution was discussed and amendments proposed; and lastly the constitution was adopted.

In addition, a critical role was played by the Congress party. It had asked a committee of experts to prepare material and proposals for the constitution as early as 4 July 1946. The committee was chaired by Nehru and had Asaf Ali, K.T. Shah, D.R. Gadgil, K.M. Munshi, Humayun Kabir, R. Santhanam and N. Gopalaswamy Ayyangar as members. Nehru drafted the Objectives Resolution and the CWC and AICC ratified it on 20 and 21 November 1946 well in time for its introduction in the first session of the Assembly. This practice continued till the constitution was adopted, with the Congressmen thoroughly discussing and examining each provision in their party forums, in addition to participating fully in the debates in the Assembly. The party's deep involvement in the process even made it open to the charge, made by one of its own members, Shibban Lal Saxena, that this reduced the proceedings in the Assembly to a formality! The overwhelming opinion, however, shared by Dr Ambedkar as well, was that its role had been all to the good as it ensured that every detail in the constitution was thoroughly scrutinized. To quote Granville Austin:[22]

> The Congress Assembly Party was the unofficial, private forum that debated every provision of the Constitution, and in most cases decided its fate before it reached the floor of the House. Everyone elected to the Assembly on the Congress ticket could attend the meetings whether or not he was a member of the party or even close to it.

Jawaharlal Nehru, who drafted the Objectives Resolution, which spelt out the philosophy and basic features of the constitution, set a formidable example by his keen involvement in every aspect of the process. Sardar Patel's interest was second, if at all, only to Nehru's. He played the decisive part in bringing in the representatives of the erstwhile princely states into the Constituent Assembly, in seeing to it that separate electorates were eliminated and in scotching any move for reservation of seats for religious minorities. Rajendra Prasad won acclaim for his impartiality and dignity as President of the Assembly. Maulana Azad brought his formidable scholarship and philosophical mind to bear on many issues of grave importance.

But perhaps above all, the Congress brought great credit to itself and enormous benefit to the nation by adopting a completely non-sectarian approach, freely recruiting the best available talent, always striving for consensus rather than imposing its will through numbers. Informed by a strong sense of its historic role in laying the foundations of independent India, the Congress party tried hard to do its best by the people it had led to freedom. In the words of Granville Austin, chronicler of the history of constitution-making in India:[23]

> The Constituent Assembly was a one-party body, in an essentially one-party country. The Assembly was the Congress and the Congress was India. There was a third point that completed a tight triangle, the government (meaning the apparatus of elected government both provincial and national), for the Congress was the government too . . . One might assume, aware of the character of monolithic political systems in other countries, that a mass party in India would be rigid and narrow in outlook and that its powerful leadership would silence dissent and confine policy and decision-making to the hands of the select few. In India the reverse was the case. The membership of the Congress in the Constituent Assembly and outside held social, economic, and political views ranging from the reactionary to the revolutionary, and it did not hesitate to voice them. The leaders of the Assembly, who played the same role in the Congress and in the Union Government, were national heroes and had almost unlimited power; yet decision-making in the Assembly was democratic. The Indian Constitution expresses the will of the many rather than the needs of the few.

The Indian Constitution: Main Provisions

The Constitution of India lays down a set of rules to which the ordinary laws of the country must conform. It provides a framework for a democratic and parliamentary form of government. The constitution also includes a list of Fundamental Rights and Directive Principles—the first, a guarantee against encroachments by the state and the second, a set of directives to the state to introduce reforms to make those rights effective.

Though the decision to give India a parliamentary system was not taken without serious debate, yet the alternative—of panchayat-based indirect elections and decentralized government—did not have widespread support. Espoused by some Gandhians, notably Shriman Narayan, this alternative was discarded decisively in favour of a centralized parliamentary constitution.

The intellectual or emotional commitment of many members to socialism also confirmed the conviction about parliamentary government. What most members desired 'was not that socialism be embodied in the constitution, but that a democratic constitution with a socialist bias be framed so as to allow the *nation in the future to become as socialist as its citizens desired* or as its needs demanded'.[24]

Adult Suffrage

The Congress had demanded adult suffrage since the 1920s. It was hardly likely to hesitate now that it had the opportunity to realize its dreams. A few voices advocated confining of adult suffrage to elections to the panchayats at the village level, and then indirect elections to higher-level bodies, but the overwhelming consensus was in favour of direct elections by adult suffrage—not a small achievement in a Brahmanical, upper-caste-dominated, male-oriented, elitist, largely illiterate, society!

Alladi Krishnaswami Ayyar, a foremost constitutional expert who played a crucial role in the framing of the constitution, said:[25]

> The Assembly has adopted the principle of adult franchise with an abundant faith in the common man and the ultimate success of democratic rule . . . The only alternative to adult suffrage was some kind of indirect election based upon village community or local bodies . . . That was not found feasible.

Austin has called direct election by adult suffrage the 'gong, the single note, whose reverberations might awaken—or at least stir—sleeping India'.[26] A very perceptive observation was also made by K.M. Panikkar who said that 'adult suffrage has social implications far beyond its political significance . . . Many social groups previously unaware of their strength and barely touched by the political changes that had taken place, suddenly realised that they were in a position to wield power.'[27] The impact of adult suffrage is even now being felt, as new groups at the lower end of the social hierarchy learn to experiment with different political parties and candidates for securing their felt needs. The beauty of adult suffrage is that it forces the most elitist of candidates to seek the favour of the vote of the humblest voter.

The extent of the leap made by the constitution can be fathomed only if it is recalled that, till the end of British rule, 'the franchise was restricted by property, educational, and other qualifications to approximately 15 per cent of the country's population'.[28]

Preamble

The basic philosophy of the constitution, its moving spirit, is to be found in the Preamble. The Preamble itself was based on the Objectives Resolution drafted by Nehru and introduced in the Assembly in its first session on 13 December 1946 and adopted on 22 January 1947. The Preamble states that the people of India in the Constituent Assembly made a solemn resolve to secure to all citizens, 'Justice, social, economic and political; Liberty of thought, expression, belief, faith and worship; Equality of status and of opportunity; and to promote among them all, Fraternity assuring the dignity of the individual and the unity of the nation.' It has been pointed out that the priority given to the concept of justice as compared to liberty, equality, fraternity, and to social and economic as compared to political justice, was deliberate. The order of the words indicates that the concept of social and economic justice was perhaps considered 'the most fundamental norm' of the Constitution of India.[29]

Fundamental Rights and Directive Principles

> The core of the commitment to the social revolution lies in parts III and IV, in the Fundamental Rights and in the Directive Principles of State Policy. These are the conscience of the Constitution.[30]

While Fundamental Rights are justiciable and Directive Principles are not, the latter are no less important for that reason. The

Universal Declaration of Human Rights also contains two sets of rights, the traditional civil and political rights and the new economic and social rights. In the Indian constitution, the first kind is included under Fundamental Rights and the second under Directive Principles. The reason for the distinction between the two is very simply that while the state could straightaway guarantee political and civil liberties contained under 'Fundamental Rights', it could only secure economic and social justice over a period of time as the economy developed and social change took place. The latter set of rights could not therefore be made justiciable, that is, a citizen could not go to a court of law in case of denial. But nonetheless, the state was enjoined upon to do its utmost to apply these precepts when making laws. By this process, rights contained in the Directive Principles could become justiciable as and when they were incorporated into laws.

The decision to have written rights, a list of rights, a declaration of rights in the constitution marked a sharp break with British constitutional tradition and practice. The British had consistently rejected Indian demands for a list of rights. Indians, on the other hand, because of their colonial experience, had developed a healthy suspicion of government and preferred rights to be written down. Their preference was in keeping with international trends as well. Following the suppression of human rights in Germany, the Soviet Union, and other places, the Atlantic Charter, and the United Nations Charter had been drawn up and the United Nations Human Rights Commission established.

The inclusion of Fundamental Rights in the constitution was imperative also because the first Constitution of India Bill framed in 1895 had contained this concept in embryo, and it had figured prominently in the Motilal Nehru Report of 1928. Further, it not only represented 'advanced democratic thought' but was also 'a convenient way of setting at rest the fears of minorities'.[31] Stung by the British claim that they had stayed on in India to protect the minorities who would otherwise be suppressed by the majority, the Congress was determined to show how patently false this assertion was. As Patel said:[32]

> It is for us to prove that it is a bogus claim, a false claim, and that nobody can be more interested than us in India, in the protection of our minorities. Our mission is to satisfy every one of them . . .

At no point did the Assembly doubt the need for Fundamental Rights. The only question was, how to distinguish between those rights that could be granted immediately, such as political rights, and those that should be there as ideals to be reached and could be granted only over time, such as social and economic rights. The solution was found by borrowing a concept from the Irish constitution and encoding the socio-economic rights as 'Directive Principles of State Policy'. These were made non-justiciable. The possibility of creating two kinds of rights, justiciable and non-justiciable, was suggested by the Sapru Report of 1945 (though not in the context of positive and negative rights) and the idea was possibly taken from there.

The Fundamental Rights are divided into seven parts: the right of equality, the right of freedom, the right against exploitation, the right to freedom of religion, cultural and educational rights, the right to property and the right to constitutional remedies. These rights, which are incorporated in Articles 12 to 35 of the constitution, primarily protect individuals and minority groups from arbitrary state action. But three of the articles protect the individual against the action of other private citizens: Article 17 abolishes untouchability; Article 15(2) says that no citizen shall suffer any disability in the use of shops, restaurants, wells, roads, and other public places on account of his religion, race, caste, sex, or place of birth; and Article 23 prohibits forced labour, which, though it was also extracted by the colonial state and the princely states, was more commonly a characteristic of the exploitation by big, semi-feudal landlords. These rights of citizens had to be protected by the state from encroachment by other citizens. Thus, the state had to not only avoid encroaching on the citizens' liberties, it had to ensure that other citizens did not do so either. A citizen whose fundamental right has been infringed or abridged can apply to the Supreme Court or High Court for relief and this right cannot be suspended except in case of declaration of Emergency. The courts have the right to decide whether these rights have indeed been infringed and to employ effective remedies including issuing of writs of habeas corpus, mandamus, prohibition, quo warranto and certiorari.

The Directive Principles, as stated earlier, have expressly been excluded from the purview of the courts. They are really in the nature of guidelines or instructions issued to future legislatures and executives. While the constitution clearly intended the Directive Principles and Fundamental Rights to be read together and did not envisage a conflict between the two, it is a fact that serious differences of interpretation have arisen many times on this issue. It is generally agreed that till 1971 the courts gave greater importance to the Fundamental Rights than to the Directive Principles, but that the 25th and 42nd Amendments in 1971 and 1976 brought in by Indira Gandhi gave precedence to the Directive Principles. In 1980, however, in the landmark judgement in *Minerva Mills Limited* v. *Union of India*, the Supreme Court held that both Fundamental Rights and Directive Principles are equally important and one cannot be sacrificed for the other (AIR 1980 SC 1789).

The essence of the Directive Principles is contained in Article 38 which lays down that 'the State shall strive to promote the welfare of the people by securing and protecting as effectively as it may a social order in which justice, social, economic, and political, shall inform all the institutions of the national life'. The state is thus to ensure that all citizens have adequate means of livelihood, that there is equitable distribution of material resources, and concentration of wealth and means of production is avoided. There is to be equal pay for equal work for men and women and the health of workers, children and pregnant women is to be protected. Workers should get a living wage and just and humane conditions of work. All citizens should have the right to work, to education and public assistance in case of unemployment, old age, sickness, etc. The Directive Principles expressed the hope that within ten years of the adoption of the constitution, there would be compulsory primary education of children up to the age of fourteen years. The objective of a common civil code was also desired. The state was to take steps to organize village panchayats, to improve standards of living and nutrition, provide free legal aid, and promote the educational and other interests of the Scheduled Castes and Tribes and other weaker sections. It was to protect and improve the environment and safeguard the forests and wildlife of the country. The state was also to promote international peace and security, maintain just and honourable relations between nations, inculcate respect for international law and treaty obligations and encourage settlement of international disputes by arbitration.

The Preamble, the Fundamental Rights and the Directive Principles read together make it clear that the constitution aimed at creating conditions for the building of an egalitarian society in which individual freedoms were secure. It did not visualize abandonment of one ideal for the preservation of the other principle. At the same time, the relationship between individual liberty and social change was rightly envisaged as dynamic. To quote Nehru:[33]

> The Directive Principles of State Policy represent a dynamic move towards a certain objective. The Fundamental Rights represent something static, to preserve certain rights which exist. Both again are right . . . Now it may be that in the process of dynamic movement certain existing relationships are altered, varied or affected. In fact, they are meant to affect those settled relationships and yet if you come back to the Fundamental Rights they are meant to preserve, not indirectly, certain settled relationships. There is a certain conflict in the two approaches, not inherently, because that was not meant, I am quite sure.

Nonetheless, conflicts did emerge and a number of amendments to the constitution had to be made in the 1950s when the implementation of zamindari and jagirdari abolition legislation was blocked in the courts on the grounds of right to property etc. During the process of the framing of the constitution as well as after it came into force, the property provisions turned out to be the most controversial. Court cases challenging the agrarian reforms began to proliferate, and the 1st Amendment to the constitution became necessary. Introduced in 1951 in the Provisional Parliament, this amendment inserted new Articles 31A and 31B and the Ninth Schedule, thus securing the constitutional validity of zamindari abolition laws by, among other things, specifying that they could not be challenged on the grounds that they violated the Fundamental Rights.

There were other cases which showed that certain articles relating to Fundamental Rights were open to interpretation in a manner that was not envisaged by the constitution framers. Accordingly, in 1951 itself, in the Provisional Parliament, the 1st Amendment was passed. This made some important changes in Articles 15, 19 and 31, dealing with the Fundamental Rights of equality, freedom of expression, and of property. The amendments ensured that the zamindari abolition legislation could not be challenged, among other things, on the ground that the right to property was a fundamental right, that the reservation of seats in educational institutions and in government jobs could not be challenged on the ground that it denied the right to equality, and that the legislation which placed reasonable restrictions on freedom of speech, the Press, association, etc., could not be questioned on the ground that it violated the right to freedom of expression etc. Further amendments had to be made in later years, as for example in 1955, in Articles 31 and 31 A, to make the quantum of compensation paid for acquired property non-justiciable as well as introduce other changes. In subsequent years as well, many important Supreme Court judgements as well as constitutional amendments continued to define and redefine the relationship between individual rights and social good, between Fundamental Rights and Directive Principles. This changing relationship is perhaps to be welcomed since it is proof of the ability of the constitution and of the other institutions it has helped flourish to adapt to the needs of new generations and to respond to the forces set in motion by the fast-changing world. It would perhaps be appropriate to conclude with Austin that the tension between the two sets of rights represents 'the classic dilemma of how to preserve individual freedom while promoting public good'.[34]

A Secular State

The constitution declares India to be a sovereign, socialist, secular and democratic republic. Even though the terms secular (and socialist) were added only by the 42nd Amendment in 1976, the spirit embodying the constitution was secular. In 1973 the Supreme Court held the secular character of the constitution to be one of the basic features of the constitution. Further, the Fundamental Rights include prohibition of discrimination on grounds of religion and right to freedom of religion including freedom of conscience and free profession, practise and propagation of religion, freedom to manage religious affairs, freedom to pay taxes for promotion of any particular religion and freedom of attendance at religious instruction or religious worship in certain educational institutions, cultural and educational rights including protection of interests of minorities and their right to establish and administer educational institutions.

The debate over the meaning of the term secular in the Indian context has been a heated one. Some people have argued that the Western context from which the term secular is borrowed is a very different one. In the West, the outcome of the struggle between the Church and the state led to the separation of the two; the Church was allowed to decide on religious rituals, the state was to regulate secular affairs. In India, the concept of secularism evolved as part of the struggle of nationalist forces against communal forces that wanted to use religion for political purposes and divide the emerging nation on the basis of religion.

Nehru put it best:[35]

> We call our State a secular one. The word 'secular', perhaps, is not a very happy one and yet for want of a better, we have used it. What exactly does it mean? It does not obviously mean a society where religion itself is discouraged. It means freedom of religion and conscience, including freedom for those who may have no religion. It means free play for all religions, subject only to their not interfering with each other or with the basic conceptions of our State.

Dr S. Radhakrishnan, the renowned scholar of Indian philosophy, who was President of India from 1962 to 1967, placed secularism within the Indian tradition:[36]

> We hold that no religion should be given preferential status of unique distinction . . . No group of citizens shall arrogate to itself rights and privileges that it denies to others. No person should suffer any form of disability or discrimination because of his religion but all alike should be free to share to the fullest degree in the common life . . . Secularism as here defined is in accordance with the ancient religious tradition of India.

5

The Architecture of the Constitution: Basic Features and Institutions

Basic Features

The constitution is supposed to have a basic structure which cannot be altered. This was spelt out by the full bench of the Supreme Court in 1973 in the majority judgement in the Kesavananda Bharati case.[1]

In the words of D.D. Basu, the judgement laid down that 'there are certain basic features of the Constitution of India, which cannot be altered in exercise of the power to amend it, under Article 368. If, therefore, a Constitution Amendment Act seeks to alter the basic structure or framework of the Constitution, the Court would be entitled to annul it on the ground of *ultra vires,* because the word "amend", in Article 368, means only changes other than altering the very structure of the Constitution, which would be tantamount to making a new Constitution.'[2] According to Justice S.M. Sikri, these basic features were the supremacy of the constitution, the republican and democratic form of government, the secular character of the constitution, the separation of powers between the legislature, executive and the judiciary and the federal structure. Some of the other features listed were the principles of free and fair elections,[3] the rule of law, the objectives specified in the Preamble, judicial review, freedom and dignity of the individual, unity and integrity of the nation, the principle of equality, the concept of social and economic justice, the balance between the Fundamental Rights and Directive Principles, the independence of the judiciary, and effective access to justice.[4]

The 42nd Amendment (1976) made during the Emergency under Indira Gandhi declared that 'there shall be no limitation' on the amending powers of parliament, and that no constitution amendment act could be 'called in question in any court on any ground'. But the Supreme Court in *Minerva Mills* v. *Union of India*[5] reaffirmed the applicability of the doctrine of basic structure by holding that 'judicial review' is a basic feature which cannot be taken away even by amending the constitution. The present position is that the court can declare *ultra vires* any amendment to the constitution if it believes that it would affect or alter any of the basic features of the constitution. 'Thus, substantive limitation founded on the doctrine of "basic features" has been introduced into our Constitution by judicial innovation.'[6]

While there has been some difference of opinion among judges about the contents of the list of basic features, there is consensus on the doctrine of 'basic features' or 'basic structure', and it can be used to check any attempts to subvert the constitution through parliamentary majorities.

Federal Structure or Unitary

The Indian constitution does not fit into any rigid definition of federal or unitary. To quote Austin:[7]

> The political structure of the Indian Constitution is so unusual that it is impossible to describe it briefly. Characterisations such as 'quasi-federal' and 'statutory decentralisation' are interesting, but not particularly illuminating. The members of the Assembly themselves refused to adhere to any theory or dogma about federalism. India had unique problems, they believed, problems that had not 'confronted other federations in history'. These could not be solved by recourse to theory because federalism was 'not a definite concept' and lacked a 'stable meaning'. Therefore, Assembly members, drawing on the experience of the great federations like the United States, Canada, Switzerland, and Australia, pursued 'the policy of pick and choose to see (what) would suit (them) best, (what) would suit the genius of the nation best . . . This process produced . . . a new kind of federalism to meet India's peculiar needs.'

The Assembly was perhaps the first constituent body to embrace from the start what A.M. Birch and others have called 'cooperative federalism'. It is characterized by increasing interdependence of federal and regional governments without destroying the principle of federalism.[8] (Interestingly, the concept of cooperative federalism was reintroduced into the political vocabulary by P. Chidambaram, when he was the Finance Minister in the United Front government in 1996–98.)

The decision of the Constituent Assembly to have a federal constitution with a strong Centre was occasioned also by the circumstances in which it was taken. A strong central government was necessary for handling the situation arising out of the communal riots that preceded and accompanied Partition, for meeting the food crisis, for settling the refugees, for maintaining national unity and for promoting social and economic development, which had been thwarted under colonial rule.

However, in the initial months of its existence, before Partition became an accepted fact, the Constituent Assembly did not express itself in favour of a strong central government. The Union Powers Committee of the Assembly, headed by Nehru, had in its first report provided for a very weak central government. But once the decision on Partition was taken and announced on 3 June 1947, the Constituent Assembly considered itself free of the restraints imposed by the Cabinet Mission Plan of 1946, and moved quickly in the direction of a federation with a strong Centre.

Dr B.R. Ambedkar, while introducing the Draft Constitution, explained why the term 'Union of States' was preferred over 'Federation of States':[9]

> The Drafting Committee wanted to make it clear that though India was to be a federation, the federation was not the result of an agreement by the States to join in a federation and that the federation not being the result of an agreement, no state has the right to secede from it. The federation is a Union because it is indestructible. Though the country and the people may be divided into different States for convenience of administration, the country is one integral whole, its people a single people living under a single imperium derived from a single source.

Indian federalism has certain distinctive features. For example, unlike the US, where a person is a citizen of the US, as well as of the state in which he or she resides, in India there is only Indian citizenship.

The constitution has also tried to minimize conflict between the Union and the states by clearly specifying the legislative powers of each. It contains three lists of subjects. The subjects listed in the Union List can only be legislated upon by the Union parliament, the ones in the State List only by the state legislatures, and those in the Concurrent List come within the purview of both, but in case of a conflict between Union and state legislation, the Union law will prevail.

While it is true that the overwhelming financial power of the Union and the dependence of the states upon the Union for grants-in-aid for discharging their functions places limits on federalism, nevertheless it would be an exaggeration to maintain, as some analysts do, that federalism has withered away in the actual working of the constitution. The most conclusive evidence of the survival of the federal system perhaps is to be found in the coexistence of state governments with sharply divergent ideological complexions: the Left Front and United Front governments in Kerala, West Bengal and Tripura, Dravida Munnetra Kazhagam (DMK) and All India Anna Dravida Munnetra Kazhagam (AIADMK) in Tamil Nadu, Telugu Desam in Andhra Pradesh, Janata Dal governments in Gujarat and Karnataka, Bharatiya Janata Party (BJP) in U.P., Madhya Pradesh, Rajasthan, Gujarat and Himachal, etc., with a Congress or Janata Dal or United Front or BJP government at the Centre. Agitations for formation of new states and demands, often successful, for more financial powers to the states, also testify that the federal impulse is alive. The Left Front government in West Bengal created history on 18 June 1998 by questioning the right of the BJP-led government at the Centre to send a fact-finding team to assess the state's law and order situation, citing that law and order is a State subject. The Communist Party of India (Marxist) (CPM) government clearly found the federal principle a useful weapon of defence in the face of BJP's attempt at applying political pressure in response to its ally, the Trinamul Congress. It also demonstrates that constitutional arguments are often occasioned by political contests and not by constitutional anomalies and further that the balance between the federal and unitary features of the constitution at every point in time is a function as much of the political balance of forces in the country as it is of constitutional developments, court judgements and the like.

It would then perhaps be fair to conclude with D.D. Basu, a leading authority on the Indian constitution, that it introduces a system 'which is to normally work as a federal system, but there are provisions to convert it into a unitary or quasi-federal system under specified exceptional circumstances'.[10] It is perhaps this flexibility, which is usually missing in purely federal constitutions, that has enabled the constitutional framework to accommodate the wide variety of Centre–state relationships encountered in the years since independence.

Institutions of Governance and their Working

The President

The executive power is vested by the constitution in the President of India but in the words of Ambedkar, he is a constitutional head who 'occupies the same position as the King under the English Constitution. He is the head of the State but not of the Executive. He represents the nation but does not rule the nation.'[11] The head of the executive is in fact the prime minister at the head of the council of ministers which is responsible to parliament. India's parliamentary form of government bears the closest resemblance to the British system, with the difference of course that India has no hereditary monarchy but an elected President as its symbolic head of state. The alternative of a Presidential form of government of the American type was rejected by the framers of the constitution as unsuited to Indian conditions.

The Indian constitution thus formally confers an enormous range of powers on the President, but these are to be exercised in accordance with the advice of the cabinet. But the President is by no means a figurehead and the political situation may provide many occasions for an activist President. This tension between his formal and real powers has been visible from the time of the first President, Dr Rajendra Prasad. Having serious reservations about the Hindu Code Bill, he tried to argue in September 1951 that the President had a greater role to play. Nehru promptly sought the opinion of Alladi Krishnaswamy Ayyar, the constitutional expert, in Madras and M.C. Setalvad, the Attorney-General. Fortunately for Indian democracy, both the experts were categorical that acceptance of President Rajendra Prasad's arguments would upset the whole constitutional structure and could lead to the President assuming dictatorial powers. Rajendra Prasad was thus persuaded to exercise a more limited role in keeping with his own earlier hope expressed in the Constituent Assembly debates that 'the convention under which in England the King acts always on the advice of his Ministers will be established in this country also and the President . . . will become a constitutional President in all matters'.[12]

The danger of a President actually using his powers is least likely when a single party commands a clear majority. But the potential for presidential activism occurs in the event of fractured electoral verdicts or splits in the ruling party, leading to unstable coalition governments. The first time this happened was in 1979 when the Janata government led by Morarji Desai fell because of a split in the ruling party. The President, Neelam Sanjiva Reddy, used his discretion in refusing Morarji Desai's request to form a new government, asking Charan Singh to prove his majority by seeking a vote of confidence by a fixed date and consulting other party leaders before accepting the new prime minister, Charan Singh's advice to dissolve the Lok Sabha. President Venkataraman acted in a similar fashion when he invited Chandra Shekhar to form the government after the resignation of V.P. Singh in November 1990. He took a whole week to accept Chandra Shekhar's advice to dissolve the Lok Sabha in March 1991 and even played around with the idea of a National Government with himself at its head.

In recent years, these worries about the President's role have intensified because of the fact that the last time any party secured a clear majority in the national elections was in 1984–85 when Rajiv Gandhi came to power after Indira Gandhi's assassination. The elections of 1989, 1991, 1996 and 1998 all created ample opportunities and need for presidential intervention. For example, in March 1998, after the election results showed that when the BJP staked its claim to form the government on the ground that it was the single largest party and had enough support from other parties to win the confidence vote in the Lok Sabha, President K.R. Narayanan insisted that Atal Bihari Vajpayee, the leader of the BJP, furnish proof in writing that his party did indeed enjoy the support of its allies. This resulted in an embarrassing wait of a few days for the prospective prime minister because one of his critical allies, J. Jayalalithaa of the AIADMK (whose desertion finally led to the collapse of the BJP government in April 1999) had many 'second thoughts' and drove hard bargains in well-advertised secret meetings before finally consenting to send the crucial missive extending the AIADMK's support to the BJP. The President's role was critical in the entire episode. He could have refused to wait endlessly for the letter of support and invited the leader of the next largest party or group, thus denying the BJP's claims which were in any case based on a wafer-thin majority. It is evident then that unstable or ambiguous political situations provide room for exercise of presidential discretion and hence potential abuse or misuse of powers.

However, even in otherwise stable situations, it has happened that presidents have, on occasion, either because of personal ambition or out of a sense of duty to the constitution, exercised discretionary power. The most vivid example is that of President Zail Singh, who was the first to use the President's power to return a bill to parliament. He also wrote at the same time to the prime minister that he was not being kept informed of important developments and this was preventing him from performing his constitutional duty of ensuring that the government was being run in accordance with the letter and spirit of the constitution. There was much speculation that he might actually dismiss the prime minister. Later in the same year, 1987, when the Bofors scandal about kickbacks in defence purchases broke, it seems that Zail Singh did actually discuss with political leaders of many hues the possibility of dismissing Rajiv Gandhi as prime minister. In the end, none of it ensued, but it is clear that the potential for the President stepping outside the conventional limits of his powers exists even when a prime minister enjoys majority support in parliament. It is to be remembered that the Congress under Rajiv Gandhi had the largest majority ever in the Lok Sabha.

Another area of debate relates to the President's role in the dismissal of state governments and imposition of President's Rule. February 1998, in the midst of the Lok Sabha elections, the governor of U.P., Romesh Bhandari, dismissed the BJP-led government of Kalyan Singh and swore in another man as chief minister. The High Court reinstated Kalyan Singh and the governor sent a report to the Centre recommending dissolution of the Assembly and imposition of President's Rule. The cabinet, after long deliberation, accepted the governor's report and prime minister I.K. Gujral recommended it to the President. But President Narayanan returned it for reconsideration to the cabinet, in a clear expression of disagreement. The governor of Uttar Pradesh accordingly resigned and Kalyan Singh continued as chief minister of Uttar Pradesh with his ragtag coalition of defectors, criminals, and others.

President Narayanan clearly had to exercise a difficult choice here. There were claims and counter-claims about the extent of support enjoyed by the Kalyan Singh ministry, there were defections and return-defections and allegations of monetary and other inducements. Nonetheless, the President decided that since the U.P. ministry had demonstrated its majority support, however unfairly acquired, on the floor of the house, he had no right to dismiss it. His critics argue that demonstration of majority support is not the only criterion on which to decide whether the constitutional machinery in a state has broken down and support achieved through intimidation or inducement can be questioned.

It is to be noted that the 44th Amendment has given him the authority to ask the council of ministers to reconsider its advice, but if the council reiterates its position, the President must accept the advice. But, as seen in the case of President Narayanan and the U.P. issue, the President's sending back the advice for reconsideration is taken very seriously and is unlikely to be ignored.

In other areas, the powers of the President are quite clearly defined. When a bill is presented to him, under Article 111, he may withhold his assent and, if he desires, return it to parliament for reconsideration. If both houses again pass it and send it back to him, he is obliged to give his assent. In the case of money bills, however, he has no discretion. In any case, he has no absolute power of veto.

The 44th Amendment in 1978 also made it explicit that the President can declare an Emergency only after receiving in writing the decision of the cabinet advising him to make the proclamation. During the period of Emergency as well, he is to act on the advice of the cabinet. It is very clear that almost all his powers, including those of appointing various high functionaries such as judges of the higher courts, governors, ambassadors, the Attorney-General, the Comptroller and Auditor-General of India, etc., are to be exercised on the advice of the cabinet. The same is true of his powers as Supreme Commander of the armed forces, and of his powers to issue ordinances when parliament is not in session.

The President is elected for five years, is eligible for re-election, and can be removed through impeachment for violation of the constitution. He is elected by elected members of both houses of parliament and of state legislative assemblies by a method of proportional representation through single transferable vote. Each Member of Parliament (MP) or Member of Legislative Assembly (MLA) has a single transferable vote, with a value corresponding to the population represented by him.

The Vice-President

If the President dies in office, or is unable to perform his duties because of absence, illness or any other cause, or is removed or resigns, the Vice-President is enjoined upon by Article 65 to act as the President. This has happened on two occasions when Presidents— Dr Zakir Hussain and Fakhruddin Ali Ahmed—died in office and Vice-Presidents V.V. Giri and B.D. Jatti had to step in. For this reason, the choice of Vice-President has to be made with great care. In normal times, the main function of the Vice-President, who is elected for five years by both houses of parliament, but is not a member of any legislature, is to act as the chairperson of the Rajya Sabha.

The Council of Ministers and the Prime Minister

The real executive power vests under the constitution in the council of ministers headed by the prime minister. The President appoints as prime minister the leader of the party that has a majority in the Lok Sabha or, if no party has a clear majority, a person who has the confidence of the majority of the members of the Lok Sabha. Other ministers are selected by the prime minister and appointed by the President. Ministers may be appointed without being members of parliament, but they must become members of any one house either by election or nomination within six months. The council of ministers is collectively responsible to the Lok Sabha and has to resign as soon as it loses the confidence of the Lok Sabha.

The prime minister is, in Nehru's words, the 'linchpin of Government'. Almost all the powers formally vested in the President are in fact exercised by the prime minister, who is the link between the President, the cabinet, and the parliament. The position of the prime minister in India has acquired its pre-eminence at least partly from the fact that the first prime minister, Jawaharlal Nehru, who retained his office for almost seventeen years, had such enormous prestige and influence that some of it rubbed off on to the office itself. Indira Gandhi was also so powerful after her election victory and the Bangladesh war in 1971 that the prime minister's position within the political system acquired enormous weight. The prime minister has full powers to choose ministers as well as recommend their dismissal. This gives the prime minister enormous powers of patronage.

The constitution does not mention different categories of ministers such as cabinet ministers, ministers of state and deputy ministers, except in Article 352 where the cabinet is defined as the council consisting of ministers of cabinet rank. In effect, however, the cabinet rank ministers who meet regularly in cabinet meetings chaired by the prime minister, are the most important as all important decisions are taken in cabinet meetings.

The constitution does not allow the possibility of breakdown of constitutional machinery and direct President's Rule at the Centre as it does in the states. There must always be a council of ministers. Even when a vote of no-confidence is passed and the council of ministers resign, they are asked by the President to continue till the new one is in place.

A new constitutional controversy arose with the refusal of the BJP-led government, which was voted out of office on 17 April 1999, to act in the spirit of a caretaker as had been the convention. Despite protests by Opposition parties, the government rejected any notion of caretaker status with the argument that there was no such provision in the constitution. However, it is arguable that this stance ignored well-established practice and was self-serving. The Chief Election Commissioner's advice to the government that it should act keeping in mind that the country was already in election mode even though the statutory period of restraint had not yet begun also fell on deaf years. (Though the Lok Sabha was dissolved in April 1999, fresh elections were delayed till September and October due to the monsoon and revision of electoral rolls.) The government at one stroke transferred eight secretary-level (the highest rank in the bureaucracy) officials, including the Home

Secretary, who is responsible for law and order, on 3 May 1999, after the Lok Sabha had been dissolved. This, despite the fact that one of the most important conventions evolved for ensuring fair elections is that officials are not transferred once elections are announced. Sadly, the letter of the constitution was used to defy constitutional practice.

The Parliament

The Indian parliament has two houses—the upper house being called the Rajya Sabha or the Council of States and the lower house the Lok Sabha or the House of the People. The Rajya Sabha has 250 members, of whom 238 are elected by elected members of the state legislative assemblies or Vidhan Sabhas via a system of proportional representation by means of single transferable vote, while another 12 are nominated by the President, on the advice of the government, to represent different fields such as education, social work, media, sports, etc. Every two years, one-third of the members of the Rajya Sabha retire; but individual members' terms are for six years, so that the Rajya Sabha is a permanent body. The Vice-President of India is the chairperson and a deputy chairperson is elected by Rajya Sabha members from amongst themselves.

The Lok Sabha is directly elected by the people for five years. It may be dissolved before its term is over. In case an Emergency is in force, the Lok Sabha can extend its term for one year at a time but not beyond six months after the Emergency has ended. In practice, only once has the Lok Sabha's term been extended for a year in 1976 when prime minister Indira Gandhi had declared the Emergency.

All Indian citizens, eighteen or above, are eligible to vote. The winning candidate is the one that is first past the post, that is, the one who gets the maximum number of votes. There is no rule that the winner must get at least 50 per cent of the votes, as is the practice in many other countries, though many thoughtful observers have been urging that this system is adopted to ensure the representative nature of the candidate elected and encourage candidates to look beyond vote-banks to wider sections of voters. There is no proportional representation.

Constituencies are territorial and single-member, and divided among states roughly in proportion to the population. A certain number are reserved for Scheduled Tribes and Scheduled Castes in proportion to their population in that particular state. This means that if, say, in Andhra Pradesh, 40 per cent of the population is Scheduled Castes and 10 per cent Scheduled Tribes, then in 40 per cent of Lok Sabha seats in Andhra Pradesh only Scheduled Caste candidates can contest and in another 10 per cent only Scheduled Tribe candidates can contest. All the voters residing in that constituency would elect these candidates—there are no separate electorates as there were before independence.

In recent years, pressure has built up for reservation of one-third of constituencies for women and a bill on those lines was also introduced in parliament in 1998, but it remains caught up in the web of claims and counter-claims of caste and religious groups who are demanding reservation within reservation, on the ground that else only upper-caste, elite, Hindu women will corner the seats reserved for women. Whatever the final outcome, the controversy has demonstrated clearly the self-propelling dynamic of the principle of reservation.

However desirable the objective, once the principle is accepted, it is virtually impossible to prevent further claims to the same benefits by other groups. The practice of reservation has also shown that it is almost impossible to reverse. The constitution had envisaged reservations as a short-term measure lasting ten years; no government has ever seriously considered not extending them every ten years, and it is now nearly fifty years! On the contrary, demands for and acceptance of reservation have only increased. Even the question— whether reservation, which per se perpetuates certain group identities, can become a barrier to the concept of citizenship as embodied in the constitution—is difficult to ask in the prevailing political climate. Disadvantaged groups, and certainly their leaders, are easily convinced that reservation is the panacea for all ills, perhaps because it enables rapid upward mobility for some visible and vocal sections of the groups or because a bird in hand is considered to be better than the invisible one in the bush of the future.

The maximum number of seats in the Lok Sabha is 552. Of these, 550 represent territorial constituencies, and two go to nominated members from the Anglo-Indian community. Members must be at least twenty-five years of age. The Lok Sabha is chaired by the speaker, and in his absence by the deputy speaker, both of whom are elected by members from amongst themselves. By convention, the speaker's post goes to the majority party and the deputy speaker's to the Opposition. But again, in recent years, fractured verdicts, unstable coalitions, claims of rival groups within and outside the government, have upset established conventions. There were fairly well-established conventions that the election of the speaker and deputy speaker would be kept free of contest to assure their non-partisan image and the speaker should be a person of considerable ability and influence capable of asserting his authority in the house. But in 1998, the BJP-led government first backed out of a promise to support a Congress nominee, P.A. Sangma, as a consensus candidate and then had elected an unknown face, Balayogi, to please its alliance partner, the Telugu Desam party. This was unfortunate, for the constitution entrusts great responsibility to the speaker: within and in all matters relating to the Lok Sabha, the speaker's word is final.

The parliament has extensive legislative powers and bills may be introduced in any house. To become law, bills must be passed by both houses, and then receive presidential assent. The President may, however, send the bills back to parliament or the government for reconsideration. If they are passed again, the President cannot withhold assent. Money-bills, however, must be introduced first in the Lok Sabha, and on the President's recommendation. They go to the Rajya Sabha, and if not returned with suggestions in fourteen days, are taken as passed. Recommendations of the Rajya Sabha may or may not be accepted by the Lok Sabha in the case of money-bills.

The constitution thus clearly envisaged parliament as an institution with great dignity and accorded privileges to its members commensurate with that position. Unfortunately, in recent years, the conduct of some members and parties who have disturbed even the President's address, indulged in unnecessary walkouts, shouting, even physical scuffles, has lowered the dignity of the parliament and delayed necessary legislative business. This has led to a popular disgust with members of parliament and a common feeling that parliament is just a big waste of taxpayers' money.

The Government in the States and Union Territories

The constitution lays down that the system of government at the state level shall also be based on the parliamentary model with the chief minister and his council of ministers exercising effective executive power while being responsible to the state legislature. The governor is meant to be a constitutional head like the President but with the very important difference that if the constitutional machinery breaks down and President's Rule under Article 356 is imposed, then the governor as the President's representative becomes the effective executive and runs the state with the help of advisers appointed by the union government.

The expectation at the time of the framing of the constitution was that governors would be 'people from outside—eminent people, sometimes people who have not taken too great a part in politics . . . an eminent educationist or a person eminent in other walks of life'.[14] But this hope has been largely belied. Governors have over the years tended more and more to be active politicians, many of whom have returned to full-time politics (if they at all gave it up as governors!) once their terms are over. They have tended to carry out the directives of the party in power in New Delhi or the one that appointed them and have sometimes even become active conspirators in murky provincial toppling games. All parties are guilty of having furthered this trend of appointing pliant governors. The convention of consulting state chief ministers before appointing governors has also lapsed though demands for its revival are growing.

There are numerous examples of misuse of governors' discretionary powers but the most notorious ones are the following. On 2 July 1984, Farooq Abdullah, the chief minister of Jammu and Kashmir, asked the governor, Jagmohan, to immediately call a session of the legislative assembly. He wanted to test his majority on the floor of the house as twelve members had deserted his party. The governor, however, dismissed his ministry from office and installed a new man, G.M. Shah, as chief minister. Abdullah campaigned against his dismissal all over the country. The incident was also cited as proof of the union government's infringement of the autonomy of the state and was thus a handy tool for stoking secessionist fires.

In a similar fashion, in Andhra Pradesh, the governor, Ram Lal, instead of summoning the Assembly as desired by the chief minister, N.T. Rama Rao (whose Telugu Desam Party had suffered a split), so that he could test his majority on the floor of the house, dismissed the chief minister on 16 August 1984. N.T. Rama Rao had asked for only two days to prove his majority; his successor was given thirty days by the governor but still could not muster the strength. Indira Gandhi made a public statement that she had no prior knowledge of governor Ram Lal's action, got him to resign, sent Shankar Dayal Sharma as the governor, and N.T. Rama Rao was again invited to form the government. In this process, however, the dignity of the governor's office suffered a severe blow.

All states have legislative assemblies, which consist of not more than 500 and not less than 60 members. A few states also have second chambers or legislative councils. States have exclusive right to legislate on items in the State List. They can also legislate on items in the Concurrent List but if there is a law passed by the parliament which is different from that passed by the state legislature, then the Union law stands.

There are also seven areas known as Union Territories, which are directly administered by lieutenant-governors appointed by the President. These territories can also have a legislature and a council of ministers, as in the case of Delhi and Pondicherry but their powers are more restricted than those of their counterparts in the states.

Local Government

The constitution did not contain provisions for the exact form that local government institutions were to take, but the Directive Principles specifically laid down that the states should take steps to organize village panchayats and endow them to function as units of self-government (Article 40). This was to allow the states the flexibility to devise forms most suited to their needs. Besides, the legacy of the freedom struggle, and especially of Gandhiji himself, who had made panchayats a part of his political programme since the Non-Cooperation movement of 1920–22, made it imperative that local self-governing bodies be set up.

However, not much progress was made in the early 1950s. The central government had concentrated its efforts for local development on the Community Development programme, which took a block of about 100 villages as a unit for promoting developmental activities with the help of village-level workers, social workers, agricultural experts, newly appointed development officials, etc. Very high hopes had been pinned on the success of this effort, and when it became apparent that it was not making much headway, a high-level committee chaired by Balwantrai Mehta, a veteran Gandhian, was asked in 1956 to make recommendations for its improvement. The Mehta Committee diagnosed the lack of democratic local bodies with real powers as the major cause of the failure of the Community Development programme. The remedy suggested was the setting up of Panchayati Raj (PR) by instituting three levels of representative bodies. The gram panchayat at the village level was to be directly elected by all adult residents of the village, and the panchayat samiti at the block level and zilla parishad at the district level were to consist of members indirectly elected from the tier below as well as cooperative movement officials, parliamentarians and others co-opted to the body.

Between 1959 and 1962, state governments in all parts of the country introduced Panchayati Raj legislation. Over the years, however, the functioning of Panchayati Raj was not up to expectations, for various reasons. State governments, whose duty it was, did not often hold local elections on time, sometimes for many years at a time, if they feared an unfavourable result. Panchayats did not have enough resources to be innovative and independent. Local bigwigs dominated panchayats and cornered benefits. A number of committees made extensive studies and gave valuable suggestions—the Asoka Mehta Committee, 1978, the G.V.K. Rao Committee, 1985, and the L.M. Singhvi Committee, 1986.

A new initiative was taken under the leadership of Rajiv Gandhi in 1988, when a committee headed by P.K. Thungon recommended that Panchayati Raj bodies should be constitutionally recognized and the constitution should have a provision to ensure timely and regular election to these bodies and their term should be five years. In 1989, the Constitution 64th Amendment Bill was introduced in parliament. The Congress did not, unfortunately, have a majority in the Rajya Sabha, and Opposition parties, suspicious of Congress intentions that this was a new device for curbing the powers of the states, blocked its passage and prevented a good measure from becoming law. That there was no principled objection in mind became clear when the National Front government of V.P. Singh introduced the same bill with minor changes within a year of the old one being blocked. History has its ironies: V.P. Singh's government collapsed before the bills could be passed and it fell to the Congress's lot to finally see through the constitution 73rd and 74th Amendment Bills in 1993.

The 73rd Amendment provides for an elaborate system of establishing panchayats as units of self-government. For the first time in the constitutional history of India, the constitution of panchayats, the duration of their term, their membership, the constitution of a finance commission to review their financial position is detailed. It also adds a new schedule to the Constitution, the Eleventh Schedule, which lists 29 subjects which are to be handled by the panchayats. With this amendment, Panchayati Raj institutions are as much a part of the structure of constitutional government in India as the Lok Sabha. The 74th Amendment does the same for the municipalities.

The Judiciary

Articles 124–147 and 214–237 of the constitution lay down the entire framework of the system of justice in India. The judiciary is to be the upholder of the constitution, after all, and no detail is too small for ensuring its independence and effectivity. The method of appointment, the years of service, qualifying conditions, powers of each court, size of the bench, pay and perquisites, and much more, are all specified in the constitution.

The Indian judicial system consists of a single hierarchy of courts with the Supreme Court at its apex. Before the Supreme Court came into being in January 1950, India had a Federal Court and further appeals lay with the Judicial Committee of the Privy Council in Britain. The jurisdiction of the Privy Council was abolished in October 1949 and the Federal Court was replaced by the Supreme Court of India in January 1950.

The Supreme Court consists of a chief justice and twenty-five other judges (seven in 1950, gradually increased by 1986 to twenty-five) appointed by the President after consultation with such of the judges of the Supreme Court and the High Courts as may be thought necessary. They hold office till the age of sixty-five. In the case of appointment of judges other than the chief justice, the chief justice shall always be consulted (Article 124). By convention, the chief justice is always the seniormost judge of the Supreme Court. In 1973 and again in 1976, this convention was flouted by Indira Gandhi when the seniormost judges (three in 1973 and one in

1976) were superseded. This action was roundly condemned as an attack on the independence of the judiciary and no government since has dared to repeat the act.

The only way a Supreme Court judge can be removed from office is if each house of parliament supported by a majority of the house as well as two-thirds of those present and voting pass a resolution in the same session and present an address to the President asking for removal on the ground of proven misbehaviour or incapacity [Article 124(4)]. To further ensure the independence of judges, there is a bar on their pleading before any court or authority in India after retirement [Article 124(7)].

The Supreme Court has original jurisdiction in appeals or writs relating to enforcement of Fundamental Rights, that is, a person can straightaway appeal to the Supreme Court without going through the normal layers of the judicial hierarchy (Article 32). The Supreme Court has original jurisdiction also in all disputes between the Union and states as well as between states. It can transfer cases from lower courts to itself. It has appellate jurisdiction in constitutional, civil and criminal cases. It has also sanctioned the practice of public interest litigation wherein a person or an organization can appeal, to the highest court, even by means of an ordinary postcard, on an issue that does not affect him or her directly but about which there is reason for concern as a citizen. A more recent trend is of 'judicial activism' by which is meant judges intervening to force executive authorities to perform their duties such as collecting garbage, placing controls on vehicular pollution, etc. While there has been some, even justified, criticism of this trend, it must be admitted that the judiciary was seen as the last refuge by a frustrated public unable to make its voice heard in other ways. The judiciary was effective precisely because of the power given to it by the constitution that all authorities must implement its decisions and orders.

The Supreme Court has played a major role in interpreting the constitution, especially with regard to the changing relationship between Fundamental Rights and Directive Principles, as discussed above. While it is limited in its powers in comparison to the US Supreme Court when it comes to declaring any law unconstitutional, since it does not have the clause of 'due process of law' or standards of natural justice, it has made up by evolving the doctrine of 'Basic Features', on the basis of which even an amendment to the constitution can be declared invalid if it is destructive of the 'Basic Features' of the constitution. It seems that Alladi Krishnaswami Ayyar, a leading member of the drafting committee of the Indian constitution, was right in his prediction that:[15]

> the future evolution of the Indian Constitution will thus depend to a large extent upon the Supreme Court and the direction given to it by that Court. While its function may be one of interpreting the Constitution, it cannot . . . ignore the social, economic and political tendencies of the times . . . On certain occasions it may appear to strengthen the union at the expense of the units and at another time it may appear to champion the cause of provincial autonomy and regionalism. On one occasion it may appear to favour individual liberty as against social or state control and another time, it may appear to favour social or state control. It is the great tribunal which has to draw the line between liberty and social control.

The High Courts in the states have powers over all the subordinate courts in their jurisdiction. Their power to issue writs or orders is wider than that of the Supreme Court as it is not restricted to cases of violation of Fundamental Rights. The High Courts have chief justices at their head and other judges as required. Their mode of appointment is similar to that of Supreme Court judges. Just as the law declared by the Supreme Court is binding on all courts in India, a law declared by a High Court is binding on all courts of that state.

The subordinate courts in each state are directly under the control of the High Court. District judges are appointed by the governor in consultation with the High Court. The lower judiciary is recruited via examinations from among those who have at least three years' experience at the Bar. Sadly, corruption is quite common at the lower levels, but happily still not common, though not unknown, at the High Court level, and rare, if not absent, in the Supreme Court. A major problem is the enormous backlog of cases and it can often take ten or even twenty years for a case to be decided. Litigation is expensive and time-consuming; as a result common people hesitate to take recourse to the courts. The judiciary is also hemmed in by a plethora of outdated laws, some more than a hundred years old. There is an urgent need for judicial reform but though subsequent chief justices of the Supreme Court have promised reform, yet not much has actually moved on the ground.

The Administrative Services

At independence, India inherited as part of the colonial legacy, an administrative structure that had been the major instrument of colonial power and perhaps the chief instrument of co-option of 'natives', from the brilliant scions of princely and zamindari families who joined the Indian Civil Service (ICS) to the Matric Fail son of the poor Brahmin priest who was happy to become a peon. British rule was bureaucratic rule, and that was what was most wrong with it. The chief culprits were the members of the ICS, a small elite group of overpaid, insensitive, mostly British men—so the nationalist argument had run *ad nauseum* before independence. Then why were the ICS given constitutional guarantees and the administrative structure left largely untouched after independence? The major reason lies in the circumstances that attended independence; Partition, transfers of population unprecedented in known history, integration of some 300 princely states, war in Kashmir, the assassination of Gandhiji. The one island of stability, of predictability, appeared to be the administrative structure. Most of the British members of the ICS had left, the few that remained were pro-India. The Indian members of the ICS, very few in number, made it clear that they were more than willing to hitch their wagons to the new regime, some out of nationalism, others as good bureaucrats whose dharma is to carry out the orders of their superiors. Perhaps national leaders had no reply to the entreaty of Sir Uma Shanker Bajpai, an outstanding ICS officer, who said with irrefutable logic: 'If I could serve so well a foreign power, how much better will I serve my own countrymen?' The ICS was therefore replaced by the Indian Administrative Service (IAS) and the pre-independence structure of all-India services, provincial or state services and central or Union government services was retained.

The constitution in 'Part XIV: Services under the Union and the States' while laying down that Union and state legislation would detail the rules for recruitment and conditions of service for Union and State services respectively, simultaneously provided constitutional guarantees against arbitrary dismissal. The constitution (Article 315) also ensures fairness in recruitment by providing for independent public service commissions (for the Union and for each state). The members of the commissions are appointed for a term of six years by the President or the governor and at least half must be civil servants with at least ten years' service. The commissions are entrusted with the task of conducting examinations for recruitment to the services and have to be consulted on all matters relating to the method of recruitment, appointment, promotion and transfer of as well as disciplinary action against civil servants.

The constitution mentions only two all-India services that were in existence at that time: the IAS and the Indian Police Service (IPS), but it provided for more by giving the power to the Rajya Sabha to resolve by a two-thirds majority to establish new all-India services. The Indian Forest Service and the Indian Engineering Service are two services set up under this constitutional provision. The all-India services have been a significant force for national integration, for typically half the cadre of each state must come from outside it. Further, each officer spends the first few years at the district or sub-district level, then some at the state level, followed by a stint at the Centre, then usually back to the state and so on, thus acquiring familiarity with all levels of administration and intimate knowledge of the work culture, strengths and weaknesses of each. The central services also perform a unifying role in that their recruitment base is the country as a whole. Officers of the Audit and Accounts Service, or Railway or Customs can be and are posted in different parts of the country even though they will work in central government offices and not in state government offices as in the case of IAS or IPS. Provincial or state service officers are posted within the state, unless they are on deputation or get promoted via internal examinations.

The constitutional safeguards were intended to encourage independence and integrity in the bureaucracy. No doubt this has ensured, there are any number of upright civil servants who have been able to resist unwelcome political pressures because of the security provided by constitutional guarantees of security of tenure. But total security has to some extent also encouraged sloth, lack of initiative and even corruption. It is so difficult to dismiss a civil servant that even gross cases of corruption are ignored because the results are not likely to be commensurate with the effort.

Politicians are also much to blame, as they often encourage or even pressurize officials to perform favours for themselves and their associates in return for monetary or other rewards. The period during the Emergency (1975–77), followed by the Janata government (1977–79), was probably the watershed in the history of the Indian bureaucracy. Mrs Gandhi had pushed the notion of a 'committed' bureaucracy, albeit with the proviso that the commitment expected was to the Directive Principles. In practice, especially with the ascendancy of Sanjay Gandhi, this tended to degenerate into commitment to a person. Those who showed 'commitment' were rewarded and those who did not were punished. With Janata coming to power in 1977, the pendulum swung all the way back. 'Victims' of the Emergency were rewarded with high posts and 'committed' officers sent into the wilderness to cool their heels. Subsequent regimes at the national level have mercifully not indulged in such visible, large-scale, playing of favourites though the slow process of the increasing politician–official nexus continues apace with caste-based parties such as the Bahujan Samaj Party (BSP) or Laloo Prasad Yadav's Janata Dal adding a new dimension by favouring officials belonging to the castes on which their electoral base rests. At the national level, the BJP's action, after it had lost the vote of confidence in April 1999, of wholesale transfers of senior officials, obviously with an eye to the impending elections, is a disturbing trend.

Conclusion

> India would do as she had done for centuries: take what she
> desired from other cultures and bend it to her needs.
> —Granville Austin[16]

The framers of the Indian constitution had borrowed freely and unabashedly from other constitutions, confident that the soil had been prepared sufficiently for exotic plants and the more homegrown ones to take root. The wisdom of the US constitution and its Supreme Court, the innovations of the Irish constitution, the time-tested conventions of the British Parliament, the administrative minutae of the Government of India Act, 1935, and much else, especially the essence of their own people's struggle for freedom— all went into the design and content of the Indian constitution.

There were many sceptics who wondered whether India could actually deliver on the freedoms she promised.

In retrospect, it may be said that the Indian constitution has not disappointed its architects, though it may have let down the sceptics. First and foremost, the institutions created by it for fashioning a democratic structure have survived and evolved to meet the changing needs. Despite stresses and strains, perhaps inevitable in a situation of rapid transition, the basic framework of responsible government, with the necessary balance between elected legislatures, functional executives, and vigilant judiciary, has acquired a legitimacy that would be difficult to erode. Notwithstanding rarified academic debates about whether Indian democracy is formal or substantive, Indians have accepted the democracy enshrined in their constitution as real enough. They are not wrong in doing so, for when they look around at their neighbours in Asia and Africa, and even at faraway Latin America, and at the troubled peoples of the erstwhile socialist world in eastern Europe, they know the worth of what they have.

The constitution has also been remarkably successful in providing a framework for protection of the Fundamental Rights of freedom of speech and expression, including the freedom of the Press, freedom of association, including the right to join political parties of one's choice and form trade unions, etc. Courts have acted as guardians of citizens' interests against encroachment by the state as well as private organizations and individuals. Courts have also been creative in expanding the meaning and scope of rights. For example, the right to life in Article 21 was expanded to include the right to livelihood in the judgement of the Supreme Court in *Olga Tellis v. Bombay Municipal Corporation*, popularly known as the 'Pavement Dwellers' Case'.[17] The right to personal liberty guaranteed in Article 21 has been interpreted to mean that a poor person cannot be imprisoned for not paying his debts. This is not to say that these rights are not violated, often with impunity, but that the institutional mechanism for their redressal exists and can be leveraged, and that the movement has been in the direction of expanding the scope of rights in the direction of a more just and caring society.

The constitution has proved sufficiently flexible in the matter of amending itself. Article 368 which contains the provisions for amendment of the constitution specifies that an amendment bill can be introduced in either house of parliament and must be passed by a clear majority with two-thirds of members present and voting. However, in the case of amendments in Article 368 itself or in articles dealing with the election of the President, the extent of the executive powers of the Union and the state governments, the judiciary, the distribution of powers, and the representation of the states in parliament, the amendment bill must also be passed by the legislatures of at least half the states. This has ensured that while amendments are not so difficult that the letter of the constitution becomes a barrier to social change, yet it is not possible to make changes unless a real consensus has been built up. Again, while Article 368 does not exclude any part of the constitution from the scope of amending provisions, the Supreme Court has in effect placed limits on the amending powers by means of the doctrine of 'Basic Structure' or 'Basic Features' of the constitution. While it is possible to argue that this is not envisaged in the constitution itself, yet it cannot be denied that the doctrine may well act as a healthy check on the ambitions of amendment-happy governments with big majorities.

Many suggestions have emanated from diverse sources over the years about changes required to be made in the constitution. Some want introduction of the Presidential system, others want proportional representation in place of or in addition to the first-past-the-post system, still others want that winning candidates should have to secure at least 50 per cent of votes, as in many other countries. A relatively recent addition is the proposal that a vote of no-confidence which brings down a government should include a vote of confidence in an alternative government—a proposal clearly inspired by rapid changes in governments and resultant fears of instability. Despite considerable opposition, the BJP-led NDA government appointed a Constitution Review Commission in 2000. The overall feeling is that most parties and most people, even when they seek important changes, are quite content to seek these within the given structure of the constitution. We cannot lay our failures at the door of the constitution; where there are failures, as indeed there are many, it is not the constitution that has failed us, it is we who have failed the constitution. As Rajendra Prasad said at the time of the framing of the constitution, a constitution can only be as good as the people who work it.

It is also significant that even those commentators who are very sharply critical of the Indian political system, and pessimistic about its future prospects, have little criticism to offer of the constitution. It is necessary to emphasize that at a time when most other institutions of governance have suffered greater or lesser erosion of legitimacy, the constitution has continued to command respect. This is not a small gain for a country with such diversity and complexity. In the turbulent times that perhaps await us in the new millennium, the constitution may well be a much-needed anchor of support. Its unambiguous commitment to a democratic, secular, egalitarian and civil libertarian society should help greatly in keeping the ship of the state tied firmly to its moorings.

The Initial Years

Fifteenth August 1947, the first day of free India, was celebrated with much exuberance and elation. The sacrifices of generations of patriots and the blood of countless martyrs had borne fruit. But this joy was tainted by despair, for the country had been divided. Large parts of the two new nations were engulfed by communal riots. There was a mass exodus of people from both states across the new borders. There was scarcity of food and other consumer goods, and a fear of administrative breakdown.

In a memorable address to the Constituent Assembly on the night of 14 August, Jawaharlal Nehru, speaking as the first prime minister of a free India and giving expression to the feelings of the people, said:

> Long years ago we made a tryst with destiny, and now the time comes when we shall redeem our pledge . . . At the stroke of the midnight hour, when the world sleeps, India will awake to life and freedom. A moment comes, which comes but rarely in history, when we step out from the old to the new, when an age ends, and when the soul of a nation, long suppressed, finds utterance. It is fitting that at this solemn moment we take the pledge of dedication to the service of India and her people and to the still larger cause of humanity . . . We end today a period of ill fortune and India discovers herself again.[1]

But independence had been accompanied by a multitude of problems, and, of course, centuries of backwardness, prejudice, inequality, and ignorance still weighed on the land. The debris of two centuries of colonialism had to be cleared and the promises of the freedom struggle to be fulfilled. The long haul had just begun. As Nehru declared in his 14 August speech, 'The achievement we celebrate today is but a step, an opening of opportunity, to the greater triumphs and achievements . . . That future is not one of ease and resting but of incessant striving so that we may fulfil the pledges we have so often taken.'[2]

There were the immediate problems of the territorial and administrative integration of the princely states, the communal riots that accompanied Partition, the rehabilitation of nearly six million refugees who had migrated from Pakistan, the protection of Muslims threatened by communal gangs, the need to avoid war with Pakistan, and the Communist insurgency. Restoration of law and order and political stability and putting in place an administrative system, threatened with breakdown because of Partition and the illogical division of the army and higher bureaucracy virtually on religious lines, were other immediate tasks. As Nehru declared in 1947, 'First things must come first and the first thing is the security and stability of India.'[3] Or, in the words of the political scientist W.H. Morris-Jones, the task was 'to hold things together, to ensure survival, to get accustomed to the feel of being on the water, to see to it that the vessels keep afloat.'[4]

In addition there were the medium-term problems of framing a constitution and building a representative democratic and civil libertarian political order, organizing elections to put in place the system of representative and responsible governments at the Centre and in the states, and abolishing the semi-feudal agrarian order through thoroughgoing land reforms.

The newly formed independent government also had the long-term tasks of promoting national integration, pushing forward the process of nation-in-the-making, facilitating rapid economic development, removing endemic poverty, and initiating the planning process. It also sought to bridge as quickly as possible the gap between mass expectations aroused by the freedom struggle and their fulfilment, to get rid of centuries-long social injustice, inequality and oppression, and to evolve a foreign policy which would defend Indian independence and promote peace in a world increasingly engulfed by the Cold War and getting divided into hostile power blocs.

All these problems had to be dealt with within the framework of the basic values to which the national movement had been committed and within the parameters of a broad national consensus.

The people and the political leadership set out to handle these short-term and long-term problems fuelled by an optimism, a certain faith in the country's future and with a *joie de vivre*. This mood was to persist for most of the Nehru years. Though many, especially on the left, were dissatisfied with and basically critical of Nehru and his policies, they too shared this feeling of hope. Those who have lived through the Nehru era often now feel that they were lucky to have done so. Nehru himself once again expressed this feeling after nearly a decade as prime minister: 'There is no lack of drama in this changing world of ours and, even in India, we live in an exciting age. I have always considered it a great privilege for people of this generation to live during this period of India's long history . . . I have believed that there is nothing more exciting in the wide world today than to work in India.'[5]

Some of this euphoria disappeared with the India–China war of 1962. The war brought in a degree of realism but even so neither Nehru nor the country experienced any sense of defeatism. Nehru had always believed that 'India's greatest need is for a sense of certainty concerning her own success'.[6] And it was this sense of excitement and of the coming success which he succeeded in imparting to the millions.

We shall discuss the short-term problems in the following sections. The long-term tasks, the maturing of the country under Nehru's stewardship, and the development of the political parties are discussed in subsequent chapters.

Independent India embarked on its tasks with the benefit of an outstanding leadership, having tremendous dedication and idealism besides the presence of a strong nationwide party, the Congress. Beside the great Nehru stood a group of leaders who had played a notable role in the freedom movement. There was his deputy prime minister, Sardar Patel, a leader who possessed a strong will and was decisive in action and strong in administration. Then there were the learned Maulana Abul Kalam Azad, the erudite Rajendra Prasad, and C. Rajagopalachari, endowed with a razor-sharp intellect. At the state level, were several leaders like Govind

Ballabh Pant in U.P., B.C. Roy in West Bengal, and B.C. Kher and Morarji Desai in Bombay, who enjoyed unchallenged authority in their states. All these leaders had skills and experience to run a modern and democratic administrative and political system which they had acquired through organizing a mass movement, building up a political party, and participating in colonial legislatures for decades. They also possessed a great deal of talent in consensus–building. The national movement had brought together different regions, sections of society and ideological currents around a common political agenda. Outside the Congress were the Socialists, Acharya Narendra Dev and Jayaprakash Narayan, the Communists, P.C. Joshi and Ajoy Ghosh, the liberal communalist, Syama Prasad Mookerjee, and the Dalit leader, Dr B.R. Ambedkar. On the periphery were Dr S. Radhakrishnan, the distinguished philosopher, Dr Zakir Hussain, the educationist, V.K. Krishna Menon, who had struggled for India's freedom in Britain, and a host of dedicated Gandhian leaders.

The leaders of independent India were persons of total personal integrity and had an austere lifestyle. No finger was ever pointed at Sardar Patel, for example, even as he performed the unenviable but necessary task of gathering funds for the Congress from the rich.

The Congress leaders also shared a common vision of independent India. They were committed to the goals of rapid social and economic change and democratization of the society and polity, and the values imparted by the national movement. Nehru's commitment to these values is well known. But, in fact, Sardar Patel, Rajendra Prasad and C. Rajagopalachari were equally committed to the values of democracy, civil liberties, secularism, independent economic development, anti-imperialism and social reforms and had a pro-poor orientation. These leaders differed with Nehru primarily on the question of socialism and class analysis of society. We may point out, parenthetically, in this context that Patel has been much misunderstood and misrepresented both by admirers and critics. The right-wingers have used him to attack the Nehruvian vision and policies, while his leftist critics have portrayed him as the archetypal rightist. Both, however, have been wrong. In any case, it is important that Nehru and the other leaders shared the belief that for the country's development the building up of a national consensus was necessary. The leadership's position was strengthened by the fact that they enjoyed tremendous popularity and prestige among almost every section of the people. On top of that, this team was headed by Jawaharlal Nehru who exercised, after December 1950, unchallenged authority in the party and the government.

Another positive feature of the Indian situation was the existence of Congress, a strong, democratically functioning, India-wide national party, with an established leadership and deep roots and strong support among the people. Except for the Communist party, its authority or legitimacy was questioned by nobody.

Even as Congress was being transformed from a movement into a party and was struggling to retain its politically all-embracing and ideologically diverse character, its leadership was aware of the fact that in the troublesome post-Partiton period the country needed a government which would represent the widest possible consensus and carry with it different shades of opinion and sections of society for implementing a common programme. So, even though the Socialists and the Communists moved into the Opposition, and the Congress was in an overwhelming majority in the Constituent Assembly and enjoyed unchallenged power, the Congress leadership widened the base of the Constituent Assembly and the government by the inclusion of distinguished and representative non-Congressmen. The government virtually became a national government. For example, the first Nehru cabinet of fourteen included five non-Congressmen: Dr B.R. Ambedkar and Syama Prasad Mookerjee, both of whom had opposed the Congress before 1947, John Mathai, C.H. Bhabha and Shanmukham Chetty. Dr B.R. Ambedkar was also made the Chairman of the Drafting Committee of the Constitution. Dr S. Radhakrishnan, the first Vice-President and the second President of India, had never been a Congressman.

Accession of the Princely States

Unifying post-Partition India and the princely states under one administration was perhaps the most important task facing the political leadership.

In colonial India, nearly 40 per cent of the territory was occupied by fifty-six small and large states ruled by princes who enjoyed varying degrees of autonomy under the system of British paramountcy. British power protected them from their own people as also from external aggression so long as they did British bidding.

In 1947 the future of the princely states once the British left became a matter of concern. Many of the larger princely states began to dream of independence and to scheme for it. They claimed that the paramountcy could not be transferred to the new states of India and Pakistan. Their ambitions were fuelled by the British prime minister Clement Attlee's announcement on 20 February 1947 that 'His Majesty's Government do not intend to hand over their powers and obligations under paramountcy to any government of British India.'[7] Consequently, rulers of several states claimed that they would become independent from 15 August 1947 when British rule ended.

In this they got encouragement from M.A. Jinnah who publicly declared on 18 June 1947 that 'the States would be independent sovereign States on the termination of paramountcy' and were 'free to remain independent if they so desired'.[8] The British stand was, however, altered to some extent when, in his speech on the Independence of India Bill, Attlee said, 'It is the hope of His Majesty's Government that all the States will in due course find their appropriate place with one or the other Dominion within the British Commonwealth.'[9]

The Indian nationalists could hardly accept a situation where the unity of free India would be endangered by hundreds of large or small independent or autonomous states interspersed within it which were sovereign. Besides, the people of the states had participated in the process of nation-in-the-making from the end of nineteenth century and developed strong feelings of Indian nationalism. Naturally, the nationalist leaders in British India and in the states rejected the claim of any state to independence and repeatedly declared that independence for a princely state was not an option—the only option open being whether the state would accede to India or Pakistan on the basis of contiguity of its territory and the wishes of its people. In fact, the national movement had for long held that political power belonged to the people of a state and not to its ruler and that the people of the states were an integral part of the Indian nation. Simultaneously, the people of the states were astir under the leadership of the States' Peoples' Conference as never before, demanding introduction of a democratic political order and integration with the rest of the country.

With great skill and masterful diplomacy and using both persuasion and pressure, Sardar Vallabhbhai Patel succeeded in integrating the hundreds of princely states with the Indian Union in two stages. Some states had shown wisdom and realism and perhaps a degree of patriotism by joining the Constituent Assembly in April 1947. But the majority of princes had stayed away and a few, such as those of Travancore, Bhopal and Hyderabad, publicly announced their desire to claim an independent status.

On 27 June 1947, Sardar Patel assumed additional charge of the newly created States' Department with V.P. Menon as its Secretary. Patel was fully aware of the danger posed to Indian unity by the possible intransigence of the rulers of the states. He told Menon at the time that 'the situation held dangerous potentialities and that if we did not handle it promptly and effectively, our hard-earned freedom might disappear through the States' door'.[10] He, therefore, set out to tackle the recalcitrant states expeditiously.

Patel's first step was to appeal to the princes whose territories fell inside India to accede to the Indian Union in three subjects which affected the common interests of the country, namely, foreign relations, defence and communications. He also gave an implied threat that he would not be able to restrain the impatient people of the states and the government's terms after 15 August would be stiffer.

Fearful of the rising tide of the peoples' movements in their states, and of the more extreme agenda of the radical wing of the Congress, as also Patel's reputation for firmness and even ruthlessness, the princes responded to Patel's appeal and all but three of them—Junagadh, Jammu and Kashmir and Hyderabad—acceded to India by 15 August 1947. By the end of 1948, however, the three recalcitrant states too were forced to fall in line.

Junagadh was a small state on the coast of Saurashtra surrounded by Indian territory and therefore without any geographical contiguity with Pakistan. Yet, its Nawab announced accession of his state to Pakistan on 15 August 1947 even though the people of the state, overwhelmingly Hindu, desired to join India.

The Indian nationalist leaders had for decades stood for the sovereignty of the people against the claims of the princes. It was, therefore, not surprising that in Junagadh's case Nehru and Patel agreed that the final voice, like in any other such case, for example

Kashmir or Hyderabad, should be that of the people as ascertained through a plebiscite. Going against this approach, Pakistan accepted Junagadh's accession. On the other hand, the people of the state would not accept the ruler's decision. They organized a popular movement, forced the Nawab to flee and established a provisional government. The Dewan of Junagadh, Shah Nawaz Bhutto, the father of the more famous Zulfiqar Ali Bhutto, now decided to invite the Government of India to intervene. Indian troops thereafter marched into the state. A plebiscite was held in the state in February 1948 which went overwhelmingly in favour of joining India.

The state of Kashmir bordered on both India and Pakistan. Its ruler Hari Singh was a Hindu, while nearly 75 per cent of the population was Muslim. Hari Singh too did not accede either to India or Pakistan. Fearing democracy in India and communalism in Pakistan, he hoped to stay out of both and to continue to wield power as an independent ruler. The popular political forces led by the National Conference and its leader Sheikh Abdullah, however, wanted to join India. The Indian political leaders took no steps to obtain Kashmir's accession and, in line with their general approach, wanted the people of Kashmir to decide whether to link their fate with India or Pakistan. (Nehru and Patel had made a similar offer in the case of Junagadh and Hyderabad.) In this they were supported by Gandhiji, who declared in August 1947 that Kashmir was free to join either India or Pakistan in accordance with the will of the people.

But Pakistan not only refused to accept the principle of plebiscite for deciding the issue of accession in the case of Junagadh and Hyderabad, in the case of Kashmir it tried to short-circuit the popular decision through a shortsighted action, forcing India to partially change its attitude in regard to Kashmir. On 22 October, with the onset of winter, several Pathan tribesmen, led unofficially by Pakistani army officers, invaded Kashmir and rapidly pushed towards Srinagar, the capital of Kashmir. The ill-trained army of the Maharaja proved no match for the invading forces. In panic, on 24 October, the Maharaja appealed to India for military assistance. Nehru, even at this stage, did not favour accession without ascertaining the will of the people. But Mountbatten, the Governor-General, pointed out that under international law India could send its troops to Kashmir only after the state's formal accession to India. Sheikh Abdullah and Sardar Patel too insisted on accession. And so on 26 October, the Maharaja acceded to India and also agreed to install Abdullah as head of the state's administration. Even though both the National Conference and the Maharaja wanted firm and permanent accession, India, in conformity with its democractic commitment and Mountbatten's advice, announced that it would hold a referendum on the accession decision once peace and law and order had been restored in the Valley.

After accession the cabinet took the decision to immediately fly troops to Srinagar. This decision was bolstered by its approval by Gandhiji who told Nehru that there should be no submission to evil in Kashmir and that the raiders had to be driven out. On 27 October nearly 100 planes airlifted men and weapons to Srinagar to join the battle against the raiders. Srinagar was first held and then the raiders were gradually driven out of the Valley, though they retained control over parts of the state and the armed conflict continued for months.

Fearful of the dangers of a full-scale war between India and Pakistan, the Government of India agreed, on 30 December 1947, on Mountbatten's suggestion, to refer the Kashmir problem to the United Nations Security Council, asking for vacation of aggression by Pakistan.

Nehru was to regret this decision later as, instead of taking note of the aggression by Pakistan, the Security Council, guided by Britain and the United States, tended to side with Pakistan. Ignoring India's complaint, it replaced the 'Kashmir question' before it by the 'India–Pakistan dispute'. It passed many resolutions, but the upshot was that in accordance with one of its resolutions both India and Pakistan accepted a ceasefire on 31 December 1948 which still prevails and the state was effectively divided along the ceasefire line. Nehru, who had expected to get justice from the United Nations, was to express his disillusionment in a letter to Vijaylakshmi Pandit in February 1948: 'I could not imagine that the Security Council could possibly behave in the trivial and partisan manner in which it functioned. These people are supposed to keep the world in order. It is not surprising that the world is going to pieces. The United States and Britain have played a dirty role, Britain probably being the chief actor behind the scenes.'[11]

In 1951, the UN passed a resolution providing for a referendum under UN supervision after Pakistan had withdrawn its troops from the part of Kashmir under its control. The resolution has remained infructuous since Pakistan has refused to withdraw its forces from what is known as Azad Kashmir.

Since then Kashmir has been the main obstacle in the path of friendly relations between India and Pakistan. India has regarded Kashmir's accession as final and irrevocable and Kashmir as its integral part. Pakistan continues to deny this claim. Kashmir has also over time become a symbol as well as a test of India's secularism; it was, as Nehru put it, basic to the triumph of secularism over communalism in India.

Hyderabad was the largest state in India and was completely surrounded by Indian territory. The Nizam of Hyderabad was the third Indian ruler who did not accede to India before 15 August. Instead, he claimed an independent status and, encouraged by Pakistan, began to expand his armed forces. But Sardar Patel was in no hurry to force a decision on him, especially as Mountbatten was interested in acting as an intermediary in arriving at a negotiated settlement with him. Time, Patel felt, was on India's side, especially as the Nizam made a secret commitment not to join Pakistan and the British government refused to give Hyderabad the status of a Dominion. But Patel made it clear that India would not tolerate 'an isolated spot which would destroy the very Union which we have built up with our blood and toil'.[12]

In November 1947, the Government of India signed a stand–still agreement with the Nizam, hoping that while the negotiations proceeded, the latter would introduce representative government in the state, making the task of merger easier. But the Nizam had other plans. He engaged the services of the leading British lawyer Sir Walter Monckton, a friend of Mountbatten, to negotiate with the Government of India on his behalf. The Nizam hoped to prolong negotiations and in the meanwhile build up his military strength and force India to accept his sovereignty; or alternatively he might succeed in acceding to Pakistan, especially in view of the tension between India and Pakistan over Kashmir.

Meanwhile, three other political developments took place within the state. There was rapid growth, with official help, of the militant Muslim communal organization, Ittihad ul Muslimin and its paramilitary wing, the Razakars. Then, on 7 August 1947 the Hyderabad State Congress launched a powerful satyagraha movement to force democratization on the Nizam. Nearly 20,000 satyagrahis were jailed. As a result of attacks by the Razakars and repression by the state authorities, thousands of people fled the state and took shelter in temporary camps in Indian territory. The state Congress-led movement now took to arms. By then a powerful Communist-led peasant struggle had developed in the Telangana region of the state from the latter half of 1946. The movement, which had waned due to the severity of state repression by the end of 1946, recovered its vigour when peasant *dalams* (squads) organized defence of the people against attacks by the Razakars, attacked big landlords and distributed their lands among the peasants and the landless.

By June 1948, Sardar Patel was getting impatient as the negotiations with the Nizam dragged on. From his sickbed in Dehradun, he wrote to Nehru: 'I feel very strongly that a stage has come when we should tell them quite frankly that nothing short of unqualified acceptance of accession and of introduction of undiluted responsible government would be acceptable to us.'[13] Still, despite the provocations by the Nizam and the Razakars, the Government of India held its hand for several months. But the Nizam continued to drag his feet and import more and more arms; also the depredations of the Razakars were assuming dangerous proportions. Finally, on 13 September 1948, the Indian army moved into Hyderabad. The Nizam surrendered after three days and acceded to the Indian Union in November. The Government of India decided to be generous and not punish the Nizam. He was retained as formal ruler of the state or its Rajpramukh, was given a privy purse of Rs 5 million, and permitted to keep most of his immense wealth.

With the accession of Hyderabad, the merger of princely states with the Indian Union was completed, and the Government of India's writ ran all over the land. The Hyderabad episode marked another triumph of Indian secularism. Not only had a large number of Muslims in Hyderabad joined the anti-Nizam struggle, Muslims in the rest of the country had also supported the government's policy and action to the dismay of the leaders of Pakistan and the Nizam. As Patel joyfully wrote to Suhrawardy on 28 September, 'On the question of Hyderabad, the Indian Union Muslims have come out in the open on our side and that has certainly created a good impression in the country.'[14]

The second and the more difficult stage of the full integration of the princely states into the new Indian nation began in December 1947. Once again Sardar Patel moved with speed, completing the process within one year. Smaller states were either merged with the neighbouring states or merged together to 'form centrally administered areas'. A large number were consolidated into five new unions, forming Madhya Bharat, Rajasthan, Patiala and East Punjab States Union (PEPSU), Saurashtra and Travancore-Cochin; Mysore, Hyderabad and Jammu and Kashmir retained their original form as separate states of the Union.

In return for their surrender of all power and authority, the rulers of major states were given privy purses in perpetuity, free of all taxes. The privy purses amounted to Rs 4.66 crore in 1949 *and were later guaranteed by the constitution. The rulers were* allowed succession to the gaddi and retained certain privileges such as keeping their titles, flying their personal flags and gun salutes on ceremonial occasions.

There was some criticism of these concessions to the princes at the time as well as later. But keeping in view the difficult times just after independence and Partition, those were perhaps a small price to pay for the extinction of the princes' power and the early and easy territorial and political integration of the states with the rest of the country. Undoubtedly, the integration of the states compensated for the loss of the territories constituting Pakistan in terms of area as well as population. It certainly partially healed 'the wounds of partition'.

Two other trouble spots remained on the Indian body politic. These were the French- and Portuguese-owned settlements dotting India's east and west coasts, with Pondicherry and Goa forming their hub. The people of these settlements were eager to join their newly liberated mother-country. The French authorities were more reasonable and after prolonged negotiations handed over Pondicherry and other French possessions to India in 1954. But the Portuguese were determined to stay on, especially as Portugal's NATO allies, Britain and the US, were willing to support this defiant attitude. The Government of India, being committed to a policy of settling disputes between nations by peaceful means, was not willing to take military steps to liberate Goa and other Portuguese colonies. The people of Goa took matters in their hands and started a movement seeking freedom from the Portuguese, but it was brutally suppressed as were the efforts of non-violent satyagrahis from India to march into Goa. In the end, after waiting patiently for international opinion to put pressure on Portugal, Nehru ordered Indian troops to march into Goa on the night of 17 December 1961. The Governor-General of Goa immediately surrendered without a fight and the territorial and political integration of India was completed, even though it had taken over fourteen years to do so.

The Communal Holocaust

Partition and the violence which accompanied it led to nearly six million refugees pouring into India having lost their all.

India was in the midst of a communal holocaust. There was senseless communal slaughter and a fratricidal war of unprecedented proportions. Unspeakable atrocities were perpetrated on the minorities in both India and Pakistan. In the span of a few months, nearly 500,000 people were killed and property worth thousands of millions of rupees was looted and destroyed. Communal violence threatened the very fabric of society. Even in Delhi, under the very nose of the central government, the looting and killing of Muslims lasted several days.

At the very outset the people and the government faced the gravest of crises. The great danger was that the atmosphere and the mentality generated by Partition and the riots might persist and strengthen communal tendencies in Indian politics. But Indian nationalism was able to withstand the test. Despite the fierce pressure of communal sentiment, which affected even some of the important Congress leaders, both at the Centre and in the states, it is to the credit of the national leadership and the people that they managed to maintain India's secular polity. This was no easy task and Nehru, particularly had to use the full force of his personality, including threats of resignation, to make this possible.

The situation was brought under control within a few months through decisive political and administrative measures. For example, during August–September, the back of communal violence in Delhi was broken by bringing the army on the streets and ordering the police to shoot at communal mobs indulging in looting and killing. In fact, in spite of many errors and weaknesses, the Government of India's record, and in particular Nehru's personal record, in dealing with the post-Partition riots was exemplary. The government also succeeded in protecting the Muslim minority in the country, so that in the end 45 million Muslims chose to remain in India.

Communalism was thereby contained and weakened but not eliminated, for conditions were still favourable for its growth. For communalism to be eclipsed a consistent struggle against it would be needed for a prolonged period. More than anyone else, Nehru was aware of this. And so he never tired of stressing that communalism was a fundamental issue of India politics and that it posed the main threat to India's integrity. 'If allowed free play,' he wrote in 1951, 'communalism would break up India.'[15] Portraying communalism as 'the Indian version of fascism', he said in October 1947: 'The wave of fascism which is gripping India now is the direct outcome of hatred for the non-Muslims which the Muslim League preached among its followers for years. The League accepted the ideology of fascism from the Nazis of Germany . . . The ideas and methods of fascist organization are now gaining popularity among the Hindus also and the demand for the establishment of a Hindu State is its clear manifestation.'[16]

Nehru carried on a massive campaign against communalism to instil a sense of security in the minorities, through public speeches, radio broadcasts, speeches in parliament, private letters and epistles to chief ministers. He repeatedly declared: 'No State can be civilised except a secular State.'[17] On Gandhiji's birthday in 1951, he told a Delhi audience: 'If any person raises his hand to strike down another on the ground of religion, I shall fight him till the last breath of my life, both as the head of the government and from outside.'[18] Democratic though he was, he even advocated a ban on political organizations based on religion and got the constitution amended to enable the government to impose 'reasonable restrictions' on the right to free speech and expression in order to curb communal speeches and writings. In his struggle against communalism, Nehru got the full cooperation of his colleagues like Sardar Patel and C. Rajagopalachari. Patel, for example, declared at the Jaipur session of the Congress in December 1948 that the Congress and the government were determined 'to make India a truly secular state'. In February 1949 he described the talk of 'Hindu Raj' as 'that mad idea'.[19] And he told his audience in 1950: 'Ours is a secular state . . . Here every Muslim should feel that he is an Indian citizen and has equal rights as an Indian citizen. If we cannot make him feel like this, we shall not be worthy of our heritage and of our country.'[20]

A major setback to the communal forces occurred with Gandhiji's martyrdom. The tragedy of the communal riots preceding and accompanying independence deeply affected Gandhiji. When the entire nation was rejoicing in August 1947, the man who had led the struggle for freedom since 1919, the man who had given the message of non-violence and love and courage to the Indian people, the man who had represented the best in Indian culture and politics, was touring the hate-torn lands of Bengal and Bihar, trying to douse the communal fire and bring comfort to people who were paying through senseless slaughter the price for freedom. In reply to a message of birthday congratulations in 1947, Gandhiji said that he no longer wished to live long and that he would 'invoke the aid of the all-embracing Power to take me away from this "vale of tears" rather than make me a helpless witness of the butchery by man become savage, whether he dares to call himself a Muslim or a Hindu or what not'.[21]

The celebrations of independence had hardly died down when on 30 January 1948, a Hindu communal fanatic, Nathuram Godse, assassinated Gandhiji or the Father of the Nation. The whole nation was shocked and stricken with grief and communalism retreated from the minds of men and women. Expressing the nation's sorrow, Nehru spoke over All India Radio:

> Friends and comrades, the light has gone out of our lives and there is darkness everywhere . . . The light has gone out, I said, and yet I was wrong. For the light that shone in this country was no ordinary light . . . that light represented something more than the immediate present; it represented the living, the eternal truths, reminding us of the right path, drawing us from error, taking this ancient country to freedom.[22]

Realizing that Rashtriya Swayamsevak Sangh's (RSS) adherence to the ideology of communalism and violence and the hatred that it had been spreading against Gandhi and secularism were the real forces behind the assassination—the RSS men had even celebrated it in many places—the government immediately banned the RSS and arrested most of its leaders and functionaries. Nehru, of course, had for some time been characterizing the RSS as a fascist organisation. In December 1947 he stated: 'We have a great deal of evidence to show that the RSS is an organisation which is in the nature of a private army and which is definitely proceeding on the strictest Nazi lines, even following the technique of organisation.'[23]

The government, however, had regard for civil liberties, even in the case of organizations like the RSS. Nehru, for example, had written to Patel on 29 June 1949: 'in existing circumstances the less we have of these bans and detentions, the better.'[24] The ban on the RSS was lifted in July 1949 after it had accepted the conditions laid down by Patel as the Home Minister. These conditions were: The RSS would adopt a written and Published *constitution, restrict itself to cultural activities* and not meddle with politics, renounce violence and secrecy, profess loyalty to India's flag and constitution and organize itself along democratic lines.

Rehabilitation of Refugees

The government had to stretch itself to the maximum to give relief to and resettle and rehabilitate the nearly six million refugees from Pakistan who had lost their all there and whose world had been turned upside down. The task took some time but it was accomplished. By 1951, the problem of the rehabilitation of the refugees from West Pakistan had been fully tackled.

The task of rehabilitating and resettling refugees from East Bengal was made more difficult by the fact that the exodus of Hindus from East Bengal continued for years. While nearly all the Hindus and Sikhs from West Pakistan had migrated in one go in 1947, a large number of Hindus in East Bengal had stayed on there in the initial years of 1947 and 1948. But as communal riots broke out periodically in East Bengal, there was a steady stream of refugees from there year after year till 1971. Providing them with work and shelter and psychological assurance, therefore became a continuous and hence a difficult task. Unlike in Bengal, most of the refugees from west Punjab could occupy the large lands and property left by the Muslim migrants to Pakistan from Punjab, Uttar Pradesh and Rajasthan and could therefore be resettled on land. This was not the case in West Bengal. Also because of linguistic affinity, it was easier for Punjabi and Sindhi refugees to settle in today's Himachal Pradesh and Haryana and western U.P., Rajasthan and Delhi. The resettlement of the refugees from East Bengal could take place only in Bengal and to a lesser extent in Assam and Tripura. As a result 'a very large number of people who had been engaged in agricultural occupations before their displacement were forced to seek survival in semi-urban and urban contexts as the underclass', and contributed to 'the process of immiserisation' of West Bengal.[25]

Relations with Pakistan

More intractable was the problem of dealing with Pakistan. Despite the Kashmir issue, Nehru and the Government of India adopted towards Pakistan a policy of non-rancour and fair dealing and of promoting conciliation and reducing mutual tensions. In January 1948, the Government of India, following a fast by Gandhiji, paid Pakistan Rs 550 million as part of the assets of Partition, even when it feared that the money might be used to finance military action in Kashmir. The governments of the two countries differed on issues raised by evacuee property, left behind by those who migrated from the two countries, but every effort was made to resolve them through negotiations.

Along with the Kashmir issue, an important source of constant tension between the two countries was the strong sense of insecurity among Hindus in East Bengal, fuelled primarily by the communal character of Pakistan's political system. This led to the steady migration of the persecuted Hindus from East Bengal to West Bengal and retaliatory attacks on Muslims in West Bengal, leading to their migration. Many urged the Government of India to intervene in East Bengal militarily to protect the minority there. But, though very concerned about the fate of Hindus in East Bengal and the rise of communal sentiment in India, Nehru and the Government of India refused to get provoked into retaliatory action. Regarding it as a human problem, the government tried to solve it through persuasion and pressure, even while taking strong action against attacks on Muslims in West Bengal. Nehru urged Pakistan to put an end to communal attacks on Hindus and to provide them with security so that they stayed on in East Bengal. He repeatedly stressed the duty of each country to protect its minorities. He even thought of resigning from office and touring East Bengal as a private person to repeat Gandhiji's approach in Noakhali.

On 8 April 1950, the prime ministers of India and Pakistan signed an agreement known as the Nehru–Liaqat Pact to resolve the issue of protection of the minorities. The pact met with the strong disapproval of the Hindu communalists and the two ministers from Bengal, Syama Prasad Mookerjee and K.C. Neogi, resigned from the cabinet in protest. It was plain sailing for the pact elsewhere in the country, given Sardar Patel's support for it. The migration of Hindus from East Bengal, however, continued despite the pact.

Notwithstanding continuous differences and acrimony, the two governments were also able to sign several agreements on trade and travel between the two countries. One of the most ticklish problems faced by the two countries was that of the distribution of canal water in Punjab. Showing a degree of generosity, the Government of India agreed to supply an undiminished quantity of water to Pakistan pending a long-term engineering solution to the problem based on mutual discussion under the World Bank's auspices.

In general, the Government of India followed the policy of trying to improve relations with Pakistan and, above all, to prevent the emergence of a climate of hostility and hatred. Nehru, in particular, repeatedly assured the people of Pakistan that India did not think of Pakistan as an enemy. One of the reasons for this policy was the effort to preserve and strengthen the secular atmosphere within India, which was being endangered by the Hindu communalists. And, undoubtedly, it did serve that purpose in the long run, even though it failed to mollify Pakistan or convince it of India's good intentions.

Nehru was voicing his own, his government's and other secular Indians' opinion when in 1950 he expressed the sentiment underlying his approach towards Pakistan:

> Ultimately we cannot go against the currents of history. I am so sure of the desire of our people that I have arrived at this conclusion. Though we may have been partitioned and we may have been divorced from each other, our own historical, cultural and other contacts, geographic, economic and every other, are so fundamentally great, despite everything that

happened, and despite all that passion and prejudice, and in spite of even gross inhumanity and killing, that ultimately the basic principles will survive. These are the things that keep us together unless, of course, India and Pakistan are terribly backward countries culturally.[26]

Nehru and the Communists

In the early post-independence period, the government was faced with another challenge; this time from the left. As we shall see in Chapter 15, the Communist Party of India (CPI) proclaimed the beginning of a general revolution in India in February 1948, declaring the Nehru government of being an agent of imperialist and semi-feudal forces. It initiated militant mass movements in various areas, the most prominent being the attempt to organize a railway strike all over the country on 9 March 1949. It also continued the armed struggle in the Telangana area of the Hyderabad state begun earlier against the Nizam. This effort at revolution continued till the middle of 1951.

Nehru was appalled, but though he was highly critical of the policy and activities of the CPI, he resisted banning it till he felt that there was enough proof of its violent activities. Even then he permitted the banning of the CPI only in West Bengal and Madras where it was most active. Being in agreement with the basic socio-economic objectives of the Communists, he believed that the best way to combat their politics and violent activities was to remove the discontent of the people through economic and other reformist measures. Even so, as soon as the CPI gave up its programme of waging armed struggle, including in Telangana, and declared its intention to join the parliamentary democratic process, Nehru saw to it that the CPI was legalized everywhere and its leaders and cadres released. It was also allowed to participate in the general elections of 1951–52.

Throughout, Nehru differentiated between the Communists and the communalists. In 1964, he said to R.K. Karanjia:[27]

Now between the parties of the Right and the Left, as you differentiate them, I would always prefer a party with some ideology built round serious social and economic thinking. You mentioned the communists. The communists, with all their faults, function in terms of serious economic solutions. What we repudiate is all the dogma and violence of their approach. If they can divest themselves of this obsession and accept the discipline of our parliamentary democracy in good faith, there is not much difference between their goal of socialism and ours. The other parties you mention, like the Jan Sangh and Swatantra, seem to be organized around plainly fascist and feudal concepts without any social or economic basis. As such, they are dangerous to the country and our values of democracy and socialism.

Consolidation of India as a Nation (I)

A major problem, perhaps the most serious one, that India has faced since 1947 has been of national unity or consolidation of the nation. The problem is also sometimes referred to as national integration or the integration of Indian people as a political community.

Unity in Diversity

The Indian nation is the product of a historical process and has been therefore in the making for very long, at least some five centuries. The roots of India's nationhood lie deep in its history and also in its experience of the struggle for independence. Pre-colonial India had already acquired some elements of common existence and common consciousness. Despite its immense cultural diversity, certain strands of a common cultural heritage had developed over the centuries, knitting its people together and giving them a sense of oneness, even while inculcating tolerance of diversity and dissent. As the poet Rabindranath Tagore put it, the unity of India is the 'unity of spirit'. Elements of political, administrative and economic unity had developed especially under the Mughals. The politics of the rulers and their territorial ambitions often cut across regions and were, at their most ambitious, subcontinental in their reach. Also, despite backward means of transport and communication, a great deal of India-wide trade, specialization of production and credit networks developed, especially during the late medieval period. A feeling of Indianness, however vague, had come into being, as testified by the currency of the concepts of Bharat Varsha and Hindustan. As pointed out in an earlier chapter, the colonialization of the Indian economy, society and polity further strengthened the process of India's unification. From the middle of the nineteenth century, Indians were more and more sharing common economic and political interests and social and cultural development even though they continued to be differentiated by language and ethnicity.

The national movement, as seen in Chapter 3, played a pivotal role in welding Indians together politically and emotionally into a nation and integrating them into 'a common framework of political identity and loyalty'. The depth, duration and deep social penetration of this movement carried the feeling of unity and nationhood to the mass of the people.

The leaders of the national movement realized that the making of the nation was a prolonged and continuous process, and one which was open to continuous challenges and interruption, disruption and even reversal. One such disruption had already occurred in 1947. As founders of the republic, these leaders were therefore fully aware that after independence too the process of unifying India and national integration was to be carefully sustained, promoted and nurtured through ideological and political endeavours. In fact, the leaders of India after 1947 saw the preservation and consolidation of India's unity as their biggest challenge. As Nehru put it in 1952, 'the most important factor, the overriding factor, is the unity of India'.[1] To quote him again: 'Personally, I feel,' he said in 1957, 'that the biggest task of all is not only the economic development of India as a whole, but even more so the psychological and emotional integration of the people of India.'[2]

India's complex diversity is legendary. It consists of a large number of linguistic, cultural and geographic-economic zones. It has followers of different religions, Hindus, Muslims, Christians. Sikhs, Parsis, Buddhists and Jews, apart from tribals with myriad belief systems. In 1950, the Indian constitution recognized fourteen major languages, besides hundreds others, many of which were spoken by just a million persons. The 1961 Census listed 1,549 languages as mother tongues. The tribals, constituting over 6 per cent of the population, are dispersed all over India.

Given this diversity, the leaders of the national movement realized that the Indian nation had to be built on a very broad foundation.

India could be unified and its segmentation overcome only by accepting this immense diversity and not counterposing it to the process of nation-in-the-making. The emergence of a strong national identity and the preservation of India's rich diversity were seen as simultaneous processes. Regional cultural identities would develop not in conflict with but as part of the all-India identity. This entire outlook was epitomized in Nehru's approach who wrote in early 1951: 'We have to remember always that India is a country with a variety of cultures, habits, customs and ways of living . . . It is very necessary, I think, for all of us to remember that this wonderful country of ours has infinite variety and there is absolutely no reason why we should try to regiment it after a single pattern. Indeed that is ultimately impossible.'[3] At the same time, the hope as well as the answer were there: 'But India is far greater, far richer and more varied than any part of it. We have to develop an outlook which embraces all this variety and considers it our very own.'[4] Thus, the differences in language, culture, religion and ethnicity were to be seen not as obstacles to be overcome, not as antithetical to national consolidation, but as positive features that were sources of strength to emerging nationhood. Consequently, the consolidation of independent India was to occur around the concept of 'unity in diversity'.

It was, however, recognized that the diversity of India could also be a source of weakness. Diversity could be used for divisive purposes and transformed into disruptive tendencies, such as communalism, casteism and linguistic or regional exclusiveness. The problem of integrating diverse loyalties was therefore quite real, especially as rapid social changes led to increase in the scale and number of social conflicts. The issues of jobs, educational opportunities, access to political power and share in the larger economic cake could and did fuel rivalries and conflicts based on religion, region, caste and language. Special efforts were necessary, different from those in other parts of the world, to carefully promote national unity. The broad strategy for national consolidation after 1947 involved territorial integration, mobilization of political and institutional resources, economic development and adoption of policies which would promote social justice, remove glaring inequalities and provide equal opportunities.

The leadership evolved a political institutional structure conducive to national consolidation. At the heart of this structure lay the inauguration of a democratic and civil libertarian polity. The argument was rejected that democracy and national integration were not compatible in the case of newly liberated and developing countries, and that an authoritarian political structure was needed to hold together such a diverse nation as India. On the contrary, precisely because India was so diverse it needed democracy rather than force or coercion to bind it. Nehru repeatedly warned his countrymen that in India 'any reversal of democratic methods might lead to disruption and violence'. India, he underlined, could only be held together by a democratic structure with full freedom as also opportunity for the diverse socio-economic, cultural and political voices to express themselves.

The constitutional structure established in 1950 encompassed *the demands of diversity as well as the requirements of unity*. It provided for a federal structure with a strong Centre but also a great deal of autonomy for the states. The makers of the constitution kept in view the difference between decentralization and disintegration and between unity and integration and centralization. The constitutional structure was not only conducive to national integration but provided the basic framework within which the struggle against divisive forces could be carried on. The political leadership was to use elections both to promote national consolidation and to legitimize its policies of integration. The parliament was the institution where basic and ultimate power resided and which acted as the open arena where different political trends could express themselves as also contend for power. Invariably, the issues and problems, as also programmes and policies, debated there were all-India in scale. As Asoka Mehta put it, the parliament acted as the great unifier of the nation.

Also, political parties acted as a great integrating force. All the major post-1947 political parties—Socialist Party, Communist Party of India, Jan Sangh and later the Swatantra Party—were all-India in character and in their organization and ideology; they stood for the unity of the country. They strove for national goals and mobilized people on an all-India basis and on all-India issues even when their capacity to do so was limited to particular regions. All this was perhaps even more true of Congress in the post-independence years. It had a strong and large organization covering almost all parts of the country. It was able to maintain internal party coherence and unity, and was also willing to play the role of a cementing force in society and polity. It is important to remember that immediately after independence, with the rapid marginalization of the communal parties, the major divide in Indian politics and among the intelligentsia was on political and ideological grounds rather than on the basis of caste, religion or language. It is also significant that the major vocal social groups and classes—the bourgeoisie, the working class and the intelligentsia—were all-India in outlook and stood for national unity. Indian nationalism, both before and after independence, had little difficulty in coming to terms with the emerging class consciousness as also class organizations such as trade unions and Kisan Sabhas on one side and the Federation of Indian Chambers of Commerce and Industry (FICCI) on the other. No section of Indian society or polity saw loyalty to a class or class organization as threatening national cohesion.

The role of the leadership and its manner of functioning in nation-making and national consolidation is quite important. The leaders of the national movement thought in national terms and were fully committed to national unity and consolidation, and this commitment was widely accepted. Further, the prominent leaders of independent India—Jawaharlal Nehru, Sardar Patel, Maulana Azad, Rajendra Prasad—were not associated with any one region, language, religion, or caste. This was also true of the prominent Opposition leaders such as Jayaprakash Narayan, J.B. Kripalani, Rammanohar Lohia, Syama Prasad Mookerjee, B.T. Ranadive and Ajoy Ghosh.

A major asset of the Congress leadership was that it was well versed in accommodative politics. As brought out in Chapter 3, it had been able to keep united diverse political and ideological trends during the anti-imperialist struggle. Following this, after 1947, despite near-total political dominance, it was willing to conciliate and accommodate, to listen to and appease the Opposition parties and dissenting groups. In particular, it was quite sensitive to popular rumblings on linguistic or other cultural issues. Reacting strongly to violence, it responded, often sympathetically, to demands pressed through non-violent means and mass backing. Nehru, for example, was willing to persuade and accommodate the Communists once they gave up recourse to violence. Other political parties too, including the CPI, came to share after some time the same means, methods and values for resolving social conflicts, differing only in rhetoric.

The Indian army and administrative services were also a force for forging national unity. India developed after 1947 a national administrative service with recruitment to its top echelons, the IAS, the IPS, and other central services, taking place on the basis of individual merit, irrespective of caste or religion, from all regions and linguistic areas. These services were all-India in character and sentiment and all officers selected were given common training and owed allegiance to the central government, which also had the ultimate power to promote or discipline them. The central services, as also the state services, were basically non-political and accepted the authority of the party which was voted to power by the people. Likewise, the army was a national force whose officers and ranks were recruited from all parts of the country.

The Indian economy, national market, and transport and communication networks were further unified after 1947. Industrial development was promoted on a national scale and dams, steel mills, fertilizer plants, cement factories, and heavy machinery and electric plants soon became symbols of national endeavour as well as national unity.

Jawaharlal Nehru and other leaders saw economic development as essential for national consolidation. Soon after independence, the government set up a Planning Commission and took active measures for planned economic development. Though the government and the Planning Commission did not succeed in putting an end to regional economic disparities, they did avoid inequality in the distribution of economic resources among states. In general, the central government followed accommodative policies towards the states. Consequently, though there was constant grumbling and plenty of grievances there was no serious discontent in the states and regions on grounds of discrimination by the central government and therefore no separatist feelings on that account.

National integration also required policies which would promote social justice and greater social and economic equality. The national movement had also linked the process of nation-in-the-making with socio-economic changes in the interests of the oppressed and the deprived. Consolidation of the nation after independence had to be judged in terms of how it affected their lives. The entire

Indian people and not merely the middle and upper classes had to benefit from the coming of independence and processes of economic development and political democracy.

The constitution laid the basis for reduction of social disparity by putting an end to any discrimination on grounds of religion, caste or sex. Redeeming the national movement's major pledge to the depressed sections of society, it provided reservations for Scheduled Castes and Scheduled Tribes in educational institutions, employment and in the legislatures. Soon after 1947, a number of social reforms and welfare laws were passed. Landlordism was abolished and there was some redistribution of land. A law was passed making untouchability an offence. Unfortunately, no struggle against the hierarchical caste system followed, so that, on the one hand caste discrimination and oppression continued, on the other, casteism or the use of caste solidarity for electoral and other political purposes began to grow. The momentum of social reform was lost by the early 1950s. Removal of social oppression and social discrimination and exploitation, based on caste, religion, language or ethnicity, and of gross economic inequality has remained the weakest part of the agenda for national integration.

From the start, the founding fathers stood for secularism as the basis for the nation. Undaunted by Partition and the accompanying riots, they remained loyal to the secular vision of the national movement. They also dealt firmly with communal violence and on the whole succeeded in protecting the religious minorities.

Independent India's foreign policy served as another unifying force. The policy of non-alignment and anti-colonialism and Nehru's growing stature as a world figure contributed to a sense of national pride in India among all sections of people all over the country and irrespective of their political alignment.

At the moment of freedom, the need for unity was urgent but also present was the problem of integrating diverse loyalties. The strategies and approaches promoting integration required time but the people were in a hurry and there was plenty of scope for conflicts. Many observers, in fact, predicted growing disunity and even break-up of the country. In the next section and the following chapters we will study some of the areas of diversity which produced conflicts and the manner in which these differences were sought to be resolved.

The Language Problem

The language problem was the most divisive issue in the first twenty years of independent India, and it created the apprehension among many that the political and cultural unity of the country was in danger. People love their language; it is an integral part of culture.

Consequently, linguistic identity has been a strong force in all societies. This is even more true of a multilingual society like India's. Linguistic diversity would inevitably give birth to strong political currents around issues linked to language, such as educational and economic development, job and other economic opportunities and access to political power.

The Indian constitution recognizes twenty-two major languages, including English and Sanskrit. In addition, there are a myriad languages spoken by the tribals and others, with or without their own scripts. The model that independent India has adopted is not that of assimilation into, or suppression of, the many languages by one of them. This is in any case impossible in a democratic polity. The feasible option is to accept and live with this 'multiplicity' in a manner that conflict situations do not emerge or persist for long.

The problem posed to national consolidation by linguistic diversity has taken two major forms. These are discussed here in two separate sections: (i) the dispute over official language of the union and (ii) the linguistic reorganization of the states.

The Official Language

The controversy on the language issue became most virulent when it took the form of opposition to Hindi and tended to create conflict between Hindi-speaking and non-Hindi-speaking regions of the country. The dispute was not over the question of a national language, that is one language which all Indians would adopt after some time, since the view that one national language was essential to an Indian national identity had already been rejected overwhelmingly by the secular majority of the national leadership. India was a multilingual country and it had to remain so. The Indian national movement had carried on its ideological and political work through the different Indian regional languages. Its demand then was for the replacement of English by the mother tongue as the medium for higher education, administration and courts in each linguistic area. Jawaharlal Nehru had clearly put across this view in 1937: 'Our great provincial languages . . . are ancient languages with a rich inheritance, each spoken by many millions of persons, each tied up inextricably with the life and culture and ideas of the masses as well as of the upper classes. It is axiomatic that the masses can only grow educationally and culturally through the medium of their own language. Therefore, it is inevitable that we lay stress on the provincial languages and carry on most of our work through them . . . Our system of education and public work must therefore be based on the provincial languages.'[5]

The issue of a national language was resolved when the constitution-makers virtually accepted all the major languages as 'languages of India' or India's national languages. But the matter could not end there, for the country's official work could not be carried on in so many languages. There had to be one common language in which the central government would carry on its work and maintain contact with the state governments. The question arose what would be this language of all-India communication? Or what would be India's official and link language? Only two candidates were available for the purpose: English and Hindi. The Constituent Assembly heatedly debated which one should be selected.

But, in fact, the choice had already been made in the pre-independence period by the leadership of the national movement, which was convinced that English would not continue to be the all-India medium of communication in free India. For example, even while appreciating the value of English as a world language, through which Indians could access world science and culture and modern Western ideas, Gandhiji was convinced that the genius of a people could not unfold nor could their culture flower in a foreign language. In fact, Gandhiji, during the 1920s emphasized that English is 'a language of international commerce, it is the language of diplomacy, it contains many a rich literary treasure, and it gives us an introduction to Western thought and culture'. But he argued English occupied in India 'an unnatural place due to our unequal relations with Englishmen'.[6] English 'has sapped the energy of the nation . . . it has estranged them from the masses . . . The sooner therefore educated India shakes itself free from the hypnotic spell of the foreign medium, the better it would be for them and the people.'[7] And he wrote in 1946: 'I love the English tongue in its own place, but I am its inveterate opponent if it usurps a place which does not belong to it. English is today admittedly the world language. I would therefore accord it a place as a second, optional language.'[8] Nehru echoed these sentiments in his 1937 article on 'The Question of Language' and also during the Constituent Assembly debates.

Hindi or Hindustani, the other candidate for the status of the official or link language, had already played this role during the nationalist struggle, especially during the phase of mass mobilization. Hindi had been accepted by leaders from non-Hindi-speaking regions because it was considered to be the most widely spoken and understood language in the country. Lokamanya Tilak, Gandhiji, C. Rajagopalachari, Subhas Bose and Sardar Patel were some of Hindi's enthusiastic supporters. In its sessions and political work, the Congress had substituted Hindi and the provincial languages in place of English. In 1925, Congress amended its constitution to read: 'The proceedings of the Congress shall be conducted as far as possible in Hindustani. The English language or any provincial language may be used if the speaker is unable to speak Hindustani or whenever necessary. The proceedings of the Provincial Congress Committee shall ordinarily be conducted in the language of the Province concerned. Hindustani may also be used.'[9] Reflecting a national consensus, the Nehru Report had laid down in 1928 that Hindustani which might be written in the Devanagari or Urdu script would be the common language of India, but the use of English would be continued for some time. It is interesting that ultimately the constitution of free India was to adopt this stand, except for replacing Hindustani by Hindi. The real debate in the Constituent Assembly occurred over two questions: Would Hindi or Hindustani replace English? And what would be the time-frame for such a replacement to happen?

Sharp differences marked the initial debates as the problem of the official language was highly politicized from the beginning. The question of Hindi or Hindustani was soon resolved, though with a great deal of acrimony. Gandhiji and Nehru both supported Hindustani, written in the Devanagari or Urdu script. Though many supporters of Hindi disagreed, they had tended to accept the Gandhi–Nehru viewpoint. But once Partition was announced, these champions of Hindi were emboldened, especially as the protagonists of Pakistan had claimed Urdu as the language of Muslims and of Pakistan. The votaries of Hindi now branded Urdu 'as a symbol of secession'. They demanded that Hindi in the Devanagari script be made the national language. Their demand split the Congress party down the middle. In the end the Congress Legislative Party decided for Hindi against Hindustani by 78 to 77 votes, even though Nehru and Azad fought for Hindustani. The Hindi bloc was also forced to compromise: it accepted that Hindi would be the official and not the national language.

The issue of the time-frame for a shift from English to Hindi produced a divide between Hindi and non-Hindi areas. The spokespersons of Hindi areas were for the immediate switchover to Hindi, while those from non-Hindi areas advocated retention of English for a long if not indefinite period. In fact, they wanted the status quo to continue till a future parliament decided to shift to Hindi as the official language. Nehru was for making Hindi the official language, but he was also in favour of English continuing as an additional official language, making the transition to Hindi gradual, and actively encouraging the knowledge of English because of its usefulness in the contemporary world.

The case for Hindi basically rested on the fact that it was the language of the largest number, though not of the majority, of the people of India; it was also understood at least in the urban areas of most of northern India from Bengal to Punjab and in Maharashtra and Gujarat. The critics of Hindi talked about it being less developed than other languages as a literary language and as a language of science and politics. But their main fear was that Hindi's adoption as the official language would place non-Hindi areas, especially South India, at a disadvantage in the educational and economic spheres, and particularly in competition for appointments in government and the public sector. Such opponents tended to argue that imposition of Hindi on non-Hindi areas would lead to their economic, political, social and cultural domination by Hindi areas.

The constitution-makers were aware that as the leaders of a multilingual country they could not ignore, or even give the impression of ignoring, the interests of any one linguistic area. A compromise was arrived at, though this led to the language provisions of the constitution becoming 'complicated, ambiguous and confusing in some respects'. The constitution provided that Hindi in Devanagari script with international numerals would be India's official language. English was to continue for use in all official purposes till 1965, when it would be replaced by Hindi. Hindi was to be introduced in a phased manner. After 1965 it would become the sole official language. However, parliament would have the power to provide for the use of English for specified purposes even after 1965. The constitution laid upon the government the duty to promote the spread and development of Hindi and provided for the appointment of a commission and a Joint Parliamentary Committee to review the progress in this respect. The state legislatures were to decide the matter of official language at the state level, though the official language of the Union would serve as the language of communication between the states and the Centre and between one state and another.

Implementation of the language provisions of the constitution proved to be a formidable task even though the Congress party was in power all over the country. The issue remained a subject of intense controversy, and became increasingly acrimonious with the passage of time, though for many years nobody challenged the provision that Hindi would eventually become the sole official language.

The constitution-makers had hoped that by 1965 the Hindi protagonists would overcome the weaknesses of Hindi, win the confidence of non-Hindi areas, and hold their hand for a longer period till such time they had done so. It was also hoped that with the rapid growth of education Hindi too would spread and resistance to Hindi would gradually weaken and even disappear. But, unfortunately, the spread of education was too slow to make an impact in this respect.

Moreover, the chances of Hindi's success as an official language were spoilt by the proponents of Hindi themselves. Instead of taking up a gradual, slow and moderate approach to gain acceptance of Hindi by non-Hindi areas and to rely on persuasion, the more fanatical among them preferred imposition of Hindi through government action. Their zeal and enthusiasm tended to provoke a counter-movement. As Nehru told parliament in 1959, it was their overenthusiasm which came in the way of the spread and acceptance of Hindi for 'the way they approach this subject often irritates others, as it irritates me'.[10]

Hindi suffered from the lack of social science and scientific writing. In the 1950s, for example, there were hardly any academic journals in Hindi outside the literary field. Instead of developing Hindi as a means of communication in higher education, journalism, and so on, the Hindi leaders were more interested in making it the sole official language.

A major weakness of the Hindi protagonists was that, instead of developing a simple standard language which would get wide acceptance or at least popularize the colloquial Hindi as spoken and written in Hindi areas as also in many other parts of India, they tried to Sanskritize the language, replacing commonly understood words with newly manufactured, unwieldy and little understood ones in the name of the 'purity' of language, free of alien influences. This made it more and more difficult for non-Hindi speakers (or even Hindi speakers) to understand or learn the new version. All India Radio, which could have played an important role in popularizing Hindi, instead took to so Sanskritizing its Hindi news bulletins that many listeners would switch off their radios when the Hindi news was broadcast. Nehru, a Hindi speaker and writer, was to complain in 1958 that he was unable to understand the language in which his own Hindi speeches were being broadcast. But the purifiers of Hindi did not relent and resisted all attempts to simplify the Hindi of news broadcasts. This led many uncommitted persons to join the ranks of the opponents of Hindi.

Nehru and the majority of Indian leaders, however, remained committed to the transition to Hindi as the official language. They believed that, though the study of English was to be encouraged, English could not continue forever as India's official language. In the interests of national unity as also economic and political development they also realized that full transition to Hindi should not be time-bound and should await a politically more auspicious time when the willing consent of the non-Hindi areas could be obtained. The non-Hindi leaders also became less and less open to persuasion and their opposition to Hindi increased with time. One result of this alienation of non-Hindi-language groups was that they too were not open to rational arguments in favour of Hindi. Instead they veered towards an indefinite continuance of English.

Sharp differences on the official language issue surfaced during 1956–60, once again revealing the presence of disruptive tendencies. In 1956, the Report of the Official Language Commission, set up in 1955 in terms of a constitutional provision, recommended that Hindi should start progressively replacing English in various functions of the central government with effective change taking place in 1965. Its two members from West Bengal and Tamil Nadu, Professor Suniti Kumar Chatterjee and P. Subbaroyan, however, dissented, accusing the members of the Commission of suffering from a pro-Hindi bias, and asked for the continuation of English. Ironically, Professor Chatterjee was in charge of the Hindi Pracharini Sabha in Bengal before independence. The Commission's report was reviewed by a special Joint Parliamentary Committee (JPC). To implement the recommendations of the Committee, the President issued an order in April 1960 stating that after 1965 Hindi would be the principal official language but that English would continue as the associate official language without any restriction being placed on its use. Hindi would also become an alternative medium for the Union Public Service Commission examinations after some time, but for the present it would be introduced in the examinations as a qualifying subject. In accordance with the President's directive, the central government took a series of steps to promote Hindi. These included the setting up of the Central Hindi Directorate, publication of standard works in Hindi or in Hindi translation in various fields, compulsory training of central government employees in Hindi, and translation of major texts of law into Hindi and promotion of their use by the courts.

All these measures aroused suspicion and anxiety in the non-Hindi areas and groups. Nor were the Hindi leaders satisfied. For example, Professor Suniti Kumar Chatterjee, an eminent linguist and a former staunch advocate and promoter of Hindi, stated in his dissenting note to the Report of the Official Language Commission that the outlook of the commission was one of the 'Hindi speakers who are to profit immediately and for a long time to come, if not forever'.[11] Similarly, in March 1958, C. Rajagopalachari, ex-president of the Hindi Pracharini Sabha in the South, declared that 'Hindi is as much foreign to the non-Hindi speaking people as English to the protagonists of Hindi'.[12] On the other hand, two major champions of Hindi, Purshottamdas Tandon and Seth Govind Das, accused the Joint Parliamentary Committee of being pro-English. Many of the Hindi leaders also attacked Nehru and Maulana Abul Kalam Azad, the Minister of Education, for dragging their feet in implementing the constitutional provisions and deliberately delaying the replacement of English. They insisted that the deadline for the changeover to Hindi laid down in the constitution must be rigidly observed. In 1957, Dr Lohia's Samyukta Socialist Party and the Jan Sangh launched a militant movement, which continued for nearly two years, for the immediate replacement of English by Hindi. One of the agitational methods adopted by the followers of Lohia on a large scale was to deface English signboards of shops and in other places.

Fully aware of the danger that the official language issue could pose to Indian polity, the leadership of the Congress took the grievances of the non-Hindi areas seriously and handled the issue with great care and caution. The attempt was to work for a compromise. Nehru, time and again made it clear that an official language could not and would not be imposed on any region of the country and that the pace of transition to Hindi would have to be determined keeping in view the wishes of the non-Hindi people. In this he was supported by the leaders of Praja Socialist Party (PSP) and Communist Party of India (CPI). PSP criticized Hindi extremism and said that it 'might severely strain the unity of a multilingual country like India'.[13]

The highlight of Nehru's approach was a major statement in parliament on 7 August 1959. To allay the fears of the non-Hindi people, he gave a definite assurance: 'I would have English as an alternate language as long as the people require it, and I would leave the decision not to the Hindi-knowing people, but to the non-Hindi-knowing people.' He also told the people of the South that 'if they do not want to learn Hindi, let them not learn Hindi'. He repeated this assurance in parliament on 4 September 1959.[14]

In pursuance of Nehru's assurances, though with delay caused by internal party pressures and the India–China war, an Official Languages Act was passed in 1963. The object of the Act, Nehru declared, was 'to remove a restriction which had been placed by the Constitution on the use of English after a certain date, namely, 1965'.[15] But this purpose was not fully served as the assurances were not clearly articulated in the Act. The Act laid down that 'the English language may . . . continue to be used in addition to Hindi'. The non-Hindi groups criticized the use of the word 'may' in place of the word 'shall'. This made the Act ambiguous in their eyes; they did not regard it as a statutory guarantee. Many of them wanted a cast iron guarantee not because they distrusted Nehru but because they were worried about what would happen after Nehru, especially as the pressure from the Hindi leaders was also growing. The death of Nehru in June 1964 increased their apprehensions which were further fuelled by certain hasty steps taken and circulars issued by various ministries to prepare the ground for the changeover to Hindi in the coming year. For example, instructions were given that the central government's correspondence with the states would be in Hindi, though in the case of non-Hindi states an English translation would be appended.

Lal Bahadur Shastri, Nehru's successor as prime minister, was *unfortunately not sensitive enough to the opinion of non-Hindi* groups. Instead of taking effective steps to counter their fears of Hindi becoming the *sole* official language, he declared that he was considering making Hindi an alternative medium in public service examinations. This meant that while non-Hindi speakers could still compete in the all-India services in English, Hindi speakers would have the advantage of being able to use their mother tongue.

Many non-Hindi leaders in protest changed their line of approach to the problem of the official language. While previously they had wanted a slowing down of the replacement of English, now they started demanding that there should be no deadline fixed for the changeover. Some of the leaders went much further. The Dravida Munnetra Kazhagam (DMK) and C. Rajagopalachari, for example, demanded that the constitution should be amended and English should be made the official language of India.

As 26 January 1965 approached, a fear psychosis gripped the non-Hindi areas, especially Tamil Nadu, creating a strong anti-Hindi movement. On 17 January, the DMK organized the Madras State Anti-Hindi Conference which gave a call for observing 26 January as a day of mourning. Students, concerned for their careers and apprehensive that they would be outstripped by Hindi speakers in the all-India services, were the most active in organizing a widespread agitation and mobilizing public opinion. They raised and popularized the slogan: 'Hindi never, English ever.' They also demanded amendment of the constitution. The students' agitation soon developed into statewide unrest. The Congress leadership, though controlling both the state and the central governments, failed to gauge the depth of the popular feeling and the widespread character of the movement and instead of negotiating with the students, made an effort to repress it. Widespread rioting and violence followed in the early weeks of February leading to large-scale destruction of railways and other Union property. So strong was the anti-Hindi feeling that several Tamil youth, including four students, burned themselves to death in protest against the official language policy. Two Tamil ministers, C. Subramaniam and Alagesan, resigned from the Union cabinet. The agitation continued for about two months, taking a toll of over sixty lives through police firings. The only eminent central leader to show concern for the agitators was Indira Gandhi, then Minister for Information and Broadcasting. At the height of the agitation she flew to Madras, 'rushed to the storm-centre of trouble', showed some sympathy for the agitators and thus became, after Nehru, the first northern leader to win the trust of the aggrieved Tamils as well as of the people of the South in general.

Efforts were made by the Jan Sangh and the Samyukta Socialist Party (SSP) to organize a counter-agitation in the Hindi areas against English, but they did not get much public support.

The agitation forced both the Madras and the Union governments and the Congress party to revise their stand. They now decided to yield to the intense public mood in the South, change their policy and accept the major demands of the agitators. The Congress Working Committee announced a series of steps which were to form the basis for a central enactment embodying concessions and which led to the withdrawal of the Hindi agitation. This enactment was delayed because of the Indo-Pak war of 1965, which silenced all dissension in the country.

With the death of Lal Bahadur Shastri in January 1966, Indira Gandhi became the prime minister. As she had already won the trust of the people of the South, they were convinced that a genuine effort would be made to resolve the long-festering dispute. Other favourable factors were the Jan Sangh's muting of their anti-English fervour and the SSP's acceptance of the basic features of the agreement worked out in 1965.

Despite facing economic problems and the weakening of the Congress's position in parliament in the 1967 elections, Indira Gandhi moved the bill to amend the 1963 Official Language Act on 27 November. The Lok Sabha adopted the bill, on 16 December 1967, by 205 to 41 votes. The Act gave an unambiguous legal fortification to Nehru's assurances of September 1959. It provided that the use of English as an associate language in addition to Hindi for the official work at the Centre and for communication between the Centre and non-Hindi states would continue as long as the non-Hindi states wanted it, giving them full veto powers on the question. A virtually indefinite policy of bilingualism was adopted. The parliament also adopted a policy resolution laying down that the public service examinations were to be conducted in Hindi and English and in all the regional languages with the proviso that the candidates should have additional knowledge of Hindi or English. The states were to adopt a three-language formula according to which in the non-Hindi areas, the mother tongue, Hindi and English or some other national language was to be taught in schools while in the Hindi areas a non-Hindi language, preferably a southern language, was to be taught as a compulsory subject.

The Government of India took another important step on the language question in July 1967. On the basis of the report of the Education Commission in 1966 it declared that Indian languages would ultimately become the medium of education in all subjects at the university level, though the time-frame for the changeover would be decided by each university to suit its convenience.

After many twists and turns, a great deal of debate and several agitations, small and big, and many compromises India had arrived at a widely accepted solution to the very difficult problem of the official and link language for the country. Since 1967, this problem has gradually disappeared from the political scene, demonstrating the capacity of the Indian political system to deal with a contentious problem on a democratic basis, and in a manner that promoted national consolidation. Here was an issue which emotionally divided the people and which could have jeopardized the unity of the country, but to which a widely acceptable solution was found through negotiations and compromise. And it was not only the national leadership provided by the Congress, with some hiccups on the way, which came up to the mark; the Opposition parties too measured up when it came to the crunch. In the end, the DMK, in whose rise to power the language issue played an important role, also helped by cooling down the political temper in Tamil Nadu.

Of course, no political problem is solved for all times to come. Problem-solving in a nation as complex as India is bound to be a continuous process. But it is significant that Hindi has been making rapid progress in non-Hindi areas through education, trade, tourism, films, radio and television. The use of Hindi as an official language has also been growing though English is still dominant. Simultaneously, English, as a second language, has been spreading fast, including in the Hindi-speaking areas. A witness of this is the number of private English-medium schools, however poor in staff and other facilities, which now dot the countryside from Kashmir to Kanyakumari. The standards of spoken and written English have fallen but the English-knowing classes have multiplied manifold. Both English and Hindi are likely to grow as link languages just as regional languages are more and more occupying the official, educational and media space. The proof of the growth of Hindi, English and regional languages lies in the rapid growth of newspapers in all of them. In fact, English is not only likely to survive in India for all times to come, but it remains and is likely to grow as a language of communication between the intelligentsia all over the country, as a library language, and as the second language of the universities. Hindi, on the other hand, has so far failed to perform any of the three roles. Of course, the ideal of making Hindi the link language of the country remains. But the way in which the enthusiastic protagonists of Hindi promoted Hindi's cause, they pushed back the chances of this happening for a long time to come.

Consolidation of India as a Nation(II): The Linguistic Reorganization of the States

The reorganization of the states on the basis of language, a major aspect of national consolidation and integration, came to the fore almost immediately after independence. The boundaries of provinces in pre-1947 India had been drawn in a haphazard manner as the British conquest of India had proceeded for nearly a hundred years. No heed was paid to linguistic or cultural cohesion so that most of the provinces were multilingual and multicultural. The interspersed princely states had added a further element of heterogeneity.

The case for linguistic states as administrative units was very strong. Language is closely related to culture and therefore to the customs of people. Besides, the massive spread of education and growth of mass literacy can only occur through the medium of the mother tongue. Democracy can become real to the common people only when politics and administration are conducted through the language they can understand. But this language, the mother tongue, cannot be the medium of education or administration or judicial activity unless a state is formed on the basis of such a predominant language.

It is for this reason that, with the involvement of the masses in the national movement after 1919, Congress undertook political mobilization in the mother tongue and in 1921 amended its constitution and reorganized its regional branches on a linguistic basis. Since then, the Congress repeatedly committed itself to the redrawing of the provincial boundaries on linguistic lines. Just five days before he was assassinated, Gandhiji, while urging the people to 'discourage all fissiparous tendencies and feel and behave as Indians', also argued that 'the redistribution of provinces on a linguistic basis was necessary if provincial languages were to grow to their full height'.[1] It was therefore more or less universally assumed that free India would base its administrative boundaries on the linguistic principle.

But the national leadership had second thoughts on the subject immediately after independence. There were various reasons for this. Partition had created serious administrative, economic and political dislocation; and independence, coming immediately after the War, was accompanied by serious economic and law and order problems. Also there was the vexed Kashmir problem and a war-like situation vis-à-vis Pakistan. The leadership felt that the most important task for the present was to consolidate national unity; and any effort undertaken immediately to redraw the internal boundaries might dislocate administration and economic development, intensify regional and linguistic rivalries, unleash destructive forces, and damage the unity of the country. Speaking on the linguistic question, Nehru clearly stated on 27 November 1947: 'First things must come first and the first thing is the security and stability of India.'[2] Hence, while still committed to linguistic states, Nehru and other leaders accorded the task of redrawing India's administrative map a low priority. The task, they felt, could wait for some years.

The question of the linguistic reorganization of India was, however, raised quite early in the Constituent Assembly. It appointed in 1948 the Linguistic Provinces Commission, headed by Justice S.K. Dar, to enquire into the desirability of linguistic provinces. The Dar Commission advised against the step at the time for it might threaten national unity and also be administratively inconvenient. Consequently, the Constituent Assembly decided not to incorporate the linguistic principle in the constitution. But public opinion was not satisfied, especially in the South, and the problem remained politically alive. To appease the vocal votaries of linguistic states, the Congress appointed a committee (JVP) in December 1948 consisting of Jawaharlal Nehru, Sardar Patel and Pattabhi Sitaramayya, president of the Congress, to examine the question afresh. This committee advised against the creation of linguistic states for the time being, emphasizing on unity, national security and economic development as the needs of the hour.

Yet, the Congress leadership would not oppose any popular demand. In the JVP report, as well as afterwards, the Congress leadership laid down that where the demand for a linguistic state was insistent and overwhelming and where other language groups involved were agreeable to it, a new state could be created. The JVP report was followed by popular movements for states' reorganization all over the country, which persisted with varying degrees of intensity till 1960. The demand for a separate Andhra state for the Telugu people was an example. The demand had been popular for nearly half a century and had the support of all political parties.

The JVP accepted that a strong case for the formation of Andhra out of the Madras Presidency existed, particularly as the leadership of Tamil Nadu was agreeable to it. But it did not concede the demand immediately, because the two sides could not agree on which state should take Madras city. The Andhra leaders were unwilling to concede Madras even though on linguistic as well as geographic grounds it belonged to Tamil Nadu.

On 19 October 1952, a popular freedom fighter, Patti Sriramalu, undertook a fast unto death over the demand for a separate Andhra and expired after fifty-eight days. His death was followed by three days of rioting, demonstrations, hartals and violence all over Andhra. The government immediately gave in and conceded the demand for a separate state of Andhra, which finally came into existence in October 1953. Simultaneously, Tamil Nadu was created as a Tamil-speaking state.

The success of the Andhra struggle encouraged other linguistic groups to agitate for their own state or for rectification of their boundaries on a linguistic basis. Nehru was not in favour at that time of continuing with the redrawing of India's internal administrative boundaries, but he was too much of a democrat to sternly and consistently oppose the demands. As Nehru's biographer, S. Gopal, has put it: 'He felt that it would be undemocratic to smother this sentiment which, on general grounds, he did not find objectionable. Indeed, a linguistic mosaic might well provide a firmer base for national unity. What concerned him were the timing, the agitation and violence with which linguistic provinces were being demanded and the harsh antagonism between various sections of the Indian people which underlay these demands.'[3]

To meet the demand halfway and to delay matters, Nehru appointed in August 1953 the States Reorganisation Commission (SRC), with Justice Fazl Ali, K.M. Panikkar and Hridaynath Kunzru as members, to examine 'objectively and dispassionately' the entire question of the reorganization of the states of the Union. Throughout the two years of its work, the Commission was faced with meetings, demonstrations, agitations and hunger strikes. Different linguistic groups clashed with each other, verbally as well as sometimes physically. As the Commissioners reported in sorrow: 'It has been most distressing to us to witness . . . a kind of border warfare in certain areas in which old comrades-in-arms in the battle for freedom have pitted against one another in acrimonious controversy . . . Deliberate attempts to whip up popular frenzy by an appeal to parochial and communal sentiments; threats of large-scale migration; assertions such as that if a certain language group is not allowed to have an administrative unit of its own, its moral, material and even physical extinction would follow as an inevitable consequence; . . . all point to an acute lack of perspective and balance.'[4] The SRC submitted its report in October 1955. While laying down that due consideration should be given to administrative and economic factors, it recognized for the most part the linguistic principle and recommended redrawing of state boundaries on that basis. The Commission, however, opposed the splitting of Bombay and Punjab. Despite strong reaction to the report in many parts of the country, the SRC's recommendations were accepted, though with certain modifications, and were quickly implemented.

The States Reorganisation Act was passed by parliament in November 1956. It provided for fourteen states and six centrally administered territories. The Telangana area of Hyderabad state was transferred to Andhra; Kerala was created by merging the Malabar district of the old Madras Presidency with Travancore-Cochin. Certain Kannada-speaking areas of the states of Bombay, Madras, Hyderabad and Coorg were added to the Mysore state. Bombay state was enlarged by merging the states of Kutch and Saurashtra and the Marathi-speaking areas of Hyderabad with it.

The strongest reaction against the SRC's report and the States Reorganisation Act came from Maharashtra where widespread rioting broke out and eighty people were killed in Bombay city in police firings in January 1956. The Opposition parties supported by a wide spectrum of public opinion—students, farmers, workers, artists, businessmen—organized a powerful protest movement. Under pressure, the government decided in June 1956 to divide the Bombay state into two linguistic states of Maharashtra and Gujarat with Bombay city forming a separate, centrally administered state. This move too was strongly opposed by the Maharashtrians. Nehru now vacillated and, unhappy at having hurt the feelings of the people of Maharashtra, reverted in July to the formation of bilingual, greater Bombay. This move was, however, opposed by the people of both Maharashtra and Gujarat. The broad-based Samyukta Maharashtra Samiti and Maha Gujarat Janata Parishad led the movements in the two parts of the state. In Maharashtra, even a large section of Congressmen joined the demand for a unilingual Maharashtra with Bombay as its capital; and C.D. Deshmukh, the Finance Minister in the central cabinet, resigned from his office on this question. The Gujaratis felt that they would be a minority in the new state. They too would not agree to give up Bombay city to Maharashtra. Violence and arson now spread to Ahmedabad and other parts of Gujarat. Sixteen persons were killed and 200 injured in police firings.

In view of the disagreement over Bombay city, the government stuck to its decision and passed the States Reorganisation Act in November 1956. But the matter could not rest there. In the 1957 elections the Bombay Congress scraped through with a slender majority. Popular agitation continued for nearly five years. As Congress president, Indira Gandhi reopened the question and was supported by the President, S. Radhakrishnan. The government finally agreed in May 1960 to bifurcate the state of Bombay into Maharashtra and Gujarat, with Bombay city being included in Maharashtra, and Ahmedabad being made the capital of Gujarat.

The other state where an exception was made to the linguistic principle was Punjab. In 1956, the states of PEPSU had been merged with Punjab, which, however, remained a trilingual state having three language speakers—Punjabi, Hindi and Pahari—within its borders. In the Punjabi-speaking part of the state, there was a strong demand for carving out a separate Punjabi Suba (Punjabi-speaking state). Unfortunately, the issue assumed communal overtones. The Sikh communalists, led by the Akali Dal, and the Hindu communalists, led by the Jan Sangh, used the linguistic issue to promote communal politics. While the Hindu communalists opposed the demand for a Punjabi Suba by denying that Punjabi was their mother tongue, the Sikh communalists put forward the demand as a Sikh demand for a Sikh state, claiming Punjabi written in Gurmukhi as a Sikh language. Even though the demand was supported by the Communist Party and a section of the Congress, it had got mixed up with religion. But Nehru, as also the majority of the Punjab Congressmen, felt that the demand for a Punjabi state was basically a communal demand for a Sikh-majority state 'dressed up as a language plea'. Nehru and the Congress leadership were clear that they would not accept any demand for the creation of a state on religious or communal grounds. The SRC had also refused to accept the demand for a separate Punjabi-speaking state on the ground that this would not solve either the language or the communal problem of Punjab. (The several powerful movements for a Punjabi state are discussed separately in the chapter on the Punjab crisis.) Finally, in 1966, Indira Gandhi agreed to the division of Punjab into two Punjabi- and Hindi-speaking states of Punjab and Haryana, with the Pahari-speaking district of Kangra and a part of the Hoshiarpur district being merged with Himachal Pradesh. Chandigarh, the newly built city and capital of united Punjab, was made a Union Territory and was to serve as the joint capital of Punjab and Haryana.

Thus, after more than ten years of continuous strife and popular struggles the linguistic reorganization of India was largely completed, making room for greater political participation by the people.

Events since 1956 have clearly shown that loyalty to a language was quite consistent with, and was rather complementary to, loyalty to the nation. By reorganizing the states on linguistic lines, the national leadership removed a major grievance which could have led to fissiparous tendencies. States reorganization is, therefore, 'best regarded as clearing the ground for national integration'.[5] Also, even though during the agitation for states' reorganization the language of warring camps was used, language has not subsequently defined the politics of the states.

Equally important, linguistic reorganization of the states has not in any manner adversely affected the federal structure of the Union or weakened or paralysed the Centre as many had feared. The central government wields as much authority as it did before. The states have also been cooperating with the Centre in planning and economic development. Hardly any person complains of discrimination in the raising or expending of resources on grounds of language. If anything, the national government has been strengthened by the creation of coherent state units. To quote W.H. Morris-Jones: 'The newly fashioned units, it is true, have a self-conscious coherence, but they are willing, thus equipped, to do business with the centre, to work as parts of a whole that is India.'[6]

Thus, states' reorganization has not only not weakened the unity of the country but as a whole strengthened it, thereby disappointing the prophets of gloom and removing the apprehensions of the friendly. To quote the political scientist Rajni Kothari: 'In spite of the leadership's earlier reservations and ominous forebodings by sympathetic observers, the reorganization resulted in rationalizing the political map of India without seriously weakening its unity. If anything, its result has been functional, in as much as it removed what had been a major source of discord, and created homogeneous political units which could be administered through a medium that the vast majority of the population understood. Indeed it can be said with the benefit of hindsight that language, rather than being a force for division has proved a cementing and integrating influence.'[7]

States' reorganization did not, of course, resolve all the problems relating to linguistic conflicts. Disputes over boundaries between different states, linguistic minorities and economic issues such as sharing of waters, and power and surplus food still persist. Linguistic chauvinism also finds occasional expression. But the reorganization has removed a major factor affecting cohesion of the country.

Minority Languages

An important aspect of the language problem has been the status of minority languages. Unilingual states were not possible in whatever manner their boundaries were drawn. Consequently, a large number of linguistic minorities, that is, those who speak a language other than the main or the official language of the state, continue to exist in linguistically reorganized states. Overall nearly 18 per cent of India's population do not speak the official language of the states where they live as their mother tongue. There is of course a great deal of variation among the states on this count. According to the 1971 census, the percentages of linguistic minorities to total population ranged from 4 in Kerala to 34 in Karnataka, 3.9 in Assam to 44.5 in Jammu and Kashmir.

From the beginning, the important point to be decided upon was the status and rights of these minorities in their states. On the one hand, there was the question of their protection, for there was the ever-present danger of them being meted out unfair treatment, on the other, there was the need to promote their integration with the major language group of a state. A linguistic minority had to be given the confidence that it would not be discriminated against by the majority and that its language and culture would continue to exist and develop. At the same time, the majority had to be assured that meeting the needs of the linguistic minority would not generate separatist sentiments or demands and that the minorities would develop a degree of state loyalty.

To confront this problem certain Fundamental Rights were provided to the linguistic minorities in the constitution. For example, Article 30 states that 'all minorities, whether based an religion or language, shall have the right to establish and administer educational institutions of their choice' and, more important, 'that the state shall not, in granting aid to educational institutions, discriminate against any educational institution on the ground that it is under the management of a minority, whether based on religion or language'. Article 347 lays down that on a demand being made on behalf of a minority, the President may direct that its language shall be officially recognized throughout the state or any part thereof for such purposes as he might specify. The official policy since 1956, sanctioned by a constitutional amendment in that year, has been to provide for instruction in the mother tongue in the primary and secondary classes wherever there is a sufficient number of children to form a class. The amendment also provides for the appointment of a Commissioner for Linguistic Minorities to investigate and report regularly on the implementation of these safeguards. On the whole, the central government has tended to play a very positive role in defence of the rights of the minorities, but the implementation of the minority safeguards is within the purview of the state governments and therefore differs from state to state. In general, despite some progress in several states, in most of them the position of the linguistic minorities has not been satisfactory. The constitutional safeguards have quite often been inadequately enforced. The Commissioner for Linguistic Minorities has in his reports regularly noted innumerable cases of discrimination against linguistic minorities in matters of schooling, admission to technical and medical institutions and employment in the state public services because of lack of proficiency in the official language of the state. However, a redeeming feature is that quite often facilities for primary education in the mother tongue of the minorities have been provided, though these may be inadequate in terms of competent teachers and textbooks. But even here the big exception is the all-round failure in the case of tribal minority languages.

Among the minority languages, Urdu is a special case. It is the largest minority tongue in India. Nearly 23.3 million people spoke Urdu in 1951. Urdu speakers constituted substantial percentages of the population in Uttar Pradesh (U.P.) (10.5), Bihar (8.8), Maharashtra (7.2), Andhra Pradesh (7.5) and Karnataka (9). Moreover, an overwhelming majority of Muslims, India's largest religious minority, claimed Urdu as their mother tongue. Urdu is also recognized as one of India's national languages and is listed in the Eighth Schedule of the constitution.

While nearly all the major languages of India were also the official languages of one state or the other, Urdu was not the official language of any state except the small state of Jammu and Kashmir where the mother tongues were in any case Kashmiri, Dogri and Ladakhi. Consequently, Urdu did not get official support in any part of the country. On the contrary, it faced official discrimination and hostility both in U.P. and Bihar. We may briefly take up the case of U.P., though the position was no different in Bihar. The U.P. government decided early on to declare Hindi as the only official language of the state; the subterfuge was that Hindi and Urdu were not two separate languages and therefore there was no need to make Urdu a second official language! In practice, Urdu began to be abolished in many primary schools. Its use as a medium of instruction was also increasingly limited. For example, in 1979–80, only 3.69 per cent of primary school students received instruction in Urdu while the number of Urdu speakers in 1981 was 10.5 per cent. The Hindi protagonists also began to eliminate Urdu words from written Hindi. The neglect of Urdu in the state led the well-known left-wing Urdu critic S. Ehtesham Husain, to complain: 'Urdu is being constantly termed as only an off-shoot or variety of Hindi, a foreign language, a language of the Muslims, an instrument of communal hatred and an enemy of

Indian unity. All these contrary things are said in the same breath, to suppress it.'[8]

Urdu speakers, therefore, were persistent in demanding that Urdu should be recognized as the second official language in the states where it had a large presence, especially in U.P. and Bihar. The U.P. government was equally consistent and successful in opposing the demand; its main justification being that the SRC had recommended that at least 30 per cent population in a state should speak a language before it could be made the second official or regional language.

Jawaharlal Nehru, in particular, was very supportive of Urdu and critical of the anti-Urdu thinking and activities of a large number of persons, including Congressmen, in northern India. 'Urdu,' he told parliament, 'is an example of integration in India, not only of languages but of minds, literatures and cultures. It is cent per cent an Indian language.'[9] He pointed out that Urdu had 'enriched Indian culture and thought'.[10] He asked the chief minister of Uttar Pradesh to declare Urdu as a second official language in districts where it was widely used and in other areas to give it the full facilities of a minority language. But even when Nehru succeeded in persuading the Uttar Pradesh government to agree to take certain steps in this regard, they were nullified by laxity in their implementation. The Uttar Pradesh government refused to pass legislation giving legal sanctity to the rights granted to Urdu on the ground that such a step might lead to communal riots.

The governments of Andhra Pradesh and Karnataka were more supportive of Urdu. In Andhra, Urdu has been recognized since 1968 as an additional language for the Telangana region. And in both the states, adequate facilities are provided for instruction through the medium of Urdu in the primary stage and for instruction in Urdu at the higher school stages.

Two other aspects of Urdu's position may be noted. First, unfortunately the question of Urdu has got entangled with the communal question. While many Muslims regard it as the language of their community as such, many Hindu communalists are hostile to it because of their anti-Muslim ideological position. Second, despite active hostility of many and official neglect, Urdu continues not only to exist but even grow in terms of literary output, journals and newspapers and especially as the language of films and television because of its inherent vigour and cultural roots among the Indian people.

Consolidation of India as a Nation(III): Integration of the Tribals

The task of integrating the tribal people into the mainstream was extremely complex, given the varied conditions under which they live in different parts of the country, and their different languages and distinct cultures. The 1971 Census recorded over 400 tribal communities numbering nearly 38 million people and constituting nearly 6.9 per cent of the Indian population. Spread all over India, their greatest concentration is in Madhya Pradesh, Bihar, Orissa, north-eastern India, West Bengal, Maharashtra, Gujarat and Rajasthan. Except in the Northeast, they constitute minorities in their home states. Residing mostly in the hills and forest areas, in colonial India they lived in relative isolation, and their traditions, habits, cultures and ways of life were markedly different from those of their non-tribal neighbours. Nevertheless, except in the Northeast, the two had for centuries interacted culturally, socially, economically and politically.

In most parts of the country, colonialism brought radical transformation of the tribals as their relative isolation was eroded by the penetration of market forces and they were integrated with the British and princely administrations. A large number of money-lenders, traders, revenue farmers and other middlemen and petty officials invaded the tribal areas and disrupted the tribals' traditional way of life. They were increasingly engulfed in debt and lost their lands to outsiders, often being reduced to the position of agricultural labourers, sharecroppers and rack-rented tenants. Many were forced to retreat further into the hills. Belated legislation to prevent alienation of land by the tribal people failed to halt the process. Verrier Elwin, who lived nearly all his life among the tribal people in central and north-eastern India and who was one of the formative influences in the evolution of the new government's policies towards the tribals, was to refer to the fate of the tribal people under British rule as follows: 'But now they suffered oppression and exploitation, for there soon came merchants and liquor-venders, cajoling, tricking, swindling them in their ignorance and simplicity until bit by bit their broad acres dwindled and they they sank into the poverty in which many of them still live today.'[1] Simultaneously, 'missionaries were destroying their art, their dances, their weaving and their whole culture'.[2]

Colonialism also transformed the tribals' relationship with the forest. They depended on the forest for food, fuel and cattle feed and for raw materials for their handicrafts. In many parts of India the hunger for land by the immigrant peasants from the plains led to the destruction of forests, depriving the tribals of their traditional means of livelihood. To conserve forests and to facilitate their commercial exploitation, the colonial authorities brought large tracts of forest lands under forest laws which forbade shifting cultivation and put severe restrictions on the tribals' use of the forest and their access to forest products.

Loss of land, indebtedness, exploitation by middlemen, denial of access to forests and forest products, and oppression and extortion by policemen, forest officials, and other government officials was to lead to a series of tribal uprisings in the nineteenth and twentieth centuries—for example the Santhal uprising and the Munda rebellion led by Birsa Munda—and to the participation of the tribal people in the national and peasant movements in Orissa, Bihar, West Bengal, Andhra, Maharashtra and Gujarat.

Roots of India's Tribal Policy

The preservation of the tribal people's rich social and cultural heritage lay at the heart of the government's policy of tribal integration. As Jawaharlal Nehru, the main influence in shaping the government's attitude towards the tribals, put it: 'The first problem we have to face there [in the tribal areas] is to inspire them [the tribal people] with confidence and to make them feel at one with India, and to realise that they are part of India and have an honoured place in it.' At the same time, 'India to them should signify not only a protecting force but a liberating one'.[3] Indian nationalism, Nehru thought, was capable of accommodating the uniqueness of the tribal people.

There were two major approaches regarding the place to be accorded to tribals in Indian society. One approach was to leave the tribal people alone, uncontaminated by modern influences operating outside their world and to let them stay more or less as they were. The second approach was that of assimilating them completely and as quickly as possible into the Indian society all around them. The disappearance of the tribal way of life was not to be regretted; it was to be welcomed for that would represent their 'upliftment'.

Jawaharlal Nehru rejected both these approaches. The first approach, of treating the tribal people 'as museum specimens to be observed and written about', was, he said, 'to insult them'.[4] The tribal people, he wrote, 'could not be left cut off from the world as they were'. Isolation was in any case impossible at this stage, for the process of penetration by the outside world had already gone too far and 'it was not possible or desirable to isolate them'.[5] The second approach of allowing them 'to be engulfed by the masses of Indian humanity',[6] or of their assimilation through the operation of normal outside forces was also wrong, according to Nehru. This would lead to the loss of the tribals' social and cultural identity and of the many virtues they possessed. In fact, he pointed out, 'if normal factors were allowed to operate, unscrupulous people from outside would take possession of tribal lands . . . and forests and interfere with the life of the tribal people'.[7] This would also 'upset their whole life and culture, which had so much of good in them'.[8]

Instead of these two approaches, Nehru favoured the policy of integrating the tribal people in Indian society, of making them an integral part of the Indian nation, even while maintaining their distinct identity and culture. There were two basic parameters of the Nehruvian approach: 'the tribal areas have to progress' and 'they have to progress in their own way'. Progress did not mean 'an attempt merely to duplicate what we have got in other parts of India'. Whatever was good in the rest of India would 'be adopted by them gradually'.[9] Moreover, whatever changes were needed would be 'worked out by the tribals themselves'.[10]

The problem was how to combine these two seemingly contradictory approaches. Nehru stood for economic and social development of the tribal people in multifarious ways, especially in the fields of communication, modern medical facilities, agriculture and education. In this regard, he laid down certain broad guidelines for government policy.

First, the tribals should develop along the lines of their own genius; there should be no imposition or compulsion from outside. The non-tribals should not approach them with a superiority complex. Rather, the understanding should be that they had an equal contribution to make to the evolution of the common culture and social and political life of the country.

Second, tribal rights in land and forests should be respected and no outsider should be able to take possession of tribal lands. The incursion of the market economy into tribal areas had to be strictly controlled and regulated.

Third, it was necessary to encourage the tribal languages which 'must be given all possible support and the conditions in which they can flourish must be safeguarded'.[11]

Fourth, for administration, reliance should be placed on the tribal people themselves, and administrators should be recruited from amongst them and trained. As few as possible outsiders should be introduced as administrators in tribal areas and they should be carefully chosen. They should have a sympathetic and understanding approach, and should not consider themselves superior to or apart from the tribal people. They should be prepared to share their life with the tribal people among whom they work.

Fifth, there should be no over-administration of tribal areas. The effort should be to administer and develop the tribals' through them own social and cultural institutions.

Nehru's approach was in turn based on the nationalist policy towards tribals since the 1920s when Gandhiji set up ashrams in the tribal areas and promoted constructive work. After independence this policy was supported by Rajendra Prasad, the first President of India, and other major political leaders.

To give shape to the government's policy, a beginning was made in the constitution itself which directed under Article 46 that the state should promote with special care the educational and economic interests of the tribal people and should protect them from social injustice and all forms of exploitation, through special legislation. The governors of the states in which tribal areas were situated were given special responsibility to protect tribal interests, including the power to modify central and state laws in their application to tribal areas, and to frame regulations for the protection of tribals' right to land and also their protection from moneylenders. The application of the Fundamental Rights was amended for this purpose. The constitution also extended full political rights to the tribal people. In addition, it provided for reservation of seats in the legislatures and positions in the administrative services for the Scheduled Tribes as in the case of the Scheduled Castes. The constitution also provided for the setting up of Tribal Advisory Councils in all states containing tribal areas to advise on matters concerning the welfare of tribals. A Commissioner for Scheduled Castes and Scheduled Tribes was appointed by the President to investigate whether the safeguards provided for them were being observed.

Legislative as well as executive action was taken by the state governments to prevent loss of tribal lands to non-tribal people and to prevent exploitation of the tribals by moneylenders. The central and state governments created special facilities and organized special programmes for the welfare and development of the tribal areas and the tribal people including the promotion of cottage and village industries and generation of employment among them. Large expenditures were undertaken and large sums set apart in the Five-Year Plans for the purpose. The funding for tribal welfare significantly increased after 1971.

In spite of the constitutional safeguards and the efforts of the central and state governments, the tribals' progress and welfare has been very slow, and even dismal. Except in the Northeast, the tribals continue to be poor, indebted, landless and often unemployed. The problem often lies in weak execution of even well-intentioned measures. Quite often there is a divergence between central and state government policies, the latter being less in tune with tribal interests. In particular, state governments have been relatively ineffective in administering the positive policies and laws laid down by the central government or by the state governments themselves, as repeatedly shown by the Commissioner for Scheduled Castes and Scheduled Tribes and in the reports of the Planning Commission. Quite often the funds allocated for tribal welfare are not spent or are spent without corresponding results, or are even misappropriated. One of the watchdogs of tribal interests, the Tribal Advisory Councils, have not functioned effectively.

Often the administrative personnel are ill-trained or even prejudiced against tribals. But sympathetic officials are also known to be quickly transferred out of tribal areas under the pressure of traders, moneylenders, forest contractors and land-grabbers.

A major handicap from which tribals suffer is denial of justice, often because of their unfamiliarity with the laws and the legal system. Laws preventing transfer of land to outsiders have continued to be evaded, leading to alienation of land and eviction of tribals. Rapid extension of mines and industries has worsened their conditions in many areas. While deforestation proceeds apace through the cooperation of corrupt officials and politicians with forest contractors, the tribals' traditional right of access to the forest and its produce is continuously curtailed. Forest laws and regulations are also used by unsympathetic and often corrupt forest officials to harass and exploit the tribal people. As a result of loss of land, deforestation and restrictions on the access to the forest, the tribal people have been facing growing unemployment and have been increasingly driven into more inaccessible stretches of hills and jungles.

The progress of education among the tribal people has been disappointingly slow. In many areas, primary education through the tribal languages has taken place, but in others the state governments have tended to neglect tribal languages and education through their medium.

Tribal society almost everywhere has also been gradually developing class differences and a class structure with those belonging to the upper crust often joining forces with the upper crust of the outsiders. Further, the major gains of whatever development takes place in the fields of education, employment in administration, economy and political patronage are reaped by the small segment of the tribal elites which has slowly emerged and grown.

On the whole, though there are a few danger signals, certain positive developments in the tribal sphere have occurred since 1947. Legislation to protect tribal rights and interests, activities of the tribal welfare departments, Panchayati Raj, spread of literacy and education, reservations in government services and in higher educational institutions, and repeated elections have led to increasing confidence among the tribal people and greater political participation by them—or at least by the growing middle classes and intelligentsia among them—in the constitutional political processes. They are now insisting on a greater and more active political role for themselves, and acquiring increasing representation in different political structures and institutions. Above all, they are demanding a greater share in national economic development.

Protest movements have sprung up among tribals out of their frustration with the lack of development and welfare. These are bound to produce positive results in time. The government policy has usually been conciliatory, though not necessarily successful in redressing tribal grievances. But some of the protest movements have taken to violence, leading to strong state action against them. Little ground has been gained by them, though they have often dramatically drawn national attention to the tribal condition.

The growing tribal antagonism towards the non-tribal people or outsiders living in tribal areas has been another unfortunate development. Undoubtedly, some of the outsiders like traders, moneylenders, landlords and government officials have been a scourge of the tribal areas, but, over decades, many other outsiders—peasants, workers, teachers, doctors and other middle- and lower-middle-class persons—have now settled there, outnumbering the tribals in almost all tribal areas outside the Northeast. The mass of the tribals and non-tribals are equally poor and have a common interest in economic and social development as also social and economic justice. Besides, most of the middle-class non-tribals, including many of the traders and industrialists, do perform useful economic functions in the tribal areas. Any undue antagonism and antipathy between the tribals and non-tribals would be inimical and even dangerous to both. It is no longer true that the only relationship that can exist between the two is an exploitative one. Tribals cannot expect to revert to isolation from their non-tribal neighbours or to prevent massive interaction with them, including their in-migration. In fact, the two can protect and promote their interests only through mutual cooperation.

Tribals in the Northeast

The tribes of north-eastern India, consisting of over a hundred groups, speaking a wide variety of languages and living in the hill tracts of Assam, shared many of the features and problems of the tribal people in the rest of the country. But their situation was different in several respects. For one, they constituted the overwhelming majority of the population in most of the areas they inhabited. Then, non-tribals had not penetrated these areas to any significant extent, though economic contacts between the tribal and the non-tribal areas had been developing over time. This was because of the British policy in the late nineteenth century.

The tribal areas occupied by the British then formed part of the Assam province but were given a separate administrative status. Their socio-political structure was not disturbed and a deliberate policy of excluding the outsiders from the plains was followed. In particular, no non-tribal plainsmen were allowed to acquire land in the tribal areas because of which the tribals suffered little loss of land.

At the same time, the British government permitted and even encouraged the Christian missionaries to move in and establish schools, hospitals and churches and to proselytize, thus introducing change and modern ideas among some of the tribal youth. The missionaries, in turn, collaborated with the colonial authorities and helped keep the nationalist influence out of the tribal areas, besides encouraging their isolation from the rest of the population of Assam and India. In fact, immediately after independence, some of the missionaries and other foreigners even promoted sentiment in favour of separate and independent states in north-eastern India.

The virtual absence of any political or cultural contact of the tribals in the Northeast with the political life of the rest of India was also a striking difference. A powerful factor in the unification of the Indian people as a nation was the common bonds forged in the course of the anti-imperialist struggle. But this struggle had little impact among the tribals of the Northeast. To quote Jawaharlal Nehru: 'The essence of our struggle for freedom was the unleashing of a liberating force in India. This force did not even affect the frontier people in one of the most important tribal areas.'[12] And again: 'Thus they never experienced a sensation of being in a country called India and they were hardly influenced by the struggle for freedom or other movements in India. Their chief experience of outsiders was that of British officers and Christian missionaries who generally tried to make them anti-Indian.'[13]

The tribal policy of the Government of India, inspired by Jawaharlal Nehru, was therefore even more relevant to the tribal people of the Northeast. 'All this North-East border area deserves our special attention,' Nehru said in October 1952, 'not only the government's, but of the people of India. Our contacts with them will do us good and will do them good also. They add to the strength, variety and cultural richness of India.'[14]

A reflection of this policy was in the Sixth Schedule of the constitution which applied only to the tribal areas of Assam. The Sixth Schedule offered a fair degree of self-government to the tribal people by providing for autonomous districts and the creation of district and regional councils which would exercise some of the legislative and judicial functions within the overall jurisdiction of the Assam legislature and parliament. The objective of the Sixth Schedule was to enable tribals to live according to their own ways. The Government of India also expressed its willingness to further amend the constitutional provisions relating to the tribal people if it was found necessary to do so with a view to promote further autonomy. But this did not mean, Nehru clarified, that the government would countenance secession from India or independence by any area or region, or would tolerate violence in the promotion of any demands.

Nehru's and Verrier Elwin's policies were implemented best of all in the North-East Frontier Agency or NEFA, which was created in 1948 out of the border areas of Assam. NEFA was established as a Union Territory outside the jurisdiction of Assam and placed under a special administration. From the beginning, the administration was manned by a special cadre of officers who were asked to implement specially designed developmental policies without disturbing the social and cultural pattern of the life of the people. As a British anthropologist who spent nearly all his life studying the tribal people and their condition wrote in 1967, 'A measure of isolation combined with a sympathetic and imaginative policy of a progressive administration has here created a situation unparalleled in other parts of India.'[15] NEFA was named Arunachal Pradesh and granted the status of a separate state in 1987. While NEFA was developing comfortably and in harmony with the rest of the country, problems developed in the other tribal areas which were part of Assam administratively. The problems arose because the hill tribes of Assam had no cultural affinity with the Assamese and Bengali residents of the plains. The tribals were afraid of losing their identities and being assimilated by what was, with some justification, seen to be a policy of Assamization. Especially distasteful to them was the attitude of superiority and even contempt often adopted by non-tribals working among them as teachers, doctors, government officials, traders, etc. There was also a feeling among them that the Assamese government failed to understand them and tended to neglect their interests. This feeling represented not so much the reality as the failure of the political leadership of Assam to redress tribal grievances in time and with deep concern.

Soon, resentment against the Assam government began to mount and a demand for a separate hill state arose among some sections of the tribal people in the mid-1950s. But this demand was not pressed with vigour; nor did the Government of India encourage it, for it felt that the future of the hill tribes was intimately connected with Assam though further steps towards greater autonomy could be envisaged.

But the demand gained greater strength when the Assamese leaders moved in 1960 towards making Assamese the sole official language of the state. In 1960, various political parties of the hill areas merged into the All Party Hill Leaders Conference (APHLC) and again demanded a separate state within the Indian Union. The passage of the Assam Official Language Act, making Assamese the official language of the state, and thus the refusal of the demand for the use of the tribal languages in administration, led to an immediate and strong reaction in the tribal districts. There were hartals and demonstrations, and a major agitation developed. In the 1962 elections, the overwhelming majority of the Assembly seats from the tribal areas were won by the advocates of a separate state, who decided to boycott the State Assembly.

Prolonged discussions and negotiations followed. Several commissions and committees examined the issue. Finally, in 1969, through a constitutional amendment, Meghalaya was carved out of Assam as 'a state within a state' which had complete autonomy except for law and order which remained a function of the Assam government. Meghalaya also shared Assam's High Court, Public Service Commission and governor. Finally, as a part of the reorganization of the Northeast, Meghalaya became a separate state in 1972, incorporating the Garo, Khasi and Jaintia tribes. Simultaneously, the Union Territories of Manipur and Tripura were granted statehood. The transition to statehood in the case of Meghalaya, Manipur, Tripura and Arunachal Pradesh was quite smooth. Trouble arose in the case of Nagaland and Mizoram where secessionist and insurrectionary movements developed.

Nagaland

The Nagas were the inhabitants of the Naga hills along the Northeast frontier on the Assam-Burma border. They numbered nearly 500,000 in 1961, constituted less than 0.1 per cent of India's population, and consisted of many separate tribes speaking different languages. The British had isolated the Nagas from the rest of the country and left them more or less undisturbed though Christian missionary activity was permitted, which had led to the growth of a small educated stratum.

Immediately after independence, the Government of India followed a policy of integrating the Naga areas with the state of Assam and India as a whole. A section of the Naga leadership, however, opposed such integration and rose in rebellion under the leadership of A.Z. Phizo, demanding separation from India and complete independence. They were encouraged in this move by some of the British officials and missionaries. In 1955, these separatist Nagas declared the formation of an independent government and the launching of a violent insurrection.

The Government of India responded with a two-track policy in line with Jawaharlal Nehru's wider approach towards the tribal people discussed earlier in this chapter. On the one hand, the Government of India made it clear that it would firmly oppose the secessionist demand for the independence of Naga areas and would not tolerate recourse to violence. Towards a violent secessionist movement it would firmly follow a policy of suppression and non-negotiations. As Nehru put it, 'It does not help in dealing with tough people to have weak nerves.'[16] Consequently, when one section of the Nagas organized an armed struggle for independence, the Government of India replied by sending its army to Nagaland in early 1956 to restore peace and order.

On the other hand, Nehru realized that while strong and quick military action would make it clear that the rebels were in a no-win situation, total physical suppression was neither possible nor desirable, for the objective had to be the conciliation and winning over of the Naga people. Nehru was wedded to a 'friendly approach'. Even while encouraging the Nagas to integrate with the rest of the country 'in mind and spirit', he favoured their right to maintain their autonomy in cultural and other matters. He was, therefore, willing to go a long way to win over the Nagas by granting them a large degree of autonomy. Refusing to negotiate with Phizo or his supporters as long as they did not give up their demand for independence or the armed rebellion, he carried on prolonged negotiations with the more moderate, non-violent and non-secessionist Naga leaders, who realized that they could not hope to get a larger degree of autonomy or a more sympathetic leader to settle with than Nehru.

In fact, once the back of the armed rebellion was broken by the middle of 1957, the more moderate Naga leaders headed by Dr Imkongliba Ao came to the fore. They negotiated for the creation of the state of Nagaland within the Indian Union. The Government of India accepted their demand through a series of intermediate steps; and the state of Nagaland came into existence in 1963. A further step forward was taken in the integration of the Indian nation. Also, politics in Nagaland since then followed, for better or for worse, the pattern of politics in the other states of the Union.

With the formation of Nagaland as a state the back of the rebellion was broken as the rebels lost much of their popular support. But though the insurgency has been brought under control, sporadic guerrilla activity by Naga rebels trained in China, Pakistan and Burma (Myanmar) and periodic terrorist attacks continue till this day.

We may also refer to one other feature of the Naga situation. Even though the record of the Indian army in Nagaland has been on the whole clean, especially if the difficult conditions under which they operate are kept in view, it has not been without blemish. Its behaviour has been sometimes improper and in rare cases even brutal. Too many times innocent people have suffered. But then it has also paid a heavy price through the loss of its soldiers and officers in guerrilla attacks.

Mizoram

A situation similar to that in Nagaland developed a few years later in the autonomous Mizo district of the Northeast. Secessionist demands backed by some British officials had grown there in 1947 but had failed to get much support from the youthful Mizo leadership, which concentrated instead on the issues of democratization of Mizo society, economic development and adequate representation of Mizos in the Assam legislature. However, unhappiness with the Assam government's relief measures during the famine of 1959 and the passage of the Act in 1961, making Assamese the official language of the state, led to the formation of the Mizo National Front (MNF), with Laldenga as president.

While participating in electoral politics, the MNF created a military wing which received arms and ammunition and military training from East Pakistan and China. In March 1966, the MNF declared independence from India, proclaimed a military uprising and attacked military and civilian targets. The Government of India responded with immediate massive counter-insurgency measures by the army. Within a few weeks the insurrection was crushed and government control restored, though stray guerrilla activity continued. Most of the hard-core Mizo leaders escaped to East Pakistan.

In 1973, after the less extremist Mizo leaders had scaled down their demand to that of a separate state of Mizoram within the Indian Union, the Mizo district of Assam was separated from Assam and, as Mizoram, given the status of a Union Territory. Mizo insurgency gained some renewed strength in the late 1970s but was again effectively dealt with by the Indian armed forces. Having decimated the ranks of the separatist insurgents, the Government of India, continuing to follow the Nehruvian tribal policy, was now willing to show consideration, offer liberal terms of amnesty to the remnants of the rebel forces and conduct negotiations for peace.

A settlement was finally arrived at in 1986. Laldenga and the MNF agreed to abandon underground violent activities, surrender before the Indian authorities along with their arms, and re-enter the constitutional political stream. The Government of India agreed to the grant of full statehood to Mizoram, guaranteeing full autonomy in regard to culture, tradition, land laws, etc. As a part of the accord, a government with Laldenga as chief minister was formed in the new state of Mizoram in February 1987.

Jharkhand

Jharkhand, the tribal area of Bihar consisting of the Chota Nagpur and the Santhal Parganas, has for decades spawned movements for state autonomy. In this area are concentrated several major tribes of India, namely, Santhal, Ho, Oraon and Munda. Unlike traditional tribes, nearly all of these practice settled plough agriculture on the basis of family farms. Economic differentiation has set in; there are a significant number of agricultural labourers and a growing number of mining and industrial workers. The landholding pattern among tribals is as unequal and skewed as among non-tribals. A large class of moneylenders has also developed among them. The tribal society in Jharkhand has increasingly become a class-divided society. Most of the tribals practise two formal religions—Hinduism and Christianity.

The Jharkhand tribes, however, share some features with other Indian tribes. They have lost most of their land, generally to outsiders, and suffer from indebtedness, loss of employment and low agricultural productivity. They organized several major rebellions during the nineteenth century; and many of them actively participated in the national movement after 1919.

In 1951, the Scheduled Tribes constituted 31.15 per cent of the population in Chota Nagpur (30.94 in 1971) and 44.67 per cent of the population in the Santhal Parganas (36.22 in 1971). Thus, nearly two-thirds of Jharkhand's population in 1971 was non-tribal. The overwhelming majority of both tribals and non-tribals were equally exploited poor peasants, agricultural labourers and mining and industrial workers. Inequality in landholding and the moneylender menace were equally prevalent among the two as was the commercialization of agriculture and commercial activity.

With the spread of education and modern activity in the tribal areas, a movement for the formation of a separate tribal state of Jharkhand, incorporating Chota Nagpur and the Santhal Parganas of south Bihar and the contiguous tribal areas of Madhya Pradesh, Orissa and West Bengal, started during the late 1930s and 1940s. Realizing that the interests of the tribal people could be best promoted and their domination by non-tribals ended if they had a state of their own within the Union of India, the Jharkhand party was founded in 1950 under the leadership of the Oxford-educated Jaipal Singh. The party achieved a remarkable success in the 1952 elections when it won 32 seats in Chota Nagpur and emerged as the main Opposition party in the Bihar Assembly. It won 25 seats in 1957.

But the Jharkhand party faced a major dilemma. While it demanded a state where the tribal people would predominate, the population composition of Jharkhand was such that they would still constitute a minority in it. To overcome this problem the party tried to give its demand a regional character by opening its membership to the non-tribals of the area and underplaying its anti-non-tribal rhetoric, even while talking of the empowerment of tribals and their dominance of the new state. The States Reorganisation Commission of 1955, however, rejected the demand for a separate Jharkhand state on the ground that the region did not have a common language. The central government also held that tribals being a minority in Jharkhand could not claim a state of their own.

By the early 1960s the rank and file of the party began to get disheartened and frustrated. The Jharkhand party could win only 20 seats to the Bihar Assembly in 1962. In 1963, a major part of the leadership of the party, including Jaipal Singh, joined Congress, claiming that by 'working from within Congress' it stood a better chance of getting its demand for a separate state accepted by the government.

Several tribal parties and movements developed in Jharkhand after 1967, the most prominent being the Jharkhand Mukti Morcha (JMM), which was formed in late 1972. The JMM revived the demand for the Jharkhand state, but it made two innovations. It recognized the hard reality that nearly two-thirds of the population of Jharkhand was non-tribal and that, therefore, a movement which appealed only to the tribal people could not acquire the requisite political strength. The JMM, thus, began to assert that all the older residents of the Jharkhand region, whether tribal or non-tribal, were exploited, discriminated against and dominated by north Bihar and the recent migrants. It put forward the demand for a separate state as a regional one on behalf of the peasants and workers of the region. Concentrating on economic issues, it also acquired the support of the non-tribal poor; several non-tribal leaders and political activists joined it, though the bulk of its following was still that of tribals. The tribal leaders felt that despite the minority character of tribals in the projected Jharkhand state, they would have a far greater representation and weight in the new state than they had in Bihar as a whole.

The JMM turned to a radical programme and ideology. Joined by other groups, especially leftist groups such as the Marxist Coordination Centre, it organized several militant agitations on issues such as recovery of alienated land, moneylenders' exploitation, employment of tribals in mines and industries and improved working conditions and higher wages in the latter, police excesses, high-handedness of forest officials and increasing liquor consumption. Shibu Soren emerged as the charismatic leader of the JMM during the early 1970s.

Cooperation with the leftists did not, however, last long; nor did the tribal–non-tribal alliance. The movement for the Jharkhand state underwent constant ups and downs and splits over the years with new groups coming up every so often. Major differences among the Jharkhand leaders pertained to the question of cooperation or alliance with the main all-India parties. Many of them believed that in parliamentary democracy, a small number of MPs or MLAs could not on their own easily get their demands accepted. Shibu Soren, his followers and some others were also aware of the futility of permanently confronting state power and the inevitable recourse to violence and armed struggle as advocated by the movement's ultra-leftist fringe.

The movement also found it difficult to shift completely from tribal to class-based regional politics, since it was basically built around tribal identity and tribal demands. In particular, the policy of reservations for tribals contained the seeds of continuing differences between tribals and non-tribals. Tribal society was also not homogeneous; it contained landlords, rich peasants, traders and moneylenders. However, for various reasons, Jharkhand finally came into existence as a state on 15 November 2000. Simultaneously Chhattisgarh and Uttaranchal were created out of Madhya Pradesh and Uttar Pradesh respectively and given the status of states on 1 November and 9 November 2002.

Consolidation of India as a Nation(IV): Regionalism and Regional Inequality

In the 1950s, many saw regionalism as a major threat to Indian unity. But, in fact, regionalism at no stage was a major factor in Indian politics and administration; over time, it tended to become less and less important. What precisely is regionalism needs to be first understood for appreciating its role in Indian politics.

Local patriotism and loyalty to a locality or region or state and its language and culture do not constitute regionalism, nor are they disruptive of the nation. They are quite consistent with national patriotism and loyalty to the nation. To have pride in one's region or state is also not regionalism. A person can be conscious of his or her distinct regional identity—of being a Tamil or a Punjabi, a Bengali or a Gujarati—without being any the less proud of being an Indian, or being hostile to people from other regions. This was put very well by Gandhiji in 1909: 'As the basis of my pride as an Indian, I must have pride in myself as a Gujarati. Otherwise, we shall be left without any moorings.'[1]

The Indian national movement too functioned on this understanding. From the beginning it functioned as an all-India movement and not as a federation of regional national movements. It also did not counterpose the national identity to regional identities; it recognized both and did not see the two in conflict.

Aspiring to or making special efforts to develop one's state or region or to remove poverty and implement social justice there, is not to be branded as regionalism. In fact, a certain inter-regional rivalry around the achievement of such positive goals would be quite healthy—and in fact we have too little of it. Also, local patriotism can help people overcome divisive loyalties to caste or religious communities.

Defending the federal features of the constitution is also not to be seen as regionalism. The demand for a separate state within the Indian Union or for an autonomous region within an existing state, or for devolution of power below the state level, may be objected to on several practical grounds, but not as regionalist, unless it is put forward in a spirit of hostility to the rest of the population of a state. If the interests of one region or state are asserted against the country as a whole or against another region or state in a hostile manner and a conflict is promoted on the basis of such alleged interests it can be dubbed as regionalism.

In this sense, there has been very little inter-regional conflict in India since 1947, the major exception being the politics of the DMK in Tamil Nadu in the 1950s and early 1960s. The role of the DMK is discussed in Chapter 22, but it may be observed that the DMK has also increasingly given up its regionalist approach over the years. Some cite the example of Punjab in the 1980s, but, as we shall see in Chapter 24, Punjab's was a case of communalism and not regionalism.

Regionalism could have flourished in India if any region or state had felt that it was being culturally dominated or discriminated against. In 1960, Selig Harrison, US scholar and journalist, in his famous work, *India—The Most Dangerous Decades,* had seen a major threat to Indian unity because of conflict between the national government and the regions as the latter asserted their separate cultural identities. But, in fact, the Indian nation has proved to be quite successful in accommodating and even celebrating—in Nehru's words—India's cultural diversity. The different areas of India have had full cultural autonomy and been enabled to fully satisfy their legitimate aspirations. The linguistic reorganization of India and the resolution of the official language controversy have played a very important role in this respect, by eliminating a potent cause of the feeling of cultural loss or cultural domination and therefore of inter-regional conflict.

Many regional disputes, of course, do exist and they have the potential of fanning interstate hostility. There has been friction between different states over the sharing of river waters: for example, between Tamil Nadu and Karnataka, Karnataka and Andhra, and Punjab and Haryana and Rajasthan. Boundary disputes have arisen out of the formation of linguistic states as in the case of Belgaum and Chandigarh. Construction of irrigation and power dams has created such conflicts. But, while these disputes tend to persist for a long time and occasionally arouse passions, they have, as a whole, remained within narrow, and we might say acceptable, limits. The central government has often succeeded in playing the role of a mediator, though sometimes drawing the anger of the disputants on itself, but thus preventing sharper inter-regional conflicts.

Economic Imbalances and Regionalism

Economic inequality among different states and regions could be a potential source of trouble. However, despite breeding discontent and putting pressure on the political system, this problem has not so far given rise to regionalism or feeling of a region being discriminated against.

At independence, the leadership recognized that some regions were more backward than others. Only a few enclaves or areas around Calcutta, Bombay and Madras had undergone modern industrial development. For example, in 1948, Bombay and West Bengal accounted for more than 59 per cent of the total industrial capital of the country and more than 64 per cent of the national industrial output. Under colonialism, agriculture had also stagnated, but more in eastern India than in northern or southern India. Regional economic disparity was also reflected in per capita income. In 1949, while West Bengal, Punjab and Bombay had per capita incomes of Rs 353, 331 and 272 respectively, the per capita incomes of Bihar, Orissa and Rajasthan were Rs 200, 188 and 173 respectively.

From the beginning, the national government felt a responsibility to counter this imbalance in regional development. Thus, for example, the 1956 Industrial Policy Resolution of the Government of India asserted that 'only by securing a balanced and coordinated development of the industrial and agricultural economy in each region can the entire country attain higher standards of living'. Similarly, recognizing 'the importance of regional balance in economic development as a positive factor in promoting national integration', the National Integration Council of 1961 urged that 'a rapid development of the economically backward regions in any State should be given priority in national and State plans, at least to the extent that the minimum level of development is reached for all states within a stated period'.[2]

From the beginning, the central government adopted a whole range of policies to influence the rates of growth in poorer states and regions so as to reduce their economic distance from the richer states and regions. A major government instrument in bringing this about was the transfer of financial resources to the poorer states. Important in this respect was the role of the Finance Commission, provided for in the constitution and appointed periodically by the President. The Commission decides the principles on which disbursement of central taxes and other financial resources from the central government to the states occurs. Various Finance Commissions have tried not only to do justice among the states but also to reduce interstate disparity by giving preferential treatment to the poorer states, by allocating larger grants to them than their population would warrant and by transferring resources from the better-off states to them.

Planning was also seen as a powerful instrument that could be used to remove regional inequality. The Second Plan reflected this objective and it was reiterated in the succeeding Plans. The Third Plan explicitly stated that 'balanced development of different parts of the country, extension of the benefits of economic progress to the less developed regions and widespread diffusion of industry are among the major aims of planned development'.[3]

For this purpose, the Planning Commission allocated greater plan assistance to the backward states. This assistance is given in the form of both grants and loans on the basis of a formula which assigns an important place to the degree of backwardness of a state. Moreover, bias in favour of backward states in the devolution of resources from the Centre to the states, in the form of both financial and Plan transfers, has tended to increase with time.

Public investment by the central government in major industries such as steel, fertilizers, oil refining, petrochemicals, machine-making, heavy chemicals and in power and irrigation projects, roads, railways, post offices and other infrastructural facilities, has been a tool for the reduction of regional inequality. India has relied heavily on public investment since the beginning of the

Second Plan in 1957 and an effort has been made to favour backward states in regard to this investment.

In the planning and location of the public sector enterprises balanced regional growth has been an important consideration, though this has entailed a certain economic cost to the enterprises concerned. Bihar and Madhya Pradesh have gained the most from such investment; Assam, Himachal Pradesh, Jammu and Kashmir and the north-eastern states have also benefited a great deal from the development of infrastructure, especially roads.

Government incentives have been provided to the private sector to invest in backward areas through subsidies, tax concessions, and concessional banking and institutional loans at subsidized rates. The system of licensing of private industrial enterprises, which prevailed from 1956 to 1991, was also used by the government to guide location of industries in backward areas.

Following nationalization of banks in 1969, the expansion of the network of their branches was used to favour backward areas. Banks and other public sector financial institutions were directed to promote investment in these areas. Also, various ministries have evolved schemes for development of backward areas. In particular, poverty eradication programmes, such as the Food for Work programme and the Integrated Rural Development Programme, adopted since the 1970s, and to some extent education, health and family planning programmes and the public distribution system have favoured poorer states.

One sector where the principle of the reduction of regional disparity has not been kept in view is that of investment in irrigation and subsidies to agricultural development. This has been especially so since the 1960s when the Green Revolution began and investment in rural infrastructure and technological innovation was concentrated in Punjab, Haryana and western U.P., namely, areas where irrigation was or could be made available readily. In particular, investment in and development of rain-fed dry land agriculture was neglected. The result was an increase in regional agricultural disparity. The spread of the Green Revolution technology during the 1970s to Andhra Pradesh, Tamil Nadu, Karnataka, eastern U.P. and parts of Rajasthan, and during the 1980s to the eastern states of Bihar, West Bengal, Orissa and Assam has redressed the regional imbalance to a certain extent.

Economic mobility of population through migration of unskilled labour from the backward regions and of skilled labour to them can also contribute to the lessening of regional disparity; and the Indian constitution guarantees this mobility. There has been a great deal of migration from one state to another. Some states—Himachal Pradesh, Orissa, Bihar and Kerala—have benefited from out-migration just as Bengal, Gujarat and Maharashtra have benefited rrom in-migration. Certain other states, like Punjab and Karnataka, have had the benefit of both out-migration and in-migration. Unfortunately, as we shall see in the next section, efforts have been made by some states to put checks on interstate migration.

It would be appropriate here to ask how far have the various efforts of the national government succeeded in reducing regional inequality. The picture that emerges is a mixed one. There has been a marginal improvement but regional inequality, especially in terms of per capita income, continues to remain a prominent feature of the Indian economy. Possibly, the situation would have been much worse but for the government's actions which has prevented the widening of the economic gap between states and regions. There are also other dimensions to be observed with regard to the impact of these policies.

For one, there has certainly been a decline in interstate industrial disparity, especially in the organized manufacturing sector. There is also less disparity in terms of social welfare as represented by life expectancy, infant mortality and literacy, though a few states like Kerala and Tamil Nadu have moved far ahead. As we have seen above, the increased disparity in agriculture is also gradually getting redressed though the rain-fed dry areas are still lagging behind. While the percentage of people below the poverty line has steadily declined in all the states, it is in the advanced states that maximum progress has been made, so that the inter-regional disparity in the distribution of poverty has been growing. Overall, while there has been economic growth in all states, the rates of growth of different states have been highly differential, leading to interstate disparities remaining quite wide.

Some backward states have managed to pick themselves up, while others have failed to do so, with the result that there has been a change in the hierarchy of states in terms of development and per capita income. Thus, Bihar, Madhya Pradesh and Orissa are still at the bottom. Kerala, Punjab and Gujarat continue to remain on the top. There has been an improvement in the position of the previously underdeveloped states of Haryana, Himachal Pradesh, Karnataka and Tamil Nadu, while there has been deterioration in that of Assam, West Bengal, Maharashtra and U.P, with U.P. moving to the bottom level and West Bengal to the middle. Andhra Pradesh and Rajasthan have stagnated, remaining just above the bottom level. On the whole, Haryana is an example of states which have improved their position and Bihar of one of those whose position has worsened.

Why then does regional inequality persist on such a wide scale? What are the constraints on its decline? Or why have Bihar and U.P. performed so poorly. It emerges that the constraint is not essentially of geography, that is, of inequality in size or natural resources. Bihar, U.P. and Orissa are, for example, very well endowed by nature; their people well known for their industriousness because of which they are welcomed in the rest of the country, and indeed overseas in the West Indies, Mauritius and Fiji to where some have migrated.

The major reason, at the all-India level, for the continuing regional disparity has been the low rate of economic growth. To make a dent on this requires a high rate of national growth so that large revenues can be raised and devoted to the development of the backward regions without adversely affecting national growth itself. The rate of growth of the Indian economy was around 3.5 per cent till the end of the 1970s and around 5 per cent in the 1980s. This was not high enough to have a significant impact on regional inequality despite policies consciously designed to favour backward regions being followed. It is only in the last few years that the rate of growth of the economy has touched 8 to 9 per cent, while population growth has also slowed down. A reduction in economic inequality may come about, provided the right type of regional developmental policies continue to be followed.

We, however, feel that the roots of some states' backwardness lie in their socio-economic and political organization itself. For example, the agrarian structure in Bihar and eastern U.P. is still quite regressive and in many parts of these states land reforms have been inadequately implemented. (This was also true of Orissa till recently.) The feudal mentality is still quite strong. Also, in Bihar and Orissa land consolidation has been tardy, though ongoing, which played an important role in the agricultural development of Punjab and Haryana.

The backward states have a lower level of infrastructural facilities, such as power, irrigation, roads, telephones, and modern markets for agricultural produce. These are essential for development and have to be developed by the states themselves being mostly State subjects.

States also have a low level of social expenditure on education and public health and sanitation, which are also state subjects. Besides, they suffer from a lack of financial resources to meet Plan expenditure. Increased central financial assistance is unable to offset this weakness. A vicious cycle is set up. A low level of economic development and production means less financial resources and limited expenditure on infrastructure, development planning and social services. And this low level of expenditure in turn leads to low levels of production and therefore of financial resources.

Political and administrative failure also bolsters backwardness. Bihar and U.P. are classic cases of states bedevilled by high levels of corruption, sheer bad administration, and deteriorating law and order. As a result, whatever central assistance is available is poorly utilized and often diverted to non-development heads of expenditure. Further, development of infrastructure, including roads and electricity, is neglected and the existing infrastructure is riddled with inefficiency and corruption. All this turns away the private sector, which is a major source of development in the advanced states. The role of greater administrative efficiency is also proved by the better rates of economic growth in the relatively better administered states of South and western India as compared to Bihar and Uttar Pradesh.

In passing, it may be mentioned that disparities in development also exist within each state. In many cases, this inequality has become a source of tension and given birth to sub-regional movements for separate states within the Indian Union, or greater autonomy for the sub-regions within the existing states, or at least special treatment and safeguards in matters of employment, education and allocation of financial resources. Examples of such sub-regional feelings are the movements in Telangana in Andhra Pradesh, Vidarbha in Maharashtra, Saurashtra in Gujarat, Bundelkhand in Uttar Pradesh, Darjeeling district or Gorkhaland in West Bengal, Bodoland in Assam, and the areas consisting of the old princely states of Orissa. It is because of these regional feelings that Uttaranchal, Jharkhand and Chhattisgarh were created out of Uttar Pradesh, Bihar and Madhya Pradesh, though the tribal and linguistic factors were also important.

Undoubtedly, regional economic inequality is a potent time-bomb directed against national unity and political stability. So far, fortunately, it has been 'digested', absorbed and mitigated because it is not the result of domination and exploitation of backward states by the more advanced states or of discrimination against the former by the national government. It is noteworthy that the politically important Hindi-speaking states of the Indian heartland—Uttar Pradesh, Bihar, Madhya Pradesh and Rajasthan, with nearly 37 per cent of the seats in the Lok Sabha—are economically backward. On the other hand, Punjab, Haryana, Gujarat and Maharashtra, with only about 17 per cent of the seats in the Lok Sabha, are the high-income states. It is, therefore, impossible for anyone who talks of the Hindi-belt states' domination of the others to be taken seriously.

On the other hand, the backward Hindi-belt states wield so much political clout that it is impossible for them to accuse the central government or non-Hindi states of dominating or discriminating against them. It is interesting that so far accusations of central domination have come from the relatively developed states of Punjab and West Bengal—obviously for political and not economic reasons. However, one hears less and less about central domination in these states too.

In the all-India services too, like the IAS, the Hindi areas are not advantaged. It is Punjab, Tamil Nadu, Kerala and West Bengal which have a higher representation than their population warrants.

Another reason for the lack of regionalism and feeling of discrimination among the poorer states has been the consciousness of their intelligentsia that their poverty and backwardness are basically the result of the actions of their own political and administrative classes. After all, feelings of deprivation and lack of progress are essentially articulated by the intelligentsia. At the same time, the vast majority of the people in the poorer states are blissfully unaware of their backwardness and poverty in comparison with other states. This leads both to absence of discontent with their position as also to a lack of effort to reach equality with the more advanced states. However, with the spread of education and the reach of the visual and print media, such as television and newspapers, this state of affairs is likely to change.

Nevertheless, as was fully realized by the founders of the Republic, it is necessary to first contain regional inequality within politically and economically reasonable and acceptable limits and then to gradually move towards its elimination, by raising the rates of growth of the poorer states by all available means including greater central assistance as also greater self-effort by them. This also, of course, means that, as Ajit Mozoomdar has argued, the national government needs to wield 'greater authority than in industrialised countries, to be able to devise and implement strategies of economic and social development, and to deal with the problems of regional disparities, which are more acute'. It also must have the authority 'to mediate and resolve conflicts between states over the appropriation of natural resources' and 'to effect significant resource transfers from richer to poorer states'.[4]

Sons of the Soil Doctrine

Since the 1950s, an ugly kind of regionalism has been widely prevalent in the form of the 'sons of the soil' doctrine. Underlying it is the view that a state specifically belongs to the main linguistic group inhabiting it or that the state constitutes the exclusive 'homeland' of its main language speakers who are the 'sons of the soil' or the 'local' residents. All others who live there or are settled there and whose mother tongue is not the state's main language, are declared to be 'outsiders'. These 'outsiders' might have lived in the state for a long time, or have migrated there more recently, but they are not to be regarded as the 'sons of the soil'. This doctrine is particularly popular in cities, especially in some of them.

Unequal development of economic opportunities in different parts of the country, especially the cities, occurred in the surge of economic progress after 1952. Demand or preference for the 'local' people or 'sons of the soil' over 'outsiders' in the newly created employment and educational opportunities was the outcome. In the struggle for the appropriation of economic resources and economic opportunities, recourse was often taken to communalism, casteism and nepotism. Likewise, language loyalty and regionalism was used to systematically exclude the 'outsiders' from the economic life of a state or city.

The problem was aggravated in a number of cities or regions because the speakers of the state language were in a minority or had a bare majority. For example, in Bombay, in 1961, the Marathi speakers constituted 42.8 per cent of the population. In Bangalore, the Kannada speakers were less than 25 per cent. In Calcutta, the Bengalis formed a bare majority. In the urban areas of Assam, barely 33 per cent were Assamese. After 1951 the rate of migration into the cities accelerated.

The important questions that arise are, why did the 'sons of the soil' movements develop in some states and cities and not in others, why were they directed against some migrants and linguistic minority groups and not others, why were some types of jobs targeted and not others, why technical and professional education *as against the so-called arts education?* Conflict between migrants and non-migrants (and linguistic minorities and majorities) was not inherent and inevitable. In general, the two have lived harmoniously in most of the states. Clearly, there were specific conditions that precipitated the conflict.

The 'sons of the soil' movements have mainly arisen, and have been more virulent, when there is actual or potential competition for industrial and middle-class jobs, between the migrants and the local, educated, middle-class youth. The friction has been more intense in states and cities where 'outsiders' had greater access to higher education and occupied more middle-class positions in government service, professions and industry and were engaged in small businesses, such as small-scale industry and shopkeeping. Active in these movements have also been members of the lower-middle class or workers, as well as rich and middle peasants whose position is unthreatened, but who increasingly aspire to middle-class status and position for their children. All these social groups also aspire to give their children higher education, especially technical education, such as engineering, medicine and commerce.

The economy's failure to create enough employment opportunities for the recently educated created an acute scarcity of jobs, and led to intense competition for the available jobs during the 1960s and 1970s. The major middle-class job opportunities that opened up after 1952 were in government service and the public sector enterprises. Popular mobilization and the democratic political process could therefore be used by the majority linguistic group to put pressure on the government to appropriate employment and educational avenues and opportunities. Some groups could then take advantage of the 'sons of the soil' sentiment for gaining political power. This was not of course inevitable. The Communist Party refused to use anti-migrant sentiments in Calcutta because of its ideological commitment, one reason why the city has not witnessed any major 'sons of the soil' movement. Similarly, though Congress may have taken an opportunist and compromising stand when faced with major 'sons of the soil' movements, it has not initiated or actively supported them.

'Outsiders' have been often far more numerous in rural areas as agricultural labourers or as workers in low-paid traditional industries, such as jute or cotton textiles, than in the cities. Here, however, the 'sons of the soil' sentiment was absent, nor hostility towards the 'outsiders' manifested because no middle-class jobs were involved. The 'locals' also did not compete with the 'outsiders' for these jobs. Consequently, there has been little conflict with the 'locals' when there has been large-scale migration of labourers from Bihar and Uttar Pradesh to Punjab and Haryana or Bombay city, or of workers from Bihar to the jute and other mills of Calcutta, or of workers from Bihar and Orissa to the tea plantations in Assam and Bengal, or of Oriya building workers to Gujarat, and domestic workers all over India. Such migrations have not posed a threat to the local middle classes; and in the last case—that of the domestic workers—the middle classes have been the chief beneficiaries as also promotees of the migration. However, more recently, because of the higher salaries and education and skill involved, competition between migrants and the 'locals' has tended to develop for employment in the technologically advanced industries.

Another factor that has influenced the emergence or non-emergence of anti-migrant movements in an area or region has been the existence or non-existence of a tradition of migration. When people of a state, especially the middle classes, have themselves migrated, there has been little opposition to immigration. This has been the case with West Bengal, Kerala, Punjab, Bihar and Uttar Pradesh; On the other hand, 'sons of the soil' movements have flourished in Maharashtra, Assam and the Telangana area of Andhra Pradesh, the people of which have not had a tradition of migration.

The Indian constitution is to some extent ambiguous on the question of the rights of the migrants. Article 15 prohibits any discrimination on the grounds of religion, race, caste, sex or place of birth. Article 16 prohibits discrimination in the employment or appointments to any office under the state on grounds of 'descent, place of birth or residence'. However, parliament, though not any state legislature, can pass a law laying down the requirement of residence within a state for appointments under that state. Under political pressure and taking advantage of the ambiguity in the constitution, many states in fact reserve jobs, or give preference for employment in state and local governments and for admission into educational institutions to local residents. The period of residence is fixed or prescribed in such cases. Also, while the constitution permits reservation or preference in state jobs only on grounds of residence and not language, some state governments have gone further and limited the preference to those local residents whose mother tongue is the state language. They have thus discriminated against long-term migrants, their descendants, and even the residents who can speak the state language but whose mother tongue is a minority language in the state. This has, of course, been in clear violation of the constitution. Many state governments have also given directions to private employers to give preference to local persons for employment in their enterprises.

The main argument put forward for reservation in employment and education for the local persons has been that in the states concerned they are socially, economically and educationally backward and are not able to compete with the more advanced migrant communities. Also, in technical colleges and universities, the more backward local students would be overwhelmed by the more advanced students from other states. It is because of this, in the post-Nehru era, even the central government has tended to support preference for residents of a state in employment in central public sector enterprises below the level of a certain technical expertise and in colleges and universities. Reservations on grounds of residence have also been approved by the courts. However, as brought out earlier, reservations for the tribal people are in a separate category.

While reservation of jobs in state administrations and seats in institutions of higher education for the backward local residents was undesirable from the point of view of national integration, some justification could be found for it. However, there was none for the anti-migrant movements of the 1960s which tried to restrict the flow of migrants from other states and which openly proclaimed antagonism and generated hostility against them. These militant anti-migrant and 'sons of the soil' movements were mainly centred in the urban areas of Assam, Telangana in Andhra, Karnataka, Maharashtra and Orissa.

The worst case was that of the movement led by the Shiv Sena which appealed to extreme regional chauvinism and assumed fascist proportions. Founded in 1966, under the leadership of Bal Thackeray, the Shiv Sena demanded that preference in jobs and small businesses should be given to Maharashtrians, who were defined as those whose mother tongue was Marathi. Raising the slogan of 'Maharashtra for the Maharashtrians', the Shiv Sena organized a militant, and often violent movement against South Indians, especially Tamils, who were declared to have a disproportionate share of office jobs such as clerks and typists in private firms and small businesses such as tea shops and eating places. In 1969, the Sena gave Bombay city a taste of fascist violence when it organized arson and terror against South Indians, looted and destroyed their tea-stalls and eating places, overturned cars of Tamils and tore off Tamil signs from shops. The Shiv Sena could not, however, sustain its hate-South Indian campaign or become a major political force outside Bombay city or get the support of any all-India political party. It, therefore, soon shifted its ideological base to Hindu communalism. Gaining a wider political constituency, it was then able to ally itself with the Bharatiya Janata Party.

The 'sons of the soil' movements in Assam and Telangana, which also assumed serious proportions and were quite complex, had some additional and distinctive features. Both these movements will therefore be discussed in the chapters on state politics.

While protective and preferential regulations have been widespread since the late 1960s, antagonism, hostility and violence against migrants have abated in recent years. The problem posed by the 'sons of the soil' doctrine is still a somewhat minor one and there is no ground for pessimism on that score. Even at its height, only a few cities and states were affected in a virulent form, and at no stage did it threaten the unity of the country or the process of nation-in-the-making. Besides, its effects on the Indian economy have been negligible: migration within the country has not been checked; interstate mobility is in fact growing. But the problem is likely to linger till economic development is able to deal effectively with unemployment, especially among the middle classes, and regional inequality.

Looking back at the divisive issues of the post-independence period, the linguistic reorganization of the states, the integration of the tribals, and regional inequality and regionalism, it is to be observed that the prophets of gloom and doom have been disproved. Linguistic states have strengthened not weakened Indian unity, even while permitting full cultural autonomy to different linguistic areas. Hindi and English are growing as all-India languages. Regional movements like the DMK have been doused after 1967 and are content to rename Madras state as Tamil Nadu and Madras city as Chennai. Tribals feel secure in the Indian Union regarding their cultural and economic autonomy, and have also gained greater strength themselves, as also political support in the country over time. The process of nation-in-the-making is being pushed forward. A national identity, that of being Indian, has come to be accepted by all on the subcontinent, and the fact of Indian unity is irreversible.

This should not suggest that all problems related to these issues have been resolved for all time. Further social and economic development, spread of education, deepening of democracy and politicization, as has been seen elsewhere, could create new sources of tension and conflict leading to disrupture tendencies. Optimism is to be tempered with a continuing concern for threats to Indian unity. Yet, India's past experience in overcoming disruptive forces may be instructive for the future. The role and legacy of the freedom struggle, the quality and wisdom of the leaders, the leadership's correct understanding of India's diversity, the leadership's rejection of secessionist demands, while respecting those within the constitutional framework, the democratic political structure, and the acceptance of the need for a strong national government within a federal structure have all contributed to promote Indian unity. Here, it must be added that a strong state should not be mistaken for an authoritarian one. A strong national government does not entail weak state governments or a national government that rides roughshod over the federal provisions of the constitution. Federalism does not mean a weak national government, rather a non-dominating national government which observes the federal features of the polity. A strong but democratic nation state is a necessity for a developing country with strong federal features. What it does with its strength depends on the political nature of the government and the ruling party of the day.

The Years of Hope and Achievement, 1951–1964

The years from 1951 to 1964 were those of maturity and achievement. They were also years marked by high hopes and aspirations, optimism and confidence. Jawaharlal Nehru could declare in April 1953:

> I shall not rest content unless every man, woman and child in the country has a fair deal and has a minimum standard of living . . . Five or six years is too short a time for judging a nation. Wait for another ten years and you will see that our Plans will change the entire picture of the country so completely that the world will be amazed.[1]

And reflecting the mood of the country, he wrote in June 1955:

> Even though we have a multitude of problems, and difficulties surround us and often appear to overwhelm, there is the air of hope in this country, a faith in our future and a certain reliance on the basic principles that have guided us thus far. There is the breath of the dawn, the feeling of the beginning of a new era in the long and chequered history of India.[2]

These were also the years when India was more or less stable, when its political system took on its distinct form, the country began to progress in all directions, and above all there was the beginning of the massive reconstruction of the polity and the economy. People experienced an advance towards the basic objectives of democracy, civil liberties, secularism, a scientific and international outlook, economic development and planning, with socialism at the end of the road. There was, of course, some discontent among the intelligentsia regarding the slow pace of development, especially with regard to the problems of poverty and employment, and the slow and unsatisfactory progress of land reforms. Among the several areas of progress and achievement, though marked by certain weaknesses and limitations, were (a) the consolidation of the nation and the solution of the language and tribal problems, (b) the initiation of the process of independent and planned economic development, (c) the evolution of an independent and innovative foreign policy, (d) the initiation of the electoral process, (e) the rooting of democracy, (f) the setting in place of an administrative structure, (g) the development of science and technology, and (h) the beginnings of the welfare state. The first three aspects are discussed in separate chapters in this volume; the last five aspects are discussed in this chapter.

The Rooting of the Electoral Process

First of all came the entrenchment of democracy—an achievement which has endured so that it is now taken for granted. The process had begun with the framing of the constitution after 1947 and its promulgation on 26 January 1950. Democracy took a giant step forward with the first general election held in 1951–52 over a four-month period. These elections were the biggest experiment in democracy anywhere in the world. The elections were held on the basis of universal adult franchise, with all those twenty-one years of age or older having the right to vote. There were over 173 million voters, most of them poor, illiterate, and rural, and having had no experience of elections. The big question at the time was how would the people respond to this opportunity.

Many were sceptical about such an electorate being able to exercise its right to vote in a politically mature and responsible manner. Some said that democratic elections were not suited to a caste-ridden, multi-religious, illiterate and backward society like India's and that only a benevolent dictatorship could be effective politically in such a society. The coming elections were described by some as 'a leap in the dark' and by others as 'fantastic' and as 'an act of faith'.

India's electoral system was developed according to the directives of the constitution. The constitution created an Election Commission, headed by a Chief Election Commissioner, to conduct elections. It was to be independent of the executive or the parliament or the party in power.

Organization of the elections was a wondrous task. There was a house-to-house survey to register the voters. With over 70 per cent of the voters being illiterate, the candidates were to be identified by symbols, assigned to each major party and independent candidates, painted on the ballot boxes (this was later changed to symbols on the ballot papers). The voters were to place the ballot papers in the box assigned to a particular candidate, and ballot was secret. Over 224,000 polling booths, one for almost every 1,000 voters, were constructed and equipped with over 2.5 million steel ballot boxes, one box for every candidate. Nearly 620,000,000 ballot papers were printed. About a million officials supervised the conduct of the polls. Of the many candidates, whoever got the plurality or the largest number of votes would get elected. It was not necessary for the winning candidate to have a majority.

In all, candidates of over fourteen national and sixty-three regional or local parties and a large number of independents contested 489 seats for the Lok Sabha and 3,283 seats for the state assemblies. Of these, 98 seats for the former and 669 for the latter were reserved for the Scheduled Castes and Scheduled Tribes. Nearly 17,500 candidates in all stood for the seats to the Lok Sabha and the state legislatures. The elections were spread out over nearly four months from 25 October 1951 to 21 February 1952. (Later this period was reduced to nineteen days in 1957 and seven to ten days in subsequent elections.)

Suitable conditions were created for the free participation of the Opposition parties in the elections, including the Jan Sangh and CPI. This was despite the fact that Jan Sangh was communal and the moving force behind it, namely, the RSS, had been banned only three years earlier for spreading communal hatred which had led to the assassination of Gandhiji. CPI had adopted an insurrectionary policy till a few months before the elections and even at the time was firmly opposed to the constitutional structure. The Opposition was, however, quite fragmented. Neither the communal parties nor the left-wing parties could come together to form electoral alliances or even arrive at adjustments among themselves.

The first general elections were marked by a vigorous election campaign by Jawaharlal Nehru. Showing remarkable energy, he covered nearly 40,000 kilometres and addressed 35 million people or a tenth of India's population during his election tour. As Nehru's biographer, S. Gopal, has pointed out, 'As before 1947, all the speeches of Nehru were part of a process of adult education, of teaching the masses that they had minds which they should use.' In fact, Nehru was at the centre stage of the election campaign. The Opposition parties too recognized his importance, and all of them, to again quote Gopal, 'joined in attacking him from every possible view point'.[3] Nehru too recognized his own centrality and wrote: 'It is true that without me in the Congress, there would have been no stable government in any State or in the Centre, and a process of disruption would have set in.'[4]

In particular, he made communalism the central issue of his campaign. The basic struggle at the time, he said, was between the secular and the communal forces, for the main danger to India's integrity came from the latter. 'If allowed free play,' he warned, communalism 'would break up India'.[5] And he declared: 'Let us be clear about it without a shadow of doubt . . . we stand till death for a secular State.'[6]

The elections were conducted in a fair, free, impartial and orderly manner with very little violence. This was widely acknowledged when Sukumar Sen, the first Chief Election Commissioner, was invited as an expert adviser on elections by several Asian and African countries. The election process was completed in May 1950 when Rajendra Prasad was elected as the President of the Republic and Dr S. Radhakrishnan as its Vice-President.

People's response to the new political order was tremendous. They participated in the polls fully aware that their vote was a prized possession. In many places, people treated polling as a festival, as a public celebration, with many decking themselves up for the occasion in festive clothing, the women wearing their silver jewellery. They also demonstrated their ability to exercise their right to vote carefully despite their poverty and illiteracy and the complicated voting procedures. For example, the number of invalid votes cast was as low as 3 to 4 per cent. There was a large turnout of voters not only in the urban areas but also in the rural areas and among the Scheduled Castes and Scheduled Tribes. A remarkable feature was the wide participation of women: at least 40 per cent of women eligible to vote did so. Thus, the faith of the leadership in the people was fully justified.

When the election results were declared, it was found that nearly 46.6 per cent of the eligible voters had cast their vote. Since then this percentage has been going up and has been comparable to the voting percentages in the United States. Party-wise the election results for the Lok Sabha and the state assemblies were as given in the table below.

Lok Sabha

Party	Seats won	Percentage of votes	Seats won in state assemblies
Congress	364	45.00	2,248
Communist and allies	23	4.60	147
Socialists	12	10.60	125
KMPP	9	5.80	
Jan Sangh	3	3.10	
Hindu Mahasabha	4	0.95	85
RRP	3	2.03	
Other parties	30	12.08	273
Independents	41	15.80	325
Total	489		3,279

Note: KMPP = Kisan Mazdoor Praja Party; RRP = Ram Rajya Parishad

The major features of this election which characterized subsequent elections till 1962 and even later were:

(i) The Congress swept the polls bagging nearly 75 per cent of the seats in the Lok Sabha and 68.5 per cent of those in the state legislatures. But in both cases it got less than 50 per cent of the votes cast. This was because of the plurality or first-past-the-post principle followed in deciding the winner. The elections represented a triumph for the Congress organization, which reached down to the village level, for the ideology of secularism, democracy and national, unity, and, above all, for the inspiring leadership of Nehru. The Congress formed the government at the Centre and in all the states. It did not get a majority on its own in four states—Madras, Travancore-Cochin, Orissa and PEPSU—but formed governments even there with the help of independents and smaller, local parties which then merged with it.

(ii) Both the parties of the left and the communal right performed poorly. The poor performance of the Socialist Party and the Kisan Mazdoor Praja Party (KMPP) (the two together won only 21 seats in the Lok Sabha) was, in fact, quite a surprise in view of their high hopes and optimistic projections. The Socialist Party won only 19 seats in the assembly in Uttar Pradesh, its strongest unit. Similarly, the three communal parties, the Jan Sangh, the Hindu Mahasabha and the Ram Rajya Parishad, won only 10 Lok Sabha seats and 6 per cent of the votes cast.

(iii) The Communist performance was better than expected. The CPI along with its allies, most of them Communists or fellow travellers in reality, emerged as the second largest group in the Lok Sabha. It was to retain this position in most of the later elections till 1977. The CPI also won a sizeable number of seats in Madras, Travancore-Cochin and Hyderabad.

(iv) The elections showed that the princes and big landlords still wielded a great deal of influence in some parts of the country. Their party, the Ganatantra Parishad, won 22.1 per cent (31 seats) of the assembly seats in Orissa. Similarly, the three communal parties won 64 of their 85 assembly seats in the former princely states.

(v) The independents and the small regional and local parties got a large number of the votes and seats both in the Lok Sabha and the state assemblies. However, the role of independents in the elections both at the Centre and in the states, started declining from 1962.

The political system that was initiated by the elections of 1951–52 has been described by many political scientists as the beginning of the one-party-dominant system. But, in fact, it represented the beginning of a multi-party system with the Congress enjoying the special status of forming the core or the focus of the system as also its stabilizing force. Despite the numerically dominant position of the Congress, the Opposition was quite effective in parliament. It used the Question Hour to great effect and maintained a high level of debate in parliament. The effectiveness of the Opposition owed a great deal to the high calibre of the few but capable Opposition members on the one hand, and Nehru's respect for the Opposition opinion on the other.

Noteworthy is the fact that though other forms of political participation, such as trade unions, Kisan Sabhas, strikes, hartals, bandhs and demonstrations, were available to the middle classes, organized working class, and sections of the rich and middle peasantry, elections were the main form of direct political participation for the vast mass of the rural and urban poor.

A few embryonic, negative features—pointers to the future—also surfaced during the first general elections. There was a scramble for tickets in the Congress and squabbles among leaders for getting safe seats for their followers. Many of the independent candidates were those rejected by the Congress and other political parties. Factionalism also made its appearance in a big way in nearly all the parties. Villages were often divided into factions irrespective of party or ideology. Vote banks also began to emerge so that some people voted according to the dictates of the influential persons on whom they were dependent economically. Of course, more legitimately, local notables such as freedom fighters, doctors, lawyers, schoolteachers also guided and decided the local voters' preferences. Caste and kinship ties also began to influence the voters significantly from this election onwards.

After 1952, during the Nehru years, two other general elections were held for the Lok Sabha and state assemblies in 1957 and 1962. In both, the voter turnout improved—while in 1951–52 it was 46 per cent, in 1957 it was 47 per cent and in 1962 nearly 54 per cent. In both elections, the Congress again gained an overwhelming majority of seats in the Lok Sabha with a minority of votes; and neither the right nor the left could pose a serious challenge to it. Both, however, made inroads into the Congress hegemony in a few states. In 1957, the Communists were able to form a government in Kerala, which was the first democratically elected Communist government anywhere in the world.

The fair and peaceful conduct of the polls was an indication that the democratic system and institutions, a legacy of the national movement, were beginning to take root. They began functioning with a fair degree of commitment to democratic values. It is also significant that partially as a result of the conduct of the elections, the framework of the constitution came to be accepted by all, including the Communists and the communalists. From then it was taken for granted that elections would decide which party would rule India, that a change in government would occur through the constitutionally provided democratic rules, that election results would be accepted by the defeated parties, however undesirable they might be from their point of view, and that elections would take place at regular intervals. The successful conduct of the polls was one of the reasons why India and Nehru came to be admired abroad, especially in the ex-colonial countries.

The elections of 1951–52 became the healthy precursors of regular and fair elections in the years to come. From 1952 to 2007 there were fourteen elections to the Lok Sabha and many more to the state assemblies with ever larger turnout of voters, especially of rural folk and women, indicating the growing political awareness among the people.

Establishment of Democratic Institutions

Building on the traditions of the national movement, the Indian leaders, and above all Nehru, further strengthened the foundations of democracy in the country by the manner of their political functioning. They gave due importance to the institutional aspects of the democratic system so that gradually attachment of people to parliamentary institutions grew. They adhered not only to the spirit but also to the forms of democratic institutions and procedures. Nehru, in particular, despite holding complete sway saw to it that political power was widely dispersed and diffused.

Civil liberties were put on a firm footing with the Press having free play, even when it criticized the government severely. The independence of the courts was carefully nurtured, even when they turned down an important piece of popular legislation, namely, agrarian reform.

Nehru treated parliament with respect and made every effort to sustain its dignity, prestige and power, even though his party enjoyed an overwhelming majority in it. He tried to make it a major forum for expression of public opinion, and made it a point to sit through the Question Hour and to attend parliamentary debates. The Opposition too played its part by respecting parliament and its procedures, functioning without fear in its portals, and keeping the standard of parliamentary debates at a high level. Moreover, parliamentary committees such as the Estimates Committee began to play an important role as critics and watchdogs of the government administration.

Under Nehru's leadership the cabinet system evolved in a healthy manner and functioned effectively. The effort was to make the cabinet the chief agent of collective policy-making. Nehru treated his cabinet colleagues with courtesy and respect. C.D. Deshmukh, India's Finance Minister from 1950 to 1956, remarked later in his autobiography: 'Nehru as head of the Cabinet was gentle, considerate and democratic, never forcing a decision on his colleagues . . . decisions were taken by a consensus and never, as far as I can remember in my time, by vote.'[7]

Despite the dominance of the Congress party the role of the Opposition was strengthened during the period. Nehru gave full play and respect to the Opposition parties and was quite responsive to their criticism. He once defined democracy as follows: 'In the ultimate analysis, it is a manner of thinking, a manner of action, a manner of behaviour to your neighbour and to your adversary and opponent.'[8] The Opposition parties, though small numerically, were able to take advantage of the fact that the Congress was not a monolithic party and encompassed within itself several political and ideological trends. They were able to influence the government policies by influencing the different ideological strands in the Congress. Nehru also respected and promoted internal democracy and debate within the Congress party and encouraged it to accommodate new social forces and trends.

Federalism, provided for in the constitution, also was established as a firm feature of Indian polity during the Nehru years, with a genuine devolution of power to the states. Respecting the states' autonomy, Nehru would not impose decisions on the state governments or interfere with their policies, though he took care to inform them of his own thinking and occasionally advise or even insist on their acceptance of a particular policy. He also permitted the state Congress parties to choose their party and government leaders. He relied upon the state leaders and governments to understand better their own intricate problems. In the process, he was willing to put up with a great deal. In fact, one reason why Nehru would not go too far in forcing the states to effect land reforms the way he conceived them was because land reforms were a State subject and he would not ride roughshod over the states' rights and powers even for a favourite cause of his. Nehru would guide and advise and urge but would not step out of constitutional boundaries; he would observe constitutional niceties in spirit and form. In fact, a major reason for the weaknesses of the agricultural, educational, health and other social welfare programmes lay in the Centre's dependence on the states for their implementation, for these were State subjects.

At the same time, Nehru did not permit any weakening of the prestige or authority of the central government. He always maintained a sharp distinction between the centralization of power or centre's domination of the states and a strong centre needed for nation-building and maintenance of the unity and independence of the country as also to keep under check disruptive and divisive forces.

A major reason that led to the development of harmonious relations between the Centre and the states and which kept in check centrifugal forces was the fact that the same party ruled in both places. The leading role of the Centre was also facilitated by the fact that some of the tallest men and women in Indian politics held office in the cabinet as well as the Congress Working Committee.

The tradition of the supremacy of the civil government over the armed forces was fully established during these years. The Indian armed forces had been traditionally non-political and had accepted civilian control and leadership. But the continuation of this role by them was not guaranteed. Nehru, in particular, was worried about the possibility of the armed forces intervening in politics and the government in case of exceptional circumstances, as happened in nineteenth-century France and Germany and in many Third World countries. To avoid such a possibility in India he took several steps in this regard. He kept the size of the armed forces relatively small, refusing to permit their expansion even after large-scale US military aid to Pakistan began in 1954. The expenditure on the defence forces was also kept extremely low, less than 2 per cent of the national income. Abandoning the British colonial practice of recruiting men in the army on the criterion of 'martial' classes, the armed forces were given a heterogeneous character, with almost every region and section of society being represented in them. India was thus protected from the danger of militarism in its formative years. The small size of the armed forces and of expenditure on them were also prompted by two other considerations: avoidance of diversion of scarce resources from economic development; and given the absence of domestic defence industries, to avoid dependence on foreign powers and the possibility of their intervention in India's internal and foreign affairs.

One blemish, though not a simple one, on the democratic record of the Nehru years occurred when the Communist government in Kerala was dismissed in 1959 and President's Rule was imposed in the state.

The Administrative Structure

Immediately after independence, it was to be decided whether the government of independent India should carry on with the administrative structure and machinery inherited from the colonial regime and 'designed to serve the relatively simple interests of an occupying power'.

The kingpin of this structure was the Indian Civil Service (ICS). If the structure was to be replaced or overhauled, the beginning had to be made with the ICS. Initially, there were differences in approach to the question between Nehru and Patel, who, as Home Minister, dealt directly with the administrative services. Nehru was a staunch critic of the ICS and bureaucracy as a whole not only because of their colonial ancestry but also because of their basic conservatism. In 1946, he had described the existing administrative structure as 'the ship of State' which was 'old and battered and slow-moving and unsuited to this age of swift change'. He declared that 'it will have to be scrapped and give place to another'.[9] Patel, on the other hand, felt that retention of the existing administrative machinery was necessary in the then troubled times when it seemed that internal stability was in danger and chaos imminent. He was not in favour of a sudden discontinuity and vacuum in administration, particularly as the ICS and other all-India services provided the only trained personnel available. Defending the all-India services in the Constituent Assembly in 1949, Patel said: 'I have worked with them during this difficult period . . . Remove them and I see nothing but a picture of chaos all over the country.' Further: 'If during the last two or three years most of the members of the Services had not behaved patriotically and with loyalty, the Union would have collapsed.'[10]

Nehru accepted Patel's position, though grudgingly, for he too realized that there was no alternative to reliance on the existing all-India services if a breakdown of administration was to be avoided. Over time he too began to rely heavily on these services, admiring their administrative efficiency, especially as he realized that the other available human resources were rather poor.

Many, following Lenin in the *State and Revolution*, have argued that the existing state administrative apparatus should have been 'smashed' or dismantled and that it was perhaps quite easy to do so in the very beginning of a new state. We think that in light of India's and other countries' historical experience there is little doubt that having well-trained, versatile and experienced civil services at the outset when the country was in turmoil was a distinct asset and advantage to India; and that they did give a good account of themselves in the troubled post-Partition years.

However, while retention of the existing bureaucracy and the administrative structure was inevitable and perhaps even sound under the circumstances, the failure to 'rebuild and transform their character' was clearly a liability. The administrative structure had been built during the colonial period largely to maintain law and order and to collect land revenue. It had to be overhauled, however gradually, to suit the needs of a democratic and developing society and made capable of executing the new economic and social welfarist policies.

Nehru in particular was fully aware of the inadequacy of the existing bureaucracy to understand the problems of the people and to implement the new tasks. As early as 1951 he complained: 'We rely more and more on official agencies which are generally fairly good, but which are completely different in outlook and execution from anything that draws popular enthusiasm to it.'[11] He was convinced that the situation could be remedied in two ways: 'One, by educating the whole machine. Secondly, by putting a new type of person where it is needed.'[12] But neither of the two steps was actually taken. Rather, the new IAS was formed very much in the old ICS mould and this pattern was followed all down the bureaucratic structure. For example, the few who joined the community development projects out of idealism and social commitment were soon frustrated when they discovered that they were being dominated, looked down upon and treated as low-paid underlings by the traditional, higher bureaucrats.

The administration not only did not improve over the years, it deteriorated further becoming more inefficient and inaccessible. The attitude of the bureaucracy, especially the police, towards the people and their problems also became increasingly unhelpful. Above all, there was the evil of corruption.

There were major signals in the Nehru era that political and administrative corruption was beginning to burgeon. In the 1950s, however, the tentacles of corruption were not yet far-reaching and checks existed in the form of a political leadership and cadres having roots in the freedom struggle and Gandhian ethos, a large, honest bureaucracy, especially in its middle and higher rungs, and a judiciary having a high level of integrity, It was, therefore, still possible to squash the evil with a certain ease.

Nehru and other leaders were aware of the problems relating to public administration. In May 1948, Nehru drew the attention of the chief ministers to complaints from the public 'about our inefficiency, inaccessibility, delays and, above all, of corruption', and added: 'I fear that many of these complaints are justified.'[13] Similarly, in his last letter to the chief ministers in May 1963, he pointed to the need to 'strengthen our Government apparatus and to fight a ceaseless war against corruption and inefficiency'. And he added:

> There is far too much talk of corruption. I think it is exaggerated a good deal but we must realise that it is there and must face that with all our will and strength. Our governmental apparatus is still slow moving and full of brakes which come in the way of all the brave schemes that we have in mind . . . I am writing about this to you because I feel strongly that we must clean up our public life . . .[14]

Nehru also took concrete action whenever a case of corruption involving his ministers was made out. But he was chary of carrying out a campaign against corruption lest it create a general atmosphere of suspicion and accusations, to which he felt Indians were already too susceptible, and thus prevent officials and ministers from taking timely decisions and assuming responsibility.

Development of Science and Technology

A major achievement of the Nehru era was in the fields of scientific research and technological education. Nehru was convinced that science and technology were crucial to the solution of India's problems. As early as January 1938, he had said in a message to the Indian Science Congress: 'It was science alone that could solve these problems of hunger and poverty, of insanitation and illiteracy, of superstition and deadening custom and tradition, of vast resources running to waste, of a rich country inhabited by starving people.'[15] This view was reiterated in the Scientific Policy Resolution passed by the Lok Sabha in March 1958 acknowledging the role of science and technology in the economic, social and cultural advancement of the country. After 1947, Nehru also became aware of the critical role that scientific research and technology would play in India's defence.

As part of the effort to promote self-sustaining scientific and technological growth, the foundation stone of India's first national laboratory, the National Physical Laboratory, was laid on 4 January 1947. This was followed by the setting up during the Nehru years of a network of seventeen national laboratories, specializing in different areas of research. To emphasize the importance of science and scientific research, Nehru himself assumed the chairmanship of the Council of Scientific and Industrial Research, which guided and financed the national laboratories and other scientific institutions.

Urgent steps were also taken to organize the training of technical personnel sorely needed by the country. In 1952, the first of the five institutes of technology, patterned ofter the Massachusetts Institute of Technology, was set up at Kharagpur—the other four being set up subsequently at Madras, Bombay, Kanpur and Delhi. The extent of the effort put in developing science and its success is revealed by the expenditure on scientific research, and science-based activities which increased from Rs 1.10 crore in 1948–49 to Rs 85.06 crore in 1965–66, and the number of scientific and technical personnel which rose from 188,000 in 1950 to 731,500 in 1965. The enrolment at the undergraduate stage in engineering and technology went up from 13,000 in 1950 to 78,000 in 1965. Similarly, the number of undergraduate students studying agriculture increased from about 2,600 in 1950 to 14,900 in 1965.

Over the years scientific research began, however, to suffer because the organization and management structure of the scientific institutes was highly bureaucratic and hierarchical, breeding factionalism and intrigue as also frustration among their personnel. This became a major factor in the brain drain of scientists that began in the late 1950s.

India was one of the first nations to recognize the importance of nuclear energy. Nehru was convinced that nuclear energy would bring about a global revolution in the social, economic and political spheres, besides affecting nations' defence capabilities.

In August 1948, the Government of India set up the Atomic Energy Commission with Homi J. Bhabha, India's leading nuclear scientist, as Chairman, in the Department of Scientific Research, which was under Nehru's direct charge, to develop nuclear energy for peaceful purposes. In 1954, the government created a separate Department of Atomic Energy under the prime minister with Homi Bhabha as Secretary. India's first nuclear reactor in Trombay, Bombay, also the first in Asia, became critical in August 1956. The ongoing and fairly well-advanced nuclear programme included the setting up of several nuclear plants to produce electricity in a few years' time. Though India was committed to the peaceful uses of nuclear power, its nuclear capacity could easily have been used to produce the atomic bomb and other atomic weapons.

India also took up space research. It set up the Indian National Committee for Space Research (INCOSPAR) in 1962 and established a Rocket Launching Facility at Thumba (TERLS). Krishna Menon, as Defence Minister, took steps to initiate defence research and development. Steps were also taken to increase India's capacity in production of defence equipment so that India gradually became self-sufficient in its defence needs. India also changed over to decimal coinage and a metric system of weights and measures, despite dire warnings that an illiterate population could not handle the change.

Social Change

The vision of the founding fathers of the Republic went beyond national integration and political stability. Indian society had to move towards social change. Article 36 of the constitution in the section on the Directive Principles of State Policy states: 'The state shall strive to promote the welfare of the people by securing and protecting as effectively as may be a social order in which justice, economic and political, shall inform all institutions of the national life.' This conception of the new social order was encompassed in 1955 by the phrase 'socialistic pattern of society' officially accepted by the Congress at its Avadi session and later incorporated as its objective in the Second and Third Five Year Plans. Consequently, several important measures of social reforms, which some have described as the beginning of a welfare state, were taken during the Nehru years. Very important measures in this respect were those of land reforms, the initiation of planned economic development and rapid expansion of the public sector which we shall examine in separate chapters of this volume. In addition far-reaching labour legislation was undertaken, including recognition of collective bargaining, the right to form trade unions and to go on strike, security of employment, and provision of health and accident insurance. There were also moves towards a more equitable distribution of wealth through progressive and steep income tax and excise tax policies. Expansion of education and health and other social services was also sought.

Nehru and other leaders were also keen to ensure that Indian social organization underwent change, leading to the social liberation of the hitherto socially backward and suppressed sections of society. As Nehru put it in 1956: 'We have not only striven for and achieved a political revolution, not only are we striving hard for an economic revolution but . . . we are equally intent on social revolution; only by way of advance on these three separate lines and their integration into one great whole, will the people of India progress.'[16]

The constitution had already incorporated a provision abolishing untouchability. The government supplemented this provision by passing the Anti-Untouchability Law in 1955 making the practice of untouchability punishable and a cognizable offence. The government also tried to implement the clauses of the constitution regarding reservations in educational institutions and government employment in favour of Scheduled Castes (SCs) and Scheduled Tribes (STs) and other weaker sections of society. Other necessary measures were taken to raise their social status, such as the provision of special facilities in the form of scholarships, hostels accommodation, grants, loans, housing, healthcare and legal aid services. A Commissioner of Scheduled Castes and Scheduled Tribes was appointed to monitor the effective implementation of all such measures and constitutional provisions. However, in spite of all these steps, the SCs and STs continued to be backward and caste oppression was still widely prevalent, especially in rural areas, where the Scheduled Castes and Scheduled Tribes also formed a large part of the landless agricultural labour, and therefore also suffered from class oppression. There was also hardly any effort to eradicate the ideology of the caste system or to remove caste inequality and caste oppression so that casteism began to spread from the upper castes to the backward castes and from the rural to the urban areas.

Participating actively in the national movement for years, women's groups and organizations were demanding revision of laws regarding women's rights in the family, and in Nehru they had a firm supporter. Already, before independence, Nehru had made his position on this issue clear and quoted Charles Fourier, the French philosopher: 'One could judge the degree of civilisation of a country by the social and political position of its women.'[17]

A major step forward in this direction was taken when the Hindu Code Bill was moved in parliament in 1951. The bill faced sharp opposition from conservative sectors of society, especially from the Jan Sangh and other Hindu communal organizations. Even though actively supported by the vocal members of the Congress party and women MPs and other women activists, Nehru decided to postpone enactment of the bill in order to mobilize greater support for it. He was, however, firm in his determination to pass the bill and made it an issue in the elections of 1951–52.

After coming back to power, the government passed the bill in the form of four separate acts which introduced monogamy and the right of divorce to both men and women, raised the age of consent and marriage, and gave women the right to maintenance and to inherit family property. A revolutionary step was thus taken for women's liberation, though its practice would take decades to take full effect. An important lacuna in this respect was that a uniform civil code covering the followers of all religions was not enacted. This would have involved changes in Muslim personal law regarding monogamy and inheritance. There was strong opposition to this from the Muslim orthodoxy. The process of social reform among Muslims had in the modern period lagged far behind that among Hindus and consequently social change had been quite slow even among middle-class Muslim women. Nehru was not willing to alarm the Muslim minority which was, he believed, even otherwise under pressure. He would make changes in Muslim personal law and enact a uniform civil code but only when Muslims were ready for it.

Education

The founding fathers were fully aware of the need for better and wider education as an instrument of social and economic progress, equalization of opportunity and the building up of a democratic society. This was all the more urgent because in 1951 only 16.6 per cent of the total population was literate and the percentage was much lower, being only 6 per cent, in the case of rural families. To remedy this situation, the constitution directed that by 1961 the state should provide free and compulsory education to every child up to the age of fourteen. Later, this target was shifted to 1966.

The government provided large sums for developing primary, secondary, higher and technical education: while the expenditure on education was Rs 198 million in 1951–52, by 1964–65 it had increased to Rs 1,462.7 million, that is, by more than seven times. Since education was primarily a State subject, Nehru urged the state governments not to reduce expenditure on primary education, whatever the nature of financial stringency. If necessary, he suggested, even expenditure on industrial development could be reduced. He told the National Development Council in May 1961: 'I have come to feel that it [education] is the basis of all and, on no account unless actually our heads are cut off and we cannot function, must we allow education to suffer.'[18]

The Nehru years witnessed rapid expansion of education, especially in the case of girls. Between 1951 and 1961 school enrolment doubled for boys and tripled for girls. From 1950–51 to 1965–66 the number of boys enrolled in classes I to V increased from 13.77 million to 32.18 million. The relevant figures for girls were 5.38 million and 18.29 million. The progress was equally rapid in the case of secondary education. Between 1950–51 and 1965–66 enrolment increased from 1.02 million to 4.08 million (by nearly four times) in the case of boys and from 0.19 million to 1.2 million (by nearly 6.5 times) in the case of girls. The number of secondary schools increased from 7,288 to 24,477 during these years.

At the time of independence there were eighteen universities with a total student enrolment of nearly 300,000. By 1964, the number of universities had increased to fifty-four, the number of colleges to about 2,500 and the number of undergraduate and postgraduate students, excluding intermediate students, to 613,000. The number of girls students increased six-fold and constituted 22 per cent of the total. However, the progress in primary education, though recognizable, did not match the needs or the intentions especially as the number of eligible students was growing fast because of the high rate of population growth. The constitutional target of free and compulsory education to all children was first shifted from 1961 to 1966 and then to a distant future. By the end of the Third Plan in 1965–66 only 61 per cent of the children between the ages of six and fourteen were in school, the figure for girls being only 43 per cent. Consequently, widespread illiteracy continued; as late as 1991 only 52 per cent of Indians were literate.

But these figures do not tell the full story. In 1965, 5 per cent of the rural population was not served by any school at all. Moreover, the facilities provided in the existing schools were very poor, with the majority of schools having no pucca building, blackboards or drinking water. Nearly 40 per cent of primary schools had only one teacher to take three or four classes. A particular malady of primary schooling was the high rate of dropouts. Nearly half of those enrolled in class I would have left school by the time they reached class IV and been rapidly reduced to virtual illiteracy again. Moreover, the dropout rate was higher in the case of girls than boys. Clearly, there was no equal opportunity in education and therefore also hardly any equalization of opportunity in work and employment for the poor and those in the rural areas who constituted the vast majority of the Indian people.

A major weakness that crept in was the decline in educational standards. Despite recognition of the problem, except for the technology sector, the educational system was left untouched and unreformed and the quality of education continued to deteriorate, first in schools and then in colleges and universities. The ideological content of education also continued to be the same as in the colonial period.

Nehru was aware of the unsatisfactory progress in education and near the end of his prime ministership began to put greater emphasis on its development, especially of primary education, which, he now stressed, should, be developed at any cost. 'In the final analysis,' he wrote to the chief ministers in 1963, 'right education open to all is perhaps the basic remedy for most of our ills.' Also, 'In spite of my strong desire for the growth of our industry, I am convinced that it is better to do without some industrial growth than to do without adequate education at the base.'[19]

Community Development programme

Two major programmes for rural uplift, namely, the Community Development programme and Panchayati Raj, were introduced in 1952 and 1959. They were to lay the foundations of the welfare state in the villages. Though designed for the sake of agricultural development, they had more of a welfare content; their basic purpose was to change the face of rural India, to improve the quality of life of the people.

The Community Development programme was instituted on a limited scale in 1952 covering 55 development blocks, each block consisting of about 100 villages with a population of 60,000 to 70,000. By the mid-1960s most of the country was covered by a network of community blocks, employing more than 6,000 Block Development Officers (BDOs) and over 600,000 Village Level Workers (VLWs or Gram Sewaks) to help implement the programme. The programme covered all aspects of rural life from improvement in agricultural methods to improvement in communications, health and education.

The emphasis of the programme was on self-reliance and self-help by the people, popular participation and responsibility. It was to be basically a people's movement for their own welfare. As Nehru stated at the very outset of the programme in 1952, the basic objective was 'to unleash forces from below among our people'. While it was 'necessary to plan, to direct, to organize and to coordinate; but it [was] even more necessary to create conditions in which a spontaneous growth from below [was] possible'. While material achievements were expected, the programme was much more geared 'to build up the community and the individual and to make the latter a builder of his own village centre and of India in the larger sense'. 'The primary matter is the human being involved,' he added. Another major objective was to uplift the backward sections: 'We must aim at progressively producing a measure of equality in opportunity and other things.'[20] In 1952 and in the later years, Nehru repeatedly referred to the Community

Development programme and the accompanying National Extension Service as representing 'new dynamism' and a 'great revolution' and as 'symbols of the resurgent spirit of India'.[21]

The programme achieved considerable results in extension work: better seeds, fertilizers, and so on, resulting in agricultural development in general and greater food production, in particular, construction of roads, tanks and wells, school and primary health centre buildings, and extension of educational and health facilities. Initially, there was also a great deal of popular enthusiasm, which, however, petered out with time. It soon became apparent that the programme had failed in one of its basic objectives—that of involving the people as full participants in developmental activity. Not only did it not stimulate self-help, it increased expectations from and reliance on the government. It gradually acquired an official orientation, became part of the bureaucratic framework and came to be administered from above as a routine activity with the BDOs becoming replicas of the traditional sub-divisional officers and the Village Level Workers becoming administrative underlings. As Nehru put it later, in 1963, while the entire programme was designed to get the peasant 'out of the rut in which he has been living since ages past', the programme itself 'has fallen into a rut'.[22]

The weaknesses of the programme had come to be known as early as 1957 when the Balwantrai Mehta Committee, asked to evaluate it, had strongly criticized its bureaucratization and its lack of popular involvement. As a remedy, the Committee recommended the democratic decentralization of the rural and district development administration. On the Committee's recommendation, it was decided to introduce, all over the country, an integral system of democratic self-government with the village panchayat at its base. The new system, which came to be known as Panchayati Raj and was implemented in various states from 1959, was to consist of a three-tier, directly elected village or gram panchayats, and indirectly elected block-level panchayat samitis and district-level zilla parishads. The Community Development programme was to be integrated with the Panchayati Raj; considerable functions, resources and authority were to be devolved upon the three-tiered samitis to carry out schemes of development. Thus, the Panchayati Raj was intended to make up a major deficiency of the Community Development programme by providing for popular participation in the decision-making and implementation of the development process with the officials working under the guidance of the three-level samitis. Simultaneously, the countryside was covered by thousands of cooperative institutions such as cooperative banks, land mortgage banks and service and market cooperatives, which were also autonomous from the bureaucracy as they were managed by elected bodies.

Nehru's enthusiasm was once again aroused as Panchayati Raj and cooperative institutions represented another radical step for change in society. They would transfer responsibility for development and rural administration to the people and accelerate rural development. They would thus act as instruments for the empowerment of the people and would not only lead to greater self-reliance, but would also act as an educative tool, for bringing about a change in the outlook of the people. Above all, they would initiate the process of creating better human beings.

However, these hopes were belied. Though adopting Panchayati Raj in one form or another, the state governments showed little enthusiasm for it, devolved no real power on the panchayati samitis, curbed their powers and functions and starved them of funds. The bureaucracy too did not slacken its grip on rural administration at different levels. Panchayats were also politicized and used by politicians to gather factional support in the villages. As a result, though foundations of a system of rural local self-government were laid, democratic decentralization as a whole was stunted and could not perform the role assigned to it by the Balwantrai Mehta Committee and Jawaharlal Nehru.

Moreover, the benefits of community development, new agricultural inputs and the extension services were mostly garnered by the rich peasants and capitalist farmers, who also came to dominate the Panchayati Raj institutions. The basic weakness of the Community Development programme, the Panchayati Raj and the cooperative movement was that they ignored the class division of the rural society where nearly half the population was landless or had marginal holdings and was thus quite powerless. The village was dominated socially and economically by the capitalist farmers and the rich and middle peasantry; and neither the dominant rural classes nor the bureaucrats could become agents of social transformation or popular participation.

Foreign Policy: The Nehru Era

The Basic Parameters

India's efforts to pursue an independent foreign policy was a highlight of post-1947 politics. A product of its long history and recent past, this policy was marked by a great deal of consistency and continuity. Despite revolutionary changes in the international situation, the broad parameters which were evolved during the freedom struggle and in the early years of independence still retain their validity. Jawaharlal Nehru stands as the architect of this not mean achievement. He realized that given her great civilization, India could not but aspire to the right to speak in her own voice. The recent, hard-won freedom from the colonial yoke would also be meaningless unless India found expression in the international arena. Being subcontinental in size, too, ruled out an assumption of client status for India. An independent voice was not merely a choice, it was an imperative.

It was Nehru who gave this voice a shape in the form of the idea of non-alignment and an organizational cohesion through the non-aligned movement. The immediate context for the emergence of this movement was the division of the world into two hostile blocs after the Second World War, one led by the US and the Western powers and the other by the Soviet Union. Nehru's understanding was that newly independent, poor countries of Asia and Africa had nothing to gain and everything to lose by falling for the temptation of joining the military blocs of the big powers. They would end up being used as pawns in contests for power of no relevance to them. Their needs were to fight poverty, and illiteracy and disease, and these could not be met by joining military blocs. On the contrary, India and other similarly placed countries needed peace and quiet to get on with the business of development. Their interests lay in expanding the 'area of peace', not of war, or hostility. India, therefore, neither joined nor approved of the Baghdad Pact, the Manila Treaty, SEATO and CENTO which joined the countries of West and East Asia to the Western power bloc.

But India went far beyond just neutrality or staying out of military blocs. Nehru was quick to reject the charge of 'immoral neutrality' hurled at India by John Foster Dulles. Non-alignment meant having the freedom to decide each issue on its merits, to weigh what was right or wrong and then take a stand in favour of right. To quote:[1]

> So far as all these evil forces of fascism, colonialism and racialism or the nuclear bomb and aggression and suppression are concerned, we stand most emphatically and unequivocally committed against them . . . We are unaligned only in relation to the cold war with its military pacts. We object to all this business of forcing the new nations of Asia and Africa into their cold war machine. Otherwise, we are free to condemn any development which we consider wrong or harmful to the world or ourselves and we use that freedom every time the occasion arises.

Non-alignment came to symbolize the struggle of India and other newly independent nations to retain and strengthen their independence from colonialism and imperialism. India being the first to become independent, rightly gave the lead to other ex-colonies in this respect. And collectively these nations counted for a great deal. In the UN, for example, whose membership had swollen with their entry, the one country, one vote system enabled the non-aligned bloc, often helped by the Soviets, to check domination by the Western bloc. Non-alignment, thus, advanced the process of democratization of international relations.

A basic objective of Indian foreign policy, that of extending support to colonial and ex-colonial countries in their struggle against colonialism, was well served by the policy of non-alignment. Another objective, that of promoting world peace, was also facilitated by it. Nehru's passionate opposition to war and the threat of nuclear conflict which loomed large after Hiroshima is well known. It grew out of his experience of non-violent struggle and his conviction in Gandhi who had resolved to make it his mission to fight and outlaw the atom bomb. Inspired by Gandhi, and supported by great intellectuals like Einstein and Bertrand Russell, Nehru made it India's role to place the goal of peace, nuclear and general disarmament before the world.

At about this time when Nehru was pointing out the dangers of world extinction through nuclear conflict, Chairman Mao, it is believed, told Nehru in a conversation that a future nuclear war was only another stage in the inevitable march towards socialism, and that if 300 million Chinese died in it, another 300 million would survive! Nehru constantly emphasized that peaceful co-existence of countries with different ideologies, differing systems, was a necessity and believed that nobody had a monopoly on the truth and pluralism was a fact of life. To this end he outlined the five principles of peaceful coexistence, or Panch Sheel, for conducting relations among countries. These were mutual respect for each other's territorial integrity and sovereignty, non-aggression, non-interference in each other's internal affairs, equality and mutual benefit, and peaceful coexistence.

While Nehru tirelessly articulated his ideas about international conduct of nations in every available forum, there were some landmark moments in his quest. Before independence, in March 1947, at his inspiration, an Asian Relations Conference attended by more than twenty countries was held in Delhi. The tone of the conference was Asian independence and assertion on the world stage. While this conference concerned itself with general issues, the next one was called in response to a very specific problem: the Dutch attempt to re-colonize Indonesia in December 1948. Nehru invited states bordering the Indian Ocean, and most Asian countries as well as Australia came. The conference resolved to deny all facilities to Dutch shipping, and sent its resolutions to the UN. Within a week the Security Council resolved that a ceasefire be declared, and the Indonesian national government be restored. The de-colonization initiative was carried forward further at the Asian leaders' conference in Colombo in 1954 and the Afro-Asian conference called by India and other Colombo powers in Bandung, Indonesia, in 1955. The conference was also a precursor to the Belgrade Non-aligned Conference, as it passed resolutions on world peace and the dangers of nuclear weapons. The pinnacle of Nehru's efforts was reached in 1961 when he stood with Nasser of Egypt and Tito of Yugoslavia to call for nuclear disarmament and peace in Belgrade. By now he was convinced that the remnants of colonialism would give way soon and the next challenge the world faced was that of preventing a nuclear war.

A major function of Indian foreign policy was to promote and protect Indian economic interests and to facilitate her on the path that she had chosen for herself. Non-alignment, by not tying India to any one bloc, enabled her to develop economic ties with countries on both sides of the divide as and when neccessary. India needed and got capital, technology, machines and food from the Western countries. She also relied, especially after 1954, on the Soviet Union for building up the public sector industries, something which the US was reluctant to do.

For military equipment, India spread the net far and wide across the ideological divide. In the Nehru years alone she bought, for example, for the Air Force, 104 Toofani aircraft from France, 182 Hunters and 80 Canberras from the UK, 110 Mysters from France, 16 AN-12s and 26 Mi-4 helicopters from the Soviet Union and 55 Fairchild Packets from the US. Two hundred and thirty Vampire aircraft were produced under licence from the UK in India. For the Navy and Army as well, similar purchases were made. In addition, efforts were made to establish a defence production base and licences were obtained from various foreign countries to produce the following equipment: Gnat interceptor aircraft from the UK, HS-748 transport aircraft from the UK, Allouette Helicopters from France, MiG interceptors from the Soviet Union, L-70 anti-aircraft guns from Sweden, Vijayanta tanks from the UK, Shaktiman trucks from Germany, Nissan one-ton trucks and Jonga-jeeps from Japan, Brandt mortars from France, 106 mm recoilless guns from the US, Sterling carbines from the UK, wireless sets from different countries.[2]

The variety of sources from which defence equipment alone was acquired shows that India succeeded in maintaining sufficiently friendly relations with a large number of countries. Spreading her net wide also ensured that excessive dependence on any one country was avoided and better bargains could be driven since potential partners knew that rivals existed. In this way, many of the inherent weaknesses of a newly independent, underdeveloped and poor country were reduced. On the same lines, India maintained an active membership of various UN bodies as well as of the IMF and the World Bank. It is no small credit to India's economic diplomacy that she has been the biggest recipient of concessional funding in absolute terms (not per capita) from multilateral international agencies.

Indian foreign policy sometimes linked apparently irreconcilable goals. For example, the Soviet Union and India initiated in 1963 and signed in August 1964, August 1965 and November 1965, major arms deals by which the Soviet Union became the largest arms supplier to India and Indo-Soviet relations entered a qualitatively new phase. At the same time, India decided to adopt the Green Revolution technology for agricultural development which was backed by the US, The arms deals with the Soviet Union and the Green Revolution which led to India becoming self-sufficient in food in a few years' time increased India's capacity to stand on her own feet and take a more independent stand in world affairs. Similarly, both the US and the Soviet Union at different times agreed to be paid in rupees, thus saving India precious hard currency.

India also maintained an active profile in multilateral bodies and sought continuously to use her presence there to her advantage. Soon after independence Nehru decided to stay within the Commonwealth for this very reason. Despite strong public opinion to the contrary, he felt that once India was independent and there was no question of Britain dominating over her, India could benefit from her presence in a multinational body. Besides, membership of the Commonwealth provided a certain security in a situation when India was yet to find out who her friends (and enemies) were going to be. India also played an active role in the UN peace-keeping forces in various parts of the world, often at heavy cost to Indian lives. A closer look at some of the international situations in which India played an active part would help illustrate the complex tasks dictated by her non-aligned foreign policy.

International Role

The Korean War

The end of the Second World War left Korea divided between a Communist North controlled by the Socialist camp and a South

Korea dominated by the Western powers. K.P.S. Menon, who was elected Chairman of the United Nations Commission on Korea in late 1947, had in his report to the UN appealed 'to the great powers to let Korea be united', warning that else 'Korea may blow up'[3] but it was to no avail. When North Korea invaded South Korea in 1950, India supported the US in the UN Security Council, condemning North Korea as aggressor and calling for a ceasefire. But American pleasure was soon to turn into anger when they found that India abstained from voting on another resolution calling for assistance to South Korea and the setting up of a unified command for this purpose. India's main concern was to prevent the entry of outside powers into the conflict. Nehru appealed to Truman and Stalin and received a warm response from the latter.

But meanwhile General MacArthur, at the head of US forces under UN command, after pushing North Korean forces out of South Korea, without the approval of the UN, crossed the 38th parallel into North Korea and continued towards the Yalu river that separated Korea from China. Chou En-lai, the Chinese prime minister, warned the Western powers through the Indian ambassador to China, K.M. Panikkar, of retaliation, but to no avail. (India was the only link between the West and East in Peking at that time.) China thereupon sent in waves of armed 'volunteers' and succeeded in pushing back American troops to South of the 38th parallel, which resulted in huge Chinese, Korean and American casualties. Nehru tried again at this point to bring about an end to the war by organizing a conference but the US queered the pitch with an ill-timed UN resolution declaring China the aggressor. India voted against it because it was clearly MacArthur and not China who was the aggressor in North Korea. A military stalemate ensued but despite India's tireless efforts it took till June 1953 to get both sides to agree to a ceasefire and evolve an acceptable formula for the repatriation of prisoners of war. It was Krishna Menon who finally succeeded in fashioning a formula that the UN General Assembly and, after Stalin's death, the Soviet bloc accepted. A Neutral Nations Repatriation Commission was set up with an Indian, General Thimayya, as its Chairman, and an Indian 'Custodian Force' under his charge was made responsible for the difficult task of repatriation of soldiers.

The Korean war had tested India's faith in non-alignment and commitment to peace to the utmost, and she had not been found wanting. She stoically faced first Chinese and Soviet hostility because she voted to declare North Korea the initial aggressor. India then endured American wrath for refusing to go along with Western intervention in the war, and for refusing to declare China the aggressor. In the midst of this, in 1950, China invaded Tibet and annexed it without any effort to keep India in the picture. Though upset, Nehru did not allow this to influence his stand on the Korean war. India continued to press the UN to recognize and give a seat to Communist China in the Security Council, especially now that the USSR had withdrawn from it in protest. India also badly needed food aid from the US to meet the near-famine conditions at home but did not allow this to blind her to US stance in Korea. India continued to press ahead even if success was not always apparent. In the end, India's stand was vindicated: both sides had to recognize the same boundary they had tried to change. The world now recognized the worth of non-alignment. It was difficult to dismiss it as mealy-mouthed, cowardly neutrality or as idealist hogwash. The USSR clearly began to see India in a different light. The Soviet prime minister, Bulganin, even told the Indian ambassador, K.P.S. Menon, that the USSR 'fully appreciated India's position in the Commonwealth and hoped that India would continue to remain in it'. This was a big change from the time when the membership of the Commonwealth was seen as final proof of India's succumbing to Western imperialism!

Indo-China

The end of the Korean war brought only momentary respite to Asia. In early 1954, Indo-China appeared to be on the brink of becoming the next theatre of the holy crusades against Communism, with the US keen to pour in massive aid to shore up the weary and hesitant French colonial power in its ongoing (since 1945) war with the Viet Minh. Nehru's initiative to appeal for a ceasefire in February 1954 was followed up by his obtaining the support of several Asian leaders at the Colombo Conference in April 1954 for his six-point proposal for a settlement. Krishna Menon was sent to explain the Asian point of view to the Geneva Conference on Indo-China (to which India was not invited as a member). These steps, besides Nehru's meeting with Chou En-lai in 1954 in Delhi, and other behind-the-scenes parleys and assurances helped prevent the further internationalization of the Indo-Chinese conflict. India obtained guarantees from China for the neutralization of Laos and Cambodia and promises from Great Britain and France to China that they would not allow the US to have bases in Laos and Cambodia. The significance of India's role in the negotiations was evident from the reference by Pierre Mendes-France, the French prime minister, to the Geneva Conference as 'this ten-power conference—nine at the table—and India'.[4] At China's request, India was appointed Chairman of the International Control Commission and its work included supervision of imports of foreign armaments into Laos, Cambodia and Vietnam. For the time being, the danger of the Chinese intervening on behalf of the Viet Minh and of the US increasing its support to the French, even to the point of introducing nuclear weapons into the region, was averted. France was tired of the war, Britain apprehensive of bellicose US intentions, and the USSR, particularly after Stalin's death, groping towards 'peaceful coexistence'. While the control commissions were later subverted through US diplomacy, and Indo-China became a major Cold War theatre, all subsequent peace efforts in fact took up solutions prescribed by Nehru.

Suez Canal

In 1956, in an impulsive reaction to US and British pressure to abandon its declared policy of non-alignment, the latest move being the Anglo-American withdrawal of the promised financial aid for building the Aswan Dam on the river Nile, Egypt nationalized the Suez Canal. This alarmed the users of the canal and Britain and France particularly demanded international control over it. India was a major user herself but she recognized that under the Constantinople Convention (1888) the Suez Canal was an integral part of Egypt. She urged both Cairo and London to observe restraint and tried at the London Conference in August 1956 to get an agreement on a formula that included Egyptian control, an advisory role for the users, and settlement of disputes in accordance with the UN Charter. The Indian proposal met with widespread approval, including from Egypt. Later, when France and Britain got Israel to attack Egypt and landed their troops in Suez, they were severely condemned by even the US, and the UN, and Nehru called it 'naked aggression' and a 'reversion to the past colonial methods'. The withdrawal took place under UN supervision and Indian troops participated in large numbers in the peace-keeping force. India continued to support Egyptian interests in subsequent negotiations leading to the settlement even while trying to ensure that British and other users' interests were protected. In time, even Britain accepted the fairness of India's approach and the episode did not leave any permanent mark on Indo-British relations.

Hungary

The Soviet Union's intrusion in Hungary in October 1956 to crush a rebellion aimed at taking Hungary out of the Soviet bloc was severely condemned by the UN and it demanded withdrawal. India abstained from joining in this formal condemnation and received a lot of flak in the West. India's stand was that while the Soviets must withdraw, the situation was not as simple as made out in the West. The existence of two zones of influence, West and East, in Europe, was a fact of post-Second World War life and any disturbance could set off a domino effect. Nothing was to be gained by humiliating the Soviets through formal condemnation, which in any case India refrained from doing as a matter of policy, as it only hardened positions and made future compromise difficult. Nehru himself criticized the Soviet action and did not send an ambassador to Budapest for two years to show his unhappiness. The Soviets reciprocated by abstaining when Kashmir next came up in the UN Security Council. Thereafter, they reverted to their usual practice of vetoing resolutions that were against Indian interests! India's situation was not an easy one but she withstood considerable pressure from both sides and did not flip in either direction.

The Congo

A very major achievement of Indian foreign policy was its role in helping maintain the integrity and independence of Congo. Congo had barely gained her independence from Belgium on 30 June 1960 when its copper-rich province of Katanga announced its independence from the Congo! Its head, Tshombe, was clearly being backed by Belgium and Belgian troops were also sent to the Congolese capital ostensibly to protect Belgian citizens. Lumumba, the prime minister of Congo, appealed to the UN, US and USSR for help, and the UN asked its Secretary-General, Dag Hammarskjold, to organize all necessary help. The next few months witnessed an unseemly drama in which foreign powers propped up their favourite local players in the mad scramble for power. The US supported the President, Kasavubu, the Soviets backed Patrice Lumumba and the Belgians blessed the army leader, Mobutu. Their tactics were eventually to lead to the murder of Lumumba. Lumumba's murder shocked the world and when Nehru forcefully demanded that the UN play a more decisive part, get rid of the mercenaries and the foreign troops, stop the civil war, convene the parliament and form a new government, and added that India was ready to commit troops for the purpose, the UN agreed. The Security Council adopted a resolution on 21 February 1961 and Indian armed forces successfully brought the civil war to a close, restoring the central government's authority over Katanga and the rest of the country by March 1963.

Dag Hammarskjold is reported to have said, 'Thank God for India,'[5] and the praise was not undeserved. It was indeed one of the finest moments for India's policy of non-alignment, of help to newly independent countries of Africa and Asia, and strengthening of the role of multilateral bodies such as the UN.

Nehru had again shown that given the will, non-alignment could work and there was not just space but also the need for the non-aligned to assert themselves on the side of newly emerging nations, who were sought after by eager superpowers for enlistment in an enterprise that could only take away their freedom even before they had had time to savour its taste.

Relations with Superpowers

USA

Indian non-alignment did not preclude, but in fact desired, a friendly relationship with the US, the leading power in the post-war world. India needed technology, machines, and aid for its development effort, food for its people, and moral support for its nation-building and democratic efforts—all of which it thought the US could provide. The US stand on Kashmir, however, shook this hope of friendship. The UN Security Council, dominated by the US and its allies, in the late 1940s and early 1950s evaded a decision on the Indian charge of Pakistani aggression even after the UN Commission reported the presence of Pakistani troops in Kashmir. All findings by UN mediators that were favourable to India were ignored, and the powerful Western media was used to spread the myth that India was not fulfilling UN directives. Indian requests for food aid were kept hanging because, it was said, Nehru never actually asked for it on his visit to the US in 1949, even though he had explained the drought situation at length. Shipments were sent only after China and the USSR stepped in to help!

The US did not appreciate India's recognition of Communist China in early 1950, nor did it like India's stand that the People's Republic of China be given representation in the UN. India's initial stand on the Korean war was welcomed, but her later position resented. Pakistan was offered some kind of military aid in 1952 itself, though it was made public only in 1953. It was ostensibly given arms against a Soviet Communist threat, but the kind of weapons it got could never cross the Hindu Kush, but could only be used against India. Indian objections were brushed aside by the US with meaningless assurances that they would not be used against India. Nehru expressed his unhappiness at the Cold War being brought to the subcontinent by the inclusion of Pakistan in CENTO, SEATO, etc. US descriptions of non-alignment as immoral did nothing to help matters either. On Goa, too, the US proved totally insensitive to Indian concerns and supported Portugal's claim in 1955 that Goa was a province of Portugal and attacked India virulently when it liberated Goa by force in 1961 after waiting patiently for fourteen years after independence.

A major reason for the difficult relationship between the world's two great democracies was of course the very different perceptions of the Cold War. The US was obsessed by Communism and could not accept that others might have an alternative set of priorities. The world looked black and white from Washington, but from Delhi it looked grey. Nehru had known Communists closely as comrades in the Indian freedom struggle, he had been deeply influenced by Marxism, and while he had his own differences with them and had even had to suppress a Communist insurgency soon after coming to power, he did not regard them as evil. Nor was India willing to line up behind the West in the Cold War for getting aid and arms, as Pakistan was, even though it hardly shared the US view of the Communist threat. Besides, India had encouraged other nations of Asia and Africa to also remain non-aligned.

It has been suggested, quite persuasively, that US antipathy to India pre-dated India's refusal to side with it in the Cold War and that the US establishment inherited, including via British intelligence officials who helped set up the CIA, the British dislike of the Congress leaders who had brought down the mighty Empire, and a positive attitude towards Muslim League/Pakistan because it was pro-British and helped in the War effort. They also inherited and then made their own, British fears (or shall one say hopes) that India would not survive as a unit. Its very diversity, the US thought, would lead to the disintegration of India. As a result, it was not considered a solid bulwark against the spread of Communism. Therefore, even if India had wanted to, it could not have become a frontline state, backed by the Western alliance, because there was a deep-rooted suspicion about her reliability and stability. It is also felt that while the 'mainspring of American policy is power—and a healthy respect for it', 'India did not have the "power" and the Indian leadership deliberately tried to denigrate it (and) accelerate the process of diminishing the utility and usability of power in international politics. The American leadership and establishment could never understand this.'[6] There was also a strong pro-colonial trend in the American establishment which had supported the French and British to return to their colonies after the war, and even supported Portuguese colonialism in Africa and the internal colonialisms of Vorster and Ian Smith in South Africa and Rhodesia. It was unlikely that India's strong anti-imperialist stance was much admired in these quarters.

This should not suggest that Indo-US relations were marked by unremitting hostility. On the contrary, people-to-people relations remained friendly. Economic ties grew as the US was the source of technology and machines. Large sections of influential opinion in India were pro-US and an important section of informed liberal opinion in the US, which included Chester Bowles, John Sherman Cooper, and Senator Fulbright, was pro-India. Towards the late 1950s there was a considerable improvement in relations, at least partly because the US was acquiring a better understanding of Indian policy and perhaps because greater Soviet friendship increased India's value. The Kennedy administration made a clear effort to improve ties by sending one of its key figures, a man who loved India and got along famously with Nehru, John K. Galbraith, as ambassador in 1961.

The Chinese attack on India in 1962, however, drastically altered the situation. Shocked beyond belief, Nehru turned to Kennedy for help. He was lucky that the awkward situation was partially eased for him because of the presence of Galbraith as the mediator.

But that is a story that is better told as part of the sad tale of China's betrayal of its great friend and well-wisher.

Soviet Union

India's relations with the Soviet Union began on a cool note but ended up acquiring great warmth. The Soviet coolness grew out of their perception of India still being under imperialist influence. Communist ambivalence towards the Indian freedom struggle and the leaders of the Congress party was transferred to Nehru's government. The Communist Party of India was engaged in an insurgency against the Indian state in Telangana. India's decision to stay in the Commonwealth was seen by the Soviets as proof of Indian surrender to imperialism, the Soviet ambassador, Novikov, calling it 'a sad day for India and the world'.[7]

Nehru had, however, from the time of his speech as Vice-President of the interim government in 1946, struck and maintained a friendly approach towards the USSR. He admired the Soviet Union and had visited it in 1927. He refused to interpret Communist insurgency in India as proof of Soviet unfriendliness, and as a special gesture offered diplomatic relations even before independence, as well as sent his sister, Vijaylakshmi Pandit, as ambassador. Characteristically, Stalin never gave her an audience.

However, possibly because of the way India conducted herself in the Korean war crisis, and her evident independence from imperialist influence, signs of a thaw began to appear by 1951-52. The Soviets, along with China, sent food shipments to tide over the drought, at a time when the US was dragging its feet. Stalin met the new ambassador, S. Radhakrishnan, future President of India, a few times, and even offered a treaty of friendship. Signs of support on the Kashmir issue at the UN began to emerge, and the CPI was told to cool off its attack on Nehru's government. The process was speeded up after Stalin's death in 1954. The USSR offered to give military equipment to India in 1954 after Pakistan joined CENTO and SEATO, but consistent with its policy of not accepting free military aid, India refused. In 1955, Nehru paid a highly successful visit to the Soviet Union, followed in the same year by an equally popular visit by Khrushchev and Bulganin. In 1956, the 20th Congress of the Comintern, the Soviet-controlled body which laid down the ideological line for all Communist parties, put its seal on the process of de-Stalinization begun after Stalin's death, and tried to soften the Cold War stance by talking of peaceful coexistence between countries belonging to different social systems. It also introduced the totally new concept in Marxism of a peaceful road to Socialism. It is another matter that the US was so taken up with its own rhetoric that it failed completely to respond to these possibilities. For Indo-USSR ties, this was a great help, for all ideological impediments to cooperation were removed. From 1955, USSR gave full support to the Indian position on Kashmir, and from 1956 used or threatened to use, its veto in the UN Security Council to stall resolutions unfavourable to India on Kashmir. The significance of this cannot be underestimated, as India was in a very awkward situation in the Security Council till the USSR started protecting India. The consistent support on Kashmir went far in binding Indo-Soviet friendship. Both countries also took a common stand against colonialism. In the UN, the USSR supported India on the integration of Goa in opposition to the US.

The path of economic development that India chose, based on planning and a leading role for the public sector in industrialization, especially in heavy industry, brought India closer to the USSR. While the Western powers, especially the US, hesitated to help, the Soviets readily came forward with assistance in the building of the Bhilai steel plant in 1956. Then followed the British in Durgapur and the Germans in Rourkela. The US was again approached for the Bokaro plant, but when it continued to remain coy, the Soviets stepped in again. In later years they played a critical role in oil exploration as well. In 1973–74, it was estimated that '30 per cent of India's steel, 35 per cent of our oil, 20 per cent of our electrical power, 65 per cent of heavy electrical equipment and 85 per cent of our heavy machine-making machines are produced in projects set up with Soviet aid'.[8]

When relations between India and China began to deteriorate from 1959 with the Dalai Lama seeking refuge in India and military clashes on the Sino-Indian border, the USSR did not automatically side with its Communist brother, but remained neutral, which itself was a great achievement at that time. Nehru was well aware of the significance of the Soviet stance, and he moved closer to the USSR. The Chinese also date the beginning of their differences with the Soviet Union to the same episode. In the same year, India and the Soviet Union signed their first agreement for military supplies and in 1960 India received 'supply dropping aircraft, helicopters and engineering equipment for the Border Roads Development Board which was to construct roads in the areas disputed by China'.[9] In mid-1962, an agreement permitting India to manufacture MiG aircraft was concluded, this being the first time the Soviets had let a non-Communist country manufacture sophisticated military equipment which even the Chinese had not been licensed to do.

The Chinese attack on India in October 1962 found the USSR again maintaining neutrality, at least partly because it occurred when the Cuban missile crisis was at its peak. Later, in December 1962, Suslov, the important Soviet leader, at the meeting of the Supreme Soviet, unambiguously declared that China was responsible for the war.

Unlike the Western powers who failed to deliver on promises of military supplies in the wake of the Indo-China war, the Soviets in 1963 signed more agreements for sale of arms and supplied interceptors and helicopters, tanks, mobile radar sets, surface-to-air missiles, submarines, missile boats and patrol ships. They helped India develop manufacturing facilities for MiG aeroplanes and to build a naval dockyard. It was this independent manufacturing base that helped India to win the 1971 war. Importantly, unlike the US, they neither stationed personnel to supervise use of equipment, nor laid down difficult conditions for deployment of equipment.

The Soviet Union too gained from this link. India was an important entry-point to the Afro-Asian world of newly independent countries who did not want to become US satellites and were open to Soviet friendship. This helped the USSR in the Cold War as well. The Soviets had, like India, a long border with China and many unresolved boundary disputes. Friendship with India kept China in check and this suited the Soviets. Indian non-alignment tilted the balance away from the West and this too was a help. Surrounded by US-inspired pacts and military bases, the USSR could do with a few friends, and therefore the relationship was one of equality. Besides, for all its faults, Marxism is anti-racist, anti-imperialist and pro-poor, and this precluded any adoption of a patronizing attitude by the Soviets, something which the Americans often tended to slip into, much to Indian annoyance. Indo-Soviet friendship thus emerged as one of the most critical elements of Indian foreign policy.

Relations with Neighbours

India's relations with her neighbours were of central concern to her and fortunately, till 1962, apart from Pakistan, she was on good terms with all her neighbours. With Nepal, she signed a Treaty of Peace and Friendship in 1950, which gave Nepal unrestricted access for commercial transit through India, and secured Nepal's total sovereignty while making both countries responsible for each other's security. With Burma, too, the problem of Indian settlers and a long uncharted border were settled amicably. The issue of Tamil settlers in Sri Lanka was not as easy of solution, and tensions remained, but these did not flare up in this period, and otherwise amicable ties were maintained. With Pakistan, however, and in later years with China, serious problems were faced, and the relations with them are discussed at length below.

Pakistan

Nehru and the Congress leaders had agreed reluctantly to the Partition of India as the solution to an intractable problem and also in the hope that this would end the hostility. But, in fact, the acrimony was only transferred to the international sphere. Communal riots and transfers of population on an unprecedented scale had in any case led to strained relations but the Pakistani invasion of Kashmir in October 1947, just two months after independence, unleashed a chain of cause and effect whose latest act was played out in Kargil. Kashmir's accession to India was a troubled one. When the British left, most of the Indian states ruled indirectly by the British but nominally by Indian princes joined up with either India or Pakistan and the very real danger of Balkanization, almost encouraged by the British, was averted. However, a few states, some of whose rulers, encouraged by British officers and Pakistan, entertained grandiose but unreal ambitions of independence, held out for some time. Among these were Hyderabad, Junagadh and Kashmir. Hyderabad and Junagadh had little real choice as they were surrounded by Indian territory.

But Kashmir had a border with Pakistan, a majority Muslim population, a Hindu ruler, and a radical popular movement for democracy led by Sheikh Abdullah and the National Conference which was very friendly with Nehru and the Congress—enough potent ingredients for whipping up a recipe for trouble. The Maharaja asked for a standstill agreement for one year to make up his mind. Pakistan formally accepted his request and though India was yet to reply, its stand had always been that the people's wishes should be ascertained by an election and therefore it was quite willing to wait and accept the verdict of the elections. However, clearly worried that the popular verdict in Kashmir was not likely to go in its favour, Pakistan decided to jump the gun and sent in so-called tribesmen from the Frontier Province, aided by regular armed forces, to invade Kashmir. The Maharaja appealed to India for help but India could only send in her armies if Kashmir acceded to India. The Maharaja signed the Instrument of Accession, the only legal requirement, as had hundreds of other rulers, and Kashmir became a part of India. Indian troops reached Srinagar just in time to save the capital city from falling into the hands of the invaders. India pushed back the Pakistani 'volunteers' to a considerable extent, and also put in a complaint with the UN against Pakistani aggression. There, instead of getting justice, India learnt her first lesson in Cold War politics. Encouraged by the British who continued to nurture a resentment of the Congress and India and a fondness for the Muslim League and Pakistan, and also for strategic reasons of wanting Pakistan as a frontline state against the USSR, the US also lined up behind Pakistan. The Soviet Union had not yet made up its mind whether India was any longer 'a running dog of British imperialism' and so it gave no support. Nevertheless, India dutifully accepted the UN resolution asking for a ceasefire, even though the military situation was to her advantage. Nehru was much criticized later for going to the UN and for offering to hold a plebiscite. But neither criticism holds, as Pakistan could have gone to the UN if India had not, and the UN could have asked for the holding of a plebiscite. India has also been often misunderstood on its later refusal to hold a plebiscite, because it is not widely known that the UN resolution of August 1948 laid down two preconditions for holding a plebiscite. One, that Pakistan should withdraw its forces from the state of Jammu and Kashmir and two, that the authority of the Srinagar administration should be restored over the whole state. These conditions were never met and in the meantime Kashmir went on to hold elections for its Constituent Assembly, which voted for accession to India and drew up a constitution which declared Kashmir an integral part of India. The Indian government now took the stand that the Constituent Assembly's vote was a sufficient substitute for plebiscite. Kashmir later participated in the Indian general elections as well as held its own state elections, thus rendering irrelevant the debate over plebiscite. In any case, India had never accepted the two-nation theory that all Muslims naturally owed allegiance to the Muslim League and all Muslim-majority areas belonged to Pakistan and on that basis Kashmir should go to Pakistan—a Pakistani argument that often appealed to Western observers unfamiliar with the history of the Indian national movement.

There was a brief period in 1953–54 when it seemed the Kashmir issue may be resolved. On Mohammed Ali Bogra becoming prime minister in 1953, following cordial visits between him and Nehru, a joint communique was issued on 20 August 1953, stating that Nehru had agreed to hold a plebiscite in Kashmir. But the brief flame of hope was snuffed out by the exigencies of Cold War politics. The US had decided after Korea that Indian non-alignment was immoral and it should give military aid to Pakistan. In the UN Security Council, while India wanted as Plebiscite Administrator someone from a small neighbouring country, the name that was proposed was of a senior US Service Officer, Admiral Nimitz. The last chance of a compromise disappeared.

The Kashmir issue continued to be used to needle India in the UN, especially as Pakistan became more and more integrated into the US-fed Western alliance system via membership of CENTO, SEATO, the Baghdad Pact and a military pact with the US in 1954. India had clearly refused to play the US game and Pakistan was more than willing. (Before independence too the Muslim League had happily played the British game; its child, Pakistan, now did US bidding. The Congress continued its anti-imperialist tradition.) In this situation, to get a solution on Kashmir would need a miracle. Only when the Soviet Union began to understand the value of Indian non-alignment and openly supported India on Kashmir could India heave a sigh of relief. From 1956 onwards, the Soviet Union used its veto powers in the UN Security Council to thwart all resolutions on Kashmir unacceptable to India.

India could, with Soviet support, ward off the international pressure on the Kashmir issue through the mid- and late 1950s and early 1960s. But the Chinese attack in 1962 which forced her to turn to the West for help, made it very difficult for her to withstand US and British pressure but Pakistan overplayed its hand by asking for almost the whole of Kashmir and lost its chance. From 1962 Pakistan also began to line up with the Chinese, thus threatening to engulf India in a pincer movement, which almost came true in 1971 but didn't, to the great disappointment of the US. In the mid-1960s, for a short while the USSR also explored the possibility of moving a little closer to Pakistan (the Tashkent initiative by Kosygin to end the Indo-Pak war of 1965 was part of that) but fortunately for India, and not without Indian encouragement, the USSR realized that Pakistan was too deeply integrated into the Western system to be of use to it.

The rancour that characterized Indo-Pak relations was a source of great sadness to Nehru and Indians in general. A common history, geography, culture, and goal of improving the condition of their poverty-stricken people should have brought about cooperation between the two countries. Nehru tried his best to remove all other irritants in the relationship, and showed great generosity on the division of pre-Partition assets, compensation to refugees and division of Indus basin waters. He even visited Pakistan in 1953. There is a little-known story about a large sum of money that India was to give Pakistan as part of the Partition settlement. When Pakistan invaded Kashmir, the Indian government held up the transfer. Gandhiji came to know of it and immediately had it sent to Pakistan, brushing aside the objections of Nehru and Patel that they were only withholding it for the time being so that it was not used for the purposes of war. At the same time, Gandhiji fully supported the Indian armed defence of Kashmir.

It is sometimes said that Pakistani foreign policy is better than ours. It may help to remember the comment of K.P.S. Menon:[10]

> The net result of Pakistan's diplomacy, however, was that Ayub Khan lost his job, Yahya Khan lost his freedom and Pakistan lost half its territory.

China

India adopted a policy of friendship towards China from the very beginning. The Congress had been sympathetic to China's struggle against imperialism and had sent a medical mission to China in the 1930s as well as given a call for boycott of Japanese goods in protest against Japanese occupation of China. India was the first to recognize the new People's Republic of China on 1 January 1950. Nehru had great hopes that the two countries with their common experience of suffering at the hands of colonial powers and common problems of poverty and underdevelopment would join hands to give Asia its due place in the world. Nehru pressed for representation for Communist China in the UN Security Council, did not support the US position in the Korean war, and tried his best to bring about a settlement in Korea. In 1950, when China occupied Tibet, India was unhappy that it had not been taken into confidence, but did not question China's rights over Tibet since at many times in Chinese history Tibet had been subjugated by China. In 1954, India and China signed a treaty in which India recognized China's rights over Tibet and the two countries agreed to be governed in their mutual relations by the principles of Panch Sheel. Differences over border delineation were discussed at this time but China maintained that it had not yet studied the old Kuomintang maps and these could be sorted out later.

Relations continued to be close and Nehru went to great lengths to project China and Chou En-lai at the Bandung Conference. In 1959, however, there was a big revolt in Tibet and the Dalai Lama fled Tibet along with thousands of refugees. He was given asylum in India but not allowed to set up a government-in-exile and dissuaded from carrying on political activities. Nevertheless, the Chinese were unhappy. Soon after, in October 1959, the Chinese opened fire on an Indian patrol near the Kongka pass in Ladakh, killing five Indian policemen and capturing a dozen others. Letters were exchanged between the two governments, but a common ground did not emerge. Then, Chou En-lai was invited for talks to Delhi in April 1960, but not much headway could be made and it was decided to let officials sort out the details first.

The 1962 Chinese Attack

On 8 September 1962, Chinese forces attacked the Thagla ridge and dislodged Indian troops, but this was taken as a minor incident. Nehru went off to London for a conference and after returning home once again left for Colombo on 12 October. A week later, the Chinese army launched a massive attack and overran Indian posts in the eastern sector in NEFA or what is now Arunachal Pradesh. The Indian army commander in NEFA fled without any effort at resistance leaving the door wide open for China to walk in. In the western sector, on 20 October, thirteen forward posts were captured by the Chinese in the Galwan valley, and the Chushul airstrip threatened. There was a great outcry in the country and a feeling of panic about Chinese intentions. It was thought that the Chinese would come rushing in to the plains and occupy Assam, and perhaps other parts as well. Nehru wrote two letters to President Kennedy on 9 November, describing the situation as 'really desperate' and asking for wide-ranging military help. He also sought Britain's assistance. Twenty-four hours later, the Chinese declared a unilateral withdrawal and, as unpredictably as it had appeared, the Chinese dragon disappeared from sight, leaving behind a heartbroken friend and a confused and disoriented people.

The Aftermath

India took a long time to recover from the blow to its self-respect, and perhaps it was only the victory over Pakistan in the Bangladesh war, in which China and the US were also supporting Pakistan, that restored the sense of self-worth. Nehru never really recovered from the blow, and his death in May 1964 was most likely hastened by it. Worse, at the pinnacle of his outstanding career, he had to face attacks from political opponents who would never have dared otherwise. He was forced to sacrifice Krishna Menon, his long-time associate and then Defence Minister. The policy of non-alignment, which he had nurtured with such care, seemed for a while unlikely to be able to withstand the body-blow delivered by a friend. The irony was that it was derailed by a Socialist country and not by a capitalist power. Right-wing forces and pro-West elements loudly criticized Nehru. They used the opportunity to block a constitutional amendment aimed at strengthening land ceiling legislation. The Third Plan was badly affected and resources had to be diverted for defence. The Congress lost three parliamentary by-elections in a row and Nehru faced in August 1963 the first no-confidence motion of his life.

India's relations with other countries were powerfully affected by the Chinese attack, as the 'China factor' loomed large in foreign policy. The US and the UK had responded positively with help in the crisis, so they could not be shrugged off once it receded.

True to form, however, with Pakistani prompting, they tried their best to use India's weakness to get her to surrender on Kashmir, hinting broadly at a quid pro quo by way of military aid, but Nehru managed somehow to withstand the pressure. Nor were these countries willing to really underwrite massive aid in return for abandoning non-alignment. The figures mentioned were in the range of $60–120 million, hardly princely sums! But there was considerable increase in US influence, especially on military affairs. US intelligence agencies developed links in the name of countering the Chinese threat, and even planting a nuclear-powered device in the Himalayas to monitor Chinese military activities. Nehru tried to counter this subtly, and pushed ahead with military agreements with the Soviets, who actually turned out to be far more willing to give India what she needed in the long term than the US, which put impossible conditions for niggardly amounts of aid. Pakistan sidled up to China, and thinking India was truly weakened, launched the 1965 war.

Whose Fault Was It?

At the time of the attack, and afterwards, in the Press and in academic writing, attempts have been made to hold Nehru responsible for Chinese perfidy. One kind of argument sees him as a naive fool who was blinded by sentiment and failed to guard Indian interests in the face of an inevitable Communist betrayal. Another view, expounded most notably by Neville Maxwell in *India's China War,* makes Nehru out to be a stubborn nationalist who, pushed by jingoist public pressure, refused to settle the borders with China on the very reasonable terms offered by the Chinese and instead followed from 1959 a 'forward policy' which provoked the Chinese to attack in self-defence. Neither view does justice to the sophistication of Nehru's understanding of China and the subtlety of his policy.

Nehru's understanding of Chinese history, of the history of revolutions, especially the Russian revolution, had convinced him that China should not be isolated and pushed into a corner, but should be brought into the community of nations and its revolution humanized. 'We know enough history to realize that a strong China is normally an expansionist China,'[11] he said, but did not want to precipitate any conflict with China as it would be as disastrous for both countries as was the French–German conflict.

Before the 1962 attack, on 7 December 1961, in the Lok Sabha he said, 'a huge elephant of a country sitting on our border is itself a fact that we could not ignore'. He added that soon after the Chinese revolution he had come 'to the conclusion that our borders were going to be, well, threatened in some way'. Nehru's long statement on 3 September 1963 in the Rajya Sabha explained at length about not wanting to spend too much on the military, about the emphasis on building one's own strength as that was the only security. 'No country that is not industrialised is militarily strong today', and 'the real thing before us is to strengthen India industrially and not superficially, by getting an odd gun or an odd aircraft'. With Pakistan already hostile, India did not need another neighbour as an enemy. Preparing for war on two fronts would have meant an end to development. Therefore, the conflict, even if inevitable, should be delayed as much as possible by adopting a friendly approach and asking others to do the same, for example by trying to get China into the UN.

He understood that the Chinese occupation of Tibet meant a common border with attendant conflicts. But he also saw that China could not think of expansionism as yet, as it had big problems to solve. After the revolt in Tibet, and the Dalai Lama's arrival, and the border clashes, he was well aware of the dangers, but what good would it have done to threaten China? In an effort to checkmate the Chinese he did make diplomatic preparations, by moving closer to the Soviets. He had never bought the line that Communist China and Communist USSR would team up, and perhaps along with Indian Communists, threaten the Indian state. He did not believe that China was a tool in the hands of the Soviets, nor did he make the mistake of thinking that the Soviet Union would back Communist brothers against Indian friends, as many in India argued.

Nehru was shocked at the scale of the attack, as he had thought that there may be occassional border skirmishes here and there, but not an invasion of this nature. He erred in not anticipating the precise nature of the attack, rather than in the foreign policy he pursued. A further mistake was the panic in appealing to the US and UK for help, as next day the Chinese withdrew. Irresponsible attacks on Nehru by sections of the Press, the Opposition parties, and even members of his own party had led to this knee-jerk response. The failure of nerve on the battlefield was compounded by that in the country at large with Nehru rather than the Chinese becoming the butt of attack! Sadly, the country showed an inability to face adversity stoically, with faith in its proven leaders, and instead fell into despair and mutual recrimination. To his credit, Nehru tried his best to retrieve the situation and get the country back to its bearings.

Most commentators are now agreed that India's defeat at China's hands in 1962 was not the result of Nehru's naive faith in Chinese friendship and Utopian pacifism and consequent neglect of India's defence preparedness. On the contrary, between 1949–50 and 1962, the strength of the Indian Armed Forces doubled from 280,000 to 550,000 and that of the Indian Air Force from seven combat squadrons in 1947 to nineteen by 1962. The war with Pakistan in 1965 was fought with the same equipment and no debacle occurred. Nehru was well aware and had been warning of the possibilities of border clashes with the Chinese since 1959. But neither the political nor the military leadership anticipated the precise nature of the Chinese attack, and were therefore taken by surprise. Apparently, the military leadership thought in terms of either border clashes or a full-scale war in the plains of Assam, but not about the possibility of a limited deep thrust and withdrawal. The Chief of Staff, General Thimayya, believed that a total war with China was unthinkable because China would have full Soviet support. He and other senior officers do not appear to have been aware of Sino-Soviet differences. Nor does he seem to have conceived of a role for the Air Force 'at a time when the Indian Air Force could have swept the skies over Arunachal Pradesh and Tibet without any opposition from the Chinese'.[12] (Nehru asked the US for an air cover without consulting his own Air Force.)

The failure was also, it is felt, due to the lack of a proper system of higher defence command and management, and because there was no system of defence planning, and the structure of civil–military relations was flawed. The chiefs of staff were not integrated into the civilian policy-making structure, but remained theatre commanders preparing for the near-term future but not for the long-term future security environment. Despite Nehru's warnings since 1959, of trouble with China, much professional thought had not gone into the planning for a war in the Himalayas. It was a failure of logistics, of intelligence, or rather of analysis of intelligence, of coordination of different wings such as the army with the Air Force, etc. It was a failure of nerve on the part of the military commander, who had an excellent record and had been decorated earlier, but withdrew without a fight, though it is believed he could have held out for at least seven days. The Chinese, on their part, withdrew as quickly as they came, having achieved their objective of humiliating India by a quick but limited thrust deep into Indian territory. Again, the Indian side had failed to anticipate the Chinese withdrawal and had now begun planning to face a full-scale war in the plains of Assam.

Maxwell's theory of Indian aggressiveness is not treated seriously by most experts, as it is too obvious that India had no inkling, leave alone intentions, of provoking a conflict. Her prime minister and Defence Minister were out of the country, the chief of staff on leave, a senior commander on a cruise. What was India to gain from provoking a war anyway? On the contrary, it can be shown that it was Chinese imperatives, of which Maxwell shows no awareness, that brought them to war, not Indian provocation. And the factors that propelled China in the direction of conflict were beyond Nehru's control.

Take Tibet. Every strong Chinese government had tried to integrate Tibet. But Tibet wanted independence. Nevertheless, Nehru accepted the Chinese position on Tibet in the 1954 Panch Sheel agreement without even getting a quid pro quo on the border, which was possibly a mistake. Only in 1959 did Chou En-lai claim territory in Ladakh and NEFA, this is in the wake of the Khampa revolt and the flight of the Dalai Lama to India with many refugees. China accused India of instigating the Dalai Lama and objected to the asylum. No Indian government could have refused asylum and India did not instigate the rebellion. Nehru did not allow a Tibetan government-in-exile, or any political activities. But he could not have prevented the Tibetan revolt!

Nor could Nehru succeed, despite his best efforts, in influencing US policy. The US refusal to accommodate China, her insistence that Formosa (later Taiwan) was the only legitimate China, which also meant that Communist China was denied a seat in the UN Security Council the attempt to checkmate her in Korea, and Indo-China, frustrated her and pushed her on the path to aggressive assertion. In fact, the US played no small role in making China paranoid about security and helping the extremist left elements to come to the fore in China.

Nor was Nehru the architect of Sino-Soviet differences which had their own role to play in increasing Chinese insecurity and pushing her in an adventurist direction. These differences had existed for some time but came into the open in 1959. When clashes took place between India and China on the border, the Soviets remained neutral. In April–May 1962, a number of incidents occurred on the Sino-Soviet border in Sinkiang. The Soviets charged the Chinese with more than 5,000 violations of the border, and the Chinese charged the Soviets with enticing tens of thousands of their citizens across the border. In 1959, the Soviets had repudiated the treaty that they had signed with China on development of nuclear weapons. In the first week of August 1962, the Soviets signed an agreement with India on the manufacture of MiG-21 aircraft. They had not done so with China. In the last week of August, the Soviets told the Chinese that they were going ahead with negotiations for a Partial Test Ban Treaty. The Chinese took this as being aimed at checking their efforts to develop nuclear weapons. This was all the more galling to the Chinese because they felt that the Soviet Union was now in a position to use its weight to secure Chinese interests in the international arena. To quote V.P. Dutt, Sinologist and foreign policy expert:[13]

> China had arrived at a new theoretical understanding of its own national interests. It had despaired of a peaceful solution to the outstanding problems with the United States and the fulfillment of its primary objectives, namely the return of Taiwan . . . acceptance of China as a great power, seat in the Security Council . . . It had now come to believe that the international balance of forces was shifting in favour of the socialist camp in view of Soviet advances in rocketry and ICBMs and that the time had come for the adoption of an uncompromising and militant line in order to compel the United States . . . to make concessions to China.

The Chinese were also upset that Afro-Asian countries were following India's line of seeking friendship and assistance from both the USSR and the US, rather than the Chinese line of keeping a distance from both. By reducing India's stature, they could hope to have their line accepted.

Therefore, it is not at all unlikely that the Chinese attack on India had little to do with issues between India and China, but was a reaction to a feeling of isolation, abandonment and frustration. By attacking India, they may have wanted to topple Nehru or at least push India into the Western camp so that the USSR could have no illusions about Indian non-alignment and would have to rethink its policy of peaceful coexistence, which, the Chinese figured, was leading to their isolation. They failed on both counts. In fact, V.P. Dutt[14] testifies that Deng Xiaoping said later to an Indian delegation of which he was a member that it was Khrushchev who was responsible for the 1962 war.

Thus, the causes of the 1962 attack were related more to China's own compulsions, that to anything that Nehru or India did or could have done. Not being able to get the recognition of the US, a UN seat, leadership of Afro-Asia, Soviet support on the nuclear issue or the border dispute with India, a leftward turn took place in Chinese politics. By humiliating India, it wanted to show that India's policy of peace and non-alignment was not feasible. Nor was the Soviet policy of peaceful coexistence. India would leave the policy of non-alignment under pressure and other countries of Asia and Africa would follow the Chinese lead. Thus, the cause of the Indian military humiliation could not be reduced to Indian foreign policy failure. It could 'only be characterized as one of those unforseeable random events of history'.[15]

If India's policy towards China was a failure, which other country's was a success? The US did a complete volte-face in 1971, and the USSR began changing, at least after 1959.

The debacle of the India–China war in no way raises doubts on the correctness of Nehru's basic thrust in foreign policy. For example, non-alignment ensured that even in the India–China war, the US and the Soviet blocs were not ranged on opposite sides and India succeeded in getting greater or lesser sympathy from both. This was an unusual occurrence in the days of the Cold War. Secondly, Nehru had been right in pursuing a policy of friendship with China, even if it ended the way it did. Especially given the hostile relationship with Pakistan (which surfaced soon after independence with the conflict over Kashmir and grew into a serious threat when it was exacerbated by the US decision in 1954 to give military help to Pakistan), it was in India's interest to try its best to avoid having another hostile neighbour and thus be caught in a pincer movement. India's espousal of China's right to have a seat in the UN was not given up by Nehru even after the

Indo-China war since he rightly believed that the Western powers' isolation of China only pushed China into becoming more irresponsible. Besides, as Nehru was most fond of pointing out, defence was not just a matter of weapons, it was also a function of economic development, of self-reliance; otherwise defence was only skin-deep. A newly independent poor country like India could have ill-afforded to divert her scarce resources into building up a massive military machine. On the contrary, by building up India's economic strength, Nehru enabled his successors to win impressive military victories.

Conclusion

The political foresight and pragmatism that informed Nehru's practice of non-alignment is testified to by the quick course correction that has had to be undertaken every time attempts have been made to move away from it.

When Indira Gandhi became prime minister in 1966, she felt that relations with the US and the West could be and needed to be dramatically improved. This was because, on the one hand, the US had a better idea of Chinese militancy and had promised help if China attacked again, and on the other, the grave food shortages caused by the drought and the critical economic situation caused by the cumulative effect of the two wars in 1962 and 1965 necessitated such help. It was in pursuance of this line that Mrs Gandhi agreed to devalue the rupee on US advice though it is another matter that it might have been in Indian interest to do so. She also visited the US in the hope of receiving economic assistance, expediting food shipments and of evolving a new relationship. She came back sadder and wiser and found that President Lyndon Johnson, despite public posturing to the contrary, deliberately delayed responding to urgent Indian requests for food and other economic help. Indira Gandhi later said that one reason for this was to pressurize India to stop criticism of US bombing of Vietnam. Indira Gandhi was, however, quick to learn her lesson. She set India firmly on the path of agricultural independence via implementation of the Green Revolution strategy and set about strengthening the non-alignment movement and Indian autonomy in international affairs—the latter being intimately tied to the former. She also gradually strengthened ties with the Soviet Union, persuading it through a vigorous diplomatic effort in 1966–67 to resile from a position of treating India and Pakistan on the basis of parity and giving military assistance to Pakistan.

The Janata government when it came to power in 1977 talked loudly about practising genuine non-alignment, but found soon that the earlier article had been genuine enough, and essentially fell back on following the Nehruvian policies. They entered into negotiations for huge arms deals with the Soviet Union which were concluded by Mrs Gandhi on her return to power in 1980. They also had to renege on their promise of cutting down defence expenditure.

Rajiv Gandhi too found very soon that his attempts to come closer to the US were not very fruitful and reverted back to the emphasis on non-alignment, nuclear disarmament, support to South Africa, and so on.

Non-alignment was not a blueprint for policy, it was an approach, a framework, a method, not a straitjacket but a lodestar by which the young nation could steer its course in the dark night. Instead of imposing any rigidity in Indian foreign policy, non-alignment let it evolve to meet the changing needs of Indian society. It did not come in the way of the close relationship that developed with the USSR from 1954 onwards. Nor did it come in the way of India joining the Commonwealth. In fact, Nehru's internationalist and humanitarian worldview did not lead to any sacrifice of Indian interests or neglect of her defence needs, as is sometimes alleged. Nor was Nehru a pacifist who refused to use force to defend Indian interests when necessary. In 1947–48, he ordered the use of force in Kashmir (with Gandhiji's approval), Junagadh and Hyderabad, and in 1961 in Goa.

The visionary nature of Nehru's understanding of international relations is shown by the fact that the rest of the world has slowly come to adopt much of what was dismissed as naive and impractical when first articulated. Nuclear disarmament has become an accepted and much-desired goal globally. Both the US and the Soviet Union agreed that a nuclear war could not be won and therefore must not be fought. In February 1972, the Americans and the Chinese signed the Shanghai Communique which declared their mutual relations to be based on the Five Principles of Peaceful Coexistence—Nehru's Panch Sheel!

It is no small consolation to India that the Chinese were forced to adopt the very same principles, expounded by the very same man, that they had betrayed so heartlessly in 1962 when they attacked India. These principles were first embodied at Nehru's instance in the Agreement on Tibet between India and China in 1954. In further vindication of Nehru, and Gandhi, the Soviet leader Mikhail Gorbachev signed with prime minister Rajiv Gandhi the New Delhi Declaration of November 1996, laying down the principle of non-violence in international relations, and in community life within nations. It is being increasingly realized that even conventional wars at the modern level of technology are too destructive. Besides, they have singularly failed either to change borders very much (as in the Iraq–Iran war) or to keep populations under occupation (as in Vietnam, Afghanistan, the West Bank, etc.) The only workable ideal is that of a nuclear weapon-free and non-violent world.

One may conclude with a quote from a letter written to Nehru by Churchill, an old foe:[16]

> I always admired your ardent wish for peace and the absence of bitterness in your consideration of the antagonisms that had in the past divided us. Yours is indeed a heavy burden and responsibility, shaping the destiny of your many millions of countrymen, and playing your outstanding part in world affairs. I wish you well in your task. Remember 'The Light of Asia'.

Jawaharlal Nehru in Historical Perspective

Jawaharlal Nehru can be justifiably considered an architect of modern India. One of the great Indians of the twentieth century, he has been variously described as a democrat, socialist, humanist and visionary, but he was all these and more. Any assessment of his role in the making of independent India would need to take cognizance of his immense stature and extraordinary personality and would, therefore, inevitably be complex and somewhat controversial.

What was it about Nehru which makes so many Indians today look back on the Nehru era with such nostalgia? That period was even more full of misery and poverty than the present. Then why did his presence make so much of a difference? What are the abiding elements of Nehru's contribution to the making of independent India; what is his legacy? What did he, and under his leadership the Indian people, achieve? What abiding values did he try to inculcate among Indians that are today treated as a guide and measure of their own and their leaders' actions, pronouncements, and ideas? And was he 'equal to his opportunities'? It is the answers to these questions which will determine his place in history and not what he failed to achieve and what remains to be done.

Space does not permit a discussion of Nehru the person here, but there was a great deal about his personality which is admirable. It is no accident that all those who came in contact with him fell under his spell. The range of his interests and concerns was wide indeed; from basic education to heavy industry, from statistics collection to world peace, from women's liberation to tribal welfare, and from art to mountain climbing and cricket. He was a veritable

Renaissance man, besides being a product of the Enlightenment with his commitment to rationality, humanity, respect for the individual, independence of spirit and secularism. Wide and generous in his outlook on every facet of life, he tried to inculcate the same among the people as also his co-workers. As he wrote to the chief ministers in 1954: 'If India is to be really great, as we all want her to be, then she is not to be exclusive either internally or externally. She has to give up everything that is a barrier to growth in mind or spirit or in social life.'[1]

A child of the Indian national revolution, Nehru was above all a nationalist. As a British political scientist put it, 'Even his enemies could never accuse him of thinking in any but national terms; caste, creed, town, tongue—none of these loyalties meant anything to him; it was India first and India last.'[2] Nehru adhered to this commitment to nationalism, national unity and national independence after 1947. It was the mainstay of his thinking and policies and is integral to any understanding of them.

For Nehru independence had to go beyond mere political independence. He was also strongly committed to change and development, the building of an equitable and egalitarian, just and democratic society—a socialist society—laying down the foundations of a democratic and civil libertarian polity and the consolidation of India as a nation. And he tried all his life—both before and after the attainment of independence—to link his dual commitment to nationalism and socialism.

This was an uncharted path. Neither Marx nor Gandhiji, two long-term influences on him, provided guidelines on how to go about building a nation. But he set upon this hard task with a degree of excitement and optimism. He had always believed that India's greatest need was 'for a sense of certainty concerning her own success'. This sense of excitement and faith in the coming success he did not abandon even after the defeat and betrayal of the India–China war of 1962. And, what is more important, he succeeded in imparting this sense to millions of Indians.

Democracy, rule of law, respect for the freedom and dignity of the individual, social equity and equality, non-violence, rationality in the guidance of human affairs and morality-based politics were the pillars of his basic approach to nation-building. Personal integrity, love for and confidence in the Indian masses were his major assets in this task.

Consolidation of Indian Independence

Maintenance, strengthening and consolidation of India's independence were among Nehru's most pressing tasks. In a world that was sharply divided between the two superpowers—the United States and the Soviet Union—which were determined to extend their hegemony over the rest of the world, Nehru resisted all pressures and refused to become their pawn. India's internal policies—right or wrong—developed outside the direct influence of the superpowers, and India remained in full control of her internal as well as her external policies. Nehru also successfully resisted penetration of India's political and economic structure and institutions by outside agencies.

Clearly, independence depended on the economic strength of a country. Given this, Nehru set out, with a great deal of success, to build an independent and self-reliant economy and made an all-out effort to break out of colonial underdevelopment and to ensure self-sustaining and self-generating growth, both in agriculture and industry. He put a great deal of emphasis on self-reliance and cautioned against dependence on other nations. Rapid industrialization, particularly growth of heavy industries, planning, development of the public sector, atomic energy and science and technology, technical modernization and the training of a large technical and scientific cadre were regarded by Nehru as necessary parts of the effort at independent economic development and self-reliance. The biggest achievement he claimed for planning and for Congress rule was the creation of 'a feeling of confidence . . . a feeling of self-reliance'.[3] This would further strengthen national independence by increasing the self-confidence and self-respect of the people.

Forging National Unity

Nehru succeeded in maintaining and strengthening the national unity forged during the freedom struggle and rendered fragile by the manner of the transfer of power in 1947. He also succeeded in checking disruptive forces, consolidating the nation and the independent state, and promoting the psychological integration of the Indian people. This was no mean task. Casteism, provincialism, tribalism, linguistic chauvinism—largely transcended during the freedom struggle—were surfacing again; the princely states were there, and, of course, there was the ever-present danger of communalism.

Nehru recognized that India was not yet a structured nation but a nation-in-the-making. He also kept in view and made allowance for India's immense variety and diversity. He constantly urged the people to develop 'an outlook which embraces all this variety and considers it our very own'.[4] A specific expression of this strategy of unity in diversity was his policy towards the tribal people. Overall, despite the persistence of many disruptive forces, at times dormant, at times active, there is no doubt that Nehru succeeded in keeping them under check, and provided the much-needed political stability and push forward to the process of national integration, of nation-building. In fact, he subordinated all other questions and issues to this task. Behind the Five Year Plans lay the concept of national unity.

Nehru also saw that in India's case unity and independence were closely related. 'We live in a dangerous age,' he wrote in 1953, 'where only the strong and the united can survive or retain their freedom.'[5]

Nurturing Democracy and Parliamentary Government

Carrying on the traditions of the national movement, Nehru carefully nurtured and entrenched democracy and parliamentary government in independent India. He fought three general elections on the basis of universal adult franchise and secret ballot and made elections the norm, not an exception.

Nehru's commitment to democracy and civil liberties was total. To him they represented absolute values and not means to an end. He would not subordinate them to any other goals, whether of social change or socio-economic development. He was aware that the parliamentary system had its weaknesses, and made efforts to remove some of them. But he would not, he declared, 'give up the democratic system for anything'.[6]

Even his immense personal power and popularity could not corrupt the democrat in Nehru. On the contrary, Nehru used this strength to reinforce the democratic process and the libertarian tradition. Though dominating politics after 1950, within the Congress party too he promoted internal democracy and open debate. He also helped create an institutional structure which was democratic and in which power was diffused: a constitution with basic civil liberties enshrined in it, a sovereign parliament elected on the basis of universal suffrage and regular elections, a free Press, a cabinet government and an independent judiciary.

This commitment to democracy was rooted in Nehru's deep and unqualified faith in and respect for the common man. 'That is enough religion for me,' he once declared.[7] He was willing to back fully 'the free market of ideas' because he believed that in the long run people could discriminate between different ideas. At the same time, he was aware of the authoritarian tendencies in the country and even in his own party. 'Our democracy,' he said in 1951, 'is a tender plant which has to be nourished with wisdom and care.'[8] And so he tried his best to instil in the commonfolk, a taste for democratic concepts. He regularly toured the land sharing his ideas with the people, trying to educate them in the ways of rational and democratic thinking. When asked what his legacy to India would be, he repeated: 'Hopefully, it is four hundred million people capable of governing themselves.'[9]

Democracy was intrinsic to Nehru's idea of social and political development. Democracy would enable the people to mobilize themselves and to exert pressure from below to achieve social justice and equality, as well as reduction of economic inequality, which over time would lead to socialism. The political party in power would either implement the popular mandate or would get swept away. He was aware that this process might take time, for parliamentary system and universal suffrage gave the right to govern but not necessarily the power to do so. But sooner or later, he believed, the power would follow the right; and he did his best to bring this about. This is one reason why he placed so much emphasis on elections, besides community development projects, Panchayati Raj, cooperatives and decentralization of all kinds of power.

Particularly, to ensure the unity of a diverse society like India's, Nehru argued, democracy was essential. No amount of force or coercion could hold India together. 'In India today,' he said in 1960, 'any reversal of democratic methods might lead to disruption and violence.'[10]

Nehru was aware of the formidable, novel and unprecedented character of his effort to develop the country economically on the basis of a democratic and civil libertarian political structure. No other country had attempted this so far. Most other nations and societies had used authoritarian and administrative measures and institutions during the period of their economic take-off. Nehru was aware that his path of development might slow down the rate of economic development. But Indian people, he felt, were willing to pay this price for the sake of a democratic political order.

Throughout his life Nehru opposed dogma and a dogmatic mentality. This was his major objection to religion and became a major ground for his favouring a scientific temper and outlook on life and its problems.

Building Socialism

Nehru rejected the capitalist developmental and civilizational perspective and, instead, worked for fundamental transformation of Indian society in a socialist direction. Clearly, he did not succeed in building a socialist society and there was a large gap between his precepts and practice. But he did, over the years, grapple with the problem of initiating socialism in an underdeveloped country with a democratic polity. It was Nehru, above all, who carried the socialist vision to millions and made socialism a part of their consciousness. Moreover, his ideas on socialism and his strategy for its establishment and development, as also his political practice, provided deep insights into the problem of socialist transformation in the modern world.

What did socialism mean to Nehru? In fact, Nehru never defined socialism in terms of a definite scheme or rigid general principles. To him, generally, socialism meant greater equality of opportunity, social justice, more equitable distribution of higher incomes generated through the application of modern science and technology to the processes of production, the ending of the acute social and economic disparities generated by feudalism and capitalism, and the application of the scientific approach to the problems of society. Socialism also meant the eventual ending of the acquisitive mentality, the supremacy of the profit motive, and capitalist competitiveness and the promotion instead of the cooperative spirit. It also meant the gradual ending of class distinctions and class domination. Socialism also laid down the large-scale social ownership or control over the principal means of production. But

Nehru insisted that, first of all, socialism concerned greater production, for there could be no equal distribution of poverty. In fact, to him socialism was equal to greater production plus equitable distribution.

In Indian conditions, Nehru regarded socialist transformation as a process and not as an event. Socialism was then not a clearly pre-defined, pre-laid-out scheme towards which the process of transformation moved. Instead, socialism was expected to go on being defined, stage by stage, as the process advanced. There was to be no sudden break but gradual change. Socialist transformation was to be viewed in terms of a series of reforms which would occur within the orbit of the existing socio-economic structure, but which would, over time and in their totality, amount to a revolution *or a structural social transformation. Nehru described these reforms* as 'surgical operations'. Socialist revolution would, thus, consist of a series of 'surgical operations' performed through the due process of law by a democratic legislature.

Nehru believed that democracy and civil liberties had to be basic constituents of socialism, and were inseparable from it.

On the basis of his experience of the national movement, Nehru came to the view that basic social change can be, and should be, brought about only through a broad societal consensus or the consent of the overwhelming majority of the people. As he told Tibor Mende in 1956: 'One has to carry people with one.' They must be willing to 'accept changes'. Parliament could, of course, legislate, but it was far more important that 'a very large section of the people must also accept it—or, at any rate, actively or passively, be ready to accept it'.[11] On another occasion he told the presidents of the Provincial Congress Committees that he was convinced of the importance of 'carrying our people along the line of progress. We are not a sectarian body consisting of the elect. We are fellow-travellers with the people of India.'[12] There were several major corollaries of this approach. First, the process of social transformation might have to be slowed down, for the process of reconciling different views inside and outside the Congress party and of winning the active or passive consent of the people was a time-consuming one. Nehru was willing to slow down the pace of socialist development in order to persuade and carry the people and his colleagues with him rather than to ride roughshod over their opinions or to ignore and show disrespect to the autonomy of the various institutions of the state. Besides, to endure and strike deep roots, socialism required popular acceptance and a democratic approach.

Learning from the experience of the rise of fascism in the 1930s, Nehru argued that in the absence of a broad societal consensus, any radical steps towards socialism would invite the danger of fascism. 'An attempt at premature leftism,' he wrote to Jayaprakash Narayan in 1948, 'may well lead to reaction or disruption.'[13] Nehru was aware of the social presence of the powerful landed elements with their social prestige and economic power and numerical strength. He was also conscious of the fact that his party had, despite his charisma and personal popularity, secured less than 50 per cent of the votes cast in the 1952 and 1957 elections. On the other hand, the different rightist political elements had together secured more than 25 per cent of the popular vote for the Lok Sabha elections in these years; and this was apart from the right-wing strength inside the Congress itself. Above all he felt that the middle strata, urban as well as rural, had to be handled with care and caution for they constituted a very large section of the people—and it was the middle strata which had formed the backbone of fascism in Germany. Any frontal attack on the propertied classes was likely to push them and the middle strata to taking a fascist position. Any effort at making a minority revolution or when the overwhelming majority of the people had not been won over was more likely to result in counter-revolution and the overthrow of democracy than in the coming of a socialist revolution. Even apart from fascism, such an effort would divide the Indian people when their unity was both essential and fragile.

India of the Nehru era was quite often criticized for being a soft state and Nehru was accused of being a weak ruler. But Nehru did not agree, for he was aware of the danger of authoritarianism posed by too strong a state and too strong a ruler. Just before his death, he said in 1964: 'One should not mistake gentleness and civility of character for weakness. They criticise me for my weakness, but this is too large a country with too many legitimate diversities to permit any so-called "strong man" to trample over people and their ideas.'[14]

One reason Nehru adopted an open-ended approach towards socialism was because of his belief that it was not possible to mobilize a large majority around a clear-cut, structured, ideological definition of socialism. A large majority could be mobilized only by uniting diverse interests and multiple views and ideological strands around a common socialist vision or broad framework.

Over time Nehru came to believe that a socialist society could be achieved through peaceful and non-violent means. While recognizing the existence and significance of the class struggle, he believed that it could be resolved through non-violent means and the rule of law.

One other aspect of Nehru's approach to politics and socialism deserves to be stressed. With the passage of time he came very close to Gandhiji in emphasizing that in building a socialist India as much importance should be attached to the means as to the ends. Wrong means, he said, would not lead to right results. His belief in the inseparability of the means and the ends was another reason why he increasingly condemned all recourse to violence even for a worthy objective like socialism.

Planning for Economic Development

Nehru looked upon rapid economic development as basic for India's independence and unity and for the removal of poverty and implementation of his social welfarist policies. In the chapter on 'Objectives of Planned Development' which he wrote for the Third Five Year Plan he observed: 'A high rate of economic growth sustained over a long period is the essential condition for achieving a rising level of living for all citizens, and especially for those in low income groups or lacking the opportunity to work.'[15] And he told the Avadi session of the Congress: 'We cannot have a Welfare State in India with all the socialism or even communism in the world unless our national income goes up greatly. Socialism or communism might help you to divide your existing wealth, if you like, but in India there is no existing wealth for you to divide; there is only poverty to divide . . . How can we have a Welfare State without wealth?'[16] In other words, production was essential whatever the nature of society—socialist or capitalist.

The three pillars of Nehru's development strategy, representing 'a fairly widespread intellectual consensus of the time',[17] were planning for rapid industrial and agricultural growth, a public sector to develop strategic industries, and a mixed economy. Nehru popularized the concept of planning and made it a part of Indian consciousness. India was to have a mixed economy as a transitional stage, with the private sector functioning for a long time to come though within the framework of planning. In the long run, the state was to occupy the commanding heights of the economy, owning or controlling all basic industries and strategic sectors of the economy. The public sector was not to be based only on state-run enterprises. Nehru was very clear that the cooperative principle should be encouraged and cooperatives in trade, industry and agriculture should play an increasingly larger role.

In the long run, the role of market forces and the profit motive was to become less significant. At the same time, Nehru was quite clear that over time the public sector must generate additional sources. According to the Industrial Policy Resolution of 1956, which he helped draft, the public sector was expected to 'augment the revenues of the state and provide resources for further development in fresh fields'. Taking a pragmatic view of the question, he also held that where the public sector performed well, it should remain, and where it did not, it was to be replaced.

Above all Nehru wanted to build an independent self-reliant economy, for independence depended on economic strength and the capacity to resist economic and political domination. Emphasis on rapid industrialization and agricultural self-sufficiency, planning, public sector and heavy, capital goods industry, minimal use of foreign capital and aid, science, technology and technical modernization, the training of a large technical and scientific cadre, and atomic energy was seen by Nehru as a necessary part of the effort at independent economic development. In achieving this, there is hardly any doubt that he was eminently successful. India did make the transition from a colonial to an independent economy, though a capitalist economy. Whatever the weaknesses that emerged later, Nehru's economic policy did prove to be the right one for India and as a result India's economic achievement was quite substantial.

Opposing Communalism

Nehru's commitment to secularism was unsurpassed and all-pervasive. Communalism went against his grain, and he fought it vigorously throughout his life. He helped secularism acquire deep roots among the Indian people; and he prevented the burgeoning forth of communalism when conditions were favourable for it. Though on almost all issues he believed in consensus and compromise, communalism was the exception, for as he said in 1950, any compromise on communalism 'can only mean a surrender of our principles and a betrayal of the cause of India's freedom'.[18]

Keeping in view India's specific situation, Nehru defined secularism in the dual sense of keeping the state, politics and education separate from religion, making religion a private matter for the individual, and of showing equal respect for all faiths and providing equal opportunities for their followers. He defined communalism as the ideology which treated Hindus, Muslims, Sikhs or Christians as homogeneous groups in regard to political and economic matters, as 'politics under some religious garb, one *religious group being incited to hate another religious group*'.[19]

Nehru was one of the first to try to understand the socio-economic roots of communalism, and he came to believe that it was primarily a weapon of reaction, even though its social base was formed by the middle classes. He also most perceptibly described communalism as the Indian form of fascism. In contrast, he regarded secularism as an essential condition for democracy.

He also did not distinguish between Hindu, Muslim, Sikh or Christian communalisms. They were, he said, different forms of the same ideology and had, therefore, to be opposed simultaneously. While he was very clear that secularism meant giving full protection to the minorities and removing their fears, at the same time, he was as opposed to minority communalisms as to the communalism of the religious majority. He also argued most convincingly that secularism had to be the sole basis for national unity in a multi-religious society and that communalism was, therefore, clearly a danger to national unity and was anti-national.

There was, however, a major lacuna in Nehru's approach to the problem of communalism, which can be seen as a certain economistic, deterministic and reductionist bias. Believing that planning and economic development and the spread of education, science and technology would automatically weaken communal thinking and help form a secular consciousness, he ignored the need for struggle against communalism as an ideology. As a result he paid little attention to the content of education or to the spread of science and a scientific approach among the people. While very active himself, he failed to use the Congress as an organization to take his own brilliant understanding of communalism to the people. He also compromised with his own stand when he permitted the Congress in Kerala to enter into an alliance with the Muslim League and Christian communal groups in 1960. Further, he was unable to persuade the state governments to take strong administrative steps against the instigators or perpetrators of communal violence. Sadly, sorrow over the large-scale communal violence marked the last years of his life.

Opposing Conservatism

Nehru did not devote much time and effort to social reform in the narrow sense of the term. But he was opposed to social conservatism; and, realizing that men and women do not live by bread alone, he regularly emphasized the necessity of bringing about changes in the social sphere along with economic and political changes. One of his greatest achievements as prime minister was the passage of the Hindu Code Bills. Another was the care with which he promoted education among girls and public employment of middle-class women.

Pursuing Foreign Policy

Nehru's foreign policy was a many-splendoured phenomenon. Nehru used foreign policy as an instrument to defend and strengthen India's newly won independence and to safeguard India's national interests and to develop the self-reliance, self-confidence and the pride of the Indian people, even while serving the cause of world peace and anti-colonialism. It is significant that successive prime ministers after Nehru, till today, have continued to follow the broad framework of his foreign policy.

Assessing Nehru

Nehru's place in history should rightly take into account his political weaknesses. This in no way diminishes him for he still emerges as a person who towered over his contemporaries.

A critical weakness of Nehru's strategy of consolidation of the Indian nation, economic development and social transformation flowed from his non-adherence to the Gandhian strategy of non-violent struggle in one crucial aspect—its emphasis on the mobilization of the people. Nehru did see the necessity of involving a large number of people in nation-building. But he had an overpowering belief in spontaneity, in the poor mobilizing on their own; he believed in the reductionist notion that the exercise of franchise would gradually educate the masses to vote in their own interest. He also harboured the nineteenth-century liberal notion that his speeches or those of other respected leaders would be enough to arouse and spur the masses.

There is no doubt that Nehru felt deeply and passionately for the people; his sway over the masses was immense as was his capacity to communicate with them, to sense their feelings and to win their love, affection and trust. But an active involvement of the people in politics and their own social liberation required organization and mobilization: a party, however loosely structured, cadres, however democratically organized, and a minimum of ideology, however broad, non-dogmatic and open-ended. In fact, Nehru's own model of development and social transformation depended on active pressure from below by the deprived, the exploited and the dominated. Such active popular participation in politics alone would enable parliamentary democracy to serve as an instrument of nation-building, social change and equity.

But Nehru failed to help create any institutions or structures or agents through which the people or even the lower-level cadres of his own party could be mobilized and politically educated. The only form of mobilization was his extensive tours through which he communicated with the people, educated them and created popular support for his policies. Before 1947, the political harvest of his tours had been gathered by the local Congress committees and the nationalist cadres. But after 1947, in the absence of any popular-level organization to follow up the outcome of his tours, the political and organizational benefits were more often than not reaped by the party bosses from the local to the state level.

The Nehruvian period, it is noteworthy, did not witness greater participation by the people in the political processes except in the form of elections. Actually, there was gradual demobilization of the people and the weakening over time of the link between politics from below and the national leadership in power as also between politics and social and constructive work; at least in the medium run—to be calculated in decades—electoral politics strengthened the hold of the local economic and political elite.

Nehru also failed to build institutions and organizational structures to implement his vision or policies or to mobilize the people behind them; he created no social instruments and this led to a general weakness in execution of his policies and ideas, and was a major reason for the shortcomings in the implementation of the land reforms, the execution of the Community Development programme and the management of the public sector.

The Congress party could have played the role of organizing secular and nationalist forces to back Nehru's policies and to popularize and to mobilize the people behind them. But Nehru also neglected party-building, even after he acquired complete control over it in 1951. He had never been a builder or organizer of the party before independence. But this weakness became a serious flaw after Gandhiji and Sardar Patel, stalwart organizers of the party before 1947, left the scene and Nehru became its sole leader. One result of this was that Congress was increasingly weakened as an organization and began to lose its role as an instrument for social change or the implementation of government policies or even education in the party ideology. Instead, it gradually veered towards machine politics.

The consequence was that Nehru increasingly started relying on government administration and bureaucracy for implementing his policies. Even the Community Development programme and the Panchayati Raj, the two great efforts to involve the people in their own development, ended up under bureaucratic control; and the village-level social worker, the kingpin in rural reconstruction, became a cog in the bureaucratic machine and spent as little time as possible in the village. Furthermore, the administrative structure and the bureaucracy remained unreformed and unreconstructed and as distant from the people as before.

Nehru also did not vigorously attack through mass mobilization and mass educational campaigns those aspects of the social structure, such as the caste system, male domination, kinship networks, economic dependence of the rural poor on the rural rich and growing corruption, which were bolstering the existing socio-economic system. He also went too far in stressing the role of consent and conversion of the dominant social classes. He had inherited this belief from Gandhiji. But, then, Gandhiji had also believed in organizing active political and ideological struggles against the current targets of his politics whether they were the British, the princes or the orthodox among the upper castes. A major part of Gandhiji's strategy had been to 'convert' them by isolating them from public opinion. Nehru did not pursue this part of his mentor's strategy.

Nehru could set goals and objectives, he could formulate people's desires, he could inspire people with a vision, he was also a skilful politician, but he lacked the capacity to design a strategic framework and to devise tactical measures to achieve the goals he set. This proved to be a failing for Nehru as a nation-builder. While strongly opposed to political opportunism and manipulation, he could replace these only with *ad hoc* political and administrative measures. This often left the field open to manipulators. This weakness was heightened by the fact that he was a poor judge of men and women. To his credit, Nehru could see the process of the political manoeuvres taking over, but could do little to counter it. And so, acting as his own leader of the Opposition, he observed and denounced the corruption, careerism, bureaucratization, and the many other emerging ills of a developing ex-colonial society, but was unable, apart from exhortations, to take the necessary concrete steps to control them. We may point to some of the large areas of neglect which have today assumed monstrous proportions: the entire educational system was left untouched and unreformed, and failed to reach the majority of the population; no worthwhile political and ideological mass struggle was waged against communalism as an ideology; the tardy and inadequate implementation of land reforms left a legacy of economic inequality, social oppression and political violence in rural India; the inadequate steps taken to curb corruption in its initial stages, later led to its assuming shocking dimensions and pervading almost every area of life, administration and politics.

To conclude, as the first prime minister of independent India, Nehru was faced with daunting tasks. In spite of this, measured by any historical standards his achievements were of gigantic proportions. He rooted certain values, approaches, objectives, goals and an outlook and made them an integral part of the ethos of the Indian people. As one of his biographers, Geoffrey Tyson, has said, 'If Nehru had been a different kind of man, India would have become a different kind of country.'[20]

Nehru and the Nehru era have receded into historical memory—only those above fifty years of age would remember him as a person. Most Indians—even those who during his lifetime were his harsh critics—hark back to the Nehru era, identify with him, and draw inspiration from his life and work, his social vision, and the values he sustained in the endeavour to build a happier and healthier society in which class, caste and gender oppression would cease to exist. The legacy he left behind is in many respects a sheet-anchor for the Indian people who are today buffeted about in a sea of despair. What more could a people ask from a leader? Has any society, any people, the right to ask a leader, however great, to solve all its problems once for all?

Political Parties, 1947–1964:
The Congress

India is virtually the only postcolonial nation to sustain a system of parliamentary government for over fifty years after independence. It is, of course, true that throughout the Nehru years Congress was dominant politically and retained power at the Centre and in almost all the states. But, simultaneously, a multi-party system based on free competition among parties and strong parliamentary institutions also developed from the beginning. The nature and working of the party system in place at the time of independence with several political parties—the Congress, the Socialist Party, the Communist Party, the Kisan Mazdoor Praja Party and the Bharatiya Jan Sangh—functioning actively and successfully in 1951–52 was crucial to the development of parliamentary democracy in India.

All the major political parties were national or all-India in character, in their structure, organization, programmes and policies, even when their political bases were limited to specific areas or classes and sections of society. They had national objectives, took up significant all-India issues, sustained an all-India leadership and put forward programmes concerned with the social, economic and political development of the country as a whole.

Though the Opposition parties remained individually quite weak compared to Congress in terms of mass support as also seats in parliament and the state legislatures, they were quite active and politically did not play just a peripheral role. They vigorously campaigned for alternative sets of economic and political policies. More significantly, non-Congress candidates polled more votes than the Congress in the general elections of 1951–52, 1957 and

1962; and, despite the first-past-the-post electoral system, they captured 26 per cent of the Lok Sabha seats in 1952, 25 per cent in 1957 and 28 per cent in 1962. They fared even better in the state assemblies where their strength was 32 per cent of the seats in 1952, 35 per cent in 1957, and 40 per cent in 1962. What is even more important, they put considerable pressure on the government and the ruling party and subjected them to consistent criticism. In practice, they also wielded a great deal of influence on public policies, in fact, quite out of proportion to their size.

Opposition parties remained weak in this period because of their inability to unite. They found they had more in common with one or the other wing of Congress than with each other. This was not accidental because except for the communal and casteist parties all the other Opposition parties had before 1947 been part of the national movement and the Congress. It was only when the left and right parties could unite, formally or informally, that they could defeat the Congress in 1977 and 1989.

The Indian National Congress was then the most important political organization in India at independence and, in fact, throughout the Nehru era. There was no alternative to it on the horizon. It enjoyed immense prestige and legitimacy as the leader and heir of the national movement. Its reach was national; it covered the entire subcontinent. Its social base extended from the metropolitan cities to the remotest of villages and from the big capitalists to the rural poor. Congress gave the country a stable government; it was a major instrument of the political stability India enjoyed for several decades.

It is axiomatic among historians and political scientists that after independence Congress was transformed from a movement into a party. But this is a half-truth, for no real break occurred immediately after 15 August 1947. In fact, this was the problem that Congress faced. In the changed circumstances it could no longer be the leader of a mass movement; but could it become a modern party for forming a government, and yet retain the character of a broad coalition for the purposes of nation-building? As a party, it had to have a certain organizational cohesion; this it secured by introducing, at Sardar Patel's initiative, a provision that no person belonging to any other political party or group, which had its own constitution and organizational structure, could be its member. (It had permitted this before 1947 when the Congress

Socialists and the Communists were its members, even while forming their own parties.) But it retained its ideological and programmatic diversity and openness as also a certain organizational looseness.

The Congress Socialists misunderstood the emerging character of Congress and assumed, especially after the Patel amendment, that it was no longer to be broad-based and was being transformed into a right-wing bourgeois party with a definite ideological and programmatic commitment to the capitalist path of development. Given these perceived differences, the Socialists decided to leave Congress. This was certainly a blow to the broad-based character of the party.

Jawaharlal Nehru, on the other hand, was convinced that it was both possible and necessary to retain the all-embracing *consensual character of Congress and that without its leadership* the country would neither be politically stable, nor capable of economic and social development. He was therefore unwilling to divide the party along left–right lines and stayed with Congress as did a large number of the Congress Socialists who saw Congress and Nehru as more effective instruments of socialism and social change. However, realizing that the departure of the Socialists would adversely affect the socialist aspirations of Congress, he made, as we shall see, several attempts to bring them back into the party or at least to get their cooperation in his nation-building efforts. He also constantly strove to reform Congress and give it a left turn, however arduous the task. He also adopted a reconciliatory approach towards political opponents other than the communalists.

Congress did, of course, become after 1947 a distinct political party, competing with other parties for political power but it did not become a monolithic party. It retained its amorphous and national consensual character with a great deal of ideological flexibility and vagueness. Though the party observed a certain degree of discipline, its functioning and decision-making remained democratic and open. There was still a great deal of debate within it as also tolerance of different viewpoints, tendencies and open dissent. The views of the party members got reflected in the All India Congress Committee (AICC) and the annual sessions of the party. The district and provincial party organizational structures also functioned effectively and conveyed to the leadership the different points of view prevailing in the party. Important in this respect was the role of Nehru who functioned as a democrat inside the party as also in relation to the Opposition parties.

Congress also remained sensitive to and functioned as the medium for the reconciliation, accommodation and adjustment of diverse and divergent class, sectional and regional interests, as it had done during the period of the anti-imperialist struggle. It also had the capacity to contain, compromise and reconcile different and competing points of view within the party. While placating the propertied and socially dominant groups, it was simultaneously able to appeal to the poor and the deprived. It was also able to accommodate new social and political forces as they gradually emerged and entered the political arena, especially as the left parties failed to represent and mobilize them.

This all-embracing, inclusive character Congress was able to retain in part because of its inheritance in the national movement but largely because of the Nehruvian notion that national consolidation, democracy and social change required the active or passive consent of the overwhelming majority of the people.

During the Nehru era, Congress remained basically a party of the Centre or middle with a left orientation—in other words, a left-of-centre party—though it had right and left minorities at its flanks. Broadly, it stood for nationalism, economic development, social justice, redistribution of wealth and equalization of opportunities encompassed by the broad idea of democratic socialism. As a centrist party it had three important features. First, the Opposition parties, other than the communal parties, were able to influence it through their mass agitations or through like-minded groups within it, for there always existed inside Congress groups which reflected the positions of the Opposition parties. Second, this conciliatory attitude led to the Opposition parties being open to absorption. Congress was able to absorb the social base, cadres, programmes and policies of the Opposition parties, and to pacify and co-opt popular movements through concessions and conciliation. Third, the Opposition parties, both of the left and the right, tended to define themselves in extreme terms in order to prevent their cadres and followers—and even leaders—from being co-opted or absorbed by Congress. This happened whenever the Socialist and Communist parties adopted realistic demands or followed a non-antagonistic approach towards Congress and its policies. But these extreme

positions also had negative consequences for the parties concerned—
they tended to isolate them further from public opinion and also
made them vulnerable to splits.

Leadership of Party versus Government

A major problem that Congress had to decide on as a party at the
very outset was what would be the precise relationship between
the leadership of the party and that of the government. In November
1946, Nehru joined the interim government and resigned from the
party presidentship on the ground that the two roles of the leader
of the government and the president of the party could not be
combined. His successor as Congress president, J.B. Kripalani,
however, demanded that the president of the party and the CWC
should have a direct role in government policy-making and that
all government decisions should be taken in consultation with
them.

Nehru and Sardar Patel and other leaders holding government
positions did not agree with Kripalani. They said that the
proceedings and the papers of the government were secret and
could not be divulged to persons outside the government. The
party, they argued, should lay down general long-term policies
and goals but should not interfere with the specific problems of
governance. The government, in their view, was constitutionally
accountable to the elected legislature; it could in no case be made
accountable to the party. In essence they argued for the autonomy
of the parliamentary wing and and even its supremacy over the
party in so far as government affairs were concerned.

Kripalani would not agree to this virtual subordination of the
party to the government and, feeling frustrated by the refusal of
the government to consult him on several important issues, resigned
from the party presidentship in November 1947 without completing
his two-year term. Explaining his resignation to the AICC delegates,
he said: 'How is the Congress to give the Government its active
and enlightened cooperation unless its highest executive or its
popularly chosen head is taken into full confidence on important
matters that affect the nation.'[1]

Kripalani was succeeded in office for one year by Rajendra
Prasad and subsequently for two years by B. Pattabhi Sitaramayya.
Neither of the two asserted the principle of organizational

supremacy or even equality and confined the functions of the party president to organizational affairs. But before the issue could be clinched, the Nehru–Tandon tussle over organizational control intervened once again and raked up this question among others.

A crisis involving differences over policies and party and government management broke out in 1950 over the question of Purshottamdas Tandon's presidentship of the Congress. With the Communists leaving the Congress in 1945 and from the end of 1947 adopting a totally hostile attitude towards Nehru and the government, and the Socialists parting ways with Congress in 1948, the radical forces in Congress were weakened. The conservative forces then decided to assert themselves and to make a bid for control over the party and the policies of the government. But before we take up this crisis, we may very briefly deal with the tension resulting from the Nehru–Patel differences.

Nehru and Patel

Sardar Patel has been much misunderstood and misrepresented. Some have used him to attack the Nehruvian vision and policies; others have made him out to be the archetypal rightist. Both have been wrong. Patel was undoubtedly the main leader of the Congress right wing. But his rightist stance has often been grossly misinterpreted. Like Nehru, he fully shared the basic values of the national movement: commitment to democracy and civil liberties, secularism, independent economic development, social reform and a pro-poor orientation. He stood for the abolition of landlordism but through payment of compensation. A staunch opponent of communalism, he was fully committed to secularism. In 1946–47 he took ruthless action against the rioters. In 1950 he declared:

> Ours is a secular State. We cannot fashion our policies or shape our conduct in the way Pakistan does it. We must see that our secular ideals are actually realised in practice . . . Here every Muslim should feel that he is an Indian citizen and has equal rights as an Indian citizen. If we cannot make him feel like this, we shall not be worthy of *our heritage and of our country*.[2]

He was also utterly intolerant of nepotism and corruption. Patel's conservatism, however, found expression with regard to the questions of class and socialism. Before 1947, he had opposed the Socialists and the Communists. After 1947, he argued successfully both for stimulus to private enterprise and the incorporation of the right of property as a fundamental right in the constitution. Thus, the right-wing stance of Patel was basically a matter of social ideology. But his positive approach to capitalism and the capitalists was combined with total personal integrity and an austere lifestyle. He collected money from the rich for the national movement but none dare offer him a paisa for his own or his family's use.

In fact, the relationship between Nehru and Patel was highly complex. Historians and political scientists have generally tended to emphasize the differences between the two and overlooked what they had in common. Certainly, their differences and disputes were real, as also significant, but they have been exaggerated to the extent of falsifying history.

Patel and Nehru had temperamental as well as ideological differences. After 1947, policy differences on several questions cropped up between them. The two differed on the role and authority of the prime minister, the manner in which the riots of 1947 were to be handled and the relations with Pakistan. The election of Purshottamdas Tandon as Congress president in 1950 created a wide breach between them. Nehru opposed, though unsuccessfully, Patel's view that the right to property should be included among the Fundamental Rights in the constitution. Several times their differences on questions of policy led to near breaches and offers of resignation from the government by one or the other. A certain tension was always present between the two.

Yet, the two continued to stick and pull together and there was no final parting of ways. This was because what united them was more significant and of abiding value than what divided them. Also, they complemented each other in many ways: one was a great organizer and able administrator, the other commanded immense mass support and had a wide social and developmental perspective. If anything, Patel buttressed Nehru's role even while challenging it in some respects. Besides, there was considerable mutual affection and respect for each other and each recognized the indispensability of the other. Gandhiji's death also made a difference; the two realized that it had made their cooperation all the more necessary. Both arrived at an agreement through the process of frank discussion on almost every major government policy decision. Patel would argue his case, sometimes strongly, would win it sometimes, but when he could not, he would invariably yield to Nehru. Throughout Patel remained Nehru's loyal colleague, assuring him of complete support for his policies. After Gandhiji's death, he repeatedly described Nehru as his 'leader'. On 14 November 1948—Nehru's birthday—he was to say: 'Mahatma Gandhiji named Pandit Nehru as his heir and successor. Since Gandhiji's death we have realised that our leader's judgement was correct.'[3] And Nehru reciprocated: 'The Sardar has been a tower of strength; but for his affection and advice I would not have been able to run the State.'[4]

Purshottamdas Tandon versus Nehru

The struggle between the right wing of the party and Nehru came to a head in August 1950 over the question of the election of the party president and lasted for over one year. The struggle involved questions of policy and ideology; but it was also important because the new office-bearers would play a decisive role in the nomination of the party candidates in the coming general elections.

The three candidates who contested the election for the party presidentship were Purshottamdas Tandon, supported by Patel, J.B. Kripalani, supported by Nehru, and Shankarrao Deo. Nehru was opposed to Tandon because of his overall conservative social, economic and political outlook. He made it clear that he would find it difficult to continue as a member of the Congress Working Committee or even of the government if Tandon were elected. Supporters of Tandon, on the other hand, hoped for his election 'to curb' Nehru, to change his foreign, economic and social policies, especially his policies towards Pakistan and the Hindu Code Bill.

In a closely fought election on 29 August 1950, Tandon won with 1,306 votes, with Kripalani getting 1,092 and Deo 202 votes. Subsequently, Tandon packed the CWC and the Central Election Committee with his men. After a great deal of internal debate and tussle, a large number of Congressmen, led by Kripalani, resigned from the party in June 1951 and formed the Kisan Mazdoor Praja Party, even though Nehru and Azad advised against the step.

Nehru now decided to give battle. Regarding the Congress as indispensable (Patel having died on 15 December 1950), he decided to intervene directly in party affairs. While keen to preserve party unity, he was not willing to let the right wing dominate the party or the coming election process. With great skill and determination and bringing into play his considerable political talents, he got the AICC to pass resolutions fully endorsing his social, economic and foreign policies. Then, on 6 August 1951, he resigned from the Congress Working Committee and the Central Election Committee asking Congressmen to choose 'which viewpoint and outlook are to prevail in the Congress—Tandon's or mine'.[5] There was no doubt as to what the Congressmen's choice would be, especially in view of the coming elections which could not be won without Nehru's leadership and campaigning. Instead of accepting Nehru's resignation, Tandon, fully realizing that Nehru's political position was stronger than his own or his friends', decided to himself resign. The AICC accepted Tandon's resignation on 8 September and elected Nehru to the Congress presidency. Nehru accepted the AICC decision, even though he was in principle opposed to the prime minister being the party president. But then he had already said earlier that 'necessity might compel' him to do so 'in special circumstances'.[6]

The entire episode led to little bitterness as Tandon resigned 'with grace and little recrimination' and Nehru graciously asked Tandon to join the Working Committee under his leadership. The offer was immediately accepted by Tandon. Nehru also asked the dissidents to rejoin the party, and several of them, including Rafi Ahmed Kidwai, did so.

Nehru now emerged as the unchallenged leader of the party—the leader who had the final word in the party as also the government and he enjoyed this position till his death in 1964. Though he failed to bring Kripalani and many other rebels back to the party, he succeeded in maintaining the pluralist, consensual as also the left-of-centre character of the Congress.

Another aspect of the conflict between Nehru and Tandon was connected to the relationship between the party organization and the parliamentary party and the government, which had cropped up earlier during, Kripalani's presidency. After his election as Congress president, Tandon had again raised the issue of the party control over the government and he and his supporters had declared that the prime minister and his cabinet must carry out the mandate given by the party and be responsible to it for the carrying out of policies. However, Tandon's resignation and Nehru's presidency confirmed the prominent role of the prime minister and the cabinet in the formulation and carrying out of the government policies; the party president and the Congress Working Committee were to concentrate on the organizational aspects of the party. Though Nehru never again became the president of the party after 1953, there was no conflict between the party and the government in his lifetime. After Nehru too, it has been widely accepted that in a parliamentary democracy where the executive is directly or indirectly elected by the people, there cannot be two centres of power and the real state power has inevitably to reside in the parliamentary wing.

But the situation in India in this respect is not like that in Britain or the US, where the party leadership plays a subsidiary role. In Congress the party president matters much more. The party plays an important role in formulating policies and in selecting the candidates for the state and parliamentary elections. Also, in a vast country like India with a largely illiterate population, the ruling party and its political workers are needed to act as links between the government and the people, to convey popular grievances to the government leaders and to explain the government policies to the people. The party alone can guarantee the proper implementation of government policies and provide a check on the bureaucracy. For example, a proper implementation of land reforms could have been achieved through an active and alive party.

Unfortunately, even while realizing the importance of the party, Nehru and his colleagues neglected the organization and failed to assign its cadre proper tasks, as also to give them their due honour and importance. Instead, there was a certain devaluing and atrophying of the party and party work. Everybody who mattered in the party wanted to be in parliament or state legislatures and then occupy ministerial chairs. Ministers and legislators took up party work only when pushed out from ministerial and legislative positions, and they often did that too so that they could manoeuvre themselves back into parliamentary positions. N. Sanjiva Reddy, who left the chief ministership of Andhra to become the president of the party, was to publicly remark that 'a junior ministership in a state government offered greater satisfaction than presidency of the Congress party'.[7]

At the same time, that the party still mattered is confirmed by the fact that almost every prime minister after Nehru either tried to have a henchman or a sycophant as the party president or herself/himself assumed the party presidency.

Intra-Congress Rivalry

Even in the early years there were signs that Congress was gradually beginning to lose touch with the people and its standards beginning to decline. A certain tendency towards deterioration is perhaps inevitable in a ruling party but the deterioration and decline should remain within reasonable bounds. This was certainly the case with the Congress in the early years after independence; but the erosion of the party values and standards was still worrisome. There were certain tendencies in the party which were fraught with danger.

There was, as a political scientist said, 'increasing corruption, disillusionment, and loss of *elan* in the Congress Party',[8] or, as Nehru bemoaned as early as 1948, 'the progressive collapse of the morale and idealistic structure that we had built up'.[9] A patronage system was initiated especially in the rural areas leading to the emergence of political brokers and middlemen and vote banks. Factions, factionalism and factional intrigues and disputes, often based on personal and group interests, though sometimes involving ideological and policy differences, emerged, leading even to non-democratic functioning at the lower levels of the organization and tarnishing the image of the party. Intense rivalry and conflict between the organization men and ministerialists in the states led to intra-party conflicts, with the former often behaving as an Opposition party, their major political objective being to dethrone the ministerialists and to occupy their seats. This tended to create among the people the image of the Congress as a party of office-seekers.

Above all, there was the increasing loss of idealism and neglect of ideology, especially as concerns social welfare and social transformation. The net result was that the Congress increasingly lost touch with the people and it no longer appealed to the intelligentsia and the younger people and was therefore unable to recruit the best of them into the party. Most of the idealist youth preferred to join the Opposition parties. The Congress was thereby failing to train a new generation of leaders to replace those thrown up by the national movement. The deterioration was beginning to affect all political parties but it affected the Congress to a much greater extent, it being the ruling party.

Nehru was, of course, aware of this state of affairs in the country and in the Congress. In a mood of disillusionment, despair and despondency, he wrote in 1948: 'It is terrible to think that we may be losing all our values and sinking into the sordidness of opportunist politics.' In 1949: 'Our standards have fallen greatly. Indeed, we have hardly any standards left except not to be found out.' And then, again in 1950: 'We have lost something, the spirit that moves and unless we recapture that spirit, all our labour will yield little profit.'[10] In 1957 he told the Congress MPs: The Congress Party is weak and getting weaker . . . Our strong point is the past. Unless we get out of our present rut, the Congress Party is doomed.'[11]

Unfortunately, Nehru was no party organizer or reformer nor did he and other tall leaders working in the government have time to devote to party organization. The important work of building the party and toning it up were neglected during the years of Nehru's total dominance of the party and the government. In fact, Nehru was compelled to rely on the state party 'bosses' for running the party machine. Nevertheless, being very much an ideologue, he made several major attempts to keep the party anchored ideologically and politically to its socialist and idealist moorings.

The Socialists and the Congress

The departure of the Socialists had weakened the radical forces in Congress and the space vacated by them was being increasingly filled by vested interests—landlords, rich peasants, and even princes. Nehru realized that Congress had been weakened ideologically by the absence of the Socialists and that he was gradually being hemmed in by conservative modes of thinking. At the same time he also felt that the Congress was indispensable and that it would be wrong and counter-productive to either divide or leave it. The answer, therefore, was to reform and improve a united Congress party despite its many weaknesses.

Nehru, therefore, tried several times to bring the Socialists back into the Congress or to at least get their cooperation in the implementation of a developmental and egalitarian agenda. He did not simultaneously woo the Communists for they were organizationally, politically and ideologically on a completely different track from that of the Congress. But he did try, with some success, to bring the Communists into the mainstream of parliamentary politics. The Socialists on the other hand, Nehru felt, had the same principles and objectives as he had. Moreover, he had a great personal regard and affection for several Socialist leaders, especially Jayaprakash Narayan, who was close enough to him for years to address him as 'Bhai' (brother).

His first attempt to bring the Socialists back into the Congress was in 1948 itself when he expressed his distress at the growing distance from them, which, he said, was 'not good either for us [the Congress] or the Socialist Party, and certainly not good either for the country'.[12] But the Socialists were still quite angry with and critical of Nehru. Jayaprakash, for example, wrote to Nehru in December 1948: 'You want to go towards socialism, but you want the capitalists to help in that.'[13] He also told Nehru in March 1949 that the proposed legislation outlawing strikes in the essential services was 'an ugly example of growing Indian fascism'.[14]

Nehru in turn felt that the Socialists 'continue to show an amazing lack of responsibility and constructive bent of mind. They seem to be all frustrated and going mentally to pieces.'[15]

Another effort by Nehru in 1951 to improve relations with the Socialists once again met with a rebuff. Believing that Nehru was shielding and supporting reactionary forces, Jayaprakash Narayan once again publicly denounced 'Nehru's naked, open fascism' and declared that his government was 'following faithfully in the footsteps of Hitler in their dealings with labour'.[16]

After winning the general elections in 1952 Nehru made his most serious effort to work together with the Socialists, hoping to build a broad political front to promote economic development and strengthen the left trend within the Congress. In 1957, he asked the Socialists to cooperate with the Congress; he also hoped to bring Jayaprakash into the cabinet. In response, Jayaprakash wanted the Congress to adopt a radical programme framed by him before he and the Socialists joined it. His 14-point programme included specific constitutional amendments, administrative and land reforms and nationalization of banks, insurance and mines.

Nehru was in agreement with many of Jayaprakash's fourteen points, but he refused to enter into a prior commitment. If he could have formulated and persuaded his party to accept and implement such a full-scale radical programme he would not have needed

Socialist cooperation. This support was needed precisely so that he could do so after strengthening the left trend in the Congress. Implementation of a radical programme would be the result of the Socialists rejoining the Congress but not a condition to be met prior to their rejoining. Nehru was prepared to strengthen the radical forces inside the Congress and not split the party in order to accommodate the Socialists. He was convinced that the Congress and the government had to go step by step towards radical transformation, that he had to build a larger societal consensus for taking steps towards socialism, that specific steps and their timing were to be determined pragmatically, and that he needed Socialist support precisely to achieve all this. But Jayaprakash could also not resile from his position for he was afraid that that would lead to a split in his own party.

From now on, while the dominant section of the Socialists continued to be convinced that Nehru and the Congress were committed to conservative policies, Nehru became increasingly contemptuous of the Socialists and felt that he would have to implement his socialist agenda alone, with the help of the left wing of the Congress and without the aid of the Socialists. His personal relations with Jayaprakash also deteriorated as he felt that the latter 'hates the Congress so much as to prefer the devil to it'.[17] With every passing year the relations between the Congress and Nehru and the Socialists went on becoming more acrimonious. In October 1956, Nehru wrote in a personal letter that Jayaprakash was saying and writing 'things which have little to do with socialism and which have much to do with nonsense'.[18] He also felt that Jayaprakash was, in the words of S. Gopal, 'willing to join forces with any group in order to defeat the Congress'. More specifically he accused Jayaprakash of supporting the Swatantra Party and encouraging the Hindu communalists. Jayaprakash in turn accused Nehru of 'having deteriorated from a national leader to a partisan of the Congress'.[19]

Clearly, this was also the beginning of the Socialist policy of anti-Congressism which went far beyond opposition to the Congress on the basis of a left or socialist critique. The other side of the medal was that this policy tended to weaken the Socialists themselves and led to splits in their rank and with every split some Socialists joined the Congress.

Socialism in the Congress

With his failure in seeking the help of the Socialists to renovate the Congress and shake it out of its staleness, Nehru decided to act on his own, by radicalizing party policies, especially with regard to the limited steps taken so far for social equality and equity as also economic development. In 1953 itself he had adopted the policy of extending land reforms from the abolition of landlordism to the fixation of ceilings on landholdings. Then came the adoption of the socialist pattern of society as the objective of the Congress at its Avadi session in January 1955. The Avadi Resolution declared:

> Planning should take place with a view to the establishment of a socialistic pattern of society, where the principle means of production are under social ownership or control, production is progressively speeded up and there is equitable distribution of the national wealth.[20]

The Second and Third Five Year Plans provided further commitment to the socialistic pattern of society. But Nehru defined this in quite a flexible manner, all the while putting strong emphasis on modernization of the economy and increased production. While placing the Second Five Year Plan before parliament, he stated: 'I do not propose to define precisely what socialism means . . . because we wish to avoid rigid or doctrinaire thinking.' And then added: 'But broadly speaking . . . we mean a society in which there is equality of opportunity and the possibility for everyone to live a good life . . . We have, therefore, to lay great stress on equality, on the removal of disparities, and it has to be remembered always that socialism is not the spreading out of poverty. The essential thing is that there must be wealth and production.'[21] In the chapter on the 'Objectives of Planned Development' which he wrote for the Third Five Year Plan document, after reiterating the objective of planning in the same terms as the Avadi Resolution, he quoted from the Second Plan: 'The socialist pattern of society is not to be regarded as some fixed or rigid pattern. It is not rooted in any doctrine or dogma. Each country has to develop according to its own genius and traditions. Economic and social policy has to be shaped from time to time in the light of historical circumstances.'[22]

An indirect result of the left turn taken by the Congress was the adverse impact on the political fortunes of the parties of the left and the right which tended to get marginalized. In particular, by stealing the thunder of the Socialists and the Communists, it also tended to promote dissensions and division among them.

The Congress moved further to the left, programmatically, when, at its Nagpur session in January 1959, it passed a resolution declaring that 'the future agrarian pattern should be that of cooperative joint farming'. Initially, service cooperatives were to be established which would ultimately be transformed into farming cooperatives on a purely voluntary basis. In addition there was to be a ceiling on landholdings and state trading in foodgrains. The Nagpur decisions faced opposition both within and outside the party and were quietly jettisoned. Land ceilings were circumvented by the state governments under the pressure of capitalist farmers and rich peasants supported by the middle peasants. The small experiments in cooperative farming were a failure, and state trading in foodgrains was soon found to be unworkable. Nehru was quite willing to learn and discard unworkable policies, and except for the land ceilings, other aspects of the Nagpur Resolution were soon abandoned. However, the commitment to socialism was once again vigorously asserted at the Bhubaneshwar session of the Congress in January 1964.

While refusing to let the Congress be divided sharply on a left–right basis, Nehru kept the Congress on a left-of-centre course. He consistently attacked the right-wing parties and individuals and treated the left parties with respect even while criticizing them and making clear his differences with them.

Decline of Congress

The stronger assertion of its commitment to socialism did not stop the rot in the Congress party. There was growing criticism of the party in the country as also disillusionment with it. Also internal divisions in the party were growing more serious. The old leaders had grown jaded while new suitable leaders were not coming forth. The party organization continued to weaken; the party had been in power too long. A large number of Congressmen were no longer satisfied with party work—they hungered for official positions, influence and patronage. Administrative corruption was beginning to go beyond tolerable limits. The Congress was drifting away from the people and losing ground to the Opposition in the states. The growing weakness of the party was revealed by the loss in 1963 of three prestigious Lok Sabha by-elections in the party strongholds. People had begun to ask the questions: After Nehru, who? And after Nehru, what?

Nehru, aided by the Madras chief minister, K. Kamaraj, now made a last effort to infuse new life into the party and restore the balance between the party and the government. This was sought to be achieved through what came to be known as the Kamaraj Plan, produced in August 1963 at a meeting of the Congress Working Committee. The essence of the plan was that a number of leading Congressmen who were in the government as Union cabinet ministers or as chief ministers in the states should voluntarily resign from their posts and take up party organizational work in order to revitalize the party. Nehru was to decide whose resignations were to be finally accepted. This would also enable Nehru to cleanse the party at the top.

The Kamaraj Plan received enthusiastic response from the party rank and file. Immediately nearly 300 resignations from ministerial posts, including those of all members of the Union cabinet and all chief ministers, followed. On 24 August, Nehru announced the acceptance of the resignations of six senior cabinet ministers— Morarji Desai, Lal Bahadur Shastri, S.K. Patil, Jagjivan Ram, B. Gopala Reddy and K.L. Shrimali—and six chief ministers.

The Kamaraj Plan had, however, come too late. Nehru was already ailing and suffered a stroke at Bhubaneshwar in January 1964 and did not have the energy to take the necessary follow-through action. The leaders relieved from government office were not assigned any party duties except for Kamaraj who became the party president in January 1964; they sulked or intrigued against political rivals in the states. The plan also failed as a means of cleansing the party of the dross. The morale of the party continued to sink, and Congressmen were as obsessed with administrative power and patronage as before. An indirect effect of the plan was to weaken Morarji Desai's position in the party. Another outcome of it was that, while failing to restore the prestige and importance of party organizational work, it increased the power of the state party bosses in central politics till Indira Gandhi cut them down to size in 1969. When Nehru died in June 1964, the Congress was continuing to go downhill.

Political Parties, 1947–1965: The Opposition

The Socialist Party

Of all the political parties that emerged immediately after independence the Socialist Party held the greatest promise. In Jayaprakash Narayan it had a leader next only to Jawaharlal Nehru in mass popularity. It had also several other brilliant leaders, for example, Acharya Narendra Dev, Achyut Patwardhan, Asoka Mehta, Dr Rammanohar Lohia and S.M. Joshi. However, the first problem the Socialists faced—and this was a problem they continued to face to the end—was that of their relationship with Congress. The Socialist Party had been born in 1934 and had remained since then a part of Congress, though it had its own separate constitution, membership, discipline and ideology.

Believing that independence could not be achieved through negotiations, the Socialist Party had boycotted the negotiations with the Cabinet Mission and refused to participate in the Constituent Assembly or the interim government or to accept membership of the Congress Working Committee. It had stoutly rejected the Mountbatten Plan for the independence and Partition of the country. Immediately after independence it had given the slogan of India's development into a socialist state and society. Most Socialists wanted Congress to make a definite programmatic and ideological commitment to socialism. They believed that by refusing to do so, it had become a right-wing bourgeois party. In early 1948 Congress framed a rule that its members could not belong to another party which had its own constitution and discipline. Since the Socialists were not willing to dissolve their own party, they decided in

March 1948 to leave Congress and also declared that their objective was to establish a democratic socialist society.

Leaving Congress proved to be a historic mistake on the part of the Socialists. Congress still retained its all-embracing character and, therefore, tolerance for diverse views; it was imposing only organizational uniformity and not an ideological one. Hence, there was no question of the Socialists being asked to give up their ideology or policies. The position was similar to that prevailing in the European labour parties. Since there was no barrier in Congress to informal organization of different trends, the Socialists could have continued to function in Congress as a loose group as the conservatives were doing, without forming a separate organization and breaking discipline.

The Socialists had assumed that with the achievement of independence, there no longer existed any common task to unite them with the non-Socialists in Congress. But, in fact, this was not so, as the material, social and political foundations of a socialist India still needed to be laid through economic development with equity, secular democracy and consolidation of national unity. And Congress was still the main organization that could fulfil this task. As Hariharnath Shastri, a member of the National Executive of the Socialist Party and a former president of the All India Trade Union Congress, put it when resigning from the party for its refusal to join the Congress-sponsored Indian National Trade Union Congress: 'The unfinished task of national revolution demands the full-fledged allegiance of all sections of the people and every progressive group in the country, including the Socialists and the Congress.'[1]

Political skill and leadership to function in a party that was practically a front lay precisely in competing with other trends in it without breaking party discipline, so as to build a broad coalition for nation-building and social change and, ultimately, socialism. True, the Socialists were a minority in Congress and were facing resistance and organizational discrimination at the party's local level. Political wisdom, as also the art of politics, lay in accepting this situation and then struggling to gradually change the balance of power between the right and the left within the Congress by pulling, inch by inch, the Centre towards the left. This is precisely what the right did throughout the period of Gandhiji's and Nehru's domination of the Congress. Instead of breaking away when Nehru committed Congress to a socialistic pattern of society, it continued inside Congress, representing an ideological and policy trend, though constantly feeling the pressure of losing out to the left. Neither the Socialists nor the Communists or the two together— an impossibility at the time—were capable of replacing Congress or bringing about socialism and social change on their own in opposition to Congress. Nehru's political acumen and historical insight lay precisely in recognizing this. At the time of the Socialist split from Congress, a large number of Socialists stayed in the parent organization perceiving itself and Jawaharlal Nehru as the more effective instruments of social change. Acharya Narendra Dev, the most erudite, mature and level-headed of the Socialist leaders, was also opposed to the decision of leaving Congress but he decided to abide by it.

The Socialists' departure from Congress seriously weakened the left inside Congress and led to Nehru being hemmed in by conservative forces in his party. It, thus, did incalculable harm to the left trend in Indian politics. On the other hand, it initiated the process of the self-destruction of the Socialist Party, leading to repeated splits within it.

The Socialists' optimism regarding the popularity of their party was to be soon belied. The general elections of 1951–52 proved to be a near disaster for the party. All its national leaders were defeated and it won only 12 seats in the Lok Sabha, though receiving 10.6 per cent of the popular vote. In the states, it won 124 of the 2,248 seats with nearly 58 per cent of its candidates losing their deposits; and its winning tally in its strongholds of Uttar Pradesh, Bihar and Bombay was 18 out of 390, 23 out of 240 and 9 out of 269 seats respectively.

Meanwhile Congress dissidents led by J.B. Kripalani had formed in June 1951 the Kisan Mazdoor Praja Party (KMPP). Claiming to be Gandhian, and being in basic agreement with Congress programme and policies, the new party promised to implement that programme. Two of its leaders, P.C. Ghosh and T. Prakasam, had been Congress chief ministers in their respective states, that is, West Bengal and Madras, while Kripalani was the Congress president till 1950 and had just lost his bid to be re-elected. The reasons for their leaving Congress were personal rather than ideological.

The KMPP too entered the general elections with high hopes and was even more disappointed with the results than the Socialist Party. It won 9 seats in the Lok Sabha and polled 5.8 per cent of the votes; but won only 77 seats in the state legislative assemblies.

Subsequently, both the Socialist Party and KMPP, having grossly miscalculated their electoral strength and being afraid of marginalization by Congress and the Communists, decided to merge and thus consolidate the Opposition forces. The leaders of the two parties felt that there were no ideological or programmatic differences between them. As Kripalani said: 'We both want a classless and casteless society free from social, political and economic exploitation. The Socialists call it the Socialist society. We call it the Sarvodaya society.'[2]

The two parties merged in September 1952 to form the Praja Socialist Party (PSP), with Kripalani as the chairman and Asoka Mehta as the general secretary. It became the largest among the Opposition parties and held the promise of being an alternative to Congress. Its two constituents had received 17.4 per cent of the popular vote in the 1952 elections. Its party organization covered the entire country and it had a large number of well-known and popular leaders at both the national and state levels. But the party could not maintain its cohesion for long.

From the beginning it was racked by ideological and factional quarrels; and it regularly underwent splits. It also suffered from widespread indiscipline among its leaders and cadres. From the outset, it was troubled by major differences over its distinct role in Indian politics as an Opposition party. The issues that tore the party apart from 1953 to 1964 concerned the attitude that it should adopt towards Congress as also the militant and extra-constitutional agitations, and the role it should play in nation-building activities. In June 1953, at the party's Betal Conference, Asoka Mehta offered his thesis that in a backward country the important task was that of economic development and that, therefore, in a constructive spirit, the Opposition should cooperate with the ruling party in that task, though not uncritically. As the Congress and PSP shared a common belief in nationalism, socialism and democracy, he said, the PSP should look for areas of agreement with Congress and oppose it only when matters of principle were involved. Mehta warned that non-cooperation with Congress and all-out opposition to it would make the PSP politically ineffective for a long time to come.

The party conference, however, rejected Mehta's thesis in favour of Dr Rammanohar Lohia's approach. Lohia stood for determined opposition to Congress and a position of equidistance from both Congress and the Communists. He also advocated the organization of militant mass opposition movements even if they were not within the legal, legislative and constitutional framework. Lohia and his followers were also not easily amenable to party discipline.

From the beginning, the PSP suffered from ineffective and unstable leadership. Over a period of time, most of its leaders had 'renounced, defected, or been expelled from the Party, each time leaving it a little weaker by taking with them their loyal supporters'.[3] Lohia and his group left the PSP at the end of 1955. Acharya Narendra Dev died in 1956. Jayaprakash Narayan withdrew from active politics in 1954 and announced that he would dedicate his life to Bhoodan and other constructive activities. After the general elections of 1957, he retired from politics, declared that party politics was not suitable to India and advocated, instead, 'partyless democracy'. In 1960, Kripalani left the party to play an independent role in politics. In 1963, Asoka Mehta agreed to become the deputy chairman of the Planning Commission and, when expelled from the party, joined Congress in the summer of 1964, taking nearly one-third of PSP cadres with him. Many state-level leaders also regularly defected to Congress—among them were T. Prakasam in Andhra, Pattom Thanu Pillai in Kerala, P.C. Ghosh in Bengal, Mahamaya Prasad Sinha in Bihar and Triloki Singh in Uttar Pradesh. Finally, in 1971, more than half of the party cadres joined Congress.

All this was reflected in the steady decline of the PSP in the general elections. The party won 19 seats in the Lok Sabha with 10.4 per cent of the total votes in 1957; 12 seats with 6.8 per cent votes in 1962; and 13 seats with 3.1 per cent of the votes in 1967. The virtual demise of the party came in 1971 when it won only 2 seats with 1 per cent share of the votes. The remnants of the party joined the Socialist Party to form the Samyukta Socialist Party.

A reason for the failure of the Socialists was their inability to distinguish themselves from Congress, especially after the Avadi Resolution committing itself to a socialistic pattern of society. In fact, they could have played a meaningful role only as a part of Congress, with which they shared a commitment to nationalism, secularism, a polity based on parliamentary democracy and civil liberties, and social change. Outside Congress they were bound to be marginalized and splintered by a bigger party with a better and more influential leader in Nehru, having the same paradigm and therefore more or less the same appeal.

After leaving the PSP, Dr Lohia formed the Socialist Party at the end of 1955. The hallmark of the new party was political militancy. It was unremittingly involved in agitations, civil disobedience movements, walk-outs from the state legislatures and disruptions of their proceedings. The party and its main leader, Lohia, were anti-Nehru in the extreme and also totally opposed to Congress. The two issues that they emphasized were first, the immediate abolition of English and its replacement by Hindi as the sole link language and second, reservation of over 60 per cent of jobs for the backward castes, the Scheduled Castes, the Scheduled Tribes and women. They accused the Nehru government of being dominated by and serving the cause of the upper castes. In many ways, they were the initiators of the casteist politics of the 1990s in so far as they started making appeals to caste as the basic feature of the party's ideology. Lohia, himself a brilliant intellectual, also encouraged a certain anti-intellectualism among his followers. Later, in 1967, Lohia and his followers were also to seek cooperation with the Swatantra Party and Jan Sangh, on the one hand, and the Communists, on the other, in order to defeat Congress. They clearly articulated and initiated the politics of anti-Congressism. The Socialist Party was also not free from dissidence, defections and splits, especially after the death of Dr Lohia in 1967. It merged with the PSP in 1964 to break free in 1965 and then to merge with it again in 1971. But by then it too had been reduced to a rump. The Lohia Socialists won 8 seats in the Lok Sabha in 1957, 6 in 1962, 23 in 1967 and 3 in 1971 when it polled only 2.4 per cent of the total votes.

The Communist Party

The Communist Party of India (CPI) was a part of Congress since 1936 but, unwilling to accept the Congress discipline, it left the party in 1945. From 1942 to 1945 it had a remarkable growth, even though it got isolated from the mainstream of the national movement and consequently suffered in terms of its hegemonic influence over the people. In 1947, the CPI started out with certain advantages: it had several able leaders and thousands of devoted, disciplined and hardworking cadres who were active among the peasants, workers, students and the intelligentsia. But, as in the case of the Socialist Party, the CPI was plagued by intense factionalism in the post-1947 years and was engulfed by internal crises every few years till it formally split in 1964. Factions in the CPI were formed, however, largely around political and ideological differences. Put simply, the CPI could not agree upon a stand on the question which P.C. Joshi, the party's general secretary from 1935 to 1948, raised as early as 1950: 'What is the political situation in India?'

The CPI had gone through a great deal of inner turmoil and division during 1947. Initially, it recognized that India had become free and advised all progressive forces to rally round Nehru against the reactionary communal and pro-imperialist forces. Later, under Soviet guidance, it declared in December 1947 that India's independence was fake (*yeh azadi jhooti hai*), 15 August was a day of national betrayal, Congress had gone over to imperialism and feudalism, Nehru had become a stooge of imperialism, the government was ruling in a fascist manner, and the constitution that was being framed was a charter of slavery. The Communists had, therefore, to take up the anti-imperialist and anti-feudal tasks, fight for freedom and democracy and initiate an armed struggle.

At its Second Congress held in Calcutta in February 1948, the party chose B.T. Ranadive in place of P.C. Joshi as its general secretary. It declared that the masses were disillusioned with Congress because of the deteriorating economic situation and the betrayal of the anti-imperialist cause and were ready to revolt. The party, therefore, gave a call for an immediate armed uprising. The CPI organized several adventurist actions, two proving to be particularly disastrous. It decided to continue the armed peasant struggle in Telangana, which had been going on against the Nizam of Hyderabad since 1946, but to direct it now against the Indian government. The result was the death of thousands of heroic party and peasant activists in the unequal and unpopular fight against the Indian army. The second major disastrous step was to declare a national railway strike on 9 March 1949 in the hope that it would lead to an all-India general strike culminating in a general, countrywide uprising. The strike was, however, a complete flop.

The party also indulged in several terrorist acts. As a consequence, the CPI was banned in several states. It gradually got isolated from Indian opinion and was organizationally decimated through expulsions and resignations, its membership declining from nearly 90,000 to about 18,000 in 1951.

Near the end of 1951, when Ajoy Ghosh became the general secretary of the party, a new programme and a new tactical line were accepted under the direct guidance of Stalin, leading to the temporary unification of the party. But this still did not represent a new understanding of the Indian social and political reality. India was still seen as essentially a colony, the transfer of power in 1947 as 'betrayal', the Indian government as subservient to imperialism and as representing landlords, princes and the reactionary big bourgeoisie collaborating with British imperialism, and the Indian political system as basically undemocratic and authoritarian with the government having established a police state. The political task was still seen to be the eventual overthrow of the Indian state through armed struggle. The new element in CPI's policy was that the overthrow of the state was to be part of the future agenda because the people were not yet ready for the task: they still suffered from 'illusions' about Congress and Nehru. Immediately, the party was, therefore, to turn away from revolution-making, to withdraw the armed struggle in Telangana, and to participate in the approaching general elections. The party was helped in making the change by the fact that Nehru was by now in full command of the government. He accepted the Communists' credentials and cleared the way for the CPI by legalizing the party all over the country.

The CPI participated enthusiastically in the first general elections. It concentrated its efforts in only those areas where it had recognizable strength, that is, in what were to become Andhra and Kerala. Along with its front organization, the People's Democratic Front in Hyderabad, it contested only 61 seats for the Lok Sabha and won 23 with 4.6 per cent share of the votes and emerged as the largest Opposition party, doing better than expected by anyone. It was to do even better in 1957 when it won 27 seats and 8.92 per cent of the votes. It won a majority in Kerala and formed the first democratically elected Communist government anywhere in the world. It also won representation in almost every state legislature. In 1962, it won 29 seats in the Lok Sabha and 9.94

per cent of the votes. By this time it had emerged as a strong political force in Kerala, West Bengal and Andhra and among the working class and the intelligentsia all over the country.

The 1952 elections promised that the party would in time be considered as the political alternative to Congress. The promise did shine bright for a few years, as it had done for the Socialists in the early 1950s, but it remained essentially unfulfilled. The truce within the party proved to be quite temporary. Almost immediately after the elections differences in the party surfaced again. Despite arriving at an agreed programme in 1951, the party was not able to maintain a consensus on such major issues as the nature of the Indian state, the role of different social classes and strata, especially the Indian bourgeoisie, the nature of the class alliance which would make the Indian revolution, the very nature and meaning of revolution in India, as also the determination of the principal enemy against whom the revolution would be directed, the attitude to be adopted towards the Congress, the government and Jawaharlal Nehru and their reformist, nation-building activities. Regarding the class alliance, there was agreement on one point: the national bourgeoisie was to be allied with—but there was no agreement on who constituted the national bourgeoisie and who represented it in Indian politics and the state. The party was torn by controversies and conflicts as it tried unsuccessfully to come to grips with the actual course of social development within the confines of the 1951 programme. It was thrown into confusion at every fresh turn of events. Gradually, the differences hardened into factions, even unity on tactics broke down and the party organization tended to get paralysed.

Over the years, the party made four major changes in its official position. First, at its Madurai Congress in 1953, it accepted that the Government of India was following an independent foreign policy though in its internal policies it was still not independent and was an agent of imperialism. Second, at its Palghat Congress held in 1956, the party accepted that India had won independence in 1947 and was now a sovereign republic. The party now held that the government's policies were directed at building capitalism but by following anti-people policies and giving concessions to the imperialists. The government was therefore basically reactionary and the party's main task was to build a 'democratic front' to replace Congress. This front, however, was not to be anti-Congress because Congress contained many democrats who had to be won over and detached from their leaders. Third, at its Amritsar Congress, in 1958, the party declared that it was possible to advance to socialism through peaceful and parliamentary means. It also declared that if it came to power it would grant full civil liberties including the right of the Opposition parties to oppose the socialist government and the socialist system through constitutional means. Fourth, at its Vijayawada Congress in 1961, the party decided to follow a policy of struggle as well as unity towards Congress. The struggle aspect would be primary but progressive policies of Congress would be supported. The expectation was that Congress would split along progressive–reactionary lines and the party would then unite with the progressive section.

The agreements at the party congresses were, however, only on the surface. The differences were in fact sharpening with time, with new issues, such as the attitude to be adopted towards the Soviet critique of Stalin, Russia–China differences and the India–China war of 1962, being added to the long list. One wing of the party supported the government wholeheartedly against the Chinese attack, the other wing while opposing the Chinese stand on the question of India–China frontiers also opposed the unqualified support to the Nehru government because of its class character. The Soviet–China ideological split also had a great deal of resonance in the CPI, and many in it were sympathetic to the Chinese position. The Chinese fuelled the differences in the CPI by giving a call to all the revolutionary elements in the Communist parties of the world to split from those supporting the 'revisionist' Soviet line.

The CPI finally split in 1964, with one party, representing the earlier 'right' and 'centrist' trends, being known as CPI and the other party, representing the earlier 'left' trend, being known after some time as the Communist Party (Marxist) or CPM. Apart from personal and factional differences, the split took mainly a doctrinal form.

According to the CPM, the Indian state was 'the organ of the class rule of the bourgeoisie and landlords, led by the big bourgeoisie, who are increasingly collaborating with foreign finance capital'.[4] Congress was the chief instrument of the ruling classes and would, therefore, have to be destroyed. The CPM did not believe that its goal of establishing a people's democratic state could be established through peaceful, parliamentary means, especially as the Indian constitution was inherently anti-democratic and 'must go lock, stock and barrel'. The party would, however, use the constitution as an 'instrument of struggle' and try to break it 'from within'. To bring about revolution in social relations, the CPM believed, it would become necessary to start an agrarian revolution and an armed struggle under the leadership of the working class and its party. The party would try to create suitable conditions for an armed struggle as soon as possible, and would use participation in parliamentary politics to create these conditions and to overcome the illusions that people still had regarding the usefulness of parliament and the constitution. A large number of those who went over to the CPM believed that it would lead them in making a revolution. In its international outlook, the CPM continued to regard Stalin as a great Marxist who was basically correct in his policies though he made some avoidable errors. It claimed to take an independent stand on Soviet–Chinese differences but was closer to the Chinese in demanding an attack on Soviet 'revisionism.'

The CPI too wanted to 'complete the anti-imperialist, anti-feudal revolution', but it would do so by forming a national democratic front which would include progressive sections of Congress. Moreover, this front need not be led by the working class or the CPI. The party also declared that transition to national democracy and then socialism was capable of being accomplished by peaceful and parliamentary means.

Both the Communist parties later split further and have more or less stagnated and remained 'small and growing', though they jointly with each other and other parties formed governments in West Bengal, Kerala and Tripura and also made their presence felt in parliament. But outside these states they have hardly a noticeable presence. In general, they have failed to conduct politics among the people and become the leaders of a broad mass movement. Like the Socialists, the Communists also failed to realize their political potential, though they did not disintegrate and disappear as the Socialist parties had done.

How is the failure of the undivided CPI and its offshoots to measure up to the challenges of independent India and to make a political breakthrough despite favourable socio-economic conditions to be explained? There was, of course, the failure of the CPI to understand the complex Indian social development and the changing mood of the people. For example, it took eight years for it to recognize that India had become free in 1947 and another nine for the breakaway CPI to accept that independent capitalism was being built. The airy debates of the 1950s and 1960s were much more theological in nature. On the other hand, the basic formulae that the economy was in crisis, the economic conditions of the people were worsening, the class contradictions were getting intensified, and the people were disillusioned with Congress were repeated in resolution after resolution without any in-depth economic or political analysis. The hope was that the party, with its committed cadres and carefully vetted members, tight discipline and correct party line, would lead the people's revolution whenever the inevitable social, economic and political breakdown occurred and a revolutionary situation developed. The result was that the party and its contending groups and factions remained stuck in grooves from which they found it increasingly difficult to extricate themselves.

Particular manifestations of the Communist failure to come to grips with the Indian political reality are related to three areas. Despite toiling hard in the anti-imperialist cause and being a part of the mainstream national movement led by Congress and Gandhiji, both before and after independence, the party failed to appreciate correctly the character of the freedom struggle as a massive national revolution, comparable to the Russian and Chinese revolutions. After independence, the CPI by and large failed to come to terms with nationalism and the problems of national development and consolidation of the nation. Nationalism had a different meaning in the ex-colonies than in the European context. Here, it was not merely or even primarily a bourgeois phenomenon or the ideological reflex of bourgeois interests. Here, it did not reflect the befogging of the people's minds by bourgeois ideology; on the contrary, it reflected the grasp of an important aspect of the reality by the people who expected a united and strong India to become a vehicle for the improvement of their social condition. Similarly, nation-building was not a bourgeois task. The Communists could not become a hegemonic or even a major force because they failed to take up the leadership in nation-building and social development of the nation as a whole, in all its aspects; from economic development and the spread of education, scientific temper, science and technology and productivity to the fight against the caste system and for equity and equality, and the guarding of the independence, integrity and security of the nation.

Next, the CPI was also not able to work out the full and real implications of a civil libertarian and democratic polity. It got repeatedly bogged down with problems posed in the abstract, such as revolutionary versus non-revolutionary path, violent versus non-violent means, parliamentary work versus armed struggle and so on. The real problem was not posed: what did it mean to be a social revolutionary in the context of post-independence democratic India? Electoral and parliamentary politics were not to be encompassed by the traditional Communist notion of using them as mere forums of propaganda and as measures of the Communist strength. Despite the bourgeois social structure underpinning it, India's democratic polity marked a historical leap; it meant a basic change in the rules of political behaviour. India's parliamentary institutions and framework had to be seen as the political channels through which social transformation was to be brought about.

The CPI did hesitatingly move towards this understanding at its Amritsar Congress in 1958, but the effort was patchy and short-lived; and inner-party contentions soon led to its being abandoned. The CPI also failed to realize that in a democratic polity, social transformation could occur only through a series of radical reforms which had to be put into practice and not pursued merely to expose the rulers and the existing social system. In other words, instead of promising what it would do after it came to power, the party had to struggle to influence existing social development in the direction of its vision. In the absence of such an approach, the CPI failed to adopt a positive and a politically viable attitude towards the nation-building and reformist measures and policies of the Nehru government. At the same time, the party failed to become an alternative to Congress, and to come up with its own agenda of national development and social justice. One result of this was that gradually the opposition space began to be occupied by reactionary communal and casteist parties.

Lastly, the CPI's centralized, bureaucratic and basically secret party structure, relying on whole-time party cadres, also did not suit a democratic and open society. Such a party could not hope to develop mass institutions and mass power. This weakness of the party was compounded in the pre-1962 years by a certain subservience to the Soviet leadership and the importation of the doctrine of ends justifying the means into inner-party disputes.

Bharatiya Jan Sangh

The Bharatiya Jan Sangh, founded in October 1951, was basically a communal party and has to be studied as such. A communal party is one which is structured around communal ideology. A communal party cannot be defined by specific policies, for it can discard any of its programmatic and policy elements and sometimes adopt the very opposite ones. Its economic, political and social policies are generally a husk or a mask which can be changed at appropriate moments to suit its electoral or other political needs, which it perceives as essential for the capture of political power, which in turn the party needs to implement its communal agenda. A communal party is not a conservative party for it is not committed to the conservation of large elements of the existing social, economic and political structure. It is, however, a right-wing party for it cannot communalize the state and society without strengthening the reactionary and exploitative elements of the economy.

The Jan Sangh could not, however, openly profess its communal ideology as it had to function within two major constraints. Being an electoral party, operating in a secular democratic polity, it had to try to cobble together an electoral majority and therefore appeal to non-communal voters, as also obey electoral laws forbidding political appeals to religion. Further, because of the firm ideological commitment of the national movement and the anti-communal sentiment in India, especially after the assassination of Gandhiji, communalism had a bad odour about it.

To understand the basic communal character of the Jan Sangh and its politics, first the Rashtriya Swayamsevak Sangh (RSS) is to be studied, for the former was a creation of the RSS, and had remained under the latter's tight ideological and organizational control since its foundation. The Jan Sangh drew its organized strength, centralized character and ideological homogeneity from the RSS. Also the grassroots workers, the well-trained and disciplined cadres and organizers, and in time nearly all the top leaders of the Jan Sangh, especially its secretaries and general secretaries, were provided by the RSS. Founded in 1925, the RSS was organized on authoritarian and militaristic lines which, functioning below the surface and glorifying violence, developed basically as an anti-Muslim organization. It did not participate in the anti-imperialist movement or wage any anti-imperialist struggle even of its own conception on the ground that it had to conserve its strength for its main task of protecting Hindus from Muslim domination. The RSS grew in northern India in the 1940s because of the communalization of politics during the war years and large-scale communal violence during 1946–47, in which it played an active role. The RSS was banned and its leaders and workers arrested after the assassination of Gandhiji.

Though not directly involved in the assassination, the RSS had been waging a campaign of hatred against Gandhiji and other Congress leaders, publicly and in its shakhas or branches, often branding them as anti-Hindu and 'traitors'. For example, referring to them, M.S. Golwalkar, the supreme head of the RSS nominated as such for life, wrote in 1939: 'Strange, very strange, that traitors should sit enthroned as national heroes.'[5]

Keen on persuading the government to lift the ban on the RSS, its leaders gave an undertaking in 1949 that it would not take part in politics. But, in fact, they were quite keen to do so. The Jan Sangh provided the perfect cover for this 'front organization'.

The basic guidelines of the RSS's communal approach towards Muslims were laid down by Golwalkar in *We or Our Nationhood Defined*, where Muslims were portrayed as a perpetually hostile and alien element within the Indian body politic and society, who must either accept total subordination to Hindus or cease being Muslims. This is evident from the passage below.

> In Hindusthan exists and must needs exist the ancient Hindu nation and nought else but the Hindu Nation . . . So long, however, as they [Muslims and other non-Hindus] maintain their racial, religious and cultural differences, they cannot but be only foreigners . . . There are only two courses open to the foreign elements, either to merge themselves in the national race and adopt its culture, or to live at the sweet will of the national race . . . The non-Hindu peoples in Hindusthan must either adopt the Hindu culture and language, must learn to respect and hold in reverence Hindu religion, . . . in one word, they must cease to be foreigners, or may stay in the country, wholly subordinated to the Hindu nation, claiming nothing, deserving no privileges, far less any

preferential treatment—not even citizen's rights . . . in this country Hindus alone are the Nation and the Moslems and others, if not actually anti-national are at least outside the body of the Nation.[6]

Golwalkar repeatedly referred to Muslims as 'our foes', 'our old and bitter enemies', 'our most inveterate enemies', and so on, and said: 'We, Hindus, are at war at once with the Moslems on the one hand and British on the other.'[7] More recently, in October 1991, Balasaheb Deoras, the successor of Golwalkar as the head of the RSS, condemned 'the aggressive and divisive mentality of the Muslims' and accused the secular parties of not hesitating 'to sacrifice national interests and to fulfil even the anti-national political aspirations of the Muslims'.[8]

In view of the carefully cultivated communal feelings among its cadres and adherents by the RSS, it was not accidental that, as the noted journalist Krishan Bhatia wrote in 1971, 'the RSS has been behind some of the worst communal riots during the past thirty years'.[9] At a more popular level, the *Organiser* and the *Panchjanya*, the unofficial organs of the RSS, continue till this day to publish articles stressing, with greater or lesser stridency, depending on the political situation, that Hindus constitute the Indian nation and emphasizing the dangers from schemes of the 'Islamization of India'.

The Jan Sangh was launched as a political party in October 1951 with Dr Syama Prasad Mukherjee as its president. Ostensibly, The Jan Sangh was an independent party in its own right and under Mookerjee it did enjoy a certain degree of independence, but even then its spearhead was the RSS and its carefully chosen cadres who were put in crucial positions in the new party. After Mookerjee's death in 1953, the fig leaf of being an independent party was gradually given up. Since 1954, when its second president, Mauli Chandra Sharma, resigned in protest against the RSS domination of the party, Jan Sangh and its later-day reincarnation the Bharatiya Janata Party (BJP), have been more openly associated with and controlled by the RSS, which has provided them with the bulk of their leaders at the top as well as the lower levels.

Though the Jan Sangh over time adopted a radical programme as befitted a petite bourgeoisie, national-socialist-type party, and supported, for example, a mixed economy based on planning and public sector (the latter controlling the commanding heights of the economy), zamindari abolition, land ceilings and land to the tiller, the cause of agricultural labour and of the working class in the modern sector, regulation of large-scale industries, nationalization of key industries, service cooperatives in the rural sector, ceilings on personal income, etc., these were merely formal positions. The issues which really mattered and on which the party and its members concentrated and exerted themselves were very different, namely, communal questions. All the party's popular slogans and everyday agitational issues were filtered through communal glasses or ideology. The party declared itself to be non-communal and secular and formally admitted Muslims as members. Initially, it also declared that its objective was to work not for Hindu Rashtra but Bharatiya Rashtra; but the latter was so defined as to stand for Hindu Rashtra. Admitting Muslims into the party was also perceived by its leaders and cadres as a mere formality and technicality—a political manoeuvre. Jan Sangh workers at the lower level, its leaders in public speeches and its journals promoted in a subtle and subterranean manner distrust and hatred of Muslims.

The Jan Sangh consistently accused the secular parties of appeasement of Muslims and pandering to their interests. Even a sober leader like Mookerjee attacked Nehru regularly for following 'a suicidal policy of appeasement of Muslims'.[10] On its part, Jan Sangh declared that it would promote national unity by 'nationalising all non-Hindus by inculcating in them the ideal of Bharatiya Culture'.[11]

The Jan Sangh was strongly anti-Pakistan. According to one of its resolutions, Pakistan's 'aim is to sustain the faith of Indian Muslims in the ultimate objective of establishing Muslim domination over the rest of India as well'.[12] In its initial years, the Jan Sangh argued for the reuniting of India and Pakistan in pursuit of its central objective of Akhand Bharat. The Jan Sangh also accused the government of consistently pursuing a policy of appeasement of Pakistan. It was only later that the slogan of Akhand Bharat was abandoned and even hostility to Pakistan was muted, especially after the Jan Sangh merged into the Janata Party in 1977 and Atal Bihari Vajpayee became the foreign minister; but hostility to Muslims as proxies for Pakistan remained as before.

The Jan Sangh emphasized the propagation of Bharatiya culture and the establishment of Bharatiya nationalism. These two terms were never defined except very vaguely as being based on non-Western and traditional values. In fact, the word 'Bharatiya' was a euphemism for the word 'Hindu' and an attempt on the part of the Jan Sangh to avoid the communal label. As communalism began to grow, Jan Sangh publications openly started using the terms Hindu culture and Hindu nationalism and continue to do so. In reality even the term 'Hindu nationalism' was a misnomer and a substitute for the term 'Hindu communalism'.

Denying the cultural diversity of India, the Jan Sangh also raised the slogan of 'one country, one culture, one nation' and asserted that all those who did not accept this one culture had imbibed 'anti-national traits'. There was also a strong element of revivalism in its talk of Bharatiya spiritual and material values; *the revival of Bharatiya culture rather than its development engaged* them. It also accused Congress of importing foreign technology and promised that instead it would aim at developing 'a self-sufficient and self-generating economy' by developing 'our own technique'.[13] A disguised opposition to parliamentary democracy and secularism was also intended when it repeatedly accused Congress of developing Indian political life on the basis of foreign ideas. However, gradually it gave up such revivalist formulations as also its talk of Bharatiya values. Their place was taken by the openly communal term 'Hindutva'.

For years, the Jan Sangh took a strident stand and an agitational approach in favour of Sanskritized Hindi and against the retention of English as an official link language of India. Later, keeping in view its need for expansion in non-Hindi areas, it quietly accepted the 1965 decision to retain English along with Hindi so long as the non-Hindi states wanted this. It also opposed the development of Urdu in U.P. and other parts of northern India. It forcefully opposed the Hindu Code Bill, and after its passage pledged to repeal this legislation.

Interestingly, the Jan Sangh opposed the linking of religion with politics and did not take up any religious issue other than that of a legal ban on cow slaughter. The reasons for the change in this respect in the 1980s will be discussed in the chapter on communalism in independent India.

In fact, significant changes in the official programme and policies as also in the social and regional base of Jan Sangh-BJP occurred over the years. Only the centrality of communal ideology remained.

And, of course, no party or leadership can be separated from the ideology with which it operates among the people. Electorally, the Jan Sangh remained throughout this phase on the margins of the Indian polity. In 1952, it won 3 seats in the Lok Sabha with 3.06 per cent of the national vote. (The combined total of the Jan Sangh, Hindu Mahasabha and Ram Rajya Parishad (RRP) was 10 seats with 6.4 per cent of the votes. Thus, the overall performance of the three Hindu communal parties was quite poor.) In 1957, the Jan Sangh won 4 seats in the Lok Sabha with 5.97 per cent of the total votes. This did not mark any real growth of communalism, for it occurred because the Jan Sangh absorbed a large part of the political base of Hindu Mahasabha and the RRP, the total score of the three parties being 5 MPs with 7.17 per cent of the votes. In 1962, the Jan Sangh won 14 seats with 6.44 per cent of the total votes—the three communal parties got 17 seats and 7.69 per cent of the votes. The high-water mark of the Jan Sangh before it became BJP was reached in 1967 when it won 35 seats with 9.35 per cent of the popular vote, with the Hindu Mahasabha and RRP having disappeared as political forces. Its tally, however, came down again in 1971 when it got 22 seats in the Lok Sabha and 7.4 per cent of the votes. Throughout, the party did not win a single seat in South India and it lost its political hold completely in West Bengal after the death of Syama Prasad Mukherjee. In fact, its political influence was mainly confined to Punjab, Haryana, Himachal Pradesh, Delhi, Rajasthan, Uttar Pradesh, Madhya Pradesh and Bihar.

The Swatantra Party

The Swatantra Party, the first authentic all-India secular conservative party, came into being in early August 1959. It had a number of distinguished leaders, most of them old Congressmen, for example, C. Rajagopalachari, Minoo Masani, N.G. Ranga and K.M. Munshi. Right-wing groups and parties had, of course, earlier existed at the local and regional levels, but Swatantra's formation was the first attempt to bring these highly fragmented right-wing forces together under the umbrella of a single party. The provocation was the left turn which the Congress took at Avadi and the Nagpur Resolutions.

Favouring the nineteenth-century conception of the 'night watchman' or laissez-faire state, Swatantra stood for free, private enterprise and opposed the active role of the state in economic development. It wanted to radically restrict centralized planning and the role of the public sector, as also state regulation of the economy. It opposed any nationalization of private enterprise and any extension of land reforms, especially fixation of ceilings on land holdings. Swatantra was fully committed to secularism and that was one reason it found it difficult to merge or form a general alliance with the Jan Sangh, though it entered into seat-sharing arrangements with it. In fact, many conservative intellectuals, businessmen and political leaders welcomed the formation of Swatantra because it provided a non-socialist, constitutionalist and secular conservative alternative to the Congress. Swatantra leaders accused Congress of accepting communist principles and trying to abolish private property. Totally misrepresenting Nehru's position, they accused him of trying to introduce collective farming and Chinese-type communes. Nehru, Rajagopalachari said, was treading 'the royal road to Communism'. Swatantra, on the other hand, was 'dedicated to saving India from the dangers of totalitarianism'.[14]

In foreign affairs, Swatantra opposed non-alignment and a close relationship with the Soviet Union and advocated an intimate connection with the United States and Western Europe. It urged the government to work for a defence alliance with non-Communist nations of the South Asian region and of Asia as a whole, including Pakistan, under the US umbrella.

The social base of Swatantra was quite narrow, consisting of (i) some industrialists and businessmen, who were disgruntled with government control, quotas and licences and attacks on the managing agency system and fearful of nationalization, besides lacking confidence in Nehru, (ii) princes, jagirdars and landlords, who were miserable and angry at the loss of their fiefdoms or lands, social power and status, and deteriorating economic conditions, and (iii) ex-landlord-turned-capitalist farmers and rich and middle peasants in some parts of the country, who had welcomed the abolition of landlordism but were fearful of losing part of their land if land reforms went any further by way of land ceiling and the growing awareness and political power of the rural poor, especially agricultural labourers. Swatantra was also joined by a few retired civil servants and disgruntled Congressmen, leading a historian to describe it as 'a holding company for local dissident groups'. The ex-landlords and rich peasants controlled the votes of many of their economic and social dependants while the erstwhile princes, jagirdars and zamindars could appeal to remnants of traditional feudal loyalties.

Swatantra did not fare badly in the 1962 elections. It won 18 seats in the Lok Sabha with 6.8 per cent of the popular vote. It emerged as the main Opposition in four states—Bihar, Rajasthan, Gujarat and Orissa. Out of 18 seats, 7 were won in Bihar, but these seven members included the Raja of Ramgarh's mother, wife, brother, sister-in-law and business manager! In 1967, the party secured 44 seats in the Lok Sabha with 8.7 per cent of the total votes. In both the elections, ex-princes, jagirdars and big landlords were in the main responsible for the party's wins. Riven with factions and defections and failing to acquire a mass following, the party rapidly declined after the death of C. Rajagopalachari in 1967. In 1971, it secured only 8 seats in the Lok Sabha with 3 per cent of the votes. Feeling a sense of hopelessness, most of the party leaders joined the Bharatiya Lok Dal in 1974, a few went back to Congress, while a small faction led by Masani carried on.

Swatantra failed mainly because there was as yet no space in Indian politics for a conservative party, for radicalization of politics was still in progress. Moreover, right-wing class interests were still quite diverse and fragmented and not easily amenable to coalescence. Also the rich and middle peasants were not yet fully and irrevocably alienated from Congress, especially as cooperative farming had been put in cold storage and land ceiling laws actually posed little threat to the existing holdings. On the other hand, they were the major beneficiaries of several government policies and measures: reduction of land revenue and extension of services including provision of rural credit, improved transport, irrigation and electrification.

The business class—the bourgeoisie whether big or small—was also as a whole not unhappy. By and large, it accepted that the government must play an active role in politics. It found that planning, the public sector and government regulations did not block its growth and, instead, in many respects, helped it to develop. The mixed economy also left enough scope for its expansion. In any case, as a propertied class, it was not willing to oppose a party—Congress—which was certain to retain power in the immediate future. Above all, though steady in pursuing its developmental and reformist agenda, the Nehru government, Congress and the broad class coalition Nehru had built up were in actual practice quite moderate in dealing with and conciliatory towards the propertied classes. They did not pose a radical or revolutionary challenge to the capitalist social order. Nehru would not antagonize the capitalist class and the agrarian bourgeoisie— the capitalist farmers and the rich peasantry—to an extent where they would feel that they were being driven to the wall. Even the princes and landlords had not been wiped out and had been consoled with compensation and other economic concessions. Consequently, in most cases their opposition remained latent and did not manifest itself in political action. Moreover, Nehru *invariably* 'responded to pressure at the margin'. Just as he had been receptive to the left in the 1950s, he now responded to the right and did not take up state trading in foodgrains or cooperative farming. Simultaneously, land ceiling laws were made quite innocuous by the state governments, which were quite receptive to the rich peasant demands.

Lastly, the Congress right realized that so long as Nehru was alive his position in the country was unassailable; it, therefore, showed no inclination to leave the shelter of the banyan tree that was Nehru. On the other hand, when Congress split in 1969 and Congress (O) emerged as a political force, the reason for the existence of Swatantra as a separate right-wing party disappeared, for the former was much more potent as a right-wing party.

Communal and Regional Parties

A large number of communal and regional parties existed between 1947 and 1964. Among the communal parties, the Hindu Mahasabha was an old party, but it soon faded from the political scene after 1952, when it had won four seats in the Lok Sabha, as it gradually lost its support base to the Jan Sangh. Same was the case with the RRP. Because of its association with the demand for Pakistan, the Muslim League lay dormant, with many of its demoralized leaders and activists joining Congress and other parties. However, it revived in parts of Tamil Nadu and in Kerala where first Congress and then the CPI and CPM gave it respectability by making it an alliance partner. The Akali Dal was another major communal party, though limited to Punjab. A large number of regional parties appeared on the scene during the period. The more important of these were the DMK in Tamil Nadu and the Jammu and Kashmir National Conference which are discussed in other chapters in this book. We have already discussed the Jharkhand party in Bihar in the chapter on the integration of the tribals. The other major regional parties were the Ganatantra Parishad in Orissa, All Parties Hill Leaders' Conference (APHLC) in Assam, and Scheduled Castes Federation in Maharashtra. There were also several small left parties, usually confined to one state: Revolutionary Socialist Party (Kerala and West Bengal), Forward Bloc (West Bengal) and Peasants and Workers Party (Maharashtra). Most of the regional left and communal groups and parties cannot, however, be discussed here, though they played a significant role in particular states and regions.

16

From Shastri to Indira Gandhi, 1964–1969

Nehru's death in May 1964 provided a test of the strength of the Indian political system. Many, both in India and abroad, predicted that it would be severely damaged, and might even break down through dissension and factional turmoil in the Congress party on the issue of succession. But the succession occurred in a mature, dignified and smooth manner and revealed the strength of Indian democracy. Perhaps, it was because of his faith in Indian democracy that Nehru had refused to name a successor.

There were two main contenders for the leadership of the Congress parliamentary party and therefore for the prime minister's job, Morarji Desai and Lal Bahadur Shastri. Desai was senior and more experienced, a sound administrator and scrupulously honest. But he was rigid and inflexible in outlook and had the reputation of being self-righteous, arrogant, intolerant and a right-winger. Moreover, he was quite unpopular with a large section of the party. Shastri was mild, tactful and malleable, highly respected and known to be personally incorruptible.

The succession occurred under the direction of a group of Congress leaders who came to be collectively known as the Syndicate. The group, formed in 1963, consisted of K. Kamaraj, the Congress president, and regional party bosses, Atulya Ghosh of Bengal, S.K. Patil of Bombay, N. Sanjeeva Reddy of Andhra Pradesh, and S. Nijalingappa of Mysore (Karnataka). Desai was utterly unacceptable to them. They favoured Shastri because, in addition to his other qualities, he had wider acceptability in the party which would keep the party united. They also hoped that he would be more amenable to their wishes and not challenge their leadership in the party.

They, as well as other party leaders, were also keen to avoid a contest, which would intensify the factionalism present in the party. Kamaraj tried to ascertain the candidate around whom there would be wider consensus among the party MPs and announced that Shastri was more generally acceptable. Though privately suggesting that the Syndicate had 'stage-managed' the decision, Desai accepted it and retired from the race in a dignified manner. Shastri, elected unopposed as the parliamentary leader by the party MPs, was sworn in as prime minister on 2 June 1964, that is, within a week of Nehru's death.

The Shastri Years

Accepting the limited character of his political mandate, Shastri did not make any major changes in Nehru's cabinet, except for persuading Indira Gandhi, Nehru's daughter, to join it as Minister of Information and Broadcasting. Under him the cabinet ministers functioned more autonomously. He also did not interfere in party affairs or with the working of the state governments. On the whole, he kept a low political profile except towards the end of his administration.

Though the country was at the time faced with several difficult problems, Shastri's government did not deal with them in a decisive manner; it followed a policy of drift instead. The problem of the official language of Hindi versus English, flared up in early 1965, but the central government failed to handle it effectively and allowed the situation to deteriorate. The problem was, however, finally resolved in early 1966. The demands for a Punjabi Suba (state) and Goa's merger with Maharashtra were also allowed to simmer.

The Indian economy had been stagnating in the previous few years. There had been a slowdown in the rate of industrial growth and the balance of payments problem had worsened. But, at that moment, the most serious problem was the severe shortage of food. Agricultural production had slowed down, there was severe drought in several states in 1965 and buffer food stocks were depleted to a dangerous extent. Clearly, long-term measures were needed to deal with the situation. But those were not taken, particularly as the chief ministers of foodgrain-surplus states refused to cooperate. After the US suspended all food aid because of the Indo-Pak war, the government was compelled to introduce statutory rationing but it covered only seven major cities. The government also created the State Food Trading Corporation in January 1965, but it did not succeed in procuring a significant amount of foodgrains. However, one positive development was the initiation of the Green Revolution strategy with the purpose of increasing agricultural output and achieving self-sufficiency in food in the long run. It was though only later, in Indira Gandhi's regime, that this strategy was pursued vigorously.

In general, Shastri was accused by critics inside and outside the party of being 'a prisoner of indecision' and of failing to give a *direction to government policies or even to lead and control his* cabinet colleagues. He felt so unsure and inadequate under pressures of government and comments of the critics that in a private chat with a newsman early in January 1965 he wondered 'whether he had been right to offer himself for the Prime Ministership and whether he had the capacity to carry the burden that the office involved'.[1]

With the passage of time, however, Shastri began to show greater independence and to assert himself, so much so that Kamaraj began to complain that he was quite often being bypassed by Shastri in important decision-making. The Indian government was among the first to criticize the US bombing of North Vietnam. Shastri also set up his own Prime Minister's Secretariat, headed by L.K. Jha, his principal private secretary, as a source of information and advice to the prime minister on policy matters, independent of the ministries. The Secretariat, which came to be known as the Prime Minister's Office (PMO) started acquiring a great deal of influence and power in the making and execution of government policy. Later, under Indira Gandhi, it emerged as a virtually alternative, independent executive. It was, however, with the brief Indo-Pak war in August–September 1965 that Shastri's moment came.

The Kashmir issue had been simmering for years, with Pakistan demanding reopening of the question and India maintaining that Kashmir being a part of India was a settled fact. In 1965, the followers of Sheikh Abdullah and other dissident leaders created a great deal of unrest in the Kashmir Valley. The Pakistani leadership thought that the situation there was ripe for an intervention, especially as Pakistan had superiority in arms, having acquired sophisticated US military equipment. Possibly, the Pakistan government wanted to face India militarily before India's efforts to improve its defences after the debacle of 1962 were still incomplete.

First came the dress rehearsal and a probe. Pakistan tested India's response to a military push by occupying in April 1965 a part of the disputed and undemarcated territory in the marshy Rann of Kutch, bordering the Arabian Sea and Gujarat. There was a military clash but, because of the nature of the terrain, India's military response was weak and hesitant. On Britain's intervention, the two sides agreed to refer the dispute to international arbitration. Unfortunately, the conflict in the Rann of Kutch sent wrong signals to the rulers of Pakistan, who concluded that India's government and armed forces were not yet ready for war. They paid no heed to Shastri's statement, given in consultation with the army chief, General J.N. Chaudhri, that whenever India gave battle it would be 'at a time and place of its own choosing'.[2]

In August, the Pakistani government sent well-trained infiltrators into the Kashmir Valley, hoping to foment a pro-Pakistan uprising there and thus create conditions for its military intervention. Taking into account the seriousness of this Pakistan-backed infiltration, Shastri ordered the army to cross the ceasefire line and seal the passes through which the infiltrators were coming and to occupy such strategic posts as Kargil, Uri and Haji Pir. Also, unlike in 1962, the entire country rallied behind the government.

In response, on 1 September, Pakistan launched a massive tank and infantry attack in the Chhamb sector in the south-west of Jammu and Kashmir, threatening India's only road link with Kashmir. Shastri immediately ordered the Indian army to not only defend Kashmir but also to move across the border into Pakistan towards Lahore and Sialkot. Thus, the two countries were involved in war, though an undeclared one. The US and Britain immediately cut off arms, food and other supplies to both countries. China declared India to be an aggressor and made threatening noises. However, the Soviet Union, sympathetic to India, discouraged China from going to Pakistan's aid.

Under pressure from the UN Security Council, both combatants agreed to a ceasefire which came into effect on 23 September. The war was inconclusive, with both sides believing that they had won significant victories and inflicted heavy damage on the other. The only effective result was that 'invasion by infiltration' of Kashmir had been foiled. At the same time, the three weeks of fighting had done immense damage to the economies of the two countries, apart from the loss of life and costly military equipment. Resources urgently needed for economic development had been drained; and the defence budgets of the two countries had begun to mount again.

Indians were, however, euphoric over the performance of the Indian armed forces which recovered some of their pride, prestige and self-confidence lost in the India–China war in 1962. Moreover, India as a whole emerged from the conflict politically stronger and more unified. There were also several other satisfactory aspects. The infiltrators had not succeeded in getting the support of Kashmiri people. And Indian secularism had passed its first major test since 1947–48 with flying colours: there was no communal trouble during the war; Indian Muslims had given wholehearted support to the war effort; and Muslims in the armed forces had disappointed Pakistan by fighting bravely alongside their Hindu, Sikh and Christian comrades. As a result of the war Shastri became a national hero and a dominating political figure.

Subsequent to the ceasefire agreement and under the good offices of the Soviet Union, General Ayub Khan, the President of Pakistan, and Shastri met in Tashkent in Soviet Union on 4 January 1966 and signed the Tashkent Declaration. Under this Declaration, both sides agreed to withdraw from all occupied areas and return to their pre-war August positions. In the case of India, this meant withdrawing from the strategic Haji Pir pass through which Pakistani infiltrators could again enter the Kashmir Valley and giving up other strategic gains in Kashmir. Shastri agreed to these unfavourable terms as the other option was the resumption of the mutually disastrous war; that would also have meant losing Soviet support on the Kashmir issue in the UN Security Council and in the supply of defence equipment, especially MiG planes and medium and heavy tanks.

The Tashkent Conference had a tragic consequence. Shastri, who had a history of heart trouble, died in Tashkent of a sudden heart attack on 10 January, having served as prime minister for barely nineteen months.

Shastri's death once again brought the issue of succession to the fore. This, the second succession in two years, was again smoothly accomplished, and affirmed the resilience of India's political system.

Morarji Desai was once again in the field. Kamaraj's and the Syndicate's dislike for Desai had not lessened, and they looked around for a candidate who could defeat Desai but remain under their shadow. Their choice fell on Indira Gandhi: she was Nehru's daughter, had an all-India appeal and a progressive image, and was not identified with any state, region, caste or religion. They also thought that Indira Gandhi, being inexperienced and a young woman and lacking substantial roots in the party, would be more pliable and malleable. It was Kamaraj who stage-managed her election. The contest was virtually decided when 12 out of 14 chief ministers threw their weight behind her, hoping to acquire greater power to run their states and also to cash in on her mass appeal and the Nehru name to attract the voters in the forthcoming elections.

There was no process of consensus this time as Desai insisted on a contest. He felt confident of winning because of his seniority and position in the party and especially when his opponent was, as he put it, 'this mere *chokri* (a young brat of a girl)'. A secret ballot in the Congress parliamentary party was held on 19 January 1966, and Indira Gandhi defeated Desai by 355 votes to 169. Her being a woman had been no handicap, for women had participated actively in the freedom struggle with thousands of them going to jail and several of them had held high positions in Congress, including its presidentship. After independence, too, they had occupied high offices, of governors and cabinet ministers at the Centre and in the states, including that of the chief minister of Uttar Pradesh, India's largest state.

Indira Gandhi: The Early Years

Indira Gandhi's government was faced with several grave problems which were long in the making but which required immediate attention and solutions. Punjab was on the boil and the Naga and Mizo areas were in rebellion. She dealt effectively with these problems by accepting the demand for Punjabi Suba and being firm with the Naga and Mizo rebels, showing willingness to negotiate with them and accepting the Naga rebels' demand for autonomy.

It was, however, the economic situation which was intractable. The economy was in recession and fast deteriorating. Industrial production and exports were declining. The rains failed for the second successive year in 1966, and the drought was more severe than in 1965, and led to galloping inflation and grave food shortages. Famine conditions prevailed in large parts of the country, especially in Bihar and eastern Uttar Pradesh The wars of 1962 and 1965 and the Pakistan–China axis had led to a sharp rise in military expenditure and diversion of resources from planning and economic development. Budget deficits were growing, endangering the Fourth Five Year Plan. The situation required hard decisions and their firm enforcement, but the government vacillated, was slow in taking decisions and, what was even worse, tardy and ineffective in implementing them. In particular, it could not reduce its own bloated administrative expenditure which the financial situation required.

The government, however, succeeded remarkably in dealing with the drought and famine situation. The problems of procurement and distribution of foodgrains and prevention of famine deaths were handled on a war footing. There were very few famine deaths as compared to the record of millions dying in the colonial period from comparative or even lesser intensity droughts and famines. This was a major achievement for Indian democracy.

The one decisive step taken by the government to deal with the deteriorating economic situation and to bolster food imports boomeranged and proved to be the most controversial of Mrs Gandhi's early decisions. As already mentioned, Indian exports were not growing and even the existing ones were being heavily subsidized by the central exchequer. Indira Gandhi's advisers argued that this was due to the rupee being grossly overvalued. If it were devalued, there would be a greater inflow of the much-needed foreign capital. India was heavily dependent for its food security on imports of wheat from the US under the PL-480 aid programme. Also, there was an urgent need for economic aid by the World Bank and the International Monetary Fund (IMF), stopped during the Indo-Pak war, to be resumed. The US, the World Bank and the IMF, however, insisted on devaluation of the rupee. Consequently, the Government of India devalued the rupee by 35.5 per cent on 6 June, barely four months after Mrs Gandhi assumed power.

There were angry countrywide outbursts against the decision. All sections of political opinion opposed the step, the most voluble critics being the left groups and parties, the majority of intellectuals and Kamaraj, who also resented the fact that he was not consulted before the decision was taken. The critics within the Congress party also felt that such a controversial and unpopular decision should not have been taken in an election year. There was also widespread resentment against the government for acting under foreign pressure. The devaluation, ironically, failed in its stated objectives of increasing exports and attracting foreign capital. Nor was there a significant increase in the flow of food and other foreign aid. Many years later, in 1980, Mrs Gandhi was to confess that the devaluation 'was the wrong thing to do and it harmed us greatly'.[3]

A few months after coming to power, Mrs Gandhi took major initiatives in the field of foreign affairs. Urgently needing American wheat, financial aid and capital investment, she initially tried to build bridges with the United States, especially during her visit to Washington in March 1966. President Johnson promised to send 3.5 million tonnes of foodgrains to India under PL-480 and give $900 million in aid. But actual dispatches to India were irregular and came in small instalments. Moreover, the President took charge of the dispatches in order to control their amount and timing on a 'tonne-by-tonne' basis and thus to ensure that 'India changed its farm policy' as also its position on Vietnam.[4] Indira Gandhi felt humiliated by this 'ship-to-mouth' approach of the United States, and refused to bow before such ham-handedness and open pressure. She also decided to get out of this vulnerable position as soon as possible. In fact, India was never again to try to come close to the US on onerous terms.

Indira Gandhi's disappointment with the US found expression in the sphere of foreign policy. She started distancing herself from that country. During her visit to Washington, in March–April 1966 she had remained silent on Vietnam. Now, in July 1966, she issued a statement deploring US bombing of North Vietnam and its capital Hanoi. In the latter part of July, in Moscow, she signed a joint statement with the Soviet Union demanding an immediate and unconditional end to the US bombing and branding US action in Vietnam as 'imperialist aggression'.

In Washington, Mrs Gandhi had agreed to the US proposal for an Indo-American Educational Foundation to be funded by PL-480 rupee funds to the extent of $300 million. She now abandoned the proposal, partially because it had been vehemently criticized by a large number of Indian intellectuals and those of leftist opinion, both inside and outside Congress, as an American effort to penetrate and control higher education and research in India.

Mrs Gandhi developed close links with Nasser of Egypt and Tito of Yugoslavia and began to stress the need for non-aligned countries to cooperate politically and economically in order to counter the danger of neo-colonialism emanating from the US and West European countries. Worried by the Soviet efforts to build bridges with Pakistan and to occupy a position of equidistance from both India and Pakistan, Mrs Gandhi assured the Soviet leaders of India's continuing friendship. She also expressed a desire to open a dialogue with China but there was no thaw in Sino-Indian relations at the time. In general, after the Washington fiasco, she followed a policy of sturdy independence in foreign affairs.

The year 1966 was one of continuous popular turmoil, of mass economic discontent and political agitations provoked by spiralling prices, food scarcity, growing unemployment, and, in general, deteriorating economic conditions. Adding to this unrest were the rising and often unfulfilled aspirations of different sections of society, especially the lower middle classes. Many were able to satisfy them but many more were not. Moreover, the capitalist pattern of development was increasing economic disparity between different social classes, strata and groups.

A wave of popular agitations—demonstrations, student strikes and riots, agitations by government servants—commenced at about the same time Mrs Gandhi was being sworn in as prime minister. These agitations often turned violent. A new feature was the bandhs which meant closure of a town, city, or entire state. Law and order often broke down as the agitating crowds clashed with lathi-wielding police. Sometimes the army had to be called in. Lathi charges and police firings brought the administration into further disrepute. Teachers and other middle-class professionals such as doctors and engineers also now began to join the ranks of strikers and agitators demanding higher pay and dearness allowances to offset the sharp rise in prices. There was growing loss of public confidence in the administration and the ruling political leadership.

Opposition political parties, especially the CPM, Socialists and Jan Sangh, took full advantage of the popular mood to continually embarrass the government and took the lead in organizing bandhs and other agitations. Some of them believed that administrative breakdown would create conditions for them to come to power through elections or through non-parliamentary, extra-constitutional means. Consequently, they often did not observe democratic boundaries or constitutional proprieties.

Jan Sangh and other communal forces also organized a fierce countrywide agitation demanding a total ban on cow-slaughter, hoping to cash in on the religious feelings of many Hindus in the coming elections. But the government stood firm against the demand because of its communal character and because many of the minorities and low-caste groups among Hindus ate beef because of its low price. Mrs Gandhi told parliament: 'This is not an attack on the Government. It is an attack on our way of life, our values and the traditions which we cherished.'[5] On 7 November, a mob of hundreds of thousands, led by naked sadhus, carrying swords, spears and trishuls (tridents), virtually tried to invade Parliament House, trying to destabilize constitutional government and burning buses and cars, looting shops, attacking government buildings on the way. They also surrounded Kamaraj's house with the intent to assault him. A clash with the police occurred leading to the death of one policeman and six sadhus. Blaming the Home Minister, Gulzari Lal Nanda, for inept handling of the situation she demanded his resignation. The movement soon fizzled out and cow-slaughter became a non-issue even in the elections that followed.

The year 1966 also witnessed the beginning of the downslide of parliament as an institution. There were constant disturbances and indiscipline in parliament with some members of the Opposition showing complete disregard for parliamentary decorum and niceties. Many a time the young prime minister was not extended the courtesy in keeping with her office. She was often subjected to heckling and harassment, vicious and vulgar personal attacks, male chauvinist and sexist references and unfounded allegations. Dr Rammanohar Lohia, in particular, missed no opportunity of ridiculing her, and described her as *'goongi gudiya'* (dumb doll).

Even in the party, Indira Gandhi had to face a rather troublesome
situation. For one, there was the erosion of popular support for
Congress. The party had been declining, becoming dysfunctional
and losing political initiative since Nehru's time. It was increasingly
ridden with groupism and factional rivalries at every level, leading
to the formation of dissident groups in almost every state.
Mrs Gandhi's own position in the party had remained weak and
insecure. On becoming the prime minister, she had not been able
to form a cabinet of her own choice, having had to leave all
important portfolios—Home, Defence, Finance, External Affairs,
and Food—undisturbed. Kamaraj, the party president, and the
Syndicate consistently tried to reassert the party organization's
position vis-à-vis the prime minister, and to restrict her freedom of
action in framing and implementing policies. They also did not let
her have much of a say in the party's internal affairs or in the
selection of candidates for the parliamentary elections. Indira
Gandhi had to tolerate all this because of 1967 being an election
year. Also, as a political leader, she suffered at this time from two
major weaknesses: she was ineffective as a leader—her opponents
quite often succeeded in isolating her in the parliamentary party
and even in the cabinet—and she lacked 'ideological moorings'.

The 1967 General Elections and State Coalitions

The fourth general elections to the Lok Sabha and the state
assemblies, held in February 1967, had a radical impact on Indian
politics. The run-up to the elections and the elections themselves
were marked by several features.

The Congress party had exhausted its mandate and lost its
character and motivation as a party of social and institutional
change. There was large-scale disenchantment, especially with its
top leaders, because of corruption and the lavish lifestyle of many
of them. Many of the regional and local Congress bosses were
perceived by the people as being devoted to loaves and fishes of
office, political wheeling-dealing and factional infighting. At the
same time people felt frustrated because there was no other party
which could replace Congress. The Opposition parties did not
raise any basic social issues during the election campaign. They
campaigned mainly on the question of defeating Congress. There
was, however, a great political awakening among the people; in

1967 the turnout of eligible voters was, at 61.1 per cent, the highest witnessed so far.

Congress had been declining since 1964. It now went into elections, under the leadership of the Syndicate, weakened, divided and faction ridden, with the leadership showing little awareness of the party's decline in public support and estimation. Earlier, factionalism had been confined to the states, now it also engulfed the Centre. Earlier, the central leadership moderated conflicts at the state level, so that the dissidents did not feel isolated. Now the central leadership supported the dominant groups in the states in order to secure its own position at the Centre. As pointed out by Zareer Masani, 'The result was a continuous power-struggle at all levels of Congress leadership and the rapid erosion of such party discipline, confidence and comradeship as Congress had built up during the Independence movement, and without which it could not hope to remain united.'[6]

Factionalism in Congress was fully reflected in the selection of party candidates. The ticket distribution was dominated by the Syndicate members who acted in a highly partisan manner. Nearly a thousand Congressmen, who had been denied tickets, now chose to stand against the official Congress candidates as independents or as members of new state-level dissident groups.

An important feature of the 1967 elections was the coming together of the Opposition parties; some of them formed anti-Congress fronts in some states. In other cases, they entered into a series of electoral adjustments by sharing seats and avoiding contests. Quite often, the dissident Congress parties and groups also joined this process. But the coalescing parties were in almost all cases ideologically and programmatically disparate, their only cement being the desire to defeat Congress. Lohia Socialists were the most promiscuous—they did not hesitate to join the communal Jan Sangh and the rightist Swatantra. Similarly, in many states the secular Swatantra and the communal Jan Sangh joined forces. In a few states, the Communist–right wing divide was also bridged. In Tamil Nadu, Swatantra, the CPM, the Muslim League and the chauvinist DMK were partners. The CPM and the Muslim League were allies in Kerala, as were the Jan Sangh, Akalis and CPM in Punjab.

The election results were dramatic and Congress suffered a serious setback. Though it succeeded in retaining control of the

Lok Sabha—it won 284 out of 520 seats—its majority was drastically reduced from 228 in 1962 to 48. Except in West Bengal and Kerala, where the left parties gained, the beneficiaries of the Congress decline were the communal, feudal, right-wing and regional parties. Congress also lost its majority in the assemblies of eight states—Bihar, Uttar Pradesh, Rajasthan, Punjab, West Bengal, Orissa, Madras and Kerala. The Jan Sangh emerged as the main Opposition party in Uttar Pradesh, Madhya Pradesh and Haryana, Swatantra in Orissa, Rajasthan, Andhra Pradesh and Gujarat, the SSP in Bihar, and the Communists in West Bengal and Kerala.

The 1967 elections revealed certain long-term trends and also had certain long-term consequences. Apart from general disenchantment with Congress because of the various factors mentioned in the previous section, defection by the rich and middle peasants from the Congress camp played a major role in the Congress debacle in the northern states.

As a result of the land reforms of the early 1950s, land ownership and social power had gradually shifted to the rich peasants. They felt that their newly acquired economic position and social status, associated with control of land, was threatened by the projected foodgrain procurement policies, the land reforms and other populist rhetoric of Congress, especially of Indira Gandhi and the Congress leftists. There was also a growing class cleavage in the countryside, and any political awakening or increase in the bargaining power of landless labour would endanger rich-peasant domination of the village. The rich peasants wanted to play a far greater, in fact, a hegemonic, role in the class alliances that Congress had forged and to get the government policies changed directly in their favour.

In South India, class and caste structure or configuration was different from that in the North and the large presence of Communists kept the rural landowners tied to Congress. Moreover, alternative rich peasant parties were non-existent. In Bihar, Uttar Pradesh and Punjab, on the other hand, alternative parties in the form of the SSP, Bharatiya Kranti Dal (BKD), and the Akali Dal were available to act as vehicles of rich-peasant interests.

In reality, Congress was nowhere anti-rich peasant but it was so perceived in North India because of its radical rhetoric. It is also true that Congress could not agree to fully satisfy rich-peasant demands without alienating the rural poor or endangering the path of economic development and industrialization it had adopted.

The rich peasants also had the advantage of carrying with them large segments of the middle and even small peasants. They shared a common ideology of peasant proprietorship and common aspirations to own and control land. To some extent, they shared common interests in terms of the prices of agricultural products and relationship with agricultural labourers. They also belonged to the same intermediate or backward castes. The rich peasants also increasingly controlled rural vote banks and therefore the vote of the marginal farmers and agricultural labourers, having gradually displaced feudal and semi-feudal landlords from that role. They also had the necessary muscle power to prevent the agricultural labourers, the large number of them being Dalits (Scheduled Castes), from going to the polling booths.

The 1967 elections heralded the era of the greater importance of rich and middle peasants in Indian politics, their hegemony over the rural social, economic and political scene, and their dislike of Congress and Communists which persists till this day. Only a coalition of small peasants and agricultural labourers could challenge this hegemony. And this is what Indira Gandhi tried to accomplish electorally in 1971 without attacking the interests of the rich peasantry.

Coalition Governments

The 1967 elections also initiated the dual era of short-lived coalition governments and politics of defection. Though the elections broke Congress's monopoly of power in the states, Congress was replaced not by a single party in any of the states but by a multiplicity of parties and groups and independents. Coalition governments were formed in all Opposition-ruled states except Tamil Nadu. In Punjab, Bihar and Uttar Pradesh, Opposition governments included Swatantra, the Jan Sangh, BKD, Socialists and the CPI. Though the CPM did not join these governments, it, too, actively supported them. Thus, these governments were ideologically heterogeneous; and the left–right or secular–communal divides were almost completely bridged in them.

Congress too formed coalition governments in some of the states where it had been reduced to a minority, allying with independents and breakaway groups from the Opposition parties.

Except the DMK government in Tamil Nadu and the Swatantra-led government in Orissa, the coalition governments in all the other states, whether formed by Congress or the Opposition, proved to be highly unstable and could not stay in power for long. All the coalition governments suffered from constant tensions and internal strains because of the heterogeneity of the partners. Most often, except in West Bengal and Kerala, the continuous bargaining among the partners was not on policies but on ministerial berths, patronage, and interest groups. This also led to bloated cabinets. These governments would get formed, break up as a result of changing loyalties of MLAs and then get re-formed again. Parties, including Congress, would topple existing governments, change partners and form new governments. In between governments, a state would sometimes undergo a period of President's Rule or even mid-term polls, which seldom changed the pattern of seats in the assembly. Thus, from the 1967 general elections to the end of 1970, Bihar had seven governments, Uttar Pradesh four, Haryana, Madhya Pradesh, Punjab and West Bengal three each and Kerala two governmental changes, with a total of eight spells of President's Rule in the seven states. In the toppling and fresh government formation game, small parties and independents came to play an important role.

The other important feature of the coalition governments of the period was the beginning of the politics of defection. Many of the governmental changes in the northern states were the result of defections or floor crossings by individual legislators, both party members and independents. Corrupt legislators indulged in horse-trading and freely changed sides, attracted mainly by lure of office or money. In Haryana, where the defection phenomenon was first initiated, defecting legislators began to be called *Aya Ram* and *Gaya Ram* (incoming Ram and outgoing Ram). Consequently, except in the case of the two Communist parties and the Jan Sangh, party discipline tended to break down. Between 1967 and 1970 nearly 800 assembly members crossed the floor, and 155 of them were rewarded with ministerial offices.

The problem of defections was to became long term and perpetual because defectors, who changed sides and toppled governments for purely personal and often corrupt reasons, were seldom punished by the voters and were elected again and again. It was only with the passage of the anti-defection law by the Rajiv Gandhi government in 1986 that a check was placed on the defection phenomenon.

Interestingly, throughout this rise and fall of many state governments, the central government remained stable despite the small majority enjoyed by the ruling party. Nor did defections take place at the Centre despite the absence of an anti-defection law. Similarly, despite at one time nearly half the states being ruled by the Opposition, the federal system continued to function more or less as before. Also, even in the states the instability of governments did not lead to the breakdown of administration.

Anti-Congressism gained ground with these elections both among the Opposition parties and a large section of the intelligentsia. Anti-Congressism as a political phenomenon is, of course, to be distinguished from opposition to Congress, which was based on differences in ideology, policies or programmes. On the other hand, anti-Congressism represented 'a weariness with Congress and a hankering after almost anything else'.[7] The anti-Congress intellectuals and the Socialists were willing to back any party from the CPM to the BKD to the Jan Sangh in order to weaken Congress. The CPM and CPI also increasingly adopted such a position. The high-priest of anti-Congressism was Rammanohar Lohia who, in the words of the political scientist Rajni Kothari, devoted himself 'to the mission of destroying the Congress monopoly of power by uniting all anti-Congress forces in the country'.[8] Lohia did succeed in polarizing the polity in 1967 along Congress versus anti-Congress lines but the results were not, and have not been, either positive or enduring.

Anti-Congressism also ignored the fact that most Opposition parties were closer to some wing or the other of Congress than to another Opposition party. The Communists and Socialists were, for example, closer to the Congress left and Swatantra to the Congress right, while the Jan Sangh was, because of its communal ideology, opposed both to Congress and other secular parties in the Opposition.

The serious Congress reverses led many commentators to predict that it was the beginning of the end of Congress domination of Indian politics. But, in fact, this was not so. Congress was still not only the largest party in the country with a majority in parliament but also the only nationwide party with a nationwide organization and following. Also, there was no cohesive Opposition, and the

Opposition parties had failed to keep power in the states where Congress had become a minority. At the same time, there is no doubt that Congress would now have to look for fresh political ways of attracting people who had had enough of promises and wanted concrete results. It could no longer get support on the basis of its role in the freedom struggle or its achievements during the Nehru era; it would have to renew itself.

The 1967 elections drastically changed the balance of power inside Congress. Its dominant leadership in the form of the Syndicate received a major blow as several Syndicate stalwarts, including Kamaraj (its president), Atulya Ghosh (West Bengal) and S.K. Patil (Bombay), bit the dust. Most of the loyal followers of the Syndicate failed to get elected to parliament and the state assemblies, leaving them in no position to control the process of government formation at the Centre as they had done in 1964 and 1966.

Paradoxically, despite the shock to Congress, Indira Gandhi's position in the party and the government was not weakened. On the contrary, it further strengthened as Kamaraj and the Syndicate, having been cut down to size, were no longer in a position to challenge her. Moreover, though not yet a popular or towering leader like Jawaharlal Nehru, she had been the star and the only all-India campaigner and vote-catcher for Congress.

Indira Gandhi's independent and strong position in the party was demonstrated by her unchallenged leadership of the Congress parliamentary party and her relative independence in the formation of her cabinet and distribution of portfolios. The only challenge to her, that from Morarji Desai, soon petered out as he shied away from a contest and, instead, bargained for a position in the cabinet as deputy prime minister. Given the party's fragile majority in parliament, Indira Gandhi agreed to Desai's demand. The designation of deputy prime minister was, however, a mere formality—it gave status but no special powers in the cabinet except those of his position as the Finance Minister.

The years 1967–69 proved to be a mere transitional stage or interregnum. The government marked time as Congress moved towards a split in 1969, which marked a new stage in Indian political development. There was, however, a major development on the left to which we will briefly turn now.

The Naxalites

The CPM had originally split from the united CPI in 1964 on grounds of differences over revolutionary politics (often equated with armed struggle) and reformist parliamentary politics. In practice, however, heeding the existing political realities, the CPM participated actively in parliamentary politics, postponing armed struggle to the day when a revolutionary situation prevailed in the country. Consequently, it participated in the 1967 elections and formed a coalition government in West Bengal with the Bangla Congress, with Jyoti Basu, the CPM leader, becoming the Home Minister. This led to a schism in the party.

A section of the party, consisting largely of its younger cadres and inspired by the Cultural Revolution then going on in China, accused the party leadership of falling prey to reformism and parliamentarianism and, therefore, of betraying the revolution. They argued that the party must instead immediately initiate armed peasant insurrections in rural areas, leading to the formation of liberated areas and the gradual extension of the armed struggle to the entire country. To implement their political line, the rebel CPM leaders launched a peasant uprising in the small Naxalbari area of northern West Bengal. The CPM leadership immediately expelled the rebel leaders, accusing them of left-wing adventurism, and used the party organization and government machinery to suppress the Naxalbari insurrection. The breakaway CPM leaders came to be known as Naxalites and were soon joined by other similar groups from the CPM in the rest of the country. The Naxalite movement drew many young people, especially college and university students, who were dissatisfied with existing politics and angry at the prevailing social condition and were attracted by radical Naxalite slogans.

In 1969, the Communist Party Marxist-Leninist (ML) was formed under the leadership of Charu Majumdar. Similar parties and groups were formed in Andhra, Orissa, Bihar, Uttar Pradesh, Punjab and Kerala. The CP(ML) and other Naxalite groups argued that democracy in India was a sham, the Indian state was fascist, agrarian relations in India were still basically feudal, the Indian big bourgeoisie was comprador, India was politically and economically dominated by US, British and Soviet imperialisms, Indian polity and economy were still colonial, the Indian revolution was still in its anti-imperialist, anti-feudal stage, and protracted guerrilla warfare on the Chinese model was the form revolution would take in India. The Naxalite groups got political and ideological support from the Chinese government which, however, frowned upon the CP(ML) slogan of 'China's Chairman (Mao Ze-Dong) is our Chairman'.

CPI (ML) and other Naxalite groups succeeded in organizing armed peasant bands in some rural areas and in attacking policemen and rival communists as agents of the ruling classes. The government, however, succeeded in suppressing them and limiting their influence to a few pockets in the country. Not able to face state repression, the Naxalites soon split into several splinter groups and factions. But the real reason for their failure lay in their *inability to root their radicalism in Indian reality*, to grasp the character of Indian society and polity as also the evolving agrarian structure and to widen their social base among the peasants and radical middle-class youth. The disavowal of the Cultural Revolution and Maoism of the 1960s and early 1970s by the post-Mao Chinese leadership in the late 1970s contributed further to the collapse of the Naxalite movement as a significant trend in Indian politics.

17

The Indira Gandhi Years,
1969–1973

Congress split in 1969. The event was the outcome of a multiplicity of factors. We have already discussed in the previous chapter the decay of the Congress party which was reflected in the electoral debacle of 1967. Discerning Congressmen realized that substantial steps had to be taken to reverse the process and rejuvenate the party and the government and that mere manipulation would not work. This also became evident when Congress fared quite badly in the mid-term elections in four states in February 1969. The split of 1969 was in part an answer to people's thinking of what should be done in these circumstances.

The deterioration in the socio-economic situation, discussed in the previous chapter, continued. The rate of economic growth had been slowing down since 1962 and planning was in a crisis. Domestic savings and the rate of investment were stagnating or even falling. US aid had shrunk in 1968 to half of what it had been in 1964–65. Corruption, the black economy and black money had grown by leaps and bounds. Consequently, there was widespread unrest in the countryside and growth of discontent in the urban areas among the lower middle classes, students and the working class. Moreover, there was a growing tendency among the discontented to take recourse to extra-constitutional and even violent means as exemplified by the growth of the Naxalite movements in different parts of the country. The emergence of a new form of industrial action called gherao under which workers' besieged the factory managers in their offices for hours or even days till their demands were met was another such example. The gherao tactic spread later to other spheres of life such as educational institutions.

The political tension inside Congress over the unsettled question of relations between its ministerial and organization wings became more pronounced. Though Indira Gandhi had acquired a certain control over the government after the blow suffered by the Syndicate in the 1967 elections, she had hardly any organizational base in the party. Moreover, after the re-election of Kamaraj and S.K. Patil to parliament in by-elections, the Syndicate members, joined by Morarji Desai, their old foe, once again asserted that the party and its Working Committee should formulate policies and the government should be accountable to the party organs for their implementation. They would also not let Indira Gandhi 'meddle' in party affairs. On Kamaraj's retirement as party president at the end of 1967, they foiled Indira Gandhi's attempt to have a friendly person elected to succeed him. Instead, the post went to the conservative Nijalingappa, an original member of the Syndicate. Indira Gandhi was also not able to have some of her people elected to the new Working Committee.

During 1968-69, the Syndicate members, following the logic of their approach, began to actively plot to dislodge Indira Gandhi from the office of the prime minister. On 12 March 1969, Nijalingappa wrote in his diary: 'I am not sure if she (Mrs Gandhi) deserves to continue as P.M. Possibly soon there may be a show down.' And on 25 April he wrote that Desai 'discussed the necessity of the P.M. being removed.'[1]

Indira Gandhi's response to the Syndicate's assertion was quite cautious and calculated. She did not want to jeopardize the unity of the party and the existence of her government by precipitating a conflict with the organizational wing, especially as the party enjoyed only a small majority in the Lok Sabha. She also realized that she had hardly any organizational base in the party. Thereupon, she tried hard to avoid an open conflict and a split and to accommodate the Syndicate and Desai in both cabinet-making and policies. But she would not compromise in regard to the supreme position and powers of the prime minister or of the government over its policies and administration. The government, she said, derived its authority from parliament and the people through elections and not from the party organization. Therefore, when faced with a direct challenge to her position, she took the plunge and fought back with unexpected strength and ruthlessness. She, too, decided to acquire a preponderant position in the party.

The inner-party struggle in Congress also acquired an ideological complexion. Very soon after the 1967 elections, two interlinked questions became significant. First, how were the growing popular protests and the accompanying violence to be handled? Second, how was the party to reverse its decline and recover its popular appeal? The party was soon divided on broadly right–left lines in addressing these questions, as also regarding the future orientation of its economic and political policies.

Though Congress had always been ideologically heterogeneous, accommodating diverse ideological strands and sectional interests, it had always leaned towards a vague radicalism, nurturing a left-of-centre image. The initial response of most Congressmen to the drubbing their party had received in the 1967 elections was to tilt to the left. Thus, in May 1967, the Congress Working Committee adopted a radical Ten-Point Programme which comprised social control of banks, nationalization of general insurance, state trading in import and export trade, ceilings on urban property and income, curb on business monopolies and concentration of economic power, public distribution of foodgrains, rapid implementation of land reforms, provision of house sites to the rural poor, and abolition of princely privileges.

But the Congress right, though always there but earlier subdued by Nehru, now grew more assertive and was willing to openly advocate more right-wing policies. Represented by Morarji Desai and Nijalingappa, the new Congress president, and other members of the Syndicate, excluding Kamaraj, it had only formally accepted the Ten-Point Programme and was determined to stall its implementation. The right wing instead advocated, (a) in the economic field, further dilution of planning, lesser emphasis on public sector, and greater encouragement to and reliance on private enterprise and foreign capital, (b) in foreign policy, strengthening of political and economic relations with the West in general and the United States in particular and (c) in the political field, suppression of the left and protest movements, especially those of the rural poor in order to get back the support of rich peasants and large landowners.

The Congress left, on the other hand, argued for a new political and economic strategy that would go back to and further develop

Nehru's socialistic agenda and further deepen the political process. It wanted that Congress should immediately implement the Ten-Point Programme and enhance its appeal to the urban and rural poor and the disadvantaged social groups such as Harijans, tribals, minorities and women on the basis of a programme of radical reforms. The Congress should neutralize working-class militancy via economic concessions rather than through administrative suppression. In general, it wished Congress should once again become the vehicle for social change and economic development. Vigorous planning and rapid industrialization, and reduced dependence on foreign collaboration should be resumed. The left put emphasis on the reconstruction of the party on the basis of democratic functioning and its reactivation at the grassroots to put an end to bossism. In foreign policy, the left advocated closer relations with the Soviet bloc and Yugoslavia, Egypt and other non-aligned countries.

As conflict between the right and the left developed within the Congress party, the right also advocated greater party discipline and reining in of the Young Turks and other leftists. The left, on the other hand, openly attacked Morarji Desai as the representative of big business and pressed for the full nationalization of banks, abolition of the privy purses of the ex-rulers, and a complete ban on company donations to political parties.

Interestingly, as the struggle between the Congress right and left intensified, both started relying on the outside support of the Opposition parties closer to them ideologically. In the words of Zareer Masani, 'the "Young Turks" . . . favoured cooperation with the Communists and other Left parties, the Syndicate leaned towards an understanding with the Right-wing Swatantra and Jan Sangh. Both sides saw "like-minded" Opposition parties as potential allies in a coalition government at the Centre in the event of the Congress splitting.'[2]

Initially, with a view to avoid organizational and ideological polarization and a split in the party, Indira Gandhi adopted a cautious, non-partisan attitude in the heated debate between the right and the left in the party. But being quite sensitive both to people's needs and to their moods, she became convinced that the party as well as the country could flourish only under left-of-centre radical programmes and policies. Gradually, over time, she began, hesitatingly and cautiously, to opt for the left's approach and economic policies.

It was the death of President Zakir Hussain in May 1969 that precipitated the events leading to the long-awaited split in Congress. While the President's position in the Indian constitution is that of a formal head of the state, in case of a hung parliament, where no party enjoyed a majority, he could play a decisive political role by inviting one of the contenders for the prime minister's office. The Syndicate was therefore determined to have their own man occupy the President's office. In the party conclave at Bangalore from 11 to 13 July, the Syndicate, enjoying a majority in the Congress parliamentary board, and despite Indira Gandhi's opposition, nominated Sanjiva Reddy, a prominent member of the Syndicate, as the Congress candidate for presidentship.

Feeling driven to the wall and aware of the Syndicate's ultimate design to oust her from office by using Sanjiva Reddy's presidency, Indira Gandhi decided to fight with no holds barred, risk all, and carry the battle to the opponents' camp with radical ideology as her main weapon. Within days of the Bangalore meeting, on 18 July, she took away the finance portfolio from Desai on the grounds that as a conservative he was incapable of implementing her radical programme. Morarji was left with no option but to resign from the cabinet. Assuming the finance portfolio herself, Indira Gandhi immediately, on 21 July, announced the nationalization of fourteen major banks through a Presidential ordinance. She also announced her plan to withdraw the special privileges of the princes. The common people welcomed her announcements enthusiastically, as did the entire left. Her popularity soared as she was seen as a champion of the masses.

The Syndicate and Desai, however, decided to swallow the humiliation, and wait for Reddy to be elected as President. But Indira Gandhi was beginning to play her cards well. Reddy was opposed by the senior statesman C.D. Deshmukh as the candidate of Swatantra and the Jan Sangh, and V.V. Giri, the Vice-President, who had decided to stand as an independent, supported by the two Communist parties, the SSP, DMK, Muslim League and a section of the Akali Dal.

Indira Gandhi wanted to support Giri, but did not know how she could go against her party's candidate whose nomination papers she had filed. At this stage the Syndicate made a major blunder. To ensure Reddy's election, Nijalingappa met the leaders of the Jan Sangh and Swatantra and persuaded them to cast their second-preference votes, once C.D. Deshmukh had been eliminated in the first round, in favour of Reddy. Indira Gandhi immediately accused the Syndicate of having struck a secret deal with communal and reactionary forces in order to oust her from power. She now, more or less openly, supported Giri by refusing to issue a party whip in favour of Reddy and by asking Congress MPs and MLAs to vote freely according to their 'conscience'. In the election, nearly one-third of them defied the organizational leadership and voted for Giri, who was declared elected by a narrow margin on 20 August.

The two sides sparred for some time, with Indira Gandhi occupying the high ground of socialism and democracy. On 8 November, in an open letter to all Congressmen, she declared: 'What we witness today is not a mere clash of personalities and certainly not a fight for power . . . It is a conflict between those who are for socialism, for change and for the fullest internal democracy and debate in the organization . . . and those who are for the status quo, for conformism . . . The Congress stands for democracy, secularism, socialism and non-alignment in international relations.'[3] The Syndicate in turn accused Indira Gandhi of hypocrisy, desiring to concentrate all power in her hands, and trying to establish a Communist dictatorship.

In the end, on 12 November, the defeated and humiliated Syndicate took disciplinary action against Indira Gandhi and expelled her from the party for having violated party discipline. The party had finally split with Indira Gandhi setting up a rival organization, which came to be known as Congress (R)—R for Requisitionists. The Syndicate-dominated Congress came to be known as Congress (O)—O for Organization. In the final countdown, 220 of the party's Lok Sabha MPs went with Indira Gandhi and 68 with the Syndicate. In the All India Congress Committee too 446 of its 705 members walked over to Indira's side.

The Congress (R) was by no means a leftist party for, like the old Congress, it still contained the entire spectrum of political, social and economic opinion. But there was one big difference. It now clearly occupied the left-of-centre position in Indian politics just as the Congress (O) did the right-of-centre. Further, Indira Gandhi was now the unchallenged leader of both the government and the new party, which soon became the real Congress. She also had the mass of the people, both the middle classes and the poor, and a large section of the intelligentsia behind her. In fact, the extent of her political power far surpassed anything that her father had ever enjoyed.

Towards the 1971 General Elections

Despite her immense popularity and clear victory over the Syndicate, Indira Gandhi was still politically vulnerable for her party did not command a majority in parliament. She was dependent on issue-based support by the two Communist parties, some Socialists, the DMK, the Akali Dal, and some independents. In spite of this, carrying on with her left-of-centre stance, she undertook several radical steps. When, in February 1970, the Supreme Court invalidated bank nationalization on the grounds that it was discriminatory and the compensation paid was inadequate, the government used a Presidential ordinance to renationalize them after overcoming the legal lacunae. It also initiated several schemes for the nationalized banks to grant loans to small-scale entrepreneurs, farmers, rickshaw and taxi drivers, etc.

In August 1970, when the government lost by one vote in the Rajya Sabha a constitutional amendment to abolish the privy purses and other privileges of the princes, it issued a Presidential order derecognizing the princes and thus ending all their monetary and other privileges. This order too was, however, immediately invalidated by the Supreme Court.

The government abolished the managing agency system, which had enabled a handful of capitalists to control a large number of industrial enterprises in which they had little or no financial stake. The government appointed a Monopolies and Restrictive Trade Practices (MRTP) Commission, under the MRTP Act passed in 1969, to check the concentration of economic power in the hands of a few leading business families. Indira Gandhi asked the chief ministers to implement more rigorously the existing land reform laws and to undertake further land ceilings legislation. The government also launched the much-postponed Fourth Five Year Plan, its investment outlay being double that of the Third Plan.

Indira Gandhi's main political achievement was that she checked the mood of despair, frustration and cynicism that had prevailed since 1962 and initiated a climate of hope and optimism. As a result of her radical and egalitarian programme and slogans, Indira Gandhi's popularity grew further; and she replenished the Congress party's social support base, especially among the rural and urban poor and, to some extent, among the middle classes. Not surprisingly, the rich peasants and the capitalists were further alienated from her.

Because hers was a minority government, Indira Gandhi felt restricted and frustrated by her dependence on other parties for getting legislation passed in the Lok Sabha. To overcome this situation, she was looking for an issue on which to go to the polls. This opportunity arose when the Supreme Court refused to let her abolish the privy purses of the princes. On 27 December 1970 she dissolved the Lok Sabha and called elections in February 1971, one year ahead of time.

The non-Communist Opposition parties—Congress (O), the Jan Sangh, Swatantra and the Samyukta Socialist Party (SSP)—formed an opportunistic, unprincipled electoral alliance known as the Grand Alliance. In the absence of any ideological coherence and positive common programme, the Grand Alliance concentrated its fire on the person of Indira Gandhi. 'Indira Hatao' (Remove Indira) became its campaign slogan and a scurrilous round of personal abuse and character assassination of Indira Gandhi the main content of its election propaganda.

In sharp contrast, Indira Gandhi refused to reciprocate in kind, avoided personal attacks and campaigned on national issues with a general emphasis on social change, democracy, secularism and socialism. More specifically she focussed on the growth of the public sector, imposition of ceiling on rural landholdings and urban property, removal of glaring disparities in income and opportunity, and abolition of princely privileges. In particular, she concentrated her fire on the Jan Sangh as a divisive communal force and the left-wing extremists for promoting violence. She appealed directly to the voters to defeat those who were coming in the way of her efforts to bring about social change. The deprived and disadvantaged groups she targeted were the landless labourers, Scheduled Castes and Tribes, minorities, women, and the unemployed and disaffected youth. She countered the slogan of 'Indira Hatao' with the more effective slogan 'Garibi Hatao' (Remove Poverty). To the middle classes and the propertied she promised a strong and stable government, action against forces of violence and disorder and full scope to the private sector to play its proper role in the mixed economy.

The results of the February elections turned out to be an overwhelming personal triumph for Indira Gandhi and a rude shock to the Opposition. Congress (R) swept the polls, winning 352 of the 518 Lok Sabha seats. This gave the party a two-thirds majority required to amend the constitution. The Grand Alliance and the right suffered a crushing defeat. The only Opposition parties to fare well were the CPM, CPI and DMK, the last two being, however, Congress allies.

The 1971 elections restored the Congress party to its dominant position in Indian politics. By voting for Congress the people had simultaneously voted for change and stability. Also, after the unhappy experience of coalition governments in the states after 1967, people did not want the unnerving drama of defections and rapid changes in party alignments to be repeated at the Centre. The elections also represented further politicization of the masses. People's votes had cut across religious, caste and regional barriers. Elections had also shown that once national issues were raised, vote banks and politics of patronage became relatively irrelevant and that increasingly people could no longer be dictated to, bullied or bought. Indira Gandhi had thus demonstrated that building a coalition of the poor and the disadvantaged around a national programme could be a viable political option.

Indira Gandhi received the mandate she had sought, and she now became the unchallenged leader of Congress and the dominant political figure in the country. Nobody would call her a *'goongi gudiya'* again. But the faith the voters, especially the poor, had reposed in her also represented a danger signal. She had raised high hopes among them; and she had now to deliver on her promises, for she had the parliamentary strength to pass any laws, to take any administrative measures, and there could be no alibis or excuses for failure.

However, the fulfilment of the mandate of 1971 was again postponed, for, on the morrow of Indira Gandhi being sworn in as prime minister, the Bangladesh crisis occurred.

The Challenge of Bangladesh

Almost immediately after the 1971 general elections, a major political-military crisis broke out in East Pakistan (now Bangladesh).

India was inevitably drawn into the fray, leading to a bloody war between India and Pakistan.

Pakistan had been created around the ideological assumption that, because of their faith, the Muslims of India constituted a separate nation. But religion was not enough to weld together the Punjabi-speaking part of West Pakistan with the Bengali-speaking East Pakistan. The West Pakistani political and economic elite soon acquired a dominant position in Pakistan's army, bureaucracy, economy and polity resulting in economic and political discrimination against East Pakistan. Moreover, in the absence of political democracy, the Bengalis had no mechanism through which to remedy the situation. Consequently, over time, the people of East Pakistan developed a powerful movement for democracy in Pakistan and greater autonomy for East Pakistan. Instead of coming to terms with this movement, the ruling elite of Pakistan decided to suppress it and which ultimately transformed it into a movement for independence from Pakistan.

In December 1970, General Yahya Khan, the military dictator of Pakistan, held free elections in which Bengal's Awami Party under the popular leadership of Sheikh Mujibur Rahman won more than 99 per cent of the seats in East Bengal and an overall majority in Pakistan's National Assembly. But the army and Yahya Khan, backed by Zulfiqar Ali Bhutto, the leading politician of West Pakistan, refused to let the Awami Party form the government. When the latter started a civil disobedience movement to enforce the constitutional provision, in a sudden move on 25 March 1971, Yahya Khan ordered a military crackdown on East Pakistan. Mujibur Rahman was arrested and taken to an unknown destination in West Pakistan. The West Pakistan army initiated a reign of terror, killing innocent citizens, burning villages and crops. Thousands of intellectuals and Bengali members of the police and army were indiscriminately but systematically eliminated in order to deprive the people of any leadership. For over six months, the army committed rape, torture, arson, brutal killings and other heinous crimes. Large sections of the East Pakistan police, paramilitary organizations and East Bengal regiments reacted by revolting. The Awami League leaders, who succeeded in escaping to Calcutta, formed a Government of Bangladesh in exile, organized the Mukti Bahini (Liberation Army) and launched a fierce underground movement and guerrilla warfare.

The brutality of the Pakistan army was specially directed against the Hindus remaining in East Pakistan who were faced with virtual genocide. They, but also a large number of Muslims, Christians and Buddhists, were forced to migrate to and seek shelter in West Bengal, Assam and Meghalaya in India. By November 1971, the number of refugees from East Bengal had reached ten million.

In India there was a wave of sympathy for the people of East Bengal and a strong demand for swift action against Pakistan. But, Indira Gandhi, though convinced that war with Pakistan was likely, opposed hasty action. Throughout the crisis, she acted with immense courage but also with abundant caution and careful and cool calculation. She did not want to strengthen Pakistani propaganda that the entire movement for autonomy in East Pakistan and the consequent revolt was not a popular uprising but an Indian conspiracy. She also did not want to do anything which would lead to India being accused of violating international law and norms.

In following a policy of restraint, Indira Gandhi had two other major considerations in view. First, if it was to be war, it should come at a time of India's choosing. Careful planning and preparations were necessary. Military operations in East Pakistan could not be undertaken during the monsoon when the large number of rivers and rivulets there would be in flood and the marshes impassable. The Himalayan passes would get snowbound only in winter making it impossible for China to intervene and send troops to aid Pakistan. The Mukti Bahini also needed time to gain enough strength to confront the Pakistani army in regular warfare.

Second, Indira Gandhi realized that international opinion had to be educated and won over to the cause of Bangladesh and made aware of India's predicament in regard to the refugees and how they were placing an unbearable burden on India, endangering its economic and political stability. This she hoped would make other countries sympathetic to India or at least not hostile to it should there be need for a military intervention. The refugees, she underlined, should return without delay, but this could only be achieved if a climate of confidence and peace was created in East Pakistan by the Pakistan government.

For the next eight months, Indira Gandhi followed a four-pronged policy. India not only gave sanctuary to the Bangladesh government in exile, but the Indian army gave military training on Indian soil and material aid in money and military equipment to the Mukti Bahini. The Indian government was also generous in providing food, clothing, shelter and medical aid to the refugees in spite of its being a tremendous strain on India's resources. Almost from the outset in April 1971, the Indian armed forces began to prepare for swift military action, though in utmost secrecy, in case a peaceful solution of the refugee problem could not be found. Moreover, the military operation had to be swift and finished before the big powers succeeded in halting the conflict and imposing a ceasefire.

India's campaign received a very positive response from the media, the intelligentsia and the students in the West and ultimately from the West European governments besides the people and the governments of the Soviet Union and other European Communist countries. But the governments of the United States and China adopted an unsympathetic and even hostile attitude towards India. Ignoring Indian protest, the US continued to supply arms to Pakistan. It also tried to pose the problem of Bangladesh primarily as an issue between India and Pakistan rather than one of Bangladesh's independence. China was fully supportive of Pakistan as it had become virtually its ally. In July–August 1971 Pakistan had helped to bring about a US–China detente.

To secure itself against a possible US–China intervention in case events led to a war, on 9 August India swiftly signed a 20-year Indo-Soviet Treaty of Peace, Friendship and Cooperation. The treaty provided for immediate mutual consultations and appropriate effective measures in case of either country being subjected to a military threat. The treaty was widely welcomed by people in India and gave a big boost to their morale.

Indira Gandhi was now full of self-confidence. In a programme on the BBC, she asserted: 'We are not dependent upon what other countries think or want us to do. We know what we want for ourselves and we are going to do it, whatever it costs . . . we welcome help from any country; but if it doesn't come, well, it is all right by us.'[4] Convinced from the beginning that a war between India and Pakistan on the Bangladesh issue and the problem of the refugees was inevitable, Indira Gandhi was prepared for it by November-end. But she was reluctant to take action first, even though the Indian army was ready and in fact 4 December had been designated as the day the Indian armed forces would directly undertake the liberation of Bangladesh. But, at this stage, Yahya

Khan obliged Indira Gandhi by pushing the button first. Equally convinced that war was coming and greatly harassed by the Mukti Bahini's stepped-up guerrilla warfare and the Indian armed forces' excursions into Bangladesh, he decided to take advantage of the first strike. On 3 December, Pakistan's air force launched a surprise attack on eight military airfields in western India, hoping to inflict serious damage on the Indian Air Force and also to internationalize the Bangladesh issue and secure UN intervention. But he was to fail in both objectives. The Indian Air Force was relatively unharmed; anticipating a Pakistani attack, the Indian Air Force had withdrawn beforehand to interior airfields.

India immediately recognized Bangladesh and gave a strong military reply. The Indian strategy was to hold the Pakistani forces in the western sector through strong defensive action, while waging a short, swift and decisive war in the east, forcing the Pakistani army there to surrender before the US, China or the UN could intervene.

Brilliantly led by General J.S. Arora, the Indian army, joined by the Mukti Bahini, virtually ran through East Bengal and reached Dacca, its capital, within eleven days, and surrounded the Pakistani garrison there. Since, in the words of Henry Kissinger, the US Secretary of State, President Nixon was 'not inclined to let the Paks be defeated',[5] the US government tried to intervene, declared India to be the aggressor and stopped all economic aid to it. But its two resolutions in the UN Security Council proposing a ceasefire and mutual troop withdrawals were vetoed by the Soviet Union, with Britain and France abstaining. The Chinese threat also did not materialize as it confined its intervention to bitter verbal denunciations. More or less in desperation and reminiscent of the gunboat diplomacy of the nineteenth century, on Nixon's orders, segments of the US Seventh Fleet, led by the nuclear aircraft carrier, *U.S.S. Enterprise*, set out for the Bay of Bengal on 9 December with the objective of forcing India to delay the fall of Dacca. But Indira Gandhi calmly ignored the American threat and, instead, asked General Manekshaw, India's Chief of Army Staff, to hurry the completion of India's military plan. The Indian armed forces, having surrounded Dacca on 13 December, forced the defeated and demoralized 93,000-strong Pakistan army in Bangladesh to surrender on 16 December.

Following the surrender in Dacca, on 17 December, the Indian government announced a unilateral ceasefire on the western front. The continuation of the war would have been hazardous both on diplomatic and military grounds. The United States, China and the UN were then likely to intervene more actively. The Soviet Union also did not favour further fighting. War on the western front would also have been very costly both in terms of men and materials. While in the east, the people had welcomed Indian troops as saviours, in the west the people and the armed forces, still intact, would fight tenaciously to defend their homes and homeland. Moreover, continuation of hostilities in the western part would have been aimless, for after all disintegration of Pakistan or annexation of any part of it was not, and could not be, an objective of Indian policy.

Pakistan readily accepted the ceasefire and released Mujibur Rahman, who came to power in Bangladesh on 12 January 1972.

India had several gains to show from the Bangladesh war. The balance of power in South Asia had been altered with India emerging as the pre-eminent power. The grave refugee problem had been solved with the ten million refugees promptly and smoothly sent back to their homes in Bangladesh. The humiliating memory of the defeat in 1962 was wiped out and India's lost pride and self-respect restored. India had not only defeated a troublesome neighbour but had asserted its independence in foreign affairs and in defence of her national interest. It had been shown that India was not a weak political entity on the world stage even if it was not yet a world power.

The war had also demonstrated the strength of Indian secularism. Hindus, Muslims, Christians, Sikhs, all had stood together as civilians or soldiers at this moment of crisis against a Muslim country. Further, a big blow had been given to the two-nation theory, the basis for Partition in 1947. Muslims in India could now see what treatment had been meted out to Bengali Muslims by the upholders of that theory.

The Bangladesh war was also, in real terms, a personal victory for Indira Gandhi. Indians admired her toughness and determination and the superb leadership qualities she had displayed throughout the crisis. Her popularity stretched phenomenally, and her prestige went up in the community of nations. She was 'at the pinnacle of her power and glory'. Many Indians referred to her as a modern-day Durga and an incarnation of Shakti or female energy. At this moment of her triumph, Indira Gandhi gladly shared her glory with Manekshaw who was made a Field Marshal, the first in India.

The war had ended; the ceasefire had come—but peace had not. India still held over 90,000 prisoners of war and was in occupation of nearly 9,000 square kilometres of Pakistani territory. Pakistan was yet to recognize Bangladesh. Indira Gandhi realized that a mutually arrived at Indo-Pak settlement was necessary for a durable peace. A hostile Pakistan would not only force India to maintain a high level of defence expenditure but also enable outside powers to interfere in subcontinental affairs. A summit conference between Indira Gandhi and Zulfiqar Ali Bhutto, the newly elected prime minister of Pakistan, was held in Simla in June 1972; a great deal of hard bargaining took place and the two signed an agreement which came to be known as the Simla Declaration. India agreed to return the Pakistani territory it had occupied, except some strategic points in Kashmir, mainly in the Kargil sector, which were necessary to safeguard the strategic road link between Srinagar and Leh in Ladakh. In return, Pakistan agreed to respect the existing Line of Control (LoC) in Kashmir and undertook not to alter it unilaterally by force or threat of force. The two countries also agreed to settle all their disputes through bilateral negotiations without any outside mediation by the UN or any other power. India also agreed to return the prisoners of war to Pakistan but this was to be contingent upon a Bangladesh–Pakistan agreement. This occurred the next year when Pakistan recognized Bangladesh in August 1973.

The justification Indira Gandhi offered to parliament in July 1972 for signing the Simla Declaration was significant. She said: 'All I know is that I must fight for peace and I must take those steps which will lead us to peace . . . The time has come when Asia must wake up to its destiny, must wake up to the real needs of its people, must stop fighting amongst ourselves, no matter what our previous quarrels, no matter what the previous hatred and bitterness. The time has come today when we must bury the past.'[6]

A Time of Success

The year 1972, which was also the twenty-fifth year of India's independence, marked the beginning of a new period in which conditions were ripe for the government to fulfil its electoral promises. There was political stability in the country; the government had a two-thirds majority in the Lok Sabha; and Indians had acquired fresh and heightened self-confidence in their own capacities and capabilities as well as faith in the political leadership.

But before this positive process could be inaugurated, the Congress leadership felt that it must acquire the levers of power in the states, which were, after all, the agencies for the implementation of much of the reforms and developmental programmes and policies. Consequently, elections were held in March 1972 for the legislative assemblies in all states except Uttar Pradesh, Tamil Nadu, Kerala and Orissa. Once again Congress won a majority in all the states. The two elections of 1971 and 1972 led to a *virtual demise of Swatantra and Congress (O)*. The political command at both the Centre and the states was now unified. Indira Gandhi had also acquired virtually complete control over the party, her cabinet, and the chief ministers.

During 1971–74, the government undertook several measures to implement its left-of-centre agenda. In August 1972, general insurance was nationalized and five months later the coal industry. Ceilings were imposed on urban landownership. The MRTP Act to check concentration of industrial enterprises in a few hands had already been passed in 1969 and an MRTP Commission appointed in 1971 to implement the Act. But Indira Gandhi refused to go any further in nationalizing industry, despite pressure from the CPI and leftists within her party; she remained fully committed to a mixed economy. Legislation to reduce ceilings on agricultural landholdings and distribute surplus land to the landless and marginal farmers was also passed in several states. The central government initiated a programme of cheap foodgrain distribution to the economically vulnerable sections of society and a crash scheme for creating employment in rural areas. It also made it compulsory for nationalized banks to open branches in underbanked areas such as small towns, rural clusters and the poorer parts of the cities and to make credit available to small industries, farmers, road transporters and self-employed persons. To reduce businessmen's influence in politics, the government imposed a ban on donations by joint-stock companies to political parties. Mrs Gandhi also tried to strengthen the Planning Commission and the planning mechanism.

The government got passed two important constitutional amendments. The Supreme Court had in two judgments in 1951 and 1965 upheld parliament's right to amend the fundamental right to property so as to make any legislation regarding it non-justiciable. But in 1967 the Supreme Court had in the Golak Nath case reversed these decisions and later set aside bank nationalization and the abolition of privy purses. The 24th Amendment to the constitution passed in 1971 restored parliament's authority to amend the Fundamental Rights. The 25th Amendment passed in the same year gave parliament the power to decide the amount to be paid as compensation and the mode of payment in case of any private property taken over for future purposes. Thus, the Supreme Court would no longer have the power to declare such compensation to be inadequate. The 24th and 25th Amendments were to rectify a situation where the courts had taken a conservative social position, come in the way of agrarian reform legislation, the nationalization of industries and other business enterprises, hindered measures to check concentration of wealth and economic power in private hands, asserted the judiciary's supremacy over parliament, and assumed powers over the constitutional amendment process which the makers of the constitution had not intended. A further, less significant, constitutional amendment abolished the privileges as well as the purses of the former princes.

India achieved a major success in terms of a breakthrough in science and technology when the Atomic Energy Commission detonated an underground nuclear device at Pokhran in the deserts of Rajasthan on 18 May 1974. The Indian government, however, declared that it was not going to make nuclear weapons even though it had acquired the capacity to do so. It claimed that the Pokhran explosion was an effort to harness atomic energy for peaceful purposes and to make India self-reliant in nuclear technology.

Since 1973, the tide had been turning against Indira Gandhi. The economy, the polity and the credibility of Indira Gandhi's leadership and the Congress government started going downhill. The disillusionment found expression in the J.P. movement of 1974. It was followed by the Emergency in 1975. Discontent and unrest marked this phase which is taken up in the next chapter.

The JP Movement and the Emergency: Indian Democracy Tested

In 1975, India experienced its greatest political crisis since independence when Internal Emergency was declared on 26 June. How did the Emergency come about? Was there no other choice, as Indira Gandhi maintained, or was it the ultimate expression of her authoritarian tendencies, as the Opposition alleged? Or did both sides indulge in obfuscation. The issue in fact, is quite complex.

The Pre-Emergency Crises

By the beginning of 1973 Indira Gandhi's popularity began to decline. People's expectations were unfulfilled. Little dent was being made in rural or urban poverty or economic inequality, nor was there any lessening of caste and class oppression in the countryside.

The immediate provocation for the rising discontent was the marked deterioration in the economic situation. A combination of recession, growing unemployment, rampant inflation and scarcity of foodstuffs created a serious crisis. The burden of feeding and sheltering nearly 10 million refugees from Bangladesh during 1971 had depleted the grain reserves and, combined with the cost of the Bangladesh war, had led to a large budgetary deficit. The war had also drained foreign exchange reserves. Monsoon rains failed for two years in succession during 1972 and 1973, leading to a terrible drought in most parts of the country and a massive shortage of foodgrains, and fuelling their prices. The drought also led to a drop in power generation and combined with the fall in agricultural production, and therefore in the demand for manufactured goods, led to industrial recession and rise in unemployment. The year 1973 also witnessed the notorious oil shock when world prices of crude oil increased four-fold, leading to massive increase in the prices of petroleum products and fertilizers. This drained foreign reserves, further increased the budgetary deficit and deepened economic recession. With all this, prices rose continuously, by 22 per cent in 1972–73 alone. The price rise, which affected both the poor and the middle classes, was accompanied by scarcity of essential articles of consumption. There were food riots in several parts of the country.

Economic recession, unemployment, price rise and scarcity of goods led to large-scale industrial unrest and a wave of strikes in different parts of the country during 1972 and 1973, culminating in an all-India railway strike in May 1974. The railway strike lasted twenty-two days but was broken in the end. Mrs Gandhi's popularity among the workers was eroded further.

Law and order deteriorated, particularly during 1974–75. Strikes, student protests and popular demonstrations often turned violent. Many colleges and universities were closed for prolonged periods. In May 1973, there was a mutiny in Uttar Pradesh by the Provincial Armed Constabulary, which clashed with the army sent to discipline it, leading to the death of over thirty-five constables and soldiers.

To tackle the deteriorating economic, political and law and order situation firm and clear leadership was needed, as exhibited during the Bangladesh crisis and in the handling of foreign affairs. But that was not forthcoming. The political situation was worsened by the play of other factors. Congress had been declining as an organization and proved incapable of dealing with the political crisis at the state and grassroots levels. The government's capacity to redress the situation was seriously impaired by the growing corruption in most areas of life and the widespread belief that the higher levels of the ruling party and administration were involved in it. The whiff of corruption touched even Indira Gandhi when her inexperienced younger son, Sanjay Gandhi, was given a licence to manufacture 50,000 Maruti cars a year.

A major new development was the growing detachment of three major social groups from Congress. While the poor continued to support it, though more passively, the middle classes, because of price rise and the stink of corruption, the rich peasantry, because of the threat of land reform, and the capitalists, because of the talk of socialism, nationalization of banks and coal mining and anti-monopoly measures, turned against Congress and Indira Gandhi. Desperation of the Opposition parties also contributed to the undermining of the political system. Utterly disparate ideologically and programmatically, the only thing uniting these parties was anti-Congressism. But they were in no position, either separately or in combination, to pose a political challenge to Congress, having been thoroughly defeated and downsized in the general elections of 1971 and state assembly elections of 1972. Unwilling to wait till the next elections to test their popularity they decided, irrespective of the consequences, to blindly support any group or movement in any form against the government at the Centre or in a state.

Gujarat and Bihar Unrest

What turned the various economic and political crises into one of the political system were two popular movements in Gujarat and Bihar against the faction-ridden Congress governments, and the leadership provided to the Bihar movement by Jayaprakash Narayan.

A major upheaval occurred in Gujarat in January 1974 when popular anger over the rise in the prices of foodgrains, cooking oil and other essential commodities exploded in the cities and towns of the state in the form of a student movement which was soon joined by the Opposition parties. For more than ten weeks the state faced virtual anarchy with strikes, looting, rioting and arson, and efforts to force MLAs to resign. The police replied with excessive force, indiscriminate arrests and frequent recourse to lathi charge and firing. By February, the central government was forced to ask the state government to resign, suspend the assembly and impose President's Rule in the state. The last act of the Gujarat drama was played in March 1975 when, faced with continuing agitation and a fast unto death by Morarji Desai, Indira Gandhi dissolved the assembly and announced fresh elections to it in June.

On the heels of the Gujarat agitation and inspired by its success, a similar agitation was started by students in Bihar in March 1974. The students, starting with the gherao of the assembly on

18 March, repeatedly clashed with the overactive police, leading to the death of twenty-seven people in one week. Moreover, as in Gujarat, Opposition parties quickly joined forces with the student agitators.

The Bihar movement was, however, characterized by two new features. Jayaprakash Narayan, popularly known as JP, came out from political retirement, took over its leadership, and gave a call for 'Total Revolution' or 'a struggle against the very system which has compelled almost everybody to go corrupt'.[1] Demanding resignation of the Congress government in Bihar and dissolution of the assembly, he asked the students and the people to put pressure on the existing legislators to resign, paralyse the government, gherao the state assembly and government offices, set up parallel people's governments all over the state, and pay no taxes. The second feature was the firm refusal of Indira Gandhi to concede the demand for the dissolution of the assembly, lest it spread to cover other parts of the country and the central government.

JP also decided to go beyond Bihar and organize a country-wide movement against widespread corruption and for the removal of Congress and Indira Gandhi, who was now seen as a threat to democracy and portrayed as the fountainhead of corruption.

JP now repeatedly toured the entire country and drew large crowds especially in Delhi and other parts of North India which were Jan Sangh or Socialist strongholds. The JP Movement attracted wide support especially from students, middle classes, traders and a section of the intelligentsia. It also got the backing of nearly all the non-left political parties who had been trounced in 1971 and who saw in JP a popular leader who would enable them to acquire credibility as an alternative to Congress. JP in turn realized that without the organizational structures of these parties he could not hope to face Indira Gandhi either in the streets or at the polls.

The fervour of the JP Movement, however, did not last long and it began to decline by the end of 1974. Most of his student followers went back to their classes. Moreover, the movement had failed to attract the rural and urban poor even in Gujarat and Bihar. Denouncing the JP Movement for its extra-parliamentary approach, Indira Gandhi challenged JP to test their respective popularity in Bihar as also the country as a whole in the coming general elections, due in February–March 1976. JP accepted the challenge and his supporting parties decided to form a National Coordination Committee for the purpose.

It appeared at this stage that the issue as to who actually represented the Indian people would be resolved through the democratic electoral process. However, this was not to be. A sudden twist to Indian politics was given by a judgement on 12 June 1975 by Justice Sinha of the Allahabad High Court, on an election petition by Raj Narain, convicting Mrs Gandhi for having indulged in corrupt campaign practices and declaring her election invalid. The conviction also meant that she could not seek election to parliament or hold office for six years and therefore continue as prime minister.

Most observers at the time noted that Justice Sinha had dismissed the more serious charges against her but had convicted her of technical and trivial, even frivolous, offences against the election law. Mrs Gandhi refused to resign and appealed to the Supreme Court. While the Supreme Court would hear her appeal on 14 July, Justice V.R. Krishna Iyer, the vacation judge of the Supreme Court, created further confusion when he decided on 24 June that, till the final disposal of her appeal by the full bench of the Supreme Court, Mrs Gandhi could stay in office and speak in parliament but could not vote in it.

Meanwhile, Mrs Gandhi suffered another political blow when the Gujarat assembly election results came on 13 June. The opposition Janata front won 87 seats and the Congress 75 seats in a house of 182. Surprisingly, the Janata front succeeded in forming a government in alliance with the same Chimanbhai Patel against whose corruption and maladministration the popular movement had been initiated.

The Allahabad judgement and the Gujarat assembly results revived the Opposition movement. JP and the coalition of Opposition parties were, however, not willing to wait for the result of Indira Gandhi's appeal to the Supreme Court or the general elections to the Lok Sabha due in eight months. They decided to seize the opportunity and, accusing Mrs Gandhi of 'clinging to an office corruptly gained', demanded her resignation and called for a countrywide campaign to force the issue. In a rally in Delhi on 25 June they announced that a nationwide one-week campaign of mass mobilization and civil disobedience to force Mrs Gandhi to resign would be initiated on 29 June. The campaign would end with the gherao of the prime minister's house by hundreds of thousands of volunteers. In his speech at the rally, JP asked the people to make it impossible for the government to function and once again appealed to the armed forces, the police and the bureaucracy to refuse to obey any orders they regarded as 'illegal' and 'unconstitutional'.

Mrs Gandhi's lightning response was to declare a state of Internal Emergency on 26 June.

The JP Movement

How did the Emergency come about, what was its legitimacy, what did it mean in practice, and why was it lifted in the end and with what consequences; these issues deserve critical attention.

The main justification of the JP Movement was that it arose to end corruption in Indian life and politics, whose fountainhead was ostensibly Mrs Gandhi, and to defend democracy which was threatened by her authoritarian personality and style of politics and administration. JP often accused Indira Gandhi of trying to destroy all democratic institutions and establish a Soviet-backed dictatorship in her hunger for power. Her continuation in office, he said, was 'incompatible with the survival of democracy in India'.[2] Later, many other critics and opponents of Mrs Gandhi expressed similar views.

Indira Gandhi justified her action in imposing the Emergency in terms of national political interests and primarily on three grounds. First, India's stability, security, integrity and democracy were in danger from the disruptive character of the JP Movement. Referring to JP's speeches, she accused the opposition of inciting the armed forces to mutiny and the police to rebel. Second, there was the need to implement a programme of rapid economic development in the interests of the poor and the underprivileged. Third, she warned against intervention and subversion from abroad with the aim of weakening and destabilizing India.

In fact, neither JP nor Indira Gandhi chose the democratic way out of the crisis. JP should have demanded and Indira Gandhi should have offered to hold fresh elections to the Lok Sabha, which were in any case due in early 1976, earlier, in October–November 1975 itself, and thus provided a practical alternative to both the demand for her resignation and the Emergency. Both JP's and Mrs Gandhi's positions need to be examined critically, in light of subsequent political developments.

The JP Movement was flawed in many respects, in terms of both its composition and its actions and the character and philosophy of its leader. Jayaprakash Narayan was justly renowned for his integrity, lack of ambition for office, fearlessness, selflessness and sacrifice and lifelong commitment to civil liberties and the establishment of a just social order. But, ideologically, he was vague. From the early 1950s he became a critic of parliamentary politics and parliamentary democracy. For years, he tried to popularize the concept of 'partyless democracy'. During 1974–75 he also advocated 'Total Revolution' *(Sampooran Kranti)*. Both *concepts were unclear and nebulous*, and at no stage was he able to delineate or explain what a political system without political parties would involve or how would the popular will get expressed or implemented in it. Similarly, the socio-economic and political content, programme or policies of the Total Revolution were never properly defined. At the same time, JP was a democrat and not an authoritarian leader. Nor was the movement he led in 1974–75 yet authoritarian or fascist, but—and this is important—it was capable of creating a space for its fascist component. JP's talk of partyless democracy and Total Revolution and the critique of parliamentary democracy, hazy and indistinctive, could also be dangerous, for it encouraged cynicism, scorn and despair towards democratic institutions. This could create a political climate favourable to authoritarianism and fascism, as happened in Italy and Germany after 1919 and in Pakistan and Indonesia in the 1960s.

The nebulousness of JP's politics and ideology is also illustrated by the fact that he took the support of political parties and groups which had nothing in common in terms of programme and policies and were ideologically incompatible. The JP Movement came to include the communal Jan Sangh and Jamaat-i-Islami, the neo-fascist RSS, the conservative and secular Congress (O), Socialists and the extreme left Naxalite groups. Almost entirely negative in its approach, the movement could not fashion an alternative programme or policies except that of overthrowing Indira Gandhi.

In its later phases, the movement depended for organization on the RSS–Jan Sangh, which alone among its constituents had a strong well-knit organization, trained cadre and branches all over the country, especially in northern and central India. Even in Bihar, the Akhil Bharatiya Vidyarthi Parishad (ABVP), a front organization of the RSS, had come to form the backbone of JP's main political vehicle, the Chhatra Yuva Sangharsha Vahini. Consequently, though JP remained the movement's chief mobilizer, it came to be increasingly dominated by the RSS–Jan Sangh. This resulted in the political character of the movement also undergoing a major change; not change of policies or of the state governments but the removal of Indira Gandhi became the movement's main goal. Furthermore, it had a potentially undemocratic character in terms both of its demands and the methods adopted or planned. Its objective was not the blocking of or bringing about changes in particular government policies but undermining first the government of Bihar and then the government at the Centre. The democratically elected legislatures and governments were to be dissolved and replaced not through elections but through extra-constitutional mass agitations mainly confined to urban areas. This amounted to a covert demand for a basic change of the political system.

The agitational methods adopted and propagated by the JP Movement were also extra-constitutional and undemocratic. Going far beyond peaceful processions, demonstrations and public rallies, in Bihar, as earlier in Gujarat, the tactic was to force the government to resign and the legislatures to be dissolved by gheraoing government offices, the assembly, and the governor and thus paralyse the government and to intimidate and coerce individual elected legislators to resign from the assemblies. This tactic was to be repeated in June–July 1975 at the Centre.

More serious was JP's incitement to the army, police and civil services to rebel. Several times during the course of the movement, he urged them not to obey orders that were 'unjust and beyond the call of the duty' or 'illegal and unjust' or 'unconstitutional, illegal or against their conscience'. The decision regarding unconstitutionality, and so on, of the orders was to be made by the individuals concerned themselves. But these various exhortations could possibly be considered more an expression of JP's hazy thinking than an actual call for rebellion.

As we have seen earlier, the climax of the JP Movement came on 25 June 1975 when a public call was given for a nationwide mass civil disobedience movement which would culminate in a gherao of the prime minister's residence, thus forcing her to resign or to enact another Jallianwala Bagh massacre—a massacre she would never be able to live down. The entire opposition game plan was made explicit by Morarji Desai in an interview later in the evening: 'We intend to overthrow her, to force her to resign. For good . . . Thousands of us will surround her house to prevent her from going out or receive visitors. We'll camp there night and day shouting to her to resign.'[3] In other words, the opposition plan had all the hallmarks of a coup d'état.

The situation that was being created by the JP Movement was that of insurrection without revolution. The tactics it evolved over time amounted to a revolution. But this was to be a revolution without a revolutionary party, organization, ideology or programme to give it direction and leadership. In fact, it was to be a revolution to be made with reliance on a mix of the ideology-less cadre of the Chhatra Vahini, the conservative cadre of Congress (O), BKD and the Swatantra Party and the communal neo-fascist cadre of the RSS–Jan Sangh.

The adoption by a popular movement of the rhetoric of revolution and of extra-legal and extra-constitutional and often violent agitational methods is not compatible with the functioning of a democratic political system. But, what is more important, when such rhetoric and methods are not part of a revolutionary design to change the socio-economic order in a fundamental manner, when masses enter into a chaotic and disorganized movement without the leadership of a properly constituted and led revolutionary party, when faith in a political system is destroyed without creating faith in an alternative system, the resultant possibility is that of the establishment of an authoritarian, often fascist, regime or of political chaos, anarchy and disintegration of the political entity. Historically, such a mix has been the hallmark not of a revolution but of a counter-revolution, as the history of the rise of fascism in Europe and dictatorial regimes in Latin America indicates.

Let me add a caveat here. The danger of authoritarianism did not come from Jayaprakash Narayan who was not planning or giving direction to an authoritarian coup d'état. But there were, as pointed out above, others around him who were so inclined and who were increasingly coming to control the movement and who could capitalize on his ideological woolliness and basically weak personality.

In any case, the proper democratic options open to the Opposition were: (i) to wait for the Supreme Court judgement and, if it went against Mrs Gandhi, to demand its implementation; (ii) to wait for the general elections to the Lok Sabha due in early 1976 and in the meantime use peaceful agitation and propaganda to erode Mrs Gandhi's standing among the people; (iii) to demand that, because the Allahabad judgement had eroded Mrs Gandhi's mandate to rule, fresh elections should be held immediately—say in October–November 1975.

In fact, those in the Opposition who wanted to defeat Mrs Gandhi at the hustings had won out in October–November 1974 when JP had accepted Mrs Gandhi's challenge to let the next general elections decide the fate of his movement's demands. But one year or even six months is a long time in politics. A popular movement could either gain or lose momentum in that period. There was also no guarantee of success in the coming elections, especially as Congress's base in South India and among the rural poor, women and the minorities seemed to be intact. Even in the Gujarat elections in early June, Congress had failed to get a majority but so had the Opposition Janata combine despite JP and Morarji Desai leading its election campaign. The Allahabad judgement marked a turning point in this respect. Sensing the real possibility of the immediate ouster of Mrs Gandhi, JP, Morarji and others went over to the coup d'état school.

The Emergency

The imposition of the Emergency by Mrs Gandhi was also flawed. She was to claim later that faced with an extra-constitutional challenge she had no other option. Resigning, she said, would have strengthened the forces that were threatening the democratic process and bringing the country to the edge of anarchy and chaos. There was, moreover, no legal, political or moral reason why she should step down during the hearing of her appeal.

But, as already indicated earlier, in reality she too had another democratic option. She could have declared that the Lok Sabha would be dissolved and fresh elections to it would be held in October–November. If JP and the Opposition had accepted her offer, the door to a democratic resolution of the political impasse through an appeal to the electorate would have been opened. If they had not, and stuck to their demand for her resignation and their declared methods to bring it about, she could legitimately declare an Internal Emergency as the only viable and available option for meeting their extra-constitutional challenge. Simultaneously, she could announce that the Emergency would be lifted as soon as the Opposition gave up its demand for her resignation, agreed to adhere to the Supreme Court or parliament's judgement, and accepted the test of elections. Interestingly, it may be pointed out, this is exactly what General de Gaulle did when faced with the much more pervasive and radical upsurge of students and workers in May 1968. And, of course, the protesting students and workers and most of their leaders accepted the challenge to face de Gaulle in elections. In any case, there was no justification for the longevity (about nineteen months) of the Emergency, once the perceived threat to law and order was over, or for the draconian character of the Emergency measures.

The political tragedy was that both the JP Movement and Indira Gandhi shunned the option of elections, which are in a democracy the vehicles for the legitimation of a political regime and for expression of popular will. This was, of course, so in part because of the manner in which the political conflict during 1974–75 had developed, with the tragic consequence that a political atmosphere had been created in which dialogue and accommodation between the two opposing forces was not possible.

Mrs Gandhi proclaimed a state of Internal Emergency under Article 352 of the constitution on the morning of 26 June, suspending the normal political processes, but promising to return to normalcy as soon as conditions warranted it. The proclamation suspended the federal provisions of the constitution and Fundamental Rights and civil liberties. The government imposed strict censorship on the Press and stifled all protest and opposition to the government. In the early hours of 26 June, hundreds of the main leaders of the Opposition were arrested under the Maintenance of Internal Security Act (MISA). Among those arrested were Jayaprakash Narayan, Morarji Desai, and Atal Bihari Vajpayee and Congress dissidents such as Chandra Shekhar. Several academics, newspapermen, trade unionists and student leaders were also put behind bars. Many of the arrested were gradually released: JP in 1975 on grounds of health and others, including Charan Singh and Vajpayee, during 1976. Several extreme communal and ultra-left organizations, including the RSS, Anand Marg, Jamaat-i-Islami and Maoist CP(ML), were banned. Arrests continued throughout the period of the Emergency though most of the arrested were released after a few days or months. In all, more than 100,000 were arrested during a period of nineteen months. Among those arrested were also a large number of anti-social elements such as smugglers, hoarders, black marketeers and known goondas.

During the Emergency, parliament was made utterly ineffective. The opposition of a few brave MPs, who had not been arrested, was nullified as their speeches were not permitted to be reported in the Press. The state governments were rigidly controlled. The two non-Congress governments of DMK in Tamil Nadu and Janata in Gujarat were dismissed in January and March 1976 despite being quite compliant. The Congress chief ministers of Uttar Pradesh and Orissa, were replaced for not being reliable enough. The Congress party was also strictly controlled. Internal democracy within the party was more or less completely snuffed. From the second half of 1976 the Youth Congress led by Sanjay Gandhi became more important than the parent organization.

A series of decrees, laws and constitutional amendments reduced the powers of the judiciary to check the functioning of the executive. The Defence of India Act and MISA were amended in July 1975 to the detriment of the citizens' liberties. In November 1976, an effort was made to change the basic civil libertarian structure of the constitution through its 42nd Amendment. Putting an end to the judicial review of a constitutional amendment, because it was said that the judiciary was obstructing pro-poor socio-economic measures such as land reform legislation in the name of defending Fundamental Rights, it was laid down that there would be no limitation whatever on the power of parliament to amend the constitution. Fundamental Rights were indirectly emasculated by being made subordinate to an expanded version of the Directive Principles of State Policy embodied in the constitution.

Thus, the Emergency concentrated unlimited state and party power in the hands of the prime minister to be exercised through a small coterie of politicians and bureaucrats around her.

Public Response to the Emergency

While a section of the intelligentsia reacted to the Emergency with marked hostility, the large majority of the people initially responded to it with passivity, acquiescence, acceptance or even, support. It was only from the beginning of 1976 that the Emergency started becoming unpopular. Why was this delayed reaction? For one, the people had no experience in recent memory, that is, since independence, of an authoritarian rule. There was bewilderment as also personal fear of the unknown. Moreover, apart from the arrest of Opposition leaders, the repressive measures were almost entirely directed either against anti-social elements or against the extreme communal right or the minuscule far left, who had enjoyed little popular support before the Emergency and who were in any case known to be averse to democracy. The number of persons arrested in the first few days in the entire country was less than 10,000. But many of the detenus were released within a short span of time. Above all, a large number of people were impressed by the positive outcome of some of the well-publicized Emergency measures most of which could, of course, have been taken without an Emergency.

With the restoration of public order and discipline, many felt relieved that the country had been saved from disorder and chaos. There was less crime in the cities; gheraos and uncontrolled, often violent, demonstrations came to an end; there was a perceptible lessening of tension in the air; there was calm and tranquillity on the campuses as students and teachers went back to classrooms. Inder Malhotra, a perceptive journalist, was to write later: 'The return of normal and orderly life, after relentless disruption by strikes, protest marches, sit-ins and clashes with the police, was applauded by most people . . . In its initial months at least, the Emergency restored to India a kind of calm it had not known for years.'[4]

There was also an immediate and general improvement in administration, with government servants coming to office on time and being more considerate to the public. Quick, dramatic and well-publicized action was taken against smugglers, hoarders, black marketeers, illegal traders in foreign currency and tax evaders, with several thousand of them put behind bars under MISA. There was a major, dramatic improvement in the economy, though only some of it was really due to steps taken under the Emergency; some of it being the result of excellent rains and some, of the policies initiated much before the Emergency. Most welcome was the dramatic improvement in the price situation. Prices of essential goods, including foodstuffs, came down and their availability in shops improved.

Popular hopes were raised and the Emergency made more palatable by the announcement on 1 July of the omnibus Twenty-Point Programme by Mrs Gandhi, its edge being the socio-economic uplift of the vast mass of the rural poor. The programme promised to liquidate the existing debt of landless labourers, small farmers and rural artisans and extend alternative credit to them, abolish bonded labour, implement the existing agricultural land ceiling laws and distribute surplus land to the landless, provide house sites to landless labourers and weaker sections, revise upwards minimum wages of agricultural labour, provide special help to the handloom industry, bring down prices, prevent tax evasion and smuggling, increase production, streamline distribution of essential commodities, increase the limit of income tax exemption to Rs 8,000, and liberalize investment procedures.

Serious efforts were made to implement the Twenty-Point Programme; and some quick results were produced in terms of reduction of prices, free availability of essential commodities, and check on hoarding, smuggling and tax evasion. But the heart of the Twenty-Point Programme was its agenda of the uplift of the rural poor. Some progress was made even there. Three million house sites were provided to the landless and the Dalits. About 1.1 million acres of surplus land was distributed to the landless; this was, however, less than 10 per cent of the surplus land. Bonded labour was made illegal but little dent was made in the practice. Laws were passed in different states placing a moratorium on the recovery of debts from the landless labourers and small farmers and in some cases to scale down or liquidate their debts. But the scale of the alternative credit provided through nationalized banks and rural cooperative institutions was small and dependence on the usurious moneylenders, who were often also the big landowners, remained. Minimum wages for agricultural labourers were enhanced but their enforcement was again tardy. On the whole, however, the rural segment of the Twenty-Point Programme ran out of steam as its progress was hindered by large landowners and rich peasants and an unsympathetic bureaucracy. Consequently, though the programme brought some relief to the rural poor, there was little improvement in their basic condition.

A major factor in the people's acceptance of the Emergency was its constitutional, legal and temporary character. It was proclaimed under Article 352 of the constitution. It was approved by parliament and legitimized by the courts. To the people, it represented an interim measure, a temporary suspension of the normal rules and institutions of democracy. They did not see it as a substitute for democracy or as an attempt to impose a dictatorship. Throughout the Emergency, Mrs Gandhi asserted that she was fully committed to multi-party democracy and a free press, that the Emergency was an abnormal remedy for an abnormal situation, and that *democratic conditions would be restored and elections held* as soon as the situation returned to normal. The Indian people tended to take Mrs Gandhi at her word.

Towards Ending the Emergency

Within a few months, however, the people started getting disillusioned with the Emergency. Popular discontent from mid-1976 reached its zenith six months later. The reasons for this are varied.

Relief to the people did not last long. Economic growth of the first year of the Emergency was not sustained. Agricultural output declined; prices rose by 10 per cent by the end of 1976. The corrupt, black marketeers and smugglers resumed their activities as the shock of the Emergency wore off. The poor were disenchanted with the slow progress in their welfare and workers were unhappy because of limits on wages, bonus and dearness allowance and restrictions on the right to strike. Government servants and teachers became discontented because they were being disciplined in their workplaces and in many cases were being forced to fulfil sterilization quotas.

In fact, no real progress along the proclaimed lines was possible, for Mrs Gandhi and Congress failed to create any new agencies of social change or organs for popular mobilization. Reliance for the implementation of the Twenty-Point Programme and other developmental programmes was placed exclusively on the same old corrupt and inefficient bureaucracy and manipulative and discredited politicians. So far as the common people were concerned, matters took a turn for the worse, for there were no avenues of protest or any other mechanism for the voicing and redressal of their grievances. Even common people and not merely intellectuals and political workers lived in an atmosphere of fear and insecurity.

The bureaucracy and the police now got increased power that 'was unchecked by criticism and exposure from the Press, courts, MLAs and MPs, political parties and popular movements. The two set out to abuse this power in usual forms. This affected all but eventually the poor were the most affected. This was particularly true in northern India. Simultaneously, the drastic press censorship and the silencing of protest led to the government being kept in complete ignorance of what was happening in the country. Also, because the people knew that what appeared in the Press or on the radio was heavily censored, they no longer trusted them. They now relied much more on rumours and tended to believe the worst regarding the government's actions or intentions.

Denial of civil liberties began to be felt by the common people as it began to impact their daily lives in the form of harassment and corruption by petty officials. Delay in lifting the Emergency began to generate the fear that the authoritarian structure of the rule might be made permanent or continue for a long time, particularly as Mrs Gandhi had got parliament to postpone elections by one year in November 1976. The intelligentsia—teachers, journalists, professionals, and small town lawyers—and the middle classes in particular viewed the 42nd Amendment to the constitution, passed in September 1976, as an effort to subvert democracy by changing the very basic structure of the constitution. The Emergency, earlier acceptable, began to lose legitimacy.

A major reason for the growing unpopularity of the Emergency regime was, however, the development of an extra-constitutional centre of power associated with the rise to political power of Mrs Gandhi's younger son, Sanjay Gandhi, who held no office in the government or Congress. By April 1976, Sanjay Gandhi emerged as a parallel authority, interfering at will in the working of the government and administration. He was courted and obeyed by cabinet ministers, Congress leaders, chief ministers and senior civil servants. Within Congress, he emerged as the leader of the Youth Congress which soon rivalled the parent party in political weight.

In July 1976, Sanjay put forward his four points which gradually became more important than the official twenty points. The four points were: don't take dowry at the time of marriage; practise family planning and limit families to only two children; plant trees; and promote literacy. Sanjay Gandhi was also determined to beautify the cities by clearing slums and unauthorized structures impeding roads, bazaars, parks, monuments, etc.

Pushed by Sanjay Gandhi, the government decided to promote family planning more vigorously and even in an arbitrary, illegitimate and authoritarian manner. Incentives and persuasion were increasingly replaced by compulsion and coercion and above all by compulsory sterilization. Government servants, school teachers and health workers were assigned arbitrarily fixed quotas of number of persons they had to 'motivate' to undergo sterilization. The police and administration added their might to the enforcement of the quotas. The most affected were the rural and urban poor who often protested in all sorts of everyday ways, including recourse to flight, hiding and rioting. Moreover, in view of press censorship, stories, true and false, of forcible vasectomies and violent resistance by the people spread quickly and widely.

Slum clearance and demolition of unauthorized structures followed the pattern of the family planning programme but were enforced with even greater callousness and cruelty, though they affected mainly Delhi and a few other cities.

Thus, the already existing climate of fear and repression, corruption and abuse of authority was further worsened by the excesses committed under Sanjay Gandhi's direction.

Surprise Elections 1977

On 18 January 1977, Mrs Gandhi suddenly announced that elections to the Lok Sabha would be held in March. She also simultaneously released political prisoners, removed press censorship and other restrictions on political activity such as holding of public meetings. Political parties were allowed to campaign freely.

The elections were held on 16 March in a free and fair atmosphere, and when the results came in it was clear that Congress had been thoroughly defeated. Both Mrs Gandhi and Sanjay Gandhi lost their seats. Mrs Gandhi issued a statement accepting the verdict of the people with 'due humility'.

Why did Mrs Gandhi announce and then hold open and free elections? After all she had got parliament to postpone elections by one year only two months before in November 1976. There is up to now no satisfactory answer to the question, though there has been a great deal of speculation. Three broad explanations are offered.

First, the favourable view is that the decision was an expression of Mrs Gandhi's underlying commitment to liberal democracy and democratic values. Mary C. Carras, her biographer, has argued that, 'Throughout her life her self-image had been that of a democrat; indeed her self-respect derives in good part from this self-image . . . She was compelled to prove to the world and, above all, to herself, that she is and always has been a democrat.'[5] In the opinion of some other writers once Mrs Gandhi became aware of the Emergency excesses and realized that matters were getting out of her control, she decided to get out of this trap by holding elections even if it meant losing power.

The unfriendly view is that Mrs Gandhi completely misread the popular temper and, misinformed by sycophants and intelligence agencies, was convinced that she would win. Isolated from public opinion, she was unaware of the extent to which her rule had become unpopular. By winning the election she hoped to vindicate the Emergency and also clear the way for Sanjay Gandhi to succeed her.

The third view is that she realized that the policies of the Emergency had to be legitimized further through elections. The imposition of the Emergency had been legitimized at the outset by the constitutional provision, but that was not enough in view of the deep-seated traditions of the Indian people. Moreover, there were clear signs of restiveness and even discontent among the people. The Emergency regime, she must have realized, was increasingly getting discredited and was quite fragile. Either the authoritarian content of the Emergency would have to be deepened, with recourse to increasing ruthlessness and brutality in suppressing dissent, or greater legitimacy and political authority acquired by changing back to a democratic system. The former option would not work in a country of India's size and diversity and also in view of its democratic traditions. The people would not accept the level of repression that it would require.

During 1975–77, many Indians and India's friends abroad had doubts about the future of the democratic system in India, though they hoped that it would survive the political crisis. The less sympathetic said that democracy in India was 'permanently in eclipse' and that India had finally joined the ranks of other post-colonial societies as an authoritarian state. Many others said that the basic changes initiated by the Emergency and the essential features of the new kind of regime would continue even if the Emergency were ended and the parliamentary system restored. Some commentators went further and argued that the shift towards authoritarianism had been going on since 1950 and was inherent in a poor and illiterate society. Others held that the democratic constitutional system established in India in 1950 was not suited to the genius of India or the needs of its people. Still others felt that it was not possible to combine economic development with democracy. Many radicals argued that, in any case, liberal democracy was only a facade hiding the underlying brutal reality of class domination and the suppression of people's struggles. The Emergency had, therefore, only removed the facade; it did not mean any basic political change except that the social and political reality was now visible to all.

There were, of course, many in India and abroad who were convinced that the Emergency was a temporary departure from the basic commitment of the people of India and its political leadership to democracy and that democracy would be sooner or later restored in the country.

The democratic system in India not only survived the JP Movement and the Emergency but emerged stronger. Since 1977, all talk of the need for dictatorship to develop economically and to end corruption has died down. Those who hold this view have been reduced to a tiny minority and that too among the middle classes; no intellectual or political leader of any stature has espoused it for several years.

In this sense, the lifting of the Emergency and the free elections that followed were a defining moment in India's post-independence history. They revealed the Indian people's underlying attachment to democratic values which were in turn the result of the impact of the freedom struggle and the experience of democratic functioning, including free elections, since 1947. As Tariq Ali pointed out, in the elections of March 1977 'the urban and rural poor demonstrated in a very concrete and striking fashion that questions of basic civil rights were not merely the preoccupations of the urban middle classes'.[6] Inder Malhotra, covering the election campaign, reported of the 'truly remarkable' manner in which 'village audiences in the remote countryside react to sophisticated arguments about civil liberties, Fundamental Rights and independence of the judiciary'.[7]

Whatever the character of the JP Movement or of the Emergency regime, there is no doubt that the decision of Mrs Gandhi to hold genuinely free elections, and her defeat and the Opposition's victory that followed were a remarkable achievement of Indian democracy. The years 1975–77 have been described as the years of the 'test of democracy'; there is no doubt that the Indian people passed the test with distinction if not full marks.

The Janata Interregnum and Indira Gandhi's Second Coming, 1977–1984

Immediately after coming out of the jails in January 1977, the Opposition leaders announced the merger of Congress (O), the Jan Sangh, Bharatiya Lok Dal (BLD) and the Socialist Party into the new Janata Party. The Congress was dealt a blow by the sudden defection from it on 2 February 1977 of Jagjivan Ram, H.N. Bahuguna and Nandini Satpathy who formed the Congress for Democracy (CFD). Along with the DMK, Akali Dal and CPM it forged a common front with the Janata Party in order to give a straight fight to Congress and its allies, the CPI and AIADMK, in the March elections to the Lok Sabha.

The Opposition front made the Emergency and its excesses, especially forced sterilizations and the restriction of civil liberties, the major issues of its election campaign. The people also treated the elections as a referendum on the Emergency. With the popular upsurge in favour of them, the Janata Party and its allies were victorious with 330 out of 542 seats. Congress trailed far behind with only 154 seats, with the CPI its ally getting 7 and the AIADMK 21 seats. Congress was virtually wiped out in North India—it won only 2 out of 234 seats in seven northern states. Both Indira Gandhi and Sanjay were defeated. The electoral verdict was, however, mixed in western India. Surprisingly in the South, where the Emergency had been less vigorous, and the pro-poor measures of the Twenty-Point Programme better implemented, Congress improved its performance, winning 92 seats in place of 70 in 1971. Janata won only 6 seats in the four southern states. The CFD merged with the Janata Party immediately after the elections.

There was a near-crisis over the issue of prime ministership between the three aspirants, Morarji Desai, Charan Singh and Jagjivan Ram. The matter was referred to the senior leaders, Jayaprakash Narayan and J.B. Kripalani, who ruled in favour of the 81-year-old Desai, who was sworn in as prime minister on 23 March.

One of the first steps taken by the new government was to try to consolidate its hold over the states. Arguing that in those states where Congress had lost in the national elections, it had also lost the mandate to rule even at the state level, the government dismissed nine Congress-ruled state governments, and ordered fresh elections to their state assemblies. In the assembly elections, held in June 1977, Janata and its allies came out victorious in these states except in Tamil Nadu where AIADMK won. In West Bengal, the CPM, a Janata ally, gained an absolute majority.

Control over both parliament and the state assemblies enabled the Janata Party to elect unopposed its own candidate, N. Sanjeeva Reddy, as the President of the Union in July 1977.

The Janata government took immediate steps to dismantle the authoritarian features of the Emergency regime and to restore liberal democracy. It restored Fundamental Rights and full civil liberties to the Press, political parties and individuals. Through the 44th Constitutional Amendment, it also modified the 42nd Amendment passed during the Emergency, repealing those of its provisions which had distorted the constitution. The right of the Supreme Court and High Courts to decide on the validity of central or state legislation was also restored.

Janata Party in Crisis

The political support to the Janata regime, however, soon began to decline and disillusionment with it set in, given its non-performance in administration, implementation of developmental policies, and realization of social justice. The political momentum of the regime was lost by the end of 1977 and the uneasy coalition that was the Janata Party began to disintegrate, though the government remained in power till July 1979. By then the lack of confidence in its capacity to govern had begun to turn into anger, for several reasons. First, the Janata Party was not able to deal with the rapidly growing social tensions in rural areas, of which the increasing extent of atrocities on the rural poor and the Scheduled Castes was one manifestation. The Janata Party's social base in North India consisted primarily of rich and middle peasants belonging mostly to intermediate castes and large landowners belonging to upper castes and the urban and rural shopkeepers, small businessmen and the petty bourgeoisie. The rural landowners felt that with the Janata governments at the Centre and the states, they had now unalloyed power in the country as a whole and in rural areas in particular. On the other hand, the rural poor, mostly landless labourers and belonging largely to the Scheduled Castes, too had become conscious of their rights and felt emboldened by the prolonged functioning of democracy and adult franchise. They also defended and asserted the rights and benefits they had obtained under the Twenty-Point Programme. In many states landowners tried to forcibly take back the plots given to them and moneylenders began to reclaim debts cancelled during the Emergency. The result was the wide prevalence of caste tensions and violent attacks on the Scheduled Castes in North India, an early instance being the killing and torching of Harijans at Belchi in Bihar in July 1977.

There was a recrudescence of large-scale communal violence. There were growing agitations, lawlessness and violence which particularly affected colleges and universities, often leading to their closure. The middle of 1979 also witnessed a wave of strikes and mutinies by policemen and paramilitary forces.

Next, the Janata regime explicitly repudiated the Nehruvian vision of rapid economic development based on large-scale industry, modern agriculture, and advanced science and technology. But it failed to evolve any alternative strategy or model of economic and political development to deal with the problems of economic underdevelopment.

Janata's economic policy merely counterposed rural development to industry-oriented growth. This policy came to be based on three pillars: labour-intensive small-scale industry, not as complementary to but in place of large-scale industry; decentralization in place of national planning; and rich-peasant-led agricultural development based on generous subsidies, reduction in land revenue, and massive shift of resources from industry to the rural sector. This shift in economic policy was a recipe for low or non-economic development.

Interestingly, the Janata Party made no effort to fulfil its earlier radical demands for land reform and payment of higher wages to agricultural labourers. The one positive economic step that the Janata government did undertake was the effort to provide employment to the rural unemployed through the 'Food for Work' programme, which was used to improve village infrastructure such as roads, school buildings, etc., and which was particularly efficiently implemented by the CPM government in West Bengal.

After the first year of Janata rule, the economy started drifting with both agriculture and industry showing stagnation or low rates of growth. Severe drought conditions and devastating floods in several states affected agricultural production in 1978 and 1979. Prices began to rise sharply, especially as foodgrain stocks had been used up in the 'Food for Work' programme. International prices of petroleum and petroleum products again rose steeply. The heavy deficit financing in the 1979 budget, presented by Charan Singh as Finance Minister, also had a marked inflationary impact. The year 1979 also witnessed widespread shortages of kerosene and other goods of daily consumption. By the end of that year, inflation had gone beyond 20 per cent.

The Janata government's tenure was too brief for it to leave much of an impact on India's foreign policy, though while continuing to function within the existing, widely accepted framework, it did try to reorient foreign policy. It talked of 'genuine non-alignment' which meant strengthening ties with the US and Britain and moderating its close relations with the Soviet Union.

Holding the party together seems to have been a major preoccupation of the Janata leaders. Already disintegrating by the end of 1977, by 1978–79, the government, lacking all direction, was completely paralysed by the constant bickering and infighting in the party both at the Centre and in the states. Each political component tried to occupy as much political and administrative space as possible. In the ideological sphere, the Jan Sangh tried to promote its communal agenda via textbooks and recruitment to the official media, educational institutions and the police. The Janata Party remained a coalition of different parties and groups and was a victim of factionalism, manipulation and personal ambitions of its leaders. The different constituents were too disparate historically, ideologically and programmatically; bound only by an anti-Indira Gandhi sentiment and the desire for power.

The Jan Sangh, its best organized and dominant component with ninety MPs, was communal and populist with umbilical ties to the RSS which provided it with cadres and ideology and which was not willing to let it be incorporated in or integrated with other parties. Congress (O) was secular but conservative and basically Congress in mentality. BLD was secular, but a strictly rich-peasant party with no all-India or developmental vision. The Socialists were largely ideology-less and rootless except in Bihar.

The Revival of the Congress

In the meantime, the Congress witnessed both a split and a revival. Feeling that Indira Gandhi was not only a spent force but, much worse, a serious political liability, a large number of established Congress leaders, led by Y.B. Chavan and Brahmanand Reddy, turned against her. She, in turn, split the party in January 1978, with her wing being known as Congress (I) (for Indira), and the other later as Congress (U) (for Devraj Urs).

Thereafter, Indira Gandhi's political fortunes began to revive and in the February 1978 elections to state assemblies Congress (I) defeated both Janata and the rival Congress in Karnataka and Andhra. There were two reasons for this revival. One was the Janata government's effort to wreak vengeance on Indira Gandhi and punish her for the happenings of the Emergency. Several commissions of enquiry—the most famous being the Shah Commission—were appointed to investigate and pinpoint the malpractices, excesses, abuses and atrocities committed by Indira Gandhi and the officials during the Emergency. In 1979, special courts were set up to try her for alleged criminal acts during the Emergency. The common people, on the other hand, began to increasingly view Indira Gandhi's persecution not as justice but as revenge and vendetta and an effort to disgrace her. They felt she had already been punished enough by being voted out of power. Moreover, deep down, the rural and urban poor, Harijans, minorities and women still considered Indira Gandhi as their saviour, their Indira Amma or Mother Indira.

However, the government remained ignorant of Indira Gandhi's growing popularity, thanks to the bias of the Press against her. A dramatic demonstration of her growing popularity came when she won a parliament seat with a large margin from the Chikamagalur constituency in Karnataka in November 1978. Ironically, soon after, on 19 December, Janata used its majority to expel her from parliament for breach of privilege and contempt of the house on a minor charge and committed her to jail for a week.

The factional struggle in the Janata government and the party took an acute form in the middle of 1979. Charan Singh, the Home Minister, had been forced to resign from the cabinet on 30 June 1978 and was then brought back as Finance Minister in January 1979. He broke up the party and the government in July with the help of the Socialists, who walked out of the party and the government on the refusal of the Jan Sangh members to give up their dual membership of the Janata Party and the RSS. Having been reduced to a minority, Morarji Desai's government resigned on 15 July. A week later, Charan Singh formed the government in alliance with the Chavan-wing of Congress (U) and some of the Socialists and with the outside support of Congress (I) and the CPI. But he never got to face parliament as, on 20 August, a day before the confidence vote, Indira Gandhi withdrew her support after Charan Singh rejected her demand for the scrapping of special courts set up to prosecute her. On Charan Singh's advice, the President dissolved the Lok Sabha and announced mid-term elections.

The elections, held in January 1980, were fought primarily between Congress (I), Congress (U), the Lok Dal, the new party floated by Charan Singh and the Socialists, and Janata, now consisting primarily of the Jan Sangh and a handful of old Congressmen such as Jagjivan Ram and Chandra Shekhar; the CPM and CPI were not in the picture except in West Bengal and Kerala. Having been disenchanted with Janata's non-governance, lack of vision and incessant mutual quarrels, the people once again turned to Congress and Indira Gandhi, perceiving her Congress to be the real Congress.

The Janata Party's main appeal consisted of warnings against the threat to democracy and civil liberties if Indira Gandhi came back to power. Charan Singh talked of 'peasant raj'. Indira Gandhi concentrated on Janata's non-governance, asking the people to vote for 'a government that works'.

The people, once again cutting across caste, religion and region as in 1971 and 1977, gave a massive mandate to Congress (I), which secured 353 out of 529 seats, that is, a two-thirds majority.

The Lok Dal with 41, Janata with 31 and Congress (U) with 13 lagged far behind. The CPM and CPI alone withstood the Congress tide and won 36 and 11 seats respectively.

After the elections, the Janata Party split once again, with the old Jan Sangh leaders leaving it to form the Bharatiya Janata Party at the end of 1980 and Jagjivan Ram joining Congress (U).

Indira Gandhi's Return

After having been out of office for thirty-four months, Indira Gandhi was once again the prime minister and Congress was restored to its old position as the dominant party. Following the wrong precedent set up by the Janata government in 1977, the Congress government dissolved the nine state assemblies in the opposition-ruled states. In the assembly elections, subsequently held in June, Congress swept the polls except in Tamil Nadu. It now ruled fifteen of the twenty-two states.

Though once again the prime minister and the only Indian leader with a national appeal, Indira Gandhi was no longer the same person she had been from 1969 to 1977. She no longer had a firm grasp over politics and administration. Despite enjoying unchallenged power, she dithered in taking significant new policy initiatives or dealing effectively with a number of disturbing problems. She did, however, still manage some success in the fields of economic and foreign policy. But, on the whole, there was a lack of direction and a sense of drift, which led to a feeling among the people that not much was being achieved. The Emergency and the Janata years had left their mark on her. She was suspicious of people around her and trusted none but her son, Sanjay. Her earlier energy, decisiveness and determination were replaced by 'an approach of hesitation and caution'. As time passed she showed signs of being a tired person.

Besides, Indira Gandhi had few political instruments to implement her election promises. Most of the well-known and experienced national and state leaders and her colleagues of the past had deserted her during 1977–78. With a few exceptions, the political leaders around her, in the Centre as also in the states, were raw untried men and women, none of whom had a political base of their own and who had been chosen more for their loyalty than for their administrative or political capacities.

Sanjay Gandhi's death while flying a stunt plane on 23 June 1980 left her shaken and further weakened. She tried to fill his place with her elder son, Rajiv Gandhi, who was brought into politics, got elected as an MP and then appointed as the general secretary of the party in 1983.

Like the first one, a major weakness of Indira's second prime ministerial innings was the continuing organizational weakness of Congress and her failure to rebuild it and strengthen its structure. This inevitably affected the performance of the government and its popularity, for a weak party structure meant the choking of channels through which popular feelings could be conveyed to the leadership and the nature and rationale of government policies explained to the people.

Despite Indira Gandhi's total domination of the party and the government, the central leadership of the party again faced the problem of continuous factionalism and infighting—in fact, virtual civil war within the state units of the party and the state governments. One result of this infighting and the consequent frequent rise and fall of chief ministers was that party organizational elections were repeatedly postponed and, in the end, not held. Another result was the erosion of the feeling that Congress could provide state governments that worked. Organizational weakness also began to erode the party's support and adversely affect its electoral performance, with dissidents often sabotaging the prospects of the official party candidates.

An example of this erosion of the party's popularity was the serious electoral defeat it suffered in January 1983 in the elections to the state assemblies of Andhra and Karnataka, the two states which Congress had ruled continuously since their inception. In Andhra, Congress suffered a massive defeat at the hands of the newly formed Telugu Desam Party (TDP), led by the film-star-turned politician N.T. Rama Rao. The Congress won only 60 seats against TDP's 202. In Karnataka, a Janata-led front won 95 seats in the 224-seat assembly, with Congress getting 81 seats.

While facing hardly any challenge at the Centre from Opposition parties, from the beginning of her second prime ministership Indira Gandhi faced certain intractable problems arising out of communal, linguistic and caste conflicts; none of these was dealt with firmly and with insight and all of them were to drag on for years. Three of the most serious of these, Kashmir, Assam and Punjab, are discussed in other chapters in this book. Communalism grew stronger because of the momentum it gained during 1977–79. Its overt manifestation was communal riots, which spanned all the years from 1980 to 1984 and beyond and which began to engulf even South India.

Similarly, atrocities on the Scheduled Castes and Scheduled Tribes continued as they began to assert their social and constitutional rights. However, administrative and judicial action, which included long terms of imprisonment, was taken in some cases against the perpetrators of the atrocities.

Though hesitatingly, India once again resumed its tasks of planning and economic development, with greater financial allocations being made for the purpose. The government also took note of the changes in world economy and their impact on India and, while making efforts to strengthen the public sector, initiated measures for what has come to be known as economic liberalization. But, the government proceeded very gradually and hesitatingly because Indira Gandhi was worried about the role of multinational corporations in eroding India's self-reliance. The government, however, succeeded in raising the rate of economic growth to over 4 per cent per year, with a large increase in agricultural and petroleum crude production, and in gradually bringing down the rate of inflation to 7 per cent in 1984.

Indira Gandhi's government also achieved some success in foreign policy. In March 1983, India hosted the seventh summit of the Non-Aligned Movement with Indira Gandhi as its chairman. As formal leader of the Non-Aligned Movement she actively worked for a new international economic order that would be more fair to the developing countries.

When on 26 December 1979 the Soviet Union sent its troops into Afghanistan to help its beleaguered government, Mrs Gandhi refused to condemn the action but, at the same time, she advised the Soviet Union to withdraw its troops from Afghanistan as speedily as possible. She, however, opposed the indirect intervention in Afghanistan's civil war by the United States and Pakistan. Mrs Gandhi's stand on the Afghanistan issue was determined by India's long-term friendship and 'special' relationship with the Soviet Union and India's strategic interest in preventing Afghanistan from having an administration hostile to India.

Indira Gandhi tried to improve India's relations with the US despite its tilt towards Pakistan. She also tried to normalize relations with China and Pakistan, despite the latter's support to the terrorists in Punjab. She did not, however, hesitate to order the army in April 1984 to deploy a brigade at the Siachen glacier along the Line of Control (LoC) in Kashmir.

On the morning of 31 October 1984, Indira Gandhi's long tenure as prime minister was brought to an end by her assassination by two Sikh members of her security guard. The Congress Parliamentary Board immediately nominated her forty-year-old son, Rajiv Gandhi, as prime minister.

Indira Gandhi—An Evaluation

Any assessment of Indira Gandhi has to acknowledge that she was a highly complex person, full of contradictions, which made her extremely controversial. During her twenty years in power she made immense contributions and exhibited many remarkable features of her political personality and approach. Of course, there were major weaknesses, but these, as well as her strengths, are to be seen in light of how she changed over the years.

Indira Gandhi possessed great political skill which she continuously developed over time as she faced new situations and challenges. Though in the habit of soliciting opinion and advice from all around her, she herself invariably made the final decision. For all of her political life, Indira Gandhi conducted herself with fierce courage. She, as also her political opponents, were quite conscious of this quality of hers. Possessed of extraordinary will, as a political fighter Indira Gandhi was tough, resolute, decisive and, when necessary, ruthless. Though quite cautious by nature and temperament, when necessary she acted boldly, swiftly, with a superb sense of timing, and decisively, as for example in the case of the Congress split in 1969, the Bangladesh crisis in 1971, the defiance of the US decision to send the Seventh Fleet to the Bay of Bengal in December 1971, the creation of the Punjabi Suba in 1966, the imposition of the Emergency in 1975, and the Janata's persecution of her through enquiry commissions during 1977–79.

A major feature of Indira Gandhi's politics was her identification with and her passionate love of the country and its people, her pride in India's greatness and confidence in its future. Indira Gandhi was acutely aware of India's national interests and committed to maintaining its prestige among the community of nations.

Fully realizing that real national greatness and independence lie in a country's inherent strength, she strove hard and successfully, in the face of many dire domestic economic and political problems, to make India economically, politically, culturally, technologically and militarily self-reliant and independent and to give the country confidence in its ability to do so. India under her leadership was one of the few countries to overcome the oil shock of the 1970s. The success of the Green Revolution made India self-sufficient in foodgrains and broke its dependence on food imports. Throughout the Nehru and Indira Gandhi years India was shielded from the recessionary cycles common in other capitalist economies.

Indira Gandhi used her firm grasp of world politics to ensure that there was no successful overt or covert foreign interference in India's internal affairs. She kept India free of both the Cold War blocs and the two superpowers. While adhering to the policy of not going nuclear, she refused to sign the nuclear non-proliferation treaty even though it was sponsored by both the United States and the Soviet Union. She strengthened the foreign policy carefully crafted by Nehru.

Indira Gandhi also actively promoted the process of nation-in-the-making, strengthened the country's unity, held it together during a difficult period, and in the end gave her life for the purpose. With all her flaws and failures, she left the country stronger and more self-confident than it was when she took command of it in 1966.

Indira Gandhi was pragmatic and lacked Nehru's ideological moorings, but she remained committed to a progressive, reformist, left-of-centre political orientation. In the economic field she remained loyal to the Nehruvian objective of rapid economic development and strengthened planning and the public sector while maintaining a mixed economy and, except for the brief period of 1971–74, a healthy private sector though under rigid state control. She, however, tried to relax this control gradually—perhaps too gradually—during 1980–84.

Ideologically, she remained true to the national movement's secular tradition and consistently opposed the communal forces, looking upon the RSS, in particular, as a great menace to the unity and integrity of the country and to its democratic polity. Her firm commitment to secularism was shown by her insistence on making Dr Zakir Hussain, a Muslim, the country's President and when she countermanded the order to remove from duty her Sikh security guards in October 1984, on the ground that India was a secular country. For the latter decision she paid with her life.

Indira Gandhi's major political asset was her empathy and affection for the poor, the underprivileged and the minorities, concern for their social condition and an unmatched capacity to communicate directly with them. The poor, in turn, almost throughout her political career, looked upon her as their saviour and gave her immense love and trust. There is also no doubt that Indira Gandhi played an important role in politicizing the people, especially in making the poor, the Harijans and tribals, the minorities and women aware of their social condition and its underlying unjust character, and in arousing consciousness of their interests and the political power that inhered in them.

However, in spite of all the power that she wielded for over sixteen years, Indira Gandhi achieved little in terms of institutional development, administrative improvement, management of the political system and far-reaching socio-economic change. Her crucial weakness as a political leader lay in the absence of any strategic design and long-term perspective around which her economic, political and administrative policies were framed. As mentioned earlier, she was a master of political tactics and their timing, without match among her contemporaries. But her brilliant tactics were at no stage components of a pre-conceived strategy. Even the imposition of the Emergency was not part of an alternative strategic design for managing the political system but merely an *ad hoc* response to a situation of crisis. But tactics, however sound, cannot suffice in themselves. They are the short-term, issue-to-issue policies through which a strategy is implemented. Without a strategy, tactics, however brilliant, hang in the air. They do not even help formulate policies which are adequate to the achievement of the proclaimed objectives of a leadership or which enable it to move a country towards the desired destination.

In economic development and foreign policy, the Nehruvian strategies were there to guide her and after some initial vacillation Indira Gandhi went back to them. For management of the political system, or even overcoming the instability of the state, or development of the administrative structure or at least preventing its downslide, there were no clear-cut or specific strategies upon which to fall back and Indira Gandhi failed to evolve any of her own. She did not creatively develop Nehru's strategy even in the field of economic policy to meet a changed national and world economic situation as is evident from her hesitant efforts to relax the licence–quota–regulation regime. Similarly, she failed to evolve a strategic framework to deal with communalism and separatism, resulting in her failure to deal effectively with the Punjab, Assam and Kashmir problems.

The consequences of Indira Gandhi's failure to evolve and function within a strategic framework were felt in several other fields also. Despite massive electoral majorities, Indira Gandhi was not able to make the institutional changes in political or governmental apparatus—parliament, cabinet, police or bureaucracy or Congress party or the educational system—needed to implement her own agenda. Not only did she not build any new institutions or make any effort to reform or strengthen old ones, much worse, she made little effort to check the erosion in most institutions and, in fact, contributed to the decay of some. As a result, increasingly over time, Indira Gandhi came to rely on personal power rather than on political and administrative institutions. She concentrated and centralized authority and decision-making in the party and the government in her hands. She systematically undermined her own party leaders who had an independent political base of their own, and chose as chief ministers persons who could not survive without her support. One result of this was that the power and influence of the chief ministers declined over the years. Moreover, not having a political base of their own, these candidates were victims of continuous factionalism in the party at the state level. Indira Gandhi was forced to replace them frequently, creating instability in the administration and the party organization in the state. Her time was taken up in day-to-day fire-fighting of problems relating to the party and government management; she had no time for evolving strategies and broader policy frameworks for dealing with the serious problems of the country or the party.

It is significant that the only major institution she built up was that of the Prime Minister's Secretariat, which she had inherited from Shastri and which became an independent bureaucratic source of policy, advice and initiative and decision-making, thus severely undermining the autonomous role of the cabinet members.

Nevertheless, despite all the concentration of power in her hands, it would be wrong to say that Indira Gandhi was undemocratic or tried or even wanted to impose an authoritarian regime. Except for the period 1975–77, she functioned within the parliamentary framework and played an important role in India remaining on the democratic path. She accepted, even when she did not like it, the authority of the judiciary. She did not tinker with the Press, even when it subjected her to calumnies, or with academic freedom, even when a large number of academic intellectuals had become severe critics of her. Even the Emergency was imposed in accord with the provisions of the constitution. Moreover, it was she who lifted the Emergency, announced and held elections, gracefully accepted the verdict of the vote and gave up power—a feat rarely, if at all, performed by dictators.

An example of Indira Gandhi's failure to build up institutions was in respect of the Congress party. She had hardly any capacity or even time for party organization, but was not willing to share the task with others. Even though she replenished the party's social support base, she failed to reorganize and revitalize it after the 1969 split. As a result, it was unable to keep contact with the people except during the elections; and as an organization it gradually decayed, especially at the local and state levels. She ruled supreme in the party—she virtually nominated the party president, members of its Working Committee, heads of its state units and other party organizations. There was also hardly any inner-party democracy and debate on issues, not to speak of criticism of the central leadership. The culture of sycophancy prevailed even after the death of Sanjay Gandhi. However, despite her total supremacy, Indira Gandhi could not prevent the prevalence of intense factionalism in the party at the local and state levels. And, many a time, sycophants turned into rebels and party-splitters when frustrated in their hopes.

Once again, political and tactical skill enabled Indira Gandhi to manage and control the party but she could not accomplish the strategic task of reinvigorating it or building it up as an organization. She did succeed in reaching out to the people and establishing direct contact with them, but only through populist measures and only during electoral campaigns and mass meetings. This could enable her and the party to have dominance in the legislatures and over the government, but it did not make it possible for the party to exercise political hegemony among the people outside the legislatures or keep for long the support gained at the polls. Consequently, through most of her prime ministerial period she was troubled and harassed by popular movements and agitations.

Even though providing some succour and benefits to the poor and oppressed, Indira Gandhi failed to fulfil her promise of bringing about radical socio-economic change or combining economic growth with social justice. In spite of her long tenure, the economy and society did not move much towards greater social and economic equality. In fact, quite the reverse; India of 1984 was more not less inequitable than India of 1966.

This incapacity to move India in the direction of greater egalitarianism was further intensified by her failure to reshape Congress into a popular instrument of political education and *mobilization and an agent of social and political transformation.* Congress continued to harbour strongly conservative as also radical elements. While the poor and the deprived gave her and Congress massive electoral support in 1971, 1972 and 1980, the composition and structure of the party continued unchanged and perhaps even worsened with the induction of black money and criminals into parties and politics.

A giant of a person, with many strengths and many weaknesses, Indira Gandhi strode the Indian political stage after independence longer than any other leader—longer than even her father—and she was fully justified in telling a friend a few days before her assassination: 'Whatever happens to me—I feel I have paid all my debts.'[1] And India and its people were surely richer for her having done so.

The Rajiv Years

Assuming Office

Rajiv, son of Indira Gandhi and grandson of Jawaharlal Nehru, became prime minister of India on the night of 31 October 1985. That morning, Indira had begun to walk from her home to her office to keep an appointment for a television interview with Peter Ustinov. Instead, she met her fate in the person of two Sikh guards who shot at her to take revenge for her ordering the storming of the Golden Temple to flush out Sikh terrorists in June 1984. By the afternoon, Indira was declared dead and, while Rajiv was away in West Bengal, senior Congress leaders had (with the concurrence of the President, Giani Zail Singh, who had rushed back from Yemen) decided to ask Rajiv to become prime minister. A reluctant Rajiv, persuading an even more reluctant Sonia, his Italian-born wife, accepted this decision which would ultimately lead to his tragic death six and a half years later at the hands of a Tamil terrorist suicide bomber.

Rajiv Gandhi, a pilot with Indian Airlines for fourteen years, had kept studiously aloof from politics till the death of his younger brother, Sanjay, in an air crash in June 1980. After Sanjay's death, Indira persuaded him to help her and in June 1981 he formally entered politics by getting elected to the Lok Sabha from Amethi, the constituency in Uttar Pradesh vacated by Sanjay's death. He was placed in charge of organizing the Asian Games in New Delhi in 1982, and by all accounts did a commendable job. In February 1983, he became one of the seven new general secretaries of the Congress, with the responsibility of rejuvenating the Congress at the grassroots, the urgency of the task having been brought home by losses in provincial elections. But the gradual apprenticeship to politics was cut short and he was catapulted into the driving seat. With elections due in a few months, Congress leaders naturally wanted someone who could rally the people. Rajiv, in their judgement, was most likely to harness the sympathy wave generated by Indira's martyrdom.

In the event, they turned out to be correct, and the Congress won by its largest ever majority in the general elections held from 24 to 27 December 1984, a little earlier than scheduled. If the seats won in the polls held later in Punjab and Assam are counted, the party garnered 415 out of 543 Lok Sabha seats. Rajiv himself won by a huge margin from Amethi in Uttar Pradesh, in the process defeating conclusively Sanjay's wife, Maneka, who wanted to establish her claim to Sanjay's legacy. The Congress election campaign had focussed on the threat to India's unity and integrity and, since Indira's death was seen by people as proof of the threat, the response was enormous. The huge majority also meant high, even unreal, expectations, which Rajiv himself once described as 'scary'.[1]

In fact, Rajiv was faced with major crises from the outset. He had hardly any time to come to terms with the personal grief of his mother's violent death. As the dignitaries from across the world were arriving in Delhi for Indira Gandhi's funeral, a horrific massacre of Sikhs in revenge for her assassination was taking place in the city, especially on its outskirts in the 'resettlement colonies' where the poorer sections lived. From 31 October, the day of Indira's death, to 3 November, many Sikhs were attacked, their businesses and houses looted and burnt, and around 2,800 killed.[2] The perpetrators were the poor, usually slum-dwellers, who looked upon Indira as their leader and sympathizer, and were disoriented by her violent death. It has also been alleged that Congress party workers and even some local-level leaders were involved in assisting and guiding the crowd, and that the police at the local level turned a blind eye to what was going on. This allegation has sometimes been enlarged into a broader charge that the Congress, with directions from the top, organized the massacre, a charge that is obviously unfounded and has been impossible to prove. It is also true that thousands of Sikhs were sheltered and protected by Hindu friends and neighbours. The government's delay in bringing the situation under control can only be explained by the confusion following Indira's assassination, with the swearing-in of the new prime minister, the responsibility of arranging the funeral, which was attended by thousands of people, and looking after the foreign guests. It also took a while for the full import of the scale of the massacre to be communicated and understood at the higher levels of the government. On 3 November, the day of the funeral, Rajiv visited some of the affected areas in the morning, and later the army was called in and the violence suppressed. Many voluntary agencies, whose personnel were generally Hindu, worked for months to bring relief to the families of victims. Similar violence, though on a smaller scale, broke out in some other North Indian cities, especially Kanpur and Bokaro.

Within two weeks of his becoming prime minister, there occurred the Bhopal gas leak tragedy, in which around 2,000 people, mostly poor slum-dwellers, lost their lives and many thousands more were taken ill because of poisonous emissions from a chemicals factory run by Union Carbide, a multinational company. The legal battle for compensation dragged on for years in Indian and US courts, and the final settlement was not a generous one, and was further bogged down in bureaucratic delays due to difficulties of identifying the sufferers.

The First Round

Despite these travails, Rajiv's administration took off on a positive note, and a number of policy initiatives were launched. At the political level, he set in motion the process that culminated in the Punjab and Assam accords, which have been discussed elsewhere in the book. But perhaps his most well-known initiative was the setting up of six 'technology missions', something that for many Indians epitomized the new, modern and technological approach of the youthful prime minister. The idea was to apply science and technology to six areas of underdevelopment in which a scientific approach would be useful in solving problems. These target-oriented projects were designated as 'technology missions' and in most cases the arrival of the millennium was set as the target date, the idea being that India must enter the new millennium as a modern nation. The most important of these was the drinking water mission, whose aim was to provide drinking water to all Indian villages, only one-fifth of which had potable water supplies. The idea was to use satellites and the disciplines of geology, civil engineering and biochemistry for identifying, extracting and cleaning water supplies. The literacy mission was aimed at attacking the serious problem of mass illiteracy which almost forty years after independence afflicted almost 60 per cent of the population. This was to be achieved by making use of and extending the television network in rural areas, as well as by using video and audio cassettes and other methods. In fact, this was probably in the long run the most significant of the missions, as the Total Literacy Campaign that it spawned made a major dent in many regions and brought the whole issue to the centre of political debate. The third mission was targeted at the immunization of pregnant women and children, again an idea that has caught on and is pursued *with greater vigour today with the mass campaign for immunization* of children against polio being a recent example. The fourth mission was to promote the 'White Revolution', or milk production, by improving the milk yield and health of cows and buffaloes, and this was remarkably successful. India imported a large quantity of edible oils, which added considerably to her foreign exchange deficit, and the fifth mission was charged with the task of expanding edible oil production. The aim of the sixth mission was to bring one telephone to every village in the country by the end of the century.

The man who inspired and helped implement the technology-mission approach was Sam Pitroda, a young US-trained Indian telecommunications expert who had made a fortune in the US from telephone switching systems. He had convinced Mrs Gandhi of the need to set up C-DOT or the Centre for the Development of Telematics, and he now became Rajiv's adviser on technology missions, and Telecom Commission chairman.

A big push was also given by Rajiv to India's computerization programme, which was already being formulated under Mrs Gandhi. Import duties on components were reduced so that domestic producers could enhance production, foreign manufacturers were allowed to enter the home market so that quality and competitive prices were ensured, and use of computers in offices and schools was encouraged. Realizing that the future was at stake, Rajiv ignored much ill-informed debate about the utility of computers in a labour-surplus society, and went ahead with the policy that has stood the country in very good stead, with computer software emerging as a major foreign exchange earner. India had missed out on the industrial revolution because of its colonial status, and it was imperative that she take part in the information and communication revolution (this was a view held by many far-sighted Indians, and Rajiv shared it and put his weight behind the effort to make it come real). Efforts at liberalization of controls in the economy as a whole, increase of exports, reduction of import duties, etc. were also made, and these have been discussed elsewhere in the book.

Much lip-service had been paid to the need for doing something to strengthen local self-government institutions. It was Rajiv and his government that took the initiative to deepen and strengthen panchayati institutions by generating debate and bringing forward legislation to make panchayat elections mandatory by giving them a constitutional sanction. This necessitated a constitutional amendment and it was Rajiv's great regret that the Opposition parties, for no good reason, blocked the passage of the bills in the Rajya Sabha where the Congress did not have a majority. As striking as the objective was the process. Between December 1987 and June 1988, Rajiv met 400 district collectors or officers in charge of districts. In July 1988 there was a meeting with chief secretaries, the highest officers of states, in January 1989 a Panchayati Raj Sammelan of 8,000 delegates, followed by a conference on Panchayati Raj for Women in May. The All India Congress Committee discussed and supported the proposals in May 1989, and a meeting of chief ministers of states was held thereafter. Rajiv could claim with some justice, as he did, that 'never before has a government at the highest level taken so carefully into account the views of so many tens of thousands of people at every level about democracy and development at the grassroots'.[3]

Another measure directed at the rural poor was the Jawahar Rozgar Yojana or Employment Plan which aimed at providing employment to at least one member of every rural poor family for 50–100 days in the year. Inaugurated to mark the birth centenary of Jawaharlal Nehru (born in 1889), the central government promised to meet 80 per cent of the cost of the scheme. The new education policy, too, had its focus on the rural areas and the poor, with its main planks being the literacy campaign, Operation Blackboard (which aimed at providing basic amenities to schools) and distance education. The much-reviled Navodaya Vidyalayas, a favourite whipping boy of Rajiv baiters, and cited *ad nauseum* as proof of the elitist nature of Rajiv's education policy, were in fact aimed at providing quality education to the children of poor rural families who were to be chosen by merit for free education and stay in the residential schools to be set up in every district.

The National Perspective Plan for Women was drafted in 1988, and among its important proposals was the reservation of 30 per cent of elected seats for women in all panchayat bodies, which was included in the Panchayati Raj legislation. It also recommended that 50 per cent of grassroots functionaries should be women. The plan addressed issues of women's health and education as well. Legislation strengthening the punishment for dowry-related offences was also passed in 1986.

The protection of the environment was a project close to Rajiv's heart as it had been to his mother's, and among other things he launched a massive effort to clean the river Ganga, the holiest of Indian rivers, which had become shamefully polluted in many parts. He created a new Ministry of Environment and environmental clearance for big projects was made mandatory. At the Non-Aligned Movement's ninth summit, he placed before it the proposal for a Planet Protection Fund to help developing countries access advanced technology for the protection of the environment.

While it became quite fashionable in certain elite circles to berate the cultural policy of the Rajiv government as catering to the West by holding very expensive festivals of India in many Western countries, it was forgotten that at the same time seven zonal cultural centres were set up in different parts of the country to shift the focus of state patronage of the arts away from the capital and encourage local and regional cultural forms. Also, whatever their criticism (there is some truth in the charge of over-enthusiasm leading to precious cultural property being transported abroad and suffering damage, though whether this was a special feature of Rajiv's regime is suspect) the festivals did succeed in placing India on the world cultural map. If one of the legitimate functions of a government is to enhance the standing of the country it governs on the world stage, then the festivals of India fulfilled that function.

There appeared to be a serious effort to clean up the political and bureaucratic system, by introducing greater openness, accountability, and taking legislative and other measures to dissuade offenders. Among these was the Anti-Defection Act, drafted after discussions with Opposition parties and passed in 1985, which laid down that one-third of the members of a political party in parliament would have to change loyalties for it to be recognized as a split in a party. Any other defections would invite expulsion from the house. This was meant to check the tendency of horse-trading and shifting party loyalties that was becoming a bane of the Indian political system. Lok Adalats, and the Consumer Protection Act were part of the same stream. Greater freedom to government media, especially the increasingly popular television, and encouragement to programmes critical of government and intended to keep ministers and bureaucrats on their toes, carried the prime minister's personal imprint.[4] V.P. Singh's much-advertised raids on business houses, which Rajiv supported, certainly in the beginning, also helped provide the ambience that gave Rajiv the Mr Clean label.

But it was his speech at the centenary celebrations of the Congress in December 1985 that really shook critics and admirers (and at that time there were more admirers than critics, as Rajiv enjoyed a honeymoon for the first eighteen months of his term). Rajiv used the occasion to launch a frontal attack on what he described as the power-brokers who had reduced the great party to a shell of its former self, and promised to rejuvenate it by removing their stranglehold. This was read as a signal to the old leaders to get their act together or else. Many partymen who were otherwise sympathetic to Rajiv's policies did not appreciate his 'disrespectful' style and thought the centenary of the grand old party an inappropriate occasion for this exercise. However, Rajiv was no more successful at holding elections within the party than was his mother or his successor as Congress prime minister. The hold of party bosses at the local level meant that they could register bogus members and manipulate elections, and in the process acquire further legitimacy by virtue of being elected! Rajiv soon also found that he needed to build links with party stalwarts and politics was different from running an efficient corporation. Over time, and partly as his own close advisers, Arun Nehru, Arun Singh and V.P. Singh, were estranged, he brought back old advisers. The process reached full circle in early 1989 with the return of R.K. Dhawan, Mrs Gandhi's close adviser, who epitomized the old system that Rajiv had vowed in his innocence in December 1985 to overturn!

Foreign Policy Initiatives

Rajiv pursued foreign affairs with the energy of an activist, travelling extensively to countries big and small, and participating in a wide range of international fora. He put his own personal stamp on foreign policy, even while pursuing the well-laid-out path of his grandfather and mother. This he did by zealously advocating the causes of nuclear disarmament and the fight against apartheid in South Africa and of Namibian independence. A little while before her death, Indira had formed the Six-Nation Five-Continent Initiative, bringing together heads of government of Argentina, Greece, Mexico, Sweden, Tanzania and India, to put international pressure on the superpowers to reduce weapons and eliminate nuclear weapons. Within a month of winning the elections, Rajiv held the first summit of the six leaders. It is important to remember that this was before Gorbachev's assumption of power and before disarmament was on the agenda of superpower relations. Rajiv met Gorbachev after he took over the reins in the USSR, and found in him a believer in disarmament. In fact, Rajiv began to hail Gorbachev as a force for peace much before the US woke up to the new leader's new ideas. In November 1986, on the occasion of Gorbachev's visit, he and Rajiv gave a call for a non-violent world, and the Delhi Declaration, as the programme came to be called, set forth a plan for disarmament. The Six Nation Initiative too matured into an Action Plan for Nuclear Disarmament, which Rajiv then presented to the UN General Assembly's third special session on disarmament in June 1988. This plan called for the elimination of all nuclear weapons by 2010.

Close to Rajiv's heart was the struggle against apartheid in South Africa. In keeping with tradition (Gandhiji was the first to take up the issue in South Africa in 1893, and Nehru the first to raise it in the UN in the late 1940s, and India the first country to apply sanctions by breaking off trade and diplomatic links), Rajiv took up the cause with fervour, even succeeding in getting the majority in the Commonwealth in favour of sanctions but failing to move an obdurate Mrs Thatcher. More successful was the setting up of the AFRICA (Action for Resisting Invasion, Colonialism and Apartheid) Fund at the Non-Aligned Summit at Harare in 1986. By the Belgrade Non-Aligned Summit meeting three years later, he was able to show a collection of half a billion dollars given by developing and developed countries to help the frontline African states overcome the losses they suffered because of sanctions against South Africa.

Namibian independence was a closely associated cause, Namibia being held as a colony by South Africa. Rajiv extended diplomatic recognition to SWAPO, the organization fighting for Namibian independence, and visited the frontline states of Zambia, Zimbabwe, Angola and Tanzania in May 1986, besides adding his voice to the cause at all international gatherings. Namibia got independence in 1990, by which time Rajiv was no longer prime minister, but he attended the celebrations, where he met Nelson Mandela, and thus was able to witness the success of two favourite causes.

Relations with the superpowers improved during Rajiv's tenure, but did not undergo any major change. Contrary to speculation based on the young prime minister's preference for open-market policies and a technocratic bias, Rajiv did not tilt towards the US. His visit to the US in 1985 was a successful one, and he got along well with Reagan, even persuading him to let India have the supercomputer India had been wanting for processing weather data. But with the US committed to supporting Pakistan to promote the Mujahideen against the USSR in Afghanistan, there was little chance of any radical shifts. With Gorbachev, however, a very close relationship developed, and the two leaders met a total of eight times in five years.

Rajiv's visit to China in 1988, the first by an Indian prime minister since Nehru's maiden visit in 1954, was remarkable in that it happened at all. It was also made memorable by television images of Deng holding on to Rajiv's hand for what seemed like an eternity, and by his referring to mistakes made by people of his generation which the new generation represented by Rajiv Gandhi should not repeat. The importance of this meeting was also because there had been a sudden dip in relations in 1986 following some border incidents. The visit was followed by efforts to solve long-standing problems on a regular basis, improvement of trade and extension of consular contacts. India even refrained from condemning the Tiananmen Square massacre of 4 June 1989, clear proof that recent improvements in relations were sought not to be jeopardized.

With immediate neighbours, relations were not very good during Rajiv's time. Bangladesh was moving in a more and more Islamic direction, and disputes over water continued. With Nepal there was trouble when it imposed heavy duties on Indian goods, gave discounts in duties to Chinese goods, received, in 1988, huge amounts of assault rifles and anti-aircraft guns from China and asked Indian residents to get work permits for working in Nepal (this when lakhs of Nepalis work and live in India without any permits). The Indian government imposed what amounted to an economic blockade in March 1989, and by September negotiations for a solution began. Maldives faced a coup attempt, asked for Indian help, which was given and the attempt scotched. With Pakistan, things were much the same despite hopes aroused by Benazir Bhutto becoming prime minister, and Rajiv visiting Pakistan (the first prime minister to do so after Nehru), what with Pakistani support to insurgency in Kashmir and Punjab continuing apace.

In Sri Lanka, however, India got involved in a messy situation from which India found it difficult to extricate herself. The problem began when thousands of Tamils from Sri Lanka fled to Tamil Nadu in India in 1983 when the Sri Lankan government launched heavy repression on Jaffna, the base of the Liberation Tigers of the Tamil Eelam (LTTE), an organization fighting for Tamil autonomy and later, independence from Sri Lanka. Public opinion in India, especially in Tamil Nadu, whose people spoke the same language as the refugees, was strongly in favour of India doing something to help the Sri Lankan Tamils. Passions were further roused when Sri Lanka imposed a blockade on Jaffna, preventing daily necessities from reaching people. India sent supplies in fishing boats but the Sri Lankan Navy stopped them. This was followed by air-dropping of supplies by Indian transport planes, which carried Indian and foreign journalists as well. Sri Lanka realized it had gone too far and permitted supplies by boat. But the problem of Tamil insurgency was continuing, and the Sri Lankan government realized that no country other than India could help. President Jayewardene approached Rajiv, and the negotiations led to an accord in July 1987 by which the northern and eastern provinces of Sri Lanka where Tamils were the majority would be merged into a single province, substantial devolution of power would take place, the LTTE would be dissolved and arms surrendered in a very short time, and the Indian army would come to the aid of the Sri Lankan government if requested by Sri Lanka. The accord failed to take off because the LTTE had given only reluctant consent, was not a signatory, did not trust the Sri Lankan government and refused to surrender. Jayewardene, in the meantime, asked for the Indian army to help implement the accord, and since it was the LTTE that was standing in the way, the army got involved in an increasingly messy fight with the Tamil guerrillas, who had an edge since they knew the terrain and had local support. The Indian army was in an unenviable position with Tamils resenting it because it was disarming the LTTE, and Sri Lankans resenting it for being a foreign army. The situation got even messier with Premadasa succeeding Jayewardene and asking the Indian government to withdraw its army. Rajiv agreed to a phased withdrawal, and the soldiers started to come home in mid-1989, but withdrew fully only after the 1989 elections. The Sri Lankan imbroglio was to cost Rajiv his life.

India played a major role in negotiating the Vietnamese withdrawal from Kampuchea (Cambodia). It was reminiscent of Nehru's days when India was called upon to play the role of the honest broker in Southeast Asia, Korea, Congo, and so on. In January 1987, Vietnam let it be known to India that it wanted to withdraw from Kampuchea which it had occupied a few years ago and that it wished India to work out the modalities in consultation with other countries. Natwar Singh, the Minister of State for External Affairs, did a lot of shuttle diplomacy in Southeast Asia, met the deposed Kampuchean ruler Prince Sihanouk a number of times in Paris, and arranged meetings between Sihanouk and Heng Samarian. As a settlement approached, the US and China got into the act and tried to sideline India. A twenty-one nation meeting was held in Paris, to which India was invited, and the settlement resulted in Vietnamese withdrawal, elections under UN auspices, and installation of a coalition government of Sihanouk and Heng Samarian.

Rajiv Gandhi gave a new life to the Non-Aligned Movement (NAM) by giving it a purpose: nuclear disarmament. He also tried to promote the idea of a G-15, a more compact version of G-77, which approximated more closely to the G-7. He placed India quite prominently on the world map, making her presence felt in a variety of fora on a number of issues. He travelled abroad on an average once a month during his five-year term, even inviting snipes from political opponents about his 'occasional visits to India'.

In keeping with his effort to build India's image in the community of nations, Rajiv was also committed to maintaining and enhancing Indian security. He gave the go-ahead to the modernization of the armed forces, which led to the doubling of the defence expenditure. The guided missile development programme, initiated by Mrs Gandhi in 1983, began to show results and two short-range missiles, Trishul and Prithvi, and one intermediate-range missile, Agni, in which Rajiv had taken great interest, were successfully tested. The Indian Navy was considerably expanded with the lease of a nuclear-powered submarine from the USSR and the purchase of a second aircraft carrier from Britain. The army got howitzer guns from Sweden and sanction for development of an all-Indian battle tank, the Arjun. In the last two years of Rajiv's tenure, defence spending was one-fifth of total government expenditure.

Bofors and Its Aftermath

Ironically, it was these very same defence purchases that were to become the proverbial albatross around Rajiv's neck. The big one was Bofors, the stink of which continues to this day, but it started with smaller scandals around Fairfax and the HDW submarine deal. Very briefly, since details are available aplenty elsewhere, the Fairfax controversy centred on the appointment by V.P. Singh, Rajiv's finance minister, who had become notorious for his 'raid raj', of an American detective agency, Fairfax, to investigate the illegal stacking of foreign exchange in overseas banks by Indians. A forged letter which suggested that the investigations included Amitabh Bachchan, a close friend of the prime minister, surfaced from nowhere, and big industrialists, Nusli Wadia of Bombay Dyeing and Ambani of Reliance, were reported to be involved in the game on opposite sides. The transfer of V.P. Singh from Finance to Defence, which Rajiv claimed was because he needed somebody capable to handle Defence at the time because of the crisis with Pakistan, was projected by the Opposition as proof that Rajiv was trying to shield his friend Amitabh. This was followed by the HDW submarine scandal. When India wanted to place a further order for two more submarines with the HDW shipyard in West Germany from which it had bought four in 1981, and asked for some price discount, the shipyard declined saying it had to pay a heavy 7 per cent commission on the sale anyway. V.P. Singh, who was Defence Minister, without speaking to Rajiv, ordered an enquiry. This was taken as an unfriendly act since Mrs Gandhi herself was Defence Minister at the time of the award of the contract in 1981, and a Congress government was in power. There was criticism of Singh's conduct in the cabinet meeting, and he soon resigned from the government. The Opposition and the Press declared this as proof of V.P. Singh's honesty and Rajiv's attempts at a cover-up. The Mr Clean label was shifted to Singh and Rajiv's honeymoon was over.

On 16 April 1987, a few days after Singh's resignation, the Bofors scandal broke. The allegations, which first appeared on Swedish Radio, were that the equivalent of Rs 60 crores was paid as bribes to Indian officials and Congress party members to secure the contract for the 410 howitzer guns to Bofors company of Sweden in the face of stiff competition from a French gun. The allegations, which were taken up in a big way by the Indian press, particularly the *Indian Express,* and later *The Hindu,* soon snowballed into a major attack on Rajiv himself with sections of the Opposition parties charging that he and his family were the recipients of the money. The situation was bad enough for Rajiv to make a public denial of his and his family's involvement. It also provided an opportunity to Giani Zail Singh, the President, to try and settle scores with Rajiv. Annoyed because Rajiv had been lax in observing the convention of regularly calling on the President to keep him informed of important developments, and also because he was not consulted about the Punjab and Mizo accords, and lured by the prospect of a second term, Zail Singh became the centre of a major conspiracy in mid-1987 to dismiss Rajiv from office. Opposition leaders and some Congress dissidents encouraged the President to dismiss Rajiv on charges of corruption or failing to fulfil the constitutional requirement of keeping the President informed. Zail Singh was almost persuaded but V.P. Singh, who was the alternative, declined to play the game and a major constitutional catastrophe was saved.

It is to Rajiv's great credit that, in the midst of scandals and conspiracies, he personally handled with great elan, from all accounts, the crisis arising out of one of the severest droughts of the twentieth century. The southwest monsoon failed in 1987 (June-September), affecting one-fourth of the population of the country, living in one-third of all districts located in eleven states. A massive effort was launched to move food and drinking water, and to start employment schemes, in affected areas. It was claimed by Rajiv with justifiable pride that not a single life was lost. This, in a country where millions died in a man-made famine as recently as in 1943, four years before independence.

But Bofors and the stink of corruption would not go away, and resurfaced in 1989, the election year. The Joint Parliamentary Committee Report had given a more or less clean chit, but the Comptroller and Auditor-General's Report cast doubts on the procedure for selection of guns and raised other issues as well. Though it said nothing of the kind, the Opposition insisted it was proof of Rajiv's guilt and demanded his resignation. They followed it up with *en masse* resignation from the Lok Sabha, which was no great sacrifice since elections were round the corner anyway, but was nonetheless an embarrassment for the government. And Rajiv went to his second general elections with the country in a mood very different from the one in his first round.

A little older and much wiser, Rajiv had much to look back upon with pride. Except for Sri Lanka, his handling of foreign affairs had met with considerable approval. India's standing in the world had been enhanced, not declined, and relations with superpowers and neighbours were on an even keel, somewhat better, certainly no worse than before. The economy had done well, registering the highest rates of growth to date, though the deficit and debt was piling up. The security and defence policy had been a sound one with the overdue modernization of the armed forces set in motion. Computerization was given a big push, a necessity if India was to remain in the reckoning in the world system. Anti-poverty programmes in general and the literacy, drinking water, immunization, and Panchayati Raj initiatives in particular, had the poor, and the rural areas as their main focus, thus giving a lie to charges of elitism.

There were several weaknesses, no doubt. Among them was Rajiv's tendency to change his mind too often. He shuffled his cabinet once every two months on an average, for example. He was also given to flashes of temper, and sometimes spoke without having thought through the consequences, as in the famous incident when he dismissed the Foreign Secretary in a press conference. Charges of inaccessibility also began to be made, and some thought that he was also becoming arrogant, but these are the usual problems of high office. The biggest problem, in fact, was his relative lack of political experience, unfamiliarity with the nuances of grassroots mobilization, party organization, etc. But most observers were agreed that he was learning fast, and that he was no more the awkward leader, that he had begun to enjoy the rough and tumble of Indian politics. Also, by 1989 he had passed a crucial test of political leadership: of having the nerves for it. He withstood Bofors, in which the most vicious personal allegations were made about him, and he was ready to endure the gruelling election campaign for a second time. Whether he won or lost, he had decided beyond doubt that he was going to be a player in the great Indian game.

Run-up to the New Millennium and After

Rajiv Gandhi had succeeded in placing the idea of preparing for the twenty-first century—the first century of the new millennium—in the minds of thinking Indians. When he asked for a mandate for the second time in November 1989, there was just a decade to go for the ambitious targets he had set before the nation, and which he hoped to have the opportunity to pursue. But running a government and winning an election are two different propositions and success in one is no guarantee of success in the other. Despite unprecedented economic growth, averaging around 5.5 per cent per annum, the highest expenditure ever on anti-poverty programmes, an almost flawless handling of the drought of 1987, significant foreign policy achievements, the 'hawa' or wind blew in the opposite direction. V.P. Singh's single-minded crusade against corruption, which he had carried on unremittingly since his expulsion from the Congress in 1987, had touched a sensitive chord. Corruption at the lower levels of the bureaucracy was an issue of everyday concern for all citizens, rich or poor, and it was widely felt that high-level corruption created conditions of legitimacy for the lower-level variety. V.P. Singh courted and won the support of a wide range of forces, which included Sarvodaya workers, trade unionists such as Datta Samant, the farmers' movement led by Sharad Joshi in Maharashtra, and some sections of radical anti-Congress intellectuals.

Apart from choosing an emotive issue, V.P. Singh also fashioned a consummate political strategy for isolating Rajiv and Congress. He first joined together with all those Congressmen who had become estranged with Rajiv for one reason or another. Among these was Arif Mohammad Khan, a young secular Muslim leader considered close to Rajiv. Arif had achieved instant fame by resigning on the issue of the Shah Bano case. This case, in which the Supreme Court granted maintenance to a Muslim woman divorced by her husband, became controversial because it was opposed by orthodox Muslims on the grounds that it interfered with the Muslim personal law. Arif, encouraged by Rajiv, had put up a brilliant defence of the judgement in parliament, but was dismayed and resigned his ministership when Rajiv, coming under enormous pressure from a powerful agitation and close advisers, agreed to introduce a bill to negate the judgement. Rajiv's stand on the Shah Bano case had first cost him Muslim support and, once he changed his mind, Hindu support as well, since he was seen as appeasing Muslims. In many ways, Arif's resignation was the beginning of the turnaround in Rajiv's fortunes. Arif was joined in the wilderness by Arun Nehru, the estranged cousin whom Rajiv had edged out when he seemed to be becoming too powerful and inquisitive as Minister of State for Home. V.P. Singh, Arif and Arun Nehru, joined by Ram Dhan, V.C. Shukla, Satpal Malik and other Congress dissidents, formed the Jan Morcha, or People's Front, on 2 October 1987. With this as the core, V.P. Singh began to build an anti-Rajiv political bloc.

He placated the left parties by calling them his natural allies and issuing statements against communalism, but made sure he had the BJP on his side by speaking from their platform and maintaining close links with Vajpayee and Advani. However, more than V.P. Singh's strategy, it was the inherent anti-Congressism of the left and the BJP that brought them to support V.P. Singh. His resounding victory in the Allahabad by-election in June 1988 against Congress, in which the Bofors gun had become the unofficial campaign symbol, had convinced them that he was the answer to their anti-Congress prayers. And though the left parties were always quick to deny any truck with the BJP, especially when it became clear later that the BJP was the main beneficiary of the electoral understanding in the 1989 elections, it is a fact that they were fully aware of V.P. Singh's dealings with the BJP. Citing Jyoti Basu's presence at a public rally held to felicitate V.P. Singh for his victory in the Allahabad by-election, in which he shared the dais with Atal Bihari Vajpayee of the BJP, V.P. Singh's biographer, Seema Mustafa, says: 'That V.P. Singh alone was not responsible for the "understanding" reached with the BJP and that it had the covert support of the Left becomes clear from this move. Indeed, eventually the Left parties told VP that they would not make an issue of any electoral agreement with the BJP, although they would not be able to support it openly.'[1]

The feeling among the left and V.P. Singh was that, as in 1977–79, the BJP would not be able to gain much as it did not have any independent strength. The BJP, on the other hand, went along, often swallowing insults that a party with less discipline would have found impossible to get its cadre to tolerate, in the conviction that the dislodging of Congress was a necessary step on its road to power. The association with left and secular forces gave it the credibility it lacked by removing the stigma of communalism that had ensured it remained on the fringes of Indian politics—a stigma that had been attached to it by the efforts of secular nationalists since the days of the freedom struggle. The BJP increased its tally from 2 in 1984 to 86 in 1989, and this jump put it on the path to power, which it achieved in 1998. To quote, 'The broad alliance [formed in 1989] was definitely one of the factors responsible for the rise of the BJP.'[2]

The strategy for Opposition unity was conceived as a three-stage process. The first stage was the unity of centrist non-Congress secular national parties, the second the formation of a National Front of all non-left secular parties, regional and national, and the third the seat adjustments with left parties and the BJP. The second stage was completed first, with the National Front of seven parties being formed on 6 August 1988. On 11 October 1988, the birthday of Jayaprakash Narayan, the Janata Dal was formed with the merger of the Jan Morcha, Congress(S), Janata and Lok Dal. The third stage was reached when the Janata Dal-led National Front and BJP agreed not to contest against each other in around 85 per cent of the seats where the two would have otherwise nominated candidates, and a similar arrangement for a smaller number of seats was reached between the National Front and the Communist parties.

The National Front Government, 1989–1990

The election results were a blow to Congress even if it was still the single largest party with 197 seats and 39.5 per cent vote share. Rajiv made it clear that Congress was not interested in trying to form a government. With the left parties and the BJP quickly declaring that they would support a National Front government from the outside, the stage was set for the second non-Congress government in post-independence India to take office. The National Front had won 146 seats and was supported by the BJP with 86 and the left parties with 52 seats.

The beginnings were not smooth, however, with Chandra Shekhar totally opposed to V.P. Singh as prime minister, and Devi Lal insisting he be made deputy prime minister at least. With elections over, all the differences caused by clashing ambitions, oversized egos, ideological preferences, came to the fore and it was with some difficulty that V.P. Singh took oath as prime minister on 2 December 1989 accompanied only by Devi Lal as deputy prime minister. The lack of trust that was to become more open later was evident even at the swearing-in ceremony where Devi Lal made a joke of himself by insisting on inserting the term deputy prime minister into the oath despite the President's gentle admonition that he should only say 'minister', as if he was not sure that the prime minister would stick to his promise!

Though V.P. Singh started out with a high-profile visit to Punjab in which he visited the Golden Temple and drove around in an open jeep, as if to heighten the contrast with the heavily guarded Rajiv, and made many noises about reversing Congress policies, it was typical of his administration that the high-sounding words did not lead anywhere. Punjab was as bad as ever at the end of his term, and Kashmir was much worse. He made George Fernandes head of the Kashmir Affairs Committee, but allowed Arun Nehru and Mufti Mohammed Sayeed to continue to interfere, and then, without consulting anybody, appointed Jagmohan the governor of Kashmir! Sure enough, Farooq Abdullah, the chief minister of Kashmir, resigned in protest, since Jagmohan was the man who had cost him his chief ministership in 1983 by encouraging defections against him. True to form, Jagmohan dissolved the assembly, and, again without consulting anyone, V.P. Singh recalled him, and made him a Rajya Sabha member to mollify him. In fact, apart from completing the withdrawal of Indian troops from Sri Lanka, and settling the trade and transit dispute with Nepal, there was little that the National Front government had to show for itself. It was also unable to use its clout with the BJP and the Muslim leaders to bring them to a resolution of the Ayodhya dispute. On the contrary, Advani's rath yatra, or chariot-ride, inflamed communal passions to fever pitch, just as Mandal aroused caste feelings as never before.

Perhaps the main reason for the inability of the government to get its act together was the enormous amount of time and energy spent on trying to resolve internal differences. Chandra Shekhar made no secret of his antipathy to the prime minister. He lost no time in supporting Farooq Abdullah when he resigned. Ajit Singh was disliked by Devi Lal, and Devi Lal by almost everybody but Chandra Shekhar. Devi Lal disliked Ajit Singh, the son of Charan Singh, who first articulated peasant interests in North India in 1967, but he loved his own son, Om Prakash Chautala, so much that he made him chief minister of Haryana in his place once he became deputy prime minister. A scandal followed Chautala's attempt to seek election from Meham, as enquiries established that large-scale rigging and physical intimidation of voters had occurred, and the election was countermanded by the Election Commission. Chautala resigned as chief minister only to be reinstated two months later. This proved too much for at least Arif and Arun Nehru and they resigned from the government. As if on cue, V.P. Singh also resigned, but was persuaded to continue after assurances of Chautala stepping down. But that was not the last trick the 'Elder Uncle' or Tau', as Devi Lal was called, had up his sleeve. He now accused Arif and Arun Nehru of corruption, and produced a letter purportedly written by V.P. Singh to the President of India in 1987, accusing them of involvement in the Bofors deal. V.P. Singh, declaring that the letter was a badly disguised forgery, dismissed Devi Lal on 1 August 1990.

Never one to take things lying down, Devi Lal gave a call for a big peasants' rally in New Delhi on 9 August to show V.P. Singh his true strength. Though V.P. Singh denies this, it is widely believed that, rattled by this threat, and wanting to divert attention, he made the most controversial decision of his rule. On 7 August, he announced in parliament that the report of the Mandal Commission, appointed by the Janata government (1977–79) and quietly ignored by Mrs Gandhi, would be implemented. The recommendations were that 27 per cent of jobs in the government services and public undertakings be reserved for candidates belonging to the 'backward castes', thus bringing the total in the reserved category to 49.5 per cent, as 22.5 per cent was already reserved for the Scheduled Castes or dalits and the Scheduled Tribes.[3] The recommendations included, as a second stage, to be implemented later, reservations in educational institutions and promotions.

The announcement was greeted with widespread dismay and anger. Even those who did not disagree with the decision in principle were upset at the sudden and arbitrary manner in which it was taken. In what was becoming an increasingly familiar pattern, V.P. Singh did not consult even close associates before making the announcement. Biju Patnaik, R.K. Hegde, Yashwant Sinha and Arun Nehru were among those unhappy with the decision for one reason or another. The left parties and the BJP were upset that they had no clue about the decision. Devi Lal and Chandra Shekhar came out in strong condemnation. The criticisms ranged from the move's timing and lack of effort to build up a consensus, to the divisive nature of the move and the faulty criteria used for identifying backward castes. The CPM wanted economic criteria to be used as the basis of reservation, and many others, including Hegde, agreed with that view. Eminent sociologists pointed out that the method of identification of backward castes was outdated and changes in social structure since independence had not been taken into account. Among those who were called 'backward castes' in the report were the sections who were the major beneficiaries of land reforms and the Green Revolution and they could hardly claim special treatment on grounds of backwardness. There were, no doubt, some sections among those identified as backward castes who were in fact not very different from Scheduled Castes in their economic and social status, and deserved special treatment, but they needed to be identified carefully and separately, for, if they were lumped together with castes who were backward only in name, they were unlikely to be able to compete for benefits.[4]

The worst aspect of the Mandal decision was that it was socially divisive: it pitted caste against caste in the name of social justice; it made no effort to convince those who would stand to lose that they should accept it in the larger interest; it encouraged the potential beneficiaries to treat all those who opposed the decision as representing upper-caste interests, and reintroduced caste as a concept and identity even in those sectors of society from where it had virtually disappeared. Further, one would have expected that forty years after reservations were first introduced for Scheduled

Castes in the constitution, a serious debate and empirical examination of their efficacy as a strategy for social justice would be in order before they were extended to new sections. The arguments that reservations were perpetuated not because they served the interests of the really disadvantaged but of the elites among the castes benefiting from reservation, that the focus on reservation as the preferred and often sole strategy for social justice prevented consideration of other equally if not more effective strategies, that politics of caste identity benefited leaders rather than the victims of the caste system—all these needed to be seriously debated and the case for extension of reservation established and public opinion built around it before such major social engineering was attempted.[5]

The strong and violent reaction of the student community in North India illustrates this.[6] In a situation where large numbers of students look upon employment in the government sector as a major career option, and one that it is still possible to avail of without using influence or money as recruitment is done via competitive examinations, the sudden blocking of almost one half of the seats for reservation, seemed patently unfair. This was especially so as they recognized that many of those who would benefit were economically and socially their equals or even superiors. This was seen as very different from reservation for Scheduled Castes, as the social and economic disability was unambiguous, and a social consensus had been built on the issue since the days of the freedom struggle. Besides, students were not innocent of the political motives that underlay the decision, as these were being loudly debated by the leaders of the National Front itself.

Anti-Mandal protest took the form of attacks on public property, burning of buses, rallies, meetings, discussions in the Press. Students were in the forefront, and were often supported by other sections of society, such as teachers, office workers and housewives. Towns and cities in North India were the locale and police firing was resorted to in Delhi, Gorakhpur, Varanasi and Kanpur among other places. From mid-September, desperate that protests were proving futile, a few students attempted self-immolation. Passions ran high, with those for Mandal condemning this as barbaric and farcical and possibly stage-managed, and those against shocked at the trivialization and lack of understanding of the depth of sentiment on the issue. The prime minister's appeals to students to desist from violence and self-immolation went unheeded. While for a major part anti-Mandal protest remained free of caste overtones, and in fact its dominant discourse was against caste as an organizing principle, there did develop a very negative tendency, especially in the later stages, and partly in reaction to being characterized as upper caste motivated, for upper-caste students to coalesce into previously unthinkable 'forward caste' associations, and for caste-flavoured abuses to be traded in college hostel corridors and dining halls. What was once a major forum for dissolving of caste identities became for some time the cradle in which they were reborn. The protest ended when the Supreme Court granted a stay on the implementation of the Mandal Report on 1 October 1990.[7]

Meanwhile, the BJP had its own agenda to complete and Mandal probably gave it the push it needed. Seeing the strong popular reaction to Mandal, the BJP had started making noises about withdrawing support. On 25 September, L.K. Advani embarked on his 6,000-mile-long rath yatra from Somnath in Gujarat to Ayodhya (to lay the foundation stone for the Ram mandir) which ended on 23 October at Samastipur in Bihar with his arrest and the withdrawal of support by the BJP. V.P. Singh could not satisfy the BJP without alienating his own party and his left allies and chose thus to break with the BJP. On 30 October, there was firing on the crowd trying to reach the spot in Ayodhya chosen for the shilanyas of the Ram temple. The rath yatra, Advani's arrest and the firing at Ayodhya aroused communal passions and the ensuing riots led to many deaths in North India. On 5 November, the Janata Dal split and fifty-eight legislators elected Chandra Shekhar as their leader. On 7 November, the second attempt at running a non-Congress government came to an end after eleven stormy months.

Chandra Shekhar to Vajpayee: A Brief Survey

The major issues that emerged in this phase have been extensively discussed in the thematic chapters; hence what is offered here is merely a brief survey of basic political changes to maintain the continuity of the narrative.

The short-lived Chandra Shekhar government which took office on 10 November 1990 with the support of Congress had only one role to perform: to hold the baby till Congress decided it wanted to go for elections. A pretext was found and support withdrawn on 5 March 1991. The elections were announced from 19 May and one round of voting was over when tragedy again struck the ill-fated family of Indira Gandhi. Rajiv Gandhi, who was rounding off one phase of campaigning with a late-night meeting in Sriperumbudur, 40 km from Madras, was blown to pieces when a young woman, who came forward to greet him, triggered a bomb that she had strapped to her waist. Widely believed, and later proven, to be the handiwork of LTTE militants, the killing of the 46-year-old Rajiv, who was regaining popularity with his sadbhavana yatras and other attempts to reach out to the people, generated a sympathy wave strong enough to give Congress 232 seats and the status of the single largest party. Narasimha Rao *formed what was initially a minority Congress government on 21* June, but which gradually achieved a majority, and lasted a full five-year term. It undertook the most radical economic reforms, and in the first year brought down the caste and communal temperature to a great extent and was successful in restoring in normality to Punjab, and improving the situation in Kashmir and Assam. It failed to save the Babri Masjid from demolition or prevent the widespread rioting that followed. All this has been discussed thematically elsewhere in this volume. Suffice it to say that Narasimha Rao's regime, despite its many achievements which are likely to be placed in a more favourable light with a longer historical perspective, tended to lose steam in the last two years, with a slowing down of economic reforms, surfacing of corruption charges and the 'hawala' scandal which led to charges, later found to be almost entirely unsustainable, of bribes and foreign exchange violations against many Congress and Opposition leaders.

The elections held in 1996 led to Congress winning only 140 seats and the BJP increasing its tally to 161 from 120 in 1991. A short-lived BJP government lasted from 16 May to 1 June, but failed to get majority support. This was followed by a United Front government with H.D. Deve Gowda as prime minister supported by Congress and the CPM in which the CPI joined as a partner and India got her first Communist Home Minister in Indrajit Gupta. Congress withdrew support on 30 March 1997, failed to form a government, and again supported a United Front government, this time with I.K. Gujral as prime minister. The support was withdrawn again and fresh elections held in February

1998 which led to the formation of BJP-led government with Atal Bihari Vajpayee as prime minister. The BJP notwithstanding getting only 182 seats, managed to secure the support of secular parties like the TDP, AIADMK and Trinamul Congress. The Congress got only 147 seats. The large number of allies prevented stability, with their competing demands, and ultimately Jayalalithaa withdrew her AIADMK from the alliance, leading to the government losing the vote of confidence in April 1999. Efforts to form an alternative Congress or secular coalition government failed and elections were announced once again. The BJP-led government continued as a caretaker government till the elections were held in September and October 1999. The election results improved the tally of the BJP and its allies to 296 from 253 though the BJP's own tally did not change, and the Congress with Sonia Gandhi at its helm was down to 134 with allies. The discrepancy in vote shares was much less, with Congress and its allies holding on to 34.7 per cent, an improvement of 3.4 per cent over 1998, as compared to the BJP and its allies' 41.3 per cent, which improved by only 1.2 per cent over 1998. A new government was formed with Vajpayee again at the helm. As always, history had its ironies, the millennium was ushered in by a government led by a party that for years had seemed to be more interested in reviving and avenging the past than in heralding the future! The coming millennium, however, with its new horizons, could yet give the indomitable Indian people the future they deserved.

The NDA Government

When the BJP came to power as the leading party in the NDA, friendly journalists and other sympathetic analysts were fond of saying that responsibility and power would smoothen the rough edges of the party, strengthen the moderates and tame the extreme elements. The BJP projected itself as a party with a difference: united, disciplined, honest and dedicated. Unfortunately, expectations were belied on both counts. The communal temperature was pushed up by the Vishwa Hindu Parishad (VHP), the Bajrang Dal and the RSS, who had no intention of being tamed, but, on the contrary, had every intention of using state power to fulfil their long-cherished desire of creating a Hindu Rashtra or nation. Despite the BJP's claim that it had put its communal agenda on the back burner in deference to the sensitivities of its coalition partners, the agitation for the building of the Ram mandir at Ayodhya reached its peak in early 2002, notwithstanding the Supreme Court's refusal to allow construction on the disputed site and the surrounding land. This agitation had a direct effect on the communal situation in Gujarat, which witnessed what many observers have called a genocide lasting for close to three months from February 2002. The ideological agenda of communalization of education was pursued with great vehemence by the RSS Minister for Human Resource Development, Murli Manohar Joshi. (We have dealt with the communal situation in a separate chapter.)

The second claim, of being a party with a difference, received severe knocks from an almost endless series of scams that seemed to be surfacing with monotonous regularity. The first big one was the exposé by Tehelka, a news-based Indian website, which laid bare the nexus between arms dealers, army men and politicians. It was a sting operation carried out by journalists posing as arms dealers, walking around defence establishments, and party offices, with suitcases which had cash as well as hidden cameras and tape-recorders. The video-tapes were aired on a television channel on 13 March 2001, and all hell broke loose. The tapes not only compromised senior army officials, but the president of the BJP, Bangaru Laxman, who was seen putting away Rs 100,000 into his table drawer. The president of the Samata Party, Jaya Jaitly, was found accepting a sum of Rs 200,000 at the official residence of the Defence Minister, George Fernandes. Laxman and Fernandes both had to go. The government also had to appoint an enquiry committee. The government's reputation also suffered because it was widely believed that Tehelka was hounded thereafter, and its staff and promoters harassed in a variety of ways, including being arrested. Even when it was revealed later that Tehelka had used means, such as hiring the services of call girls, which most agreed were unethical, the government's attempt to use this to cast doubts on the veracity of the original exposé did not cut much ice.

The Unit Trust of India scam, in which millions of small investors lost their savings, also tarnished reputations as names of officials close to the prime minister and from his household were talked about. Similarly, in 2002, Ram Naik, the Petroleum Minister, came under a cloud because his ministry had allotted over 3,000 petrol pumps, gas agencies and kerosene dealerships to BJP and RSS leaders and their relatives. Parliament was stalled for days and allotments cancelled. This was followed by revelations that the largest number of allotments of prime land in the heart of Delhi since 1999 had been made to organizations affiliated to the RSS.

The 'mini-general elections' in May 2001 in which Kerala, Pondicherry, Assam, Tamil Nadu and West Bengal went to the polls had returned the Congress to power in the first three, the AIADMK, its ally, in Tamil Nadu, and the Left Front in West Bengal. With this, the number of Congress chief ministers went up to eleven. The BJP had failed to make any gains. In fact, the only election won by the BJP in this period was in Gujarat, and that in very exceptional circumstances, which hardly added to its credibility. In 2003, it lost Himachal Pradesh as well, which was considered a stronghold, to the Congress. Later, it won Madhya Pradesh, Chhattisgarh and Rajasthan, and such was the optimism generated by this that the general elections, due only after October 2004, were advanced by about six months to April–May. The economy was thought to be in such good shape, with large foreign exchange reserves, and low inflation, that the Finance Minister went on a pre-election binge. The NDA launched what it thought was an unbeatable campaign: 'India Shining'. But large numbers of Indians thought otherwise, and the result was described as the biggest upset since 1977, when the Congress was swept out of power in the elections following the Emergency.

The UPA Government

The Congress was now the largest party with 146 MPs, and with the support of its allies and the Left Front, had no difficulty forming a government. Sonia Gandhi as party president was the obvious choice, and received support from all concerned, but despite enormous pressure from party cadres and colleagues, refused to accept the post of prime minister. Instead, she named Manmohan Singh, eminent economist and former Finance Minister, a man with a reputation of total probity, who had overseen the crucial economic reforms in 1991 when Narasimha Rao was prime minister. Sonia's sacrifice was widely appreciated, and served to enhance her stature among the people and increased her influence in the party.

The Hindu newspaper expressed the views of many when it described the election verdict as 'clearly a vote against the NDA's policies—its highly divisive policies pursued most viciously in Gujarat and Uttar Pradesh and also in the educational arena'. It also explained why the India Shining campaign failed to take off: 'by seeming to mock the deprivations of the mass of voters in rural as well as urban areas, it opened up a huge credibility gap for the ruling party.' The new government sought to give expression to popular sentiment by emphasizing that it would follow a strategy of reforms with a human face, and that it believed in inclusive growth. A National Advisory Council, with Sonia at the head, was set up with representatives of civil society groups, intellectuals and experts as its members, to assist the government in policy formulation.

Beginning with education, the process of communalization was sought to be reversed. The task was not easy, for it is easier to destroy than to build. Heads of many institutions, who had been taking a blatantly partisan approach, were changed, governors of many states replaced, school textbooks, particularly history books, sent for review, and Prevention of Terrorism (POTA) repealed. However, not everybody was satisfied at the pace of what came to be called 'detoxification', and sections among the left and civil society groups were often quite critical of the government's approach. The UPA government also set up a new Ministry for Minority Affairs, as well as a committee headed by Justice Sachar to make recommendations for the welfare of economically and educationally backward sections among the minorities. It also introduced the Communal Violence (Prevention, Control and Rehabilitation of Victims) Bill in parliament.

There were major developments in the economic sphere and in foreign policy which are dealt with elsewhere in the book, but we need to mention here some important developments in the sphere of public policy. Largely at the initiative of the National Advisory Council, and with the strong support of Sonia Gandhi, a national Right to Information (RTI) Act was passed in October 2005. This legislation superseded the few state-level acts that were already in place, and bestowed on citizens the right to get information from any public authority within a period of thirty days. The legislation was regarded as among the most progressive in the world, and refusal to comply entailed penalties. The Centre as well as the states were obliged to set up Information Commissions which had powers to hear complaints and punish officials for non-compliance with the law. An interesting feature of the Indian law was that it came about as a result of a popular mass movement which began in Rajasthan under the leadership of the Magsaysay award winner Aruna Roy and the Mazdoor Kishan Shakti Sangathan (MKSS), and grew into a National Campaign for People's Right to Information (NCPRI), with Shekhar Singh as the Convenor, and was not simply a government initiative. The popular response to the Act has been tremendous, as it has been welcomed by a public sick of corruption, and official high-handedness. Officials, who earlier refused to heed any complaints, have been reported to have rushed to do the needful and at times even visit the homes of citizens who took recourse to the Act to seek information on missing rations, bad roads, forged muster rolls, delayed passports, and the like.

Another progressive measure that was taken, again at the prodding of the National Advisory Council and its Chairperson, as well as in response to a long-standing campaign on the issue, was the passing of the National Rural Employment Guarantee Act (NREGA) in September 2005, under which the government is obliged to provide hundred days of employment per annum to one member of every poor rural family. Initially covering the two hundred most backward districts, it is to be extended to the entire country in five years' time. The scheme has enormous potential, for it can increase the bargaining position of the poor in rural society, and, especially if the Right to Information Act is used to keep a check on the possibilities of corruption, it can besides providing livelihoods, empower the poor to fight for their rights.

On the women's front, while the legislation for reservation of one-third seats in the legislatures for women continued its endless wait for political consensus, other useful measures were put on board. The Protection of Women from Domestic Violence Act, 2005, was passed, and it was a big leap forward for it recognized the existence of emotional, psychological and physical violence in the home. Another radical measure gave Hindu women inheritance rights in coparcenary property equal to men's in all the states. The Sexual Harassment of Women at Work Place (Prevention, Prohibition and Redressal) Bill was also on the anvil. Women were guaranteed one-third of the jobs made available under the NREGA.

Another positive initiative which started well but lost steam was the Right to Education Bill. The Central Advisory Board of Education (CABE) took two years to deliberate and propose a bill, but when the time came in the summer of 2006 to get it passed, the Human Resource Development (HRD) Ministry sent it to the states as a model bill on the plea that the Finance Ministry had expressed its inability to find the necessary funds for its implementation. The state governments in their turn sent it back to the Centre on the ground that they had no funds either! This was typical of the way the issue of compulsory education has been treated by almost all governments since independence. It was never a top priority, even though it was evident that it was the single most important measure that empowered the poor. However, the movement for Right to Education continued to press for the enactment of the bill, and it was hoped that its efforts would meet with success.

Higher education, on the other hand, was promised liberal increases in funding to neutralize the opposition to the 27 per cent reservation for Other Backward Castes (OBCs) which was legislated to be initiated from 2007, as institutions of higher learning were told to increase seats in all courses to ensure that general category seats were not reduced. The Supreme Court, however, stayed the implementation of the order, in response to petitions questioning the measure on various counts. This provided some respite to the institutions which were hard put to increase capacity, given the already dismal situation regarding availability of faculty and infrastructure. However, this initiative of the government also raised the larger issue of autonomy of educational institutions, autonomy from government and autonomy from populist political pressure, which were a prerequisite for pursuit of excellence. Was it possible for institutions, such as the IIMs and IITs, which achieved world recognition, to continue to deliver their best, if they did not even have the autonomy to decide on the numbers they were to admit?

Foreign Policy in the 1990s

New Challenges: Today and Tomorrow

Indian foreign policy faced a big challenge with the demise of the Soviet Union, the end of the Cold War, and the shift to the economic strategy of liberalization and globalization. The two events coincided in the case of India in the year 1991, and the consequences of both were not dissimilar. India had to re-order her relationship with the US and the Western world. She needed the capital, the technology and the markets for export and there was, in any case, no Soviet Union to fall back upon. Her success also critically depended upon how quickly and well she could use the new strategy to achieve rapid economic development, because ultimately, in today's world, it is those with the largest economic clout who carry the greatest political weight in international affairs. In the words of V.P. Dutt:[8] 'If one were asked to identify just one most notable trend in the world, one would say that the economic struggle had taken primacy over the political struggle.'

While it was true that the good old days of Indo-Soviet friendship were over, there still existed a tremendous reservoir of goodwill and loyalties in the countries of the erstwhile Soviet Union. Russia may have been going through a period of crisis, but she was a great power with a strong sense of her own position and was bound to make a comeback. It was in India's interest to maintain good relations with Russia. Other countries of Central Asia that had broken out of the Soviet Union also had tremendous potential as friends and allies. They were rich in natural resources, were strategically placed and were already being courted by the US and other Western powers. Fortunately, they too had old links with India dating back to the Soviet era and the Indian government had been actively building upon them.

India's stock in the Middle East had been high since she had always supported the Arab struggle for Palestine and did not have any diplomatic relations with Israel. In recent years, while maintaining support for the PLO, India had also opened up ties with Israel. India had also succeeded in maintaining friendly ties with Iran and had refused to fall in line with US policies of total ostracism of Iraq and Iran. As a result, Pakistan's efforts to use the Organisation of Islamic Unity (or States) against India were not very successful. By refusing to join in the hysteria against Iraq let loose during the Gulf War by the US, India had also retained her goodwill, built over many years of economic partnership, with Iraq.

Indian diplomacy also had to tread some new paths. Much of the world today was getting organized into new trade or economic blocs, ASEAN, EEC, NAFTA, etc. India had shown insufficient interest and awareness of this trend. She made little effort to become part of ASEAN at the right time and had only lately become a dialogue partner. SAARC was yet to emerge as a serious economic bloc, though efforts in that direction were being made. The move to bring together countries of the Indian Ocean, in which India played an active part, was a welcome one, especially as it included South Africa, an old friend with great potential as an economic partner.

India needed to learn to look eastwards as well. To Japan, which was the largest donor in the world, with the biggest surpluses of investible capital and with whom India had no history of colonial domination or border wars or economic arm-twisting and whose long-term strategic interests to keep China in check dovetailed with India's. India needed to develop closer economic and political ties with other countries of Southeast Asia with whom she had historically good relations—with Indonesia whom India supported in Indonesia's struggle against Dutch colonialism, with Vietnam, whom India supported in her struggle against French and American colonialism, with Thailand, Cambodia and Malaysia with whom India had old cultural ties, with Singapore which was the powerhouse of Southeast Asia and had shown how modern technology enabled a tiny city state to become an economic superpower.

This was also necessary if India was to contribute to the making of a multipolar world and the democratization of international relations, all of which was in her enlightened self-interest. The sure way of preventing the crystallization of a unipolar world was by gently encouraging countries which had achieved economic strength to assert themselves in international affairs. Japan and at least some of the East Asian tigers which had too long been in the habit of silently endorsing US hegemony could well begin to want to express their own view of the world. All breaches in unipolarity and in favour of plurality were in India's and the world's interest and were to be encouraged, as was done so successfully via the NAM in the 1950s Cold War. In this respect the strong support received for continuation of NAM at its tenth annual summit in 1992 in Jakarta from member states, despite the many problems it had been facing, was very encouraging. Prime Minister Mahathir of Malaysia, who had emerged as a strong independent voice in world affairs, expressed himself very firmly in favour of NAM, as did Suharto of Indonesia who was in the chair. The summit demanded democratization of the UN, more open multilateral trading systems, greater financial flows to developing countries, and other such measures.

On the flip side was the increasing tendency of the US to interfere in the name of self-determination and human rights, with Kosovo being an example. Countries like India and China and even Russia with large ethnically diverse populations were vulnerable to attention of this nature. No wonder that they protested against the US and NATO role in Kosovo. The technologization of war the made such interference possible as it reduced the human costs to the aggressors to negligible proportions. Both the Gulf War and Kosovo demonstrated this to the hilt.

India had to adapt her foreign policy to this new situation. Keeping intact its goal of retaining independence of action in international affairs, and seeking to find a respectable place for herself in the community of nations, India had to constantly evaluate the changing nature of in iternational alignments and find the means to secure her objectives. The world order was in flux, and likely to remain so for some time, and in this fluid situation India needed to evolve a creative foreign policy.

We take a closer look at two of the most important events in recent years that had international implications: India's nuclear tests in 1998 and the near-war with Pakistan in 1999.

Pokhran II

India's conduct of another round of nuclear tests on 11 May 1998 and declaring herself a nuclear weapons state is a complex question that has to be examined in the context of the changing world environment and the position adopted by India since independence on the nuclear issue.

From the days of Nehru, India had maintained a principled and sustained position, arguing for nuclear disarmament and a nuclear weapons-free world. This position was forcefully and actively pursued by Rajiv Gandhi when he tried to initiate global action towards phased nuclear disarmament. On the other hand, once again pioneered by Nehru, India laid great emphasis on development of science and technology, particularly on keeping abreast with developments in the field of nuclear science. Subsequent governments kept abreast with developments. The first nuclear tests were conducted successfully in October 1974 when Indira Gandhi was the prime minister. The governments of Rajiv Gandhi, Narasimha Rao, Deve Gowda and I.K. Gujral were in full readiness for exercising the nuclear option and in fact it is said that Narasimha Rao in 1995 was about to give the go-ahead for tests similar to the 1998 ones but the Americans got to know of it and put enough pressure for Rao to stay his hand. Thus, India till the May 1998 tests, while maintaining her position in favour of nuclear disarmament, had kept herself ready for exercising the nuclear option. This dual position was maintained for several reasons.

First, there existed after the Second World War an extremely iniquitous world order on the nuclear front. The Nuclear Non-Proliferation Treaty (NPT) was essentially conceived to ensure that four countries, the US, Soviet Union, Britain and France, remained the only nuclear weapons-owning countries in the world. China forced its way into this elite club and joined the other four in the clamour to restrict the nuclear monopoly now to the 'Big Five'. The Comprehensive Test Ban Treaty (CTBT) which the nuclear powers had been pressurizing non-nuclear countries to sign was equally discriminatory as its aim was again to keep other countries from going nuclear while refusing *any* commitment on the part of the nuclear powers towards nuclear disarmament, not even within a fifty-year time-frame. India's efforts to get such a commitment included in the CTBT were brushed aside, forcing her to refuse to sign the CTBT as she did the NPT. The message was clear. Non-nuclear countries have no voice.

Second, India was surrounded by nuclear weapons. On one side there was China (a country which invaded India in 1962) with a major nuclear armoury of 400 to five 500 nuclear warheads and a sophisticated long-distance delivery system, including intercontinental ballistic missiles (ICBMs), and nuclear bases in Tibet. On the other, US nuclear ships cruised the seas around India with a base in Diego Garcia. Also, Kazakhstan, Ukraine and Russia had major nuclear weapons. Moreover, with open Chinese collusion and help, Pakistan (a country that forced India into war three times and maintained a consistent low-intensity hostility almost continuously) had developed not only considerable nuclear capability but also a substantial long-distance missile programme. A surface-to-surface ballistic missile with a range of 1,500 km named rather provocatively, Ghauri (presumably after the notorious invader into India centuries ago), had been successfully launched before the Indian nuclear tests of May 1998. Soon after the Indian tests, Pakistan conducted its tests and announced the explosion of its bomb which is widely suspected to have been 'mothered' by China. The growing China–Pakistan nuclear axis, given their collusion diplomatically and in war against India, was a matter of serious concern.

The iniquitous world nuclear order and the security concern posed by some of its immediate neighbours go a long way in explaining why all regimes in India saw the necessity of it maintaining nuclear preparedness, and why there had been for quite some time considerable support within the country for going ahead and exercising the nuclear option.

It was in this situation that the BJP-led government headed by Atal Bihari Vajpayee gave the go-ahead (rather hurriedly, within a few weeks of assuming power) for the nuclear tests that were conducted in May 1998. On 11 May three underground tests, one of them thermonuclear (showing, it was claimed, a hydrogen bomb capability with a 45 kiloton yield), were conducted in Pokhran, the same site used in 1974. Two days later another two tests were conducted at the same site. These were tests with a lower yield aimed at generating data for computer simulation and the capacity to carry out sub critical experiments in the future if necessary. There was no talk this time of tests for 'peaceful purposes' as Indira Gandhi had maintained earlier. Vajpayee declared, following the tests, that India was now a nuclear weapons state. The indigenously developed Prithvi and Agni surface-to-surface missiles could now carry nuclear warheads.

The country, by and large, with the exception of sections of the left and some small anti-nuclear groups, welcomed the tests and particularly the achievements of the scientific team led by A.P.J. Abdul Kalam and R. Chidambaram, the Chief Scientific Adviser and the head of the Department of Atomic Energy. The Opposition leader, Congress president Sonia Gandhi, praised the achievement of the scientists and engineers, expressed pride in Congress having kept India's nuclear capability up to date and reiterated the commitment of Congress to a nuclear weapons-free world and peace with her neighbours.

However, the manner in which the BJP government exercised the nuclear option and particularly its handling of the situation after the tests was widely disapproved of. It was suspected that the government hurriedly went in for the tests without adequate preparation with an eye on the political advantage it could reap at home. The suspicion appeared to be justified when the BJP resorted to open jingoism, talking of building a temple at Pokhran and making threatening noises regarding neighbouring countries. In fact, one of the most important national dailies in India had to editorially express 'the strongest possible condemnation' of an article which appeared in *Panchjanya,* the mouthpiece of the RSS, where 'an implicit case for an Indian nuclear attack on Pakistan' was made.[9] Having done the tests what India needed was to reassure the world and particularly its neighbours of her peaceful intent through skilful diplomatic moves, but the government did *just the opposite. Also, seen as political disasters were the Defence* Minister, George Fernandes's pronouncement, a week before the tests, naming China as 'potential threat number one' and prime minister Vajpayee's letter to President Clinton, which was published in *The New York Times,* defending the blasts by naming China and Pakistan as security threats. By unnecessarily naming specific countries and suggesting that the nuclear capability was being built against them, the wrong message was sent out. China (with whom India's relations were being improved with sustained hard work by previous Congress and United Front governments) had initially reacted moderately to the tests but now it adopted an almost vicious tone.

The response from the West and Japan was, as expected, negative and the tests were widely condemned. The US went further and immediately announced the imposition of sanctions. Japan, Norway, Sweden, Denmark, the Netherlands and Canada suspended aid to India. The US, however, did not succeed in getting the G-8 countries to take collective action against India. France, Russia and Germany continued their normal economic links with India. Britain as the current President of the European Union (EU) failed to get the EU to adopt a strong, anti-India stance.

While the long-term fallout of the sanctions and how long they would last was not clear immediately, what was certain was that India's nuclear tests posed a major challenge to the iniquitous nuclear world order in which the nuclear haves blatantly resorted to double standards. Witness the fuss made by the US about the Indian tests and its insistence that India sign the CTBT when not enough support could be generated within the US to ratify the CTBT. As the Secretary-General of the UN, Kofi Annan, put it, 'You cannot have an exclusive club (whose members) have the nuclear weapons and are refusing to disband it and tell them (India and Pakistan) not to have them.'[10]

Kargil

After Pokhran, Pakistan carried out its own nuclear tests and there was much sabre-rattling on both sides. In early 1999, when the atmosphere appeared more congenial, Vajpayee initiated the 'bus diplomacy' (travelling on the first bus service between India and Pakistan), aimed at making a major breakthrough in improving relations with Pakistan. However, as later events revealed, from long before the much-hyped bus ride to Lahore, soldiers of the Pakistan Army and Pakistan-backed Mujahideen (religious militants and mercenaries), were busy infiltrating into Indian territory. In fact, by May when the whole crisis blew up it was discovered that Pakistani armed forces had intruded deep across the LoC in Kashmir and had occupied key strategic peaks in the Kargil area. India had to mount a massive and extremely difficult counter-offensive from a disadvantageous military position, which was extremely costly particularly in terms of human lives, in order to evict the intruders. Pictures of body bags of hundreds of Indian soldiers and officers killed in the Kargil operations began to appear regularly in Indian newspapers in a manner not witnessed before.

The international reaction to the Kargil crisis was, somewhat unexpectedly, almost unanimous in favour of India. Even the US, Britain and China—long-time allies of Pakistan—put pressure on Pakistan to withdraw from Indian territory. Pakistan's claim that it had no regular army men on the Indian side of the border but only provided moral support to militants was not taken seriously by anybody. The US stance can be partly explained by the growing fear of international Islamic terrorism. Troops from the personal bodyguard of the Saudi Islamic fundamentalist Osama bin Laden, who was suspected to be behind the bomb attacks on US consulates in Africa in 1998 costing several 'American lives', were reported to be involved in the Pakistan operations in Kargil. China's being soft on India could be related to China finding India as the sole ally (apart from Russia) in questioning growing American hegemonism, witnessed starkly in the Kosovo crisis in early April–

May 1999 where, disregarding the UN, the US had taken upon itself the role of playing the world's policeman.

The domestic fallout was complex. At one level, it proved extremely useful for the BJP in the elections that followed a few months after the end of the Kargil crisis. However, the crisis raised some fundamental questions for the Indian state. Once it became known that infiltration by Pakistani armed personnel was occurring from as early as the autumn of 1998, the question arose why nothing was done about it for so many months. Could it have been such a total intelligence failure in one of the most sensitive areas on India's border or was it more than that? A very senior officer of the Indian army, Brigadier Surinder Singh, commander of the Kargil-based 121 Brigade, alleged, including in court, with documentary evidence (part of which was published by the major Indian magazine *Outlook*), that intelligence about intrusion and setting up bases inside Indian territory was available for many months and repeated warnings were given (from as early as August 1998) and these warnings were reached not only to the highest levels within the army but even to the government. This has raised doubts whether the BJP government deliberately allowed the situation to fester so that it could at an electorally opportune time come down with a heavy hand and project a 'victory' against the enemy— that is, use the Indian soldiers' lives as cannon fodder to gain political advantage. If this were to be proved true, it would certainly mark the lowest depths Indian politics ever reached. In any case, the government was compelled to institute a high-level enquiry committee to look into the matter.

The other disturbing aspect was that the BJP's actions upset the long-cherished traditions of keeping the armed forces in India out of politics. Chiefs of the military services were asked by the government to come to meetings of BJP party members. Large cut-outs of senior officers of the armed forces decorated podiums where BJP leaders were to address meetings. Elements from within the BJP combine such as the VHP landed up in the defence headquarters in South Block with thousands of rakhis for soldiers, and priests were sent to Kargil to bless the soldiers—moves which could not be seen to be innocent in the context of the multi-religious nature of the Indian armed forces. The Muslim, Sikh and Christian soldiers who gave their lives in Kargil to defend India were excluded. All this, on top of the well-known efforts of the party to woo retired services personnel into active party politics and to even try and influence serving personnel with communal ideology, caused considerable alarm. Such acts have been sharply criticized in India, as any move which could politicize the armed forces and threaten the secular and democratic traditions nurtured over the past fifty years (particularly within the armed forces) would not be acceptable.

The fallout of the Kargil episode in Pakistan was that Nawaz Sharif, the elected prime minister, was deposed on 13 December 1999, in a *coup d'etat* by General Musharraf, whom Sharif had appointed Chief of the Army Staff. The US President intervened to save Sharif's life, and he was exiled to Saudi Arabia. Musharraf first became Chief Executive and later President. Though Musharraf claimed later that Sharif was in the know about the Kargil plan, it is clear from a telephonic conversation between him and his deputy General Aziz, which was intercepted by Indian Intelligence, that in fact Sharif had been kept in the dark.[11]

The Kandahar Incident

Indo-Pak relations took another nose-dive with the Kandahar incident. An Indian Airlines plane on its way from Kathmandu to Delhi on Christmas Eve of 1999 was hijacked by terrorists who demanded the release of thirty-six captured militants and a ransom. Strangely, the plane was allowed to take off from Amritsar in Indian Punjab where it had landed and stayed for a full forty minutes. It finally landed in Kandahar in Afghanistan, and one passenger was killed by the hijackers to make their intent clear. Negotiations were conducted with the help of the Taliban and finally, to the shock and disbelief of the entire nation, the Minister for External Affairs Jaswant Singh, personally escorted Maulana Masood Azhar, a major leader of the terrorists, and two others, in a special plane to Kandahar. The hijackers as well as the released terrorists were all Pakistan based, and this did not help improve matters between the two countries.

The Agra Summit

Meanwhile, the situation in Kashmir was continuing to be a cause of anxiety, despite attempts at talks with political elements. At this stage, Musharraf showed an inclination for engaging in dialogue, and Vajpayee invited him to Agra for a summit in July 2001. However, not enough groundwork had been done in advance, and while Vajpayee wanted wide-ranging talks, Musharraf wanted to talk only about Kashmir. Ultimately, there could be no agreement on the joint statement, because Pakistan wanted to include a reference to Kashmir as a core issue, and India wanted to include cross-border terrorism. Pakistani reports claimed that a joint draft in which Kashmir was mentioned without the word 'core', and terrorism put in without the adjective 'cross-border', was okayed by Vajpayee and Jaswant Singh, the Foreign Minister, but vetoed by the Home Minister, L.K. Advani, possibly in deference to the RSS.

The summit, held in full media glare, with TV channels covering it round the clock, was used to great effect by Musharraf and his aides to put forward their point of view before the Indian public. Musharraf held a much-watched breakfast meeting with senior Indian editors in which he termed the terrorism in Kashmir as an indigenous freedom struggle. The Indian establishment, on the other hand, did not share any information with their own media, and failed to project their point of view. As a public relations exercise, the Agra Summit was a great success for Musharraf and a disaster for India.

Relations with Pakistan did not improve substantially after that. At times, they deteriorated, as after the terrorist attack on the Indian parliament on 13 December 2001, when India amassed huge numbers of troops on the border for no evident reason. The terrorist attack in the US on 11 September, 2001, after which Pakistan was chosen as the frontline state in the war against terrorism, exerted some pressure on Musharraf to condemn terrorism, but Pakistan remained unwilling and/or unable to call off the militants. India's credibility vis-à-vis Kashmir improved greatly after the successful holding of elections in Jammu and Kashmir in September 2002, despite stepped-up militant violence. Conducted by the Election Commission under the leadership of James Lyngdoh, and the watchful eye of the diplomatic community and the international media, they were universally accepted as being free and fair. The contrast with the elections to the National and Provisional Assemblies of Pakistan a month later, which seemed to have convinced neither foreign nor indigenous observers about their fairness, was glaring indeed. The SAARC summit at Islamabad in January 2004 provided an opportunity for Vajpayee and Musharraf to meet on the sidelines, and the freeze that had set in since the attack on the Indian parliament thawed somewhat. Nor was any real breakthrough achieved by the Manmohan Singh government, despite meetings with Musharraf, and various confidence-building measures such as the starting of a bus service from Srinagar to Muzaffarabad. Terrorist attacks in Delhi, Varanasi, Bangalore and Mumbai, as well as Kashmir, killing hundreds, continued to sour relations. A positive feature was the emergence of public opinion on both sides of the border which favoured friendship and removing of restrictions on travel and communication.

Indo–US Relations and the Nuclear Agreement

The sanctions that were imposed on India by the US after the Pokhran nuclear tests were removed in October 2001 in the wake of the new situation created by 9/11. Even before that, Clinton visited India in March 2000, responding to a growing feeling in the US that it must engage with India as it was an important emerging economic power and a democracy. Also, the Indian community in the US had become a factor to be reckoned with, as it consisted mostly of highly educated professionals working in crucial sectors of US society. The new regime in the US under George Bush was fairly well-inclined towards India, whatever its other predilections. Even when it propped up Pakistan as a front-line state in the campaign against the Al-Qaida in Afghanistan by giving it a huge economic package and military supplies, it kept its relationship with India on course.

On the Indian side, there seemed to be an overanxiety to please the US, with Jaswant Singh making all kinds of offers in his Track 2 diplomacy with Strobe Talbot. If Talbot's account is accurate, Jaswant Singh made incredulous offers such as that India could sign the CTBT if sanctions were withdrawn, and that the LoC in Kashmir could be accepted as the international border. When 9/11 happened, again Jaswant Singh shot off his mouth by offering India as a base for operations, forgetting that geography was a hindrance, as India had no border with Afghanistan. When its focus shifted to Iraq after the invasion in March 2003, the government wanted to send troops in response to a request by the US, but public opinion was strongly opposed, and the government wisely desisted. It was also generally believed that the US had been allowed to assume an informal intermediary role on the Kashmir issue, something which India had consistently refused to any outsider, on the ground that this was a bilateral matter.

Building on the lifting of sanctions, a dialogue had also begun in 2002 on civilian nuclear technology, nuclear safety, and high-tech trade. In January 2004, Bush and Vajpayee even issued a joint statement pledging cooperation in these areas. These discussions were taken to a new stage altogether during the tenure of the Manmohan Singh government which took office in May 2004. The turning point was a visit by Condoleezza Rice, US Secretary of State, in March 2005, during which she is reported to have told the prime minister that it was 'the policy of the United States to help India become a major world power in the 21st century'. Manmohan Singh's visit to the US resulted in a joint statement on 18 July 2005 which spelt out that the US would work to adjust US laws and international regimes to enable full civilian nuclear energy cooperation and trade with India, including provision of fuel supplies for the Tarapur nuclear reactors. On its part, India agreed to identify and separate civilian and military nuclear facilities and programmes in a phased manner, place its civilian nuclear facilities under International Atomic Energy Agency (IAEA) safeguards, continue its unilateral moratorium on nuclear testing, ensure non-proliferation, etc.

The agreement aroused a great deal of debate and discussion in India. The critics became more strident when India voted at the IAEA general body meeting in favour of a resolution warning Iran that it would get reported to the UN and face possible sanctions if it did not cooperate fully with IAEA investigations into its alleged efforts at enrichment of uranium towards development of a nuclear device. The Indian vote was under US pressure, it was said, and against Indian interest. The government stand was that Iran, being a signatory to the NPT, had been in a position different from that of India when it undertook its nuclear tests. They also argued that the vote was cast only after an assurance that reporting to the UN would be postponed.

Others have pointed out that Iran was part of the nexus of beneficiaries of the Pakistan nuclear scientist A.Q. Khan's illegal nuclear trade. Further, Iran had voted innumerable times against India on the Kashmir issue in the Organization of Islamic Countries. In 1996, in a move rare in diplomatic history, it had even cancelled the then Foreign Minister, I.K. Gujral's visit to Iran, on the ground that India was oppressing Muslims in Kashmir. Besides, the real difficulty was that Iran could not make up its mind what it wanted to do, including whether it wanted to accept the various proposals made by Russia, China and EU countries. On the other hand, it was true that the US was unreasonably hostile to Iran, and this pushed Iran more and more into extremist positions.

To return to the discussion on the Indo-US nuclear agreement and the legislation passed by the US Congress with reference to this agreement, there were many concerns expressed by commentators, including by scientists associated with the nuclear programme. One major concern was about what would happen if India at any time in the future wanted to suspend its voluntary moratorium and undertake a nuclear test. The US would be obliged according to its laws to stop supply of fuel and technology, and ask for return of all material supplied to India's civilian nuclear programme. The second concern was with regard to what was to happen to spent fuel, as the Act did not specify this. The issue of whether or not the civilian and military programmes could be separated was also raised. The larger issue at stake was whether India's foreign policy would become subservient to US needs.

The government countered by saying that India would be bound only by those items that it signed in an agreement, and not by US law. India needed the uranium, it needed to step up its civilian nuclear programme for its burgeoning energy needs. The agreement meant that India was accepted as a de facto nuclear weapons state, and that was a huge gain. The prime minister assured the nation that Indian foreign policy was its own, and cited his public and private statements in the US that India was opposed to the Iraq war. He has also maintained that India will not accept any additional conditionalities. The deal was still being negotiated and it was not certain whether the final agreement will go through.

At the end of July 2007, the draft agreement was finally concluded. A joint statement issued by External Affairs Minister Pranab Mukherjee and US Secretary of State Condoleezza Rice simultaneously in Washington and New Delhi on 27 July 2007 said: 'The United States and India have reached a historic milestone in their strategic partnership by completing negotiations on the bilateral agreement for peaceful nuclear cooperation.'

The National Security Adviser Narayanan, Atomic Energy Commission (AEC) Chairman Anil Kakodkar and Foreign Secretary Shivshankar Menon jointly addressed a press conference to allay any public apprehensions about the deal. AEC Chairman Anil Kakodkar, some of whose earlier statements showed concerns over certain aspects of the agreement, said that he was 'satisfied' with the final document: 'What I said earlier was the national position. What I am saying now is the national position and what we have got is consistent with our national position. I have no reason to unhappy.'[12]

In Washington, during a briefing, US Under Secretary of State for South Asia Nicholas Burns said the 123 Agreement was 'the single most important initiative between the United States and India' He went on to say that the agreement was so significant and complex that 'the US will never offer (it to) any other country in the world'.[13]

The broad details of the agreement revealed certain unique provisions which the US has not conceded to any other country with which it has signed 123 agreements so far. These can be categorized as

(i). Enrichment and reprocessing: India has 'advance right to reprocess' US-origin safeguarded spent fuel.

(ii). Fuel supplies guarantee and strategic fuel reserve: The US has made commitment for uninterrupted fuel supplies to Indian reactors. It would also support India to build a strategic fuel reserve with the help of other supplier countries.

(iii). Non-hindrance clause: The US will not hinder the growth of India's nuclear weapons programme. The agreement also does not prescribe that India should not test a nuclear device, which most other 123 agreements have.

The agreement received widespread support in the media and other sections of civil society. However, the left parties, who support the UPA government from outside, raised their voice of protest over the deal citing certain provisions in the text which, they thought, would make India's foreign policy subservient to that of the US. The negotiations between the government and the left parties had yet to yield any fruitful result when this book went to press. The government was not left with much of a choice. It can press for the completion of the deal only at the risk of its own survival. A debate on the issue slated for the winter session of parliament is likely to clarify the issue further.

Politics in the States (I): Tamil Nadu, Andhra Pradesh and Assam

Functioning within the political and economic framework of the Indian Union, politics in various states have a great deal in common, but their pattern and achievements vary considerably. Each state has a different constellation of class, caste, social and cultural forces and levels of social and economic development, and which, in turn, influence its politics.

It is, therefore, not accidental that changes in the social bases of politics, whether of caste, class, tribe, status groups, religion, region, or gender, are first reflected at the state level. Patronage networks, extending into small towns and villages, are also initiated and built up at this level. Basic nation-building and human resource development measures, relating to changes in agrarian structure, agricultural and industrial development, health, roads, power, irrigation, are implemented primarily by state administrations. Despite the many centralizing features of Indian polity as it has developed over the years and the Centre's ability to interfere with and encroach upon the powers of the states, the central government basically relies on the state governments for carrying out its important decisions; the effectiveness of the central developmental programmes also depends on the performance of the states. Even when the same party rules in the Centre and the states, the capacity of the central government to get its plans and policies executed is quite limited. Witness, for example, the varying fate of land reforms in different Congress-ruled states in the 1950s. In fact, the difference in the competence of various state governments explains to a large extent the wide divergence in their performance and the rates of social, cultural and human resource development.

Unfortunately, we do not have the space to discuss most of these aspects of state politics or the politics of each one of the states as they have developed since independence. Instead, we have chosen as case studies a few states—Tamil Nadu, Andhra Pradesh, Assam, West Bengal and Jammu and Kashmir—and that too to illustrate some aspect of their politics that makes these states distinct.

We have discussed Punjab separately in the chapter 'The Punjab Crisis' as an example of both communal politics and minority communalism ultimately assuming a separatist form.

Constraints of space also prevent us from taking up the case of Bihar where, since the 1960s, casteism both of the upper castes—Bhoomihars, Brahmins, Rajputs and Kayasthas—and the backward castes—Yadavas, Kurmis and Koeris—has gradually eroded and seriously damaged the administration, economy, educational system, and culture of the people. This is particularly depressing as the state had a hoary past, militant traditions of the national, peasant and tribal movements and produced in recent times political leaders of the calibre of Sachidanand Sinha, Rajendra Prasad, Mazhar-ul-Haq, Jayaprakash Narayan and Swami Sahajanand Saraswati, and intellectual giants like the economist Gyan Chand, historian R.S. Sharma, political scientist B.B. Mazumdar, historian, philosopher and writer Rahul Sankritayan, novelist Phanishwar Nath Renu, and poets Nagarjun and Ramdhari Singh Dinkar.

The DMK in Tamil Nadu

A study of the Dravida Munnetra Kazhagam (DMK) illustrates how a strong separatist regional strain in Indian polity was overcome and co-opted.

The DMK emerged in the 1950s as a party and a movement which thrived on strong caste, regional and even secessionist sentiments. It was the heir to two strands of the pre-independence period movements in Tamil Nadu: the non-Brahmin movement, which had led to the formation of the pro-British Justice Party in 1920, and the strongly reformist anti-caste, anti-religion Self-Respect Movement led by E.V. Ramaswamy Naicker, popularly known as Periyar (Great Sage).

In 1944, Naicker and C.N. Annadurai established Dravida Kazhagam (Federation) or DK which split in 1949 when Annadurai founded the Dravida Munnetra (Progressive) Kazhagam (DMK).

But, significantly, in contrast to the Justice Party and Naicker, Annadurai had taken up a strongly anti-imperialist, pro-nationalist position before 1947.

Annadurai was a brilliant writer, a skilful orator and an excellent organizer. Along with M. Karunanidhi and M.G. Ramachandran (MGR) and other film personalities—actors, directors and writers—Annadurai used dramas, films, journals, pamphlets and other mass media to reach out to the people and over time succeeded in building up a mass base, especially among the youth with a rural background, and a vibrant political organization.

The DMK was strongly anti-Brahmin, anti-North and anti-Aryan— southern Brahmins and North Indians being seen as Aryans, all other South Indians as Dravidas. It raised the slogan of *opposition to the cultural, economic and political domination of the South by the North*. Naicker and others had in 1938 organized a movement against the decision of the Congress ministry to introduce Hindi in Madras schools, labelling it to be an aspect of Brahminical North Indian cultural domination. The DMK also decided to oppose what it described as expansion of Hindi 'imperialism' in the South. Its main demand, however, was for a homeland for the Dravidas in the form of a separate independent South Indian state—Dravidnadu or Dravidasthan—consisting of Tamil Nadu, Andhra, Karnataka and Kerala.

During the 1950s and 1960s, however, there were several developments which gradually led to a change in the basic political thrust of the DMK. Naicker gave up his opposition to Congress when, in 1954, Kamaraj, a non-Brahmin, displaced C. Rajagopalachari as the dominant leader of Congress in Tamil Nadu and became the chief minister. The DMK leadership too gradually lessened its hostility to Brahmins and started underplaying its anti-Brahmin rhetoric. It also gradually shifted its emphasis from race to Tamil consciousness, to pride in Tamil language and culture and in being a Tamil. It, however, retained its opposition to Hindi and its emphasis on radical social reforms, especially in terms of the removal of all caste distinctions and the inculcation of a rational and critical approach towards the classical 'Hindu' scriptures.

There was also a gradual change in the DMK's secessionist plank as it began to participate in elections and in parliamentary politics, and also because the other southern states refused to support secessionism. The DMK did not participate in the 1952 elections, but it tested its electoral appeal by helping nearly thirty MLAs to win. It participated in the 1957 and 1962 elections. That a change was coming became visible when, in the 1962 elections, it entered into an alliance with Swatantra and the CPI and did not make a separate Dravidnadu a campaign issue though it was still a part of its manifesto. Later still, during the India–China war, it rallied to the national cause, fully supported the government, and suspended all propaganda for secession.

A further and final change came when, as a result of Nehru's determination to deal firmly with any secessionist movement, the 16th Constitutional Amendment was passed in 1962 declaring the advocacy of secession a crime and requiring every candidate to parliament or state assembly to swear 'allegiance to the Constitution' and to 'uphold the sovereignty and integrity of India'. The DMK immediately amended its constitution and gave up the demand for secession. From secessionism it now shifted to the demands for greater state autonomy, more powers to the states, while limiting the powers of the central government, an end to the domination and unfair treatment of the South by the Hindi-speaking North, and allocation of greater central economic resources for the development of Tamil Nadu. The DMK gradually developed as a state-wide party with appeal in urban as well as rural areas and with a programme of radical economic measures, social change and development of modern Tamil language and culture. It also further softened its anti-Brahmin stance and declared itself to be a party of all Tamils, which would accommodate Tamil Brahmins.

With each election the DMK kept expanding its social base and increasing its electoral strength. In 1962 it had won 50 seats in the state assembly and 7 in the Lok Sabha. Two subsequent events enabled it to take off in the 1967 elections. First, fierce anti-Congress sentiments were aroused by the anti-Hindi agitation of early 1965, and the DMK was the main beneficiary. Second, the DMK fought the 1967 elections in alliance with Swatantra, the CPM, PSP, SSP and the Muslim League. Consequently, it captured 138 of the 234 seats in the assembly, with Congress getting only 49. The DMK formed the government in the state with Annadurai as chief minister. Congress was never to recover from this defeat. The DMK, on the other hand, began to follow the trajectory of a 'normal' regional party.

After Annadurai's death in February 1969, M. Karunanidhi became the chief minister. Later, the DMK supported Indira Gandhi in her struggle against the Syndicate. Its support, along with that of CPI, enabled Indira Gandhi to remain in power after having been reduced to a minority in the Lok Sabha. In the 1971 elections to the Lok Sabha and the state assembly, the DMK teamed up with the Indira-led Congress (R), which surrendered all claims to assembly seats in return for DMK's support to it in 9 parliamentary seats which it won. The DMK won 183 out of the 234 assembly seats and 23 Lok Sabha seats.

In 1972, the DMK split, with MGR forming the All-India Anna DMK (AIADMK). The two-party system now emerged in Tamil Nadu, but operated between the two Dravida parties, with both parties alternating in power in the state since then.

Participation in electoral politics, assumption of office, and greater integration of Tamil Nadu with the national economy led to the DMK being transformed from a secessionist movement into an integral part of India'a democratic and secular political system and a 'politically mature and pragmatic' regional, or rather one-state, party.

Just like the other mainstream parties, the DMK also split into two main, and later, several small parties. The DMK and AIADMK (and their offshoots) in turn, at one time or the other, allied with Congress, the CPI, CPM, Janata and Janata Dal and other all-India parties. In recent elections, the AIADMK in 1998 and the DMK in 1999 joined forces with the BJP, the party they had earlier accused of representing the Aryan North and Hindi domination at their worst. The two also gradually diluted their anti-North and anti-Hindi stance. They have given up the idea of Dravidnadu or even of the unification of the four southern states within the Indian Union. They have put the goal of the annihilation of the caste system in cold storage with the result that the Scheduled Castes and other downtrodden castes have been turning away from them. In fact, the anti-Brahmin movement has, as a whole, failed to make much of a dent in the Brahminic caste order and caste domination; its only success has been in driving out Brahmins from Tamil Nadu to the rest of India and the United States, thereby affecting science and technology, and intellectual and academic life in Tamil Nadu. Caught in a cleft between the rich and middle peasantry and the rural landless, the DMK and AIADMK have also virtually given up their agrarian radicalism. Their social radicalism has in the main taken the form of providing large-scale reservation in education and government services to backward castes and classes, which has resulted in long-term damage to administration, educational standards and development without significantly removing economic disparities based on caste and class.

Of course, the most important reason for the transformation of the Dravida parties has been the realization that (i) secession was not possible and the Indian state was strong enough to suppress any move towards it, (ii) there was no real contradiction between a regional identity and the overall national identity, (iii) India's federal and democratic system of government provided both the state and the individual Tamils economic opportunities, and a great deal of political and administrative freedom to develop and undertake social reforms, (iv) the Indian political system and national integration were based on acceptance of cultural pluralism, and (v) the states have complete cultural autonomy, including control over language and other cultural affairs. In short, the Dravida parties and the people of Tamil Nadu have come to realize over time that the concept of 'unity in diversity' is quite workable and an integral part of the Indian polity and ethos.

Telangana versus Coastal Andhra Pradesh

Andhra's is a case of a single linguistic cultural region being engulfed by political conflict and sub-regional movements based on disparity in development and presumed inequality in economic opportunities.

As we have seen, Andhra was created as a separate state in October 1953 and in November 1956 the Telugu-speaking Telangana area of Nizam's Hyderabad state was merged with it to create Andhra Pradesh. The hope was that being part of a large unilingual state would cement the Telugu people culturally, politically and economically. Even at that time certain Telangana Congress leaders, as also the States Reorganisation Commission, had some reservations about the merger because of Telangana being relatively more underdeveloped, its level of development being nearly half that of the coastal districts of Andhra Pradesh. Telangana's per capita income was Rs 188 compared to Rs 292 in the coastal districts; the number of hospital beds per lakh population was 18.6 while it was 55.6 in the coastal districts. The literacy rate in Telangana was 17.3 per cent as against 30.8 in the rest of Andhra Pradesh. Similarly, Telangana had only 9 miles of roads per 100 square miles, the comparative figure being 37 miles for coastal Andhra. Unlike coastal Andhra, Telengana's sources of irrigation were scanty, consisting mostly of rain-fed tanks and wells.

A powerful movement for a separate state of Telangana developed in 1969 based on the belief that because the politics and administration of the state were dominated by people from the Andhra region (Andhrans), the Andhra government had neglected Telangana, had done very little to remove the regional economic imbalance, and Andhrans were exploiting the Telangana region. For example, it was believed that in rural electrification the ratio of the Andhra region and Telangana was 4:1 during the Second Plan and 5:1 in the Third Plan. Similarly, in the matter of irrigation schemes, the Andhra region was stated to have been favoured at the cost of Telangana. Further, the revenue surpluses being generated in Telangana because of free sale of liquor were supposed to be diverted to Andhra which had prohibition. All these allegations were refuted by the spokespersons of the government but the people of Telangana were not convinced.

But, above all, the separatist sentiment was based on the notion of injustice and discrimination in employment in state institutions. While the number of educated job-seekers had been growing as a result of sharp increase in education, employment, especially in the government services, was contracting all over the state as a result of the difficulties in the implementation of the Third Plan. But the political leaders and the unemployed middle-class youth put the blame for the growing unemployment in Telangana and Hyderabad city on the governmental bias in favour of the Andhra region.

The major issue in this context became the implementation of what came to be known as the Mulki Rules. The Nizam's government in Hyderabad had accepted as early as 1918 that in all state services those who were born in the state or had lived there for fifteen years (i.e., Mulkis) would be given preference, while restrictions would be imposed on the employment of outsiders. At the time of the merger of Telangana with Andhra in 1956 the leaders of the two regions had evolved a 'gentlemen's agreement' providing for the retention of the Mulki Rules in a modified form, a fixed share of places in the ministry for Telangana leaders, and preference for students from Telangana in admission to educational institutions including to Osmania University in Hyderabad. The discontented in Telangana accused the government of deliberately violating the agreement while the government asserted that it was trying its best to implement it. The latter argued that sometimes properly qualified persons were not available from the Telangana region because of educational backwardness in the old Hyderabad state. For example, expansion of education in Telangana made it necessary to bring in a large number of teachers from the Andhra region.

Towards the end of 1968, the students of Osmania University went on a strike on the question of discrimination in employment and education. The strike soon spread to other parts of Telangana. Fat was added to the fire by a Supreme Court judgement in March 1969 declaring the reservation of posts under the 1956 agreement to be constitutionally invalid. A massive, often violent, agitation demanding separation of Telangana from Andhra Pradesh now spread all over Telangana where schools and colleges remained closed for nearly nine months. The agitation was soon joined by organizations of non-gazetted government employees, who went on an indefinite strike, and a large number of teachers, lawyers, businessmen and other sections of the middle classes.

To lead the movement for a separate Telangana state in an organized manner, the Telangana Praja Samiti (TPS) was soon formed. A large number of disgruntled and dissident Congress leaders joined the TPS and occupied a dominant position in it. All the major national parties opposed the demand for a separate Telangana state; the two Communist parties looked upon it as an effort of the vested interests to misguide and misdirect popular anger against the landlord-bourgeois system. A large number of local leaders of Swatantra Party, Samyukta Socialist Party and Jan Sangh, however, supported the demand. Indira Gandhi and the central Congress leadership strongly resisted the demand though; trying to play a mediatory role, they urged the Andhra government to adopt a sympathetic attitude towards Telangana's economic demands and to redress its grievances.

Because of the central government's firm opposition to the break-up of the state, the failure of the movement to mobilize the peasantry, and the inevitable fatigue from which any mass movement suffers if it is not able to achieve success when it is at its height, the movement for a separate Telangana began to lose steam and to peter out after the summer of 1969. In July, the economically hard-pressed non-gazetted employees called off their strike. The students too went back to their studies before the examinations to be held in December 1969. Still the TPS succeeded in winning 10 out of 14 Telangana seats in the 1971 elections to the Lok Sabha.

After the 1971 elections, a compromise was worked out under the aegis of the central government, under which the Mulki Rules were to continue and a Telangana regional committee with statutory powers was to be formed. The compromise satisfied the disgruntled middle-class youth. The TPS merged with Congress in September 1971 after Brahmanand Reddy, the chief minister, resigned and was replaced by P.V. Narasimha Rao from Telangana.

It was, however, now the turn of the middle classes of the Andhra region to express anger. They were convinced that the Mulki Rules, however much amended, would adversely affect recruitment of Andhrans to state services. The political storm broke when the Supreme Court gave a judgement in October 1972 sanctioning the continuance of Mulki Rules. And, as in the case of Telangana, students and non-gazetted employees unions took the initiative in organizing meetings, strikes and demonstrations, which sometimes turned violent, and demanded the repeal of the Mulki Rules and other acts of alleged discrimination against Andhran government employees. Once again, doctors, who argued that medical funds were being diverted to Hyderabad city, lawyers, who wanted a High Court in the Andhra region, and businessmen, who opposed ceiling on urban wealth proposed by the state government, joined the agitation. An important difference from the Telangana agitation was that the big landowners and rich peasants, too, took an active part in the agitation because they were opposed to the land ceiling legislation passed by the state legislature in September 1972.

The prime minister announced a compromise formula on 27 November, according to which the Mulki Rules would be further modified and would continue in Hyderabad city till the end of

1977 and in the rest of Telangana till the end of 1980. The formula was seen as favourable to Telangana and the Andhra agitation now turned against both the central government and the concept of a united Andhra Pradesh. On 7 December, the Andhra non-gazetted employees went on an indefinite strike. Encouraged by Swatantra, the Jan Sangh and some independents, the agitators now demanded the creation of a separate state for the Andhra region. Once again the demand for division of the state was firmly opposed by the Communists, with the result that most of the trade unions and Kisan Sabha organizations stayed away from the agitation. Many Congressmen, however, supported it. Nine members of the Narasimha Rao cabinet resigned from it, though others remained integrationists. The movement turned violent in many places with attacks on the railways and other central government property and clashes with the police. The Central Reserve Police Force and the army had to be brought in at many places.

Once again Indira Gandhi took a firm stand in favour of a united Andhra Pradesh. On 21 December the Lok Sabha passed the Mulki Rules Bill. On 17 January 1973, she asked Narasimha Rao to resign and then imposed President's Rule in the state. The situation was gradually brought under control. Faced with a determined central government and as 'agitation fatigue' set in, the separatist movement subsided, especially as it could not mobilize the mass of the peasantry and the working class. Moreover, the epicentre of the movement remained in the coastal districts. Though the Rayalaseema region was opposed to the Mulki Rules it did not feel strongly about the demand for a separate state. As in the case of the upsurge in Telangana, non-gazetted government employees called off their strike in March and the students too returned to their classes. Finally, in September, the central government put forward a six-point formula which did away with the Mulki Rules but extended preference in employment and education to all districts and regions of the state over outsiders. The 32nd Constitutional Amendment was passed to enable the implementation of the formula. This satisfied most of the Congressmen of the two regions. In December, President's Rule was lifted and J. Vengal Rao, who became the consensus chief minister, was asked to implement the new formula. Thereafter, the demand for division of the state gradually petered out in both parts of Andhra Pradesh, though the Jan Sangh and later the BJP adopted it as a part of their programme.

In the case of both the Telangana and Andhra regions, the central government firmly and successfully opposed the demand for bifurcation of the state as it was apprehensive of similar demands being raised in other parts of the country. At the same time, what made it possible in the end to accommodate the two regional demands in Andhra was the fact that they were entirely economic and did not involve communal or cultural differences. Another lesson learnt from the two movements was that it is necessary not only to alleviate economic disparities between different states but also to promote integrated development within a state and that mere linguistic and cultural unity was not enough to inculcate a feeling of oneness and solidarity among a state's people.

Turmoil in Assam

In terms of population Assam is a small state. Political turmoil racked the state for years because its people feared the weakening or loss of their identity as Assamese. At no stage, however, did their politics take a secessionist turn. Several components constituted this fear, shaping the nature of demands made and movements launched.

(i) The Assamese had a strong and persistent grievance that the severe underdevelopment of Assam was due to unfair treatment being meted out to it by the central government, which had not only neglected its development but also discriminated against it in allocation of central funds and location of industrial and other economic enterprises. Much worse, the Centre was seen as having deprived Assam of its due share of revenues from its crude oil and tea and plywood industries. Assam's revenues had been pumped out and utilized elsewhere in the country. Assam's economic backwardness was also ascribed to control of its economy and resources, particularly the production and sale of its tea, plywood and other commodities by outsiders, mostly Marwaris and Bengalis. Moreover, the labour force in tea, plywood and other industries was also mostly non-Assamese.

Several times since independence, Assam has witnessed protest movements. There were demands for a greater share for Assam in the revenues derived from tea and plywood industries, a higher royalty for its crude oil, larger central financial grants and plan allocation, location of oil refineries in Assam, construction of more bridges over the Brahmaputra river, upgrading of the railway link between Assam and the rest of India, greater effort at industrialization of the state by both the state and the central governments, and greater employment of Assamese in central government services and public sector enterprises located in the state.

(ii) For historical reasons, which we do not have the space to discuss here, throughout the colonial period and for several years after independence, Bengalis settled in Assam occupied a dominant position in government services, in teaching and other modern professions and in higher posts in the public and private sectors. Being more backward in education, the Assamese-speaking youth felt disadvantaged in competition with the Bengali-speaking middle classes for jobs. There was also a strong feeling among the Assamese speakers that Bengali predominance in education and middle-class jobs also posed a threat to the Assamese language and culture.

The lack of job opportunities, the significant role of 'outsiders' in Assam's industry and trade, and the fear of being culturally dominated produced a sense of deprivation in the minds of middle-class Assamese. They started a movement in the 1950s demanding preference for Assamese speakers in recruitment to state government services and making Assamese the sole official language and medium of instruction in schools and colleges. Bengalis, who formed a majority in Cachar district and had a large presence in the rest of Assam, felt that the practice, initiated in 1871, of having both Assamese and Bengali as official languages should continue.

The movement for a change in the official language led to the gradual building up of hostility between Bengali and Assamese speakers. In July 1960, it erupted in tragic language riots. Bengalis were attacked *en masse* in both urban and rural areas, their houses were looted and set on fire. A large number of Bengalis had to take shelter in Cachar and Bengal. This led to a counter-agitation in Cachar and an angry, sometimes chauvinist, reaction in West Bengal.

Very soon, in 1960 itself, the state assembly passed a law, against the wishes of Bengali speakers and many tribal groups, making Assamese the sole official language, though Bengali remained the additional official language in Cachar. In 1972, Assamese was made the sole medium of instruction also in colleges affiliated to Guwahati University.

This effort to impose the Assamese language became one of the factors which hampered the process of evolution of the Assamese identity, prevented it from encompassing the entire state and led to many of the hill tribes demanding separation from Assam.

(iii) Over the years, the demographic profile of Assam underwent a change as a result of migration from other parts of India and, above all, from East Bengal-Bangladesh. However, the main grievance that was to develop into a massive anti-foreigners movement in 1979, was the large-scale illegal migration in a relatively short span of time from Bangladesh and to some extent from Nepal.

Migration of outsiders into Assam has a long history. The British administration had encouraged migration of thousands of Biharis to work on the tea plantations and of hundreds of thousands of Bengali peasants to settle on the vast uncultivated tracts of Assam. Assamese landlords had welcomed the hardworking Bengali tenants in the sparsely populated Assam. Between 1939 and 1947 Muslim communalists encouraged Bengali Muslim migration to create a better bargaining position in case of partition of India. Partition led to a large-scale refugee influx from Pakistani Bengal into Assam besides West Bengal and Tripura. In 1971, after the Pakistani crackdown in East Bengal, more than a million refugees sought shelter in Assam. Most of them went back after the creation of Bangladesh, but nearly 100,000 remained. After 1971, there occurred a fresh, continuous and large-scale influx of land-hungry Bangladeshi peasants into Assam. But land in Assam had by now become scarce, and Assamese peasants and tribals feared loss of their holdings. However, this demographic transformation generated the feeling of linguistic, cultural and political insecurity, that overwhelmed the Assamese and imparted a strong emotional content to their movement against illegal migrants in the 1980s.

Since the late nineteenth century and especially after independence, a certain cultural renaissance took place enhancing people's pride in language, culture, literature, folk art and music in Assam. Even while becoming a part of the Indian nation-in-the-making, a distinct Assamese linguistic and cultural identity emerged. The process was a complex one, given the state's cultural, linguistic and religious diversity. Many Assamese felt that the development and consolidation of a wider Assamese identity, by the gradual assimilation of Assamese tribes, was prevented by the central government's decision to separate large tribal areas from Assam and create small non-viable states such as Meghalaya, Nagaland, Mizoram and Arunachal Pradesh.

The demographic transformation of Assam created apprehension among many Assamese that the swamping of Assam by foreigners and non-Assamese Indians would lead to the Assamese being reduced to a minority in their own land and consequently to the subordination of their language and culture, loss of control over their economy and politics, and, in the end, the loss of their very identity and individuality as a people.

There was undoubtedly a basis for these fears. In 1971, Assamese-speaking persons constituted only 59 per cent of Assam's population. This percentage covered a large number of Bengali speakers, many of whom had in the course of time and as a result of generational change also learnt Assamese and had given the census enumerators Assamese as their mother tongue because of pure political expediency. Moreover, Assamese speakers lacked a majority in Guwahati and several other towns, which are the main habitat of literature, the Press, culture, modern economy and politics.

Though illegal migration had surfaced as a political matter several times since 1950, it came to the fore as a major issue in 1979 when it became clear that a large number of illegal immigrants from Bangladesh had become voters in the state. Afraid of their acquiring a dominant role in Assam's politics through the coming election at the end of 1979, the All Assam Students Union (AASU) and the Assam Gana Sangram Parishad (Assam People's Struggle Council), a coalition of regional political, literary and cultural associations, started a massive, anti-illegal migration movement. This campaign won the support of virtually all sections of Assamese speakers, Hindu or Muslim, and many Bengalis.

The leaders of the movement claimed that the number of illegal aliens was as high as 31 to 34 per cent of the state's total population. They, therefore, asked the central government to seal Assam's borders to prevent further inflow of migrants, to identify all illegal aliens and delete their names from the voters list and to postpone elections till this was done, and to deport or disperse to other parts of India all those who had entered the state after 1961. So strong was the popular support to the movement that elections could not be held in fourteen out of sixteen parliamentary constituencies.

The years from 1979 to 1985 witnessed political instability in the state, collapse of state governments, imposition of President's Rule, sustained, often violent, agitation, frequent general strikes, civil disobedience campaigns which paralysed all normal life for prolonged periods, and unprecedented ethnic violence. For several years there were repeated rounds of negotiations between the leaders of the movement and the central government, but no agreement could be reached. It was not easy to determine who were the illegal aliens or 'foreigners' or how to go about detecting or deporting them. There was also lack of goodwill and trust between the two sides.

The central government's effort to hold a constitutionally mandated election to the state assembly in 1983 led to its near-total boycott, a complete breakdown of order, and the worst killings since 1947 on the basis of tribal, linguistic and communal identities. Nearly 3,000 people died in state-wide violence. The election proved to be a complete failure with less than 2 per cent of the voters casting their votes in the constituencies with Assamese majority. The Congress party did form the government, but it had no legitimacy at all.

The 1983 violence had a traumatic effect on both sides which once again resumed negotiations in earnest. Finally, the Rajiv Gandhi government was able to sign an accord with the leaders of the movement on 15 August 1985. All those foreigners who had entered Assam between 1951 and 1961 were to be given full citizenship, including the right to vote; those who had done so after 1971 were to be deported; the entrants between 1961 and 1971 were to be denied voting rights for ten years but would enjoy all other rights of citizenship. A parallel package for the economic development of Assam, including a second oil refinery, a paper mill and an institute of technology, was also worked out. The central government also promised to provide 'legislative and administrative safeguards to protect the cultural, social, and linguistic identity and heritage' of the Assamese people.

The task of revising the electoral rolls on the basis of the agreement was now taken up in earnest. The existing assembly was dissolved and fresh elections held in December 1985. A new party, the Assam Gana Parishad (AGP), formed by the leaders of the anti-foreigners movement, was elected to power, winning 64 of the 126 assembly seats. Prafulla Mahanta, an AASU leader, became at the age of thirty-two the youngest chief minister of independent India. Extreme and prolonged political turbulence in Assam ended, though fresh insurgencies were to come up later on, for example that of the Bodo tribes for a separate state and of the secessionist United Liberation Front of Assam (ULFA).

Experience in Assam since 1985 has shown that while it was and is necessary to stop the entry of foreigners, massive detection and deportation of the existing illegal entrants is not easy and perhaps not possible. Expulsion of old or recent minorities of all types is not the answer. Rather their gradual integration and assimilation into the Assamese identity is the only long-term and realistic solution. Chauvinism, whether in the form of their exclusion or their forceful elimination would only disturb and weaken the historical process of Assamese identity-in-the-making.

It is noteworthy that the Assam anti-foreigners movement was not communal or secessionist or disruptive of the nation in any form. It was therefore possible for the central government and the all-India political parties to negotiate and accommodate its demands, even though they were sometimes exaggerated and unrealistic.

There were elements in the Assam movement, such as the RSS, which wanted to give it a communal twist because most of the illegal aliens were Muslims. Similarly, some others wanted to give the movement a chauvinist, xenophobic, Assamese colour. The movement, however, succeeded in avoiding both these eventualities because of the non-communal cultural tradition of the Assamese, the role of the national parties such as the CPI, CPM and large parts of Congress, and the wide base of the movement and leadership among Assamese Muslims and Bengalis. Undoubtedly, the movement suffered from many weaknesses; but, then, no movement is generated and develops according to a blueprint.

The conflict in Assam and its resolution again showed that while communal and secessionist movements disruptive of the nation cannot be accommodated and have to be opposed and defeated, it is quite possible and, in fact, necessary to accommodate politics of identity based on language or culture, or economic deprivation and inequality, for they are quite compatible with progressive and secular nationalism.

Politics in the States (II): West Bengal and Jammu and Kashmir

West Bengal presents the case of a Communist government that came to power through the parliamentary process and has functioned according to the rules of a democratic and civil libertarian polity and under conditions of a capitalist economy, though with the presence of a strong public sector. This government has ruled the state for nearly thirty-seven years, winning five state elections so far in a row, and given people on the whole an effective, reformist government.

The Congress government in Bengal had not performed badly till the early 1960s. Despite dislocation and disruption of the economy due to the partition of Bengal and the refugee influx of over 4 million coming from East Bengal till 1965, the government had been able to provide economic stability. West Bengal had maintained its position for industry in the hierarchy of states. There was marked progress in the public health programme, electricity generation and road construction. The government, however, had failed on two major fronts: unemployment among the educated and the rural landless grew continuously, and, while the zamindari system had been abolished, the power of the intermediary jotedars and landlords over sharecroppers and tenants was not curbed.

Political Mobilization and the CPI/CPM

Since 1930 the Communist party had enjoyed significant support among intellectuals and workers in Calcutta, and it emerged as a major political force in Bengal by 1947. The united CPI in the

1950s and CPM in the 1960s and 1970s organized a large number of mass movements and trade union struggles, including gheraos during 1967–69, and combined them with an effective use of the legislature to 'expose the government's misdeeds'. As a result there was a steady growth of the united CPI and later the CPM, both electorally and organizationally. Congress was defeated in the state elections of 1967 and 1969 and United Front governments led by breakaway groups from Congress and with CPM participation were formed. Both United Front governments broke up because of internal contradictions but they added to the CPM's popularity. During these years the CPM was also able to organize massive agrarian movements of tenants and sharecroppers and thus extend its political base to rural areas.

During the decade of 1967–77, West Bengal witnessed increasing violence and chaos, a crisis of governability, heightened factionalism and splits in Congress, which ruled the state directly or through President's Rule from 1969 to 1977. Unprecedented levels of state repression were especially directed against the Naxalites and the movements of the rural poor. In the end the CPM's popularity, combined with the mass reaction against the Emergency, was transformed into an electoral victory in 1977, and the CPM, along with its left allies, was able to form the government. Since then the CPM has further consolidated its power and entrenched itself, especially among the peasantry. It has succeeded in maintaining the left coalition as well as control of the government during the last thirty years, and through seven assembly elections.

CPM: Record of Successes

Two significant achievements of the CPM are worthy of analysis, in terms of improving the conditions of the rural poor. The first one has been in the field of land reform or rather tenancy reform. Though the Congress government had done away with the zamindari system in the 1950s it had allowed two aberrations: jotedars (intermediaries for rent collection between zamindars and sharecroppers who were the actual cultivators) were permitted to stay, and many large landowners allowed to retain above-ceiling land through benami transactions.

After coming to power the CPM launched the programme called 'Operation Barga' which reformed the tenancy system in the interests of the bargadars (sharecroppers), who constituted nearly 25 per cent of the rural households. For decades, sharecroppers had suffered from the two ills of (1) insecurity of tenure, for their tenancy was not registered, though law provided for permanency of tenure, and (2) high, illegal levels of the share of the crops they had to give to jotedars as rent. Through Operation Barga, which included politicization and mobilization of sharecroppers by the party and peasant organizations, the government secured legal registration of sharecroppers, thus giving them permanent lease of the land they cultivated and security of tenure, and enforced laws regarding the share of the produce they could retain, thus improving their income.

The decision to drastically reform the jotedari system in the *interests of the sharecroppers but not end it in toto* was a brilliant political tactic. Jotedars were of all sizes. The small and middle-sized jotedars were large in number. Moreover, many of them were simultaneously cultivators on their own land as rich and middle peasants. Some of them were petty shopkeepers in villages, or teachers, clerks, chaprasis, etc., in towns and cities. As such, in terms of both socio-political power and electoral clout and the interests of increased agricultural production they mattered—they could not be totally antagonized. Their economic power and income could be limited by reducing their crop share and giving permanency of tenure to sharecroppers, but their rent share and therefore income and ownership of land could not be completely abolished. After all, elections can be won only by a broad coalition, i.e., on the basis of broad-based political support, which would have to include, and at least not permanently and completely alienate, a significant section of rural society, consisting of small jotedars, who also happened to be rich and middle peasants and small shopkeepers. This strata was, moreover, capable of politically influencing and mobilizing a large number of small peasants and the rural and urban lower-middle classes. The party therefore treated only the large and absentee landowners as permanent 'class enemies'.

Significantly, reform of the jotedari system provided the incentive to all concerned to increase production. It became a contributory factor in the ushering in of the Green Revolution and multi-cropping, leading to increase in income of both sharecroppers and jotedars. It also enabled those jotedars who were cultivators to concentrate on increasing production.

For political and administrative reasons, the CPM government took up the tasks of unearthing benami above-ceiling land and its distribution to the landless with great caution, spread over several years, lest the rich peasants went over *en bloc* to the Opposition. The government supplemented tenancy and land reform measures with programmes for providing cheap credit to sharecroppers and small peasants, saving them in the bargain from the clutches of moneylenders. The Congress government at the Centre had evolved several schemes for providing subsidized low-interest loans through nationalized and cooperative banks to peasants and specially to landless labourers and small peasants for investment in Green Revolution technologies. The West Bengal government was one of the few state governments which successfully implemented these schemes with the help of panchayats and party and peasants' organizations.

The second major achievement of the West Bengal government has been its restructuring and transformation of the Panchayati Raj institutions, through which the rural poor, the middle peasants and the rural intelligentsia were empowered, or enabled to share in political power at the local level.

The Panchayati Raj experiment of the 1960s had failed in West Bengal as also in the whole of India because of the domination of its village, taluka and district institutions by the economically or socially privileged sections of rural society and by the local and district bureaucracy. It had yielded no benefits to weaker sections.

The CPM government and the party ousted the large landowners and other dominant social groups from the Panchayati Raj institutions—district-level zilla parishads, block-level panchayati samitis and village-level gram panchayats—involved the rural lower and lower-middle classes, teachers, and social and political workers, brought the bureaucracy under their control, and strengthened their authority and financial resources.

In addition, the CPM government took several other steps to improve the social condition of the landless. Its record of implementing centrally financed anti-poverty and employment generating schemes was not unblemished but was better than that of other states. The 'Food for Work' programme in particular was implemented effectively to generate jobs for the landless. Moreover, the West Bengal government took up projects such as road construction, drainage and cleaning of irrigation channels and village tanks which were meaningful from the point of view of the lower classes in the villages and tried to implement them through the reformed Panchayati Raj institutions so that the opportunities for corruption were drastically reduced.

The CPM also speeded up the organization of agricultural labourers and regularly organized mass struggle for higher wages. Interestingly, rather than concentrate on taking away land from rich peasants and distributing it among agricultural labourers and thus equalizing landownership, the CPM concentrated on enhancing the latter's capacity to struggle for higher wages. The success of the Green Revolution strategy and multi-cropping also resulted in greater employment as well as increase in wages in the countryside throughout the 1980s and 1990s.

The CPM government's record in containing communal violence has been one of the best in the country. Despite having a high ratio of Muslims in the population and the large influx of Hindu refugees from East Bengal, West Bengal remained relatively free of communal violence. In 1984, it successfully contained the communal fallout of Indira Gandhi's assassination and in December 1992 of the Babri Mosque's demolition. The CPM also did not permit the growth of casteism and caste violence in West Bengal.

In 1986, the Gorkha National Liberation Front (GNLF) organized, under the leadership of Subhash Gheising, a militant, often violent, agitation in the hill district of Darjeeling in West Bengal around the demand for a separate Gorkha state. Following negotiations between GNLF and the central and state governments, a tripartite accord was signed in Calcutta in August 1988, under which the semi-autonomous Darjeeling Gorkha Hill Council, within the state of West Bengal, came into being. The Council had wide control over finance, education, health, agriculture and economic development.

Overall, the CPM has succeeded in giving West Bengal a moderately effective and on the whole non-corrupt, and relatively violence-free government, especially in rural areas. It has also held its alliance with other smaller left parties, i.e., the CPI, the Revolutionary Socialist Party and the Forward Bloc. The worst of poverty and naked oppression by the dominant classes in rural areas has been mitigated in some measure. The CPM has also successfully checked and even reversed the role of the police and lower bureaucracy as the tools of the rural rich and as the oppressors and exploiters of the rural poor. The support of the rural poor is the reason why the party has remained in power in West Bengal for as long as it has.

Problem Areas

The urban sector and the field of industrial development have emerged as the vulnerable areas of the CPM government. Unlike in the countryside, it has been unable to find suitable structures or forms to work properly the institutions through which civic problems could be solved and the urban people involved in civic affairs. There has been no replica of Panchayati Raj in the cities. Before 1977, the CPM had organized struggles of urban citizens for higher wages and salaries and cheaper urban facilities such as transport. These struggles could obviously not continue for long under a CPM administration. Consequently, the deterioration in urban infrastructural facilities as well as in the quality of life that began under Congress rule has continued under CPM rule in most of West Bengal's towns and cities.

But the most important failing of the CPM government has been the inability to develop industry and trade because of the absence of any theory or strategy of economic development, of industrialization, of large-scale creation of jobs in a situation where a state is ruled by a Communist party while the country as a whole is not. There can be no removal of poverty, or long-term improvement in the living conditions of the mass of rural landless, or large-scale redistribution of wealth, or a meaningful dent in the burgeoning urban and rural unemployment without rapid industrialization and significant overall economic development and the resultant creation of jobs in industry, trade and services.

This is particularly true of West Bengal where the landless and marginal farmers constitute nearly half the rural population who cannot be absorbed on any significant scale in agriculture. But how can this economic development be integrated with the socialist orientation of the government and the ruling party? The CPM did not even undertake to find an answer to this pressing issue, what to speak of taking up the task.

Large-scale flight of capital from West Bengal had taken place during 1967–75 as a result of near-total administrative anarchy, gheraos and bandhs and labour militancy. After coming to power in 1977, the CPM did try to deal with the problem of capitalist investment in the state in a pragmatic manner. It began to restrain labour militancy, so much so that in a few years West Bengal came to have more industrial peace than most other parts of the country. West Bengal under the CPM displayed one of the best records in the maintenance of law and order. The CPM no longer threatened property owners; on the contrary the government began offering numerous incentives to capitalists, both Indian and foreign, to invest in West Bengal. But the capitalists did not respond and were not inclined to come back to West Bengal and to make fresh investments there in the field of industrial activity.

An important reason for the capitalists' staying away from the state has been the lack of a work culture and accountability, a malaise that has been difficult to cure. The real problem, however, has been that potential investors are not willing to trust a Communist government and a Communist party. Most of them believe that the leopard can disguise its spots but not change its nature. The problem is intractable and the party's dilemma is inherent in a situation where it is committed to the abolition of capitalism, however gradually, and has acquired partial and limited power in a state of the Union. This difficulty could have been foreseen.

The CPM, however, failed to take cognizance of the problem and look for innovative solutions suited to the circumstances in which the party was ruling in West Bengal. This was in part because the party assumed that its rule would not last long, as it would be overthrown by the central government. The party would, therefore, use its short-lived power to 'unleash' popular, revolutionary forces by freeing them from the fear of police and bureaucracy, hold the fort in West Bengal and Kerala for a short period and wait for the rest of India to catch up with them. Social development in general, and economic development in particular, would have to wait till an all-India revolution took place. As Jyoti Basu, chief minister of West Bengal put it as late as 1985: 'The aim of our programmes is to alleviate the sufferings of the rural and urban people and to improve their conditions to a certain extent. We do not claim anything more, as we are aware that without structural changes in the socio-economic order it is hardly possible to bring about any basic change in the conditions of the people.'[1] In other words, social and economic development was not and could not be on the CPM agenda in West Bengal.

414 Index Since Independence

What the CPM did not foresee was that if, by chance, it continued to rule for decades then it would have to deal with problems of urban decay, rural poverty, and growing unemployment among the educated youth, both in cities and villages, and the rural landless. All this would require high rates of economic growth under conditions where it would not be possible to rely upon capitalists to undertake the task. The real problem has, therefore, been of the CPM's failing to evolve an alternative strategy of development on the basis of the state and cooperative sectors, aided by small and medium entrepreneurs. That it is not a problem only of West Bengal but of economic development under and by a Communist state government is borne out by similar economic stagnation in Kerala.

Perhaps, the failure to innovate theoretically and strategically goes further. The CPM has now functioned as a political party within the framework of a democratic polity and a capitalist economic system since 1964. It has held political power in West Bengal continuously since 1977 and off and on in Kerala since 1957. It also no longer looks upon parliamentary democracy as a bourgeois ploy or the Indian constitution as a hoax to be attacked and exposed. Instead it defends the constitution, the Fundamental Rights enshrined in it, and its democratic institutions from attacks by anti-democratic forces. It only argues that the existing democracy should be further deepened both politically and socially and economically. Its political practice has been described by a sympathetic political scientist, Atul Kohli, as social democratic and reformist in orientation.[2]

In recent years, the CPM has attempted to change its industrial policies and invite, with some success, Indian and foreign capitalists to invest in West Bengal. But perhaps that is where lies the crunch. The CPM's reformism and social democratism have been pragmatic and not arrived at theoretically. The party has refused to theoretically analyse its own political practices and to then advance further on that basis.

The CPM has also failed to analyse the implications of its politics for its organizational structure and then to make innovations in this regard. Undoubtedly, its centralized and disciplined democratic-centralism party structure helped it withstand state repression, to acquire political power, and, to a certain extent, implement its agrarian policies. But, clearly, this party structure has now become a drag. It tends to promote monopolization of power by party cadre so that the people start depending on it to get everything done. Bureaucratization, patronage, privilege, abuse of power, and partisan behaviour have been taking a toll on the party and its popularity. Party cadres, panchayat leaders and trade union functionaries have started developing vested interests in the perks of power.

A basic class approach and pro-poor orientation together with a tight organizational structure enabled the CPM to come to power in West Bengal and to adopt several pro-rural-poor measures. But the government's failure to innovate theoretically and organizationally has contributed to its political stagnation. It increasingly finds itself in a Catch-22 situation. As a result of growing unemployment, failure to arrest urban decay, and develop the state, the CPM and its allied left parties have been losing support in the cities, especially Kolkata. This erosion of support is now spreading to rural areas, where the memory of Operation Barga, land reform and other ameliorative measures is beginning to recede. For several years the CPM has been winning elections mainly because of the absence of a viable alternative and the continuing loyalty of the poor. But the Opposition is being increasingly successful in gradually whittling down its support.

The future of the CPM in West Bengal is, of course, not yet foreclosed. With its wide popularity among the common people, especially among the rural poor, and a strong base in loyal and committed party workers and supporters, it has the possibility of making a theoretical and political leap forward. Only time will tell whether it does so or not. But there is no doubt that its future in West Bengal and the rest of India depends on this happening.

The Kashmir Problem

Kashmir has been an intractable problem so far as Indo-Pak relations are concerned. It has also posed a constant internal problem for India with forces of integration with India and secession from it being in continuous struggle.

An overriding factor in the situation is that Kashmir has become over the years a symbol as well as a test of India's secularism. If in 1947 Kashmir had acceded to Pakistan, Indians would have accepted the fact without being upset. But once, as a result of the invasion of Kashmir by Pathan tribesmen and Pakistani troops and the persuasion of its popular leader, Sheikh Abdullah, the state of Jammu and Kashmir acceded to India, the situation became different. Pakistan claimed Kashmir on the ground that it was a Muslim-majority state. This was unacceptable to secular India, which did not accept the two-nation theory. For India the question of Kashmir became not merely one of retaining a small part of its territory; it impinged on the very basic character of the Indian state and society.

As Nehru and other Indian leaders had seen clearly, separation of Kashmir from India would pose a serious danger to Indian secularism. If Kashmir seceded from India on grounds of religion, the two-nation theory would seem to have been vindicated. It would strengthen the Hindu communal forces and pose a serious threat to millions of Muslims, whose number in India is larger than even that in Pakistan, making their position in India quite untenable. The position was grasped quite clearly by many knowledgeable non-Indians too. For example, Josef Korbel, a member of the United Nations Commission on India and Pakistan, wrote in 1954:

> The real cause of all the bitterness and bloodshed, all the venomed speech, the recalcitrance and the suspicion that have characterised the Kashmir dispute is the uncompromising and perhaps uncompromisable struggle of two ways of life, two concepts of political organisation, two scales of values, two spiritual attitudes, that find themselves locked in deadly conflict in which Kashmir has become both symbol and battleground.[3]

Immediately after Kashmir's accession in October 1947, India had offered a plebiscite under international auspices for the people of Kashmir to take a final decision on it. But there was a rider: Pakistan's troops must vacate Kashmir before a plebiscite could be held. Till the end of 1953, the Government of India was willing to abide by the results of a plebiscite if proper conditions were created for it. But a plebiscite could not be held, partly because Pakistan would not withdraw its forces from Pakistan-held Kashmir, and partly because Indo-Pak relations got enmeshed in the Cold War. During 1953–54, the United States entered into a virtual military alliance with Pakistan. This also encouraged Pakistan to take a non-conciliatory and aggressive approach based on a 'policy of hatred' and animosity.

By the end of 1956, the Indian government made it clear to Pakistan and the international community that the situation in Kashmir and Indo-Pak relations had changed so completely that its earlier offer had become absolute and Kashmir's accession to India had become a settled fact. Since then, so far as India is concerned, Kashmir has been an irrevocable part of the nation. However, without openly saying so, Nehru and his successors have been willing to accept the status quo, that is, accept the ceasefire line or Line of Control (LoC) as the permanent international border.

Special Status of Jammu and Kashmir

Under the Instrument of Accession signed in October 1947, the state of Jammu and Kashmir was granted a temporary special status in the Indian Union under Article 370 of the Indian constitution. The state ceded to the Indian Union only in defence, foreign affairs and communications, retaining autonomy in all other matters. The state was permitted to have a Constituent Assembly and a constitution of its own, to elect its own head of the state called Sadr-e-Riyasat, and to retain its own flag. Its chief minister was to be designated as prime minister. This also meant that the Indian constitution's section on Fundamental Rights did not cover the state, nor did institutions such as the Supreme Court, the Election Commission, and the Auditor-General have any jurisdiction there. However, Article 370 dealt with the relations of the state with the Centre and not with its accession to the Union, which was complete.

In 1956, the Constituent Assembly of Jammu and Kashmir ratified the accession of the state to India. Over the years, the state's special status was considerably modified—one might even say liquidated. The jurisdiction of Union institutions such as the Supreme Court, the Auditor-General and the Election Commission and the constitutional provisions regarding Fundamental Rights had extended to the state. Parliament's authority to make laws for the state and the President's authority over the state government, including the power to impose President's Rule, had also been extended. The state's services were integrated with the central and all-India services. Symbolic of the changes were that in the nomenclature of the Sadr-e-Riyasat to Governor and of the state prime minister to chief minister.

A sizeable section of Kashmiris resented this erosion of the provisions relating to the state's autonomy. On the other hand, Article 370 gave birth to a powerful movement in the Jammu region of the state for full accession to India, a greater share for Jammu in government services and even for separation of Jammu from Kashmir. The movement soon acquired communal colours with the danger of the state being divided on religious lines— Kashmir being Muslim majority and Jammu being Hindu majority. The agitation in Jammu was led by the Jammu Praja Parishad which later merged with the Jan Sangh, which raised the agitation to an all-India level. An unfortunate event was the death of Jan Sangh president Syama Prasad Mookerjee due to a heart attack in a Srinagar jail, on 23 June 1951. He had gone to the state in violation of a government order. The Praja Parishad agitation played into the hands of communal pro-Pakistan elements in Kashmir. It tarnished India's secular image and weakened India's case on Kashmir. It also unsettled Sheikh Abdullah, and made him doubt the strength of Indian secularism.

The Politics of Sheikh Abdullah

India's internal problems in regard to Kashmir began with Sheikh Abdullah, a man of remarkable courage and integrity, having a mass appeal, but who was also autocratic, wayward and arbitrary. Pressed by communal elements in the Kashmir Valley demanding merger with Pakistan and harassed by communalists in Jammu demanding full integration with India, Abdullah began to veer towards separation. Exaggerating the strength of communal forces and the weakness of secularism in India, he increasingly talked of the limited character of the accession of the state to India and of 'full' autonomy for the state. He even hinted at Kashmir's independence to be achieved with the help of the US and other foreign powers. He also began to appeal to communal sentiments among Kashmiri Muslims. Nehru pleaded with him for sanity and restraint but with little effect. By the middle of July 1953, Abdullah publicly demanded that Kashmir should become independent. The majority of his colleagues in the cabinet and his party opposed his new political position and asked the Sadr-e-Riyasat to dismiss him on charges of 'corruption, malpractices, disruptionism and dangerous foreign contacts'. Abdullah was consequently dismissed and Bakshi Ghulam Mohammed installed as prime minister. The new government immediately put Abdullah under arrest. He, however, remained a martyr and a hero for many Kashmiris. Nehru was unhappy with the turn of events but would not interfere with the state government.

Abdullah's political career, closely interwoven with that of Kashmir's, had a chequered history from 1953 till his death in 1982. Under Nehru's pressure, he was released on 8 January 1958 but was rearrested three months later as he continued with his separatist campaign and appeals to communal sentiments.

Nehru got Abdullah released again in April 1964. Abdullah, however, continued to claim that Kashmir's accession to India was not final and that he would fight to secure for the state the right of self-determination. But since he was also against the state's merger with Pakistan, he was frontally opposed by pro-Pakistani political groups led by Moulavi Farooq and the Awami Action Committee. Abdullah was put under house arrest and again deprived of his liberty in May 1965. The restrictions on him were removed only in 1968.

Bakshi Ghulam Mohammed ruled Jammu and Kashmir with a heavy hand and with large-scale corruption and misuse of patronage and government machinery. He was succeeded by G.M. Sadiq and then by Mir Qasim, who were men of integrity but not effective administrators or skilful politicians. The state government under these leaders never acquired wide popularity, though the pro-Pakistan forces remained weak.

The Bangladesh war and the break up of Pakistan in 1971 had a significant impact on Kashmir; the Pro-Pakistani Awami Action Committee and the secessionist Plebiscite Front suffered a severe political jolt. Abdullah now got into a better frame of mind, did some rethinking and adopted a more conciliatory approach towards the central government. Indira Gandhi, in turn, extended a hand of friendship, lifted all restrictions and opened a dialogue with him. He informally agreed not to raise the question of self-determination or plebiscite and to limit his demands to that of greater autonomy within the Indian Union. Finally, in February 1975, he once again became chief minister and the leader of the

National Conference. In the July 1977 mid-term poll in the state he won hands down. His son, Farooq Abdullah, succeeded him as chief minister, on his death in 1982.

Farooq Abdullah, Insurgency and Terrorism

Since 1982 the state has either been ruled mostly by Farooq Abdullah or been under President's Rule. Farooq won a comfortable majority in the mid-term elections in June 1983; but acrimony soon developed between him and the central government. In July 1984, in a coup against Farooq, his brother-in-law, G.M. Shah, split the National Conference. Acting at the behest of the central government, the governor, Jagmohan, dismissed Farooq as chief minister and installed G.M. Shah in his place.

G.M. Shah was both corrupt and inept and, as he failed to control communal attacks on Kashmiri Pandits, his government was dismissed in March 1986 and President's Rule imposed in the state. Subsequently, Rajiv Gandhi entered into an alliance with Farooq Abdullah for the assembly elections in early 1987. But Farooq, who won the election, was unable to manage the state politically or administratively. Thereafter, the movement for secession stepped up in the Valley. Both Hizbul Mujahideen and other fundamentalist, pro-Pakistan groups and those for independence led by the Jammu and Kashmir Liberation Front (JKLF) took to violent agitations and armed insurgency. All these groups were actively financed, trained and armed by Pakistan, and carried on a campaign of murders, kidnappings and torture of political opponents and of attacks on police stations, government offices and other public buildings. They also attacked Kashmiri Pandits, most of whom were forced to leave their homes and move to refugee camps in Jammu and Delhi. To contain terrorism and insurgency, V.P. Singh at the Centre dismissed Farooq Abdullah's government, which had lost control over the Valley to the terrorist groups, and imposed President's Rule in the state. Farooq, however, made another political comeback by winning the long-delayed elections in 1996. In the 2002 state elections, he lost power and the state came to be ruled by an alliance of the People's Democratic Party, headed by Mufti Muhammed Sayeed, and the Congress party.

The all-party Hurriyat (Liberation) Conference and the JKLF which stands for Kashmir's independence and the pro-Pakistan Mujahideen have lost steam in recent years, mainly because of the Mujahideen and JKLF's terrorist depredations against the people of the state, but Pakistan-supported and organized terrorism continues to be a menace affecting normal politics in Jammu and Kashmir.

The Way Out

From the early 1950s to date, Kashmir has been bedevilled by several major ills, leading to the alienation of the people of Jammu and Kashmir from the state's rulers as also India as a whole. There has been an absence of good and sound administration; the government and its various departments have been mired in corruption and nepotism. Most elections, starting with the very first one in 1951, have been rigged and marred by electoral fraud, leading to loss of faith in the legitimacy of the electoral process and the political system as a whole among the people, who have therefore not hesitated to take recourse to extra-constitutional means. Even otherwise, democracy has functioned quite imperfectly from the beginning and politics and administration in the state have assumed an authoritarian character. With the passage of time and as Pakistan-sponsored insurgency and terrorism have grown, human rights have taken a beating in Kashmir. A large role for the army in Kashmir has been a necessity in view of Pakistani military threat and subversion; but this has also meant a high cost in terms of the functioning of a civil libertarian polity.

Kashmir has also suffered from near-perpetual instability which has often led to, and has often been caused by, repeated central intervention and political manipulation, dismissal of governments and replacement of one set of incompetent and corrupt ministers by another similar set, and imposition of President's Rule. As a result the people of the state have tended to regard centrally-supported rulers as puppets and governors as mere agents of the central government. It is, however, widely acknowledged that the 1996 and 2002 elections in the state were more or less fair and widely representative of the people of the state.

Jammu and Kashmir's accession to India is irreversible, though India is not likely to regain control over Pakistan-occupied Kashmir.

It is clear that while it is necessary to take stern action against terrorism and insurgency, such action should not adversely affect the civil liberties and human rights of the people. The estranged Indo-Pak relations will continue to cast a deep and dark shadow over Jammu and Kashmir; but that makes it even more necessary that Kashmir is given a clean, sound and democratic government, free of excesses by the police and paramilitary forces.

The extent of local autonomy is a contentious issue that will have to be resolved keeping in view the sentiments of the people of the state and the federal constitutional structure of India. We believe, however, that more significant is the issue of how the democratic process in the state develops with the fuller participation of the people. It would not be difficult to resolve the Kashmir problem if two important parameters are kept in view. No democracy would easily permit secession of any of its parts, and no democracy can afford to ignore for long the wishes of any part of its people.

The Punjab Crisis

During the 1980s, Punjab was engulfed by a separatist movement which was transformed into a campaign of terror and which has been aptly described by some as a low-intensity war and a dangerous crisis for the Indian nation.

The genesis of the problem lay in the growth of communalism in Punjab in the course of the twentieth century and, in particular, since 1947, and which erupted into extremism, separatism and terrorism after 1980. Before 1947, communalism in Punjab was a triad with Muslim, Hindu and Sikh communalisms, opposing one another, and the latter two often joining forces against the first. After August 1947, Muslim communalism having disappeared from the Punjab, Hindu and Sikh communalisms were pitted against each other.

From the beginning the Akali leadership adopted certain communal themes which became the constitutive elements of Sikh communalism in all its phases. We may discuss them briefly, as they developed before 1966 when the present Punjabi-speaking state of Punjab was created.

Denying the ideal of a secular polity, the Akalis asserted that religion and politics could not be separated as the two were essentially combined in Sikhism. They also claimed that the Akali Dal was the sole representative of the Sikh Panth which was defined as a combination of the Sikh religion and the political and other secular interests of all Sikhs.

A second theme put forth by the Akalis was that Sikhs were being continuously subjected to discrimination, oppression, persecution, humiliation and victimization, and that there were all sorts of conspiracies against them. There was also constant anti-

Hindu rhetoric. Hindus were accused of designs to dominate Sikhs, of imposing Brahminical tyranny over them, and of threatening their 'Sikh identity'. The Congress and the 'Hindu' Nehru, 'who ruled from Delhi', were made special targets of Akali anger for representing the Hindu and Brahminical conspiracy against Sikhs. Above all, echoing the Muslim League credo of the 1940s, the Akalis raised the cry of Sikh religion in danger.

While the relatively extreme Akali leaders were more virulent, even the more moderate leaders were not far behind in articulating these communal complaints. Moreover, with the passage of time, the extremists' influence kept on growing, and was in any case met with little criticism or disavowal from the more moderate Akalis. For example, addressing the All India Akali Conference in 1953, Master Tara Singh, who dominated the Akali Dal as well as the Sikh Gurdwara Parbandhak Committee (SGPC) at the time, said : 'Englishman has gone [sic], but our liberty has not come. For us the so-called liberty is simply a change of masters, black for white. Under the garb of democracy and secularism our *Panth,* our liberty and our religion are being crushed.'[1]

Interestingly, no evidence other than that of the denial of the Punjabi Suba was offered for this long list of grievances. The only concrete allegation regarding discrimination against Sikhs in government service was found to be baseless by a commission appointed by Nehru in 1961. The political scientist Baldev Raj Nayar was to point out in 1966 that though Sikhs 'are less than 2 per cent of the Indian population, they constitute about 20 per cent of the Indian army, have double their proportionate share in the Indian administrative services, and that in the Punjab their share in the services, as also in the legislature, the cabinet, and the Congress Party organisation, is higher than their proportion in the population (of the state)'.[2]

Another significant feature of Akali politics during this period was the use and manipulation of the institutions and symbols of the Sikh religion in order to harness religious sentiments and fervour to communal appeal. Significant in this respect was the Akali use of the SGPC, which controlled over 700 Sikh gurudwaras, to promote Akali politics and to organize Akali political movements. In particular, consistent use was made of the Golden Temple at Amritsar.

Akali politics also witnessed factionalism resulting in intense rivalry and competition between different Akali groups with regard to communal extremism, and also the control of the gurudwaras and the Golden Temple. This rivalry also led to constant multiplication and escalation of demands and the more moderate among the Akalis consistently yielding to the extremist and emerging groups.

Hindu communalism was also very active in Punjab during the Nehru years. Though not as strident or wedded to religion as Sikh communalism, it continuously acted as a counter-point to the latter.

Secular Response to the Punjab Problem

Before we discuss the two major issues around which communal politics in Punjab revolved till 1966, let us briefly consider how the secular parties dealt with Punjab's communal problem. As we have brought out earlier, Nehru adopted three basic rules for dealing with militant agitations and their demands: no negotiations or political transactions with the leaders of a movement or acceptance of their demands if they had secessionist tendencies, if they took recourse to violence, or based their movement or demands on religion or communalism. Nehru was more than aware of the fascist character of extreme communalism, including its Akali variety under Master Tara Singh's leadership.

At the same time, Nehru, being very sensitive to the feelings of the minorities, tried to conciliate the Akalis by accommodating, as far as possible, their secular demands. This approach led him to sign pacts with the Akali Dal twice in 1948 and 1956 when it agreed to shed its communal character. The accommodative strategy failed, however, to stem the growth of communalism in Punjab. New leaders soon emerged and resurrected the Akali Dal on a more extreme ideological and political basis, formulating and putting forward new lists of demands and grievances. Simultaneously, the Congress accommodation of the Akalis strengthened Hindu communal forces.

Nehru gave full support to Pratap Singh Kairon, Punjab's chief minister, as he was dealing firmly with both Hindu and Sikh communalisms. Neither Nehru or Kairon, however, took steps to check the communalization of Punjabi society through a mass ideological campaign or to confront communalism frontally at a time when it was not difficult to do so.

The CPI was quite strong in Punjab and a very strong force for secularism. It also opposed the Hindu and Sikh communalisms, politically and ideologically, throughout the 1950s. However, after 1964, its two offshoots, the CPI and the CPM, formed alliances with the Akali Dal for making electoral gains, thus giving Akali politics a certain legitimacy.

Roots of Post-1947 Communalism

Two major issues, which were in themselves secular but were communalized by Sikh and Hindu communalists, dominated Punjab politics till 1966. The first issue was that of state language: to decide what was to be the language of administration and schooling in bilingual Punjab. The Hindu communalists wanted this status for Hindi and the Sikh communalists for Punjabi in the Gurmukhi script. The government tried to resolve the problem by dividing Punjab into two—Punjabi and Hindi—linguistic zones. But the Hindu communalists opposed the decisions to make the study of Punjabi, along with Hindi, compulsory in all schools and Punjabi being made the only official language for district administration in the Punjabi linguistic zone. Even more contentious was the problem of the script for Punjabi. Traditionally, for centuries, Punjabi had been written in Urdu, Gurmukhi and Devanagari (Hindi) scripts. However, dissociating Punjabi from its common cultural background, the Akalis demanded that Gurmukhi alone should be used as the script for Punjabi. The Hindu communal organizations insisted on Devanagari also being used along with Gurmukhi. The issue was given a strong communal complexion by both the Sikh and Hindu communalists.

The second issue—that of the Punjabi Suba—proved to be more emotive and divisive. After the SRC was set up in 1955, the Akali Dal, the CPI, many Congressmen and Punjabi intellectuals put before it a demand for the reorganization of the state on linguistic lines, which would lead to the creation of Punjabi-speaking Punjab and Hindi-speaking Haryana. The SRC rejected the demand on the grounds that there was not much difference between Hindi and Punjabi and that the minimum measure of agreement necessary for making a change did not exist among the people of Punjab. After a great deal of haggling, an agreement was arrived at in 1956 between the Akali Dal and the Government of India leading to the merger of Punjab and Patiala and East Punjab States Union (PEPSU).

However, the Akali Dal under the leadership of Master Tara Singh soon organized a powerful agitation around the demand for the formation of a Punjabi Suba. Giving the demand a blatantly communal character, the Akali Dal alleged that the non-acceptance of the demand was an act of discrimination against Sikhs. It argued that the Sikhs needed a state of their own in which they could dominate as a religious and political community because of their population preponderance. The Jan Sangh and other Hindu communal organizations and individuals strenuously opposed this demand on the ground that it represented an effort to impose Sikh domination and Sikh theocracy on Punjab. They denied that Punjabi was the mother tongue of Hindus in the Punjabi-speaking part of the state and asked the latter to register themselves as Hindi-speaking in the Census of 1961.

Interestingly, the Harijan Sikhs, known as Mazhabi Sikhs, who were mostly landless agricultural labourers, also opposed the demand for a Punjabi Suba because they were afraid that the new state would be dominated by their class opponents, the rich peasants, who as Jat Sikhs were the main supporters of the Akali Dal.

Nehru refused to concede the demand for a Punjabi Suba mainly because of its communal underpinnings. He felt that the acceptance of a communal demand would threaten the secular fabric of the state and society. Nor was there a broad consensus in the state on the demand. Apart from a large section of Hindus, two stalwart Sikh leaders of the Congress, Pratap Singh Kairon and Darbara Singh, were bitterly opposed to the demand, as it was communal. Nehru should perhaps have accepted the demand as it was inherently just, especially as it was also being supported on a secular basis by the CPI, the PSP and a number of intellectuals and as, by 1960, the rest of India had been reorganized on a linguistic basis.

However, the way for the creation of a Punjabi Suba in consonance with Nehru's criteria was cleared by two later developments. First, Sant Fateh Singh, who ousted Master Tara Singh from the leadership of the SGPC and the Akali Dal, declared that the demand for a Punjabi Suba was entirely language based. Second, major political and social organizations in Haryana demanded a separate Hindi-speaking state and those in Kangra asked for its merger with Himachal Pradesh. Consequently, in

March 1966, Indira Gandhi, the prime minister, announced that Punjab would be split into two states: Punjabi-speaking Punjab and Hindi-speaking Haryana, with Kangra being merged with Himachal Pradesh.

But one question still remained: Where would Chandigarh go? To settle the matter, Indira Gandhi appointed the Punjab Boundary Commission, whose terms of reference were accepted by both sides. The Commission by a majority of two to one awarded Chandigarh along with the surrounding areas to Haryana. The Akali Dal, however, refused to accept the award. Indira Gandhi, not willing to displease the Akalis, announced that Chandigarh would be made a Union Territory and would serve as a capital both to Punjab and Haryana. Dissatisfied, the Akali Dal launched, immediately after the creation of the new state in November 1966, a vigorous agitation for the inclusion of Chandigarh in Punjab. However, after some time, its leadership agreed to submit the question to arbitration by the prime minister and to abide by her decision. Once again Indira Gandhi yielded to Akali pressure and, in 1970, awarded Chandigarh to Punjab with two Punjab tehsils (subdivisions), Fazilka and Abohar, having Hindu majority, being transferred to Haryana. This decision, too, was not implemented because of the Akali Dal's refusal to agree to the transfer of the two tehsils.

The acceptance of the Punjabi Suba demand was, we believe, a correct step, but it should not have been seen as a solution of the Punjab problem. The heart of that problem was communalism and unless that was eradicated the problem would remain, though it might take ever newer forms.

Akali Politics and Militancy

With the creation of the Punjabi Suba, all the concrete major demands that the Akali Dal had raised and agitated for over the years had been accepted and implemented; no real, meaningful demands were left which could enthuse its followers for long and therefore be sustained for long. It was, therefore, faced with the problem of where to go politically. The option of giving up communal politics and becoming either a purely religious and social organization or a secular party appealing to all Punjabis was seen by the Akali leaders as committing political harakiri.

Akali communalism therefore inexorably moved towards separatism as was the case with the Muslim League after 1937. The fact is that the logic of minority communalism, especially when it is repeatedly 'satisfied' is separatism, just as the logic of majority communalism is fascism.

Another problem was that of acquiring power through democratic means and the electoral process. Even in the newly created Punjabi Suba the Akali Dal failed to secure a majority in the 1967 and later elections. For one, the population arithmetic did not favour it as the Sikhs constituted less than 60 per cent of Punjab's population. Second, the Scheduled Caste Sikhs, constituting 25 to 30 per cent of the Sikh population, had, as agricultural labourers, a basic class contradiction with the rich and middle peasants, who were the main social base of the Akali Dal. They, therefore, voted for the Congress and the Communists till 1980. Third, and most important of all, Sikhs did not vote exclusively along communal lines. Most often, a good majority of Sikhs voted for the Congress and the Communists.

In fact, from 1952 to 1980, the Akali votes hovered between 35 and 45 per cent of the Sikh votes. The only time the Akali Dal was able to form the government in Punjab was in 1967 in alliance with the Jan Sangh, the Hindu communal party which had bitterly opposed the demand for a Punjabi Suba, and in 1977 in alliance with the Janata Party whose major constituent in Punjab was the Jan Sangh. In the 1980 elections to the Punjab assembly, just before launching its most militant and communal movement, the Akali Dal secured only 26.9 per cent of the total vote. This meant that less than 50 per cent of Sikhs voted for it and that the majority of Sikhs rejected the Akali politics and ideology.

Having lost the elections in 1980 and in order to widen their support base among Sikhs, the Akalis began to intensify the communal content of their politics and to continuously escalate their demands, the so-called moderate leaders keeping in step with the extremists. In 1981, the main Akali Dal, headed by Sant Longowal, submitted to the prime minister a memorandum of forty-five religious, political, economic and social demands and grievances, including the issue of the sharing of Punjab's river waters between Punjab, Haryana and Rajasthan and the question of the transfer of Chandigarh to Punjab, and launched a virulent campaign around them. Very soon, implementation of the Anandpur

Sahib Resolution (ASR), adopted in 1973, became the most prominent demand. The resolution, which had many versions, was openly communal and separatist in all its versions.

Simultaneously, the Akalis took up in a more blatant and strident manner all the communal themes we have discussed above. There was a more open use of religion as a mobilizing tool. Gurudwaras were the focal points of the Akali movements.

Thus, the logic of the communal ideology and politics of the Akalis since 1947 was separatism and the demand for a sovereign theocratic state. After 1981, the terrorists were to follow this logic to its conclusion. The failure of Akali agitations, which did not and could not succeed to the full, along with the heightened, unrequited sense of deprivation being preached for over thirty years, led to the belief among the more honest believers that violence offered the only remedy; and if organized mass violence was not possible and the militant mass movement had proved futile, then terrorist violence was the only answer.

Also, clearly, in practice, the Akali view was that the Akali demands had to be necessarily met, negotiations being only a matter of form. Moreover, often, the Akalis would accept an award, only to reject it later if found inconvenient. After a demand was met they would mount a fresh agitation around a new set of demands. Any agreement with them provided only a temporary and short-lived respite. Their basic approach was that Punjab, because of being a 'Sikh' state, and the Akali Dal, being a 'Sikh' party, were above the political norms and structure of the country, or the interests of the other neighbouring states, or a democratic, federal mechanism for the resolution of interstate disputes.

Terrorism in Punjab

Parallel to Akali militancy, terrorism made its appearance in Punjab in 1981 as a partial culmination of communal politics since 1947 and the policy of appeasement towards communalism followed by the Punjab Congress leadership, especially since the early 1970s. The initiator of terrorism was Sant Jarnail Singh Bhindranwale, who emerged in the late 1970s as a strong campaigner of Sikh orthodoxy. In this campaign he received the tacit support of the Punjab Congress led by Giani Zail Singh, who hoped to use him to undercut the Akalis. He was, however, to soon become a Frankenstein and turn against his erstwhile patrons.

The terrorist campaign by Bhindranwale and the All India Sikh Students Federation, headed by Amrik Singh, began on 24 April 1980 with the assassination of the head of the Nirankari sect. This was followed by the killing of many Nirankaris, dissident Akalis and Congress workers. In September 1981, Lala Jagat Narain, editor of a popular newspaper and a critic of Bhindranwale, was killed. Bhindranwale was shielded from government action by Giani Zail Singh who had in 1980 become the home minister at the Centre. To protect himself, Bhindranwale moved in July 1982 to the sanctuary of Guru Nanak Niwas, a building within the Golden Temple complex from where he directed the campaign of terrorism in Punjab. He now emerged as a central figure in Punjab politics.

Till September 1983, terrorist killings were confined to Nirankaris, petty government officials and Sikhs who disagreed with Bhindranwale. Bhindranwale was, however, since 1981, carrying on a verbal campaign of hatred against Hindus and 'fallen' Sikhs, that is, members of reformist Sikh sects, and inciting violence against them, especially through widely circulated audio cassettes.

A new dimension to terrorist activity was added when from September 1983 he started targeting Hindus on an increasing scale, and indiscriminate killing of Hindus began; this could be done with relative impunity as the Punjab administration and police were in a run-down condition and the Government of India was hesitant to take action against terrorism. He also organized the looting of local banks, jewellery shops and home guard armouries, the killing of Nirankaris and government officials and random bomb explosions. In April 1983, A.S. Atwal, a Sikh deputy inspector-general of police, was killed just as he was coming out of the Golden Temple after offering his prayers. From now on there was a marked and continuous increase in terrorist operations as also communal passions among Sikhs and Hindus. Bhindranwale also gave a call for a separation from and an armed struggle against the Indian state, emphasizing the separateness and sovereignty of Sikhs.

Fearing arrest, in December 1983, Bhindranwale moved into the safe haven of the Akal Takht within the Golden Temple and made it his headquarters and armoury, and a sanctuary for his terrorist followers, many of whom were criminals and smugglers. He smuggled on a large scale light machine-guns and other sophisticated arms into the temple, and set up workshops there for fabricating Sten-guns, hand grenades and other arms. He erected pillboxes in and around the Akal Takht and other buildings, where he provided weapons training to new recruits and from where he sent out death squads and conducted his campaign of murders, bombings and loot. A large number of other gurudwaras were also used as sanctuaries and bases for terrorist activities.

Led by Bhindranwale, the Khalistanis, the extremists, the militants, the terrorists—by whatever name they may be called—hoped to gradually transform terrorism into a general insurgency and an armed uprising. They were fighting for political and ideological hegemony over the people of Punjab. All their activities were designed to prove that the Indian state was not capable of ruling in Punjab and, therefore, separation from India was a realizable objective. Their bullying of the Press and the judiciary, their killing of police officials (and their families) and those suspected of cooperating with the police and administration, their successful diktats to administrators to do their bidding, their collection of 'parallel taxes', their silencing of intellectuals and political workers, their coercion of the peasants in giving them shelter, and their random killings—all were designed not only to facilitate their activities but also to convince the people of Punjab that they had the capacity to challenge the Indian state and that they were the rulers of tomorrow. To achieve this objective, they made no distinction between Sikhs and Hindus. Nearly 55 per cent of those killed from 1981 to 3 June 1984 were Sikhs.

Terrorists and the Akalis

The attitude of the Akali leadership towards the terrorists was ambivalent. While not joining them and even harbouring a certain hostility towards them, they kept quiet out of fear, and even supported them out of expediency. The moderation of the party's majority wing was also not backed by political action, positions and statements. There was no open stand against the terrorists or unequivocal condemnation of their activities or the senseless killings or the vitriolic propaganda of Bhindranwale. Instead, even the moderate Akali leaders defended, directly or indirectly, those accused of terrorist acts. They condemned every concrete action of the police against the terrorists. They objected to any government action against Bhindranwale. Longowal, for example, said in 1981: 'Entire Sikh community supported Bhindranwale.'[3] When, on rare occasions, the Akali leaders did condemn violence and individual killings, they put the blame on the government and the Congress, accusing them of organizing the violence and killings in order to tarnish the Sikh image. They took no action against the occupation and desecration of the gurudwaras and the Golden Temple by the terrorists. In fact, feeling that their leadership of the Sikh masses was in danger, they tried to keep up with Bhindranwale. As they lost ground to the latter, they took up more and more extreme positions, competing with him in demands and aggressive political and ideological posturing.

What made it difficult for the Akali leaders to oppose *Bhindranwale was the fact that they shared a common political* ideology with him and the extremists, even though they had tactical and strategic political differences. The Akalis equally whipped up communal feelings; and the public manifestations of the Akali ideology were indistinguishable from those of Bhindranwale and the extremists and, in fact, echoed them.

Indira Gandhi and Terrorists

Instead of boldly confronting the communal and separatist challenge to the Indian polity, Indira Gandhi gave way to indecisiveness; her response, uncharacteristic of her political style, was to dither and vacillate between a policy of appeasement and tactical manoeuvring and firmness. She refused to take strong action against terrorist killings for three long years, from 1981 to 1984, or to fight extreme communalism, ideologically and politically, and to counter communal propaganda effectively. She also did not realize that there was a basic difference between paying heed to minority feelings and appeasing minority communalism.

Indira Gandhi carried on endless negotiations with G.S. Tohra, Parkash Singh Badal and H.S. Longowal. Knuckling under the Akali and terrorist threats, she failed to evolve what the situation demanded, namely, a strategy of combating communalism, secessionism and terrorism. She also did not realize that when it came to a crunch she would not be able to unilaterally accept the Akali demands and ignore the strong and unanimous opinion of the people and political parties of Haryana and Rajasthan.

The result of the weak-kneed policy followed by Indira Gandhi was to send wrong signals to secessionists and the terrorists as well as to the people of Punjab. As K.P.S. Gill, former director-general of police in Punjab who directed the successful phase of the anti-terrorist campaign there, has pointed out: 'Nothing encourages the terrorists to greater audacity than the spectacle of weakness in the political leadership, and of confusion in the security forces.'[4]

Important in this respect was the failure of the government to act at the time of A.S. Atwal's murder in April 1983 within the precincts of the Golden Temple itself and which left the people of Punjab outraged. Atwal, a deputy inspector-general of police, had come to the temple to offer prayers when he was shot and killed in broad daylight.

The situation in Punjab deteriorated rapidly in 1984. Akali militancy grew by leaps and bounds. The leadership called for a fresh round of militant agitations starting from 3 June. It also increasingly and publicly expressed solidarity with Bhindranwale.

An increasingly dangerous feature of the situation was Pakistan's growing involvement in Punjab affairs. As a part of its strategy of waging low-intensity warfare against India, Pakistan had started providing training, weapons, ideological indoctrination, safe areas for hiding, and military guidance to terrorist organizations. Certain extremist Sikh groups abroad were also giving increasing encouragement to the secessionists and helping them with money and weapons.

By June 1984, the situation had reached an explosive point as terrorist activity escalated. There was in Punjab and in the country as a whole an intense feeling of danger to the peace and unity of the country. Fear and panic were spreading among Hindus in Punjab with an increasing number leaving the state. More and more gurudwaras were being fortified and turned into arsenals. Clearly, a situation of insurgency was building up in Punjab. At the same time, the government was losing its prestige and getting discredited.

One of the most worrisome features of the situation was the increasing Hindu–Sikh divide in Punjab and the spread of Hindu communalism in the rest of the country, especially in North India. A warning came from Haryana when anti-Sikh rioting broke out in February.

By the end of May, it was clear that decisive action against terrorists could no longer be put off and that the use of drastic force to flush out the terrorists holed up in the Golden Temple and other gurudwaras had become necessary. And so, finally faced with a dead end so far as political manoeuvres were concerned, the Government of India undertook military action, code-named Operation Blue Star. While there was no alternative to military action once the situation had worsened to the extent it had, there is no doubt, as later events were to show, that the operation was hastily conceived, undertaken without adequate information and proper planning and poorly executed, with the result that its political and emotional cost proved to be far higher than its planners had anticipated.

On 3 June the army surrounded the Golden Temple. It entered the temple on 5 June. There it found that the terrorists were far greater in number and also far better armed than the government sources had assumed. Rather than lasting an hour or two, as a surgical operation, the military operation turned into a full-scale battle, with the army having to deploy tanks in the end. What was worse, over a thousand devotees and temple staff were trapped inside the temple and many of them died in the crossfire. Moreover, the buildings in the temple complex were severely damaged, with the Akal Takht being virtually razed to the ground. Harmandir Sahib, the most hallowed of the Sikh shrines, was riddled with bullet marks, even though the army had taken special care at the cost of the lives of its soldiers not to damage it. Among the dead were Bhindranwale and many of his followers.

Operation Blue Star produced a deep sense of anger and outrage among Sikhs all over the country. It was seen by most of them as a sacrilege and an affront to the community rather than as a necessary though unpleasant effort to deal with Bhindranwale and the terrorists. While much of the hostile reaction to the operation represented an emotional outburst, there was a great deal to be said for its critics who held that some other way than the military storming of the temple should have been found. Later, critics were to point to the success of the skilfully planned and executed Operation Black Thunder in 1988 which forced the terrorists, once again occupying the temple in a manner similar to that of 1984, to surrender to the police in a relatively bloodless fashion.

However, despite its many negative repercussions, Operation Blue Star had certain positive features. It established that the Indian state was strong enough to deal with secession and terrorism; it put an end to the charismatic Bhindranwale and his gang; and it created that minimum of law and order which enabled secular parties such as the Congress, CPI and CPM to move among the angry people and counter communal politics by explaining to them that the real responsibility for the Punjab situation lay with Bhindranwale, the terrorists, and the Akali communalists.

Operation Blue Star and After

Following Operation Blue Star, the terrorists vowed vengeance against Indira Gandhi and her family for having desecrated the Golden Temple. On the morning of 31 October 1984, Indira Gandhi was assassinated by two Sikh members of her security guard. Earlier she had rejected her security chief's suggestion that all Sikhs be removed from her security staff with the comment: 'Aren't we all secular.'

The assassination of the popular prime minister, in an atmosphere of heightened communalization in North India during 1981–84, led to a wave of horror, fear, anger and communal outrage among people all over the country, especially among the poor. This anger took an ugly and communal form in Delhi and some other parts of North India, where anti-Sikh riots broke out as soon as the news of the assassination was announced and the highly exaggerated rumour spread that many Sikhs were celebrating the event. In particular, for three days from the evening of 31 October itself mobs took over the streets of Delhi and made Sikhs targets of their loot and violence. There was complete failure of the law and order machinery in giving protection to Sikhs and their property. The three-day violence in Delhi resulted in the death of over 2,500 people, mostly Sikhs, with the slums and resettlement colonies of Delhi being the main scenes of carnage. The November riots further alienated a large number of Sikhs from the government.

Rajiv Gandhi succeeded Indira Gandhi as prime minister on 1 November 1984. He moved quickly after the general elections in December 1984 to tackle the Punjab problem. In January 1985, the major jailed leaders, including the Akali Dal president,

H.S. Longowal, were released. A month later Rajiv Gandhi ordered an independent judicial enquiry into the November riots. The political tide in Punjab was also turning in a positive direction despite Operation Blue Star and the November riots. The terrorists were down and out and the Akalis had lost a great deal of their credibility. Moreover, though the Akalis were not willing to fight the terrorists, they were no longer helping them.

Rajiv Gandhi soon initiated negotiations with the Akali leaders in the belief that a settlement with them would provide a lasting solution to the Punjab problem. The result of this policy, however, was that the advantage accruing from Operation Blue Star was lost, the fight against terrorism and communalism virtually abandoned, and the latter given a new lease of life.

After their release the Akali leaders were divided, confused and disoriented. On the one hand, many of them, including Longowal, tried to consolidate their position *vis-à-vis* the terrorists by taking recourse to militant rhetoric. On the other hand, it was clear to most Akali leaders that mass agitation could no longer be revived nor could militant politics be carried on. Longowal, therefore, even while talking tough, entered into secret negotiations with the government.

Finally, in August 1985, Rajiv Gandhi and Longowal signed the Punjab Accord. The government conceded the major Akali demands and promised to have others reviewed. In particular, it was agreed that Chandigarh would be transferred to Punjab, a commission would determine which Hindi-speaking territories would be transferred from Punjab to Haryana, and the river water dispute would be adjudicated by an independent tribunal. Elections to the state assembly and the national parliament were to be held in September 1985.

On 20 August, the day Longowal announced that the Akalis would participate in the elections, he was assassinated by the terrorists. The elections were, however, held on time. Over 66 per cent of the electorate voted as compared with 64 per cent in 1977 and 1984. The Akalis secured an absolute majority in the state assembly for the first time in their history.

The Akali government, headed by Surjit Singh Barnala, was, however, from the beginning riven with factionalism and, consequently, immobilized. Its most important administrative step was the release of a large number of persons accused of terrorist crimes, most of whom rejoined the terrorist ranks, giving terrorism a major fillip.

The Akali government found that it could not agree to the transfer of any of Punjab's territories to Haryana as compensation for the loss of Chandigarh; the Haryana government, however, would not agree to the latter without the former. The Akali leadership also went back in regard to the judicial adjudication of the river water dispute. The major terms of the accord were thus once more under dispute. The fact is that the accord had been, as was the case with Operation Blue Star, prepared in haste without considering its feasibility.

The militant groups soon regrouped taking advantage of the soft policies of the Barnala government. There was, over time, a resurgence in terrorist activities, and the state government, riven with factionalism, was unable to contain them. Consequently, the central government dismissed the Barnala ministry and imposed President's Rule in Punjab in May 1987.

The fact is that the Akali Dal and an Akali government, sharing the ideological wavelength of the extremists and the terrorists, were incapable of confronting or fighting communalism and separatism. It was, therefore, a strategic error on the part of the Rajiv Gandhi government to stake all on Barnala and his supporters and see them as the frontrunners in the campaign to decommunalize Punjab, separate religion from politics and fight commmunal terrorism.

Also, Rajiv Gandhi regarded the Punjab Accord as the solution to the terrorist problem rather than as the opening gambit in, or the gaining of an opportunity for implementing, a long-term strategy of which a political-ideological struggle against communalism would form a basic part. Simultaneously, there had to be the realization that separatism, terrorism and violence had to be firmly dealt with. Besides, even the moderate communalists had to be first rescued and protected from the terrorists before they could function politically in their own communal mode. It is quite significant in this respect that Longowal spoke openly against terrorism and then signed the accord with Rajiv Gandhi only after Operation Blue Star had eliminated Bhindranwale, destroyed the myth of the invincibility of the terrorists and checked terrorism to a large extent. Likewise, the Akalis boycotted the elections in 1992 when terrorism was still ravaging Punjab, but agreed to participate in them in 1997 when it had been brought to a virtual end.

Resolving Terrorism

Despite President's Rule, terrorism in Punjab went on growing, going through phases of waning and resurgence, especially as after 1985 it had begun to be openly funded, supported and even directed by Pakistan.

We need not discuss at length the growth of terrorism and despoliations after 1985 since they have been dealt with at length by K.P.S. Gill in his *Punjab—The Knights of Falsehood*. Increasingly, most of the terrorist gangs took to extortion, robbery, smuggling, drugs, abduction and rape, land grabbing, murder of innocents, and a lavish lifestyle. From 1987, they also began a systematic campaign to acquire political and ideological hegemony over the people. Their ban on meat, liquor, tobacco, and the use of sarees by women, their effort to determine the dress of schoolchildren, their restrictions on marriage rites and practices, their hoisting of the Khalistani flag on public buildings, their collection of parallel taxes, were all designed to convince the people that they were the rulers of tomorrow. Periodic statements by well-meaning persons, sometimes repeated by the prime minister himself, advocating negotiations, conditional or unconditional, between the central government and various groups of the terrorists tended to have the same impact.

Imposition of President's Rule in Punjab in 1987 was a short-term measure to salvage a rapidly deteriorating situation. It should have been seen as a tactical part of a long-term strategy which had to be based on the understanding (i) that no soft options were available in Punjab since 1982 when communalism entered a stage when it had either to be conceded or defeated, (ii) that moderate communalists could not be depended upon to fight extreme communalism or terrorism and (iii) that a policy of firmness combined with political ideological struggle would yield results only if it was followed for a sufficient length of time and was not interrupted by efforts to appease the terrorists and the communalists. The perspective had to be of years and not months. After 1986, the Rajiv Gandhi government several times came near getting an upper hand over the terrorists, but it lacked the determination to run the full course; and, misguided by weak-kneed advisers, it talked of and even initiated negotiations with one or the other secessionist groups. It, thus, lost the advantage gained by strong state action, and inevitably led to higher levels of state violence against terrorism every time.

The policy of 'solving' the Punjab problem through negotiations with and appeasement of the terrorists and extreme communalists was followed even more vigorously by the governments of V.P. Singh and Chandra Shekhar during 1990 and 1991. In the meantime the number of the victims of terrorism went on increasing.

The state did finally take strong action. A preview of such action was Operation Black Thunder, undertaken by the Punjab police and paramilitary forces in May 1988, which succeeded in flushing out the terrorists from the Golden Temple.

A hard policy towards terrorism was followed from mid-1991 onwards by the Narasimha Rao government at the Centre and after the February 1992 elections by the Congress government led by Beant Singh in Punjab. The police, often aided by the rural people, became increasingly effective though a large number of policemen—over 1,550 from 1988 to 1992 alone—lost their lives in its operations. Also, the leaders and cadres of the two Communist parties, the CPI and CPM, and a large number of Congressmen played an active and courageous role in fighting terrorism, often paying a heavy price in terms of life and property. By 1993, Punjab had been virtually freed of terrorism.

An Assessment

Despite the depredations of the terrorists for over ten years, there were several redeeming features in the situation. Though there was some degree of a psychological divide between Hindus and Sikhs, especially in the urban areas, and a few incidents of Hindu–Sikh clashes, there was not even one major communal riot in Punjab throughout the years of the terrorist sway; on the whole the people of Punjab remained secular. The mass of Hindus did not support the efforts of the Shiv Sena and other Hindu communal organizations to create a volunteer corps of Hindus alone to fight terrorism. Similarly, the majority of Sikhs offered strong resistance to the terrorists in many areas.

The refusal of the people of Punjab to imbibe the values and ideology of the terrorists and the extreme communalists was mainly because the secular tradition was quite strong in Punjab, thanks to the work and influence of the Ghadr Party and the Ghadri Babas, Bhagat Singh and his comrades, Kirti Kisan groups, the Communists and the Socialists, the militant peasant movement and the Congress and the national movement.

The mass of Sikhs refused to accept that the separatists and the terrorists were fighting in defence of Sikh religion and Sikh interests. To most Sikhs it gradually became clear that the terrorists were abusing and betraying their religion, debasing Sikh institutions and the teachings of the Sikh gurus and defiling the gurudwaras. Of the 11,700 killed by the terrorists in Punjab during 1981–93, more than 61 per cent were Sikhs.

The Punjab experience is quite relevant to the country as a whole as it could face similar problems in the future in other parts of it. There are important lessons to be learnt. First, communalism has to be confronted both politically and ideologically; separation of religion from politics has necessarily to be enforced. In particular, the Punjab experience emphasizes the centrality of the struggle against communal ideology. The major weakness of the struggle against terrorism was the failure to grasp that the real and the long-term problem in Punjab was not terrorism but communalism. The roots of the former lay in the latter. Extremism and terrorism were directly linked to the Akali communal ideology and the blatant use of religion by the Akalis for political ends. As already indicated, communalism cannot be appeased, placated or assuaged—it has to be opposed and defeated. Appeasement of communal forces can at most provide temporary respite. The time thus gained has to be used to counter communalism among the people; otherwise communalism gets strengthened and pushed towards extremism.

Second, communal violence in all its forms, including as terrorism, has to be handled firmly and decisively and suppressed as quickly as possible through the full and timely use of the law and order machinery of the state. No amount of popular will and opposition can defeat violence and terrorism on its own; it can play an important role only in support of and as a supplement to the measures of the state and its security forces.

Third, communalists, however moderate, cannot be expected to or depended upon to fight extreme communalism or communal terrorism despite real political differences between the two because the two share a common communal ideology.

25

Indian Economy, 1947–1965: The Nehruvian Legacy

The Nehruvian Consensus

A meaningful appraisal of India's development experience after independence would have to place it both in a historical and comparative context. The level and stage from which the beginning was made, and the uniqueness of the effort to undertake an industrial transformation within a democratic framework need to be taken into account; the achievements should be measured with other countries at a comparable stage of development.

We have seen in the chapter 'The Colonial Legacy', the pitiful condition of the India that we inherited at independence after colonialism had ravaged the economy and society for nearly two hundred years and deprived it of the opportunity of participating in the process of modern industrial transformation occurring in other parts of the world. Apart from extreme poverty, illiteracy, a ruined agriculture and industry, the structural distortions created by colonialism in the Indian economy and society (such as the rupture of the link between various sectors of the Indian economy and their getting articulated with the metropolitan economy in a dependent manner) made the future transition to self-sustained growth much more difficult.

It is this legacy of colonial structuring which independent India had to undo so that conditions could be created for rapid industrial development. The task of attempting a modern industrial transformation, two hundred years after the first industrial revolution and nearly a hundred years after several other countries had industrialized, was a stupendous one. Besides this handicap created by colonialism and the several built-in disadvantages faced by the latecomer, India had to confront political and economic conditions which had changed radically. New and innovative strategies were called for if success was to be achieved.

While undertaking this difficult and complex task, India, unlike many other post-colonial societies, had certain advantages. First, a small but independent (Indian owned and controlled) industrial base had emerged in India between 1914 and 1947. This was achieved, amongst other things, by the Indian capitalist class seizing the opportunities created during this period by the weakening of the imperialist stranglehold during the two world wars and the Great Depression of the 1930s. By the time India gained political independence in 1947 Indian entrepreneurs had successfully competed with European enterprise in India and with foreign imports, in the process capturing about 75 per cent of the market for industrial produce in India. Indian capitalists had also acquired dominance over the financial sphere, i.e., banking, life insurance, etc.[1]

By independence, therefore, India had, 'in spite of and in opposition to colonialism', developed an *independent* economic base from which to attempt a take-off into rapid independent industrialization.[2] She did not, like many other post-colonial countries, get pushed into a neo-colonial situation where, while formal political independence was achieved, the erstwhile colony's economy continued to be essentially dominated by metropolitan interests.

A mature indigenous entrepreneurial class, which could serve as the *agency* for carrying out a substantial part of the post-independence planned development was an asset to India. Further, a high degree of concentration and consolidation had led, during the colonial period itself, to the emergence of large business conglomerates like the Birlas, Tatas, Singhanias, Dalmia-Jains, etc., with interests in different areas like trade, banking, transport, industry and so on. Such conglomerates, like the *zaibatsu* in Japan or the *chaebol* in South Korea, were extremely important in enabling late entrants to world capitalism to successfully compete with the already established foreign capital and especially multinational corporations. The absence of the *agency* of a mature, indigenous entrepreneurial class was sorely felt in many of the post-colonial African states and can be seen as a critical drawback even today, for example in most parts of the former Soviet Union.

Second, India was fortunate to have a broad societal consensus on the nature and path of development to be followed after independence. For example, the Gandhians, the Socialists, the capitalists as well as the Communists (barring brief sectarian phases), were all more or less agreed on the following agenda: a multi-pronged strategy of economic development based on self-reliance; rapid industrialization based on import-substitution, including of capital goods industries; prevention of imperialist or foreign capital domination; land reforms involving tenancy reforms, abolition of zamindari, introduction of cooperatives, especially service cooperatives, for marketing, credit, etc., growth to be attempted along with equity, i.e., the growth model was to be reformist with a welfare, pro-poor orientation; positive discrimination or reservation, for a period, in favour of the most oppressed in Indian society, the Scheduled Castes and Tribes; the state to play a central role in promoting economic development, including through direct state participation in the production process, i.e., through the public sector, and so on.

Most important, there was agreement that India was to make this unique attempt at planned rapid industrialization within a democratic and civil libertarian framework. All the industrialized countries of the world did not have democracy and civil liberties during the initial period of their transition to industrialism or period of 'primitive accumulation'. Nehru and others including the capitalists were acutely aware that they had chosen an uncharted path. Yet, they were committed to it. Nobody in India ever argued for a variant of the model followed in parts of Latin America, East Asia, etc., where an authoritarian government in partnership with the capitalists would push through a process of rapid development in a hothouse fashion. It is this consensus, a product of the nature of the national movement in India, which enabled India, virtually alone among the post-colonial developing nations, to build, retain and nurture a functioning democracy.

Planning and the Public Sector

As early as the late nineteenth century, in the economic thinking of the early nationalists such as M.G. Ranade and Dadabhai Naoroji, the state was assigned a critical role in the economic development of India. This trend of seeking state intervention and not leaving economic forces entirely to the market got further crystallized and acquired widespread acceptance in the inter-war period, partly due to the influence of Keynesian economic ideas, the experience of the New Deal in the US and the Soviet experiment. In 1934, N.R. Sarkar, the president of the Federation of Indian Chambers of Commerce and Industry (FICCI), the leading organization of Indian capitalists, proclaimed: 'The days of undiluted laissez-faire are gone for ever.' Voicing the views of the leadership of the capitalist class, he added that, for a backward country like India, a comprehensive plan of economic development covering all aspects of the economy, agriculture, industry, power, banking, finance, and so on, chalked out and coordinated by a high-powered 'National Planning Commission', was essential for India to make a structural break with the past and achieve her full growth potential. In 1938, under the leadership of Jawaharlal Nehru, the greatest champion of planned economic development for India, the National Planning Committee (NPC) was set up, which through its deliberations over the next decade, drew up a comprehensive plan of development, its various subcommittees producing twenty-nine volumes of recommendations.

Apart from the general recognition of the need for state planning, there was a wide consensus emerging around the notion that the role of the state would not only involve the proper use of fiscal, monetary and other instruments of economic policy and state control and supervision over the growth process, but would also have to include a certain amount of direct participation in the production process through the public sector. The famous Karachi Resolution of Congress in 1931 (as amended by the AICC) envisaged that 'the State shall own or control key industries and services, mineral resources, railways, waterways, shipping and other means of public transport'.[4] Indian business leaders were also, along with Nehru and the NPC, among the early proponents of the public sector and partial nationalization. The critical reason for business support to the public sector was elaborated in the *Plan of Economic Development for India,* popularly called the Bombay Plan, authored by business leaders in 1945. The Bombay Plan saw the key cause of India's dependence on the advanced countries to be the absence of an indigenous capital goods industry. Anticipating a basic element of the Second Plan strategy, the Bombay Plan declared, 'We consider it essential that this lack (of capital goods industries) should be remedied in as short a time as possible. Apart from its importance as a means of quickening the pace of industrial development in India, it would have the effect of ultimately reducing our dependence on foreign countries for the plant and machinery required by us and, consequently, of reducing our requirement of external finance.'[5] It was felt that in the development of capital goods industries and other basic and heavy industries, which required huge finances and had a long time lag for returns, the public sector would have to play a critical role. While Nehru and the left nationalists on the one hand and the capitalists on the other were agreed on this issue of the need for the public sector to reduce external dependence, they differed on its scope and extent. The former saw planning and the public sector as a step in the socialist direction, whereas the latter saw it as an instrument of promoting independent capitalism and of pre-empting socialism by helping combine equity with growth. This tension between the two approaches was to persist for some time, particularly in the early years.

In 1947, for example, when the Economic Programme Committee appointed by the AICC and headed by Jawaharlal Nehru not only laid down the areas, such as defence, key industries and public utilities which were to be started under the public sector but also added that 'in respect of existing undertakings the process of *transfer from private to public ownership should commence after a period of five years*',[6] the capitalists were alarmed and howls of protest ensued. Signs of accommodation were seen in the 1948 Industrial Policy Resolution (IPR) which, while delineating specific areas for the public and the private sectors, added that the question of nationalizing any existing industry would be reviewed after ten years and dealt with on the basis of circumstances prevailing at that time. Even after the Indian parliament in December 1954 accepted 'the socialist pattern of society as the objective of social and economic policy' and Congress in its Avadi session (1955) elaborated the sharp leftward swing on these lines, the 1956 IPR and the Second Plan, while considerably expanding the scope of the public sector, made no mention of nationalizing existing industries.[7] In fact, the model projected was of a 'mixed economy' where the public and the private sectors were not only to coexist but were to be complementary to each other and the private sector was to be encouraged to grow with as much freedom as possible within the broad objectives of the national plan. It is another matter that the great emphasis on heavy and capital goods industries in the Second Plan by itself led to a major shift towards the public sector as these were areas which, it was commonly agreed, could be basically developed by this sector.

It may be noted that Nehru refused to push his own ideological positions beyond a point, much to the disappointment of sections of the left, still under the influence of a Stalinist type of orthodox Marxism or, 'Stalin-Marxism'. In the evolution of Nehru's thought, from as early as the late 1930s, socialism had become inseparable from democracy. Therefore, any step in that direction, such as planning and the public sector, had to be introduced in a democratic manner, capable of carrying society along in the effort. Planning for Nehru had to be *consensual*, and not a *command* performance, even if it meant toning down many of his objectives.

This was the perspective with which the Planning Commission (established on 15 March 1950) functioned, despite the enormous *de facto* power it exercised with Nehru himself as its chairperson. The First Plan (1951–56) essentially tried to complete projects at hand and to meet the immediate crisis situation following the end of the war. Independence had come along with the dislocation caused by Partition, including the massive problem of refugees resulting from the largest mass migration in history in the space of a few years. It is with the Second Plan (1956–61) that the celebrated Nehru–Mahalanobis (Professor P.C. Mahalanobis played a leading role in drafting the Second Plan) strategy of development was put into practice and it was continued in the Third Plan (1961–66). A basic element of this strategy was the rapid development of heavy and capital goods industries in India, mainly in the public sector. (Three steel plants were set up in the public sector within the Second Plan period.) Import substitution in this area was seen as an imperative not only because it was thought to be critical for self-reliance and reduction of external dependence but also because it was assumed that Indian exports could not grow fast enough to enable the import of the necessary capital goods and machinery—an export pessimism which has been criticized in later years, though it was quite commonly accepted at that time. The model also saw some foreign aid and investment as essential in the initial phase to finance the massive step-up in investment though the objective was to do away with this need as soon as possible by rapidly increasing domestic savings. (In fact, in the initial years after independence, Nehru had tried to woo foreign investments into India, much to the chagrin of, as yet not too confident, Indian capitalists.)

The shift in favour of heavy industry was to be combined with promoting labour-intensive small and cottage industries for the production of consumer goods. This, as well as labour-absorbing and capital-creating community projects in agriculture, promoted by community development programmes and agricultural cooperatives were seen (too optimistically, as later events showed) as the immediate solutions to the escalating problem of unemployment, without the state having to make large investments in these areas.

Another critical element of the Nehru–Mahalanobis strategy was the emphasis on growth with equity. Hence, the issue of concentration and distribution in industry and agriculture was given a lot of attention though perhaps not with commensurate success. It may be added that the strategy did not posit equity against growth but assumed that higher growth enabled higher levels of equity and was critical for meeting the challenge of poverty; utmost attention was therefore given to rapid growth.

State supervision of development along planned lines, dividing activity between the public and the private sectors, preventing rise of concentration and monopoly, protecting small industry, ensuring regional balance, canalizing resources according to planned priorities and targets, etc.—all this involved the setting up of an elaborate and complicated system of controls and industrial licensing, which was done through the Industries Development and Regulation Act (IDRA) of 1951. Further, the balance of payments crisis and acute shortage of foreign exchange that occurred in 1956–57, at the very start of the Second Plan, led to the imposition of stringent import and foreign exchange controls. The seeds of the Kafkaesque web of licence quota rules and regulations were thus laid and in later years it was found that it was not easy to dismantle a system that had acquired a vicious stranglehold over the Indian economy. The bureaucracy–politician nexus and certain sections of business that were beneficiaries of the system resisted such a change.

Achievements

We shall now briefly review some of the bold beginnings made in the Nehru years during which the first three Plans were conceived, though the full impact of many of the initiatives was to be felt in the years following his death.

Considerable progress on several fronts was made during the first phase of the development effort, spanning the first three Five-Year Plans, i.e., by the mid-1960s. The overall economy performed impressively compared to the colonial period. India's national income or Gross National Product (GNP) grew at an average rate of about 4 per cent per annum, between 1951 and 1964–65 excluding the last year of the Third Plan, i.e., 1965–66, which saw an unprecedented drought and a war). This was roughly four times the rate of growth achieved during the last half century of colonial rule. The rate of growth achieved by India after independence compared favourably with the rates achieved by the advanced countries at a comparable stage, i.e., during their early development. To quote eminent economist Professor K.N. Raj:[8]

> Japan is generally believed to be a country which grew rapidly in the latter part of the 19th and the first quarter of the 20th century; yet the rate of growth of national income in Japan was slightly less than 3 per cent per annum in the period 1893–1912 and did not go up to more than 4 per cent per annum even in the following decade. Judged by criteria such as these the growth rate achieved in India in the last decade and a half (1950–65) is certainly a matter for some satisfaction.

Stepping up the rate of growth required a substantial increase in the investment rate. An important achievement in this period was the rise in the savings and investment rates. On the basis of rather rudimentary data, the draft outline of the Fourth Plan estimated that domestic savings and total investment in the Indian economy were both 5.5 per cent of national income in 1950–51, rising to savings of 10.5 per cent and investment of 14 per cent in 1965–66. The gap between domestic savings and investment in later years was met partly by liquidating the foreign exchange reserves (mainly the huge sterling balances, about Rs 16 billion, that England owed India in 1947, because of the forced credit England had extracted from India during the war) and partly through foreign borrowing and aid. It has been estimated that the total investment in 1965–66 was nearly five times the 1951–52 level in nominal terms and more than three times in real terms.

On the agrarian front, the comprehensive land reform measures initiated soon after independence, the setting up of a massive network for agricultural extension and community development work at the village level, the large infrastructural investment in irrigation, power, agricultural research, and so on, had created the conditions for considerable agricultural growth in this period. During the first three Plans (again leaving out 1965–66), Indian agriculture grew at an annual rate of over 3 per cent, a growth rate 7.5 times higher than that achieved during the last half century or so of the colonial period. The growth rates achieved compared very favourably with what was achieved by other countries in a comparable situation, say China or Japan. For example, Japan achieved a growth rate of less than 2.5 per cent between 1878 and 1912 and an even lower growth rate till 1937. What was particularly creditable was that India, unlike most other countries (such as China, Japan, Korea, Taiwan, Soviet Union, Britain, etc.) achieved its land reforms and agricultural growth in the context of civil liberties and a modern democratic structure. However, the commendable agricultural growth achieved during this period was not sufficient to meet the growing demand of agricultural produce, necessitating increasing imports of foodgrains throughout the first three Plans. Since 1956, India had to rely heavily on food imports from the US under the controversial PL-480 scheme. It was only after the process of the Green Revolution took off, since the late sixties, that this dependence on imports ceased. (The whole issue of land reforms and agricultural growth which affected the lives of not only the vast majority of the Indian population dependent on agriculture but the Indian economy as a whole has been dealt with separately in later chapters.

Industry, during the first three Plans, grew even more rapidly than agriculture, at a compounded growth rate of 7.1 per cent per annum between 1951 and 1965. The industrial growth was based on rapid import substitution, initially, of consumer goods and particularly, since the Second Plan, of capital goods and intermediate goods. The emphasis on the latter since the Second Plan was reflected in the fact that 70 per cent of Plan expenditure on industry went to the metal, machinery and chemical industries in the Second Plan and 80 per cent in the Third Plan. Consequently, 'the *three-fold* increase in aggregate index of industrial production between 1951 and 1969 was the result of a 70 per cent increase in consumer goods industries, a *quadrupling* of the intermediate goods production and a *tenfold increase* in the output of capital goods,' a stupendous growth of the capital goods sector by any standards.[9]

Tables 25.1 and 25.2 reflect this growth pattern (over a longer period) in which intermediate and capital goods industries like basic metals, chemicals, transport equipment and electrical and non-electrical machinery grew very rapidly and much faster than consumer goods industries like textiles, particularly between 1951 and 1971.

Table 25.1: Indices of Industrial Production in India: 1951–1979

1960 = 100 (for 1951–1971) and 1970 = 100 (for 1978–79)

Industrial Group	1951	1961	1971	1978–79
General	55	109	153	186
Textiles	80	103	106	110
Basic Metals	47	119	209	144
Machinery	22	121	373	208
Electrical Machinery	26	110	405	162

Source: India: A Reference Annual, *GOI, New Delhi, 1980, p. 312, cited in B.L.C. Johnson*, Development in South Asia, *Harmondsworth, 1983, p. 136.*

This growth pattern went a long way in reducing India's near-total dependence on the advanced countries for basic goods and capital equipment, which was necessary for investment or creation of new capacity. At independence, to make any capital investment, virtually the entire equipment had to be imported. For example, in 1950, India met 89.8 per cent of its needs for even machine tools through imports. In contrast to this, the share of imported equipment in the total fixed investment in the form of equipment in India had come down to 43 per cent in 1960 and a mere 9 per cent in 1974, whereas the value of the fixed investment in India increased by about two and a half times over this period. In other words, by the mid-1970s, India could meet indigenously more than 90 per cent of her equipment requirements for maintaining her rate of investment. This was a major achievement, and it considerably increased India's autonomy from the advanced countries in determining her own rate of capital accumulation or

Table 25.2: Rates of Growth in Indian Manufacturing: 1951–52 to 1982–83 (per cent)

Industry Group	1951–52 to 1959–60	1960–61 to 1969–70	1970–71 to 1982–83
Textiles	2.98	0.70	5.36
Rubber, Petroleum and Plastic Products	17.54	10.40	3.82
Chemical Products	7.90	8.39	5.76
Basic Metal and Alloys	6.52	7.01	5.46
Non-electrical Machinery	21.02	17.00	16.09
Electrical Machinery	17.64	14.01	6.17
Transport Equipment	14.83	7.66	3.34

Estimates are trend growth rates based in semi-log functions and relate to the factory sector of Indian manufacturing.

Source: Selected from Sukhamoy Chakravarty, Development Planning: The Indian Experience, *Delhi, 1987, Table 13, p. 111.*

growth. It was this, and the food security India was able to achieve once the process of the Green Revolution took off, which explains India's ability to retain an independent foreign policy, by withstanding enormous external pressures.

Dependence on external resources, foreign aid or foreign private investment, was kept quite low. Net aid utilized by India was only 0.4 per cent of Net National Product at factor cost during the First Plan, rising to 2.25 and 3.17 per cent during the Second and Third Plan and again falling drastically since the end-1960s. Also, external resources came mainly as official aid, and according to one estimate net aid and net foreign private investment came in the ratio of 6:1 between 1948 and 1961. More than 71 per cent of the foreign aid in the First Plan was used for wheat loans, whereas in the Second and Third Plans foreign aid was used overwhelmingly, nearly 98 per cent, to fund iron and steel projects and general industrial development, transport and communication and power. Overall, in the first three Plans, industry, transport and power utilized about 95 per cent of the foreign aid. (The counterpart funds generated by the PL-480 food aid from the US were allocated to the above areas.)[10] Soviet aid came in the Second Plan priority areas, i.e., core and basic industries and that too in the public sector.

The weight of the public sector in the overall economy increased rapidly, and it captured the 'commanding heights' of the economy, further marginalizing the presence of an already small foreign sector. (In India, unlike certain Latin American countries, the public sector did not grow in collaboration with foreign private capital or multinational corporations.) The total paid-up capital in government companies as a proportion of the total paid-up capital in the entire corporate sector rose from 3.4 per cent in 1951 to 30 per cent in 1961. In the early 1970s the proportion had risen to about 50 per cent and by 1978 it had reached a whopping 75 per cent.

Apart from industry and agriculture, the early planners gave utmost priority to the development of infrastructure, including education and health, areas greatly neglected in the colonial past. The average actual Plan expenditure on transport and communication during each of the first three Plans was about Rs 13 billion, accounting for an average of about 26 per cent of the total Plan expenditure in each Plan. The corresponding figures for social/community services and power were Rs 9.4 billion and 19.9 per cent and Rs 6.16 billion and 10.6 per cent respectively. Over time, Plan investment in these areas (and in irrigation) was to prove critical both in stepping up private investment and improving its productivity, as was seen so clearly in the case of agriculture with the coming in of the Green Revolution.

Table 25.3 shows the rapid per capita increase in the availability of some of the infrastructural and social benefits as they grew several times faster than the population. In 1965–66, as compared to 1950–51, installed capacity of electricity was 4.5 times higher, the number of town and villages electrified was 14 times higher, hospital beds 2.5 times higher, enrolment in schools was a little less than three times higher and, very importantly, admission capacity in technical education (engineering and technology) at the degree and diploma levels was higher by 6 and 8.5 times respectively. The population had increased only by a little over one-third during the same period.

Jawaharlal Nehru and the early Indian planners were acutely aware of India's backwardness in science and technology (an area left consciously barren in the colonial period) and therefore made massive efforts to overcome this shortcoming. Nehru's 'temples of modern (secular) India' consisted not only of steel and power

Table 25.3: Growth in Infrastructure, Health and Education

Item	Unit	1950–51	1960–61	1965–66	Percentage change between 1950–51 and 1965–66
Electricity: Installed capacity	Million KW.	2.3	5.6	10.2	393.5
Towns and villages electrified	'000	3.7	24.2	52.3	1,313.5
Railways: Freight carried	Million tonnes	93	156	205	120.4
Surfaced roads	'000 km	156	235	284	82.0
Hospital beds	'000	113	186	300	165.5
Enrolment in schools	Million	23.5	44.7	67.7	188.1
Technical Education: Engineering and technology (admission capacity)					
(a) Degree level	1000	4.1	13.8	24.7	502.4
(b) Diploma level	1000	5.9	25.8	49.9	745.8
Population	Millions	357	430	490	37.3

Source: J. Bhagwati and P. Desai, India: Planning for Industrialisation, *London, 1970, p. 74.*

plants, irrigation dams, etc., but included institutions of higher learning, particularly in the scientific field. During the First Plan itself, high-powered national laboratories and institutes were set up by the Council of Scientific and Industrial Research for conducting fundamental and applied research in each of the following areas: physics, chemistry, fuel, glass and ceramics, food technology, drugs, electro-chemistry, roads, leather and building. In 1948 the Atomic Energy Commission was set up, laying the foundations of the creditable advances India was to make in the sphere of nuclear science and related areas. This was in addition to the unprecedented increase in the educational opportunities in science and technology in the universities and institutes. National expenditure on scientific research and development kept growing rapidly with each Plan. For example, it increased from Rs. 10 million in 1949 to Rs 4.5 billion in 1977. Over roughly the same period India's scientific and technical manpower increased more than 12 times from 190, 000 to 2.32 million. A spectacular growth by any standards, placing India, after the dissolution of the Soviet Union, as the second country in the world in terms of the absolute size of scientific and technical manpower. This was a major achievement despite the fact that the quality of education in general, and particularly in the university system, tended to deteriorate over time and there was massive brain drain, mainly to the US, of a significant part of the best talent produced in the country. Yet, it is an achievement of considerable significance, as increasingly today 'knowledge' is becoming the key factor of production and there is a global awareness of the necessity to focus on education and human resource development. That India can even think of participating in the globalization process in today's world of high technology, with any degree of competitiveness and equality, is largely due to the spadework done since independence, particularly the great emphasis laid on human resource development in the sphere of science and technology.

In the enthusiasm to support the very necessary economic reforms being undertaken by India today (since 1991), it has become fashionable in some circles to run down the economic achievements of the earlier periods, particularly the Nehruvian era. Nothing could be more short-sighted and ahistorical. It is the Nehruvian era that created the basic physical and human infrastructure, which was a precondition for independent modern development. Today's possibilities are a function of the achievements of the earlier period; they have not arisen despite them.

Also, the Nehruvian phase has to be seen in the global historical context of that period. As Dr Manmohan Singh, India's prime minister and brilliant economist, who as finance minister inaugurated the structural adjustment programme for India in 1991, was to acknowledge: 'In 1960, if you had asked anybody which country would be on top of the league of the third world in 1996 or 1997, India was considered to be the frontrunner.'[11] There was a consensus among a wide variety of economists, including prominent ones in the West—W.W. Rostow, Rosenstein-Rodan, Wilfred Mandelbaum, George Rosen, Ian Little, Brian Reddaway, to name just a few—that the direction of the Indian planning effort was a very positive one with great potential. (It was common to eulogize the democratic Indian path as opposed to the model followed by totalitarian China.) There was, in fact, a dialectical relationship between the evolution of contemporary development theory and the Indian experience. As reputed economist Sukhamoy Chakravarty noted, 'Dominant ideas of contemporary development economics influenced the logic of India's plans, and correspondingly, development theory was for a while greatly influenced by the Indian case.'[12]

Surely, over time, changes needed to be made, learning from the experience of this novel effort to bring about industrial transformation in the modern (mid-twentieth century) environment of a post-colonial backward country, while fully maintaining a functioning democracy. Clearly, some of the policy instruments— industrial licensing, price and distribution controls, import restrictions shielding inefficient domestic producers, dependence on an increasingly inefficient public sector, etc.—needed to be given up or amended. Also, changes in the nature of world capitalism called for novel ways of seeking economic opportunity, which, *inter alia,* involved a greater opening up to the world economy. However, the possibility of such a change got short-circuited by a series of crises faced by India in the mid-1960s and changes in the international and internal political situation which forced her to move further in a protectionist, inward-looking and dirigiste direction. We look more closely at this aspect in the next chapter.

26

Indian Economy, 1965–1991

The Mid-1960s: Crisis and Response

The significant achievements during the first three Plans notwithstanding, the Indian economy was in the grip of a massive crisis in many respects by the mid-1960s, which rapidly changed India's image from a model developing country to a 'basket case'. Two successive monsoon failures of 1965 and 1966, added to the burden on an agriculture which was beginning to show signs of stagnation, and led to a fall in agricultural output by 17 per cent and foodgrain output by 20 per cent. The rate of inflation which was hitherto kept very low (till 1963 it did not exceed 2 per cent per annum) rose sharply to 12 per cent per annum between 1965 and 1968 and food prices rose nearly at the rate of 20 per cent per annum. The inflation was partly due to the droughts and partly due to the two wars of 1962 (with China) and 1965 (with Pakistan) which had led to a massive increase in defence expenditure. The government consolidated (state and Centre) fiscal deficit peaked in 1966–67 at 7.3 per cent of GDP.

The balance of payments situation, fragile since 1956–57, deteriorated further, with foreign exchange reserves (excluding gold) averaging about $340 million between 1964–65 and 1966–67, enough to cover less than two months of imports. The dependence on foreign aid, which had been rising over the first three Plans, now increased sharply due to food shortages as well as the weakness of balance of payments. Utilization of external assistance, which was 0.86 per cent of Net National Product (NNP) at factor cost in 1951–52, increased to 1.05 per cent in 1956–57, 2.37 per cent in 1957–58, 2.86 per cent in 1960–61 and 3.8 per cent in 1965–

66. Amortisation and interest payments as percentage of exports (debt service ratio) rose sharply ftom 0.8 up to the end of the First Plan to 3.9 during the Second Plan, 14.3 during the Third Plan to 20.6 in 1966–67 and a whopping 27.8 in 1966–67. Given the overall situation, long-term planning had to be temporarily abandoned and there were three annual Plans between 1966 and 1969 before the Fourth Five Year Plan could commence in April 1969.

It was at this most vulnerable time for the Indian economy—with high inflation, a very low foreign exchange balance, food stocks so low as to threaten famine conditions in some areas, calling for large imports, and nearly half the imports having to be met through foreign aid—that the US, the most important donor at that time, decided to suspend its aid in response to the Indo-Pak war (1965) and India's stand on Vietnam and refused to renew the PL-480 (wheat loan) agreement on a long-term basis. Also, the US, in President Johnson's words, wanted to keep India 'on a short leash' so that India did not stray too much from the policies preferred by it, which they now sought to pressurize India to accept.

The US, the World Bank and the IMF wanted India to (a) liberalize its trade and industrial controls, (b) devalue the rupee and (c) adopt a new agricultural strategy. While there was considerable indigenous support for a new initiative in agriculture (which was successfully implemented), there was plenty of suspicion over trade and industrial liberalization and particularly over devaluation. As it happened, the devaluation of the rupee (nominally by 36.5 per cent though effectively much less) and the trade liberalization that was initiated by prime minister Indira Gandhi in the mid-1960s got associated with the continuing recession in industry, inflation, and the failure of exports to pick up, all of which was at least partly caused by 'exogenous' circumstances like the second major drought of 1966–67 and partly by the inadequate manner in which these policies were initiated. In any case, these policies were condemned before their long-term effect could be realized.

The perceived failure of the devaluation and liberalization of controls on trade and industry combined with the resentment at the 'arm-twisting' resorted to by external agencies in favour of these policies, using India's economic vulnerability, led to an 'economic nationalist' response based on a reversal to (and often considerable accentuation of) the earlier policies of controls and state intervention. The immediate imperative was seen to be the restoring of the health of India's balance of payments situation, creation of sufficient foreign exchange reserves and the removal of dependence on food imports by improving agricultural production and creating food reserves.

The method chosen for meeting the balance of payments crisis and reducing the fiscal deficit (the two being linked) was a severe tightening of the belt, involving drastic cuts in government expenditure rather than increases in tax levels. The cut fell mainly on government capital expenditure, which in real terms decreased by about 50 per cent between 1966–67 and 1970–71. This was an important factor in the continued industrial recession in this period. The industrial slowing down continued till the mid-1970s, the industrial growth rate coming down from an average of 7.8 per cent per year between 1951 and 1966 to 4.99 per cent per year between 1966 and 1974.

Further, the political developments in this period had important implications for economic policy. In the 1967 elections, the Congress party received a major setback at the Centre and particularly in the states. The prime minister responded by adopting a radical stance which led to differences within the Congress and eventually a split in November 1969. After the split Mrs Gandhi could retain the government only with the support of the Communist parties and some regional parties, and this accentuated the radical left turn in her policies. In December 1970, she called for a general election and, campaigning on the slogan of *garibi hatao* and promising radical socialist policies, she romped to power with a landslide victory in March 1971.

The post-1967 period therefore saw the launching of a series of radical economic policies which were to have long-term effects on India's developmental effort. Some of these policies accentuated the shortcomings that had begun to emerge during the first phase of planning itself, that is, in the 1950s and early 1960s, others created new distortions. The major private commercial banks in India were nationalized in 1969. The same year the Monopolies and Restrictive Trade Practices (MRTP) Act, severely restricting the activities of large business houses, was passed. After the 1971 election victory, a series of further such measures increasing government control and intervention were introduced with the active support of left radical intellectuals like P.N. Haksar, D.P. Dhar and Mohan Kumaramangalam. Thus, insurance was nationalized in 1972 and the coal industry was nationalized in 1973. A disastrous effort was made to nationalize wholesale wheat trade the same year, which was abandoned after a few months. The Foreign Exchange Regulation Act (FERA) was passed in 1973, putting numerous restrictions on foreign investment and the functioning of foreign companies in India, making India one of the most difficult destinations for foreign capital in the world. The government also decided to take over and run 'sick' companies, such as a number of textile mills, rather than allow such loss-making companies to close down.

The debilitating long-term effects of many of these measures on the overall economy have been discussed later in this chapter.

It must be remembered, though, that the new policies, which were partially a result of the historically specific economic and political situation, met many of the critical problems faced by the country at that time. They pulled India out of the economic crisis most creditably and restored her independence and dignity *vis-á-vis* the advanced countries. We shall briefly review these achievements in the next section.

The Achievements

In the considerable economic achievements between the mid-1960s and the end-1980s, Indira Gandhi (often too easily dismissed as populist) played a major role. These achievements are to be viewed in light of the series of formidable internal and external shocks witnessed during this period. For example, following the crisis of the mid-1960s discussed above, there was the genocide in East Pakistan (Bangladesh) resulting in the huge burden of over 10 million refugees from that region (nearly half the population of a country like Australia!) taking shelter in India, the 1971 war with Pakistan, two droughts of 1972 and 1974, the major oil shock of 1973 leading to a quadrupling of international oil prices and hence of cost of oil imports, the oil shock of 1979 when oil prices doubled, the disastrous harvest of 1979–80 caused by the worst drought since independence, and the widespread successive droughts of 1987 and 1988.

Concerted efforts were made after the mid-1960s to, *inter alia,* improve the balance of payments situation, create food security, introduce anti-poverty measures and reduce dependence on imports for critical inputs like oil. These enabled India to weather the impact of the droughts, war and the oil shocks without getting into a debt crisis and a recessionary spin as happened in the case of a number of developing countries, especially in Latin America in the 1980s, and without serious famine conditions, let alone the huge number of famine deaths that occurred in Communist China in the late 1950s.

On the food front the situation improved rapidly. The adoption of the Green Revolution strategy of introducing a package of high-yield variety (HYV) seeds, fertilizers and other inputs in a *concentrated manner to some suitable select areas* paid immediate dividends in creating food security and poverty reduction. Between 1967–68 and 1970–71 foodgrain production rose by 35 per cent. Net food imports fell from 10.3 million tonnes in 1966 to 3.6 million tonnes in 1970, while food availability increased from 73.5 million tonnes to 89.5 million tonnes over the same period. Food availability continued to increase sharply to 110.25 million tonnes in 1978 and 128.8 million tonnes in 1984 and food stocks crossed the 30 million tonnes mark by the mid-1980s, putting an end to India's 'begging bowl' image and creating considerable food security even to meet extreme crisis situations. For example, the economy was able to absorb the massive successive droughts of 1987–88 without undue pressure on prices of food or imports. In fact, the rural poverty index continued to show a decline in these crisis years as rural employment and incomes were maintained through government programmes using the surplus food stocks. This was the first time since independence that rural poverty was not exacerbated during a drought or a poor harvest.

Apart from food self-sufficiency, certain other features emerged that pointed towards a greater autonomy of the Indian economy and increased self-reliance. The fiscal deficit was brought down sharply from 7.3 per cent of GDP in 1966–67 to 3.8 per cent in 1969–70. The balance of payments situation improved considerably with reduced food and other imports, a certain improvement in exports and particularly with the surge in remittances made by Indian workers from the oil-boom rich Middle East. By 1978–79, foreign exchange reserves had risen to a peak of about $7.3 billion (including gold and SDKs), more than nine months of imports cover compared to the less than two months covered in 1965–66.

Given the arm-twisting of the donors, self-reliance was seen as the need to reduce dependence on foreign aid not only in crisis situations such as those created by drought or other natural disasters, but also on aid as a short-term means to develop key capabilities, as was envisaged in the earlier Nehru–Mahalanobis strategy. Partly as a result of this shift in perspective, foreign aid began to decline rapidly. Net aid as a proportion of NNP, which had peaked to an average of 4.22 per cent during the Third Plan (the last few crisis years of the Plan partly accounting for this high rate), came down to 0.35 in 1972–73 and rose only slightly after the 1973 oil crisis, but yet averaged not more than 1 per cent of NNP till 1977–78. The debt service ratio, that is, the annual outflow of interest and repatriation of principal due to existing debt as a proportion of exports of goods and services, fell to a low and easily manageable 10.2 per cent in 1980–81 from an estimated 23 per cent in 1970–71 and 16.5 per cent in 1974–75.

We have already seen that the rapid expansion in the indigenous capital goods industry, which started in the Nehru years, had greatly reduced India's dependence on the external world for maintaining her rate of investment (and growth) as the share of equipment that needed to be imported in the total fixed capital investment in India had fallen from 43 per cent to 9 per cent between 1960 and 1974.

Private foreign investment continued to be very low in proportion to total investment. Unlike many Latin American and some East Asian countries, foreign capital or multinational corporations played a very minor role in India. In 1981–82, only about 10 per cent of value added in the factory sector of mining and manufacturing was accounted for by foreign firms which included FERA companies with diluted foreign shareholding. Till the 1980s, most foreign collaborations were technological collaborations not involving any foreign share or equity capital. For example, in 1977–80, 86.5 per cent of technology import agreements did not involve any foreign equity. Foreign capital was marginal in the financial sphere as well. It was negligible in the insurance sector and foreign banks accounted for only 8.9 per cent of total deposits in the organized banking sector in 1970. Between 1969 (the year of bank nationalization) and 1981, while the number of branches of all commercial banks in India rose from 8,262 to 35,707, the number of branches of foreign banks rose from 130 to 132. By 1992, the corresponding figures were 60,601 and 140. (It may be noted here, as an aside, that more than 60 per cent of the massive branch expansion of the Indian banks was in the rural areas, not only creating a much wider base for mopping up savings but also for extending credit, and thus enabling priority credit to agriculture, and that too increasingly to the poorer households as part of the second wave of land reform and the *garibi hatao* campaign.

Thus, while the volume of foreign private investment remained marginal and foreign aid declined and the ratio of foreign savings to total investment fell and remained low throughout the 1970s, the rates of domestic savings and investment increased rapidly. As Table 26.1 shows, from an average savings rate of 10.58 per cent and a rate of Gross Domestic Capital Formation or investment of 11.84 per cent in the 1950s, the savings and investment rates nearly doubled to 21.22 per cent and 20.68 per cent respectively between 1975–76 and 1979–80. The 1980s and 1990s saw further increases in the rates of domestic savings and capital formation, making them comparable to several high-growth economies.

A new feature of the 1980s was the phenomenal increase in new stock market issues, the stock market thus emerging as an important source of funds for industry. It has been estimated that in 1981 the capital market accounted for only 1 per cent of domestic savings, whereas by the end of the 1980s this proportion had increased by about seven times. The new stock issue in 1989 was Rs 6,500

Table 26.1: Gross Domestic Savings and Gross Domestic Capital
Formation

(As per cent of GDP at current market prices)

Annual Average	Gross Domestic Savings	Gross Domestic Capital Formation (Adjusted)
1950–51 to 1959–60	10.58	11.84
1960–61 to 1969–70	13.53	15.63
1970–71 to 1979–80	18.92	19.06
1975–76 to 1979–80	21.22	20.68
1980–81 to 1989–90	20.03	21.99
1990–91 to 1995–96	23.80	25.35

Source: Calculated from Economic Survey, 1996, Government of India.

crore, which was about 7.25 per cent of Gross Domestic Savings of 1989–90. Another estimate shows that in 1990 Indian companies raised an unprecedented Rs 12,300 crore from the primary stock market.

The early 1980s also saw a highly successful breakthrough in the import substitution programme for oil under the supervision of the Oil and Natural Gas Commission (ONGC), a public sector organization. The large loan received from the IMF in this period helped this effort considerably. In 1980–81, domestic production of oil was 10.5 million tonnes and imports 20.6 million tonnes, the oil import bill taking up 75 per cent of India's export earnings! With new oil finds at the Bombay High oil fields, by the end of the Sixth Plan (1980–85), the target of indigenous production of 29 million tonnes was achieved. As a result, in 1984–85, the net import of oil and oil products was less than a third of the domestic consumption and the oil import bill was also down to a third of export earnings.

By the mid-1970s, the industrial growth rate also started picking up from a low of about 3.4 per cent between 1965 and 1975 to about 5.1 per cent between 1975 and 1985. If the crisis year of 1979–80 was omitted, then the industrial growth rate during 1974–75 to 1978–79 and 1980–81 to 1984–85 was about 7.7 per cent per annum. In the 1980s as a whole the industrial growth rate maintained a healthy average of about 8 per cent per year. Again it was in the 1980s that the barrier of the low, so-called 'Hindu rate of growth' of 3 to 3.5 per cent that India had maintained over the previous two decades was broken and the economy grew at over 5.5 per cent. By one estimate the average real GDP growth rate between 1980 and 1989 was an impressive 6 per cent.[1]

Long-term Constraints: The Need for Reform

While on the one hand the Indian economy in the 1980s seemed to be doing quite well, on the other hand there were certain long-term structural weaknesses building up which were to add up to a major crisis by 1991 when the country was on the verge of defaulting. It is this crisis which brought home to the country the immediate necessity of bringing about structural adjustment and economic reforms.

Broadly, there were three sets of problems which had gathered strength in the Indian economy over time and which needed urgent reform.

The first set of problems related to the emergence of structural features that bred inefficiency. The import-substitution-industrialization (ISI) strategy based on heavy protection to indigenous industries was, as we saw earlier, very effective in deepening and widening India's industrial base and giving the economy a lot of freedom from foreign dependence. However, over time, the excessive protection through import restrictions started leading to inefficiency and technological backwardness in Indian industry.

This situation was further accentuated by the so-called 'Licence Quota Raj', that is, a whole plethora of rules, regulations and restrictions which stifled entrepreneurship and innovation. The MRTP Act and the reservation of sectors for small-scale industry are cases in point. The MRTP Act went against the basic principle of economies of scale, which is at the heart of capitalist development (or for that matter of socialist production). It also punished efficiency, as any company which expanded due to efficient production, good management and research and development (R&D), would face severe restrictions, including refusal of permission to increase capacity once it crossed a prescribed limit. It has been pointed out that the combination of the ISI strategy focusing on the domestic market together with restrictions on large industry from fully exploiting the domestic market through MRTP restrictions was particularly damaging for growth. Industry could neither expand in the domestic market nor were the ISI policies encouraging them to exploit foreign markets.

Again, reserving certain areas (the list kept growing) for small-scale industries meant excluding these areas from the advantages of scale and larger resources for R&D activities. This made the sector often internationally uncompetitive, leading to India losing out to its competitors in many areas. Also, the policy towards small-scale industry forced entrepreneurs in the reserved areas to remain small, as any expansion as a result of efficient and profitable functioning would deny the enterprise the special incentives and concessions. This inhibited efficiency and innovation in this sector. Further, industrial licensing cut off domestic competition just as import control cut off external competition and the two combined left little impetus for indigenous industry to be efficient.

The large public sector in India, which controlled 'the commanding heights' of the economy, also began to emerge as a major source of inefficiency. The early emphasis on the public sector was critical to India's industrial development. It is the public sector which entered the core areas, diversified India's industrial structure, particularly with regard to capital goods and heavy industry, and reduced India's dependence on foreign capital and foreign equipment and technology. However, over time, political and bureaucratic pressure on the public sector undertakings gradually led to most of them running at a loss. They were overstaffed, often headed by politicians who had to be given sinecures, became victims of irresponsible trade unionism and were unable to exercise virtually any efficiency accountability on their employees. State-run utilities like electricity boards and road transport corporations were notorious for incurring enormous losses. Apart from rampant corruption and lack of accountability, these enterprises, under populist pressure, often charged rates that did not cover even a small fraction of the actual costs. The extreme case of course was of the recent (1997) Punjab government decision to distribute electricity *free* to farmers! Even the critical banking and insurance sectors, which after nationalization had expanded phenomenally, mopping up huge resources, soon began to suffer from the public sector malaise of inefficiency and political interference. Many banks started running at a loss and the insurance sector remained inefficient and covered only a fraction of its enormous potential market.

Licensing, MRTP Act, small-scale reservation and the like made entry or expansion of business very difficult; since the mid-1970s virtually no exit was possible for inefficient loss-making companies as they could not close down or retrench without government permission. Powerful trade unions, which had led to a dramatic increase in collective bargaining, the index number of man-days lost rising from 100 in 1961 (base year) to 891.6 in 1980, made such closures very difficult. The government ended up taking over many 'sick' companies which otherwise needed to be closed down—the National Textile Corporation which took over a number of 'sick' textile mills becoming a major contributor to the total losses incurred by the public sector.

All this led to the investment efficiency in India being very low or the capital-output ratio being very high. A 1965 study shows that the public sector Heavy Electricals Limited was set up in Bhopal with a capital-output ratio of between 12 and 14—with no questions being asked or enquiry set up! Though this is an extreme case, estimates for the economy as a whole show that the capital used per unit of additional output or the incremental capital-output ratio (ICOR) kept rising, it being a little over 2 during the First Plan and reaching 3.6 during the Third Plan. According to one estimate, between 1971 and 1976 the ICOR had touched a high of 5.76. This explains why despite substantial increases in the rate of investment (see Table 26.1) there was an actual decrease in the overall growth rates of aggregate output or GDP between the 1950s and 1970s. The ICOR started declining in the 1980s though it still remained around 4 in the 1990s. Even during the 1980s, one estimate shows that the (simple) average rate of financial return on employed capital in public sector enterprises was as low as 2.5 per cent. Actually, the rate of return was much lower if the fourteen petroleum enterprises were excluded, as these accounted for 77 per cent of the profits in 1989–90.

The controls, restrictions, interventions etc., discussed above were paradoxically often resorted to in the name of introducing 'socialist' principles and equity but actually ended up building a distorted, backward capitalism, as they went against the basic laws of capitalism such as the need for continuous expansion on the basis of innovation and efficient investment. Low efficiency or low productivity levels are of critical consequence in today's 'post-imperialist' world, where economic superiority is established and transfer of surplus from one country to another occurs not through direct political or economic domination but through processes such as unequal exchange occurring between countries with different productivity levels. Economic thinkers of the left and the right are agreed on placing the question of productivity at the centre of any national development. In today's context of rapid globalization, pursuing excessively autarchic policies in search of autonomy (something a section of the Indian left and the newly discovered Swadeshi path of the right, such as the RSS, still argues for) may, through fall or stagnation of productivity levels, destroy precisely that autonomy and push the country towards peripheralization.

This brings us to the second set of weaknesses that emerged in the Indian economy and which relate to the continuation of the inward-oriented developmental path followed by India since independence. India failed to make a timely shift from the export

468 India Since Independence

pessimism inherent in the first three Plans, a pessimism which, one must recognize, was shared widely by development economists the world over in the 1950s. The failure lay not in adopting the policies that emerged from the wisdom of the 1940s and 1950s but in the inability to quickly react to changes occurring in the international situation and to world capitalism after the Second World War, particularly since the 1960s and 1970s.

Some of the important changes that needed to be taken cognizance of are mentioned here: first, the nature of foreign capital and multinational corporations was changing. A process of 'internationalization of production' had started. Multinational corporations, instead of just looking for markets or sources of raw material, now looked for cheaper production areas. Instead of creating enclaves in the backward countries, which had backward and forward linkages with the home country (this was the typical colonial pattern), they were now bringing in investments which had major multiplier effects on the local economy, including of technology transfer. It became common for multinational companies to 'source' a large part of the components that went into the final product from all over the developing world and even shift entire production plants to the developing countries. Then, along with, and partially as a result of, the above process, there were massive capital transfers between countries, reminiscent of the capital transfers of the nineteenth century at the height of colonial expansion, but very different in character. The above two processes contributed to another major international development, that of an unprecedented explosion of world trade. Between the 1950s and 1970s, world output of manufactures increased four times but world trade in manufactures increased ten times. The percentage of world produce that went for export doubled between 1965 and 1990. What is most significant is that while there was a massive increase in global industrial exports, the Third World was able to rapidly increase its share of total industrial exports, especially since the 1970s, from about 5 per cent in 1970 to double the figure in 1983.[2]

The East Asian Miracle, that is, the rapid industrialization of the East Asian countries, beginning in the 1960s, which gradually shifted the industrial base of the world from the West to the East, took advantage precisely of these kinds of opportunities of capital and market availability. Japan's example of explosive post-Second

World War growth was being repeated by South Korea, Taiwan, Singapore, Hong Kong and, more recently, Thailand, Malaysia, China and Indonesia. The four Asian Tigers, South Korea, Hong Kong, Singapore and Taiwan increased their share in world export of manufactures from 1.5 per cent in 1965 to 7.9 per cent in 1990. Even the newly industrializing economies (NICs), Indonesia, Malaysia and Thailand increased their share from 0.1 per cent to 1.5 per cent over the same period.[3] South Korea's manufactured exports, which were negligible in 1962, amounted to four times those of India by 1980. Again South Korea was exporting $41 billion worth of manufactured goods to the OECD countries in 1990 to India's mere $9 billion.

India did reasonably well till the mid-1960s, basing herself on an inward-oriented, import-substitution-based strategy. However, India failed to respond adequately to the new opportunities thrown up by the changing world situation despite the availability of the East Asian experience. In fact, after the crisis of the mid-1960s, India got pushed by immediate circumstances to take a tighter 'protectionist' and inward-looking turn in the late 1960s and early 1970s instead of taking advantage of the globalization process.

In fact, the restrictions on multinational corporations and suspicion of foreign capital increased in this period. No advantage could be taken of the internationalization of production and of the increased international flow of funds. As for exports, though successful efforts were made to diversify them, both in terms of commodity composition (e.g., the rapid shift to manufactured exports, it being 50 per cent of total exports in 1980–81 rising to 75 per cent in 1989–90) and in terms of geographical spread, the quantitative expansion or the increase in volume of exports lagged far behind the potential created by the world expansion of trade, which was successfully exploited by the East Asian countries. In fact, India's share in world exports actually shrank from about 2.4 per cent in 1948 to 0.42 per cent in 1980, rising to a still paltry 0.6 per cent by 1994. The volume of India's manufactured exports in 1980–81 was half that of China's, one-third of Brazil's and a quarter of South Korea's.

India was thus unable to use the opportunities provided by the changed world situation to rapidly industrialize and transform its economy, increase income levels and drastically reduce poverty levels, as did many of the East Asian countries. South Korea, for example, had a per capita income level comparable to India's in the 1960s (based on purchasing power parity) and today South Korean income levels are knocking at the doors of levels achieved by advanced countries, while India is still pretty much near the bottom of the heap. Even China changed track in 1978, opening up its economy, participating in the globalization process, welcoming foreign investment, pushing up its exports, and so on, leading to a current growth rate much higher than India's. Between 1980 and 1989, China's real GDP, by one estimate, grew at an average rate of 9.4 per cent, considerably faster than did India's over the same period. Though the figures for China are not fully reliable, yet economists agree that China was well ahead of India in this respect.

One may add here that India's poor growth in exports had implications regarding the productivity levels achieved in the country. In fact, countries like Japan and South Korea have effectively used export obligation on the part of various enterprises as a mechanism of enforcing international competitiveness through maintenance of high productivity levels. Enterprises or business houses which failed to meet the export obligation because of lack of competitiveness were blacklisted and suffered serious consequences, sometimes leading to bankruptcy.

The third set of problems which overtook the Indian economy were primarily the result of certain political imperatives, and which were related to the manner in which the Indian state structure and democratic framework evolved. More and more sections emerged which made strong, articulate demands on state resources. Governments, however, were increasingly unable either to meet these demands fully or diffuse the clamour for them. This resulted in the gradual abandoning of fiscal prudence from about the mid-1970s. A situation was created where the macroeconomic balance, which was maintained in India (unlike many other developing countries) with great caution for the first twenty-five years or so after independence, was being slowly eroded. The macroeconomic imbalance that now emerged tended to be long term and structural in character as distinct from the short-term imbalances created by shocks such as those of the mid-1960s or the 1970s, related to oil.

The gradual erosion of fiscal prudence was reflected in government expenditure rising consistently, mainly because of the proliferation of subsidies and grants, salary increases with no relationship to efficiency or output, overstaffing and other 'populist' measures such as massive loan waivers. Growing political instability and political competition, as the Congress party's sole hegemony began to erode, led to competitive populism with each party trying to outdo the other in distributing largesse. Also, it has been argued that with the prestige of Congress waning, it was no longer able to stand above competing groups pressing for an immediate increase in their share of the national cake and rein them in with the promise of rapid growth and a just income distribution in the future if current demands were subdued. Further, with Mrs Gandhi increasingly centralizing power in her hands, democratic functioning within the Congress party declined, with the party gradually losing its organizational links with and control over the grassroots. Political bargaining between sections of society was now not done within party structures but through budget allocations. Lastly, with parties clearly representing sectional interests, such as those of the rich and middle peasants, coming to power in several states after the 1967 elections and even beginning to have a say in the Centre after 1977, huge budgetary allocations were often made which were in the nature of sectional subsidies at the cost of an expenditure pattern best suited to overall development.

How did these political imperatives translate into real economic terms? As we saw earlier, the, response to the mid-1960's crisis was fiscal and balance of payments caution. However, a certain relaxation of fiscal discipline began after 1975 and particularly during the Janata regime of 1977–79. Food subsidies doubled between 1975–76 and 1976–77 from Rs 2.5 billion to Rs 5 billion. The fertilizer subsidy multiplied ten times from Rs 0.6 billion in 1976–77 to Rs 6.03 billion in 1979–80. The export subsidy multiplied by about four and a half times from Rs 0.8 billion to Rs 3.75 billion between 1974–75 to 1978–79. During 1977–79 (the Janata period) procurement prices for foodgrains were increased without corresponding increases in issue prices, taxes on a wide range of agricultural inputs were decreased and budgetary transfers to loss-making public sector units increased. In fact, the 1979 budget has been described by eminent economists Vijay Joshi and I.M.D. Little as a 'watershed marking the change from previous fiscal conservatism'.[4]

The fiscal profligacy continued through the 1980s and particularly during the second half, reaching absurd limits where, for example, the V.P. Singh-led National Front government that came to power in 1989 announced a loan waiver for farmers which would cost the exchequer more than Rs 100 billion. The direct subsidies from the central budget on only food, fertilizer and exports in 1980–81 have been estimated to exceed Rs 15 billion, an amount equal to half of the total gross capital formation in manufacturing in the public sector that year! While there was this explosive growth of government spending, the savings generated by the government or public sector kept falling with their growing losses. The result of fiscal profligacy was that the consolidated government (Centre and states) fiscal deficits rose sharply from 4.1 per cent of GDP in 1974–75 to 6.5 per cent in 1979–80, 9.7 per cent in 1984–85, peaking at 10.4 per cent in 1991. Governments in this period tended to seek ways and means of increasing their domestic and foreign borrowing to meet this deficit rather than either trying to increase government savings or reduce government expenditure. In fact, the gap between public (government) investment and public savings widened threateningly. After the crisis of mid-1960s the gap had been brought down to 3.6 per cent of GDP between 1968–69 and 1971–72, but rose to 5.3 per cent in 1980–81 and 9 per cent by 1989–90.

The growing government saving–investment gap and the fiscal deficit had a negative impact on the balance of payments and debt situation. From a situation of balance of payments surplus on the current account in 1977–78 of $1.5 billion (1.4 per cent of GDP), by 1980–81 there was a deficit in the current account to the tune of $2.9 billion (1.7 per cent of GDP). The deficit increased to $3.5 billion (1.8 per cent of GDP) in 1984–85 and rose very sharply thereafter to $9.9 billion (3.5 per cent of GDP) in 1990–91. It must be noted that the rapid worsening of the balance of payments situation, especially in the late 1980s, was neither due to any major external shock nor due to import liberalization. In fact, the second half of the 1980s saw an actual improvement in trade balance with exports growing rapidly at an average of about 14 per cent per year in dollar terms. The overall economy's savings–investment gap which had risen to an average of about 2.5 per cent of GDP between 1985 and 1990 (as the huge public savings–investment gap could not be fully compensated by the substantial excess of household and private corporate savings over private investment) and the consequent necessity of heavy borrowing had caused the balance of payments deficit.

It must be noted that the 1980s were a period of high growth. Between 1985 and 1990, on an average, India's GDP grew at over 5.5 per cent per year, industry at over 7 per cent, capital goods at 10 per cent, consumer durables at 12 per cent and so on. However, this growth was not a result of any step-up of savings and investment; in many ways it was a result of over-borrowing and overspending. The growth was both debt led (like Latin America of the 1970s) and the result of an explosion of domestic budgetary spending. This kind of growth was naturally not sustainable as the macroeconomic imbalances were bound to reach a point where a crash could no longer be averted—as happened in Latin America in the 1980s and in India almost a decade later.

The deteriorating fiscal and balance of payments situation had *led to a mounting debt problem, both domestic and foreign, reaching* crisis proportions by the end of the 1980s. Total government (Centre and state) domestic debt rose from 31.8 per cent of GDP in 1974–75 to 45.7 per cent in 1984–85 to 54.6 per cent in 1989–90. The foreign debt situation also became very precarious with debt rising from $23.5 billion in 1980–81 to $37.3 billion in 1985–86 to $83.8 billion 1990–91. The debt service ratio (i.e., payment of principal plus interest as a proportion of exports of goods and services) which was still a manageable 10.2 per cent in 1980–81 rose to a dangerous 35 per cent in 1990–91. Moreover, the proportion of concessional debt to total debt also fell from over 80 per cent to about 40 per cent in this period, that is, increasingly, the debt consisted of short-term commercial borrowing. The prejudice against foreign direct investment (FDI), which still remained, led to this excessive dependence on foreign debt rather than foreign equity capital, and inadequate returns on the borrowings led to an unsustainable debt service burden.

India's foreign exchange reserves fell from $5.85 billion in 1980–81 to $4.1 billion in 1989–90, and in the next year (1990–91) they fell drastically by nearly half to $2.24 billion enough only for one month's import cover. The Iraqi invasion of Kuwait in August 1990, leading to an increase in oil prices and a fall in Indian exports to the Middle East or Gulf region, partly contributed to this alarming foreign exchange situation. India's international credit rating was sharply downgraded and it was becoming extremely difficult to raise credit abroad. In addition, non-resident Indian (NRI) deposits in foreign exchange began to be withdrawn rapidly. In such a situation, where foreign lending had virtually dried up, the government was forced to sell 20 tonnes of gold to the Union Bank of Switzerland in March 1991 to tide over its immediate transactions. By July 1991 foreign exchange reserves were down to a mere two weeks' import cover despite loans from the IMF. The country was at the edge of default.

This is the situation (June 1991) in which the minority Congress government of Narasimha Rao took over power and with Manmohan Singh as finance minister attempted one of the most important economic reforms since independence.

27

Economic Reforms Since 1991

The long-term constraints that were building up over a few decades and debilitating the Indian economy combined with certain more recent and immediate factors led to a massive fiscal and balance of payments crisis that climaxed in 1991. The crisis pushed India into initiating a process of economic reforms and structural adjustment. The reforms, which in the Indian context were almost revolutionary in nature, were ironically started by a minority government led by Narasimha Rao, and guided by one of the most distinguished economists of post-independence India, Manmohan Singh, as finance minister.

Reform of the dirigiste, controls-ridden and inward-looking Indian economy was long overdue. As early as the early 1960s, Manmohan Singh had argued (quite bravely, given the intellectual climate of the period) that India's export pessimism at that time was unjustified. He advised more openness and a less controlled economy.[1] Other eminent Indian economists such as Jagdish Bhagwati were among those who urged reform in the early stages. An attempt at reform was made in the mid-1960s but it got stymied for a variety of reasons discussed elsewhere leading to a further recoiling into restrictionist policies. The 1970s witnessed some, what has been described as, 'reform by stealth', with the rupee being allowed to depreciate in response to market conditions not by an outright devaluation, which was then politically unviable, but by pegging it to a depreciating sterling. Indira Gandhi, particularly after her return to power in 1980, tried to bring in liberalization measures, mainly in the area of deregulation of industrial licensing and reduction of restrictions on large 'monopoly' enterprises. Though by the standards of the post-1991 reforms these efforts would appear puny, a glance at the newspapers of the 1980s would suggest that they were seen as quite path-breaking (particularly by the critics) at that time. Rajiv Gandhi, when he took over in 1984, attempted reform at a relatively quicker pace towards industrial deregulation, exchange rate flexibility and partial lifting of import controls. The major issue of the emerging macroeconomic imbalance, calling for stabilization of the fiscal and balance of payments deficits, was, however, left unattended, despite the express intentions to the contrary. Reforms of the financial and labour markets and the public sector also essentially remained untouched. Even these piecemeal attempts at reforms made by Rajiv Gandhi got abandoned after some time mainly due to the political crisis centred on the Bofors allegations and the desertion of V.P. Singh and others.

Though the need for reform had been recognized early enough, its comprehensive implementation could not occur for various reasons. Governments, especially when in a vulnerable situation (e.g., Rajiv Gandhi after the Bofors scandal, Indira Gandhi with the Punjab crisis, and later even Narasimha Rao following the destruction of the Babri Masjid), were extremely wary of initiating or sustaining reforms which would involve introducing unpopular measures like attempts to regain fiscal discipline, change in labour laws, steps which in the initial phase were bound to be painful. Also, there was (and still remains) persistent opposition to reform from vested interests such as the bureaucracy and even sections of business who benefited from the existing system of controls, using them to earn a sort of 'rent'. Last, and certainly not the least, a strong ideological opposition from the orthodox left, strangely oblivious to the changing global reality, continued to play a role in obstructing reform.

The crisis in 1991, with the country at the edge of default, enabled the Narasimha Rao government to break through the traditional mindset and attempt an unprecedented, comprehensive change at a time when both the ideological opposition and the resistance of the vested interests was at a weak point. Thus, though late, nearly thirteen years after China changed course, a programme of economic reform was initiated in 1991. One reason why the shift took so long and, even when it took place, was not as sharp a turnaround as it was in China in 1978 or the Soviet Union after the mid-1980s was that in a democracy the change from one kind of societal consensus (such as the Nehruvian consensus) to a new consensus (say around reforms) had to be a process and not an event, which had its own dynamic, very different from that operating in a non-democratic or totalitarian society.

The process of reforms started in 1991, involved, *inter alia*, an immediate fiscal correction: making the exchange rate more realistically linked to the market (the rupee underwent about a 20 per cent devaluation at the very outset); liberalization of trade and industrial controls like freer access to imports; a considerable dismantling of the industrial licensing system and the abolition of the MRTP Act; reform of the public sector including gradual privatization; reform of the capital markets and the financial sector; removing a large number of the restrictions on multinational corporations and foreign investment and welcoming them, particularly foreign direct investment, and so on. In short, it was an attempt to free the economy from stifling internal controls as well as equip it to participate in the worldwide globalization process to its advantage.

The record of the first few years of reform was creditable by any standards, though a lot of problems and challenges still remained. India performed one of the fastest recoveries from a deep macroeconomic crisis. Moreover, the process of structural adjustment, particularly the fiscal reining in (done initially), was achieved with relatively minimal pain—without it setting off a prolonged recessionary cycle leading to massive unemployment and deterioration of the condition of the poor as was feared and as occurred in the case of several other economies in a similar situation attempting structural adjustment.

For example, the growth rate of India's GDP which had fallen to a paltry 0.8 per cent in the crisis year of 1991–92 recovered quickly to 5.3 per cent by 1992–93 and rose further to 6.2 per cent in 1993–94 despite the major disturbances in 1992–93 triggered by the Ayodhya crisis. More important, over the next three years, the Indian economy averaged an unprecedented growth rate of over 7.5 per cent, a rate closer to the high performers of East Asia. Despite the crisis and the necessary structural adjustment, the Eighth Plan (1992–97) averaged a growth rate of nearly 7 per cent (6.94), higher, and on a more sustainable basis, than the Seventh Plan (1985–90) average of 6 per cent. Gross Domestic Savings averaged over 23 per cent between 1991 and 1997, higher than the Seventh Plan average of 20.6 per cent. Gross Domestic Capital Formation (Investment) and Gross Domestic Fixed Capital Formation between 1992 and 1997 also maintained a respectable average of 25.2 per cent and 22.3 per cent of GDP respectively, considerably higher than the Seventh Plan average of 21.8 and 19.8 per cent.

Industrial production, which showed a dismal, less than 1 per cent, growth rate in 1991–92 (it was negative in manufacturing), picked up to 2.3 per cent in 1992–93 and 6 per cent in 1993–94, peaking at an unprecedented 12.8 per cent during 1995–96. The capital goods sector, which had demonstrated negative growth rates for a few years, bounced back to nearly 25 per cent growth in 1994–95, allaying early fears that import liberalization would hit the domestic capital goods industry adversely. The small-scale sector too grew faster than overall industrial growth, suggesting that abolition of the MRTP Act did not have an adverse effect on it and perhaps encouraged its growth. Agriculture, too, after recording a fall in 1991–92, picked up the following year and by and large maintained till 1996–97 the high rate of growth of over 3 per cent which it had been experiencing for some years.

The central government's fiscal deficit, which had reached 8.3 per cent of GDP in 1990–91, was reduced and averaged roughly 6 per cent between 1992–97. The important thing was that out of the total fiscal deficit of 5.2 per cent in 1996–97, 4.7 per cent was accounted for by interest payments which was a liability emanating from past fiscal laxity. The primary deficit, that is, fiscal deficit net of interest payments, which represents current fiscal pressures or overspending, was only 0.6 per cent in 1996–97; it was systematically brought down from 4.3 per cent of GDP in 1990–91 and 2.9 per cent in 1993–94.

The external sector also showed considerable improvement. Exports, which registered a decline of 1.5 per cent in dollar terms during 1991–92, recovered quickly and maintained an average growth rate of nearly 20 per cent between 1993–96. Very significantly, India's self-reliance was increasing to the extent that a considerably larger proportion of imports were now paid for by exports, with the ratio of export earnings to import payments rising from an average of 60 per cent in the 1980s to nearly 90 per cent by the mid-1990s. The current account deficit in balance of payments, which had reached an unsustainable 3.2 per cent of

GDP in 1990–91, was brought down to 0.4 per cent in 1993–94 and rose to 1.6 per cent in 1995–96. Yet the average deficit between 1991–92 and 1997–98 was about 1.1 per cent, significantly lower than the Seventh Plan (1985–90) average of about 2.3 per cent. The foreign exchange reserves (including gold and SDRs) had grown to a respectable $30.4 billion at the end of January 1999, providing cover for about seven months of imports as compared to a mere two weeks in July 1991.

The debt situation had also started moving away from a crisis point. The overall external debt–GDP ratio for India fell from a peak of 41 per cent in 1991–92 to 28.7 per cent in 1995–96. The debt service ratio also fell from the peak of 35.3 per cent in 1990–91 to 19.5 per cent in 1997–98. It is, however, still quite high compared to China, Malaysia and South Korea, which all had (till 1997) debt service ratios below 10 per cent.

Reforms and liberalization of the stock market since the 1980s and particularly after 1991 produced dramatic results. The total market capitalization on the Indian stock markets as a proportion of GDP rose from a mere 5 per cent in 1980 to 13 per cent in 1990 and, following further reforms in 1991, it rose rapidly to 60 per cent of GDP by the end of 1993. By 1995, the Indian stock market was the largest in the world in terms of the number of listed companies—larger even than the US. Measures such as the repeal of the Capital Issues Control Act of 1947 (through which the government used to control new issues and their prices) and the external liberalization (which, *inter alia*, allowed foreign institutional investors to buy Indian corporate shares and enabled Indian companies to raise funds from foreign markets) considerably increased the Indian companies' ability to raise funds from the stock market (including in foreign exchange) to finance their development and growth. The amount of capital Indian companies could raise in the primary market in India increased from Rs 929 million in 1980 to Rs 2.5 billion in 1985 and Rs 123 billion in 1990. By 1993–4 the figure had reached Rs 225 billion—a nearly 250 times increase since 1980.[2] A substantial 12.8 per cent of the country's Gross Domestic Savings was accounted for by new corporate securities in 1993–94, up from about 1 per cent in 1981. Also, permission to access the international market enabled Indian companies, during 1994–95, to raise $2.03 billion through 29 Euro issues of Global Depository Receipts (GDRs) and Foreign

Currency Convertible Bonds (FCCBs). Up to December 1995, Indian firms had raised $5.18 billion through 64 issues of GDRs and FCCBs.

The encouragement to foreign investment bore fruit with FDI increasing at nearly 100 per cent per year between 1991 and 1996, it being $129 million in 1991–92 and $2.1 billion in 1995–96. Total foreign investment including portfolio investment increased from $102 million in 1990–91 to $4.9 billion in 1995–96. Considerable improvement, no doubt, but yet a far cry from what was being achieved by the East Asian countries. China alone had been absorbing more than $30 billion of FDI every year for some years, the figure for 1996 being $40.8 billion. One positive sign, however, was that one of the most stubborn mindsets—the xenophobia about foreign capital—seemed to have eroded, with the Common Minimum Programme (CMP) of the coalition government (following the defeat of the Congress in 1996), to which even the Communists were a party, desiring that the FDI in India should rise to $10 billion per year. However, the danger emanating from the relatively volatile nature of foreign portfolio investments, with the possibility of their sudden withdrawal (as happened in Mexico and more recently, in the late 1990s, Southeast Asia) due to often unpredictable extraneous factors, was understood by successive governments and efforts made to control short-term capital inflows and capital flight.

Critics of reform, mainly from the orthodox left, made the charge that reform was anti-poor, a major (and perhaps the only somewhat credible) plank of their arguments. However, studies of a large number of countries have shown that barring a few exceptions, rapid economic growth has been associated with fall in poverty levels. India too witnessed significant fall in poverty levels with the relatively faster economic growth of the 1980s. The proportion of population below the poverty line (the poverty ratio) fell from 51.3 per cent in 1977–78 to 38.9 per cent in 1987–88. Countries like China and Indonesia, which had much higher poverty ratios of 59.5 and 64.3 in 1975 compared to India's 54.9 in 1973–74, were able to reduce their poverty levels to much below India's in the span of twenty years. These countries maintained a much higher rate of growth than India during this period and their poverty ratios fell dramatically to 22.2 and 11.4 respectively by 1995, while India's had fallen only to 36 by 1993–94.[3]

To the extent, therefore, that the economic reforms were designed to put India on a higher-growth path, it would be expected that poverty levels would decline as well. The key question remaining was what would be the impact on poverty in the transitional phase, especially when the necessary stabilization had to take place with the attempts to improve the balance of payments position and reduce the fiscal deficit, leading to a possible fall in government expenditure. India's initial stabilization programme was said to be 'extraordinarily successful' causing 'remarkably little suffering' when 'compared with most other countries which were forced to effect a large and rapid reduction in their current external account deficits'.[4] Calculations based on several different indicators of poverty show that poverty, mainly rural poverty, marked a *significant rise only in 1992–93 and its causation was* linked mainly to a drought and fall in foodgrain output in 1991–92, leading to a rise in food prices, and very weakly to the stabilization programme. Even this was perhaps avoidable to a great extent. The government's failure in not anticipating the situation and maintaining expenditure on rural employment programmes, its not refraining from making any cuts (in real terms, there being a nominal increase) in the anti-poverty Social Services and Rural Development (SSRD) expenditure in 1991–92 to achieve fiscal stabilization, was criticized even by the supporters of reform. However, all the poverty indicators showed that by 1993–94 there was much improvement in the poverty situation. The poverty levels, both rural and urban, were significantly lower in 1993–94 than in 1992, by nearly six percentage points, and were lower than the pre-reform average of the five years 1986–87 to 1990–91.[5] Thus, it may be noted that the stabilization under the reforms had little negative impact, if any, on poverty levels. Other aspects of structural reform, it is generally agreed, do not threaten the poor and in fact would improve their condition by releasing the full growth potential of the economy.

The improvement in the poverty situation was helped by the fact that the government increased the overall Social Services and Rural Development expenditure from 1993–94. It rose from 7.8 per cent of total government (Central) expenditure in 1992–93 to an average of nearly 10 per cent between 1993 and 1998. Real agricultural wages, which had decreased by 6.2 per cent in 1991–92, grew in the next two years at over 5 per cent per year and by 1993–94 surpassed the pre-reform level. After the low of 1991–92, additional employment generated in the total economy rose to 7.2 million in 1994–95, averaging about 6.3 million jobs every year between 1992–93 and 1994–95, considerably higher than the average annual increase of 4.8 million in the 1980s. Moreover, inflation, which hurts the poor the most, was kept under control. The annual rate of inflation, which touched a high of 17 per cent in August 1991, was brought down to below 5 per cent in February 1996.

But this does not complete the picture. Though on the whole the reform initiatives looked quite successful, there was still a long way to go. Continued political instability, aggravated by no clear majority emerging in parliament of any political party, made it difficult for any government to move away from populist measures and take tough but necessary decisions.

That is why no serious efforts were made to increase public savings and reduce government expenditure and the problem of high fiscal deficits continued. The public savings–investment gap remained at a very high average of 7.1 per cent of GDP between 1992 and 1996. The foodgrain subsidy actually increased from Rs 28.5 billion in 1991–92 to Rs 61.14 billion in 1996–97 (revised estimate). The fertilizer subsidy also increased from Rs 32.01 billion in 1988–89 to Rs 45.42 billion in 1989–90 and Rs 62.35 billion in 1995–96. The huge subsidies contributed towards a tendency for real investment in agriculture to fall because of lack of resources. C.H. Hanumantha Rao, eminent agricultural economist, noted in 1992, 'the annual subsidy on fertiliser alone amounts to nearly as much as the annual outlay on agriculture by the Centre and states put together'.[6] A similar example was the government subsidy on diesel, kerosene and cooking gas amounting to Rs 93.6 billion in 1995–96. The oil pool deficit (dues owed to oil companies by government which partly enabled the huge subsidy) in 1996–97 was Rs 98 billion making the cumulative deficit in that year about Rs 155 billion. The result was that the oil companies were unable to make the absolutely necessary investments in the oil sector.

Similarly, little was achieved with regard to reform of the public sector, particularly of state-owned utilities like electricity boards, transport corporations, etc. While the Punjab government went to the absurd limit of actually distributing electricity and water free to the farmers, several other states were not much better as they charged rates which covered only a small fraction of the costs. Therefore, state electricity boards and transport corporations ran at huge losses at a time when availability of power and proper transport infrastructure threatened to be critical bottlenecks, slowing down the projected rate of growth of the economy.

Also, there was no significant move towards reform of the labour market and creating possibilities of exit for loss-making enterprises. After the few years of initial success, the tempo of economic reform in India seemed to be waning. Moreover, the economy began witnessing a slowdown, from 1997. The GDP growth rate had decelerated significantly to 5 per cent in 1997–98, down from 7.8 per cent in 1996–97. Exports, which were growing at over 20 per cent, slowed down for the third year in succession since 1996 and were negative in 1998–99 (April-December). There was a slowdown in industry after 1995–96 and it was growing at less than half the rate achieved that year over the next three years. Very importantly, there was been a slowdown in the critical infrastructure sector, which was emerging as a major bottleneck. Flows of external capital, both FDI and portfolio investment, declined sharply, the latter turning negative in 1998–99 (April–December).

One of the most dangerous reversals was in the sphere of fiscal deficit, where the primary deficit which had been brought down to 0.6 per cent of GDP in 1996–97 (0.5 per cent in the new series data used in the Economic Survey of 1998-99) more than doubled to 1.3 per cent in 1997–98 and for the Centre and states together it was estimated to be 2.4 per cent (revised estimate). The selective acceptance of the Fifth Pay Commission recommendations by the United Front (Gujral) government in 1997, whereby the government expenditure on salaries was to increase very sharply without any compensatory savings, as the measures suggested by the Commission to achieve such savings were not accepted, put further pressure on the fiscal deficit. The situation reached a point where, 'given the serious fiscal slippage', even the Economic Survey of the Government of India of 1998–99 was constrained to argue, 'the time has perhaps come to reconsider the issue of *constitutional limits* on the deficit'.[7]

The slowing down of the economy from 1996–97 was partly because of the East Asian crisis, with Japan in recession and South Korea, Indonesia, Thailand and others showing negative growth rates. Other parts of the world such as Russia and Brazil were also facing crisis situations. There was a slowing down of world growth and particularly world trade growth in 1998. The crisis adversely affected world flows of capital, and exports, partially explaining the fall in Indian receipts of foreign investment and Indian exports. However, the fact that the deceleration in Indian exports was greater than that of the 'developing countries' as a whole is indicative of the failure of the reform process in addressing some structural factors which inhibited Indian exports such as poor infrastructure (power, transport, port facilities, etc.), archaic labour laws, continued trade restrictions and so on. It is this which enabled China and not India to occupy the space vacated by Korea, Taiwan, Hong Kong, etc., in the sphere of exports of labour-intensive goods, as labour costs in the latter countries rose.

Also, the economic sanctions imposed on India because of the nuclear tests (which the BJP government hurried into clearly with an eye on the domestic political scene) had a dampening effect on the economy. Political instability, opportunistic coalition governments with partners having widely divergent world-views, the BJP's 'double face' in economic matters, as in politics, with the RSS, their mother organization, talking of 'Swadeshi' which inhibited India's reforms and participation in the globalization process, while the BJP continued to swear by reform, all partially explain the tardy progress of reform.

Yet, it was a positive development of enormous significance in a democracy, that there was a broad consensus among all political parties from the right to the left (barring the extremists at both ends) that the reform process had to continue, a consensus reminiscent of the one around the Nehruvian programme at independence.

The consensus was suggestive of the fact that economic reforms or liberalization did not mean a change of goals set at independence by the Indian people, such as rapid growth, industrialization, self-reliance, removal of poverty and so on. Liberalization and participation in the globalization process was not the 'final surrender' to international capital or imperialism or the IMF–World Bank combine as has been argued *ad infinitum* by sections of the orthodox left. On the basis of the experience with various controls and state intervention at home, of changes occurring in the world such as the collapse of the Socialist bloc, the new globalization process after the Second World War and the experience of various fast-growing economies in the recent past, the aspiration towards the same goals set out at independence required an altering of strategy.

However, this is not to say that the earlier 'Nehruvian' strategy was wrong. That strategy had its historical significance. As we saw, it gave the Indian economy a certain depth and spread, increased its bargaining power and independence, and lent the Indian economy and society the dignity it did not possess after the colonial experience. But, over time, certain negative features developed. That, and the response to the changed world conditions, required a shift in strategy for the achievement of the same goals. To give just one example, if self-reliance and rapid growth in the 1950s, required import substitution, today capital and technology flows, and through that, keeping up efficiency or productivity levels was the route to self-reliance and rapid growth.

It was no accident that so many of the very people who created, outlined or subscribed to the earlier strategy over time saw the necessity of reform. We have, for example, apart from Indira Gandhi herself, the radical economist of the Nehruvian era K.N. Raj, the Marxist economist Lord Meghnad Desai, the Nehruvian Narasimha Rao, left economists like Sukhamoy Chakravarty, C.H. Hanumantha Rao, Arjun Sengupta and Nobel laureate Amartya Sen, and practising Communist and chief minister for the longest tenure since independence, Jyoti Basu, all implementing or arguing for economic reforms involving liberalization and participation in the globalization process, though with different approaches and in varying degrees. Even the BJP, despite the strong resistance of the RSS-supported Swadeshi Jagran Manch, was essentially committed to pressing on with reforms.

There was, in other words, a growing recognition in India of the imperative to be responsive to the external changes and internal experience and change strategy so that this great country could come into its own and realize its enormous potential rather than fritter away the considerable achievements made since independence. It is this which gave hope that India would enter the new millennium ready for her 'tryst with destiny', strengthened by the journey since independence so dramatically started by the people of India with Nehru in the lead.

28

The Indian Economy in the New Millennium

The great promise that the process of economic reforms had held out, especially after the major reforms in 1991, was to a considerable degree met in the years of the new millennium. The future prospect of the Indian economy in 2007, the sixtieth year of the country winning independence from colonial domination, perhaps looked brighter than it had ever looked in its recent history. However, many of the problem areas confronted in the first phase of reform persisted and the related issue of the sustainability of the rapid progress made in several directions remained. A critical bottleneck was on the equity front with India's ranking in the global Human Development Index (HDI) actually falling even as the economy registered spectacular growth for several years. These issues, and the new problems that emerged as India integrated further with the global economy, constituted the challenges faced by the country in the new millennium.

The Breakthrough in Growth

The slowdown experienced by the Indian economy in the late 1990s, partially due to the East Asian and Southeast Asian crisis and a global slowdown, continued at the turn of the century. The first few years of the new millennium were turbulent with oil price hikes, the 9/11 terrorist attack in the US and a further global slowdown. Despite this, the Ninth Plan period, 1996–97 to 2000–01, experienced an average GDP growth of 5.5 per cent per annum. Though the growth rate was lower than the Plan target of 6.5 per cent, it nevertheless demonstrated the post-reform Indian economy's ability to ride through crisis years without too much damage, maintaining growth rates well above the so- called 'Hindu rate' of 3 to 3.5 per cent which the country had got accustomed to.

The Tenth Plan too started off poorly with the first year, 2002–03, recording a growth of only 3.8 per cent. This deceleration was essentially 'agriculture pulled' with agriculture and allied sectors showing a negative growth rate of 7.2 per cent that year. Indian agriculture, which was already experiencing a slowdown in the late 1990s, was faced with a monsoon failure in 2002–03, leading to a fall in agricultural production by 15.6 per cent. In fact the overall performance of the agricultural sector during the Plan period, 2002–03 to 2006–07, remained rather poor, showing an average growth rate of only 2.3 per cent, a rate significantly lower than the 3.4 per cent rate achieved between 1980–83 and 1992–95, or the rate achieved in the first five years of the new millennium (2001–02 to 2005–06) of about 3 per cent.[1]

However, despite the low GDP growth in the first year of the Tenth Plan and the poor performance of agriculture in the Plan period, the overall economy showed a robust growth with the GDP growing at an average of 7.6 per cent during the Plan period 2002–03 to 2006–07. Though it was slightly below the Plan target of 8 per cent, yet it was an unprecedented achievement. At no point in the past had the Indian economy sustained such a growth rate over a five-year period. A forecast made in 2004 that the Indian economy could achieve a growth path of 7 per cent annual GDP growth and 5.6 per cent per capita growth for the next twenty years no longer seemed a pipe dream.[2] Eminent economist Jeffrey D. Sachs had gone one step further and had, along with Nirupam Bajpai, advised the Indian prime minister as early as 2000 that he should look at the next decade as one in which 'India would double its per capita income' because, as he put it, 'A doubling of per capita income in a decade, as had been achieved by Japan in the 1960s, Korea in the 1970s, and China in the 1980s and 1990s, requires an *annual average growth rate of 7 per cent per capita for a decade, a rate of growth that we believed to be within India's reach.*'[3]

In fact the last four years of the Tenth Plan proved more than equal to these expectations, registering an impressive average growth of 8.6 per cent. This, and the fact that the Indian economy grew at 9.4 per cent during 2006–07 on top of the 9 per cent growth in the previous year (with per capita income growing at 8.4 per cent in 2006–07), raised the question whether the Indian economy was now ready for 'take-off' to a different growth trajectory of 9 per cent or more (with per capita growth of more than 8 per cent) as compared to the average of 6 per cent achieved in the 1990s.[4] The Planning Commission had in fact for the Eleventh Five Year Plan (2007–08 to 2012–13) set a target of an annual average growth of 9 per cent. Should India achieve that or more, then the transformation that Japan achieved in two decades, from the 1950s when it grew at an unprecedented rate of 8 per cent per annum per capita to catapult itself into becoming the second largest economy of the world, would appear replicable for India, with much more significant implications given India's much larger size.

The Indian economy was perhaps poised in the new millennium for a historic breakthrough. Angus Maddison's monumental work shows that India was the world's largest economy through the thousand years of the first millennium accounting for as much as nearly 30 per cent of the world's GDP. As late as 1700 India continued to be the largest economy in the world. After this, as India came under colonial domination, the share of the Indian economy in world GDP fell continuously and dramatically for over 200 years accounting for a mere 4.2 per cent in 1950 when India had just achieved independence. In the next fifty years the Indian economy was again beginning to slowly grow to a greater share of the global economy, reaching 5.4 per cent in 2001. This India was able to do by registering an annual growth rate of 5.12 per cent between 1973 and 2001, a growth rate second only to China's and much higher than the global growth rate of 3.05 per cent in that period.[5] Since then, as mentioned above, India had moved on to a much higher growth trajectory, growing, from 2003–04 onwards, at 8.6 per cent annually, nearly two to three times faster than the advanced economies including the US, Japan and the Euro area and way above the global growth rate of about 5 per cent.[6] If this growth rate was maintained, then the forecast that India would in the not-too-distant future overtake Japan to become the third largest economy in the world after the US and China could turn out to be correct.[7]

Is the Growth Sustainable?

It is necessary to examine certain other parameters of the economy in recent years to ascertain whether the high growth rates achieved were sustainable. A critical aspect in this connection is the savings and investment generated by the economy. A very good sign was the consistently increasing rate of Gross Domestic Savings and Investment as a proportion of GDP in the new millennium, bringing them close to the high East Asian levels. Gross Domestic Savings increased sharply from 23.4 per cent of GDP in 2000–01 to 32.4 in 2005–06 and the corresponding figures for Gross Domestic Investment were 24 and 33.8. In fact it was investment rather than consumption which became the main source of GDP growth in the high growth rate achieved during 2004–05 and 2005–06. The rising rates of saving and investment were powered by increases in the private and especially the private corporate sector. A new feature since 2003–04 was that the public sector began to show positive savings after showing negative rates for the previous six years. As a result, the public Saving–Investment gap somewhat narrowed and the impact on the aggregate Saving–Investment gap was more telling. In fact, for three consecutive years, 2001–02 to 2003–04, savings were in *excess* of investments, leading to the period 2000–01 to 2005–06 as a whole witnessing a marginal average annual *surplus* of about 0.2 per cent of GDP, instead of a Saving–Investment gap. A considerable change from the average aggregate gap of about 1.9 per cent of GDP between 1980–81 and 1990–91 which somewhat improved after the 1991 reforms to an average gap of 1.2 per cent of GDP between 1991–92 and 1999–2000.[8]

Apart from the virtuous cycle of higher growth inducing higher savings and the new dynamism of the private sector, it has been pointed out that the 'demographic dividend' in the form of high savings rate was going to continue as the already high proportion of the Indian population in the working age group 15–64, which stood at 62.9 per cent in 2006, was projected to go up to 68.4 per cent in 2026. In other words, a higher savings rate was likely to be *sustained* by the declining dependency ratio (ratio of non-working population to working population), projected to go down from 0.62 in 2000 to 0.48 in 2025. By one estimate, 'this 14 percentage point decline in dependency ratio (would) translate into roughly an equivalent rise in private and aggregate savings, from about 25 per cent of GDP (in 2000) to 39 per cent (in 2025).'[9]

The fiscal deficit situation of the central and state governments began to show some improvement since 2003–04. The fiscal deficit issue had been a matter of much concern not only in the pre-reform period, especially in the 1980s, but continued to be a major bottleneck through the 1990s. The central government's fiscal deficit had come down from 6.6 per cent of GDP in 1990–91 to 4.1 per cent in 1996–97 but again gradually crept back to 6.2 per cent by 2000–01. Not only was the fiscal deficit coming back to high unsustainable levels, the proportion of revenue deficits (consisting, *inter alia*, of interest payments, subsidies, defence expenditure, salaries, etc.) to total deficit was also rising, from 49.4 per cent in 1990–91 to 74.8 per cent in 1998–99, reaching a high of 79.7 per cent in 2003–04. This meant that less and less was being spent on capital asset creation. As we saw earlier the situation had become so bad that, by the end of the 1990s, the government itself was talking in terms of putting constitutional limits on the deficits incurred by the central and state governments due to their fiscal profligacy.[10]

Such a step was indeed taken with the passing of the Fiscal Reforms and Budget Management Act (FRBMA) in August 2003. The Act and the rules were notified to come into effect from 5 July 2004. The Act was aimed at ensuring fiscal prudence. The rules of the Act required that revenue deficits be reduced by half per cent or more of the GDP every year and be eliminated altogether by 31 March 2009. The fiscal deficit was to be reduced by 0.3 per cent or more of the GDP every year and by 31 March 2009 it was to be no more than 3 per cent of GDP.

There was some success in reversing the trend particularly after the FRBMA came into effect in 2004. The central government fiscal deficit gradually came down from 6.2 per cent of GDP in 2001–02 to 4 per cent in 2004–05, to a budget estimate (BE) of 3.8 in 2006–07. Revenue deficits also fell from 4.4 per cent of GDP in 2000–01 to 2.5 per cent in 2004–05 and a BE of 2.1 per cent in 2006–07. This led to the revenue deficit as a proportion of fiscal deficit declining by 27 percentage points, from 79.7 per cent in 2003–04 to 57 per cent BE in 2006–07. The fiscal situation of the states also improved significantly. The fiscal deficit of states, having actually risen from 3.3 per cent in 1990–91 to 4.5 per cent in 2003–04, subsequently fell to 3.2 per cent in 2005–06 (revised estimate) and 2.6 per cent in 2006–07 (BE). The revenue deficits had also risen from 0.9 per cent in 1990–91 to 4.5 per cent in 2003–04 and subsequently fell to 0.5 per cent in 2005–06 and it was budgeted to be zero in 2006–07. The FRBMA-mandated targets for fiscal and revenue deficits were thus set to be achieved by the states two years ahead of schedule. The combined improvement in the central and state budget deficits led to the consolidated general government deficit, which had risen from 9.4 per cent of GDP in 1990–01 to 9.9 per cent in 2001–02, to fall to 7.5 per cent in 2004–05 and 6.3 per cent in 2006–07 (BE). It is significant that the 2006–07 figure was only marginally higher than the 6 per cent figure which the Twelfth Finance Commission had declared as a sustainable ratio of combined fiscal deficit to GDP, to be equally shared between the Centre and the states.[11]

On the revenue side of the fiscal equation, the government was unable to substantially raise the tax–GDP ratio. In fact, in the early years of reform, with the reduction in direct taxes (personal income tax and corporate tax) as well as indirect taxes (customs, excise and service tax), the total tax–GDP ratio fell from 10.1 per cent in 1990–01 to 8.2 per cent in 2001–02. Thereafter it slowly crept back to levels a little higher than in 1990–91, that is, 10.3 per cent in 2005–06 (provisional) and 10.8 per cent in 2006–07 (BE).

However, the overall revenue figures do not tell us about a substantial change occurring in the Indian tax framework. Despite drastic cuts in the rates, the total volume of personal and corporate (or corporation) taxes grew rapidly. Personal income tax as a proportion of total tax revenue nearly doubled from 9.3 in 1990–91 to 17.1 per cent in 2000–01, with the BE for 2006–07 being 17.5 per cent. Corporation tax as a proportion of total revenue showed an even more dramatic increase, more than doubling from 9.3 per cent in 1990–01 to 19.6 per cent in 2001–02 and nearly tripling the 1990–91 figure by 2004–05 by reaching 27.1 per cent. The BE for 2006–07 was an even higher 30.1 per cent. Thus the proportion of direct tax (personal plus corporation) to total tax revenues increased from 19.1 per cent in 1990–01 to 47.6 per cent in 2006–07 (BE).[12] This was a significant change in a progressive direction which critics of reform need to note.

The problem, however, was on the expenditure side. About 86 per cent of the revenue receipts were committed to expenditure on interest payments, subsidies, pay, pensions and defence in 2005–06. Interest payments alone, due to heavy government borrowing in the past (total government debt–GDP ratio had reportedly reached unsustainable levels of about 90 per cent),[13] used up over 38 per cent of total revenue and major subsidies another 13 per cent in 2005–06.[14] The pattern of fiscal profligacy powered by populist pressures in which governments, in order to meet various sectional demands, committed expenditures through subsidies (often in the name of the poor but not benefiting them), salary concessions, etc., a problem inherited from the late 1970s and 1980s, had continued through the post-1991 economic reform years (sometimes even been getting exacerbated) except for a brief improvement in the early 1990s under IMF pressure. As a result, government *capital* expenditure as a proportion of total revenue receipts and of GDP had actually started declining from 2003–04,[15] at a time when the need for Government investment in infrastructure (such as roads, ports and electricity), agricultural development, education and health was crying out for urgent attention. Despite some improvement in the fiscal deficit situation since the enactment of the FRBMA, analysts were agreed that India would have to introduce far greater discipline and not keep on hoping to offset government dissaving by the large overseas savings abroad. Also, government expenditure had to be directed and managed in a much better fashion if the country was to maintain the high growth levels it had begun to achieve.

A much more positive trend in the new millennium was the recovery of industrial growth, which had been facing a downturn since the late 1990s. The industrial sector picked up from a low growth rate of 2.7 per cent in 2000–01 to a double-digit 10 per cent growth in 2006–07. More important, it averaged a growth rate of nearly 8.8 per cent for five successive years ended in 2006–07, at no point falling below 7 per cent. This was an unprecedented feat since 1951.[16] The Eleventh Plan (2007–12) target for annual industrial growth was 10 per cent.

Within industry, manufacturing was growing the fastest. It is significant that the capital goods sector which had slowed down at the turn of the century, even showing negative growth for 2001–02, causing much concern, bounced back to double-digit growth for the next five years, averaging about 13.5 per cent between 2002–03 and 2005–06. In fact the growth rate of the capital goods sector had not only caught up with the consumer durables sector which had been growing much faster between 1993 and 2003 but had overtaken it by 2005.

The services sector, which had been maintaining a high rate of growth since the 1980s (higher than industry), continued to do very well, contributing as much as 68.6 per cent to the total growth in GDP between 2002–03 and 2006–07. The rest of the contribution to growth came almost entirely from industry as agriculture grew slowly in this period. As a result of the long-term differential growth rates of these three sectors, the shares of these sectors in India's GDP altered considerably, with services accounting for 55.1 per cent, industry 26.4 and agriculture only 18.5 per cent in 2006–07.[17] The corresponding figures for the tertiary, secondary and primary sectors for 1950–51 and 1970–71 were 27.5, 13.3, 59.2 and 32.1, 21.6, 46.3 respectively.[18] The fact that the services sector, which constituted more than 55 per cent of India's GDP by 2006–07, was also the fastest growing had important implications for the maintenance of high overall growth rates for the economy.

Relationship with the External World

The changes in the new millennium with regard to India's relationship with the external world have been by and large very promising. The Indian economy since the economic reforms, which involved liberalization and globalization, was getting rapidly integrated into the global economy. One indicator of that was the rapid increase in India's external trade (imports plus exports in goods and services) as a proportion of India's GDP, rising from just above 10 per cent in 1974 to 15.71 per cent in 1990 as a result of the hesitant steps taken towards economic reform. Thereafter as a result of the reforms since 1991 it jumped to 32.6 per cent in 2004, more than double the 1990 figure. India's external trade as a proportion of GDP was 30.8 per cent in 2002, a proportion higher than that of the US's 23.6 per cent and Japan's 21 per cent, though as yet much lower than China's 54.8 per cent and South Korea's 69.1 per cent.[19]

India's exports, in merchandise or commodities alone (the services story is even more dramatic), appear to have moved on to an unprecedented high trajectory since 2002, growing, in US dollar terms, at over 20 per cent consistently for five years ended 2006–07. The average rate of growth for exports between 2002–03 and 2005–06 was about 24 per cent and in the first nine months of 2006–07 it was 36.3 per cent. By 2005–06 India's exports had crossed the $ 100 billion mark, doubling in value in less than five years, a feat which took 23 years (1949–72) during India's early phase of independent development. Indian exports were growing faster than China's (the star performer in recent years) and at more than double the global export rate since 2005 (up to August 2006). As a result, India's share in global exports, which had fallen to a miserable 0.43 per cent in 1981, began to increase consistently, reaching 0.67 per cent in 2000 and crossing the 1 per cent mark in 2005. The targeted share for 2009 was 1.5 per cent.[20] It is important to reiterate that the exports growth was led by petroleum products, ores and minerals and manufactured goods, particularly engineering goods like machinery and instruments, transport equipment and chemical products, including drugs and pharmaceuticals.

While exports grew rapidly in the new millennium, imports grew even faster. The increase in the imports bill was partially due to the investment boom leading to the rise in the import of capital goods, and the high international petroleum prices. Petroleum products continued to be the largest item in India's imports, constituting over a third of the total imports in April–October 2006, followed by capital goods accounting for about 12 per cent of total imports. The negative trade balance in commodities was, however, to a great extent offset by the positive balance in invisibles due to the excellent performance of the services sector in exports. As a result, the current account deficit remained moderate at an average of 0.75 per cent of GDP between 2004–05 and 2005–06, after having shown a surplus of an average of 1.4 per cent for the previous three years.[21] The moderate current account deficit, however, was easily compensated by rising capital receipts, as we shall presently see.

India's services exports have been growing rapidly and faster than merchandise exports in past few years. They were worth $4.9 billion in 1992, $25 billion in 2003 and $61.4 billion in 2005–06. The Economic Survey of the Government of India, 2006–07, summarized the recent experience in this sphere, stating that services 'exports have increased threefold during the last three years: in 2005–06 with a growth of 42 per cent, it reached US$61.4 billion. Growth has been particularly rapid in the miscellaneous service category, which comprises of software services, business services and communication services. In 2005, while India's share and ranking in world merchandise exports were 1 per cent and 29, respectively, its share and ranking in world commercial services' export was 2.3 per cent and 11 respectively. By growing faster than merchandise exports, services exports constituted almost 60 per cent of merchandise exports in 2005–06.'[22]

Within services exports, software exports showed tremendous buoyancy, growing at an annual compounded rate of 36 per cent between 1995–96 and 2003–04. The share of software in total services exports in this period rose from about 10 per cent to nearly half, 48.9 per cent. Impressive as this growth would appear, the potential for sustained future growth in this sphere was enormous as services accounted for more than 60 per cent of world GDP and trade in services had grown faster than in merchandise since 1985 and the market share of India in global IT spending was estimated at a mere 3.4 per cent in 2003–04.

Apart from software a relatively new development was the explosive increase in export of business services including professional services, which grew by 216 per cent in one year to reach $ 16.3 billion in 2004–05, and by 181 per cent in the first half of 2005–06 to reach a level of $ 15.4 billion, surpassing the value of software services exports. In offshore IT services and business processes outsourcing (BPO), India accounted for 65 per cent and 46 per cent of the global market in 2004–05. However, all countries put together were estimated to have tapped only 10 per cent of the potential offshore and outsourcing market. Therefore, the potential for growth for India, one of the largest players in this field, was enormous.[23] The transformation of India in this respect was truly remarkable. As Jeffery Sachs put it, 'Who would have guessed twenty-five years ago that impoverished India would burst upon the world economy in the 1990s through high-tech information services? Nobody.'[24]

However, the largest contributor to inflows of invisibles into India has been (since as early as the 1970s) remittances by Indian migrants abroad. This, to a great extent, compensated for the very large negative trade balance in commodities, and kept the current account deficits within manageable limits. In fact in terms of capital inflows these remittances in the current account were much larger in volume compared to the net inflows in the capital account based on foreign direct investment (FDI) and portfolio investment put together. These remittances, along with the number of migrants, have grown dramatically since the 1990s with the onset of the IT revolution. From an average annual inflow of about $2.5 billion between 1980 and 1990, they rose to an average of $7.4 billion between 1991 and 2000. The new millennium saw the average annual inflow rise to more than $17.5 billion between 2001 and 2004. In 2004 inward remittances into India were $21.7 billion, making India the highest remittance receiving country in the world, followed by China ($21.3 billion), Mexico ($18.1 billion), France ($12.7 billion) and the Philippines ($11.6 billion). Out of total global remittances of $225.8 billion in 2004, India's share alone was almost 10 per cent. As a proportion of GDP, remittances into India increased from 0.7 per cent in 1990–91 to 3.2 per cent in 2003–04.[25]

A new feature of the nature of migration was that while earlier the bulk of the migration was of low-skilled Indian workers to the Gulf and the Middle East, increasingly, higher-earning, more technically qualified workers and professionals (especially in IT areas) were moving towards the West, the US, Europe and Canada. As a result remittances too were no longer mainly from the Middle East but were from the West. Indians living in the US alone were reportedly sending in about half the total remittances into India.[26] Various incentives and facilities for transferring funds to India as well as the robustness of the Indian economy and its capital markets had made India an attractive destination for repatriating money.

The flows into India on the capital account also showed an overall healthy growth in the new millennium. Capital account surpluses not only comfortably financed the deficit in the current account which had started appearing since 2004–05 but were leading to accumulation of increasing foreign exchange reserves, causing if anything 'problems of plenty'. Skilful monetary management was required, for example, to ensure that the rupee did not appreciate too much, and thereby affect India's competitiveness in the global markets. Foreign exchange reserves rose dramatically from $42.3 billion in 2000–01 to $185.1 billion in February 2007, a more than four times increase in just six years.[27] It was a sea-change from the earlier situation where foreign exchange reserves in 1980–81 were $5.8 billion and in 1990–91 a mere $2.24 billion.

Among capital flows, net FDI flows which had been consistently rising since the 1990s, averaging about $2.5 billion per year between 1995 and 1999, rose to an average of $3.7 billion per year over the next six years from 2000–01 to 2005–06. The rising trend continued during 2006–07. From April to September 2006 the net FDI according to provisional data had already reached $4.2 billion, almost twice the level for the corresponding period in the previous year. The FDI growth is significant compared to India's past record though it is still way below the levels achieved by China, which attracted net FDI several times more than the Indian levels clocking, for example, $49.3 billion in 2002.

While looking at net FDI coming into India one must keep in mind the relatively new phenomenon of outward FDI flows, which were reaching significant levels of about $3.2 billion in 2005–06. With Indian companies making major investments, mergers and acquisitions abroad, such as the recent (2007) much-talked-about acquisitions by the Tata group of the Anglo-Dutch-owned steel giant Corus for reportedly $12.2 billion, or aluminium firm Hindalco buying Canada's Novelis, Inc. for $5.9 billion, a qualitatively new process appears to have started unfolding.[28] It is claimed by one report that Indian companies could end up spending $35 billion in acquisitions and mergers abroad in 2007.[29] That Indian business was increasingly becoming global is seen from a December 2005 report that twenty of India's top hundred companies, ranked by market capitalization, derived more than 50 per cent of their revenues from sales abroad.[30]

Portfolio investments (PFI) constitute capital flows into the Indian capital market through foreign financial institutions (FIIs) and resources mobilized by Indian companies through American Depository Receipts (ADRs) and Global Depository Receipts (GDRs). It was only since 1992 that the Government of India permitted foreigners through FIIs to invest in Indian primary and secondary securities market, though with certain restrictions. Since then PFIs into India through FIIs have grown, averaging about $2.3 billion per year for the ten years from 1993 to 2002. Since 2003, net PFI into India increased manifold, 2005–06 seeing a record high of $12.5 billion. ADR and GDRs which were part of the PFI flows rose to $2.6 billion in 2005–06, up from $0.62 billion the previous year. The dramatic rise in foreign portfolio investment into India reflects the bullish sentiments in the Indian capital markets. The Indian capital market had matured beyond recognition. The market capitalization of the Indian stock market as a proportion of GDP rose from a mere 5 per cent in 1980, 13 per cent in 1990, 60 per cent in 1993 to 91.5 per cent in January 2007, reaching a figure comparable not only to emerging market economies but also to Japan (96 per cent) and South Korea (94.1 per cent).[31]

The rapid rise in PFI came with its costs: a greater vulnerability of the domestic economy to global financial fluctuations. But then this was one of the costs of participating in the globalization process and benefiting from it. The issue was how to protect the domestic economy from this instability. The gradual and careful manner in which the various regimes in power during the entire post-reform period have tried to deal with the issue of full capital account convertibility is evidence of the common concern that PFI should not have a destabilizing effect on the Indian economy.

A positive development in India's relationship with the external world was that its external debt levels were reaching more manageable levels and so was India's capacity to service them. On all counts of the four debt sustainability indicators, that is, debt-GDP ratio, debt service ratio, short-term debt to total debt ratio and concessional debt to total debt ratio, India's performance was creditable. India's external debt as a proportion of GDP fell from 28.7 per cent in 1990–91 to 22.5 per cent in 2000–01 and further to 15.8 in 2005–06. Equally significantly, debt servicing as a proportion of external current receipts, or the debt service ratio, which is a measure of a country's ability to service her debts without getting into a debt trap, also fell from a high of 35.3 per cent in 1990–91 to 17.1 per cent in 2000–01 to a comfortable 6.1 per cent in 2004–05.

India had moved down from the third rank of the top ten debtor countries in 1991 to eighth rank in 2004 in terms of total volume of debt. But more important, among these countries (see table 28.1) only China had a lower debt–GDP and debt service ratio than India in 2004, of 12.9 per cent and 3.5 per cent respectively, as compared to India's 17.9 and 6.1. The Indian figures compare extremely favourably with the debt–GDP and debt service ratios of other countries in this list of ten, such as Brazil (38 per cent and 46.8 per cent), Turkey (53.6 and 35.9), Indonesia (56.5 and 22.1) and Hungary (66.8 and 25.2). The debt service ratio for India, however, rose again to 10.2 per cent in 2005–06 mainly due to the one-off redemption payments of India Millennium Deposits. As for the proportion of short-term debt to total external debt, it was only 6.1 per cent for India, which was the lowest among the debtor countries, with China registering 47.2 per cent. Similarly, India was able to raise the highest proportion of concessional debt to total debt at 35 per cent, way above China's 15.5 per cent.[32]

Table 28.1: International Comparison of External Debt, 2004

No. Country	Total external debt (US$ billion)	Debt to GNI	Debt Sustainability Indicators		
			Debt service	Short-term debt to total external debt	Concessional debt to total debt
1. China	248.9	12.9	3.5	47.2	15.5
2. Brazil	222.0	38.0	46.8	11.4	1.5
3. Russian Fed.	197.3	34.7	9.8	17.6	0.0
4. Argentina	169.2	117.4	28.5	16.2	0.8
5. Turkey	161.6	53.6	35.9	19.7	2.9
6. Indonesia	140.6	56.5	22.1	17.4	27.7
7. Mexico	138.7	20.8	22.9	6.6	1.0
8. India	122.7	17.9	6.1	6.1	35.0
9. Poland	99.2	41.7	34.6	17.0	6.4
10. Hungary	63.2	66.8	25.2	19.5	0.3

Source: Global Development Finance 2005, The World Bank, quoted in *Economic Survey 2006–07*, Government of India, p. 132.

The improved debt scenario underscores the point that since the reforms of 1991 India had got on to a higher-growth path with greater sustainability. Unlike the growth of the 1980s which was based on overborrowing and overspending leading towards a debt crisis and an unsustainable fiscal deficit, a much higher domestic savings rate, a somewhat improved fiscal deficit situation and a considerably improved external debt situation characterises the post-reform rapid growth of the Indian economy, particularly in the new millennium.

Is it Dependent 'Neo-colonial Development'?

Critics of economic reforms or the liberalization and globalization process have seen in this path of development a threat to India's sovereignty, of India moving towards virtually a neo-colonial direction of dependent development, abandoning the Nehruvian consensus of growth with self-reliance and equity. They argue that the opening up of the Indian economy and the pursuance of 'neo-liberal' policies dictated by the 'Washington consensus' would lead to indigenous industrial stagnation if not de-industrialization, swamping of indigenous industry and economy in general by 'metropolitan' capital or multinational corporations, etc.[33]

None of these apprehensions appear to hold good. As discussed above, the Indian economy witnessed a major step up in its growth rate with a declining dependence on foreign debt or aid. Indian industrial growth had also picked up and it was not the typical 'neo-colonial' import-intensive consumer goods-based industrial development, but a diversified industrial development, including of capital goods industries. Foreign imports and foreign companies operating in India did not swamp indigenous industry and the Indian market. Despite a much higher inflow of FDI, foreign interests did not appear to have acquired substantial, leave alone dominant, control over the Indian economy. A study of a sample of large private sector companies showed that the share of foreign firms in total value added and total sales in Indian manufacturing increased from 9.5 per cent and 11.26 per cent respectively in 1990 to merely 12.63 per cent and 13.77 per cent in 2001. The study excluded from its analysis public sector manufacturing companies and the non-large private sector units where foreign capital presence was either nil or negligible. Thus if the entire economy was looked at, the share of foreign interests in Indian manufacturing would be even smaller.[34] Indian industry was in fact now not only successfully competing in the international market in highly competitive areas like the automobile industry (automobile exports grew at an annual average of 35 per cent for six years from 2000–01 to 2005–06, with the industry exporting about 18 and 16 per cent of its domestic production of three wheelers and passenger cars respectively in 2005–06)[35] and pharmaceuticals but was doing acquisitions and mergers of major global multinational companies.

The Indian economy and industry may not have grown as fast as that of China but, as has been argued, 'India's growth and exports have a much higher domestic content, domestic ownership and are sold under domestic brands. In an increasingly open economic environment, Indian firms have displayed the ability [to] internationalize their operations with exports and by investing in businesses abroad in a variety of manufacturing and service industries.'[36] The fact that (in 2003) India's FDI stock as a proportion of GDP at 5.4 per cent, and share of FDI inflows in gross fixed capital formation at 4 per cent, was only one-seventh and less than one-third the corresponding figures for China, and that mergers and acquisitions by cross-border investors were much higher in China than India, has led Baldev Raj Nayar to argue that 'China and India can indeed be regarded as two distinct growth models, the former driven by foreign capital and the latter principally reliant on local capital'.[37] Food for thought for those who counterpoise China's independence to India's succumbing to the 'Washington consensus'!

The fact that India was able to demonstratively profit by participating in the globalization process, including by opening its doors considerably to flows of foreign goods, services and capital, without being overwhelmed by it, and that China had continued to follow this path with greater enthusiasm and with remarkable success, further cemented the consensus around the need for change in the direction of economic reform that had emerged in India by 1991. Though much eroded, resistance to this, by now virtually globally accepted need for change, continued in a section of the orthodox leftist academia and a section of the cadres of the Communist parties, as the daring Communist reformer, chief minister of West Bengal, Budhhadeb Bhattacharya was to discover, much to his chagrin. While virtually all shades of political opinion now vied with each other for greater economic reforms, increased private investment including foreign investment, etc., it was not as if the challenges that the reform process faced when it commenced were all sorted out.

It is to these challenges that we shall now turn.

Challenges in the New Millennium

The greatest challenge that India continued to face was that of poverty. There has been much debate among economists on whether economic reforms had speeded up the process of poverty eradication or slowed it down. While there is general agreement that poverty did fall substantially between 1983 and 1993, from 44.5 per cent of the population living below the poverty line to 36 per cent, the controversy centres on what happened thereafter, particularly in the 1990s. Data generated by the 55th round of the National Sample Survey (NSS) showed that there was a sharp fall in poverty to 26.1 per cent in 1999–2000. The method used for conducting this survey was, however, not comparable to the one adopted in the earlier surveys and has added to the confusion on this question. The 61st round of the NSS fortunately generated separate sets of data for 2004–05, which were comparable to the 1993 data and 1999 data. The data that were comparable to the 1993 data show a fall in the poverty level from 36 to 27.8 per cent between 1993 and 2004–05. Using a method comparable to the one used in 1999–2000 the poverty figures fall from 26.1 to 22 per cent between 1999–2000 and 2004–05.[38]

Here again what is not disputed is that poverty did decline between 1993 and 2004–05 from 36 to 27.8 per cent. The debate centred on what happened in the 1990s, though there appears to be a consensus that poverty did decline quite rapidly in the new millennium, between 1999–2000 and 2004–05. Using various strategies to surmount the comparability problem, Angus Deaton argued that there was a 'very substantial poverty reduction in the 1990s' with rural poverty declining by 1.3 percentage points per year and urban poverty by 0.9 per cent per year between 1993–94 and 1999–2000.[39] Sundaram and Tendulkar broadly endorsed this estimate, claiming further that there was 'greater point to point average annual reduction in poverty during the last six years of the 1990s than in the preceding ten and a half year period'.[40] Others like Himangshu, Mahendra Dev and C. Ravi have contested this.[41] They claim that poverty fell faster, at 1.1 per cent per annum between 1973 and 1988, compared to 0.6 per cent per annum between 1987 and 2005, and 0.7 per cent between 1993 and 2005.[42] However, they are agreed that most of the fall in poverty between 1993 and 2005 was accounted for by a sharp fall in poverty between 1999–2000 and 2004–05 suggesting that the 1990s was the 'lost decade of poverty reduction'.[43]

While the rate at which poverty decreased in the 1990s may be debatable, it is generally agreed that poverty reduction in the new millennium showed considerable improvement: 1.8 per cent per annum rural and 0.8 per cent urban by one estimate,[44] and 1.13 per cent rural and 0.73 per cent urban during the period 1999–2005 by another estimate.[45] It is interesting that rural poverty showed a sharp decline in this period precisely when agriculture took a downturn. This could have been due to the increased growth of employment, particularly non-farm employment and a successful check on inflation, in fact a fall, compared to the earlier period, in the 1990s. Another, positive aspect is that the proportion of the very poor (those below 75 per cent of the poverty line) to the total poor showed a substantial decline from 55.2 per cent in 1983 to 43.2 per cent in 1993–94 to 36.5 per cent in 2004–05.[46]

However, despite the definite improvement in poverty levels, in the sense of the proportion of the poor falling, especially since the Indian economy moved on to a higher-growth path in the 1980s, the absolute number of the poor was still intolerably large in India, about 300 million in 2004–05. This made the size of the poor population nearly as large as what the size of the total Indian population was at independence (361 million in 1951). Clearly, economic growth was not fast enough. Also, rising inequality did not allow the benefits of growth to reach the poor adequately. One study shows that while the higher growth rates in the years 1993–2005 made an important contribution to reduction in poverty, the rise in inequality in this period limited this process. It is calculated that, had the inequality levels (GINI) remained the same, then poverty levels would have fallen by 2.8 per cent more in rural areas and 4.3 per cent in urban areas over this period.[47]

India's chief failure still remained on the equity front. Illiteracy was rampant and over a third of the children aged between six to fourteen did not go to school. A very large percentage of those that did go, ended up learning very little, as recent studies have shown. (The tall claims of the government that after launching the Sarva Shiksha Abhiyan, into which considerable resources were poured in, a great degree of 'Sarva Shiksha' or universal education was achieved were widely disputed by scholars and activists.) This meant education, *the chief source of social mobility for the poor*, was not accessible to an astonishingly large proportion of the poor. While India experienced spectacular economic growth over the last couple of decades, shockingly, the benefits of this growth were barely reflected in improvement of the quality of life of the most vulnerable sections of society, particularly children of the poor, in terms of immunization, health and education.[48] The 2006 National Family Health Survey (NFHS 3) showed an immunization coverage of only 44 per cent—an improvement of only 2 per cent in the last eight years, compared to the 1998 NFHS 2 data. Similarly, 46 per cent of the children under three were underweight in 2006, again a fall of only 1 per cent in the last eight years.[49] It was small wonder that India's position in the global Human Development Index (HDI) had actually gone down from a lowly 124 in 2000 to 126 in 2004, Sri Lanka ranking much higher at 89.[50] Also, though there was rapid growth in industries and services, agricultural growth remained sluggish in the new millennium. This had serious implications for the poor as about 55 per cent of the total workforce in India was still engaged in agriculture though the share of agriculture in GDP had fallen to 18.5 per cent in 2006–07. Employment growth in agriculture faced 'a near collapse' between 1994 and 2005 causing severe distress in rural areas.[51]

Clearly, just growth, which from Jawaharlal Nehru's time was correctly seen as a necessary condition for equity, was not sufficient by itself. This was recognized at the highest level, with prime minister Manmohan Singh making repeated statements on the need for making growth more inclusive and for addressing the agrarian distress urgently.[52] However, what was true of the Nehru–Mahalanobis strategy of growth with equity is true for the post-reforms period as well: the benefits of growth, or of progressive legislation, etc., reach the poor only when there is popular mobilization from below. India had much higher growth rates in the last twenty years than it did in the first twenty years after independence, but in terms of the change in the lives of the common poor, perhaps the early period still stands out as more successful. The urgency of reaching the benefits of growth to the ordinary citizen in the new millennium cannot be overstated. The existence of democracy in India and the presence of a significant left ensured that the issue of poverty and equity was constantly foregrounded and no regime could ignore it. Yet, much more needed to be done.

Some grassroots level popular movements emerging from within civil society were showing the way. Movements in Rajasthan led by Aruna Roy and in other parts of the country have mobilized the poor for the right to information, and used this right to see that resources allocated for the poor are not misappropriated. Similarly, movements for the right to employment led to countrywide efforts to have employment guarantee schemes for the rural unemployed. Movements in Andhra Pradesh led by Shantha Sinha, through an organization called the M.V. Foundation (MVF), for protection of child rights, particularly children's right to education, mobilized the village community to protect and secure this right for their children in village after village, bringing over 300,000 working children to regular schools. This movement was spreading in other parts of the country. The right to food campaign has also been gaining ground. The issue remains of how to bring these diverse movements on to the national agenda. The day these movements get adopted by mainstream political parties and their millions of cadres would be the day of rejoicing for India's toiling millions.

The UPA government led by Manmohan Singh, responding to these urges, enacted the Right to Information (RTI) Act and the National Rural Employment Guarantee Act (NREGA), two very important measures in the direction of deepening India's democracy. The National Advisory Council chaired by Sonia Gandhi played a seminal role in foregrounding these issues and getting these legislations through.

The NREGA was notified in September 2005 and the scheme launched in February 2006. Two hundred backward districts were identified in the initial stage and all the districts of the country were to be covered under this Act within five years. In fact, as early as September 2007 the government announced the extension of the scheme to all districts in the country.[53] The Act provided that 'every State Government shall, by notification, make a scheme for providing not less than 100 days of guaranteed employment in a financial year to every household in the rural areas covered under the scheme and whose adult members volunteer to do unskilled manual work . . .'[54] The Act attempted to reach benefits to the most needy through 'self selection' without dividing the poor into caste and other categories, as is repeatedly done, not so much to reach benefits to the most needy, but to seek short-term political dividends on a communal or caste basis. In combination with the RTI Act, the NREGA had tremendous potential in ensuring that funds meant to reach the rural landless unemployed, one of the most vulnerable sections of society, did reach them (and did not get lost in the proverbial bottomless pit of corruption, callousness and unaccountability that has got created in the bureaucratic structure of the country) and that necessary rural infrastructure got built in the bargain. The short experience with the Act already shows that in areas where the poor were somewhat empowered through popular mobilization the Act was getting implemented far better than in other areas where they remain uneducated and unmobilized.

The setting up of the National Commission for the Protection of Child Rights and appointment of Shantha Sinha as its chairperson in early 2007 gave a glimmer of hope that the issue of child rights would be taken up in right earnest and the MVF experiment particularly in the sphere of education would be replicated on a national scale. So far the record in meeting perhaps the most insistent demand of the poor, a right to a decent education, has been dismal. For example, the right to education bill was not passed in 2007 citing financial difficulties!

In fact, the whole manner in which the education policy was being framed at a time when the world was moving towards a knowledge society where knowledge was increasingly becoming the key factor of production left much to be desired and could have critical economic consequences. It has now become common-sense knowledge among economists of all hues that rapid growth in primary and basic education as well as in higher education is critical in providing access to a better life to the poor, in sustaining high growth rates which require an enormous increase in educated manpower and in maintaining global competitiveness in research and development. The IT sector was already facing severe skilled manpower shortages which NASSCOM predicted was going to increase manifold in coming years. China's rapid progress in providing basic education widely and a very ambitious expansion of higher education reflected in a manifold increase in research papers produced and patents filed by Chinese scientists should have instilled an immediate sense of urgency for India in this respect. The setting up of the Knowledge Commission by prime minister Manmohan Singh was reflective of that sense of urgency but it could not make much headway. While the lasting impact in the education front during the NDA regime was the communalization of education, the recent (2006–07) initiatives led by Arjun Singh, Education Minister in the UPA government, of reserving 27 per cent seats for the backward castes in institutions of higher learning (significantly not in primary schools) appeared to be aimed more at playing 'backward caste' politics than at meeting either the needs of the millions of the poor who did not even get to see the face of a school, or of producing skilled manpower in sufficient numbers or of producing globally competitive research in various critical disciplines. The Knowledge Commission lost its thrust with critical members resigning from it in protest. Lack of urgent action in this area of education at various levels could create a major bottleneck which resurgent India can ill afford.

The challenge before the country in the new millennium, unlike in the early decades after freedom, was not so much of trying to achieve high levels of economic growth. The challenge was of effective governance that would harness this growth, create institutions and structures that would make this growth sustainable, and inclusive. The challenge was for civil society movements and political parties to ensure that the state apparatuses delivered and the growth that India was witnessing translated into improvement in the quality of life of its vast millions. As an economist actively involved in making and commenting on India's economic reforms put it at the beginning of the millennium, 'if we have the will, and we are able to realise even half our potential in the next 20 or 25 years, India's poverty would have become a distant memory'.[55] There is today a historic opportunity for India to meet its tryst with destiny and not squander it in petty communal and caste squabbles and narrow gains for its political and bureaucratic elite.

29

Land Reforms (I): Colonial Impact and the Legacy of the National and Peasant Movements

Indian Agriculture at Independence: The Colonial Impact

Colonialism had a devastating effect on Indian agriculture. This when Indian agriculture, like in any other pre-industrial society, accounted for the preponderant share of the country's total output.

Colonialism shattered the basis of traditional Indian agriculture without bringing in any dynamic new forces. Commercialization of agriculture and differentiation within the peasantry occurred on an unprecedented scale. However, unlike independent societies undergoing transition from pre-industrial and pre-capitalist to capitalist mode of production, in India commercialization and differentiation did not mark the shift towards capitalist commodity production and the rise of the rich peasant/capitalist farmer.

Commercialization of agriculture in colonial India facilitated the extraction of surplus from the peasantry (through land revenue demand in cash) and the transfer of this surplus from India to Britain by bringing agricultural produce to the export market. The 'unrequited' export surplus being the size of the surplus extraction or 'drain' from India.

Similarly, differentiation of the peasantry in India by and large did not lead to the rise of the rich peasant/capitalist farmer but to the creation of a rentier landlord class. Thus, while Indian agriculture was transformed, it was done in a 'colonial' manner which had a long-term enervating effect on it.

The typical features that emerged in Indian agriculture under colonialism put an unbearable burden on the bulk of the Indian peasantry. First, the colonial state made a very high tax demand on agriculture. In the early colonial period the state made permanent settlements with zamindars (the zamindari or Permanent Settlement) fixing the land revenue rates at a very high level. The zamindar was the intermediary between the state and the direct cultivator. He committed to pay fixed land revenue to the state while he collected rent from the actual producers. However, since land revenue was fixed, the colonial state discovered that it was not able to mop up the rise in agricultural income caused by the rise in agricultural prices that occurred over time. The surplus or the increase in income was being largely appropriated by the *intermediaries*.

Consequently, all subsequent land tax or revenue settlements made by the colonial rulers were temporary settlements made directly with the peasant, or 'ryot' (e.g., the ryotwari settlements). In ryotwari areas and other areas under very similar tenurial system comprising over 40 per cent of British territories, the land revenue rates were periodically enhanced pushing them up to the maximum limit the economy or polity could bear. Contrary to British claims the actual land revenue collections under the British were generally much higher than those under the traditional indigenous rulers. Being rigid and inflexible in crisis years of low production or low income due to crash in prices, such as during the Great Depression of the 1930s, the land revenue collections could equal 75 per cent of the whole of the net produce of the peasant! Till the turn of the twentieth century land revenue constituted more than half of the total revenue raised by the colonial state.

Second, under colonialism Indian agriculture experienced the growth of landlordism and rack renting on a very wide scale. In the zamindari areas absentee landlordism and subinfeudation was rampant. So high were the rents and other exactions from the peasant that the gap between what was collected from the peasant and the land revenue paid to the state was in some areas able to sustain scores of layers of intermediaries between the state and the direct cultivator!

In the ryotwari areas, too, despite the direct settlements between the state and the peasant producer, landlordism and tenancy became widespread over time. By one estimate the landlord holdings in ryotwari areas covered 40 to 50 per cent of the total land. On the eve of independence roughly 60 to 70 per cent of the total cultivable land in British India (including zamindari areas) was owned by landlords.

The colonial situation created ideal conditions for tenancy and rack-renting. The destruction of traditional handicrafts and artisanal industry and the absence of a rapid growth of modern industry created an enormous population pressure on agriculture and an adverse land–man ratio of about 0.92 acre per capita at independence. Further, the growing differentiation of the peasantry and the consequent concentration in landownership was adding rapidly to the number of landless hungering for land in the context of unavailability of virtually any alternative employment. Such was the concentration of landownership at independence that over 60 per cent of rural households either owned no land or were semi-proletarian in the sense that they owned small fragments of less than an acre or uneconomic and marginal holdings of a hectare or less. The total land owned by them was only 8 per cent of the total area. Another estimate has it that nearly 75 per scent of the rural population was landless, consisting of landless tenants and agricultural labour.

No wonder then that levels of rent in cash or kind were generally higher than 50 per cent of the crop and in some areas such as in Punjab and in Tanjore in Tamil Nadu it went up to 80 to 85 per cent of the crop respectively! In fact in Punjab in the late 1930s the peasant movement demanded a rate of 50 per cent for tenants and in Tanjore an ordinance of 1952 lowered the landlord's share to 60 per cent of the crop.[1] Further, the landlord mostly paid only the land revenue making the tenant bear the entire cost of production. Also, the level of rents tended to move upwards much faster than the price increases.

In addition to the rent demand the landlords resorted to numerous illegal exactions in cash, kind or labour (begar), which put a severe burden on the peasant. The report of the U.P. Zamindari Abolition Committee pointed out, for example, that in parts of U.P. the number of such illegal exactions added up to as many as fifty in number! In fact a common and persistent feature of peasant movements all over the country in the colonial period was the struggle against such 'semi-feudal' illegal exactions.[2]

Given the above situation it made much more economic sense for the large landowners to give out either their entire land, or the lands in excess of that which could be cultivated by their family, on tenancy, extracting very high rents and other illegal dues from landless peasants competing for land, rather than go in for large-scale capitalist agriculture using hired wage labour under their direct supervision. It was not because of any allegedly inherent 'feudal' mentality of the Indian peasants or landlords that capitalist agriculture did not emerge. Typically, therefore, the large landowners in zamindari and ryotwari areas leased out their lands in small pieces to tenants who continued to cultivate them with traditional techniques. Despite high concentration in landownership the operated holdings in India remained by and large small and often very tiny. Petty commodity production with traditional techniques rather than large-scale modern capitalist farming was the typical production pattern in colonial India.

Studies conducted shortly after independence estimated that about 60 per cent of the family holdings in India were less than 5 acres each and about 40 per cent of the holdings were less than 2.5 acres each.

The problem of small holdings was further accentuated by their fragmentation, that is, these being held in dispersed small plots. One estimate is that the average holding in the country had approximately 6 plots of 1.1 acres each. The average hides the extreme cases of fragmentation. The Royal Commission of Agriculture, 1928, for example, reported cases in Ratnagiri where plots were as small as $1/160$ of an acre or in Punjab where mile-long strips which were only a few yards wide were held as plots. When subdivision of family holdings occurred among the successors, each fragment was further subdivided as they varied in quality and productivity. The efforts of the colonial state to handle this problem of subdivision and fragmentation proved very meagre.

The heavy demands on the cultivator made by the colonial state and the dominant sections in rural society led to a third major feature of colonial agriculture: extreme indebtedness of the peasantry. Bonded labour or debt bondage became a common feature in large parts of the country. The overwhelming bulk of the peasants' debt was contracted at usurious rates from private moneylenders. The Reserve Bank of India (RBI)-commissioned Rural Credit Survey Committee reported in 1954 that 93 per cent of the credit needs of agriculturists were supplied privately with the government accounting for 3 per cent, cooperative societies for another 3 per cent and commercial banks for a mere 1 per cent. S.J. Patel using data from the All India Rural Credit Survey made a rough estimate for 1950–51 that about Rs 6,500 million was the interest paid by cultivators on their debt. The total burden on the peasant of interest payments on debt and rent on land could be estimated at a staggering Rs 14,200 million or about $5 billion per year towards about the end of the colonial period.[3]

Given the above conditions where the bulk of the Indian peasantry was drained of any resources, living close to or below subsistence level, and where the upper sections of rural society found rent and usury more profitable than capitalist agriculture as a source of income, very little agricultural investment and improvement actually took place. The colonial state too did not put back a fraction of what it extorted from agriculture. Indian agriculture therefore remained at a very backward level. Nearly 97 per cent of the ploughs used in India as late as 1951 were still wooden ploughs; only 3 per cent were iron ploughs! Use of improved seeds, artificial fertilizers, etc. remained extremely low and scanty.

It is not surprising, therefore, that Indian agriculture, which was facing long-term stagnation, began to show clear signs of decline during the last decades of colonialism. Yields per acre of principal crops showed a significant decline between 1936–38 and 1950. Similarly, between 1901 and 1941 per capita agricultural output *declined* by 14 per cent and foodgrain output by 24 per cent.

No wonder, at independence India was faced with an acute food shortage which created near-famine conditions in many areas. Between 1946 and 1953 about 14 million tonnes of foodgrains worth Rs 10,000 million had to be imported, seriously affecting India's planned development effort. After all, the value of food imports was nearly half of the total capital investment in the First Five Year Plan (1951–56).

The challenge before the independent regime in 1947 was to try to reverse the long-term distortions in Indian agriculture which had emerged during the colonial period and to put Indian agriculture on a high-growth path. A multi-pronged attempt was made to reduce the various kinds of legal and illegal burdens on the peasant producer, remove the large 'semi-feudal' intermediaries, improve the terms of tenancy, provide cheap credit, step up investment in agriculture and necessary infrastructure, generate scientific agricultural research and so on. An attempt, in other words, to bring about comprehensive institutional and technological reform in Indian agriculture. Also, attainment of food self-sufficiency was to be a matter of 'first concern so as to put an end to dependence on foreign aid in this respect'.[4]

The main thrust of and the parameters within which the reform initiatives were to be taken after independence were understandably to a considerable extent laid down by the ideas and practice generated during the Indian national movement. It is this legacy of the national movement we shall now briefly turn to.

Legacy of the National and Peasant Movements and Agricultural Transformation

Since the late nineteenth century the early nationalists had been highlighting the backwardness of Indian agriculture under colonialism, 'its overcrowding due to de-industrialisation, its failure to modernise and use modern techniques of production, the declining trend in productivity and the vast unemployment and underemployment in the rural sector'.[5]

They saw the link between excessive competition for land caused by colonialism and rack-renting of tenants, the subdivision of land and so on. They were particularly critical of the high land revenue collected by the colonial state which not only deprived the peasant of any capacity to save and invest in agricultural operations but even cut into his very subsistence. The Indian National Congress, virtually since its inception in 1885, demanded year after year that there should be a low permanently fixed land tax and permanent settlement of land revenue demand even in the temporary settled areas so that periodic enhancement of revenue demand could not occur.[6]

While generally the early nationalists focussed on state exploitation of agriculture, some among them criticized the oppressive landlord–tenant relationship and the problem of usury and argued for change. G.V. Joshi, for example, argued for the establishing of small peasant farming which would be maintained through vigorous tenancy legislation in both the ryotwari and the zamindari areas, giving protection and permanent tenure for the actual cultivator, availability of cheap credit, and a permanent and low land tax.

Justice Ranade, rather precociously, went a step further and was among the first to argue for a structural change which would replace the existing semi-feudal agriculture with capitalist agriculture. Showing remarkable prescience, to some extent anticipating the actual developments that were to occur after independence, more than half a century later, he argued for a mixed model of capitalist agriculture. He envisaged on the one hand a class of wealthy large-scale Junker-style farmers who were to be created by the transformation of the existing rentier landlords into capitalist landlords and by transforming the upper strata of the peasantry or the rich peasants into capitalist farmers. On the other hand he envisaged a vast mass of independent peasant proprietors free from landlord oppression, with access to cheap credit, and subject only to a low fixed land tax. In Ranade's words, 'A complete divorce from land of those who cultivate it is a national evil, and no less an evil is it to find one dead level of small farmers all over the land. High and petty farming . . . this mixed constitution of rural society is necessary to secure the stability and progress of the country.'[7] In fact 'this policy of replacing landlordism by rich and middle peasants (and capitalist landlords), while keeping the small, subsistence farmer-cum-commodity producer intact so that there was no proletarianization and disintegration of the peasantry' proved to be the most viable one given the political and economic context at independence and was by and large 'accepted by the Congress Party and Government of India after 1947',[8] though a number of alternative strategies were also advocated, as we shall see later.

At the level of active agitation at the national level, on the whole, the national movement continued till about the turn of the twentieth century to focus on curtailment of the colonial state's demand on agriculture and to some extent on some ameliorative measures for tenants and the indebted peasantry. There were, however, peasant and tenant movements emerging in various parts of the country fighting for their specific demands without directly confronting colonialism and the colonial state. In Bengal, for example, in the 1870s 'agrarian leagues' or 'combinations' were formed which organized rent strikes against enhanced rents demanded by zamindars. Again in the 1880s, during the discussions on the Bengal Tenancy Bill, peasants were mobilized on a large scale demanding occupancy rights, permanent fixation of rents, etc. Similarly in Maharashtra a powerful movement emerged in the 1870s against moneylenders. In both cases nationalist organizations like the Indian Association and Poona Sarvajanik Sabha extended support to the peasants.[9]

The twentieth century saw the emergence of a much firmer linkage between the peasant movements and the wider anti-imperialist movement, each deriving and giving strength to the other. The national movement got more broad based and began to take up wider agrarian issues and the peasant movements now emerged through modern, and over time, national-level organizations articulating their class demands more effectively.

The 1920s saw peasant movements emerging in Uttar Pradesh and Malabar in close association with the Non-Cooperation and Khilafat movements raising demands like security of tenure for tenants, decrease in rent, abolition of illegal exactions in cash, kind or labour and so on. The Bardoli Satyagraha (1928) in Gujarat of course marked the coalescence of the peasant movement and the national movement to an unprecedented level with leaders like Sardar Patel and Mahatma Gandhi playing a direct and active role in it.[10]

The 1930s and 1940s saw the rapid radicalization of the Indian national movement and the growing influence of the left within it. The peasantry moved further centre stage in the nationalist agenda and the peasant movement now grew as an integral part of the national movement.[11] The Civil Disobedience movement, the most powerful mass movement launched by the Indian National Congress, took on the form of no-tax and no-rent campaigns in many parts of the country such as Uttar Pradesh and Andhra. Gandhiji himself issued a manifesto to the Uttar Pradesh kisans (peasants) asking them to pay only 50 per cent of the legal rent.

Taking a bold and clear stand, the Indian National Congress at its famous Karachi session in 1931, included in the list of 'Fundamental Rights and Economic Programme' that it wanted to be provided for in any future constitution of independent India, the following:[12]

(a) Substantial reduction in agricultural rent or revenue paid by the peasantry and in case of uneconomic holdings, exemption for rent for such periods as may be necessary.

(b) Relief of agricultural indebtedness and control of usury—direct and indirect.

(c) Labour to be freed from serfdom or conditions bordering on serfdom.

(d) Peasants and workers shall have the right to form unions to protect their interests.

(e) Imposition of a progressive income tax on agricultural income above a fixed minimum.

In the meantime a Kisan Conference in Allahabad in 1935, presided over by Sardar Patel, passed a resolution which in unequivocal terms called for the abolition of zamindari. A system of peasant proprietorship without the intervention of any intermediaries was advocated. The Bihar Kisan Sabha also adopted the slogan of zamindari abolition the same year. The Communists and Socialists joined the kisan organizations and strengthened them considerably. The culmination of the efforts of such peasant bodies was the formation of the All India Kisan Congress (later renamed All India Kisan Sabha) in 1936. Jawaharlal Nehru was one of the participants in the first session of the Kisan Congress.

A kisan manifesto was issued by the Kisan Congress and the influence of this manifesto was seen in the agrarian programme adopted by the Indian National Congress at its Faizpur session in Maharashtra in December 1936. The second session of the Kisan Congress presided over by N.G. Ranga was held along with the Indian National Congress session at Faizpur. The Faizpur Agrarian Programme reiterated the demand made at Karachi for substantial reduction in both rent and revenue. It further demanded: a substantial decrease in canal and irrigation rates, all feudal dues and levies and forced labour be made illegal, fixity of tenure with heritable rights, a moratorium on debts and steps to provide cheap credit, a living wage and suitable working conditions for agricultural labour. Quite significantly, it also recommended that an effort be made to introduce cooperative farming—an issue which was to raise a strong debate in the years to come.[13]

The Congress election manifesto for the 1937 provincial elections described 'the appalling poverty, unemployment and indebtedness of the peasantry' as the *'most important and urgent problem of the country'*, which it argued was 'fundamentally due to antiquated and repressive land tenure and revenue systems'. While it was understood that 'the final solution of this problem inevitably involved the removal of British imperialistic exploitation' and a thorough structural reform of the land tenure, rent and revenue systems the manifesto also saw the need for immediate relief with regard to the revenue, rent and debt burden.[14]

During the twenty eight months between 1937–39, when the Congress formed ministries in most of the provinces of British India, valiant efforts were made to implement the agrarian programme and the election pledge.[15] The task was difficult given the limited powers available to the ministries in the colonial context and the constraint of time as the ministries were short-lived and also the need to maintain anti-imperialist unity by carefully balancing mutually clashing interests of classes which were allies in the struggle against imperialism. Yet much was achieved. A *series of legislations were passed by the various ministries on* issues concerning tenancy rights and indebtedness. For example, in Bihar tenancy legislations were passed in 1937 and 1938 which abolished all increases in rent since 1911, effectively reducing rent by about 25 per cent, gave under-ryots occupancy rights after twelve years of cultivating the land, prohibited all illegal exactions and so on. Similar laws improving the condition of the tenants were passed in United Provinces, Bombay, Central Provinces, NWFP, Orissa, Madras and so on. In Orissa the British governor refused assent to a bill which would have effectively reduced the zamindar's income by 50 to 60 per cent. In Madras a committee headed by the Revenue Minister T. Prakasam made a recommendation which would have reduced rents by about two thirds and virtually ended the zamindari system. The Madras assembly and the chief minister, C. Rajagopalachari, supported the report, with the latter rejecting any question of compensating the zamindars. However, before a bill could be drafted on the basis of this report, the ministry resigned. Most provinces passed laws regulating the activity of the moneylenders and providing debt relief. In Bombay 40,000 tied serfs or bonded labour were liberated. In a sense this brief interlude of Congress rule served as a mirror of the future for both the dominant classes in rural India and the oppressed and both learnt their lessons though perhaps somewhat unevenly.

The radicalization of Mahatma Gandhi in the 1930s and 1940s, particularly on the agrarian question was of great importance as he, more than anyone else, both created and reflected accurately the balance of class forces in the Indian political scene and at the ground level. In 1937 he said, 'land and all property is his who will work it', not too far from the notion of land to the tiller. In June 1942, in his famous interview with Louis Fischer, Gandhiji predicted that the peasants would seize the zamindar's lands and, while there could be some violence, but the zamindars could also 'cooperate by fleeing'. He added that it would be fiscally impossible to compensate the landlords. Again, he told Mira behn in jail (he was arrested in August 1942) that after independence the zamindars' land would be taken by the state either through their voluntary surrender or through legislation and then distributed to the cultivators.[16]

After the war ended in 1945, the peasant movements, which had subsided during the war, emerged with renewed vigour, in anticipation of freedom and a new social order. The demand for zamindari abolition was now pressed with greater urgency. Militant anti-landlord movements sprang up in various parts of the country like the Telangana movement in Hyderabad state and the Tebhaga movement in Bengal. As has been argued, 'perhaps the most important contribution of the peasant movements that covered large areas of the subcontinent in the 30s and 40s was that . . . they created the climate which necessitated the post-independence agrarian reforms'.[17]

The critical link between the long history of the national and peasant movements in India and the nature and intensity of the land reform initiatives taken after independence has to be underlined. The failure to fully appreciate this link has led no less a person than the eminent economist and among the most cited scholars of India's land reforms, A.M. Khusro, to make the astounding argument that 'the elaborately conceived and many-sided programme of land reform launched in the country during the 1950s could be said in a considerable degree to be a *gift of the administration* to the peasantry', and not the product of a national or peasant movement![18]

In fact in the immediate years preceding independence, reflecting the long history of the national and peasant movements, a consensus on the agrarian question seemed to have emerged among a broad spectrum of Indian political opinion and on some issues among a wide section of the peasantry. For example, the National Planning Committee (formed in 1938 with Jawaharlal Nehru as chairman and deliberated through the 1940s) which was deeply influenced by left opinion, the Bombay Plan (a plan of Economic Development for India 1944–45, prepared by the leading representatives of the Indian capitalist class) and the election manifesto issued by the Congress Working Committee in 1945 were more or less agreed on the following basic issues:[19]

> An urgent reform of the land system to be undertaken which involved the abolition of intermediaries between the peasant and the state i.e., the Zamindars and Talukdars, they could be paid compensation that was considered necessary and desirable; problem of rural indebtedness had to be addressed and cheap credit made available; while individual farming or peasant proprietorship was to continue in large parts of the country cooperative farming on privately owned lands and collective farming on state lands was to be encouraged.

While on zamindari abolition the consensus in the countryside (barring, naturally, the zamindars) was clear, it was not so on the issue of cooperativization. Sufficient mobilization among the peasantry had not occurred on this issue and this idea had not taken root among them. The National Planning Committee, the capitalists and the Congress showed awareness of this question. The careful wording of the Congress election (1946) manifesto on this issue is significant: 'while individualist farming or peasant proprietorship should continue, progressive agriculture as well as the creation of new social values and incentives require some system of cooperative farming suited to Indian conditions. *Any such change can however be made only with the goodwill and agreement of the peasantry concerned.*'[20] A certain disjunction between the agrarian programme put out by the political leadership or the Congress and the preparedness of the peasantry at whom it was aimed, which was to emerge shortly, was as yet absent.

After the 1946 provincial elections once again the Congress swept the polls. An interim government headed by Nehru was formed at the Centre and the Congress governments in the provinces set up committees to draw up bills for abolition of the zamindari system.

Shortly after independence, in November 1947, the AICC appointed a special committee to draw up an economic programme for the Congress. The programme was to be based on the December 1945 election manifesto and a set of stated principles which, *inter alia*, would meet the great challenge of building 'real democracy in the country . . . based on equality and social justice', enable central planning along with decentralization of political and economic power; provide 'an alternative to the acquisitive economy of private capitalism and the regimentation of a Totalitarian state'.[21] This was indeed a complex agenda without any pre-existing model to follow. The committee which was to draw up such a programme was headed by Jawaharlal Nehru and had as members other stalwarts like Maulana Azad, N.G. Ranga, G.L. Nanda, Jayaprakash Narayan, J.C. Kumarappa, Achyut Patwardhan and Shankarrao Deo—a fair mix of 'Gandhians' and socialists.

The committee (also called the Economic Programme Committee) made a twenty-point recommendation for agriculture.[22] Some of the points may be highlighted here. Clause 2 of the recommendations read: 'All intermediaries between the tiller and the state should be eliminated and all middlemen should be replaced by non-profit making agencies, such as cooperatives.' While the first part of the clause clearly referred to abolition of zamindari, the second part about middlemen was a bit ambiguous. Some have read it to mean 'elimination of all private money lenders and traders'.[23]

While this strand of argument was perhaps present among some Congressmen, the Economic Programme Committee did not seem to be taking such an extreme position. All that was agreed to at this stage was setting up of multi-purpose cooperatives, which would 'cut down the costs of agricultural credit, processing and marketing' and presumably thus replace the moneylender and trader.

As for cooperative farming or production cooperatives the committee recommended that 'the state should organise *pilot schemes for experimenting* with cooperative farming among small holders and should set up cooperative colonies on *Government unoccupied . . . lands*, and should also directly own and run farms for purposes of *experiment and demonstration*'. No compulsion was visualized as yet either for production or even service cooperatives. [24]

The committee also introduced the notion of land ceiling, it seems for the first time as an official Congress position. It argued: 'The maximum size of holding should be fixed. The surplus land over such a maximum should be acquired and placed at the disposal of the village cooperatives.' Apart from this some of the other recommendations were: present land revenue system to be replaced by progressive agricultural income tax, remunerative prices for agricultural produce and equitable terms of trade between agriculture and industry, and the consolidation of small holdings and the prevention of further fragmentation. It was also recommended that: 'Statutory Village Panchayats should be organised . . . for self governing purposes with well defined powers and adequate financial resources, and with supervisory jurisdiction over all other institutions in the locality.'[25] An effort to properly implement this recommendation required an amendment to the constitution (73rd Amendment in 1993) nearly half a century later.

As we shall see, many of the other clauses especially those regarding cooperatives, ceilings, agricultural income tax, etc., did not have an easy passage either. Key subjects relating to the rural sector such as land reforms, agricultural credit, land revenue assessment, taxation of agricultural income, etc., were all included in the State List, that is, it was not the central government but the provincial governments which could act on these issues and implement them. This meant that the nature of the programme legislated at the state level and especially the manner of its implementation was a function of the nature of provincial politics, the strength of peasant mobilization, that is, the balance of class forces at the level of the provincial political parties and at the grassroots level, the nature of the administration especially at the lower levels and of course the role of the judiciary.

A dichotomy soon began to emerge between the recommendations made by the central government and what the states and the various administrative apparatuses were willing or able to implement. This occurred particularly when recommendations emanating from the Centre, for example, those made by the Congress Agrarian Reforms Committee (Kumarappa Committee) in July 1949 or by the 1959 Nagpur Congress, on many issues went way beyond what was acceptable to the states, the peasantry or the people as a whole. These were issues such as the introduction of a degree of compulsion for promoting cooperative farming and for replacing private trade and moneylending with state or cooperative organizations, implementing land ceilings and so on. Resistance to such programmes occurred in various ways, some overt and others subterranean but equally effective.

It is keeping in mind this tension—the stuff of any democracy—as a backdrop that we shall examine the actual success and failures of the land reform effort in post-independence India—a historically unique effort at transformation of agrarian relations within a democratic framework.

30

Land Reforms (II): Zamindari Abolition and Tenancy Reforms

The process of land reform after independence basically occurred in two broad phases. The first phase which started soon after independence and arguably continued till the early 1960s focussed on the following features: (1) abolition of intermediaries—zamindars, jagirdars, etc., (2) tenancy reforms involving providing security of tenure to the tenants, decrease in rents and conferment of ownership rights to tenants, (3) ceilings on size of landholdings, (4) cooperativization and community development programmes. This phase has also been called the phase of institutional reforms. The second phase beginning around the mid- or late 1960s saw the gradual ushering in of the so-called Green Revolution and has been seen as the phase of technological reforms. The two phases are not to be divided into rigid watertight compartments. In fact, they were complementary to each other and there was a fair degree of overlap in the programmes followed during these phases. In the following chapters therefore we shall not strictly follow the chronology of the two phases and will often discuss programmes which cut across them.

Zamindari Abolition

Within a year or two of independence, that is, by 1949, zamindari abolition bills or land tenure legislation were introduced in a number of provinces such as Uttar Pradesh, Madhya Pradesh, Bihar, Madras, Assam and Bombay with the report of the Uttar Pradesh Zamindari Abolition Committee (chaired by G.B. Pant) acting as the initial model for many others.

In the meantime, the Constituent Assembly was in the process of framing India's constitution. There was, however, widespread apprehension, including among Congress leaders deeply committed to zamindari abolition like Jawaharlal Nehru, G.B. Pant and Sardar Patel, that the zamindars could try to stymie the acquisition of their estates by moving the courts, raising issues like the violation of right to property or 'unjustness' of the compensation. After prolonged discussion the relevant provisions of the constitution were framed in a manner that the leaders felt assured that the zamindari abolition bills pending in the state assemblies would go through on the basis of compensation recommended by the state legislatures as these recommendations were made non-justiciable, requiring only Presidential assent which meant ultimately the support of the Union cabinet. The compensation recommended by the legislatures was of course expected to be small and reasonable from the tenants' point of view. It is significant that there was a wide consensus on giving the legislatures the authority to prescribe principles of compensation on expropriation of the zamindars. The acquisition of commercial or industrial property continued to require an entirely different set of principles.

However, belying the expectation of the framers of the constitution, the zamindars in various parts of the country challenged the constitutionality of the law permitting zamindari abolition and the courts, as for example the Patna High Court, upheld the landlords' suit. The Congress government responded by getting constitutional amendments passed. The 1st Amendment in 1951 and the 4th Amendment in 1955 were aimed at further strengthening the hands of the state legislatures for implementing zamindari abolition, making the question of violation of any fundamental right or insufficiency of compensation not permissible in the courts. Though the zamindars continued to make numerous appeals to the High Court and Supreme Court, if for no other purpose but to delay the acquisition of their estates, yet, the back of their resistance was broken by the mid-1950s. It may be reiterated that, contrary to a view often put forward, the framers of the constitution, including the so-called 'right wing', were not participating in a design to stymie land reforms but were in fact trying to complete the process within a democratic framework.

A major difficulty in implementing the zamindari abolition acts, passed in most provinces by 1956, was the absence of adequate land records. Nevertheless, certainly by the end of the 1950s (though essentially by 1956) the process of land reform involving abolition of intermediaries (the zamindars of British India, and jagirdars of the princely states now merged with independent India) can be said to have been completed. Considering that the entire process occurred in a democratic framework, with virtually no coercion or violence being used, it was completed in a remarkably short period. This was possible partly because the zamindars as a class had been isolated socially during the national movement itself as they were seen as part of the imperialist camp. But reforms which threatened the interests of sections of the upper peasantry who were very much part of the national movement and had considerable societal support were far more difficult, and sometimes impossible to achieve, as we shall see later.

The abolition of zamindari meant that about 20 million erstwhile tenants now became landowners. The figures for area and number of households under tenancy are highly unreliable partly because in many areas a very large proportion of tenancy was 'oral' and therefore unrecorded. Yet, scholars agree that there was some decline in tenancy after the reforms started, one rough estimate being that area under tenancy decreased from about 42 per cent in 1950–51 to between 20 and 25 per cent by the early 1960s. However, the decline in tenancy and the considerable increase in self-cultivation was not a result only of tenants becoming landowners but also of eviction of existing tenants by landowners, as we shall see presently.

The compensation actually paid to the zamindars once their estates were acquired was generally small and varied from state to state depending upon the strength of the peasant movement and consequent class balance between the landlords and the tenants and the ideological composition of the Congress leadership and of the legislature as a whole. In Kashmir, for example, no compensation was paid. In Punjab, the occupancy tenants of Patiala paid nothing and even the inferior tenants paid a negligible amount, often just the first instalment of the total compensation to be paid over a number of years. Most states followed a variation of the model worked out in Uttar Pradesh, where, very significantly, the compensation paid was inversely related to the size of the land which came under a zamindar. The small zamindars (they were often hardly distinguishable from the well-to-do peasants; land reform initiatives were quite consciously not directed against them) who used to pay land revenue of up to Rs 25 were to receive about twenty times their net annual income as compensation whereas the big zamindars who paid land revenue ranging between Rs 2,000 and Rs 10,000 were to receive merely two to four times their net annual income. Moreover the payment of compensation, was to stretch over a long period, in some cases forty years. It is estimated that the big zamindars who did receive compensation found that their incomes from alienated land, through compensation, would fetch them only one-fortieth of their earlier income.

Out of a total due of Rs 6,700 million, the compensation actually paid till 1961 was Rs 1,642 million, a small figure considering that India spent, by one estimate, more than six times the amount, Rs 10,000 million in just food imports between 1946 and 1953.

Weaknesses in Zamindari Abolition

There were, however, certain important weaknesses in the manner in which some of the clauses relating to zamindari abolition were implemented in various parts of the country. For example, in Uttar Pradesh, the zamindars were permitted to retain lands that were declared to be under their 'personal cultivation'. What constituted 'personal cultivation' was very loosely defined '(making) it possible for not only those who tilled the soil, but also those who supervised the land personally or did so through a relative, or provided capital and credit to the land, to call themselves a cultivator'.[1] Moreover, in states like Uttar Pradesh, Bihar and Madras, to begin with (i.e., till land ceiling laws were introduced) there was no limit on the size of the lands that could be declared to be under the 'personal cultivation' of the zamindar. This, despite the fact that the Congress Agrarian Reforms Committee (Kumarappa Committee) in its report of 1949 had clearly stipulated that 'only those who put in a minimum amount of physical labour and participate in actual agricultural operations' could be said to be performing 'personal cultivation'. Also, the committee had envisaged a limit or ceiling on how much land could be 'resumed' for 'personal cultivation', under no circumstances leading to the tenant's holding being reduced to below the 'economic' level.[2]

The result in actual practice, however, was that even zamindars who were absentee landowners could now end up retaining large tracts of land. Further, in many areas, the zamindars in order to declare under 'personal cultivation' as large a proportion of their lands as possible often resorted to large-scale eviction of tenants, mainly the less secure small tenants. (This was to be followed by further rounds of evictions once the land ceilings and tenancy legislations came into being, cumulatively leading to a major blot in the record of land reforms in India.)

Many of the erstwhile essentially rent-receiving zamindars, however, did actually begin to manage the lands declared under their 'personal cultivation'. They invested in them and moved towards progressive capitalist farming in these areas, as this was indeed one of the objectives of land reform.

Retaining large tracts under 'personal cultivation' was only one way through which the landlords tried to avoid the full impact of the effort at abolition of the zamindari system. Several other methods were used to resist the bringing in of zamindari abolition legislation and their implementation. Since such legislation had to be passed by the state legislatures, the landlords used every possible method of parliamentary obstruction in the legislatures. The draft bills were subjected to prolonged debates, referred to select committees and repeated amendments were proposed so that in many states like Uttar Pradesh and Bihar several years passed between the introduction of the bills and the laws being enacted.

Even after the laws were enacted the landlords used the judicial system to defer the implementation of the laws. As we saw earlier, they repeatedly challenged the constitutionality of the laws in the courts, going right up to the Supreme Court. In Bihar, where the landlords put up the maximum resistance, they tried to block the implementation of the law even after they lost their case in the Supreme Court twice. They now refused to hand over the land records in their possession, forcing the government to go through the lengthy procedure of reconstructing the records. Further, implementation of the law was made difficult and, as much as possible, skewed in favour of the zamindar, by the collusion between the landlords and particularly the lower-level revenue officials. Such collusion was helped by the fact that in zamindari areas many of the revenue officials were former rent-collecting agents of the zamindars. At all levels involving the legislative, judicial and executive arms of the state, the landlords put up resistance.

The Congress responded by repeatedly reiterating its resolve to complete the process of zamindari abolition as quickly as possible. This resolve was seen in AICC resolutions (e.g., that of July 1954), in the conference of the chief ministers and presidents of PCCs (April 1950), in the First Plan document and most of all in the Congress election manifestos. Democracy with adult franchise on the one hand reduced the political weight of the zamindars, and on the other increased the urgency of meeting the long-standing demands of the peasantry. The Congress itself had over the years mobilized the peasantry to make these demands. The Congress also took necessary administrative and legislative steps, such as getting the constitutional amendments of 1951 and 1955 passed by parliament, which would meet the challenge put up by the landlords.

Despite the resistance of landlords, the process of zamindari abolition was essentially completed, as noted earlier, except in certain pockets of Bihar, within a decade of the formation of the Indian Republic. The typically large 'feudal' estates were gone. While the big landlords, who lost the bulk of their lands, were the chief losers, the main beneficiaries of zamindari abolition were the occupancy tenants or the upper tenants, who had direct leases from the zamindar, and who now became landowners. Such tenants were generally middle or rich peasants who sometimes had sub-leases given out to lower tenants with little rights, often called 'tenants at will'.

Tenancy Reforms

The issue of continuing tenancy in zamindari areas, oral and unrecorded, therefore remained even after abolition of zamindari was implemented. Such tenancy existed in the lands of the former zamindars now said to be under their 'personal cultivation' as well as in the lands sub-leased by the former occupancy tenant who now became the landowner. Moreover, at independence only about half the area was under zamindari tenure. The other half was under ryotwari where too the problems of landlordism and an insecure, rack-rented tenantry were rampant.

The second major plank of the land reforms envisaged was, therefore, concerned with tenancy legislation. The political and economic conditions in different parts of India were so varied that the nature of tenancy legislation passed by the different states and the manner of their implementation also varied a great deal. Yet, there were certain commonly shared objectives of the various legislations and over time some common broad features emerged in the manner of their implementation in most parts of the country. It is an examination of only these common aspects rather than of the myriad differences that is possible within the scope of this study.

Tenancy reforms had three basic objectives. First, to guarantee security of tenure to tenants who had cultivated a piece of land continuously for a fixed number of years, say six years (the exact number of years varied from region to region). Second, to seek the reduction of rents paid by tenants to a 'fair' level which was *generally considered to range between one*-fourth and one-sixth of the value of the gross produce of the leased land. The third objective was that the tenant gain the right to acquire ownership of the lands he cultivated, subject to certain restrictions. The tenant was expected to pay a price much below the market price, generally a multiple of the annual rent, say eight or ten years' rent. For example, in parts of Andhra Pradesh the price he had to pay was eight years' rent, which was roughly 40 per cent of the market price of the land.

It needs to be added here that while attempting to improve the condition of the tenants, tenancy legislation in India by and large sought to maintain a balance between the interest of the landowner, particularly the small landowner, and the tenant. The absentee landowners' right of resumption of land for 'personal cultivation', which was granted in most parts of India, as well as the tenants' right to acquire the lands they cultivated, was operated through a complex and variable system of 'floors' and 'ceilings' keeping this balance in view.

The landowner's right of resumption was limited (this was aimed at the large landowners) to his her total holding after resumption not exceeding a certain limit or ceiling prescribed by each state. The First Plan suggested a limit of three times the 'family holding'. A family holding, *inter alia*, was defined as a single plough unit. Also, while resuming land the landowner could not deprive the tenant of his entire lands. In some states like Kerala, Orissa, Gujarat, Himachal Pradesh, Maharashtra, Karnataka and Tamil Nadu, the tenant had to be left with at least half his holding. In some other states like Bihar the floor was half the holding of the tenant or a minimum of 5 acres (in West Bengal 2.5 acres), whichever was less.

Conversely (and this was aimed at the small landowner), the tenants' right to acquire the landowner's lands was restricted by the condition that the landowner was not to be deprived of all his lands and that the tenants' holding after acquisition was not to exceed the ceiling prescribed by each state.

It was recognized, as the Second Plan noted, that, 'The economic circumstances of small owners are not so different from those of tenants that tenancy legislation should operate to their disadvantage.'[3] The Plan therefore envisaged that very small landowners could resume their entire holding for self-cultivation. However, the actual experience of implementation of the tenancy laws was more complicated. As P.S. Appu, who headed the Planning Commission Task Force on Agrarian Relations (which reported in 1973), noted, the provisions introduced to protect the small landowners were misused by the larger landlords with the active connivance of the revenue officials.[4] The Third Plan also pointed out the abuse of such provisions by large landowners transferring their lands in the names of a number of relatives and others so as to enter the category of 'small landowner' and then evicting tenants from such lands by exercising the right of resumption given to small owners.[5]

In fact, the right of resumption and the loose definition of 'personal cultivation' referred to earlier (initially only Manipur and Tripura made personal labour by the landowner a condition of resumption for personal cultivation) was used for eviction of tenants on a massive scale. The process of eviction had actually begun in anticipation of the imminent tenancy legislations. The inordinate delays in enacting and implementing the legislations were engineered by vested interests enabling them to evict potential beneficiaries before the law came into force.

Even after the tenants got legal protection against eviction, large-scale evictions occurred. For example, the Planning Commission's Panel on Land Reforms noted in 1956 that between 1948 and 1951 the number of protected tenants in the state of Bombay declined from 1.7 million to 1.3 million, that is, by more than 23 per cent; in the State of Hyderabad between 1951 and 1955 the number declined by about 57 per cent. Another detailed study of Hyderabad showed that out of every 100 protected tenants created in 1951, after four years, that is, by 1954, only 45.4 per cent maintained that status; 12.4 per cent became landowners by exercising their right to acquire land; 2.6 per cent were legally evicted; 22.1 per cent were illegally evicted; and 17.5 per cent 'voluntarily' surrendered their claims to the land. Voluntary surrenders by tenants was really a euphemism for illegal eviction as most often the tenant was 'persuaded' under threat to give up his tenancy rights 'voluntarily'. So common was the practice that the Fourth Plan was constrained to recommend that all surrenders should only be in favour of the government, which could allot such lands to eligible persons. However, only a handful of states acted upon this recommendation.

Before proceeding further on the failures of tenancy legislation in providing security of tenure to a large section of tenants, it is extremely important to also recognize that a substantial proportion of tenants did acquire security and permanent occupancy rights. The detailed study of Hyderabad referred to in the previous paragraph after all shows that 45.4 per cent of the tenants remained protected tenants and 12.4 per cent became owners, that is, in sum about 67.8 per cent of the tenants brought under the legislation no longer suffered from insecurity. This was an important development with ramifications on levels of investment and improvement in productivity in the lands of such 'secure' tenant cultivators.

In many cases tenancy legislations led to tenancy being pushed underground, that is, it continued in a concealed form. The tenants were now called 'farm servants' though they continued in exactly the same status. In the early years of land reform, tenants were often converted to sharecroppers, as surprisingly the latter were not treated as tenants and therefore were not protected under the existing tenancy legislation in some states such as Uttar Pradesh Only cash rent payers were treated as tenants and not those who paid fixed produce rents or those who paid a proportion of total produce as rent, that is, sharecroppers. In West Bengal sharecroppers, known as bargadars, received no protection till as late as July 1970 when the West Bengal Land Reforms Act was amended to accord limited protection to them. A spurt in the practice of share-cropping in the immediate years after 1951 can partially be explained by this factor, that sharecroppers had no tenancy rights.

Perhaps what contributed most to the insecurity of tenants was the fact that most tenancies were oral and informal, that is, they were not recorded and the tenants therefore could not benefit from the legislation in their favour. However, going only by the recorded tenancies, the 1971 Census reached absurd conclusions such as that 91.1 per cent of cultivated area in India was owner operated and that Bihar had the largest percentage of area under owner cultivation among the states, that is, 99.6 per cent, and that in Bihar tenancies constituted only 0.22 per cent, of operational holdings and 0.17 per cent of total cultivated area! This, when it is commonly accepted that Bihar had a very high proportion of tenancy, the 1961 Census quoting a figure of 36.65 per cent. The discrepancy between the 1961 and 1971 Census figures would suggest that an overwhelming majority of the tenancies were unrecorded and consequently the tenants remained insecure. The 1961 Census estimated that 82 per cent of the tenancies in the country were insecure!

The absence of proper records, for example, was seen as a major impediment in the implementation of the Zamindari Abolition and Land Reform Act in Uttar Pradesh in the initial years after independence. A massive drive had to be launched by Charan Singh, the then Revenue Minister, to get a few million records corrected or newly inscribed.

In later years, in certain areas, other such drives were launched, often under the hegemony of left forces, and the targeted beneficiaries were no longer only the upper and middle tenantry but also the poor, totally insecure and unprotected sharecroppers and tenants at will. Some celebrated examples of such efforts were seen in Kerala and West Bengal.

In the late 1960s a massive programme of conferment of titles to lands to hutment dwellers and tenants was undertaken in Kerala. The programme, which achieved considerable success, was launched with the active participation of peasant organizations.

The Left Front government in West Bengal which came to power in June 1977 launched the famous Operation Barga in July 1978 with the objective of, in a time-bound period, achieving the registration of sharecroppers, so that they could then proceed to secure for them their legal rights, namely, permanent occupancy and heritable rights and a crop division of 1:3 between landowner and sharecropper. Out of an estimated 2.4 million bargadars in

West Bengal only 0.4 million were recorded till June 1978. However, after the launching of Operation Barga the number of those recorded rose from 0.7 million in October 1979 to about 1.4 million in November 1990.

A significant aspect of the Operation Barga experiment in West Bengal was that, like in Kerala, an effort was made to mobilize the support of the rural poor and especially the targeted beneficiaries (the bargadars) and their active participation was sought in the implementation of the reform measures. This went a long way in neutralizing the lower-level revenue officials like patwaris, etc. who often acted as major impediments in the successful implementation of government programmes. An innovative move of the West Bengal government aimed at both giving a voice to the rural poor and changing the attitude of the revenue officials was to start a number of orientation camps while launching Operation Barga, 'where 30 to 40 agricultural workers and sharecroppers and a dozen and a half officers of Land Reform and other related departments were made to stay together, eat together and discuss together in the same premises in distant rural areas'.[6]

Though Operation Barga did lead to recording of a large number of sharecroppers and consequently providing them with security of tenure, the process could not be completed and it reached more or less a stalemate after a little more than half the sharecroppers had been covered. This was because of some significant reasons. First, it was found politically unviable, just as it was ethically indefensible, to proceed with Operation Barga when faced with 'landlords' who themselves were cultivators with holdings only marginally larger, if even that, than those of the sharecroppers; landlords who were entitled to only one-fourth of the produce, the rest being the sharecroppers' share. As it has been noted that in West Bengal where over time the overwhelming majority of the cultivators were small cultivators controlling less than 5 acres, a further redistributive thrust was difficult. 'The "class enemy" had dissolved into a sea of small holdings.'[7] The dilemma was the same as the one that was faced in other parts of India, that is, the need to balance the interest of the small landowner and the tenant. As mentioned before, tenancy legislation in India generally anticipated this aspect and had provisos built into the legislation which addressed the problem.

The other problem was that such was the land–man ratio in Bengal that the landlord was often able to rotate a piece of leased land among two or more sharecroppers or bargadars, that is, for each piece of land there could be more than one bargadar claiming tenancy rights. Registering anyone would permanently oust the other. Also, if all the bargadars were registered in such a situation the size of the holdings per cultivator would threaten to go way below the optimum. There were, thus, political and economic limits to how far Operation Barga could be carried; the objective situation did not permit the full implementation of the notion of 'land to the tiller' or even the provision of full security of tenure to each cultivator.

Limitations of Tenancy Reform

Thus, the first objective of tenancy legislation in India, that of providing security of tenure to all tenants, met with only limited success. While a substantial proportion of tenants did acquire security (many even became landowners, as we shall see presently) there were still large numbers who remained unprotected. The partial success 'stories such as those of Kerala and West Bengal notwithstanding, the practice of unsecured tenancy, mostly oral, whether taking the form of sharecropping or the payment of fixed produce or cash rent, continued in India on a large scale. It is the continued existence of large numbers of insecure tenants which, *inter alia*, made the successful implementation of the second major objective of tenancy legislation, that of reducing rents to a 'fair' level, almost impossible to achieve. The market condition, for example, the adverse land–man ratio that developed in India during colonial rule, led to high rents. Legal 'fair' rents in such a situation could only be enforced in the case of tenants who were secure and had occupancy rights, that is, they could not be removed or changed.

Legislation was enacted in all the states regulating the rent payable by cultivating tenants. Most states fixed maximum rents at levels suggested by the First and Second Plans, that is, to 20 to 25 per cent of gross produce. Some states like Punjab, Haryana, Tamil Nadu and Andhra Pradesh (coastal areas) fixed maximum rents somewhat higher, ranging between 33.3 and 40 per cent. In practice, however, the market rates of rent almost in all parts of the country tended to be around 50 per cent of gross produce. In addition the tenant often ended up bearing the cost of the production inputs either fully or to a substantial extent. Further, the Green Revolution which started in some parts of India in the late 1960s aggravated the problems, with land values and rentals rising further and reaching, for example, in parts of Punjab, rates as high as 70 per cent. What made matters worse was the fact that it was only the poor insecure tenants or sharecroppers who paid the market rates of rent. Only the upper stratum of the tenantry, which had secured occupancy rights, and was often indistinguishable from a landowner, was able to enforce the payment of legal rates of rent.

As for the third objective of tenancy legislation in India, that is, the acquisition of ownership rights by tenants, this too was achieved only partially. As we saw above, in some detail, the use of the right to resumption by landowners, legal and illegal evictions, 'voluntary' surrenders, shift to oral and/or concealed tenancy, etc., eroded the possibility of achieving this objective adequately. Yet, it must be noted, quite a substantial number of tenants did acquire ownership rights.

Unfortunately, detailed data on this aspect for the whole country are not available. However, certain case studies of specific regions may serve as an indicator. P.S. Appu wrote in 1975 that, according to 'latest information', in Gujarat out of about 1.3 million tenants, ownership rights had been purchased by more than half, namely, about 0.77 million; and in Maharashtra out of 2.6 million tenants, again about half, namely, 1.1 million had acquired ownership rights. In other states, too, a substantial number of tenants did become owners, their numbers adding up to a few million.[8] (It must be remembered that this is in addition to the 20 million-odd tenants who became landowners as a result of the abolition of intermediaries in zamindari areas.) It has been argued that one reason why an even larger number of tenants did not acquire ownership rights was that for a large number of tenants who had acquired permanent occupancy rights and achieved rent reduction, there was hardly any motivation to try and acquire full ownership which would involve not only raising capital (albeit only a fraction of the market value of land) but legal and other complications. These superior tenants were for all practical purposes virtual owners.[9]

The cumulative effect of abolition of zamindari, tenancy legislation and ceiling legislation in the direction of meeting one of the major objectives of land reform, that is, creation of progressive cultivators making investments and improvement in productivity, was considerable. A very perceptive observer of India's land reforms, economist Daniel Thorner noted, as early as 1968, that despite all the evasions, leakages, loopholes, and so on, 'many millions of cultivators who had previously been weak tenants or tenants-at-will were enabled to become superior tenants or virtual owners'.

If one lists certain changes together, the cumulative impact can be easily ascertained. Abolition of zamindari led to about 20 million tenants, the superior occupancy tenants, becoming landowners and many absentee zamindars actually turning to direct cultivation in the lands 'resumed' for 'personal' cultivation. In the ryotwari areas nearly half the tenants, for example, in Bombay and Gujarat became landowners. Further, about half (in Bombay about 70 per cent) of the lands from which tenants were evicted were used by the landowners for direct cultivation, that is, they were not leased out again in a concealed manner. Also, a very substantial number of inferior tenants in former ryotwari areas got occupancy rights (about half in Gujarat and Maharashtra). Even in former zamindari areas such as West Bengal, nearly half the sharecroppers got occupancy rights. To this may be added between 3–5 million landless cultivators who got land which was declared surplus under ceiling laws.

Now the tenants and sharecroppers who got occupancy rights and paid reduced fixed rents, the tenants who acquired ownership rights, the landless who got land which was declared surplus over ceiling limits, absentee landowners who became direct cultivators, all had the motivation, and many the potential, of becoming progressive farmers based on their own resources or on credit from institutional sources which became increasingly available even to the poorer peasants.

31

Land Reforms (III): Ceiling and the Bhoodan Movement

Land Ceilings

A major plank of the land reform effort in India was the imposition of ceilings on the size of landholdings, with the objective of making land distribution more equitable. On this question, however, societal consensus was weak, if not non-existent, and that was reflected in the extreme difficulty in implementing this programme with even a reasonable degree of success.

The All India Kisan Sabha had supported the demand for a maximum limit of landownership of 25 acres per landholder in 1946. The Congress, perhaps for the first time, officially introduced the notion of land ceiling soon after independence. In November 1947, the AICC appointed a committee, which drew up the economic programme of the Congress. The committee headed by Jawaharlal Nehru had recommended, 'The maximum size of holdings should be fixed. The surplus land over such a maximum should be acquired and placed at the disposal of the village cooperatives.'[1] Similarly, the Congress Agrarian Reforms Committee, chaired by J.C. Kumarappa, which submitted its report in July 1949, also recommended a ceiling on landholding which was to be three times the size of an economic holding. (An economic holding was defined as that which would give a reasonable standard of living to the cultivator and provide full employment to a family of normal size and at least to a pair of bullocks.)

The First Plan (1951–56) too expressed itself 'in favour of the principle that there should be an upper limit to the amount of land that an individual may hold'. Though the Plan broadly accepted the upper limit suggested by the Kumarappa Committee as 'fair', it was nevertheless stated that the exact upper limit was to be 'fixed by each State, having regard to its own agrarian history and its present problems'. Moreover, it was stated, 'The census of land holding and cultivation, which it is proposed to hold during 1953, will give the data relevant to this decision.' Clearly, there was no immediate programme of implementing ceilings and the First Plan anticipated that 'two to three years would be necessary' to even undertake the necessary survey and set up a machinery which would enforce ceiling legislation effectively.[2]

It was a matter of no surprise, therefore, that despite the early statements of intentions and recommendations, not much progress on the question of ceilings occurred in the initial years after independence. This was recognized by the Congress, and the AICC in its session in Agra in 1953 urged, 'The State Governments should take immediate steps in regard to collection of requisite land data and the fixation of ceilings on land holdings, with a view to redistribute the land, as far as possible, among landless workers.'[3] This position was reiterated repeatedly by the CWC and the AICC over the next few years. In 1957 the Standing Committee of National Development Council (NDC) adopted a decision to complete the imposition of ceilings in the few states where such legislation had been passed by the end of 1960 and decided that other states should pass such legislation by 1958–59 (The NDC was created in 1952. It was a forum where all the chief ministers of the states would assemble, under the chairmanship of Nehru, to discuss critical issues relating to development.)

In the meantime, opposition to ceilings was building up in large parts of the country, in the Press, in parliament, in the state legislatures and even within the Congress party. A threat to the right to private property was perceived by the rural landowners as well as urban interests. Matters came to a head at the Nagpur session of the Indian National Congress in January 1959. Despite opposition from prominent Congressmen at the AICC and the Subjects Committee meeting preceding the open session, the Nagpur Congress (January 1959) passed a resolution stating that 'in order to remove uncertainty regarding land reforms and give stability to the farmer, ceilings should be fixed on existing and future holdings and legislation to this effect . . . should be completed in all States *by the end of 1959*'. Further, the land declared surplus, that is, above ceiling limits, was to 'vest in the panchayats . . . and (be) managed through cooperatives consisting of landless labourers'.[4]

A wave of criticism was to follow in the months after the Nagpur session. N.G. Ranga, secretary of the Congress parliamentary party who had already, in December 1958, sent to Nehru a letter signed by a hundred Congress MPs, critiquing the idea of ceilings, resigned from the Congress in February 1959. The Nagpur Resolution contributed considerably towards the consolidation of the right-wing forces both in the rural and urban sectors of the country. N.G. Ranga and C. Rajagopalachari, alarmed at the moves towards land ceilings and threats of compulsory cooperativization, now joined hands with Minoo Masani, an important leader of the Forum for Free Enterprise which campaigned against the threat of nationalization and the public sector swamping the private sector, to form the Swatantra party in June 1959, with Ranga as president. The campaigners and beneficiaries of zamindari abolition, the tenants who had now become landowners, also ranged themselves against the next step in land reform, an attempt at redistribution of land-ownership through imposition of land ceilings.

The opponents of the ceilings legislation were, however, to have their real victory at the state level, as it was the states which had to formulate and implement the legislation. The state legislatures, which met shortly after the Nagpur session, showed no haste in implementing the Nagpur Resolution. The ceilings issue thus dragged on and most states passed the enabling legislation only by the end of 1961, that is, nearly fourteen years after the idea was officially mooted.

Weaknesses in Land Ceiling Legislation

The long delay, as well as the nature of the legislation, ensured that the ceilings would have a very muted impact, releasing little surplus land for redistribution. By and large the ceiling laws in most states had certain major shortcomings. First, in a situation where more than 70 per cent of landholdings in India were under 5 acres, the ceiling fixed on existing holdings by the states were very high. For example, in Andhra Pradesh, it varied from 27 to 312 acres (depending on the class of land), Assam 50 acres, Kerala 15 to 37.5 acres, Punjab 30 to 60 acres, West Bengal 25 acres,

Maharashtra 18 to 126 acres and so on. Moreover, in most states, initially, the ceilings were imposed on individual and not family holdings, enabling landowners to divide up their holdings 'notionally' in the names of relatives merely to avoid the ceiling. Further, in many states the ceiling could be raised, for example, by 67 per cent in Kerala, 90 per cent in Madhya Pradesh, 100 per cent in Bihar, Madras and Maharashtra, 140 per cent in Tripura and so on, if the size of the family of the landholder exceeded five. Andhra Pradesh had no limit, allowing 6 to 72 acres (depending on the nature of land) per 'extra' member of the family. Very few landed families would have holdings that exceeded these liberal limits. Only in some states, where very few holdings exceeded the ceiling limit such as Jammu and Kashmir, West Bengal, Himachal Pradesh and Punjab, no allowance was made for the size of the family.

Second, a large number of exemptions to the ceiling limits were permitted by most states following the Second Plan recommendations that certain categories of land could be exempted from ceilings. These were tea, coffee and rubber plantations, orchards, specialized farms engaged in cattle breeding, dairying, wool raising, etc., sugarcane farms operated by sugar factories and efficiently managed farms on which heavy investments had been made.[5] The intention was clearly to promote and certainly not hinder progressive or capitalist farming done on a large scale, while at the same time ending absentee landlordism indulged in by large landowners through tenants and sharecroppers.

However, the exemptions were often carried to absurd limits with Tamil Nadu reportedly permitting twenty-six kinds of exemptions. In any case, criteria such as 'efficiently managed farm' were sufficiently vague for large numbers of landholders to evade the ceilings by simply getting themselves declared 'efficient'. Similarly, exemption to land held by cooperatives, as proposed by the Madras government, was open to great misuse with landlords transferring their lands to bogus cooperatives. On the other hand, however, the ceiling laws led to at least some landowners shifting to direct 'efficient' farming in order to avoid alienation of their lands.

Finally, the long delay in bringing in ceiling legislation to a large extent defeated its purpose. The large landowners had enough time to either sell their excess lands, or make malafide transfers in the names of relatives and even make benami transfers. Further, the landowners also resorted to mass eviction of tenants, resuming their lands at least up to the ceiling limit, and claiming, often falsely, to have shifted to progressive farming under their direct supervision. Thus, by the time the ceiling legislations were in place, there were barely any holdings left above the ceiling and consequently little surplus land became available for redistribution. This was recognized by the Congress leadership and the Third Plan also admitted it.

In fact, despite the ceiling legislations which were passed by most states by 1961, till the end of 1970 not a single acre was declared surplus in large states like Bihar, Mysore, Kerala, Orissa and Rajasthan. In Andhra Pradesh, a mere 1,400 acres was declared *surplus but no land was distributed. Only in Jammu and Kashmir* were ceiling laws fully implemented and by the middle of 1955 about 230,000 acres of surplus land had been handed over to tenants and landless labourers, that too without having to pay any compensation. However, taking India as whole, only 2.4 million acres was declared surplus by the end of 1970, and the area distributed constituted only about half the surplus land, constituting a mere 0.3 per cent of the total cultivated land of India.

The dismal record in using ceiling legislation for a more equitable distribution of land combined with a sharply increasing polarization in the countryside since the mid-1960s called for a new initiative in land reform. The Indian countryside saw the growing consolidation of the owner cultivator/rich peasant interests (similar to what the Rudolphs call 'Bullock capitalists') and their finding a distinct political voice in formations such as the BKD (formed by Charan Singh after he brought down the C.B. Gupta-led Congress government in Uttar Pradesh in 1967). The BKD later merged with Swatantra and other parties to become BLD in 1974 and the BLD was the principal component of the Janata Party which came to power in 1977, after the Emergency, bringing the strong influence of the owner cultivator/rich peasant interests, which was hitherto felt mainly at the state level, to the central or national level.

In the wake of the political and economic crisis of the mid-1960s, inflation, devaluation, the Indo-Pak war, and so on, there emerged a strong strand of agrarian radicalism in large parts of the country. The Naxalite movement led by the CPI (ML) peaked in West Bengal and parts of Andhra Pradesh, Orissa and Bihar towards the end of the 1960s. The year 1970, and in some cases like in West Bengal the preceding few years, saw a widespread 'land grab' movement by the landless in many parts of the country under the leadership of the Communist and Socialist parties. Disturbances were reported from Assam, Andhra Pradesh, Bihar, Gujarat, Punjab, Rajasthan, Tamil Nadu, Uttar Pradesh, and West Bengal in 1969–70. The total amount of land seized was not very significant and most of it was government wasteland, land taken over by the government but not distributed, and to some extent homestead land. The movement was effectively suppressed. About 20,000 political activists were arrested. However, despite the very limited success in land seizure and the quick suppression of the movement, on the whole the movement had a significant symbolic effect. The nation's attention was drawn dramatically to the agrarian question.

This was the context in which the second spurt of land reform efforts was to occur in the 1960s and early 1970s. The Land Reform Implementation Committee of the National Development Council met in June 1964 and made sustained efforts to put pressure on the chief ministers to plug the loopholes in the land reform legislations and implement them effectively. With the political shift of Indira Gandhi to the left in the late 1960s, particularly after 1969, these efforts received a further momentum. At a land reform conference of the chief ministers called by her in September 1970, she forcefully argued that social discontent and violence in the countryside had erupted because:[6]

> The land reform measures implemented have failed to match the legitimate expectations which were first fostered among millions of cultivators during the national movement . . . In short, we have yet to create institutional conditions which would enable small farmers, tenants, and landless labourers to share in the agricultural New Deal.

Reduction of ceiling limits was one of the main issues discussed at the conference with most of the chief ministers rejecting such a proposal outright. The matter was referred to the Central Land Reforms Committee, which was to look into this and other contentious issues that emerged at the conference. In August 1971, the committee made a series of recommendations including a substantial reduction in the ceiling limits, withdrawal of exemptions such as those in favour of 'efficient' or mechanized farms and making ceilings applicable to the family as a unit and not to individuals as was the case in most states.

The Congress, now further strengthened after the electoral victories of 1971 and 1972, was able to get the chief ministers' conference held in July 1972 to approve new national guidelines following months of bitter opposition. The new guidelines were based essentially on the August 1971 recommendations of the Central Land Reforms Committee. Some of the important features of the July 1972 guidelines, which marked a break in the history of ceiling legislation in India, were:

(i). The ceiling for double-cropped perennially irrigated land was to be within the range of 10–18 acres, it was 27 acres for single-cropped land and 54 acres for inferior dry lands.

(ii). A ceiling was to be applicable to a family as a unit of five members (husband, wife and three minor children). Additional land per additional member could be permitted for families which exceeded this number but up to a maximum limit of double the ceiling for the five-member unit.

(iii). In the distribution of surplus land, priority was to be given to landless agricultural workers, particularly those belonging to the Scheduled Castes and Scheduled Tribes.

(iv). Compensation payable for surplus land was to be fixed well below market price so as to be within the capacity of the new allottees.

Following the 1972 guidelines most states (barring some north-eastern states and Goa which had no ceiling laws) passed revised ceiling legislation, lowering the ceiling limits within the range prescribed in the guidelines. Resistance to the ceiling laws and efforts to evade the ceiling continued in a variety of ways. A common method was to seek judicial intervention on a number of grounds. Hundreds of thousands of ceiling cases were filed in courts all over the country. One estimate mentions 500,000 pending cases in Andhra Pradesh alone!

In an attempt to stem this menace the government got the 34th Amendment to the constitution passed in parliament in August 1974, getting most of the revised ceiling laws included in the Ninth Schedule of the constitution so that they could not be challenged on constitutional grounds.

While the renewed effort of the 1970s did lead to some progress in surplus land being redistributed, the overall results were still far from satisfactory. As a result of the ceiling laws of the 1970s, an additional area of about 2.27 million acres of land was distributed by the early 1980s, but, quite symptomatic of the entire effort at ceiling reform, an estimated 32.25 million acres of land was wilfully dispersed to avoid ceilings.

Nevertheless, by March 1985, 7.2 million acres was declared surplus out of which 4.3 million acres was distributed to about 3.3 million beneficiaries. Moreover, more than half, 54.6 per cent of the beneficiaries, were members of the Scheduled Castes and Scheduled Tribes who received about 43.6 per cent of the area distributed. The objective set out in the 1947 economic programme of the Congress, of distributing surplus lands to village cooperatives or of even using such lands to start new cooperatives did not achieve any success. Out of the land declared surplus but not distributed, nearly 1.6 million acres was under litigation.

There was wide regional variation in the implementation of ceiling laws, with the states where greater political mobilization of the targeted beneficiaries occurred, or where greater political will was shown by the government, achieving a much higher level of success. For example, it is estimated that West Bengal, which had only less than 3 per cent of the cultivated area in India, contributed about a quarter of the total land declared surplus under ceiling laws all over India.

By the middle of 1992, the area declared surplus was 7.3 million acres (it was 2.4 million acres in 1970) and the area distributed was about 5 million acres (it was 1.2 million acres in 1970) and the beneficiaries numbered about 4.7 million. The increase in the number of beneficiaries particularly between 1985 and 1992 was far greater than the increase in area distributed, 1.4 million beneficiaries and 0.1 million acres respectively. This suggests that the new beneficiaries would be receiving only tiny plots or homestead lands.

Thus, while there was a distinct improvement after 1972, yet, the total area declared surplus that could be distributed among the landless constituted only about 2 per cent of the cultivated area. Again, while it is true that more than 4.5 million people, mostly landless, did receive some land (however poor its quality and however small the size of the holding), the inequities in Indian agriculture, which the ceiling laws were intended to address, persisted to a very large extent.

An important impact of the ceiling laws, and perhaps in the long run the most critical one, was that it killed the land market and prevented an increasing concentration in landholdings through de-peasantization. As the eminent scholar of Indian agriculture and policy-maker C.H. Hanumantha Rao put it, 'The law discouraged concentration of landownership beyond the ceiling level and thus prevented the possible dispossession of numerous small and marginal holders which would probably have occurred through a competitive process in the land market in the absence of a ceiling on landholdings.'[7]

Also, though the opportunity to acquire large areas of surplus lands for redistribution was missed because of defective and delayed ceiling laws, in the long run the high population growth and the rapid subdivision of large holdings over several generations (in the absence of the practice of primogeniture for inheritance in India) led automatically to little land remaining over the ceiling limits. In fact, the number of holdings and the area operated under the category of large holdings, 25 acres or above (even 15 acres and above) kept falling in the decades since independence right up to the 1990s. Except in certain small pockets in the country, very large landholdings of the semi-feudal type are now things of the past. Inequality among landowners was no longer a key issue, as landholding was not very skewed any more. By one estimate, by 1976–77 nearly 97 per cent of the operated holdings were below 25 acres and 87 per cent of the holdings were below 10 acres.[8] The problem of the landless or the near landless, who it is estimated constituted nearly half the agricultural population, still required urgent attention.

However, any further attempt at land redistribution through lowering of ceilings does not appear to be politically feasible or even economically viable. Given the adverse land–man ratio in India and particularly given (unlike many other countries with similar ratios) the fact that a very high proportion of the population continues to be dependent on agriculture (nearly 67 per cent of the total workforce was engaged in agriculture in 1991) and that consequently the number of potential competitors for land is very large, any attempt to further reduce ceilings to provide land for landless labourers would vastly increase the number of uneconomic and unviable holdings. Also, it would range the entire, now politically very important, landowning classes, powerfully mobilized under the 'new' farmers' movement, against any regime which tried to do so. As an eminent radical journalist said to us recently, 'Only a Pol Pot can try to do land redistribution on the basis of land to the tiller today.'

Perhaps the only viable programme left for the landless was the one which has been to some extent taken up in recent years, of distributing homestead lands or even just home sites, ensuring the payment of minimum wages, as well as providing security of tenure and fair rents to sharecroppers and tenants.[9] Other answers are to be found in increasing off-farm employment in rural areas, in increasing animal husbandry and other activities associated with cultivation but not requiring land.

The Bhoodan Movement

Bhoodan was an attempt at land reform, at bringing about institutional changes in agriculture, like land redistribution through a movement and not simply through government legislation. Eminent Gandhian constructive worker Acharya Vinoba Bhave drew upon Gandhian techniques and ideas such as constructive work and trusteeship to launch this movement in the early 1950s. Unfortunately, its revolutionary potential has generally been missed.

Vinoba Bhave organized an all-India federation of constructive workers, the Sarvodaya Samaj, which was to take up the task of a non-violent social transformation in the country. He and his followers were to do padayatra (walk on foot from village to village) to persuade the larger landowners to donate at least one-sixth of their lands as bhoodan or 'land-gift' for distribution among the landless and the land poor. The target was to get as donation 50 million acres, which was one-sixth of the 300 million acres of cultivable land in India. The idea was that each average family of five should give up to one-sixth of their land accepting the poor landless man as a member of the family.

The movement, though independent of the government, had the support of the Congress, with the AICC urging Congressmen to participate in it actively. Eminent former Congressman and a prominent leader of the Praja Socialist Party, Jayaprakash Narayan withdrew from active politics to join the Bhoodan movement in 1953.

Vinoba received the first donation of land on 18 April 1951 in the village of Pochampalli in the Telangana region of Andhra Pradesh, where the reverberations of the Communist Party-led armed peasant revolt were still being felt. In less than three months he had covered about 200 villages in this region and received 12,200 acres as donation. The movement then spread to the North, particularly Bihar and Uttar Pradesh. In the initial years the movement achieved a considerable degree of success, receiving over 4 million acres of land as donation by March 1956. After this the movement lost momentum and very little new land was received as donations.

Also, a substantial part of the land donated was unfit for cultivation or under litigation. Perhaps this was one reason why out of the nearly 4.5 million acres of Bhoodan land available only about 654,000 acres was actually distributed among 200,000 families by the end of 1957. By early 1961, about 872,000 acres of land had been distributed.

Meanwhile, towards of the end of 1955, the movement took a new form, that of Gramdan or 'donation of village'. Again taking off from the Gandhian notion that all land belonged to 'Gopal' or God, in Gramdan villages the movement declared that all land was owned collectively or equally, as it did not belong to any one individual. The movement started in Orissa and was most successful there. By the end of 1960 there were more than 4,500 Gramdan villages out which 1,946 were in Orissa, 603 in Maharashtra, 543 in Kerala, 483 in Andhra Pradesh and about 250 in Madras. It has been argued that this movement was successful mainly in villages where class differentiation had not yet emerged and there was little if any disparity in ownership of land or other property, such as those inhabited by certain tribal communities. Vinoba is said to have picked such villages for this movement.

By the 1960s the Bhoodan/Gramdan movement had lost its elan despite its considerable initial promise. Its creative potential essentially remained unutilized. The programme, however, appeared to drag on indefinitely, essentially forgotten but for rude reminders such as the Bihar government decision of June 1999 to dissolve the State Bhoodan Committee for its inability to distribute even half the Bhoodan land available over the past thirty-eight years![10]

A proper assessment of the movement particularly its potential is still to be made. It has been too easily dismissed as not only

'Utopian' but also as being reactionary, class collaborationist and aimed at preventing class struggle. As one historian of agrarian reforms in India put it, its purpose was to 'serve as a brake on the revolutionary struggle of the peasants'.[11] This is not surprising as far more successful movements led by Gandhiji continue to be wrongly characterized in this fashion by some sections for having based themselves on similar principles.

There were, however, some very significant aspects of the Bhoodan movement that need to be noted. First, the very fact that it was one of the very few attempts after independence to bring about land reform through a movement and not through government legislation from the top is in itself very significant. Second, the potential of the movement was enormous, based as it was on the idea of trusteeship or that all land belonged to God. If the landlords failed to behave as trustees or as 'equal' sharers of property, then a satyagraha, in the Gandhian mould, could be launched against them. This, for example, was precisely what the Tamil Nadu Sarvodaya leaders proposed to do in 1961: 'Start satyagraha against landlords who refused to cooperate in Gramdan villages and went back on their promises to donate land.'[12] There were some including a section of Socialists influenced by Gandhian thought and practice (many of them were in the PSP in the early 1950s) who wanted to realize the revolutionary potential of the notion of trusteeship and of constructive work through the technique of satyagraha by launching mass civil disobedience against injustice. The Sarvodaya Samaj, however, on the whole failed to make this transition: to build an active large-scale mass movement that would generate irresistible pressure for social transformation in large parts of the country.

Yet, the movement made a significant contribution by creating a moral ambience, an atmosphere, which, while putting pressure on the landlords, created conditions favourable to the landless. This was recognized even by the noted Communist leader E.M.S. Namboodiripad. Citing an article by Namboodiripad titled 'Sarvodaya and Communism', Kotovsky wrote:[13]

> the Bhoodan and Gramdan movement . . . has . . . to a certain extent stimulated political and other activity by the peasant masses and has created a favourable atmosphere for political propaganda and agitation for redistribution of the

land, for abolition of private ownership of land and for the development of agricultural producers' cooperatives.

This, ironically, is perhaps the best appreciation of the significance of the Bhoodan movement coming from those who have been its major critics.

Cooperatives and an Overview of Land Reforms

Cooperatives

A wide spectrum of the national movement's leaders including Mahatma Gandhi, Jawaharlal Nehru, the Socialists and Communists were agreed that cooperativization would lead to major improvement in Indian agriculture and would particularly benefit the poor. Cooperativization was therefore seen as an important element in the agenda for institutional changes sought to be achieved through land reform. However, as in the case of the land ceiling issue, there was no general consensus, particularly among the peasantry, on the question of cooperatives. Correctly reflecting this situation, the Congress at independence made very tentative proposals—like the state making efforts to organize '*pilot schemes for experimenting with cooperative farming* among small holders on government unoccupied but cultivable lands'.[1] Further, it was clarified that any move towards cooperativization was to be through persuasion, by getting the goodwill and agreement of the peasantry. No force or compulsion was visualized.

The recommendations in July 1949 of the Congress Agrarian Reforms Committee, called the Kumarappa Committee after its chairman, showed the first signs that the Congress could push beyond the existing consensus. The committee recommended that 'the State should be *empowered to enforce* the application of varying degrees of cooperation for different types of farming. Thus, while the family farmer *will have* to make use of the multipurpose co-operative society for marketing, credit, and other matters, the below-basic holder (i.e., peasant with small uneconomic holding) *will have* to cultivate his farm jointly with such other holders'.[2] For the first time there was a suggestion of compulsion being used to promote cooperatives and the committee assumed the 'gradualness of the programme, intelligent propaganda, liberal state aid and its judicious implementation by a specially trained cadre would to a great extent reduce the psychological hesitation of the farmer to take to the co-operative patterns recommended by the committee'.[3] This was a hasty assumption, as later events were to show.

The First Plan approached the issue more judiciously and recommended that small and medium farms in particular should be *encouraged and assisted* to group themselves into cooperative farming societies. The Plan did not talk of any enforcing powers to the state though it did envisage some amount of compulsion when it suggested that if majority of the owners and occupancy tenants in a village, owning at least half the land of the village, wished to enter upon cooperative management of the land of the village, then their decision should be binding on the village as a whole.

The early planners had hoped that the village panchayat activated by motivated party workers and aided by the trained workers of the newly launched Community Development programme (in October 1952) would not only help implement rural development projects but would help bring about critical *institutional changes* in Indian agriculture, for example, by assisting in the implementation of land reforms, by organizing voluntary labour for community work and by setting up of cooperatives. Further, there was a high and growing level of expectation, in the initial years, regarding how much such institutional changes, particularly cooperativization, would substitute for investment outlay in agriculture, in achieving the planned targets of rapid increases in agricultural production.

The Second Plan reflected this expectation by declaring that 'the main task during the Second Five Year Plan is to take such essential steps as will provide sound foundations for the development of cooperative farming so that *over a period of ten years or so a substantial proportion of agricultural lands are cultivated on cooperative lines*'.[4] However, even the ambitious plan (considering that no coercion was envisaged) of having a 'substantial' proportion of agricultural lands under cooperatives within ten years soon appeared to be too modest once exaggerated reports started pouring in of the dramatic increases in agricultural output achieved by China through measures such as cooperativization. (It was many years later, after Mao's death in 1976, that this myth was destroyed. By one estimate, China's agricultural growth rate between 1954 and 1974 was only 2 per cent, which was actually lower than India's, which was 2.5 per cent.)

In the middle of 1956 two Indian delegations (one of the Planning Commission, the other of the Union Ministry of Food and Agriculture), consisting of leaders of the cooperative movement in India, MPs, bureaucrats involved with cooperatives, technical experts and planners, were sent to China to study how they organized their cooperatives and achieved such rapid increases in agricultural output. Underlying these visits was the feeling that the targets of agricultural growth envisaged by the Second Plan were inadequate and required an upward revision and the Chinese experience could show how these targets could be achieved without significant increases in outlay.

The two delegations arrived at quite similar conclusions. It was reported that China had achieved remarkable increases in foodgrain production and extension of the agricultural infrastructure through cooperativization. They both recommended (barring the minute of dissent by two members of one committee) a bold programme of extending cooperative farming in India. Jawaharlal Nehru, who was deeply committed to the idea of cooperativization, started putting pressure on the states to emulate the Chinese example and commit to higher food production on the basis of institutional changes in agriculture, that is, without demanding additional funds for investment in agriculture. The National Development Council and the AICC now set targets even higher than the one envisaged by the Second Plan, proposing that in the next five years agricultural production be increased by 25 to 35 per cent if not more, mainly by bringing about major institutional changes in agriculture such as cooperativization. The states, however, resisted any large-scale plan for cooperativization, agreeing only to experiments in cooperative farming and that too if they remained strictly voluntary.

The Congress under Nehru's persuasion continued to mount pressure in favour of an agricultural strategy based critically on institutional change. The Congress pressure culminated in the famous

Nagpur Resolution passed at the party's Nagpur session in January 1959. The Nagpur Resolution clearly stated that 'the organisation of the village should be based on village panchayats and village cooperatives, both of which should have adequate powers and resources to discharge the functions allotted to them'. Further, the Resolution stated:[5]

> The future agrarian pattern should be that of *cooperative joint farming*, in which the *land would be pooled for joint cultivation*, the farmers continuing to retain their property rights, and getting a share of the net produce in proportion to their land. Further, those who actually work on the land, whether they own the land or not, will get a share in proportion to the work put in by them on the joint farm.

> As a first step, prior to the institution of joint farming, service cooperatives should be organised throughout the country. This stage should be completed within a period of three years. Even within this period, however, wherever possible and generally agreed to by the farmers, joint cultivation may be started.

A big leap was involved here. Not only did the Nagpur Resolution visualize an agrarian pattern based on joint cooperative farming in the future, it specified that such a pattern was *to be achieved within three years*. The proposal for introducing cooperatives, which was being made since the mid-1940s, could no longer be treated as just another radical recommendation with no concrete programme for its implementation. A wave of opposition, both within and outside the Congress, followed this recommendation.

The press and parliament, which was convened shortly after the Nagpur session, argued that the Resolution was the first step towards ending private property and eventual expropriation of the landed classes and that it would lead to forced collectivization on the Soviet or Chinese pattern. From within the Congress party senior leaders like C. Rajagopalachari, N.G. Ranga and others like Charan Singh mobilized opinion in the party and outside and mounted an open attack saying that a totalitarian, Communist programme was being thrust upon the country.

Faced with serious division within the party, Nehru struck a conciliatory note, assuring parliament in February 1959 that there was no question of using any coercion to introduce cooperatives and that no new law or act was going to be passed by parliament on this question. He only reiterated his personal conviction that cooperative farming was desirable and that he would continue to try and convince the peasants, without whose consent the programmme could not be implemented.

The Chinese repression in Tibet in March 1959, and more so the Chinese encroachments inside the Indian border a few months later, were not only a personal loss of face and prestige for Nehru but also made any plan which smacked of the China model automatically suspect and very difficult to push publicly. A further retreat became inevitable and the Congress put forward a position in parliament which essentially argued for setting up *'service cooperatives'* all over the country ever the next three years and left the issue of setting up cooperative farms sufficiently vague. Cooperative farms were to be set up *voluntarily* wherever conditions became mature.

The Congress was aware that even the task of setting up service cooperatives all over the country in three years was a gigantic effort requiring the setting up of 6,000 new cooperatives every month for a period of three years! The AICC decided to establish a training centre for Congress workers who would play a key role in organizing service cooperatives, and the PCCs were directed to do the same. The provincial Congress leaders simply ignored the directive and despite the efforts of the Congress president, Indira Gandhi, the AICC training programme did not get off the ground and was eventually altogether abandoned after June 1959.

The Third Plan, in sharp contrast to the Second, reflected the mellowed position regarding cooperativization and took a very pragmatic and cautious approach. As regards cooperative farming, it accepted a modest target of setting up ten pilot projects per district. At the same time it put in the caveat that 'cooperative farming has to grow out of the success of the general agricultural effort through the community development movement, the progress of cooperation in credit, marketing, distribution and processing, the growth of rural industry, and the fulfillment of the objectives of land reform'.[6] This sounded like a wishful platitude not a plan of action.

Limitations of Cooperativization

Given the policy stalemate reached, it is not surprising that the progress that the cooperative movement made in India by and large fell far short of the goals set by its early proponents. Most of the weaknesses that Daniel Thorner, the noted economist, had observed during his survey of 117 of the 'best' cooperatives all over India between December 1958 and May 1959 remained largely true in the years to come. Another economist and observer of India's land reforms, Wolf Ladejinsky, made similar observations for the 1960s and 1970s.

As for joint farming, two types of cooperatives were observed. First, there were those that were formed essentially to evade land reforms and access incentives offered by the state. Typically, these cooperatives were formed by well-to-do, influential families who took on a number of agricultural labourers or ex-tenants as bogus members. Forming a cooperative helped evade the ceiling laws or tenancy laws. The influential members got the lands tilled by the bogus members who were essentially engaged as wage labour or tenants. Moreover, forming these bogus cooperatives enabled the influential families to take advantage of the substantial financial assistance offered by the state in the form of a subsidy, as well as get priority for acquiring scarce agricultural inputs like fertilizers, improved seeds and even tractors, etc.

Second, there were the state-sponsored cooperative farms in the form of pilot projects, where generally poor, previously uncultivated land was made available to the landless, Harijans, displaced persons and such underprivileged groups. The poor quality of land, lack of proper irrigation facility, etc., and the fact that these farms were run like government-sponsored projects rather than genuine, motivated, joint efforts of the cultivators led them to be generally expensive unsuccessful experiments. The expected rise in productivity and benefits of scale, which is a major *raison d'être* of cooperative farming, was not in evidence in these farms.

In any case, the hope that the service cooperatives would facilitate the transition to cooperative farming was completely belied. Cooperative farming had spread to negligible levels beyond the government projects and the bogus cooperatives.

The service cooperatives, which fared much better than the farming cooperatives, also suffered from some major shortcomings.

To begin with, the service cooperatives not only reflected the iniquitous structure of the Indian countryside but also tended to reinforce it. Typically, the leadership of the cooperatives, that is, its president, secretary and treasurer, consisted of the leading family or families of the village which not only owned a great deal of land but also controlled trade and moneylending. These well-to-do families, the 'big people' or the 'all in alls' of the village, were thus able to corner for themselves scarce agricultural inputs, including credit. In fact, quite often, low interest agricultural credit made available through cooperative rural banks was used by such families for non-agricultural businesses, consumption and even moneylending! It was a case of public subsidy being used by a non-target group for private investment. To the extent that Congress and other political formations with similar objectives, viz., the Socialists and the Communists, failed to use the political space provided at the grassroots level by the panchayats, the Community Development programme and the cooperatives in favour of the underprivileged in the countryside, by mobilizing them into action, these institutions were taken over by the dominant sections in the village, who used them to further buttress their economic and political influence.

The village poor, the landless, got little out of these institutions in the early years. An example at hand is the constant refusal to implement the elaborate recommendation made by the Reserve Bank of India (RBI) in 1954 that rural credit cooperatives were to give credit to the cultivator as the producer of a crop and not as the owner of land. This refusal of the cooperatives to issue 'crop loans' or loans in anticipation of the crop being produced, and their insisting on credit being given against land as security, meant that the landless were essentially excluded from this scheme. In 1969, the RBI observed that tenant cultivators, agricultural labourers and 'others' secured only 4 to 6 per cent of the total credit disbursed. The report of the All India Credit Review Committee, 1969, and the Interim Report on Credit Services for Small and Marginal Farmers produced by the National Commission on Agriculture, 1971, confirmed the virtual exclusion of the landless and added that the small and marginal farmers were also at a considerable disadvantage vis-à-vis the bigger cultivators in accessing credit from the cooperatives and even from the nationalized banks. As we shall see presently, it required a special targeting of these groups through programmes like the Marginal Farmers and Agricultural Labourers (MFAL) Scheme and the Small Farmers Development Agency (SFDA) under the broad rubric of the *garibi hatao* campaign launched by Indira Gandhi, for this bias to be considerably mitigated.

A common shortcoming of the cooperative movement was that instead of promoting people's participation it soon became like a huge overstaffed government department with officials, clerks, inspectors, and the like, replicated at the block, district, division and state levels. A large bureaucracy, generally not in sympathy with the principles of the cooperative movement and quite given to being influenced by local vested interests, instead of becoming the instrument for promoting cooperatives, typically became a hindrance.

Yet, over time, the service cooperatives, particularly the credit cooperatives, performed a critical role for Indian agriculture. After all, while in 1951–52, the Primary Agricultural Credit Societies (PACS), which were village-level cooperative societies, advanced loans worth only about Rs 23 crore (Rs 230 million), in 1960–61 about 212,000 such societies disbursed nearly Rs 200 crore (Rs 2 billion). By 1992–93, these societies were lending as much as Rs 4,900 crore (Rs 49 billion).

As Table 30.1 shows, in 1951–52, cooperatives supplied only 3.3 per cent of the credit requirements of the cultivator, whereas by 1981 they supplied nearly 30 per cent. It is found that in 1951 the cultivator was dependent on non-institutional and generally rapacious sources of credit such as the moneylender, trader or landlord for 92.7 per cent of his credit requirements. By 1981,

Table 32.1: Different Sources of Credit for the Cultivator, 1951–1981

(figures in per cent)

	1951–52	1971	1981
Moneylender, trader, landlord, etc.	92.7	68.3	36.8
Cooperatives	3.3	22.0	29.9
Commercial banks	0.9	2.6	29.4
Government	3.1	7.1	3.9

Source: All India Debt and Investment Survey, 1961–62, 1981. (Cited in Ruddar Datt, et.al., Indian Economy, p. 469.)

however, low-cost institutional credit looked after over 63 per cent of the cultivator's requirements. Nearly 30 per cent was met by the cooperatives and another nearly 30 per cent was met by commercial banks which, after their nationalization in July 1969 by Indira Gandhi, were prevailed upon to provide credit to agriculture on a priority basis.

The cooperative credit societies, however, suffered from a major drawback, that of failure to repay loans and, consequently, a very large percentage of overdues. Between 1960 and 1970, overdues of the primary societies rose from 20 to 38 per cent of the credit disbursed. The situation continued to deteriorate with the all-India average of overdues rising to 45 per cent in the mid-1970s and many provinces reaching totally unviable figures, like 77 per cent in Bihar. Quite significantly, it has been observed that the defaulters were not necessarily the poor and small farmers but more often the well-to-do ones. With the growing political and economic clout of the well-to-do peasant, the problem of overdues had reached dangerous proportions, affecting the viability and growth rate of rural credit institutions. Populist measures like the decision of V.P. Singh's National Front government in 1990 to write-off all rural debts up to Rs 10,000 not only put a heavy burden on the national exchequer but further eroded the viability of rural credit institutions.

As already mentioned, a larger proportion of cooperative and bank credit started becoming available, particularly to the small and marginal farmers in the 1970s. In 1979–80 about 34 per cent of the short-term loans given by scheduled commercial banks went to households holding less than 2.5 acres, when such households constituted only 33 per cent of the total households. Similarly, 57 per cent of such loans went to households owning up to 5 acres, while the proportion of households in that category was only 49 per cent. No longer was institutional rural credit the preserve of the rural elite. Policy initiatives were to follow which led to the rural banks giving a much higher proportion of the credit to the weaker sections. As for the cooperatives (PACS), those with holdings up to 5 acres received 34 per cent of the credit and those holding above 5 acres received 62 per cent. The situation of the landless, however, remained the same: only 4 per cent of the credit went to them.[7]

It is thus evident that service cooperatives had started to play a very important role in rural India. Their role in making available a much increased amount of cheap credit to a wider section of the peasantry was critical. They not only helped in bringing improved seeds, modern implements, cheap fertilizers, etc., to the peasants, they also provided them with the wherewithal to access them. And, in many areas they also helped market their produce. In fact, in many ways they provided a necessary condition for the success of the Green Revolution strategy launched in the late 1960s, which was based on intensive use of modern inputs in agriculture. It is not surprising then that Wolf Ladejinsky, who was fully aware of all the shortcomings of the cooperative movement in India, was to record in his annual note to the World Bank in May 1972: 'Millions of farmers have benefited from them (cooperatives) and rural India without this landmark is hard to visualise.'[8]

Milk Cooperatives: Operation Flood

The story of the cooperative movement in India, however, cannot be complete without a description of the most successful experiment in cooperation in India, which was a class apart from any other effort of the kind. This experiment, which started modestly in Kaira (also called Kheda) district of Gujarat eventually became the harbinger of the 'White Revolution' that spread all over India. Here, space permits only a brief description of the Anand experiment.[9]

Peasants of Kaira district, which supplied milk to the city of Bombay, felt cheated by the milk traders and approached Sardar Patel, the pre-eminent nationalist leader, who hailed from this district, for help. At the initiative of Patel and Morarji Desai, the farmers organized themselves into a cooperative union and were able to pressurize the Bombay government, albeit with the help of a 'milk strike', to buy milk from their union. Thus, the Kaira District Cooperative Milk Producers' Union Ltd, formally registered in December 1946, started modestly in Anand, a small town on the highway between Ahmedabad and Baroda, supplying 250 litres of milk every day.

The Gandhian freedom fighter Tribhuvandas K. Patel, who patiently roamed the villages on foot to persuade farmers to form milk cooperatives, became the first chairman of the union in

January 1947 and continued to be elected to this position for over twenty-five years. Dr Verghese Kurien, the brilliant engineer from Kerala and later the heart and soul of the White Revolution in India, was the celebrated and proud employee of the Kaira farmers, and the chief executive of the union from 1950 to 1973, though he has continued his close association with the union till today. The union, which started with two village cooperative societies with less than a hundred members each, by 2000 had 1,015 societies with 574,000 members. From 250 litres of milk a day, it was by then handling nearly 1 million litres of milk a day and had an annual turnover of Rs 487 crore or Rs 4.87 billion.

In the process of this rapid growth, the union greatly diversified its activities. In 1955, it had set up a factory to manufacture milk powder and butter, partly to deal with the problem of the greater yields of milk in winter not finding an adequate market. The same year the union chose the name of 'Amul' for its range of products. This was a brand name which was to successfully compete with some of the world's most powerful multinationals like Glaxo or Nestle and soon become a household word all over India.

In 1960, a new factory was added which was designed to manufacture 600 tonnes of cheese and 2,500 tonnes of baby food every year—the first in the world to manufacture these products on a large commercial scale using buffalo milk. In 1964, a modern plant to manufacture cattle feed was commissioned. Over time, sophisticated computer technology was used by the union to regularly, even daily, do a cost–benefit analysis of the prices of the various inputs which go into cattle feed and their nutritional value to arrive at the 'optimum' mix of the balanced feed concentrate which was made available to the farmers. In 1994–95 the union sold 144,181 tonnes of cattle feed through its branches.

Any community development work necessarily involves an integrated approach. The Kaira Cooperative Union was a model case of how the union's own activities kept expanding, and how it spawned other organizations, bringing within its scope wider and wider areas of concern to the ordinary peasant. An efficient artificial insemination service through the village society workers was introduced so that the producers could improve the quality of their stock. In 1994–95, about 670,000 such inseminations were performed through 827 centres. A 24-hour mobile veterinary service with twenty-nine vehicles fitted with radio telephones was available to the farmers at nominal cost. Cattle owned by cooperative members were provided with insurance cover should anything happen to this major source of their livelihood. High quality fodder seeds for producing green fodder were made available. Even manufacture of vaccines for the cattle was started, again taking on multinational pharmaceutical companies in a struggle over turf which had all the ingredients of a modern thriller. A regular newsletter was published in an effort to educate the peasants about modern developments in animal husbandry. A special effort was made to educate women who generally looked after the animals in a peasant household. At the other end of the spectrum, an Institute of Rural Management (IRMA) was founded in Anand for training professional managers for rural development projects, *using the Amul complex and the Kaira Cooperative* as a live laboratory. As the 'Anand Pattern' gradually spread to other districts in Gujarat, in 1974, the Gujarat Cooperative Milk Marketing Federation Ltd, Anand, was formed as an apex organization of the unions in the district to look after marketing.

The existence of the cooperative had considerably improved the standard of living of the villagers in Kaira district, particularly the poor farmers and the landless. According to one estimate, as a result of the activities of the cooperative, nearly 48 per cent of the income of the rural households in Kaira district came from dairying. Some of the profits of the cooperative also went to improve the common facilities in the village including wells, roads, schools, etc.

A crucial feature of the cooperative movement associated with the 'Anand Pattern' was the democratic mode of functioning of the cooperatives, with a conscious effort being made by the management to keep its ear to the ground and not overlook the interest of the humblest of the cooperative members including the 'low' caste and the landless. In fact, the structure of the cooperative was such that it involved the direct producer in the planning and policy-making process. The only necessary condition for membership of a village cooperative society was of being a genuine primary milk producer who regularly supplied milk to the cooperative. The villager, irrespective of caste, class, gender or religion who queued up at the milk collection centre of the cooperative in the village, day after day, to sell milk and collect the payment for the sale made on the previous occasion *typically had one or two buffaloes,* not

562 India Since Independence

large heads of cattle like the big landlords. In fact, by one estimate, one-third of the milk producers were landless.

It is such producers who became members of the cooperative with a nominal entrance fee of Re 1 and the purchase of at least one share of Rs 10. The members would elect a managing committee by secret ballot with each member having one vote irrespective of the number of shares owned by him. The committee would elect the chairman and work for the cooperative in an honorary capacity. The work of the committee involved policy formulation and supervision while paid staff was employed for the routine work of the cooperative. The chairman, along with a third of the committee by rotation, would retire every year and fresh elections would be held. The elections were eagerly contested with very high polling figures, reaching even up to 99 per cent. The district-level union managed by a twelve-member board of directors had six members elected from among the chairmen of the village societies. The board would elect a chairman annually *from among the village representatives* and appoint a managing director who in turn would appoint supporting professionals etc. This cooperative was unique in effectively combining the initiative and control of the direct producer with the use of modern technology and the hiring of the most advanced professional help, managerial, technical or scientific, that was available in the country. The structure of the cooperative engendered such a combination.

The Kaira Cooperative success made the movement's spread to the rest of the country inevitable. In 1964, Lal Bahadur Shastri, the then prime minister of India, wrote to the chief ministers of all the states about the proposed large programme to set up cooperative dairies on the 'Anand Pattern'. To perform this task the National Dairy Development Board (NDDB) was created in 1965 at his initiative. Kurien with his proven dynamism was to be at its helm as its honorary chairman, proudly continuing to draw his salary as an employee of the Kaira milk producers. At his insistence the NDDB was located in Anand and not in New Delhi and acquired a structure not of yet another inefficient government department but one which was more suitable to its objectives. Drawing heavily from the Kaira Union for personnel, expertise and much more, the NDDB launched 'Operation Flood', a programme to replicate the 'Anand Pattern' in other milksheds of the country. By 1995 there were 69,875 village dairy cooperatives spread over 170 milksheds all over the country with a total membership of 8.9 million farmers. Though the expansion was impressive, yet, by one estimate, Operation Flood represented only 6.3 per cent of total milk production and 22 per cent of marketed milk in India. The potential for further expansion thus remains immense.

A study done by the World Bank (evaluation department) of Operation Flood details how the effort to replicate the 'Anand Pattern' paid rich dividends. A brief summary of the findings of this study show how the complex multi-pronged benefits, similar to those achieved in Gujarat, now spread to other parts of the country.[10]

First, the obvious impact of Operation Flood was the considerable increase in milk supply and consequent increase in income of the milk producers, particularly the poor. While national milk production grew at 0.7 per cent per annum till 1969, it grew at more than 4 per cent annually after the inception of Operation Flood. 'In constant (1995) Rs., the annual payment by the cooperative system (to) dairy farmers has risen from Rs. 2.1 billion in 1972 to Rs. 34 billion in 1995.'[11] Further, village-level enquiries showed that dairying was increasingly becoming an important activity of the farmer and in some cases becoming the main source of income, particularly among the poor. It was estimated that '*60 per cent of the beneficiaries were marginal or small farmers and landless*', and it was further stated that 'the extent to which such benefits (were) reaching the extremely poor and needy (destitute, widows, landless, and near landless) in certain "spearhead" villages (was) unusually noteworthy'.[12] Milk cooperatives thus proved to be a significant anti-poverty measure.

In this connection, the World Bank report highlighted an important 'lesson' learnt from Operation Flood, a lesson with major politico-economic implications. The 'lesson' was that 'by focusing a project on a predominant activity of the poor, *"self-selection"* is likely to result in a major portion of the beneficiaries being poor' thus reaching 'target' groups which generally prove 'elusive to reach in practice'.[13] Further, it may be added the Anand-type milk cooperatives reached the poor irrespective of caste, religion or gender, without targeting any of these groups specifically. Similar objectives were met by the Employment Guarantee Scheme (EGS) first launched in rural Maharashtra in the mid-1970s, followed by a few other states including Andhra

Pradesh. The chief beneficiaries of this scheme were the landless who were predominantly from among the Scheduled Castes or Scheduled Tribes, that is, they got 'self-selected', though the scheme did not exclusively target these groups. Such programmes had the important advantage of reaching certain deprived sections without exclusively targeting them. This prevented an almost inevitable opposition or even a backlash among the groups excluded, which has so often been witnessed in schemes in India as well as in other countries, such as the US, where benefits were sought to be given exclusively to a particular community or group.

Second, as in the case of Anand, the impact of the milk cooperatives and Operation Flood went way beyond just increase in milk supply and incomes. As the World Bank study reported, 'A by-product impact of Operation Flood and the accompanying dairy expansion has been the establishment of an indigenous dairy equipment manufacturing industry (only 7 per cent of dairy equipment is now imported) and an impressive body of indigenous expertise that includes animal nutrition, animal health, artificial insemination (AI), management information systems (MIS), dairy engineering, food technology and the like.' The indigenization of the infrastructure and technology and the training of rural labour for performing a wide range of technical functions is said to have considerably lowered costs, making it possible to procure and account for minute quantities of milk brought in by the producers, without raising costs to an unviable level.

Third, Operation Flood spread and even intensified the impact of the milk cooperatives on women and children and on education. Realizing the potential of empowering women through this movement, Operation Flood in cooperation with NGOs like the Self-Employed Women's Association (SEWA), established about 6,000 women dairy cooperative societies (WDCS) where only women were members and the management committees also were constituted exclusively of women. These cooperatives were seen to be generally more efficiently run than male-dominated cooperatives. They gave women greater control over their lives through the milk income accruing to them and also enabled them to participate in decision-making outside their homes, giving full play to their managerial and leadership potential. Further, field-level observation showed that the milk income in the poorer villages often made it possible for children to attend school, while in better-off villages it contributed to children staying in school longer, that is, it reduced the dropout rate. In still wealthier villages, where all children went to school, a part of the earning of the cooperative was used to improve the facilities in the local school. The field surveys also confirmed that increased school attendance for girls was perceived as a very common effect of the dairy cooperative societies. Greater family income and the woman involved in dairying being able to stay at home instead of going out for wage labour relieved children from having to earn a wage or look after household chores. Instead, they attended school.

The spread of the 'Anand Pattern' was not to be limited to milk. Cooperatives for fruits and vegetable producers, oilseeds cultivators, small-scale salt makers and tree growers were started at the initiative of the NDDB. Again the Kaira Union provided the technology as well as the trained personnel to help this process. Often the resistance from vested interests, particularly the powerful oilseeds traders, was vicious. In some regions of the country, the NDDB team which tried to make the initial moves towards setting up cooperatives was threatened with physical violence and there were cases where workers died in 'mysterious' circumstances. Yet, the movement has progressed. In many parts of the country cooperative outlets of fruits and vegetables are beginning to be as common as milk outlets. The 'Dhara' brand of vegetable oils, a child of the NDDB effort, is beginning to represent in the area of vegetable oils what 'Amul' does in the area of milk and milk products.

This has been one of the major achievements of post-independence India. The search for cooperatives led to Indian delegations going to China in the mid-1950; today scores of countries send delegations to India to study and learn from the Anand experience. An indication of the impact this experiment had at the grassroots level was the statement made to the present authors by a poor farmer in a village near Anand in 1985, 'Gujarat is fortunate to have one Kurien; if only God would give one Kurien to every state, many of India's problems would be solved.'

This poor Gujarat peasant who in his personalized way was trying to explain to us the magnitude of the success of this experiment with reference to Kurien, a Syrian Christian from Kerala, will surely feel out of tune with the Hindu communal upsurge his state witnessed in early 1999, where Christians were hounded and attacked, their religion presumably making them anti-national!

Land Reforms: An Overview

India witnessed the unique phenomenon of wide-ranging land reforms being implemented within a modern democratic structure without any violence or use of authoritarian force. There was no forced collectivization as in the Soviet Union or forcible expropriation of land and pushing of peasants into communes as in China, processes that had cost millions of lives. Nor was there any external army of occupation undertaking the task of land reforms among a defeated people as in Japan. India had to attempt this task with adult franchise, full civil liberties to the Opposition and an independent judiciary. Yet, basing itself on the heritage of long, powerful national and peasant movements, independent India successfully transformed the colonial agricultural structure (with all its semi-feudal characteristics) which it had inherited. The legacy of nearly half a century of agrarian stagnation was reversed. Institutional and infrastructural changes were put in place, which were to enable the bringing in of modern, progressive or 'capitalist' farming in more and more parts of the country with the ushering in of the next phase, that of technological reforms associated with the Green Revolution.

Large, semi-feudal, rapacious landlords rack-renting the peasantry as well as extracting illegal cesses in cash, kind or labour (begar) had by and large become a thing of the past. State demand from the peasant, the other major burden on the agriculturist, also gradually virtually disappeared. Many states scrapped land revenue. Elsewhere the real value of land revenue fell sharply as agricultural prices rose steeply while the land revenue rates remained constant for decades. While in the colonial period the burden of land revenue was very high, often adding up to half the net income from agriculture, it gradually declined to negligible levels, below 1 per cent of the net income from agriculture. The stranglehold of the moneylender over the peasantry was also considerably weakened with the growing availability of cooperative and institutional credit. Loans advanced by such institutions increased from Rs 0.23 billion in 1950–51 to Rs 3.65 billion in 1965–66 and Rs 7.75 billion in 1972–73. This credit was becoming increasingly available to the poorer sections. Gradually, but surely, democracy, the poorest having an equal vote, kept the pressure on the government as well as the rural elite (for their political survival) to try and reach benefits to the lower sections of the peasantry. The resources available to the peasantry as a whole for agricultural improvement thus increased significantly.

The motivation or incentive for agricultural improvement was now present among a much wider section of the agrarian classes. Large numbers of zamindars and jagirdars who were formerly absentee landlords now took to modern capitalist farming in the lands that they could retain for personal cultivation. Similarly, the tenants and sharecroppers who either got ownership rights or security of tenure were now prepared to make far greater investment and improvements in their lands. The landless, who received ceiling-surplus or bhoodan lands or previously unoccupied government land distributed in anti-poverty programmes, were ready to put in their best into lands which they could now, typically for the first time, call their own. As discussed earlier, the cumulative effect of the various land reform measures in creating progressive cultivators, making investments and improvements in productivity was considerable, on a national scale.

Further, the state, instead of extracting surplus from agriculture, as in the colonial period, now made major efforts at agricultural improvement. Community Development projects were started in rural areas and Block Development Officers (BDOs), Agricultural Extension Officers and Village Level Workers (VLWs) became a routine feature in hundreds of thousands Indian villages, trying to inculcate improved farming methods, supply seeds and implements, promote small-scale public works and so on. Major investments were made in scientific agricultural research, irrigation projects, electricity generation, and general infrastructure. Availability of chemical fertilizers increased from 73,000 tonnes of nutrient in 1950–51 to 784,000 tonnes in 1965–66 and 2,769,000 thousand tonnes in 1972–73. All this had a major impact on agriculture. As Daniel Thorner, one of the keenest observers of Indian agriculture since independence, noted:[15]

> It is sometimes said that the (initial) five-year plans neglected agriculture. This charge cannot be taken seriously. The facts are that in India's first twenty-one years of independence more has been done to foster change in agriculture and more change has actually taken place than in the preceding two hundred years.

The results speak for themselves. During the first three Plans (leaving out 1965–66, the last year of the Third Plan) Indian agriculture grew at an annual rate of over 3 per cent. This was a growth rate 7.5 times higher than that achieved during the last half century or so of the colonial period—the rate of growth between 1891 and 1946 being estimated as only 0.4 per cent per year. Further, the growth rate achieved during the first three Plans was a function not only of extension of area but also of increases in yields per acre, nearly half the agricultural growth was explained by the latter. Also, the agricultural growth achieved in this period was higher than what was achieved by many other countries in a comparable situation. For example, Japan achieved a growth rate of less than 2.5 per cent between 1878 and 1912 and an even lower growth rate after this till 1937.

It is generally agreed that as a result of land reform in India, self-cultivation became the predominant form of cultivation in most parts of the country. Moreover, over time, the vast mass of owner cultivators were small and medium farmers. By one estimate, by 1976–77, nearly 97 per cent of the cultivators had operational holdings of less than 25 acres and they operated 73.6 per cent of the total area. (86.9 per cent of the cultivators had operational holdings of 10 acres or less and they operated 43.4 per cent of the total area.) On the other hand, along with this vast mass there were the large landowners operating above 25 acres, though they constituted only 3 per cent of the holdings and 26.2 per cent of the operated area. Further, the share of the large landowners, both in the proportion of holdings and area controlled, kept declining steadily over time.[16] Very large estates of over 100 acres were very few and rare, and they were generally run on modern capitalist lines. The picture that emerged was remarkably similar to what Ranade had envisaged several decades earlier.

However, the problem of the landless (India, unlike most other countries, had through the caste system inherited a large category of landless since ancient times) or the near landless, constituting nearly half the agricultural population has persisted. The high rate of population growth and the inability of the industrialization process to absorb a greater proportion of the agricultural population has made it difficult to deal with this situation. Providing agricultural land to all the landless is not, and perhaps never was, a politically or economically viable solution in Indian conditions. (After all, even West Bengal with a Communist government for decades has never taken up seriously the question of land to the tiller, the major 'success' there being limited to getting security of tenure for about half the sharecroppers or bargadars.) Efforts at improving the working conditions of the landless and providing them with non-farm employment in rural areas have had uneven results in various states and have left much to be desired in large parts of the country.

The effort at cooperative joint farming failed as one way of solving the problems of rural poverty, inequity and landlessness. Other efforts aimed at the underprivileged in the countryside were often appropriated by the relatively better off. Despite Nehru, despite the Avadi session (1955) adoption of 'Socialistic Pattern of Society' as the objective of the Congress (and its inclusion in the Directive Principles of the Constitution of India), despite the Nagpur Congress recommendations, Indian agriculture did not move in the direction of socialism. Again, as Daniel Thorner put it very succinctly, 'To the extent that the Government of India ever intended to— (introduce) socialism in the countryside, we may say that it has been no more successful in that direction than was the British regime in introducing capitalism.'[17] Perhaps, it is possible now with more information available on the fate of the disastrous Soviet and Chinese attempts to introduce socialism in agriculture to ask whether this was not a lucky 'failure' ensured by the democratic nature of the Indian political system. Yet, independent India did succeed in essentially rooting out feudal elements from Indian agriculture and put the colonial agrarian structure that it inherited on the path of progressive, owner cultivator-based capitalist agricultural development; a development the benefits of which trickled down to the poorer sections of the peasantry and to some extent even to agricultural labourers.

The considerable progress made in the early years was, however, inadequate for the growing needs of the country. The rapid rise of population at about 2.25 per cent per annum after independence, the rise in per capita income, the attempt at rapid industrialization in a hothouse manner, two major wars with neighbours, all put demands on Indian agriculture difficult to meet. Import of foodgrains kept rising, from 12 million tonnes during the First Plan to 19.4

and 32.2 million tonnes during the Second and Third Plans respectively. On the basis of the institutional reforms already completed and the major infrastructural investments made the country was by the mid-1960s poised for the next phase of agrarian breakthrough, the Green Revolution, based on technological reforms.

Agricultural Growth and the Green Revolution

In popular parlance, the phenomenon of the Green Revolution is identified with India's being catapulted from a chronically food-short country, with a begging-bowl image, to one which was self-sufficient and which became over time even surplus in food. The change follows the major technological reforms that occurred in Indian agriculture, particularly from the mid-1960s. There has been much debate on the timing and the political and economic factors behind the ushering in of the New Agricultural Strategy which led to the Green Revolution. Its impact on the nature of agricultural growth, on the changing position of various agrarian classes, particularly the poor, and on the class balance of governments has also generated lively controversy. The brief overall description of this phenomenon given here is inevitably laced with elements of this controversy.

The view that in the 'Nehru years', that is, from independence till his death in 1964, Indian agriculture was neglected or that the focus was only on institutional reforms and not on the technological base for agriculture has increasingly been abandoned. Nehru was well aware of the centrality of agricultural development in meeting his dream of rapid industrialization. The plan outlays on agriculture from the First Plan itself were substantial by any standards. Apart from the First Plan, where the outlay on agriculture and irrigation was 31 per cent of the total, in all the Plans that followed, the outlay was between 20 and 24 per cent, irrespective of the changes in regimes. It is true, that in the initial years, during the first two Plans, the expectations of output increases on the basis of institutional reforms, particularly when accompanied by cooperative farming, were quite high and proved to be misjudgements. However, simultaneously, with the efforts at institutional reforms, Nehru from the very beginning placed great emphasis on creating the physical and scientific infrastructure necessary for modern agriculture. Massive irrigation and power projects like the Bhakra-Nangal, numerous agricultural universities and research laboratories, fertilizer plants, etc., took their due place along with steel plants as the 'temples of modern India' in the Nehruvian vision.

Over time, by the late 1950s and early 1960s, as the benefits from the land reforms that could be carried out in Indian conditions had begun to peak and the possibilities of agricultural growth based on extension of agriculture, that is, bringing more area under cultivation, were also reaching their limit, Nehru's focus inevitably shifted further towards technological solutions. (After all, countries like Japan and China which had carried out more far-reaching land reforms also had to follow the path of making modern technological improvements in agriculture to keep up their growth rates.) Even the New Agricultural Strategy of picking out select areas with certain natural advantages for intensive development with a package programme the Intensive Agricultural Districts Programme (IADP) was launched in fifteen districts, one for each state, on an experimental basis during the Third Plan in Nehru's lifetime—a practice which was to be generalized on a large scale a few years later. As one of the major scholars of the Green Revolution, G.S. Bhalla, says:[1]

> The qualitative technological transformation in India—the Green Revolution . . . came about not during his lifetime but soon after his death. But the foundations for the technological development were laid during Nehru's time.

However, by the mid-1960s, the impact of certain long-term trends, as well as several immediate imperatives coincided with critical scientific breakthroughs to create a conjuncture which called for and enabled a big push towards the New Agricultural Strategy.

Despite the very creditable growth of agricultural output between 1949 and 1965 of about 3 per cent per annum, India had been facing food shortages since the mid-1950s and in the mid-1960s India was in the throes of a crisis. Agricultural growth had begun to stagnate in the early 1960s. The massive jump in population growth rates after independence, to about 2.2 per cent per annum from about 1 per cent in the previous half century, the slow but steady rise in per capita income, and the huge (and rising with each Plan) outlay towards planned industrialization, put long-term pressures on Indian agriculture, creating, for example, a demand for food which Indian markets were not able to meet fully. From the mid-1950s, food prices state to rise. To meet the food shortage and to stabilize prices India was forced to import increasing amounts of food. The alternative was to go in for large-scale forced procurements from the countryside at huge human cost, a path which was unacceptable in India but was adopted by other countries like Russia or China which did not have democracy as a safeguard. The controversial agreements made by India to import food from *the US under the PL-480 scheme started in 1956*. Nearly 3 million tonnes of foodgrains were imported under this scheme in the very first year and the volume of imports kept rising thereafter, reaching more than 4.5 million tonnes in 1963.

In this situation came the two wars with China (1962) and Pakistan (1965) and two successive drought years in 1965–66 leading to a fall in agricultural output by 17 per cent and food output by 20 per cent. Food prices shot up, rising at the rate of nearly 20 per cent per annum between 1965 and 1968. India was forced to import more than 10 million tonnes of foodgrains in 1966. It is in this moment of crisis, with famine conditions emerging in various parts of the country, especially in Bihar and Uttar Pradesh, that the US threatened to renege on commitments of food exports to India. The Indo-Pak war, India's stand on Vietnam and the desire to arm twist India into accepting an economic policy package favoured by the US had convinced President Johnson that India should be put 'on a short leash' and what better way to do it than to cynically use India's desperate dependence on the US for food!

Given this scenario of the mid-1960s, economic self-reliance and particularly food self-sufficiency became the top priority objectives of Indian economic policy and for that matter of foreign policy. The New Agricultural Strategy began to be implemented in right earnest. The then prime minister, Lal Bahadur Shastri, Food Minister, C. Subramaniam, and Indira Gandhi, who followed Shastri in 1966 after his brief tenure, all gave full support to and crafted this basic transition in the strategy for developing Indian agriculture. The World Bank-appointed Bell Mission recommended such a transition and the US pressed in its favour, but they appear to have been 'leaning on open doors', as a considerable consensus in favour of such a change had emerged within India. Critical inputs like high-yield variety (HYV) seeds (the suitability to Indian conditions of the high-yielding Mexican dwarf wheat proved to be an extremely timely scientific breakthrough), chemical fertilizers and pesticides, agricultural machinery including tractors, pump-sets, etc., soil-testing facilities, agricultural education programmes and institutional credit were concentrated on areas which had assured irrigation and other natural and institutional advantages. Some 32 million acres of land, about 10 per cent of the total cultivated area, was, thus, initially chosen for receiving the package programme benefits on top priority.

Government investment in agriculture rose significantly. Institutional finance made available to agriculture doubled between 1968 and 1973. The Agricultural Prices Commission was set up in 1965 and efforts were made to see that the farmer was assured a market at sustained remunerative prices. Public investment, institutional credit, remunerative prices and the availability of the new technology at low prices raised the profitability of private investment by farmers and as a result the total gross capital formation in agriculture began to grow faster. This was reflected in, for example, the rate of increase in the gross irrigated area rising from about 1 million hectares per annum in the pre-Green Revolution period to about 2.5 million hectares per annum during the 1970s. Also, between 1960–61 and 1970–71 the number of electric and diesel pumpsets increased from 421,000 to 2.4 million, tubewells increased from 90,000 to 460,000 and tractors from 31,000 to 140,000. Also, consumption of chemical fertilizers, nitrogen, phosphorus and potassium, increased from 306,000 metric tonnes in 1960–61 to 2,350,000 in 1970–71. Most of this increase occurred in the second half of the period.

The results of this new strategy began to be witnessed within a short period. Between 1967–68 and 1970–71 foodgrain production rose by 35 per cent. Again, between 1964–65 and 1971–72 aggregate food production increased from 89 to 112 million tonnes, calculated to be a 10 per cent per capita increase. Net food imports fell from 10.3 million tonnes in 1966 to 3.6 million tonnes in 1970, while food availability increased from 73.5 million tonnes to 99.5 million tonnes over the same period. It has been estimated that 'but for the new agricultural strategy India would have to import a minimum of about 8 to 10 million tons of wheat yearly at a cost of $600 to 800 million'.[2] Food availability continued to increase sharply to 110.25 million tonnes in 1978 and 128.8 million tonnes in 1984, putting an end to India's 'begging-bowl' image. By the 1980s, not only was India self-sufficient in food with buffer food stocks of over 30 million tonnes, but it was even exporting food to pay back earlier loans or as loans to food-deficit countries. It was this comfortable situation which enabled India to successfully deal with the severe and widespread droughts of 1987 and 1988 without large-scale foreign help as was needed in the mid-1960s. By the end of the 1990s, foodgrain production in India was nearly 200 million tonnes, up from 51 million tonnes in 1950–51, a growth rate of about 3 per cent, ahead of the high population growth rate of 2.1 per cent.

A major impact of the Green Revolution strategy was that through increases in agricultural yields India was able to maintain, once again, the high rate of agricultural growth achieved since independence. The average rate of growth achieved between 1949–50 and 1989–90 was about 2.7 per cent per annum. In the pre-Green Revolution period, 1949–50 to 1964–65, about 51 per cent of the growth in agricultural output was accounted for by increase in area (which grew at 1.61 per cent per year) and 49 per cent by increase in yield (which grew at 1.5 per cent per year), that is, both area and yield increases were equally important in maintaining growth levels. Once the possibilities of area increases reached saturation point rapid yield increases became necessary if a similar growth rate was to be maintained. This is what the Green Revolution strategy succeeded in doing. Between 1967–68 and 1989–90 about 80 per cent of the growth of agricultural output was explained by increases in yields per acre (which grew at 2.5 per cent per year) while increase in acreage (which grew only at 0.26 per cent per year) accounted for only 20 per cent. In fact, in recent years, virtually the entire output growth has been attributed to increases in yield, as agricultural acreage has remained stagnant and even shrunk.

It must be recognized that, apart from the maintaining of the agricultural growth rates, the critical impact of the Green Revolution was that it generated a rapid increase in the marketable surplus of foodgrains. This aspect has perhaps not been sufficiently highlighted. A number of factors explain why the New Agricultural Strategy generated large marketable surpluses; the fact that the initial breakthrough in food production occurred in the relatively developed regions in north-western India and parts of southern India where food consumption levels were already high meant that a large proportion of the additional output was marketed; the use of labour per unit of output tended to decline, creating a marketable surplus from the rural areas to the extent that the proportion of the output which had to be set aside for consumption by labour declined; and the fact that output increases occurred mainly as a result of yield increases and not increases in acreage led to a fall in the need for foodgrain as seed per unit of output.

It was the marketed surpluses as a result of the Green Revolution (and not any unprecedented rise in aggregate all-India growth rates) which enabled internal procurement of food by the government and the building up of large food stocks. The food requirements generated by a strategy of rapid industrial development, the rapidly growing urban and general population and the periodically food-deficit areas could now be met internally. The liberation from dependence on PL-480 or other imports for the above was a major step in the direction of self-reliant independent development for India.

However, doubts about the New Agricultural Strategy began to be expressed from the very early stages of its implementation. One persistent argument had been that by concentrating resources on the regions that already had certain advantages the Green Revolution strategy was further accentuating regional inequality. Clearly, the solution to such fears lay in spreading the Green Revolution further and not opposing it per se. The research of scholars like G.S. Bhalla show that instead of promoting further inequality, the Green Revolution has over time actually spread to large parts of the country bringing prosperity to these regions.[3] In the first phase of the Green Revolution, 1962–65 to 1970–73, an all-India compounded growth rate of 2.08 per cent per year was achieved but it was mainly the result of sharp increases in yield in wheat in the north-western region of Punjab, Haryana and western Uttar Pradesh, which grew at a much faster rate than the average, Punjab registering a stupendous rate of 6.63 per cent. In the second phase, 1970–73 to 1980–83, with the extension of HYV seed technology from wheat to rice, the Green Revolution spread to other parts of the country, notably eastern Uttar Pradesh, Andhra Pradesh, particularly the coastal areas, parts of Karnataka and Tamil Nadu and so on. Regions like Maharashtra, Gujarat, Andhra Pradesh now grew much faster than the all-India growth rate of 2.38 per cent per year. The third phase of the Green Revolution, 1980–83 to 1992–95, showed very significant and encouraging results. The Green Revolution now spread to the erstwhile low-growth areas of the eastern region of West Bengal, Bihar, Assam and Orissa, with West Bengal achieving an unprecedented growth rate of 5.39 per cent per annum. Other regions, particularly the southern region and Madhya Pradesh and Rajasthan of the central region grew rapidly as well. In fact, for the first time, the southern region registered a higher rate of growth than the north-western region. By the end of the third phase, the coefficient of variation of the output growth levels and yield (per hectare) levels between the various states fell substantially compared to earlier decades. This period, therefore, saw not only a marked overall (all-India) acceleration of the growth of agricultural output touching an unprecedented growth rate of 3.4 per cent per year, but also witnessed a much more diversified growth pattern, considerably reducing regional inequality by increasing the spread of rural prosperity.

In the early stages of the Green Revolution, particularly the early 1970s, a considerable opinion emerged that the Green Revolution was leading to class polarization in the countryside. It was argued that rich peasants and capitalist farmers were getting strengthened partly at the expense of the small peasants, tenants, etc., who, unable to access the modern inputs, were being pushed into the rank of the landless, that is, a process of de-peasantization was in progress. Further, the mechanization of agriculture was displacing labour, leading to increasing unemployment and a fall in wages of agricultural labour. In other words, on the whole, a process of relative immiseration of the rural poor and for some sections even absolute immiseration was taking place, creating conditions for agrarian unrest and revolt. 'The Green Revolution will lead to the Red Revolution' was the catchy slogan doing the rounds in some circles in the late 1960s and early 1970s.

Later events and recent scholarship has shown most of these misgivings were unfounded, as were the reservations about regional inequality. From the very beginning of the initiation of the New Agricultural Strategy there was an awareness that steps would have to be taken to ensure that the poor farmers could access the benefits of the new technology and the agricultural labourers' interests were protected. (It may be noted that the immediate, though somewhat alarmist, warning signals put out by sections of the Indian intelligentsia regarding the negative effects of the new strategy on the poor perhaps contributed to the early consciousness and efforts to prevent such a denouement.) Shortly after the strategy was fully on course a concerted effort was made once again, as part of the *garibi hatao* campaign launched by Indira Gandhi in the late sixties and seventies, to reach the rural poor, small farmers and the landless. A series of programmes such as the Rural Works Programme (RWP), SFDA, MFAL, Crash Scheme for Rural Employment (CSRE), EGS in Maharashtra, were launched. The SFDA and the MFAL, for example, identified more than a million small farmers and over half a million marginal fanners who were given short-, medium-and long-term loans. Small and marginal farmers were also assisted by government subsidies of 25 per cent and 33.3 per cent of the investments for which they borrowed, respectively. Millions of poor farmers also benefited from the massive increase in institutional credit made available to agriculture, through cooperative societies, land development banks, nationalized commercial banks, the Agricultural Refinance Corporation, etc., with a special effort, which was considerably successful, to see that the credit reached the poorer sections as well.

With all their weaknesses and loopholes these programmes had a considerable cumulative effect. So much so that eminent economist Raj Krishna reported in 1979 that 'small farmers, as a class, command more productive assets and inputs per unit of land than large farmers'.[4] Though the small farmers, with operational holdings of 5 acres or less, cultivated only 21 per cent of the total cultivated area, their share of net irrigated area was 31.4 per cent, of total fertilizer use 32 per cent and of total agricultural credit 33 per cent. The new Green Revolution technology proved to be not only scale neutral but appears to have evolved an inverse relationship between scale and productivity. Small farmers applying more inputs per unit of land compared to large farmers were able to produce 26 per cent of the value of agricultural output with 21 per cent of the land.

The Green Revolution, far from pushing the small farmer into the ranks of the landless, actually enabled him to survive. With the adoption of the new technology, improved seeds and other agricultural inputs, the small farmer became relatively more viable and did not have to sell out to the large farmer in distress. Studies such as those of G.S. Bhalla and G.K. Chadha have confirmed this phenomenon.[5] In fact, the share of the large landowners operating 25 acres or more in the total number of holdings and in the total area cultivated has consistently declined over the years since independence. And the number of holdings and the area controlled by the marginal, small and medium landowners has remained stable or risen over the years. The Green Revolution notwithstanding, India has remained a country dominated by small and medium farmers. In 1980–81, cultivators operating holdings of 25 acres or less constituted nearly 98 per cent of the total operational holdings, cultivating 77.2 per cent of the total area, and cultivators operating holdings of 10 acres or less constituted 88.5 per cent of the total operational holdings, cultivating 47.5 per cent of the total area.

Tenants and sharecroppers, who did not have security of tenure, were perhaps the only losers. These sections came under pressure as rents and land values rose rapidly in areas where the Green Revolution spread. Also, in these areas the owners tended to get rid of the unprotected tenants in order to resume self-cultivation with hired labour and modern equipment. 'Secure' tenants and sharecroppers were, however, like landowning small peasants, beneficiaries of the new technology.

Fears of the Green Revolution leading to increasing rural unemployment because of labour-displacing mechanization proved to be baseless. On the basis of a field trip made as early as February 1969 in Punjab, Wolf Ladejinsky (who advised General MacArthur in planning land reforms in Japan during the period of Allied occupation after the war and after that was closely associated with land reforms in Taiwan, South Vietnam, Nepal, Indonesia, the Philippines and India) reported that with the spread of the new technology 'the demand for casual labour has increased and so have wages and the landless labourer is somewhat better off than in the past'.[6] The 'victims' of tractorization were bullocks not labour. The net impact of tractorization, taking into account increase in cropping intensity etc., was an increased demand for labour. The fear that indiscriminate mechanization in the next, post-tractorization phase, such as large-scale introduction of combine harvesters and threshers would lead to displacement of labour also does not appear to have materialized on a significant scale in any part of the country till today. In Punjab, for example, the number of agricultural labourers is said to have trebled between 1961 and 1981, while the number of landless agricultural households declined. The additional demand for labour was met through large-scale migration of labour from the poorer districts of eastern Uttar Pradesh and Bihar.

It has been argued, however, that in the later phases of the Green Revolution the *rate* of increase in employment in agriculture, which accompanied agricultural growth, tended to slacken, that is, the employment elasticity of output growth declined. The complaint, however, was about the failure to generate sufficient additional employment. There was no question of any displacement of labour.

Besides, the general experience of the Green Revolution in region after region—Punjab, Haryana, coastal Andhra, Maharashtra, Tamil Nadu, etc.—has been that apart from the growth in agricultural employment, it has generated non-agricultural rural and semi-urban employment, through the development of agro-industries, rapid increase in trade and warehousing of agricultural produce and agricultural inputs like fertilizers and pesticides, massive growth of the transport industry, manufacturing of a large range of farm implements and other inputs, heavy demand for repairs and servicing of trucks, tractors, electric and diesel pumps and other modern agricultural equipment and machinery and so on. Since over time almost all the agricultural machinery and equipment was produced indigenously, mechanization in agriculture created urban factory employment. Also, the increase in rural incomes following the Green Revolution led to increased demand for masons, carpenters, tailors, weavers, etc. in the rural areas and for factory-produced consumer durables from transistor radios, watches, cycles, fans, televisions, washing machines, motorcycles, sewing machines to cars and air conditioners. Since the rural demand for some of these commodities began to exceed the urban demand, forcing their manufacturers to turn towards the countryside, its impact on generating urban employment is not inconsequential. It is significant that Punjab saw a striking increase of about 50 per cent in urban employment between 1971 and 1981, partly reflecting the impact of development in agriculture in the non-agricultural sector.

However, all the employment generated by the Green Revolution was still not sufficient to meet the employment requirements of the rapidly growing population, a large proportion of which lived in the countryside. Urgent short-term and long-term steps were therefore necessary to deal with this situation. Here, too, the Green Revolution proved critical. The surplus stocks of foodgrain that became available as a result of the agricultural breakthrough made it possible to launch employment-generating poverty alleviation programmes on a considerable scale, particularly in the agriculturally backward areas. As the agricultural expert and policy-maker C.H. Hanumantha Rao put it:[7]

> From about 20 million person-days of employment generated in the mid-1960s, the employment generated under such programmes in the country as a whole amounted to 850 million person-days in 1988–89. These employment programmes, together with the income generated under the Integrated Rural Development Programme (IRDP), seem to make up for about half the deficiency in employment generation in agriculture in the post-green revolution period . . . These programmes were made possible because of the increased availability of foodgrains from internal procurement.

The Green Revolution did, however, contribute to an increase in inequality in the countryside. But the poor too benefited in absolute terms though their well-to-do neighbours did far better relatively. Yet, pursuing a strategy which was more 'equitable' and 'politically correct' but left the rural poor, already living at the edges of survival, worse off would be cruel. Some of the earliest reports of the impact of the New Agricultural Strategy, such as those of Daniel Thorner based on field visits to coastal Andhra, Thanjavur in Tamil Nadu, parts of Haryana, western Uttar Pradesh, etc., in 1966 and 1967–68 and those of Ladejinsky from Punjab in 1969 confirm that, while inequity increased, the poor including the small peasant and the landless agricultural labourer benefited. Real wages of agricultural labour consistently rose in areas where the Green Revolution spread. Increase in wages in the high-growth areas, such as Punjab, would have been much sharper but for the migration of labour from low-wage areas of Bihar and Uttar Pradesh But then not only were the migrant labourers beneficiaries of considerably higher wages, the wage levels in the areas they came from also tended to rise. Interstate disparities in agricultural wages began to decline from the mid-1970s, partly because of the migration of labour from the backward regions to the Green Revolution areas.

In summary, then, the Green Revolution had a major impact on rural poverty levels through its impact on food availability, decline in relative prices of food (the most important item of expenditure for the poor), generating of agricultural and non-agricultural employment, rise in wages and so on. The link between the spread of agricultural growth or the Green Revolution in an area and the fall in the numbers of the rural population living below the poverty line in that area is now widely accepted and can be seen to be operating in a large and growing part of the country. With the majority of the Indian population still dependent on agriculture the critical importance of spreading the Green Revolution type of development as an anti-poverty measure has been widely recognized. (The slowing down in recent years of public investment in irrigation and other infrastructure, which is critical for the spread of rapid agricultural growth, has been widely criticized for this reason.)

The Green Revolution, therefore, has not spawned any 'Red Revolution' in the countryside. Peasant protest and even peasant militancy has been on the rise but then these are not movements of the lowest strata demanding a systemic overthrow but of small, medium and large peasants who are beneficiaries of the system and want more via higher prices for their produce and lower input costs through state subsidy. In fact, over the years the political clout of these sections has increased and the governments of the day have felt compelled, to a greater or lesser degree, to make concessions to them, which were often not economically viable. Most states, for example, provide electrical power for agricultural purposes at prices far below the cost of production, with some states like Punjab providing it free! Such developments have in the long run adversely affected the overall health of the Indian economy including that of agriculture.

A major and pressing issue that has surfaced in recent years relates to the question of environmental degradation and the long-term sustainability of agricultural growth. The negative environmental impact of excessive use of chemical fertilizers and pesticides, as well as the plateauing of the growth rates in areas using such technology over a long period, such as Punjab, has been well-documented. The excessive withdrawal of groundwater for irrigation, which is taking place in many Green Revolution areas without adequate recharging of the subsoil aquifers, is also environmentally unsustainable. However, there are no easy answers to this problem. While agricultural growth with this technology is throwing up problems, absence of agricultural growth throws up other critical environmental problems apart from the obvious economic and political ones. It has been argued that in India the ecological degradation occurs *mainly* due to the extension of cultivation to the marginal and sub-marginal dryland and to deforestation and it has also been noted that 'across different states in India, the extension of areas under cultivation and the denudation of forests seems to be high *where the progress of yield-increasing technology is slow*',[9] and the poor are forced to depend on marginal lands, village commons and forests, etc. The renowned agricultural expert M.S. Swaminathan, has estimated that to produce the current level of foodgrains output with the pre-Green Revolution yields per hectare of wheat and rice would require an additional 80 million hectares of land, that is, it would require an impossible increase of about 66 per cent in the existing cultivable area![10] Clearly, yield-increasing technology has been critical for forest-saving in a situation where India's forest cover has depleted to dangerous levels.

Given this situation, any blind opposition to agricultural growth with the existing modern technology would be unsustainable and counter-productive. However, it has become necessary to make a major effort in educating the farmers so that excessive and improper use of chemical fertilizers and pesticides, wasteful irrigation practices, etc., are checked and they are acquainted with the necessity of retaining biodiversity and of learning from traditional methods of retaining the ecological balance while using modern technology. Partly, the answer lies in the direction of further scientific breakthroughs, particularly in the area of biotechnology. It is felt that top priority needs to be given to research in this frontier area, if India is to achieve sustainable growth with self-reliance in the emerging world context today, as she has been able to do in the past with the Green Revolution technology.

Agrarian Struggles Since Independence

The years since independence have seen agrarian struggles of enormous variety, ranging from the legendary Telangana peasant movement and the PEPSU tenants' movement which continued from the pre-independence years to the Naxalite or Maoist movement in the late 1960s and the 'new' farmers' movements of the 1980s. Interspersed in between are many lesser-known struggles, such as the Kharwar tribals' movement in Madhya Pradesh and Bihar in 1957–58, the Bhils' movement in Dhulia in Maharashtra from 1967–75, or the Warlis' struggle led by the Kashtakari Sanghatna headed by the Marxist Jesuit Pradeep Prabhu since 1978. The SSP and PSP launched a land grab movement in 1970, as did the CPI. In Punjab and Andhra Pradesh, peasants protested against betterment levies imposed for covering costs of irrigation schemes, for better prices for crops, and other similar issues. The CPI set up the first nationwide agricultural labour organization, Bharatiya Khet Mazdoor Union, in Moga in 1968. In Tanjore and Kerala, movements of agricultural labour and tenants took place, as did numerous others all over the country.[1] The trajectory of these movements in many ways maps the process of agrarian and social change since independence. A shift is discerned from immediate post-independence concerns bequeathed by colonialism and feudalism to issues arising out of the Green Revolution and other processes of agrarian change including the aspirations aroused by the struggles for and policy of land reform. Constraints of space do not permit an exhaustive account of these struggles; the choice has inevitably fallen on the more dramatic ones, while many quieter stories must await their turn.

In anticipation of independence and the accompanying changes in agrarian relations, the period between 1945 and 1947 witnessed a sharp increase in agrarian struggles all over the country. Some of these, such as Tebhaga in Bengal and the Canal Colonies tenants' movements in Punjab were disrupted by the rising tide of communalism that preceded and accompanied Partition. But in two areas, both located in princely states undergoing the process of integration into India, the movements continued into the post-independence years. One was the Telangana area of Hyderabad state and the other the Patiala area of PEPSU. Both were led by Communists and provide important insights into their politics at the time.

Telangana Peasant Struggle

The Telangana or Telugu-speaking area of Hyderabad state ruled by the autocratic Nizam had been experiencing political opposition since the late 1930s under the influence of nationalist and democratic organizations such as the State Congress and the Andhra Mahasabha. From the early 1940s, the Communists emerged as a major force and when the ban on the CPI was lifted by the British in 1942 due to their pro-war line, they quickly expanded their influence and established their control on the Andhra Mahasabha. The peasants in Telangana suffered extreme feudal-type oppression at the hands of jagirdars and deshmukhs, some of whom owned thousands of acres of land. The Communists began to organize the peasants against the hated forced grain levy imposed by the government, and veth begar or forced labour extracted by landlords and officials. From 1945, helped along by a few incidents in which the Communists heroically defended the poor peasants, the peasant movement began to spread rapidly.

The Nizam of Hyderabad was among the very few rulers who refused to join the Indian Union at independence in the vain hope, encouraged by Pakistan and some British officials, that he could hold out and stay apart The people of the state grew restless at his delaying tactics and started a movement for integration under the leadership of the State Congress. Camps were set up on the borders of Hyderabad with Maharashtra, coastal Andhra, etc., and arms were also sent in to help the resisters withstand the attacks of the Razakars, armed gangs of Muslim militia let loose on the predominantly Hindu population. The Communists participated actively in the anti-Nizam, pro-integration movement, and it is in this phase, August 1947 to September 1948, when they rode the anti-Nizam pro-India wave, that they registered their greatest successes, establishing a firm base in the Nalgonda, Warangal and Khammam districts. Landlords and officials mostly ran away to the towns, leaving the field free for the Communists in the villages. The Communists organized the peasants into gram sabhas and formed guerrilla bands or dalams, for attacking Razakar camps and protecting villages. Armed mostly with slings, sticks and stones and later crude country guns they established control over a large number of villages (the numbers mentioned by them are 3,000), and used the opportunity to reorder land relations. Lands that had been taken over by landlords in lieu of debt claims in large numbers during the Great Depression of the 1930s were returned to the original owners, government-owned uncultivated waste and forest land was distributed to the landless, wages of agricultural labour were sought to be increased, and women's issues such as wife-beating were also taken up. As confidence grew, 'ceilings' on landlords' land were declared, first at 500 acres and then at 100 acres, and the 'surplus' land distributed to landless and small peasants. It was found that the greatest enthusiasm was for recovering lands lost to landlords in living memory, followed by occupation of government waste and forest land. Occupation of the landlords' surplus land, even when it was offered in place of land lost to the landlord but which could not be restored because it had in the meantime been sold to some other small peasant, was not really popular with peasants. Clearly, they believed strongly in their claim to their own ancestral land and even to uncultivated land but felt little claim to the landlords' land even when it was surplus land. They also probably calculated quite wisely that they had a greater chance of retaining land to which they had some claim or to which nobody else had a claim (and there was also a customary traditional sanction for claim of ownership of the person who brought uncultivated wasteland under cultivation). In fact, this is what happened after the movement declined. Peasants were able to by and large hold on to these categories of lands, but not to the 'surplus' lands.[2]

On 13 September 1948, after having waited for more than a year for the Nizam to see the writing on the wall, and once the anti-Nizam resistance movement had shown clearly what the people desired, the Indian army moved into Hyderabad. The people greeted it as an army of liberation and within days the Nizam and his troops surrendered. The army then moved into the rural areas to clear out the Razakars and was greeted enthusiastically by peasants. However, the Communists in the meantime had decided that they were not going to give up their arms and disband their guerrilla bands but were going to fight a liberation war with the pro-imperialist, bourgeois-landlord Nehru government. As a result, the dalam or guerrilla squad members were told to hide in the forests and attack the Indian army just as they had the Razakars. They seemed to have not noticed that this army was a modern, well-equipped force with high morale unlike the hated Razakars armed with medieval weapons. An unnecessary and tragic conflict ensued with the army successfully flushing out activists from villages in a few months, but in the process causing great suffering to thousands of peasants. Communist activists who had hidden in the forests continued to make efforts to re-establish links and build new bases among the tribes in the forests, but with diminishing success. Officially, the movement was withdrawn only in 1951, once the CPI changed its line after endless debates and a visit by its leaders to Moscow, but in effect only a few comrades remained in hiding in forests by then. Many, perhaps around 500, had died and about 10,000 were in jail.

The government was quick to respond to the issues raised by the movement. The Jagirdari Abolition Regulation was laid down in 1949 itself, and the Hyderabad Tenancy and Agricultural Lands Act was passed in 1950. Over 600,000 tenants covering over one-quarter of the cultivated area were declared 'protected' tenants with a right to purchase the land on easy terms. Land ceilings were also introduced in the mid-1950s. It was also found that land reforms were much better implemented due to the high level of political consciousness of the peasants. Landlords who returned after the movement collapsed were not able to go back to the old ways. They often agreed to sell land at low rates, were subject to pressure for higher wages, did not try very hard to recover peasants' own lands or wastelands, but only the 'surplus' lands. The movement had broken the back of landlordism in Telangana, but this had already been done as part of the anti-Nizam, pro-integration liberation struggle, when their position as leaders of the popular upsurge provided Communists the opportunity to articulate radical peasant demands as well. The costly adventure thereafter was not dictated by the imperatives of the peasant movement but was entirely a consequence of misguided revolutionary romanticism, of which some Indian Communists appeared to be enamoured.

Patiala Muzara Movement

The muzara or tenants' movement that was going on in Patiala (the largest princely state in Punjab, that had become notorious for its repressive and rapacious maharaja) at independence had its origins in the late nineteenth century. Biswedars (the local term for landlords), who earlier had only some mafi claims or revenue-collecting rights, due to their growing influence in the administration, succeeded in claiming proprietary status (imitating the pattern in British India where zamindars or revenue collectors with customary rights only to retain a share of the revenue had been made into landowners) and relegated the entire body of cultivating proprietors of roughly 800 villages, comprising one-sixth the area of the state, to the position of occupancy tenants and tenants-at-will. The new tenants regarded the new landlords as parvenus, who had no *legitimate* right to the land which had belonged to the tenants for generations, and not in the manner in which a traditional tenantry might regard their old, established, feudal landowners, whose right to the land had acquired a certain social legitimacy by virtue of its very antiquity.

The grievance festered, but the opportunity for expression came only with the new wave of political awareness brought by the national movement and its associated movements such as the Akali and the Praja Mandal movements in the 1920s. But the repressive atmosphere in Patiala made any political activity extremely difficult, and it was only in the late 1930s with the change in the political atmosphere brought about by the formation of Congress ministries in many provinces that it became possible for a movement to emerge. By then, Communists were quite active in the peasant movement in the neighbouring British Punjab, and they soon emerged as the leading force in the muzara movement as well.

From 1939, a powerful movement emerged and from 1945 it escalated into an open confrontation between muzaras and biswedars, with the state intervening mainly to institute cases of non-payment of batai (rent in kind) and criminal assault. Numerous armed clashes took place at different places, some over forcible possession of land, others over forcible realization of batai. The Praja Mandal, which spearheaded the anti-Maharaja democratic movement, under the influence of Brish Bhan, who was sympathetic to the Communists and the tenants' cause, extended support. This gave strength to the tenants as the Praja Mandal had the weight of the Congress behind it.

With the coming of independence, Patiala joined the Indian Union, but made no moves to grant responsible government. The Maharaja, in fact, isolated by the opposition of all political groups, launched severe repression on the muzaras, leading to appeals to the Ministry of States in Delhi by the Praja Mandal on behalf of the tenants. The repression decreased after the formation of the PEPSU in July 1948, a new province comprising the erstwhile princely states of Punjab.

However, with the state unable to assert its authority, the situation was increasingly beginning to resemble that of a civil war in which the contending classes or political groups were left, by and large, to settle the issue between themselves as best as they could. Increasingly, as some landlords began to use armed gangs, the necessity arose for the movement to resist this armed onslaught by organizing its own armed wing. The decision to organize an armed volunteer corps was given a concrete form by the formation in 1948 of the Lal Communist Party, by Teja Singh Swatantar and a breakaway group of Punjab Communists, mostly belonging to the 'Kirti' group which originated in the Ghadr movement and had always had an uneasy relationship with the CPI.

Thus, by the end of 1948, this small band of armed men was in place, whose duty was to rush to the aid of muzaras who were threatened with physical, especially armed, assault by the biswedars and their organized gangs. The fear of the 'armed force' helped to keep biswedars in check. However, quite contrary to popular notions, and Communist mythology, the size of this 'armed force' was never more than 30 or 40 people, the largest estimate being 100. This armed force was also not meant to take on the forces of the state, as was clearly shown by the Kishangarh incident in January 1949, in which four members of the armed force lost their lives. Anticipating an assault by the government forces, since a policeman had died in an earlier clash, the Communist leaders had wisely decided to send away the main body of the force, maintaining only a token presence so that the people did not feel abandoned. Dharam Singh Fakkar and others who were arrested in this incident were acquitted after a defence was organized by the left-wing Congressmen led by Brish Bhan.

The situation changed radically with the formation of a new, purely Congress ministry in 1951, in which Brish Bhan was deputy chief minister and his group had a strong presence. An Agrarian Reforms Enquiry Committee was set up to make recommendations and, till such time as the legislation could be enacted, the PEPSU Tenancy (Temporary Provision) Act was promulgated in January 1952 which protected tenants against eviction. In the meantime, the general elections intervened, and the Congress failed to secure a majority on its own in PEPSU. Now was the chance for the three Communist legislators to pay back some of the debts they owed to Brish Bhan and his group, but they chose instead to support Rarewala, the Maharaja's uncle, on the specious plea that they secured some minor reduction in compensation to be paid to biswedars. Other accounts suggest a deal by the CPI (with whom the Lal Communist Party had merged) with the Akalis in Punjab for seat-sharing in the elections.

Rarewala's ministry also collapsed without passing the agrarian legislation, and it was the introduction of President's Rule that brought about a qualitative change in the situation, as the President issued the PEPSU Occupancy Tenants (Vesting of Proprietary Rights) Act (1953). Under this act, occupancy tenants could become owners of their land by paying compensation amounting to twelve times the land revenue, an amount which (given the wartime and post-war inflation and the fact that land revenue continued to be assessed at the pre-war rates) was none too large. This legislation, though it did not meet fully the Communists' demand of transfer of proprietary rights without compensation, was obviously found acceptable by the tenants, and no further resistance was reported.

The Communists continued, however, to condemn the new agrarian legislation as inadequate because the biswedars' lands were not being confiscated without compensation. This resulted in their growing isolation from the peasants, a process that was also furthered by their desertion of their erstwhile comrades-in-arms in the muzara movement and the Praja Mandal, the left-wing Congress group led by Brish Bhan. In the long run, the Communists were also the losers in this game, because they were too weak to struggle effectively on their own against the gradual ascendancy of the Akalis and other communal and semi-communal and right-wing groups. This was most poignantly expressed by an 85-year-old grassroots Communist worker to the authors in 1981: 'These people for whom we fought so hard do not even offer us a drink of water these days.'[3]

Naxalite Peasant Movement

Naxalbari, West Bengal

On 2 March 1967, the first non-Congress United Front (UF) government was sworn in West Bengal, comprising the CPI, CPM, and Bangla Congress, a breakaway group from Congress. It decided to expedite the implementation of land reforms. Harekrishna Konar, veteran CPM peasant leader, as land revenue minister announced a programme of quick distribution of surplus land among the landless and an end to eviction of sharecroppers. He also called for peasants' initiative and organized force to assist the process of implementation. This raised expectations among the poor but also frightened many middle and small owners that their land would be given to sharecroppers. There were many problems with distribution of land, however, as much of it was under litigation, and, once in office, the CPM could not ignore the legal constraints. Besides, verification of claims, adjusting of rival claims, grant of pattas, was a time-consuming process, which the party was only now about to learn. Some comrades, however, had other ideas, and had no desire to learn. Among these was the group in Naxalbari.

The Naxalbari area of Darjeeling district in north Bengal had been organizing sharecroppers and tea estate labour, mostly to the Santhal, Oraon and Rajbansi tribal communities, since the 1950s. The sharecroppers worked for jotedars or landlords under the 'adhiar' system, in which the jotedars provided the ploughs, bullocks and seeds and got a share of the crop. Disputes over shares followed by evictions were commonplace and increased with the coming of the UF government because of the fear that sharecroppers would be given the land. Tea garden labour also often worked as sharecroppers on tea garden owners' paddy lands, which were shown as tea gardens to escape the ceiling laws on paddy lands.

Charu Mazumdar was a major leader of this area and it had been clear for some time, at least since 1965, that his ideas about agrarian revolution and .armed struggle, apparently based on Mao Zedong's thoughts, were different from the official CPM position. He not only did not believe that land reform was possible through legal methods, but argued this path only deadened the revolutionary urges of the peasants. To be politically meaningful, land had to be seized and defended through violent means. To concretize their ideas, he and his associates, Kanu Sanyal and the tribal leader Jangal Santhal, organized a peasants' conference under the auspices of the Siliguri subdivision of the CPM in Darjeeling district only sixteen days after the UF government had come to power. They gave a call for ending of landlords' monopoly on land, land distribution through peasant committees and armed resistance to landlords, the UF government and the central government. According to some claims, all the villages were organized between April and May 1967. Around 15,000 to 20,000 peasants became full-time activists, it is said, and peasants' committees formed in villages became the nuclei of armed guards, who occupied land, burnt land records, declared debts cancelled, delivered death sentences on hated landowners, and set up a parallel administration. Bows, arrows and spears were supplemented by whatever guns could be seized from landlords. Hatigisha, Buraganj, and Chowpukhuria under Naxalbari, Kharibari and Phansidewa police stations respectively were the reported rebel strongholds.

CPM leaders could easily see that the Naxalbari peasants were being led into a suicidal confrontation with the state, of which Communists were now a part. The CPM could not remain in the government and sanction the action of the Naxalbari comrades. Persuasion was tried first, and Harekrishna Konar went to Siliguri and, according to his version, got the leaders to agree to surrender all persons wanted by the police and to stop all unlawful activities and to cooperate in the legal distribution of land in consultation with local peasant organizations. The local leaders denied any agreement and, anticipating repression, began to incite the peasants against the police. After this, things took their predictable and inexorable course, with a vicious circle of attacks on police, police reprisals, further clashes, and so on. The CPM was in an unenviable position, trying for some time to steer a middle course between support for rebels and police repression, and making further attempts at conciliation by sending a cabinet mission of the UF government. It appears from some sources that the peasants did want to negotiate, but were brushed aside by Charu Mazumdar. The CPM had to ultimately condemn and expel the dissident leaders or resign from the government. It chose the former and this triggered the process of the coming together of the extreme left forces, first into a committee to help the Naxalbari peasants, and later in the CP(ML).

Meanwhile, repression had its effect, and by July the peasant movement was over and most of its activists and leaders including Jangal Santhal in jail. The Naxalite movement then remained only in the towns with students as its main force, and it came increasingly to be characterized by street warfare between armed gangs of Naxalite and CPM or Congress youth supporters. A far cry from the romantic visions of peasant revolution!

Srikakulam, Andhra Pradesh

But in faraway Srikakulam, another group of romantic revolutionaries claiming to be inspired by Mao Zedong were about to lead another group of tribals into a suicidal confrontation with the Indian state. Strangely, it never occurred to them to ask the Naxalbari tribal peasants what they thought of a leadership that used them as guinea pigs for experiments with revolution and pushed them, armed with only bows and arrows and spears, to face a modern police force. The Srikakulam tribals, mostly illiterate, living deep in forests, with little exposure to the outside world, had no way of knowing about the tragedy of Naxalbari when they began to enact their own.

Srikakulam, the northernmost district in Andhra Pradesh, bordering on Orissa, was among the least developed. The local tribal population, comprising the Jatapu and Savara tribes, had been organized by Communists working in the Parvatipuram, Palakonda, Patapatnam and Kottur areas since the early 1950s. From 1957–58 to 1967, a movement that organized tribals into Girijan Sanghams and Mahila Sanghams had secured many gains, including restoration of land illegally taken over by non-tribal moneylenders and landlords, wage increases, better prices for forest produce, reduction of debts, and free access to forests for timber for construction of houses and other daily needs. Tribals had gained in self-confidence and participated in rallies in nearby towns with enthusiasm. There is no evidence that there was any push from within the tribals or Girijan (forest people) towards greater militancy or use of violence.

As in Naxalbari, extremist dissident CPM leaders, who were unhappy with the party line, decided to shift over to a line of armed struggle, guerrilla warfare, and later, much more than in Naxalbari, annihilation of individual 'class enemies'. Inspired by Naxalbari, but ignoring its experience, the movement began well after Naxalbari had been suppressed. Beginning in November 1967, it reached an intense mass phase between November 1968 and February 1969. Girijans armed with bows and arrows and stones and sometimes crude country guns chased away police parties that came to arrest activists. Communist revolutionaries roamed the villages asking the people to form village defence squads (dalams) and get whatever arms they could. In April 1969, with the decision at the national level to form the CP(ML), a new party of extreme left activists, a fresh turn was taken with emphasis shifting from mass line to guerrilla action and individual annihilation. According to government sources, about forty-eight people were annihilated by the extremists; the rebels claimed about double that figure. These included landlords, moneylenders, police and forest officials. Inevitably, repression too intensified from November 1969 and by January thirteen leaders were killed and several arrested. By mid-June 1970, a massive police operation was launched in which 1,400 were arrested. On 10 July 1970, V. Satyanarayana and Adibhatla Kailasam, the two major leaders were killed, and that brought the movement to an end. Feeble attempts were made by some Maoist factions to revive the movement from 1971 onwards but, by 1975, these seem to have died out. Groups of Maoist youth continue even today in remote, backward pockets, often inhabited by tribals or very poor low-caste cultivators and agricultural labourers, in Andhra Pradesh, Bihar and Madhya Pradesh, trying to build their model of revolution. But now this effort appears to have violence as its sole motif.

'New' Farmers' Movements

The farmers' movements burst onto the national political stage in 1980 with the road and rail roko agitation in Nasik in Maharashtra led by the Shetkari Sangathana of Sharad Joshi. Nearly 200,000 farmers blockaded road and rail traffic on the Bombay–Calcutta and Bombay–Delhi route on November 10 demanding higher prices for onions and sugarcane. Thousands were arrested, two killed in police firing, and prices of onions and cane enhanced. The leader was an ex-UN official, Sharad Joshi, who articulated the ideology of the movement in terms of India versus Bharat or urban, industrial India versus rural, agricultural Bharat. In 1986, in Sisauli village in Muzaffarnagar district of Uttar Pradesh, Mahinder Singh Tikait, a middle-school-educated, medium-size peasant, Jat by caste, and head of the Jat caste panchayat or khap, presided over a gathering of lakhs of villagers before which the chief minister of Uttar Pradesh had been forced to appear in person to announce his acceptance of their demand for reduction of electricity charges to the old level. These were only the more dramatic moments in what had emerged in the 1980s as a widespread grassroots mobilization of rural dwellers. Led by the Vivasayigal Sangam in Tamil Nadu, the Rajya Ryothu Sangha in Karnataka, Bharatiya Kisan Union (BKU) in Punjab and Uttar Pradesh, Khedut Samaj and Kisan Sangh in Gujarat and the Shetkari Sangathana in Maharashtra, farmers in thousands and lakhs, at different times for different demands, stopped traffic on highways and train routes, withheld supplies from cities, sat on indefinite dharnas at government offices in local and regional centres, gheraoed officials, prevented political leaders and officials from entering villages, especially at election time, till they agreed to support their demands, refused to pay enhanced electricity charges, and interest on loans, and cost of irrigation schemes, resisted confiscation proceedings in lieu of debt, and even de-grabbed confiscated goods and land.

The basic understanding on which the movements rested is that the government maintains agricultural prices at an artificially low level in order to provide cheap food and raw materials to urban areas, and the consequent disparity in prices results in farmers paying high prices for industrial goods needed as inputs into agriculture and receiving low returns for their produce. As a result, farmers are exploited by urban interests, and are victims of internal colonialism. They need not pay back loans or charges for infrastructure costs as they have already paid too much and are in fact net creditors. This basic philosophy is articulated in different forms by all the leaders and organizations; it provides the legitimacy for the movement in the farmers' consciousness, along with the traditional propensity of the Indian peasants to resist what they perceive as 'unjust' government demands. (The most common issue on which resistance surfaced among the landowning peasants in the colonial period was payment of one or another government demand. This is also true of peasants in other parts of the world.[4])

These 'new' farmers' movements that have attracted much media and political attention, especially in the 1980s, have focussed mainly on demanding remunerative prices for agricultural produce, and lowering or elimination of government dues such as canal water charges, electricity charges, interest rates and principal of loans, etc. This has brought on them the charge that they are mainly vehicles for demands of rich or well-to-do agriculturists most of whom are beneficiaries of post-independence agrarian development, including the Green Revolution, and have little or no room for the concerns of the rural poor. This is hotly denied by the leaders and ideologues of the movement, who point as proof to the diverse social base of the movement among medium and small peasants, as well as some other features such as inclusion of demands for higher minimum wages for agricultural labour and the insertion of women's and dalits' issues, for example, by the Shetkari Sangathana of Maharashtra. The fact, however, remains that, apart from the Shetkari Sangathana, no other organization has really gone beyond what can be described as landowning peasants' issues. These organizations have shown scant concern for the landless rural poor or rural women. It is, however, true that they are broad based among the peasantry and not confined to the upper sections, as alleged by some critics, for smaller-holding peasants are as much interested in higher prices and lower rates of government dues since they too produce for the market and pay government dues.

While there is often justice in the demands for higher prices and better facilities, the basic rural versus urban or Bharat versus India ideology is essentially flawed, and can only lead the farmers into a blind alley of mindless resistance and state repression of which inevitably the smaller peasants are likely to be the chief victims. In fact, this is what happened in Tamil Nadu in 1981 where a very strong movement was killed by state repression brought on by refusal to repay loans and consequent forcible confiscation by government. All efforts by Naidu to revive the movement he had

nursed for almost two decades, including the founding of the
Toilers and Peasants Party in 1982, came to nought and he died
a disappointed man in 1984. It appears that the lessons of the
Tamil Nadu movement were not learnt by others, else one would
not have come across suicidal decisions such as the one taken in
1984 to ask the Punjab peasants to reduce foodgrain production,
in order to hold the country to ransom, a decision mercifully never
implemented for other reasons. Leading movements is as much
about knowing when and where to stop as it is about knowing
when and how to begin, as Gandhiji knew so well. But despite
many claims by the leaders to be following in Gandhi's footsteps,
there is little evidence of lessons learnt from him, especially about
the awesome responsibility of leadership.

These movements are often referred to as 'new', the suggestion
being that they are part of the worldwide trend of 'new' non-class
or supra-class social movements which have emerged outside the
formal political party structures, examples being the women's and
environmental movements.[5] Let us examine the claim. As stated
above, apart from the Shetkari Sangathana, no other organization
has shown signs of really trying hard to become a social movement.
The Karnataka movement has been concerned with the environment,
and Tikait to some extent with social reform, but little else. This
does not bring them into the category of 'new' social movements
defined as non-class movements, concerned with women's issues or
child labour or environmental issues that are outside the framework
of the traditional party structure. The 'new' farmers' movements
are not all that new as similar demands were made by peasant
organizations earlier as well, but without the regressive rural versus
urban ideology. In Punjab, for example, a big movement was
launched by the Kisan Sabha under the CPI's direction against the
imposition of a betterment levy or irrigation tax in 1958. Demands
for remunerative prices were made by all peasant organizations and
most political parties or peasant lobbies within parties. The emergence
of Charan Singh and the BLD in Uttar Pradesh in 1967 was widely
regarded as the coming of age of a landowning peasantry that had
benefited from post-independence agrarian change. Movements of
Backward Castes were also seen as part of the same process.

The other ground on which 'newness' is asserted is that these
movements are not linked to political parties, whereas earlier
organizations were wings of parties. This is only partially correct.

While it is true that none of the organizations were started by political parties, it is also true that over time they have inexorably got linked to politics. The Tamil Nadu organization was the first to openly become a party and this led to the disarray in the All-India BKU which Naidu, the Tamil Nadu leader, had helped found, as distance from political parties had been enunciated as a basic principle of the organization. The Karnataka Ryothu Sangha (KRS) put up candidates in elections. The Punjab BKU has retained the character of a farmers' lobby more than any other, but did link up with Akalis when it suited them. The Shetkari Sangathana was involved in politics from the 1984 Lok Sabha elections when it put out a list of forty-eight candidates, one for each constituency in Maharashtra, who were most likely to defeat the Congress candidates. It asked its followers to vote for them. From 1987, Sharad Joshi openly allied with V.P. Singh in his anti-Congress mobilization and in 1989 was rewarded with a cabinet-level post to formulate a new agricultural policy. Joshi's links with V.P. Singh led to his estrangement with Tikait, and hopes of an all-India unity of farmers were dashed on 2 October 1989 when Tikait and his men almost dragged Joshi and other leaders off the stage at the Boat Club lawns after making them wait for two hours in front of a crowd of lakhs that had collected for what was to be a joint rally. But Tikait's loud protestations about staying off politics began to sound hollow once his not-so-clandestine support to the BJP in the wake of the hotting up of the Ayodhya issue in 1990 became apparent. The Gujarat Kisan Sangh's links to the BJP are well known.

Ideologically as well, the movement is deeply divided. Sharad Joshi now favours liberalization, with the farmer being linked to the world market. The KRS is dead against multinationals and has been carrying on protests against their entry. Organizational and ideological unity have thus eluded the movement. Also, there has been a distinct loss of momentum in the 1990s and, by the index of longevity, the movement may be ranked quite low. The movement no doubt touched a vital chord among peasants by drawing attention to the neglect and backwardness of rural areas, its problem remained that instead of focusing on redressal, it began to pit peasants and villagers against town dwellers in a fratricidal war.

Revival and Growth of Communalism

Communalism and communal parties and organizations are very much a part of today's political environment. The communal appeal is used on a large scale for electoral mobilization. For the last nearly three decades the country has been regularly racked by a spate of communal riots. Communalism is today the most serious danger facing Indian society and polity. It is undermining secularism, has become a menace to the hard-won unity of the Indian people and threatens to unleash the forces of barbarism.

To discuss the problem of communalism in independent India, the terms secularism and communalism first need to be defined. Secularism, basically, means separation of religion from the state and politics and its being treated as a private, personal affair. It also requires that the state should not discriminate against a citizen on grounds of his or her religion or caste.

Communalism is an ideology based on the belief that Indian society is divided into religious communities, whose economic, political, social and cultural interests diverge and are even hostile to each other because of their religious differences. Communalism is, above all, a belief system through which a society, economy and polity are viewed and explained and around which effort is made to organize politics. As an ideology it is akin to racialism, anti-Semitism and fascism. In fact, it can be considered the Indian form of fascism. Further, the relationship between communal ideology and communal violence needs to clarified. The basic thrust of communalism as an ideology is the spread of communal ideas and modes of thought. Though communal violence draws our attention to the communal situation in a dramatic manner, it is not the crux of the problem. The underlying and long-term cause of communal violence is the spread of the communal ideology or belief system.

Communal violence usually occurs when communal thinking that precedes it reaches a certain level of intensity and the atmosphere is vitiated by the building up of communal fear, suspicion and hatred. Communal ideology can thus prevail without violence but communal violence cannot exist without communal ideology. In other words, communal ideology and politics are the disease, communal violence only its external symptom. Unfortunately, the presence of communal ideology as a prelude or prologue to communal violence is generally ignored; awareness of communalism registers only when violence breaks out. Communalists are also, therefore, primarily interested in spreading the communal belief system and not necessarily communal violence. In fact, the major purpose of those who inspire and organize communal violence is not genocide but to create a situation which communalizes the masses.

Secularism: Its Roots

It was one of the great triumphs of the Indian national movement that, despite the Partition of India and the barbaric riots that accompanied it, the Indian people accepted secularism as a basic value, enshrined it in the constitution, and set out to build a secular state and society. The legacy of the freedom struggle, Gandhiji's martyrdom, Nehru's total commitment to secularism and the active support extended to Nehru by Sardar Patel, Maulana Azad, C. Rajagopalachari and other leaders in the struggle against communalism, led to its becoming dominant in the 1950s. Communal parties made a poor showing in the elections of 1952, 1957 and 1962 and for years remained a marginal force in Indian politics. Consequently, people became complacent and came to believe that economic development and spread of education, science and technology would automatically weaken and extinguish communal thinking.

Communalism, they believed, would gradually disappear from the Indian scene. It was not realized by the people or their leaders that communalism can have passive and active phases, depending on circumstances, but that it would not disappear without an active struggle. Moreover, even while communal politics lay dormant, communal ideologues continued their work and communal organizations such as the RSS, Jan Sangh, Jamaat-i-Islami, Muslim League, Akali Dal and various Christian communal groups in Kerala continued to function. Communalism became active in the 1960s, gaining in strength as seen in the rising communalization of Indian society. In the late 1950s itself, there was a series of communal riots. The number of persons killed in riots increased from 7 in 1958 to 41 in 1959 and 108 in 1961. In particular, the riot in Jabalpur in 1961 shook the whole nation. Nehru reacted by immediately forming the National Integration Council. The Chinese aggression in 1962 aroused feelings of national unity among all sections of the people and communal sentiments had to retreat. But this interlude proved to be short-lived.

Once again, in the mid-1960s, the disruptive forces of communalism were on the upswing in Indian politics and large sections of the common people became susceptible to communalism and casteism. The Jan Sangh increased its strength in parliament from 14 in 1962 to 35 in the general elections of 1967. It participated in coalition ministries in several North Indian states and began to attract considerable support in the rural areas of Uttar Pradesh, Madhya Pradesh and Rajasthan. The incidence and severity of communal riots also increased, the number of riots being 1,070 in 1964, 520 in 1969 and 521 in 1970; the number of those killed being 1,919, 673 and 298 respectively. There was some respite from communalism and communal riots from 1971 to 1977. The number of communal riots did not exceed 250 in any of those years and the number of killed did not exceed 1,000, as Indira Gandhi consolidated her power in the parliamentary election of 1971. In elections, the Jan Sangh's strength in parliament was reduced from 35 in 1967 to 22 in 1971. The Bangladesh war at the end of 1971 also gave a major blow to both Hindu and Muslim communalisms. However, communalism and communal violence began to once again increase from 1978 and has become endemic since then, assuming alarming proportions.

A worrisome aspect of the growth of communalism and communal violence has been its widespread character. It has covered almost all parts of the country and all the major cities, embracing even areas such as Kerala, Tamil Nadu, Andhra Pradesh, West

Bengal and Orissa which were earlier believed to be immune to riots. Communal riots have also spread to villages and involved all religious groups. Increasingly, communal violence has been pre-planned and well organized and of longer duration. Some of the communal riots have lasted weeks and even months. Also, rioters have been provided with ample funds, firearms and other destructive materials. It is interesting that when, during the Emergency from 1975 to 1977, all the major leaders and most of the activists of the RSS, Jan Sangh and Jamaat-i-Islami were arrested, communal violence, as well as the level of communal propaganda, came down drastically, for few were left to organize riots or to promote communal hatred. On the other hand, during the period of the Janata government, there was an increase in communalism and communal violence because of the strong influence of the RSS and Jan Sangh in the Janata Party and the government. So strong was the momentum given to communalism during this period that even the return of Indira Gandhi to power in 1980 failed to check its growth. Communalism in the country has remained quite strong since then.

Characteristics of Communalism

Like all ideologies and politics, communalism has a concrete social base or roots; it is the product of and reflects the overall socio-economic and political conditions. But this happens in a distorted manner, defeating any accurate diagnosis of the situation, its causes and remedies. Thus, communalism does not reflect any social truth: what it declares to be the social reality is not the social reality; what it declares to be the causes of social discontent are not the causes; and what it declares to be the solutions of the social malady are not the solutions—in fact it is itself a social malady. Communalism is, thus, no answer to any of the problems leading to its generation and growth. Instead, it undermines the real struggle for changing social conditions. While the society and polity of India after independence have been secular, the logic of the socio-economic system has continued to provide favourable soil for the spread of communalism. Especially important in this respect have been the social strains which have arisen out of the pattern of economic development. Indian economic development after 1947 has been impressive but the problems of poverty, unemployment, and inequality arising out of colonial underdevelopment have been only partially tackled, especially in the context of the population explosion. These problems breed frustration and personal and social anxiety among the people and generate unhealthy competition for the inadequate economic and social opportunities. In fact, capitalist development has generated sharp and visible economic inequality and the position in this regard has been worsening over the years. Though, overall, there are greater economic opportunities available for the people, there is far greater inequality than before in regard to access to them. Also, the aspirations of the people are rising faster than their possible fulfilment. The soil for the growth of communalism (and casteism) is thus always ready.

The social dilemma described above has affected the middle classes or the petty bourgeoisie with particular force. In recent years, the petty bourgeoisie have been faced with the constant threat of unemployment and adverse socio-economic conditions. Moreover, its growth has constantly outpaced economic development. The situation is further aggravated by the fact that after independence the spread of education, the pattern of social change and rapid population growth have led millions of peasant and working-class youth to look for jobs in the cities and in administration and to joining the ranks of the petty bourgeoisie, at least as far as aspirations are concerned. This line of analysis also explains why communalism remained relatively dormant till the early 1960s. Independence and the three Five-Year Plans did open up a wide range of opportunities for the middle classes because of the Indianization and expansion of the officer rungs of the armed forces and private firms, immense expansion of the administrative apparatus, the rapid development of banking, trading and industrial companies, the growth of school and college education and other social services, and the phenomenal expansion in the training and recruitment of engineers, doctors and scientists. But this initial push to middle-class employment was exhausted by the mid-1960s. Besides, the pattern and rate of economic development were such that they failed to generate large-scale employment in the industrial and commercial sectors and also placed limits on the expansion of social services. The petty bourgeoisie was now back to a situation of job scarcity, competition, rivalry and discontent. Moreover, changes in agrarian relations threw up new strata of rich and middle peasants and capitalist farmers, that is, rural bourgeoisie and petty bourgeoisie, who provided a fertile ground for the germination and spread of communal and casteist ideologies, movements and parties.

Communalism was, however, no answer to the economic problems of the petty bourgeoisie; it did not serve the interests of this social stratum in any way. Unable to understand the reasons for their economic or social distress, growing social and economic disparity and insecurity, their anxiety tended to take a communal or casteist form. The other religious or caste groups were seen as the cause of their problems.

The communal problem did not, however, lie merely in the economic realm. For several generations Indians have been undergoing a social transition; they have been losing their old world without gaining the new. The process accelerated after independence. Old, traditional social institutions, solidarities and support systems—of caste, joint family, village and urban neighbourhood—have been rapidly breaking down. The new institutions and solidarities of class, trade unions, Kisan Sabhas, youth organizations, social clubs, political parties and other voluntary associations have, on the other hand, made tardy progress and have not been able to take their place to a significant extent. In this situation, many turn to communal organizations as an alternative focus of unity and solidarity. Also, old values and social mores, which cemented together different segments of society have been disappearing under the hammer blows of the profit motive, capitalist competitiveness, careerism, and the philosophy of the winner takes all and let the devil take care of the hindmost. The result has been a moral and cultural vacuum which is highly conducive to ideologies based on fear and hate. Individuals, groups and parties are taking the quick and easy route to political power by arousing communal sentiments and passions.

Another aspect of the communal problem has been the inevitable exhaustion of the political idealism generated by the national movement which inspired the people, particularly the youth, and gave impetus to secular ideas. After 1947, people needed a new unifying, anti-divisive goal or vision which could generate hope for the future, kindle healthy national feelings, inspire and unite them in a common nationwide endeavour, and strengthen the secular content of society. Unfortunately, such a vision has been lacking, especially after the 1970s. There is, thus, every danger that without radical social change and the sway of an inspiring developmental and egalitarian ideal, communalism and communal-type movements may succeed in destroying India's unity and hampering all efforts at social and economic development. It is, therefore, necessary to eliminate the social conditions which favour the growth of communalism.

A warning may, however, be sounded in this context. Great care has to be exercised in making a social analysis of communalism, which should be based on serious empirical and theoretical research. At present, it is not easy to assign communal motives to various classes except in the case of the petty bourgeoisie. There is, for example, so far no evidence that the capitalist class *in India backs communalism. But, of course, it cannot be asserted* that it would never do so in the future.

Long-term and Short-term Causes

Just as we distinguish between communalism as an ideology and communal violence, we have to distinguish between the long-term causes of communalism and the immediate and short-term causes of communal riots and other forms of communal violence. The causes of communal violence have often been conjunctural; they have been local, specific and accidental, such as some minor religious issue or dispute, or teasing of a girl, or even a violent quarrel between two persons belonging to different religious groups. These causes have invariably become operative only when there has been prior communalization of the area concerned. These conjunctural causes at the most act as sparks which light the communal fire for which ground had already been prepared by the communal groups, parties and ideologues. There are also a few other factors which have been important in communal violence. Communal violence has often actively involved the urban poor and lumpen elements whose number has grown rapidly as a result of lopsided economic development and large-scale migration into towns and cities from rural areas. Rootless, impoverished and often unemployed, millions live in overcrowded areas without any civic facilities in terms of health, education, sanitation and drinking water. Their social anger and frustration, fed by horrid living conditions, makes them easy victims of the purveyors of communal hatred and finds expression in spontaneous violence and loot and plunder whenever a communal riot provides the opportunity. In more recent years, criminal gangs engaged in lucrative illegal activities, such as smuggling, illicit distillation and sale of liquor, gambling, drug pushing and kidnapping have used communal riots to settle scores with their rivals.

An important feature of Indian politics and administration in the last few decades has been the growing laxity of the state apparatuses, especially the police, in their treatment of communal violence. After all, the state alone possesses the instruments to successfully counter communal violence, and immediate and effective state action is the only viable way of dealing with it. However, in recent years, the administration has seldom acted firmly and decisively and in time and with the full force of the law and order machinery. Communal violence is, moreover, invariably preceded by the intensive spread of different forms of inflammatory propaganda. Yet, seldom has action been taken even under the existing laws against the instigators of communal hatred and organizers of communal violence. Also, communalists and communal ideology have been making serious inroads into the state apparatuses over the years. Consequently, many of the officials at different levels have betrayed communal tendencies and encouraged, overtly or covertly, communal forces. In particular, communalized sections of the police force have often made the situation worse by their inaction and sometimes even partisanship in dealing with communal riots.

Another major factor in the growth of communalism since the 1960s has been the political opportunism towards communalism practised by secular parties, groups and individuals. They have often permitted the intrusion of religion into politics and have tended to vacillate and retreat in the face of the communal onslaught. They have compromised with and accommodated communal forces for short-term electoral gains or as a part of the policy of anti-Congressism. And, far worse, they have sometimes associated and entered into alliance with communal parties. Congress was the first to do so by allying with the Muslim League in Kerala in the early 1960s. In turn, Communist parties allied with the Muslim League in Kerala and Akali Dal in Punjab in the late 1960s, justifying their action by declaring that minority communalism was understandable and democratic, and even justifiable, and in any case not as bad and dangerous as majority communalism. In 1967, the Socialists and other secular parties and groups did not hesitate to join the communal Jan Sangh first in seat adjustment in elections and then in forming non-Congress governments in several states in North India. In 1974–75, Jayaprakash Narayan permitted the RSS, Jan Sangh and Jamaat-i-Islami to become the backbone of his movement of 'Total Revolution' against Congress and Indira Gandhi. In 1977, the Jan Sangh became a part of the Janata Party. In November 1989 elections, the Janata Dal, under the leadership of V.P. Singh, formed an indirect electoral alliance with the BJP and then formed a government at the Centre with its support. The Communist parties sanctioned both steps, though indirectly.

The soft approach towards communal parties and groups has had the extremely negative consequence of making them respectable and legitimizing communalism. This policy has tended to whittle down one of the major contributions of the national movement and the Nehru era, of making communalism a dirty word even when failing to root it out. The secularists have also in recent years tended to pander to communal sentiments through all types of concessions. For example, Rajiv Gandhi did so by reversing the Supreme Court judgement in the Shah Bano case, through a constitutional amendment, and by opening the gates of the disputed Ayodhya mosque-temple in 1986. V.P. Singh did so by declaring the Prophet's birthday a holiday in his Red Fort speech on Independence Day in 1990. These concessions to Muslim and Hindu communalisms did not lessen communal tensions but only aggravated them.

It is, however, significant that, despite their crass opportunism, most of the Indian political parties and intellectuals—whether of the right, left or Centre—have themselves not been communal. This has so far prevented the rapid growth of communalism and has kept India basically secular. The Indian state has also been basically secular and opposed to communalism so far despite being ruled by the National Democratic Alliance (NDA) from 1999 to 2004 in which the BJP was the dominant power. However, the quality of the secularism of the Indian state and most of the political parties has had many weaknesses and has, in fact, seldom been very sturdy. Still, a major saving feature of the Indian social and political situation has been the absence of active state support to communal ideology and communal forces. Though till 1998, the state was lacking in the political will to deal firmly with communalism and communal violence, it had not promoted communal ideology through its myriad channels, from textbooks and mass media to administrative measures. Our experience in the colonial period, the experience of Pakistan and Bangladesh, and the experience of fascist movements in Italy, Germany, Japan and Spain (where they succeeded), on the one hand, and France and the US (where they failed) on the other, clearly indicate that communal and communal-type movements cannot prevail without state support or at least the neutrality and passivity of state power. A few points may be made parenthetically at this stage. First, a sharp distinction has to be made between communal parties and parties which are basically secular but adopt an opportunistic attitude towards communalism. A communal party is one which is structured around communal ideology. Such parties have since their inception promoted communal thinking and often whipped up communal passions. Though the secular-opportunist parties have tended to vacillate and retreat in the face of communal onslaught, it is still very important that they have themselves not been communal. This fact has been a major obstacle in the burgeoning forth of communalism. Second, it is to be noted that there is no difference between majority (Hindu) communalism and minority (Muslim, Sikh, Christian) communalisms—they are merely variants of the same communal ideology and are equally dangerous. However, while minority communalisms can end up in separatism, as Muslim communalism did before 1947 and Sikh communalism did in Punjab in recent years, majority communalism can take the form of fascism. Also, in recent years, as also in the past, different communalisms have fed on and supported and strengthened each other with dangerous implications.

Hindu and Muslim Communalisms

Since the early 1960s, communalists in India have been taking recourse to religious issues to impart passion and intensity to their politics. Muslim communalism flourished in the 1940s in colonial India on the basis of the cry of Islam in danger, but Hindu communalism remained weak in India and a marginal force in Indian politics as it had not been able to appeal to religion or arouse religious passion. Hindu communalists raised the cries of Hindus or their culture being in danger but were not able to arouse Hindus emotionally as effectively as Muslim communalists. This was because of several factors: Hinduism is not an organized religion—it is not based on the sanctity and authority of a single sacred book or a hierarchical priestly class. Hindus do not have one God or one set of beliefs—consequently there is immense religious diversity among them—in fact, there are no strict rules determining who is a Hindu. Hindus also have a long tradition of religious tolerance and broad-mindedness. It was also not easy to convince Hindus, who constituted the large religious majority in India, that their religion was in any danger. Hindu communalists found that without the strong emotional appeal to religion or a *religious issue the progress of communal politics was tardy*. Taking a leaf out of the pre-1947 Muslim League politics, they began from the late 1970s to grope for a religious issue around which to develop their politics. Such an opportunity was presented to them in the early 1980s in the Babri Masjid (mosque)–Ram Janmabhoomi (birthplace of Ram) issue, which could inflame Hindus, for Ram occupies a unique place in India. He is the incarnation of the values that a Hindu, in fact an Indian, cherishes. His name touches the hearts and minds of millions. Over the years, the BJP and its sister organizations, the Vishwa Hindu Parishad (VHP) and Bajrang Dal, all carefully nursed by the RSS, succeeded in using this issue and its religious appeal to gain influence with a large number of Hindus all over the country and to weaken their resistance to communalism. A brief history of the controversy follows.

A mosque was built by a governor of Babur at Ayodhya (in Uttar Pradesh) in the early sixteenth century. Some Hindus claimed in the nineteenth century that it was built over a site which was the place where Ram was born and where a Ram temple had existed. But the issue did not take a serious turn till December 1949 when a communal-minded district magistrate permitted a few Hindus to enter the mosque and instal idols of Sita and Ram there. Sardar Patel, as the home minister, and Jawaharlal Nehru condemned the district magistrate's action, but the Uttar Pradesh government felt that it could not reverse the decision. However, it locked the mosque and barred it to both Hindus and Muslims. The situation was more or less accepted by all as a temporary solution for the period of the dispute in the court. The resulting quiet lasted till 1983 when the VHP started a whirlwind campaign demanding the 'liberation' of the Ram Janmabhoomi, which would entail the demolition of the mosque and the erection of a Ram temple in its place. The secular parties and groups did not do anything to counter the campaign; they just ignored it. Suddenly, on 1 February 1986, the district judge, probably at the prompting of the Congress chief minister of Uttar Pradesh, reopened the mosque, gave Hindu priests its possession, and permitted Hindus to worship there. As a result, religious and communal passions were aroused leading to communal riots all over the country; sixty-five persons were killed in Uttar Pradesh towns alone. Soon, powerful Hindu and Muslim communal groups led by the VHP and the Babri Masjid Action Committee were ranged against each other. The Hindu communalists demanded the demolition of the mosque and the construction of a Ram temple on its site; the Muslim communalists demanded the restoration of the mosque to Muslims. The secular and nationalist-minded persons, parties and groups now suddenly woke up to the enormity of the problem. Even then the issue was allowed to fester so that both communalisms got consolidated. Clearly, over the years, certain necessary steps should have been taken. In a country with centuries of history there are bound to be problems of this nature—there are bound to be prolonged perceived periods and instances, real or otherwise, of injustice, oppression, suppression, discrimination, and so on, just as there is the immense tradition of tolerance, of the development of a composite culture, of happy common living. But, clearly, the present cannot be used to set right what went wrong in the past.

The initiative soon passed into the hands of the Hindu communalists. In 1989, the VHP, keeping in view the impending Lok Sabha elections, organized a massive movement to start the construction of a Ram temple at the site where the Babri mosque stood. As a part of that objective, it gave a call for the collection of bricks, sanctified by water from the river Ganges, from all over the country—villages, towns and cities—to be taken to Ayodhya. The Lok Sabha elections took place in an heightened communal atmosphere. There was also an indirect alliance of the Janata Dal and its left allies with the BJP, which increased its strength from two in 1984 to eighty-six in 1989. Moreover, the new government at the Centre formed by V.P. Singh relied on outside support, of the CPI and CPM as well as the BJP. To consolidate its increased popular support, the BJP now officially adopted as its objective the construction of the Ram temple at Ayodhya. To popularize the objective, it organized in 1990 an all-India rath yatra headed by its president, L.K. Advani. The yatra aroused fierce communal passions and was followed by communal riots in large number of places. Thousands of BJP–VHP volunteers gathered at Ayodhya at the end of October 1990, despite the Uttar Pradesh government, headed by Mulayam Singh Yadav, banning the rally. To disperse the volunteers and to prevent them from harming the mosque, the police opened fire on them, killing and injuring over a hundred persons.

The BJP thereafter withdrew its support to the V.P. Singh government, resulting in its fall. Elections to a new Lok Sabha were held in 1991. The BJP with 119 MPs emerged as the main opposition to Congress. It also formed governments in four states— Uttar Pradesh, Madhya Pradesh, Rajasthan and Himachal Pradesh. To consolidate and further enhance its political gains, the BJP– VHP organized a huge rally of over 200,000 volunteers at the site of the mosque on 6 December 1992, with the major leaders of the two organizations being present. To allay the fears of injury to the mosque, the BJP chief minister of Uttar Pradesh, Kalyan Singh, had given an assurance to the Supreme Court that the mosque would be protected. The assurances had been repeated by the BJP leaders in parliament. In spite of these assurances, the BJP–VHP volunteers set out to demolish the mosque with hammer blows, while BJP leaders looked on. The central government also lay paralysed. The entire country was shocked by this event which had other disastrous consequences. Communal riots, the worst and the most widespread since 1947, broke out in many parts of the country, the worst hit being Bombay, Calcutta and Bhopal. The riots in Bombay lasted for nearly a month. In all more than 3,000 people were killed in the riots all over India. Even though the good sense of the Indian people has since asserted itself and communal passions have abated, the Babri Masjid–Ram Janmabhoomi issue has continued to fester like a running sore in the country, and the communal forces have continued to grow politically. In the 1996 elections to the Lok Sabha, the BJP won 161 seats, while in 1998 and 1999 it succeeded in winning 182 seats and forming governments with the help of its allies. The biggest blot on the NDA government, led by Atal Bihari Vajpayee, was the communal carnage in Gujarat during 2002 and the failure of the Vajpayee government to suppress it.

This section may be concluded by pointing out that though on the surface the Babri Masjid–Ram Janmabhoomi issue appears to be a religious one, in reality this is not so. In fact, the communalists are not interested in religion; they are interested only in the manipulation and exploitation of religion and religious identity for the communalization of the people for political ends. Religious differences as such are neither responsible for communalism nor its root cause. Communalism is not the same as religious-mindedness. In fact, the moral and spiritual values of all religions go against communal values. It is the intrusion of religion into politics and affairs of the state which is undesirable. As Gandhiji put it in 1942: 'Religion is a personal matter which should have no place in politics.'[1]

Conclusion

Despite the growth of communalism and communal parties and groups in recent years, and being ruled by the NDA under BJP's hegemony, India still is a basically healthy secular society. Even though communalism is perhaps the most serious challenge facing Indian society and polity, it is not yet the dominant mode of thought of the Indian people. Even when the communalists have succeeded in utilizing communalism as the quick and easy route to political power and have won elections, the people who have voted for them have done so to express their discontent with the existing state of political and economic affairs. They have not yet imbibed communal ideology significantly. The Indian people are still basically secular, and the believers in communal ideology constitute a fringe. Even in areas where communal riots have occurred, there does not exist a permanent divide between Hindus and Muslims or Hindus and other minorities. In no part of the country is 'an aggressive majority arranged against a beleaguered minority'. In fact, popular consciousness has posed a major barrier to the spread of communalism to a significant extent in the rural areas and to large parts of urban India. This also explains why communalism, making a beginning in the last quarter of the nineteenth century, has still failed to strike deep roots in large parts of the country and has taken such a long time to acquire even its present strength.

Communalism and the Use of State Power

The assumption of political power for the first time since
independence by an avowedly communal party at the national
level in 1998 was a new experience for the Indian people. The
mask of Gandhian socialism worn in 1980 when the Jan Sangh
was reborn in a new avatar as the BJP had been stripped off in
full public view when the Babri Masjid was demolished on 6
December 1992 by Hindutva-inspired volunteers in the presence of
top BJP leaders. Almost 3,000 people had lost their lives in the
communal violence that followed, and communalization of popular
consciousness had reached new heights.[1] The usual tactic of
whitewashing the crimes of the party by blaming them on 'extreme
elements', and projecting the top leadership as distressed, unhappy,
and shocked at the mayhem was tried once again. When the BJP
came to power in 1998, and then again in 1999, as the leader of
the National Democratic Alliance (NDA), it was to be seen whether
or not the argument that power would mellow the extreme elements,
strengthen the moderates, and thus mainstream the party, was
valid. Or whether the secular stand that it was extremely dangerous
to allow state power in the hands of communal/fascist forces, as
it could and would be used by them to rapidly spread communal
ideology, was closer to reality.

The actual experience was that the communal temperature was
pushed up by the VHP, the Bajrang Dal and the RSS, which had
no intention of being tamed, but, on the contrary, had every
intention of using state power to fulfill their long-cherished desire
of creating a Hindu Rashtra or nation. The ideological agenda of
communalization of education was pursued with great vehemence

by the Minister for Human Resource Development (HRD), Murli Manohar Joshi, who remained true to his RSS affiliations, and was also quite keen to please his RSS mentors. Amid strong protests, including by the leader of the Opposition, Sonia Gandhi, the portrait of V.D. Savarkar, whom the Justice Jiwan Lal Kapur Commision had held guilty of the conspiracy to assassinate the Mahatma,[2] was installed in the Central Hall of parliament, facing the portrait of his victim. Despite the BJP's claim that it had put its communal agenda on the backburner in deference to the sensitivities of its coalition partners, the agitation for the building of the Ram temple at Ayodhya reached its peak in early 2002, notwithstanding the Supreme Court's refusal to allow construction on the disputed site and the surrounding land. The situation got so bad that the prime minister asked the RSS to intervene and persuade the VHP to slow down. This agitation had a direct effect on the communal situation in Gujarat, which witnessed what many observers have called a genocide lasting for close to three months from February 2002. In the following pages we take a closer look at the communalization of education and the tragedy of Gujarat.

Communalization of Education

Despite the fact that the BJP was in power only as part of the NDA coalition, there was no doubt that it would attempt to spread its ideology of Hindutva through every possible means. The RSS, which provided the organizational and ideological ballast to the BJP, was not going to be satisfied with anything less. Political power at the state level had been used consistently in the 1990s to put in place school textbooks which preached the sectarian and divisive view of Indian history and society. The models were already there in books prepared by the Vidya Bharati for the RSS-run Saraswati Shishu Mandirs functioning since the early 1950s. In Uttar Pradesh, Madhya Pradesh, Rajasthan, Gujarat, wherever the BJP came to power, books demonizing Muslims, and describing minorities as foreigners, and valorizing Hindu civilization were made part of the curriculum. The National Council for Education, Research and Training (NCERT) during the period of the Narasimha Rao government had in fact appointed a high-level committee to enquire into the issue of communalization of textbooks and the report of this committee had revealed the grave extent of the problem in various state-level school textbooks.

The focus of the ideological onslaught was on history textbooks, since the heart of communal ideology was the communal interpretation of history. While the RSS/Hindu communal effort to spread a communal interpretation of history had been around for many years, the new and more dangerous trend, after the BJP came to power at the Centre, was the *attempt to use government institutions and state power* to attack scientific and secular history and historians and promote an obscurantist, backward-looking, communal historiography through state-sponsored institutions at the national level. The last time the RSS came close to power at the Centre was when the Jan Sangh had merged with the Janata Party and the Janata Party came to power in 1977. At that time an effort was made to *ban* school textbooks which the NCERT had persuaded some of the tallest historians of India, such as Romila Thapar, R.S. Sharma, Satish Chandra and Bipan Chandra, to write. A countrywide protest, including from within the NCERT and other autonomous institutions, put paid to this attempt and it had to be abandoned.

This time round the lessons of the previous experience were well learnt by the BJP. Anticipating resistance from autonomous institutions like the NCERT, UGC, ICSSR and the ICHR, the government first took great care to appoint those who were willing to serve as its instruments as directors, chairpersons and council members. Having achieved that, the BJP government gave the Education Minister, Murli Manohar Joshi, full backing in implementing the RSS ideological agenda in education. For the RSS combine, there was no pulling back in the ideological sphere unlike what was done in the economic, political and even foreign policy spheres. The demands of the trade union or peasant fronts of the Sangh were often set aside, the Swadeshi Jagran Manch's objections to economic reforms could be essentially ignored but not the RSS agenda in spreading communal ideology.

Murli Monohar Joshi now presided over the systematic destruction of the academic edifice built up painstakingly over decades. The NCERT director introduced a new National Curriculum Framework (NCF) in 2000, without attempting any wide consultation, leave alone seeking to arrive at a consensus. This when education is a concurrent subject (involving partnership between the Centre and the states) and virtually since independence the tradition had been to put any major initiative in education through discussion in parliament and the Central Advisory Board of Education (CABE), a body which includes among its members the education ministers of all states and Union territories. The NCERT arrived at the New Curriculum, which was widely seen by professional academics as introducing the Hindu communal agenda, without any reference to the CABE, thus violating both tradition and procedural requirements.

This was followed by deletions of passages from the existing NCERT history books written by eminent secular historians of the country without any reference to the authors, violating all copyright norms. As mentioned above, these authors had been persuaded by the NCERT on the recommendation of the National Integration Council to write textbooks for children which would correct the existing colonial and communal bias in history books. The deletions were decided not by any recognized committee of professional historians but by the RSS, with the RSS view put on record in a published volume a few months before the NCERT was ordered to carry them out![3]

It was repeatedly claimed that the deletions were in deference to the religious sentiments, especially of minorities. The NCERT director even asserted that he 'would consult *religious experts* before including references to any religion in the textbooks, to avoid *hurting the sentiments* of the community concerned'.[4] This extremely dangerous move was supported by the Education Minister, Murli Manohar Joshi, who stated that 'all material in textbooks connected with religions should be cleared by the heads of the religions concerned before their incorporation in the books'.[5] Once such a veto over what goes into textbooks is given to religious leaders or community leaders, as the government had started doing, it would become impossible to scientifically research and teach not only history but other disciplines, including the natural sciences. Deletions had already been made from textbooks for pointing out the oppressive nature of the caste system in India, presumably because some 'sentiments' were hurt. The dangerous implications of such a practice, especially in a multi-religious country like India, were pointed out by a very wide range of critics.

However, at this point an alarming trend began of branding as anti-national those who did not agree with the kind of interpretations promoted by the Hindu communal forces. The RSS Sarasanghachalak, K.S. Sudershan, called those who were resisting the revisions of the NCERT textbooks 'anti-Hindu Euro-Indians'[6]. Vigilante groups demanded that the historians Romila Thapar, R.S. Sharma and Arjun Dev be arrested. The HRD minister, Murli Manohar Joshi, at whose residence this group had collected, defended the deletions from their books and called for a 'war for the country's cultural freedom'.[7] The minister went one step further and added fuel to this fascist tendency of trying to browbeat or terrorize the intelligentsia which stood up in opposition by branding the history written by these scholars as '*intellectual terrorism unleashed by the left*' which was '*more dangerous than cross-border terrorism*'. He exhorted the BJP stormtroopers to counter both types of terrorism effectively.[8]

There were a lot of protests from the secular forces at this attempt at communalizing the education system. Historians, the secular media and a very wide section of the Indian intelligentsia voiced their protests unambiguously. The government's attempts were resisted with reason and argument. It was pointed out that civilized societies cannot ban the teaching of unsavoury aspects of their past on the grounds that it would hurt sentiments or confuse children or it would diminish patriotic feelings among its children, as the government was trying to do. Nor could India fabricate fantasies to show India's past greatness and become a laughing stock of the world. Should America remove slavery from its textbooks or Europe the saga of witch hunting and Hitler's genocide of the Jews, it was asked? India should stand tall among civilised nations and not join the Taliban in suppressing history as well as the historians.

The argument with the communalists was joined with great persuasion by the Nobel laureate Amartya Sen in his Presidential Address to the Indian History Congress in January 2001. Arguing that attempts to distort Indian history and to give it a narrow sectarian colour obfuscated the truly remarkable aspects of India's past of which any society in the world could be justifiably proud he pointed to 'India's persistent heterodoxy' and its 'tendency towards multi-religious and multi-cultural coexistence' which had important implications for the development of science and mathematics in India. Emphasizing that the history of science is integrally linked with heterodoxy, Sen went on to say that 'the roots of the flowering of Indian science and mathematics that occurred in and around the Gupta period (beginning particularly with Aryabhatta and Varahamihira) can be intellectually associated with persistent expressions of heterodoxies which pre-existed these contributions. In fact Sanskrit and Pali have a larger literature in defence of atheism, agnosticism and theological scepticism than exists in any other classical language.' He went on to say that rather than the championing of 'Vedic Mathematics' and 'Vedic sciences' on the basis 'of very little evidence', 'what has . . . more claim to attention as a precursor of scientific advances in the Gupta period is the tradition of skepticism that can be found in pre-Gupta India—going back to at least the sixth century B.C.— particularly in matters of religion and epistemic orthodoxy'. [9] He could well have added that the tradition of scepticism in matters of religion and epistemic orthodoxy was continued by Mahatma Gandhi, when he argued that, 'It is no good quoting verses from Manusmriti and other scriptures in defense of . . . orthodoxy. A number of verses in these scriptures are apocryphal, a number of them are meaningless.' Again he said, 'I exercise my judgement about every scripture, including the Gita. I cannot let a scriptural text supercede my reason.' [10]

However, despite nationwide protests, particularly from the academia (including the widely respected, more than sixty-year-old, Indian History Congress, the national organization of professional historians) and the media, this process, of what the editor of the *Hindustan Times*, Vir Sanghvi, called the 'Talibanisation' of education, was continued. A new syllabus based on the NCF 2000 was adopted, again without proper procedures being followed. The process culminated in the existing NCERT history books written by eminent scholars (from which deletions were made) being withdrawn altogether and being replaced by books written by people whose chief qualification was their closeness to the Sangh ideology and not recognized expertise in their field of study. The Indian History Congress published a volume called *History in the New NCERT Text Books: A Report and an Index of Errors*. [11] The volume ran into 130 pages just listing the major mistakes and distortions introduced in these books. To quote from its findings:

> Often the errors are apparently mere products of ignorance; but as often they stem from an anxiety to present History with a very strong chauvinistic and communal bias. The

textbooks draw heavily on the kind of propaganda that the so called Sangh Parivar publications have been projecting for quite some time . . . With such parochialism and prejudice as the driving force behind these textbooks, it is clear that these cannot be converted into acceptable textbooks by a mere removal of the linguistic and the factual errors pointed out in our Index . . . These textbooks are therefore beyond the realm of salvage, and they need to be withdrawn altogether.

A major controversy arose when it was discovered that in the first edition of Hari Om's *Contemporary India* for Class X, a book dealing with the twentieth century, Gandhiji's assassination was not even mentioned! When there was a national furore on this question, including in parliament, a reprint edition was brought out with the addition of this bare sentence:

> Gandhiji's efforts to bring peace and harmony in society came to a sudden and tragic end due to his assassination by Nathuram Godse on January 30 1948, in Delhi while Gandhiji was on his way to attend a prayer meeting. (p. 57)

No mention was still made of who Godse was, and of his strong links with the RSS and the Hindu Mahasabha, particularly its leader Savarkar.

That the communalization of textbooks had long-term dangerous consequences was shown by the way communal violence flared up in Gujarat. Activists familiar with Gujarat had been pointing out for some time the extremely objectionable material in school textbooks. For example, children reading the Gujarat State Social Studies text for Class IX would have learnt that minorities are foreigners:

> apart from the Muslims even the Christians, Parsees and other *foreigners* are also recognised as the minority communities. In most of the states the Hindus are in minority and Muslims, Christians and Sikhs are in majority in these respective states.

In the Gujarat State Social Studies textbook for Class X, which virtually eulogizes fascism and Nazism, the children are taught how to deal with these 'foreigners' who are making the Hindus a minority in their own country:

Ideology of Nazism: Like Fascism, the principles or ideologies for governing a nation, propounded by Hitler, came to be known as the ideology of Nazism. On assuming power, the Nazi Party gave unlimited total and all embracing and supreme power to the dictator. The dictator was known as the 'Fuhrer'. Hitler had strongly declared that 'the Germans were the only pure Aryans in the entire world and they were born to rule the world'. In order to ensure that the German people strictly followed the principles of Nazism, it was included in the curriculum of the educational institutions. The textbooks said, 'Hitler is our leader and we love him'.

Internal Achievements of Nazism: Hitler lent dignity and prestige to the German government within a short time by establishing a strong administrative set-up. He created the vast state of Greater Germany. He adopted the policy of opposition towards the Jewish people and advocated the supremacy of the German race. He adopted a new economic policy and brought prosperity to Germany. He began efforts for the eradication of unemployment. He started constructing Public buildings, providing irrigation facilities, building Railways, roads and production of war materials. He made untiring efforts to make Germany self-reliant within one decade. Hitler discarded the Treaty of Versailles by calling it just 'a piece of paper' and stopped paying the war penalty. He instilled the spirit of adventure in the common people.

That in order to maintain the purity and supremacy of the 'Aryan' race millions of Jews were butchered is not even thought worthy of mention.

A generation brought up on glorification of Nazism and trained to think of minorities as foreigners was probably easy to mobilize into acting as stormtroopers for communal/fascist forces and participating in an unprecedented targeting of a minority community, as was done in Gujarat in 2002.

Genocide in Gujarat

'A black mark on the nation's forehead' which had 'lowered India's prestige in the world' is how Atal Bihari Vajpayee, then prime minister of India, described the ongoing violence in Gujarat on

March 2002 in a televised address to the nation in which he also
endorsed the appeal for peace made by an all-party meeting a day
earlier.[12] That the government over which he presided failed to
quell the violence to which he referred is evident from the fact that
it not only continued unabated for almost three months but also
spread to new areas and from towns to villages, in the process
lowering 'India's prestige in the world' even further. When the fury
spent itself, most (unofficial) estimates placed the number of dead
at over 2,000, and the number of refugees in camps at around
200,000.

The gruesome story began on the morning of 27 February at
Godhra, a small town in Gujarat, where 58 people, including 15
women and 20 children, burnt to death in a fire that engulfed a
bogey of the Sabarmati Express. The victims were all Hindus,
karsevaks or volunteers, returning from participating in a yagya
or religious ceremony at Ayodhya. They were part of the thousands
of volunteers being brought to Ayodhya by the VHP, a militant
Hindu organization, as part of its campaign for the construction
of the Ram temple at the site of the Babri Masjid which had been
demolished by a communally aroused crowd on 6 December 1992.
The BJP had promised construction of the temple and now that it
had been in power for over three years, its stormtroopers were
getting restless. This heightened communal feeling was bound to
lead to conflagration sooner or later, and sure enough it did in
Godhra. The actual incident, as has emerged from various enquiry
reports, was of a quarrel between karsevak passengers and Muslim
vendors at the station, probably caused by some taunting of the
Muslims by the Hindu militants. In some reports, it is said that
the Muslims were asked to shout slogans in praise of Lord Ram,
and when they refused, their beards were pulled. The altercation
escalated as word reached the nearby Muslim neighbourhood and
groups of ten or fifteen people rushed towards the train and pelted
stones. The train, however, moved out of the station, but stopped
on its outskirts. At this stage, one of the coaches in which the
karsevaks were travelling caught fire and the tragedy unfolded.

The most popular theory that was current was that the Muslim
mob had poured some inflammable substance into the bogey and
set fire to it. All later forensic reports as well as the U.C. Banerjee
Enquiry Report have shown that this could not have been the case
and that the fire was possibly accidental, or caused by some

inflammable material such as kerosene or diesel being carried in the train itself, and that the thick black smoke reported by all survivors which possibly caused the maximum casualties was due to the rubber vestibule catching fire. But at that time, the anger against 'Muslims' was legitimized by responsible people clearly pointing fingers.

The chief minister of Gujarat, a BJP-ruled state, Narendra Modi, an RSS man, was an ardent votary of Hindutva, the sectarian ideology espoused by the BJP, of which the core was antipathy to Muslims, in the same way as the core of Nazism was antipathy to the Jews. He immediately announced a state funeral for the victims of the fire. The bodies were to be brought to Ahmedabad and the time of their arrival was announced on the radio. Television channels and Gujarati-language newspapers carried pictures of the burning train. The chief minister declared that the attack on the train was organized by Pakistan's Inter-Services Intelligence, thus clearly suggesting that the fire was part of a pre-planned attack by Muslims. The VHP openly put the blame on Muslims, and called for a statewide bandh on 28 February, which also received the support of the government.

On 28 February began a wave of communal carnage which lasted for almost three months. From the beginning, the new pattern that emerged was of large mobs of Hindu youth with saffron bands tied round their heads attacking and looting Muslim neighbourhoods, setting fire to homes, burning people to death and slaughtering them in cold blood, molesting, raping and sexually torturing women, while the police and administration looked the other way or even connived and helped. Considerable evidence surfaced that officials were instructed by the highest political authorities not to intervene to stop the violence. Not surprising then that the violence spread from Ahmedabad and Vadodara, to many more towns and even to villages. At one time, forty towns had to be put under curfew. The pattern, scale and persistence of violence suggests that it was by no means spontaneous. The attackers often had lists of business establishments owned by Muslims which they identified, targeted, looted and burnt by releasing and lighting cooking gas from cylinders they had carried with them. A very large number of religious places, including many of historical value, such as the dargah of Wali Gujarati, a famous Urdu poet, revered by Hindus and Muslims, were destroyed. In the new pattern of communal violence it was noticed that the violence spread to villages, where people who had lived together for generations suddenly became enemies. This led to a large-scale exodus from affected villages. Also, Dalits and tribals were very active participants in the assaults, along with the upper castes.

Many observers have remarked that what distinguished the events of 2002 was that, unlike a typical riot situation in which two groups engage in, usually spontaneous, violence, the assault was one-sided, premeditated, brutal, and supported or facilitated by the state. The terms that have been frequently used to capture the nature of the violence are 'genocide' and 'ethnic cleansing'. No doubt, after the first shock was over, there were also instances of violence being initiated by minority groups in areas where they had numerical preponderance, but this remained a relatively minor phenomenon. The communalization of Gujarati society had clearly reached very far, as social activists had been warning for some time and as testified by the frequent outbreak of communal riots in the previous two decades, when both Hindu and Muslim communalists had been active. Gujarati children had for many years been reading textbooks in which Hitler was a hero and Muslims the villains of Indian history. In 1998, the Hindu communal forces had unleashed widespread attacks on Christians in Gujarat on the plea of preventing conversions, and it was popular knowledge that they saw it as a 'trailer' of the main story which was yet to come. Thus Godhra was in many ways a convenient pretext for putting into action a plan that had been in the making for quite a while.

The Gujarat events shook the conscience of the nation. The national media, print as well as visual, played a sterling role in bringing the truth about Gujarat into the open. The Opposition parties, led by the Congress, put enormous pressure on the Vajpayee government to get the state government to act. The government was obliged to ask the National Human Rights Commission to send a team to enquire into the situation. The NHRC's report was a big blow to the Government, since it held that the Modi Administration failed in its duty to protect the rights of the people of Gujarat by not exercising its jurisdiction over non-state players that may cause or facilitate the violation of human rights.

More blows were to follow. On 29 April, one day before the censure motion tabled by the Opposition was to come up in parliament, Ram Vilas Paswan, the Coal Minister, and a major Dalit leader, resigned from the cabinet, and withdrew his Lok Janshakti Party from the NDA. He said this was in protest against the failure of the Gujarat government in controlling the communal violence and continuation of the state chief minister, Narendra Modi.[13] Further ignominy awaited the prime minister and his party colleagues in the Lok Sabha the following day. As reported in *The Hindu* newspaper on 1 May 2002, 'what became obvious during the course of the speeches, the sparring, and the shouting was that the allies and the parties "friendly" to the National Democratic Alliance were one with the Opposition in their strong condemnation of the continuing murder and arson in Gujarat and their demand for the removal of the chief minister, Narendra Modi'. The National Conference decided to abstain from the voting, and Omar Abdullah, its representative in the NDA government, offered to resign. The TDP leader, Yerran Naidu, and Mamata Banerjee of Trinamul Congress, both allies of the NDA, asked for Modi's ouster. The former prime minister, Chandra Shekhar, charged that the cabinet minister, Uma Bharti of the BJP, had spoken more like a 'Nazi volunteer' than a 'sanyasin', thus implying that the BJP in Gujarat was attempting to do what the Nazis did in Germany. The Samajwadi Party leader, Mulayam Singh Yadav, asked the prime minister: 'How many more bodies have to be counted in Gujarat, and how many more incidents of arson you want before you act?' The issue at hand was 'not the survival of one government or another, but the survival of the nation', he said. The CPI(M) leader, Somnath Chatterjee, who later became Speaker of the Lok Sabha, went so far as to say that Gujarat was witnessing a 'State-sponsored genocide, masterminded by Narendra Modi'.[14]

Intervening in the parliamentary debate, the leader of the Opposition and Congress president Sonia Gandhi, started out by describing in some detail incidents of rape and murder perpetrated in Gujarat. She then proceeded to make the following demands: one, that the Gujarat chief minister, Narendra Modi, should be 'immediately and quickly' removed; two, the state government be put on notice under Article 355; three, a commission of enquiry headed by a sitting judge of the Supreme Court be set up. She also said that the central government must act firmly and promptly to control the situation in Gujarat. She further added that this must include immediate implementation of all the recommendations of the NHRC and other statutory bodies, prompt action against the guilty and a massive rehabilitation and relief programme for the victims.[15]

While speaking of the 'need to move from polarisation to reconciliation, from discord to dialogue, to rebuild Gujarat', Sonia Gandhi questioned Vajpayee's claim that the violence in Gujarat could have been prevented if the Godhra carnage had been condemned in parliament. It was a 'falsehood' that parliament did not condemn it, she said. 'I was the first to condemn the terrible Godhra tragedy in the strongest possible terms on the 27th itself,' she added. But repeating falsehood so that it eventually passed off as truth was a favourite tactic of the RSS and the Sangh Parivar just as it was during those 'obnoxious times in Germany', she said, in a blunt reference to Nazi Germany. She went on to quote from an official BJP document on Vajpayee's Goa speech about Muslims and accused him of 'doublespeak': 'One day he offers sympathy, the next day he condemns the whole community, one day he pleads for tolerance, the next day he plays on divisive prejudices. When the prime minister indulges in doublespeak, what can the nation expect from this Government.' Nevertheless, she said, 'It is still not too late. The situation can still be redeemed.' Appealing to his 'nobler instincts', she called on the prime minister to 'rise above party affiliations and respond to his responsibilities and obligations to the people of India, irrespective of religion and faith'.[16]

The sharp attack in the Lok Sabha was followed up by Sonia Gandhi's speech in Porbandar, Gandhiji's birthplace, in which she alleged that Gandhi's Gujarat was being turned into Godse's Gujarat.[17] The President had already publicly expressed his anguish at the situation a few days earlier.[18] Badly cornered, and faced with the prospect of a defeat in the Rajya Sabha in which the NDA was in a minority, the BJP-led government changed strategy and chose to accept the Opposition-sponsored motion—urging the Centre to intervene effectively in Gujarat under Article 355 of the constitution—under Rule 170, which entails voting. This did not, however, save it from very strong criticism in the upper house, with Lalu Prasad Yadav, Rashtriya Janata Dal (RJD) leader, and former chief minister of Bihar, even suggesting that he 'suspected' the RSS's hand behind the Godhra incident and demanding that Narendra Modi be 'arrested under POTA'.[19]

Deserted by its allies, ridiculed by the Opposition, and faced with a hostile Press and public opinion, the government took the first step as part of a direct central initiative to stem the continuing violence in Gujarat, and appointed Punjab's former Director-General of Police, K.P.S. Gill, as the Security Adviser to the state chief minister, Narendra Modi.[20] Gill had successfully tackled communal incidents during his tenure as the Assam police chief and later effectively curbed terrorist violence in Punjab. The Gujarat government was clearly unhappy with this decision, and initially adopted a posture of non-cooperation. However, it had no choice but to eventually accept the Centre's directive. The situation began to improve thereafter and violence began to subside.

By early July, the Modi government decided that it should go in for early elections to the assembly, presumably to take advantage of the high communal temperature. It declared that the situation was normal, sent Gill back to Delhi, and dissolved the assembly, and asked the Election Commission to organize early polls. But it had not bargained for the fact that the Election Commission, led by J.M. Lyngdoh, an extremely independent and upright civil servant, had a mind of its own. At a meeting held on 16 August 2002, the Commission not only unanimously refused to bend to the Gujarat government's wish and NDA's pressure, but made many observations which amounted to a severe indictment of the Gujarat government and were a major setback for the BJP. It said that the law and order situation in the state was 'still far from normal' and that the 'wounds of communal divide following the riots have not yet healed'. In its view, the return to normality was being delayed by the slow pace of relief and rehabilitation work, as well as by the fact that the guilty were not being arrested and punished and there was a fear of a communal backlash. It said that 'similar feelings are shared by persons from the majority community living in minority-dominated areas. The people have lost confidence in the local police, civil administration and political executive.' What was needed was confidence-building measures, and 'foremost among these would be to arrest and punish the guilty, irrespective of their status and rank for their crimes', it said. Election campaigns by evoking passions would only shatter the fragile peace, it held.

The Commission referred to the report of its nine-member team that visited Gujarat earlier in the month and found that there was still a sense of insecurity among the victims. This was followed up by a visit of the full Commission to Gujarat, so that it could gather first-hand information. What emerged from this visit was extremely disturbing, as it revealed the full extent of the affected areas to be much larger than understood earlier. Out of 25 districts, 20 were 'affected areas'. It quoted the statement of the Additional Director-General of Police, R.B. Sreekumar, that 151 towns and 993 villages, covering 154 out of 182 assembly constituencies in the state and 284 police stations out of 464 were affected by the riots. 'This evidently falsifies the claims of the other authorities that the riots were localised only in certain pockets of the State,' the Commission observed. The Commission said that on-the-spot inspections had revealed that a substantial majority of electors who left their homes and fled from their villages to escape the arson and carnage in the wake of the Godhra massacre of February 27 had not yet returned, hence the electoral rolls could not be updated. Reminding the government that the drought situation in the state was widespread and serious, it wondered, 'which would be a greater priority for the State Government—holding Assembly elections in the midst of drought and thereby disrupting relief work or (doing) relief work'.[21] It would be difficult to find another example in the history of independent India when a constitutional body such as the Election Commission has used such strong language when talking about a state government.

The BJP suffered more loss of legitimacy when the Supreme Court turned down the appeal by the government against the Election Commission's decision. The appeal argued that elections must be held immediately because according to the constitution six months cannot lapse between two sessions of a legislative assembly. The Supreme Court upheld the right of the Election Commission to decide on the date of the elections and said that the six-month rule applied only to an assembly that was alive and not to one that had been dissolved. The Election Commission then announced that the elections would be held in mid-December.[22] Meanwhile, a terrorist strike on 24 September killed roughly thirty people at the famous Akshardham temple in Gandhinagar, further inflaming passions. The elections were held and showed further how deeply divided Gujarat society had become on religious lines.

The BJP won an overwhelming majority of seats and Modi was back as chief minister. Electoral success strengthened the hardliners and whetted their appetite, as is evident from the battle-cry of Praveen Togadia, easily the most aggressive VHP leader, who declared: 'Hindu Rashtra could be expected in next two years . . . we will change the Indian history and Pakistan's geography by then.'[23]

The Gujarat experience in many ways brought out the best and the worst in Indian society and polity. On the one hand there was the continuation of victimization of the Muslims through economic boycott, via refusal of employment and hounding of Muslim-owned businesses. There was also the refusal to take back Muslim residents by villages unless they promised not to pursue cases against them. The recourse to the law was consistently blocked by the police not filing FIRs, not framing charge-sheets, withdrawing cases, etc. Activists were threatened, and sought to be physically intimidated. The families of those who died in the Godhra train tragedy were given Rs 200,000 as compensation but others only Rs 100,00 the distinction being a communal one, as in the former case all the dead were Hindus, whereas in the later instances, the majority were Muslims. The state government first refused to set up refugee camps for victims, and then insisted on shutting down camps to prove that there was normality. The POTA was used to terrorize Muslims by picking up 'suspects' who had supposedly conspired to set fire to the train at Godhra. There was an inevitable ghettoization as a consequence of all these developments, and even middle-class Muslims were forced to gravitate towards mono-religious habitats. Most significantly, there was a pervasive climate of fear, of the state, of the police, of the communal bands that roamed untamed, which only the very brave could defy.

On the other hand there were civil society groups, such as Citizens for Justice and Peace, Anhad, Communalism Combat, Sahmat, and many others, and activists, such as Fr. Cecil Prakash, the lawyer Mukul Sinha, Shabnam Hashmi, Teesta Setalvad and Harsh Mander, who worked fearlessly and tirelessly to give succour and help in getting justice for the affected people. An independent Citizen's Tribunal collected evidence, human rights and feminist groups conducted enquiries, journalists kept public interest alive, and film makers such as Rakesh Sinha produced documentaries and campaigned with them all over the country. A very moving feature film, *Parzania*, was also made.

A major focus of the resistance was to secure legal redress, and the NHRC and the Supreme Court played a sterling role in this process. In May 2003, the NHRC, responding to complaints of threats received by witnesses, asked the Director-General of Police to report on measures taken 'to protect the safety, physical and psychological well-being, dignity and privacy of victims and witnesses'. On 15 March 2004, the Supreme Court conveyed its lack of faith in the state government when it asked the central government to identify key witnesses in nine Gujarat riot cases, and deploy central police or paramilitary forces to protect them. The Supreme Court judgement in the famous Best Bakery case was also a landmark one, for it ordered fresh investigations and retrial outside Gujarat of individuals who had been acquitted in a widely-criticized trial for setting on fire and killing fourteen people at a bakery in Vadodara. A similar retrial outside Gujarat was ordered in the case of Bilkis Yakub Rasool Patel by the Supreme Court. But perhaps the biggest victory for the resistance was the Supreme Court response to the application filed by Amicus Curiae Harish Salve, former Solicitor General of India, stating that of the 4,252 cases registered by the police in connection with the Gujarat violence, nearly 2,100 had been closed. On 17 August 2004, it ordered the state government to set up a panel of senior police officials to review cases where the local police had filed closure reports instead of charge-sheets and asked the Director-General of Police, Gujarat, to report every three months on the progress made by the review committee. It further desired that all acquittals in riot trials be re-examined to see whether reviews could be filed.

Meanwhile, in May 2004, the NDA lost to the Congress-led alliance in the general elections. Most analysts believed that the events in Gujarat contributed significantly to the loss of legitimacy of the NDA government, leading to the defeat in the elections. It certainly helped in rallying the secular forces behind the Congress for they had seen the writing on the wall. This also meant that there were high expectations from the UPA government. A complex situation arose when Narendra Modi was refused a visa by the US for a visit in March 2005, largely as a result of a consistent campaign by US-based secular groups who came together in a Campaign Against Genocide, as well as a resolution by a bi-partisan group of prominent Congressmen and a recommendation of the US Commission on International Religious Freedom. The

UPA government attracted much criticism for taking a legalistic position and protesting against this refusal and even the left was reported to be ambivalent because a supposed national insult was involved. Activists pointed out with great persuasion that Modi had been indicted by some forty reports by all kinds of organizations, and that the refusal of the visa was a victory for all those who had resisted the communal onslaught of the Sangh combine. Further loss of face for the BJP and its friends was in store as the UK followed suit with a refusal of visa! The campaign for the repeal of POTA was only partially successful since it was repealed but not with retrospective effect, and thus those already detained under it could be kept in custody.

The deep mark that the Gujarat genocide has left on India's body politic is far from erased. The BJP continued to rule the state with Narendra Modi at the helm, though factional squabbles within the party contributed considerably to the erosion of his position. Revelations in April–May 2007 of custodial killings and fake encounters involving an alleged underworld Muslim don and his wife by senior Gujarat police officers reminded the nation that all was not well in the benighted province. In Baroda University, in April 2007, an art student was arrested, and his professor who stood up for him dismissed from his deanship, at the behest of Hindu vigilante groups who complained to the vice-chancellor that his painting, which was part of his examination and not for public display, violated their religious feelings. A sting operation by the *Tehelka* magazine, which was shown to shocked viewers on prime time television on 25 October 2007, caught major Hindutva politicians, including the MLA representing Godhra and the lawyer representing the Gujarat government before the Nanavati Commission, boasting and providing gory details about their role in the post-Godhra violence and testifying to the active support of chief minister Narendra Modi.

Hindu communal parties and groups may have been pushed on to the back foot, but they are neither repentant nor defeated. In the Gujarat assembly elections of 2007 Modi was re-elected as chief minister. Gujarat is yet to return to the path of its greatest son, Mohandas Karamchand Gandhi, whose spirit inspires all those who have kept the flame of hope and humanity alive in its darkest days.

Caste, Untouchability, Anti-caste Politics and Strategies

The caste system in India originated about 2,500 hundred years ago. It is prevalent not only among Hindus but also among Sikhs, Christians and Muslims. While it has many aspects, here we are concerned with the aspect of hierarchy, of high and low, of touchable and untouchable, which has provided legitimation for the unequal access to resources, and to the exploitation and oppression of lower castes, besides the discrimination against lower castes by higher castes.

The most obnoxious part of the caste system was that it designated certain groups as untouchables and outcastes, and then used this to deny them ownership of land, entry into temples, access to common resources such as water from the village tank or well. Non-untouchable castes, including the lowest among them, were not to have any physical contact with untouchables. They could not accept water or food from their hands.

In the villages, the untouchable castes performed all the menial jobs such as those of scavengers, water-carriers, skinners of hides of dead animals, leather-workers, as well as, of course, agricultural labour. Under the jajmani system, they received a fixed share of the produce from the landowning families as payment for their services.

From the middle and late nineteenth century onwards, breaches began to appear in the system described above. Economic changes, especially the commercialization of agricultural production and agrarian relations, emergence of contractual relations, new employment opportunities outside the village in factories, mandis, government service, the army (aided by education), all contributed to a shift in the position of the untouchables. Social reform movements, such as those of Jyotiba Phule in Maharashtra and Sri Narayana Guru in Kerala, also began to question the caste system and caste inequality. From 1920 onwards, Gandhiji integrated the issue of abolition of untouchability into the national movement and major campaigns and struggles, such as the Vaikom (1924–25) and Guruvayur satyagrahas (1931–32) were organized.[1] Gandhiji's effort was to make the upper castes realize the enormity of the injustice done via the practice of untouchability and to persuade them to atone for this wrong. He opposed the British attempt to treat the Depressed Classes, as untouchables were then called in official parlance, as separate from Hindus, and grant them reserved seats in legislatures, based on separate electorates in the Communal Award of 1932, because once they were separated from the Hindus, there would be no ground for making Hindu society change its attitude towards them.

Dr B.R. Ambedkar, a brilliant lawyer, educated in the United States with the help of a scholarship given by the Maharaja of Baroda, emerged as a major leader of the Depressed Classes by the late 1920s. He was a Mahar, a major untouchable caste of Maharashtra. In 1932, after Gandhiji went on a fast against the Communal Award, he agreed to the Poona Pact by which the Depressed Classes (later Scheduled Castes or SC) were given reserved seats from within the general Hindu category. But by 1936, he argued that conversion to another religion was necessary and even chose Sikhism. But the conversion was deferred since the British government would not promise that the benefits of reservation would be continued in the case of conversion. In 1936, he formed the Independent Labour Party which sought to combine with peasants and workers and contested and won a few seats in the 1937 elections to the Bombay Legislative Assembly. By the early 1940s, Ambedkar realized that his effort to build an alliance against the Congress was not making much headway, and he decided to focus on the SCs alone and formed the All India Scheduled Castes Federation in 1942. He also cooperated, politically, with the colonial government on the understanding that he could get more benefits for the SCs. His loyalty won him a seat on the Viceroy's Executive Council (the equivalent of the cabinet) in the 1940s.

Other strands also emerged in different regions; in Punjab the Ad-Dharm, in Uttar Pradesh the Adi-Hindu and in Bengal the Namashudras. Interestingly, in both Punjab and Bengal, they allied with the pro-British Unionist Party and Krishak Praja Party respectively. In Bihar, Jagjivan Ram, who emerged as the most important Harijan Congress leader, formed the Khetmajoor Sabha and the Depressed Classes League. The main demands of Harijan organizations before independence were freedom from the begar or caste-specific imposed labour, grant of forest or wastelands for cultivation, and removal of legal disabilities from owning land, such as those imposed by the Punjab Land Alienation Act, 1900, which did not include SCs among agriculturist castes. Many individual Gandhians and Gandhian organizations were very active in this respect.

With independence, major initiatives in the area of removing caste injustice and inequality were to be attempted. The constitution extended political rights to all citizens irrespective of religion, caste, sex, language, race and this included the SCs. But it also specifically in Article 17 declared that: '"untouchability" is abolished and its practice in any form is forbidden. The enforcement of any disability arising out of "untouchability" shall be an offence punishable with law'. In 1955, parliament passed the Untouchability (Offences) Act which further specified that any offences were punishable with a fine, and/or cancellation of licences and public grants. In 1976, the Protection of Civil Rights (Amendment) Act was passed which provided for enhanced and stringent punishment, appointment of officers and special courts to deal with offenders, legal aid for victims, etc. The constitution also made provisions for reservation of seats in legislatures and educational institutions and of government jobs for SCs. The reservations were initially made for a period of ten years but have been extended continuously since then.

Dr Ambedkar was a party to the constitutional and legal initiatives as, despite their differences in the pre-independence days, he was chosen by the Congress as the chairman of the Drafting Committee of the Constitution and was the law minister in Nehru's cabinet. However, differences emerged, and he left the government to form the All India Scheduled Castes Federation, which contested elections but its candidates mostly lost to Congress candidates in reserved seats. In 1956, he reverted to his position of conversion being necessary and, with himself at the head, led half a million people (some say 6 million), mainly Mahars, his own community, to become Buddhists. He could probably do this because reservations were not denied to Buddhist converts as they were to SCs who converted to Christianity and Islam. Some other untouchable groups, such as the Jatavs of Agra, also followed him, but many others did not.

Ambedkar died soon after, in 1956, leaving no second line of leadership. However, on the basis of a letter written by him, published posthumously, the Republican Party was founded in 1957 and it fought the elections to the Bombay Legislative Assembly in the same year and won a few seats. Personality clashes and other issues soon led to splits and in a few years most factions joined or allied with the Congress, which under Y.B. Chavan made special efforts to accommodate them.[2]

In the early 1970s, a new trend identified as the Dalit Panthers (Dalit, meaning downtrodden, being the name by which the SCs now prefer to call themselves in various parts), emerged in Maharashtra as part of the countrywide wave of radical politics. It was first reflected in creative literature and then in politics. Established as a political organization in 1972, the Dalit Panthers leaned ideologically on Ambedkar's thought, and had their base mainly among youth and students in urban centres. They talked about revolution, but there is little evidence of any concrete strategy being evolved. The agitation for renaming Marathwada University as Ambedkar University resulted in the anti-Dalit riots in 1978 in the rural areas of Maharashtra in which the main aggressors were the middle-caste Maratha Kunbi non-Brahmin peasants.

By the 1980s, the Dalit Panthers had developed serious differences over issues such as whether or not to include non-Dalit poor and non-Buddhist Dalits, primacy of cultural versus economic struggle, as well as over personalities, for example, Raja Dhale versus Namdeo Dhasal. Splits began to occur and most factions, as in the case of the Republican Party twenty years earlier, joined or allied with Congress over time. Prakash Ambedkar, grandson of B.R. Ambedkar, in 1990 made an effort to unite all Dalit organizations for contesting the Maharashtra State Assembly elections and a huge morcha of 500,000 people was organized in Bombay but later differences cropped up again.

In North India, a new party, the Bahujan Samaj Party (BSP) emerged in the 1980s under the leadership of Kanshi Ram (and later Mayawati, who became chief minister of Uttar Pradesh) which declared electoral power as its basic aim and strategy. Though initially there was talk of Dalit and Backward Castes and minorities coming together as a bahujan samaj, in practice the BSP has become a Dalit-based party willing to ally with any political force, BJP, Congress, Janata, Samajwadi Party, as long as it advances its vote share and gets political power. Such a deal with the BJP got Mayawati her chief ministership in Uttar Pradesh in 1995 and, much to the annoyance of those who regarded V.P. Singh as the messiah of social justice, the BSP happily dropped him to support Devi Lal and Chandra Shekhar in 1990. The BSP has succeeded in securing a sufficient base among the SCs in Uttar Pradesh, Punjab and Madhya Pradesh for it to become a significant factor in electoral calculations of other parties and the lack of dominance of any one party has given it an importance it might not have had otherwise. A marked feature of its ideology has been a strident and often abusive stance towards upper castes in general, though proximity to power appears to be already exercising its mellowing effect.

In May 2007, Mayawati led the BSP to a clear majority in the assembly elections in Uttar Pradesh. This was a major achievement, because even though she had been chief minister of Uttar Pradesh earlier on three occasions, June to October 1995, March to September 1997, and May to August 2003, this was the first time a Dalit party had come to power on its own, without support from other parties. The BSP won 206 out of 403 seats. The most significant feature of the BSP victory is that Mayawati managed to attract support from across India's complex caste spectrum. Brahmins, Thakurs, Muslims and OBCs voted for the first time for a Dalit party, because BSP had offered seats to people from these communities. As usual, this was accompanied by a colourful slogan: *Haathi nahi, Ganesh hain, Brahma, Vishnu, Mahesh hain*: The elephant (BSP logo) is really the wise Ganesh, the trinity of gods rolled into one. After being sworn in as chief minister of Uttar Pradesh for the fourth time, on 13 May 2007, she announced that her agenda is focussed on social justice through laws and other means for weaker sections, providing employment instead of distributing money to unemployed and her slogan is to make Uttar

Pradesh into an Uttam (excellent) Pradesh. In keeping with the policy of attracting the votes of upper castes, she also talked about a policy for poverty-based reservations rather than caste-based reservations.

Non-Dalit parties and groups taking up issues of concern to Dalits have also played a significant role in their empowerment. The agricultural labour unions set up by different parties and NGOs that have taken up agricultural labour issues such as wage demands, demands for employment guarantee schemes, right to work, house sites, abolition of child labour, right to education, etc., have all contributed to a new Dalit self-confidence. Exclusively Dalit organizations have also mushroomed. Dalit youth in rural areas have organized Ambedkar Sanghams. In urban areas, students, teachers, youth and office workers have been organized into associations, but these are more concerned with advancing the interests of their members and have little link with rural areas or the urban poor.

It must, however, be recognized that despite all the efforts of Dalit parties and other political groups, the majority of Dalits still vote for the Congress. It is this simple but overwhelming ground reality that has propelled Dalit leaders over the years towards the Congress and not simplistic explanations based on theories of co-option or betrayal. If their aim is to change this, Dalit ideologues will have to understand the underlying causes.

Sociologists have found that despite the claims of the leaders of the Dalits, Buddhist converts in the villages have not given up their old Hindu gods and goddesses, but have only added photographs of Ambedkar and the Buddha, in that order, to the pantheon. Buddhist converts in villages show their newfound confidence by celebrating Hindu festivals, especially ones earlier barred to them, such as Gauri puja and Ganapathi puja, with great gusto and public display, by cooking prohibited religious foods, etc. The upper castes are angered not by their having become Buddhists—they are able to accommodate that quite easily—but precisely by their defiance of traditional Hindu norms and emulation of Hindu religious practices. Thus, despite conversion, we find that Dalits feel equality with caste Hindus only when they are able to practice the same religious rites and customs which the upper castes had denied to them. Gandhiji's understanding and strategy of struggle against the Dalit problem, which emphasized gaining religious equality via temple entry, stands validated. The fate of converts to Christianity, who continue to have separate Dalit churches, or separate places within churches, who face discrimination, including denial of promotions within Church hierarchy, denial of right to perform ceremonies, refusal by priests to accept water from their hands, etc., also proves that conversion has only transferred the problem of caste-based discrimination from Hinduism to Christianity. The same is true of Muslims, with low-caste Muslim converts being treated by high-caste Ashrafs in a similar manner.

Similarly, reservation of jobs and seats in educational institutions at a higher level could only make a marginal difference. Given that, in the total population, only about 3 per cent get higher education and can have access to government jobs, the percentage of SCs who could possibly benefit is much smaller, as they are mostly poorer, more rural, etc. Reservation of seats for SCs in legislatures has had some effect, with electoral imperatives forcing representatives to take up issues of concern to their constituents, but the tendency for co-option and personal aggrandizement among representatives of SC origin has not been any lower than that among those belonging to higher-caste groups. A more recent problem is the competition between different SC castes, such as Mahais and Mangs in Maharashtra, Malas and Madigas in Andhra Pradesh, Chamars and Chuhras in North India. As the benefits of reservation are inevitably availed of by the better-off castes among the SCs, the disadvantaged ones begin to demand quotas within quotas, and intra-SC hostility is becoming increasingly politically visible. This is the logic of reservation—once reservation is secured, the only way of further improving one's prospects is by trying to secure a larger slice of the apportioned cake for one's group.

The overall position of SCs has improved considerably, nevertheless. But the causes are not to be found mainly in either conversion or reservation, the two highly visible strategies. The more invisible processes of social and economic change, of industrialization, of agricultural growth leading to growth of rural employment, of urbanization, have all helped. The extension of primary education and health facilities, the anti-poverty programme, the rural employment guarantee schemes, rural income-generating schemes such as subsidies and loans for dairying and goat rearing, the literacy campaign, the campaign for abolition of child labour, have all been crucial. The provision of house sites in villages, begun by Indira Gandhi, has been particularly important since it has removed a major instrument of coercion from the hands of the upper castes who could earlier threaten to throw out the recalcitrant members from the village land. Adult franchise, which makes the vote of even the poorest and the lowest caste valuable, has had its own consequences. Distribution of land, where it has occurred, has also helped in improving status by removing the stigma of landlessness and raising living standards. An innovative new scheme started in Andhra Pradesh enables SCs to purchase land on the market with the help of grants and loans provided by the government. The breakdown of the jajmani system, and the increasing delinking of caste from traditional occupation, has also been critical.

As a result of all these and many other similar processes, untouchability in urban areas has virtually disappeared and in rural areas has declined drastically. In the more prosperous rural areas, where employment opportunities for low castes have expanded untouchability has decreased. When employers have to seek out labour, they can ill-afford to flaunt their higher-caste status. In factories and offices, caste-based discrimination is rare, though old casteist prejudices may linger. Atrocities against SCs continue to occur, but they are usually a reaction to open defiance of upper-caste norms, such as a lower-caste boy eloping with an upper-caste girl, or lower castes allying with extremist political groups, as in Bihar, to challenge upper-caste authority. As such, the atrocities, though worthy of condemnation in the strongest terms, are to be understood as proof of increasing assertion by lower castes.

However, great inequalities still remain in access to education, to employment, to other economic and social opportunities. The link between caste and literacy is strong, with studies showing that in villages where upper castes have had near-universal adult literacy for several decades, lower castes could have literacy rates close to zero, particularly for women.[3] In 1991, in India as a whole, while literacy rates for men were 64 per cent and for women 39 per cent, for SC men they were 46 and for SC women only 19. In Uttar Pradesh, the comparable figures were 56 and 25 and 39 and 8. In Kerala, however, the gap is much narrower, with the general figures being 94 and 86 and SC figures being 85 and 73.[4] The regional contrast shows how it is possible to reduce inequality through positive social measures such as provision of elementary education. Even the benefits of the policy of reservation cannot be utilized without education as is shown by the general inability to fill quotas reserved for SCs at every level.

In the future, too, the emphasis on anti-poverty strategies such as rapid economic development and employment, and income expansion via employment guarantee schemes and other similar measures needs to continue. Education has been found to be a major vehicle for social mobility and therefore emphasis on providing universal primary and even secondary education is an imperative. This must include a special emphasis on female education, given the direct impact observed on fertility rates. This also shows the need for greater emphasis on equal opportunities for quality education from the primary level itself as education has been found to be a critical vehicle for social mobility.

The issue of the Backward Classes or Castes, which came to a head with the Mandal report in the anti-Mandal agitation in 1990, is quite different from that of the SCs, though efforts are made at the political level to equate or collapse the two.[5] The so-called Backward Castes are really the intermediate castes whose position in the ritual hierarchy was below that of the Brahmins and the Kshatriyas and above that of the untouchables. They did suffer from certain ritual disabilities as compared to the upper castes, but they were in no way comparable to the SCs since they often had access to land and other economic resources. Nor did they suffer from untouchability. Besides, the category includes great disparities, with some castes or sections of castes being very powerful economically and socially and others being quite disadvantaged with a ritual position just above that of the SCs.

Sociologists have shown that Backward Castes such as the Ahirs, Yadavas, Kurmis, Vokkaligas, Lingayats and Lodhas have gained considerable economic advantage via post-independence land reform which gave land rights to ex-tenants of zamindars. This new found strength increased their political clout and representation and they are now seeking to use this clout to secure greater advantages for themselves in jobs, education, etc. In rural areas, they are the biggest exploiters of the SCs who are agricultural labourers and there is little in common between them. The Mandal report has been shown by scholars to be based on faulty methodology and a weak database. The Mandal judgments have also been subjected to severe criticism by sociologists who have argued that caste has undergone such drastic changes since independence but the judiciary is still working on the basis of outdated and ill-informed Western notions of caste. In fact, the politics of reservations for Backward Castes has more to do with sharing the loaves and fishes of office and power than with a struggle for social justice.

Indian Women Since Independence

Beginnings

Dramatic changes have taken place in the legal, political, educational and social status of women since independence. This was not unexpected since the question of the improvement of the position of women had been at the heart of the social reform movement from the first quarter of the nineteenth century when Ram Mohan Roy started his questioning of social orthodoxy. Besides, the freedom struggle since the 1920s and especially since the 1930s had partaken amply of the creative energies of Indian women. Gandhiji's statement in the mid-1930s to Mridula Sarabhai, a valiant fighter for his causes of women and freedom, 'I have brought the Indian women out of the kitchen, it is up to you (the women activists) to see that they don't go back,'[1] was no empty boast and no thoughtless exhortation. The national movement by treating women as political beings capable of nationalist feelings and as, if not more, capable of struggle and sacrifice as men resolved many doctrinal debates about the desirability of women's role in the public sphere. If women could march in processions, defy the laws, go to jail—all unescorted by male family members— then they could also aspire to take up jobs, have the right to vote, and maybe even inherit parental property. Political participation by women in the massive popular struggles from the 1920s onwards opened up new vistas of possibilities that a century of social reform could not. The image of the woman changed from a recipient of justice in the nineteenth century, to an ardent supporter of nationalist men in the early twentieth, to a comrade by the 1930s and 1940s. Women had participated in all streams of the national movement—from Gandhian to Socialist to Communist to revolutionary nationalist. They had been in peasant movements and in trade union struggles. They had founded separate women's organizations as well as the All India Women's Conference, founded in 1926, being the most important of these.

After independence, when the time came to consolidate the gains of the hard-fought struggle, the attention naturally turned to securing legal and constitutional rights. The constitution promised complete equality to women. It fulfilled the promise made many years ago by the national movement: women got the vote, along with men, without any qualification of education or property or income. A right for which women suffragettes fought long and hard in many Western countries was won at one stroke by Indian women!

In the early 1950s, Nehru initiated the process of the enactment of the Hindu Code Bill, a measure demanded by women since the 1930s. A committee under the chairmanship of B.N. Rau, the constitutional expert who prepared the first draft of the Constitution of India, had already gone into the matter and submitted a draft code in 1944. Another committee, chaired by B.R. Ambedkar, the law minister after independence, submitted a bill which raised the age of consent and marriage, upheld monogamy, gave women the rights to divorce, maintenance and inheritance, and treated dowry as stridhan, or women's property. Strong opposition from conservative sections of society, and hesitation on the part of some senior Congress leaders, including President Rajendra Prasad, led to the bill being postponed, despite strong support from a majority of Congressmen and from women activists and social reformers. Ultimately, sections of the bill were passed as four separate acts: the Hindu Marriage Act, the Hindu Succession Act, the Hindu Minority and Guardianship Act, and the Hindu Adoption and Maintenance Act.

The extension of legal rights to Hindu women was not sufficient but it was a big step forward. This is seen from the stiff opposition encountered by the government in its attempts to extend legal rights in the case of other religious communities. The Shah Bano case is a good example. In 1985, about forty years after Hindu law was reformed, the Supreme Court granted a pittance as maintenance to Shah Bano, a divorced Muslim woman. There was a furore among the conservative Muslim sections and sufficient pressure was put on the Rajiv Gandhi government for it to wilt and introduce a bill to negate the Supreme Court judgement. It is no doubt easy and even necessary to castigate the government for its cowardice but it should be remembered that while the Opposition brought hundreds of thousands of people into the streets, the supporters of Shah Bano could muster only hundreds. While criticizing Nehru for not pushing through a more radical civil code for Hindus and for not passing a uniform civil code applicable to all citizens, it should be remembered that while Nehru did face opposition, he could also muster considerable support because among Hindus the process of social reform had gone much further than among Muslims, as evidenced by the Shah Bano case thirty years later.

While some legal rights have been exercised, others have remained on paper. The right to vote has been taken very seriously and women are keen voters, acutely conscious of the power of the vote. This is particularly true of rural women. But in other respects, especially with regard to right to inheritance of parental property, legal rights are by and large not claimed. It is still common in most parts of the country for women, both rural and urban, to forgo their rights in parental property. The custom of partilocal residence (residence in husband's home) is very largely responsible for this. This is also one reason women have refused to give up dowry because it is their only chance of getting a share of their parental property. The legal right to divorce has been increasingly used in urban areas, though the stigma attached to divorce is still prevalent, and the difficulties of setting up as a single woman immense.

Women's Movements: Post-1947

A positive development is that women's issues have been taken up by women's organizations as well as by mainstream political parties and grassroots movements. As expected, attention has been focussed on the more visible forms of gender injustice such as dowry deaths, rape, and alchohol-related domestic violence. From the 1970s onwards, through the 1990s, various movements were launched, sometimes localized, sometimes with a bigger spatial reach, on these issues, and public awareness of these has therefore heightened.[2]

After independence, with different political forces in the national movement going their own ways, the women's movement too diversified. Many women leaders became involved in government-initiated and other institutional activities for women's welfare, including rehabilitation and recovery of women lost or abandoned as a result of the mass migration and riots accompanying Partition, setting up working women's hostels in cities, and women's vocational centres. In 1954, Communist women left the All India Women's Conference to form the National Federation of Indian Women, which became a party forum and not a broad united platform for women. Perhaps inevitably, there was not much evidence of women's 'struggles' in the 1950s and 1960s, which led to a view that there was no women's movement after independence till the new initiative in the 1970s. But such a perception fails to comprehend the inevitable phases of consolidation and quiet constructive work that follow phases of intense struggles as being integral parts of the movement. The Indian women's movement went through precisely such a phase after independence.

Women have also played an important role in peasant, tribal, farmers', trade union and environment movements and this has also enabled them to raise women's issues within them. In the Tebhaga peasant movement in Bengal in 1946–47, women had organized themselves on a separate platform of the Nari Bahini and they ran shelters and maintained lines of communication. Communist women activists also mobilized rural women on specifically women's issues such as rights to finance and property, and village-level Mahila Atma Raksha Samitis (women's self-defence committees) were formed which also took up the issue of domestic violence or wife-beating. In another major Communist peasant struggle of that time in the Telangana area of Hyderabad state from 1946 to 1950, women's participation was also quite significant, and the leadership did pay attention to women's issues such as wife-beating. But there is no evidence of women's organizations emerging. It is also said that women were discouraged from joining the guerrilla force and, when they did succeed in joining, felt they were not totally accepted. Communist women in other areas also complained later that they were strongly encouraged to marry men comrades and edged into working on the 'women's front', rather than integrated into the leadership as members in their own right.[3]

In the late 1960s and early 1970s, there was a new political ferment in the country which gave rise to a host of new political trends and movements, such as the Naxalite movement, the JP Movement, the Chipko movement, and the anti-price rise movement. In the anti-price rise movement of 1973–75, which was organized by Communist and Socialist women in the urban areas of Maharashtra, thousands of housewives joined in public rallies and those who could not leave their houses joined by beating thalis (metal plates) with lathas (rolling pins). The movement spread to Gujarat where it meshed into the Nav Nirman movement influenced by Jayaprakash Narayan's 'Total Revolution'. Though neither of these directly addressed what are called women's issues, the very fact of mass participation of women had a liberating effect and enabled women to gain the self-confidence needed for moving on to more complex issues of patriarchy and women's oppression. Meanwhile, in Gujarat, a very important new development was the founding of a women's wing of the Textile Labour Association (TLA), an old Gandhian organization, called SEWA or Self-Employed Women's Association, which eventually became independent of the TLA. It was unique in that it took up women in the unorganized sector who worked as vendors and hawkers and at home in the putting-out system and organized them into a union which along with collective bargaining provided training, credit and technical help. SEWA spread to Indore, Bhopal, Delhi and Lucknow and even today under the able leadership of Ela Bhatt is among the top success stories of Indian women.

A very different kind of movement emerged in the Shahada tribal area of Dhulia district in Maharashtra in 1972. Led initially by Gandhian Sarvodaya workers and later also by Maoist activists, the movement for drought relief and land in which the Bhil tribal women were very prominent culminated in a militant anti-liquor campaign in which women, who saw liquor as the main cause of wife-beating, broke liquor pots in drinking dens and marched to punish in public, men who beat their wives. In Uttarakhand, in the hill areas of Uttar Pradesh in the early 1960s, a similar movement had taken place under the influence of Gandhians such as Vinoba Bhave, Gandhiji's followers Sarla behn and Mira behn, who had set up ashrams in Kumaon after independence, and the local Gandhian leader Sunderlal Bahuguna, who became famous in the Chipko agitation. Women had come out in large numbers to picket liquor vendors and demand prohibition of sale of liquor. Anti-liquor movements have continued to erupt from time to time in different parts, the most recent being in Andhra Pradesh in the mid-1990s, when a powerful wave of anti-liquor protest by poor rural women led to a policy of prohibition and later restriction of liquor sales. Clearly, Gandhiji had understood a very important aspect of women's consciousness when he made liquor boycott an integral part of the nationalist programme and entrusted its implementation to women.

From 1974, women in Uttarakhand were again very active in the Chipko movement which got its name from the actions of women who hugged trees in order to prevent them from being cut down by timber contractors. It became famous as the first major movement for saving the environment and gave rise to the understanding that women had a special nurturing role towards nature, and that environment issues were very often women's issues because they suffered most from its deterioration, as when forests disappeared and they had to walk for miles to collect fuelwood, fodder and water.[4]

In Chhattisgarh in Madhya Pradesh, women were very militant in the Chhattisgarh Mines Shramik Sangh which was set up in 1977 in the tribal belt to protest against the Bhilai steel plant's policy of mechanization, which was seen as being specially detrimental to women's employment; the Mahila Mukti Morcha developed as a new platform. In 1979, the Chhatra Yuva Sangharsh Vahini, an organization influenced by the ideas of Jayaprakash Narayan, which was leading a struggle of agricultural labourers against temple priests in Bodh Gaya in Bihar, and in which women activists and ordinary women were playing a major role, raised the demand that land should be registered in the names of women as well. This idea caught on in later years and in some states pattas, or title deeds for land distributed by government, and even tree pattas were given only in the name of women.

The Bhopal Gas Peedit Mahila Udyog Sangathan played the leading role in the effort to secure justice for the victims of the chemical gas leak in the Union Carbide factory in Bhopal in 1984. In the mid-1980s, the Samagra Mahila Aghadi emerged as the women's wing of the Shetkari Sangathana, which was spearheading the farmers' movement in Maharashtra from 1980. Over 100,000 women attended its session in November 1986 and took a stand against brutalization of politics which affects women more than other sections of society and also decided to put up all-women panels for the panchayat and zilla parishad elections.

Another stream of the women's movement took the form of what have been called 'autonomous' women's groups. These mushroomed in the urban centres from around the mid-1970s. Many of these consisted of women who had been active in or influenced by the Maoist or Naxalite movement, and its decline in the early 1970s triggered a process of debate and rethinking in which the issues of gender relations and the place of women in political organizations were prominent. Among the earliest of these was the Progressive Women's Organization in Osmania University in Hyderabad in 1974, and the Purogami Stree Sangathana in Pune and the Stree Mukti Sangathana in Bombay in 1975. The declaration by the UN of 1975 as the International Women's Year probably contributed to a flurry of activity in Maharashtra in 1975 with party-based and autonomous organizations celebrating 8 March as International Women's Day for the first time and a women's conference being attended in October in Pune by women from all over the state belonging to Maoist groups, the Socialist and Republican parties, CPM and Lal Nishan Party.

After the Emergency in 1977, another spurt of activity began. A women's group in Delhi began what turned out to be one of the most enduring institutions of the women's movement. *Manushi,* a journal which has documented and analysed the women's movement, told its history, presented literature by women, and much else, has continued till today under the able leadership of Madhu Kishwar, undoubtedly among the most original, self-reflective and fearless voices in the women's movement.

The women in the Janata Party, mostly Socialists, formed the Mahila Dakshata Samiti and played a major role in initiating the campaign against dowry in which the Delhi-based Stri Sangharsh was also very active.[5] The issue of dowry harassment and dowry deaths was taken up from 1979 in a big way through street rallies and plays, demonstrations outside houses of dowry victims, and demands for legal reform. The Janwadi Mahila Samiti, a wing of the CPM women's wing, the All India Democratic Women's Association set up in 1981, conducted a door-to-door campaign on the issue. A bill to amend the Dowry Prohibition Act (1961) was sent to a Joint Select Committee of parliament and throughout

1981 and 1982, women's organizations and other activists presented evidence before the committee as it toured the country. The amendments strengthening the law against perpetrators of dowry-related crimes were passed in 1984; a few minor ones followed later. The movement declined after this, leaving behind a feeling that the victories have not meant much, given the persistence of dowry and difficulty in securing convictions of offenders.

The other major campaign issue that emerged was rape, especially police rape. A number of cases, the Rameeza Bi case in 1978 in Hyderabad, the Mathura case in Maharashtra and the Maya Tyagi case in western Uttar Pradesh in 1980, brought the whole issue to public attention. Women's groups and organizations, along with mainstream political parties, took up the issue in a big way and a bill was introduced in 1980 itself to amend the existing law on rape. Passed in 1983, the main change that it brought about was that custodial rape was treated as a more heinous crime than other forms of rape and the burden of proof was shifted from the victim to the accused and this made a sea-change in the possibility of bringing about convictions of offenders. The campaign had subsided in the meantime, having shown up in its course the sharp divisions in the women's movement, which were caused as much by struggles over turf as by differences of ideology and strategy. The prompt response of the government also left many activists feeling that their agenda had been hijacked or 'appropriated' by the government. The inherent weakness in a strategy that does not have room for absorbing reformist gains was revealed starkly.

The anti-dowry and anti-rape agitations seemed to have dissipated the energies of the movement for some time, and while there were protests around the Shah Bano case in 1985–86, there was not the same enthusiasm or unity. The issue was also less clear, being complicated by the overall communal atmosphere in which issues of Muslim identity got entangled with the simpler issue of women's rights, and the Hindu communalists' enthusiasm for Muslim women's rights often left women's rights activists confused and helpless.

The agitation against what was called the sati but looked like the murder of Roop Kanwar, a young woman in Deorala in Rajasthan, was also on the same lines, with the issues being muddled by Hindu communal groups portraying it as an attack on

Indian tradition and putting women on to the streets to defend their right to sati. Interestingly, some of the more effective opposition to sati came from Arya Samajists like Swami Agnivesh, who toured the rural areas of Rajasthan and Haryana mobilizing opinion against sati, and also challenged the head priests of the Puri and Benares temples to a debate on their claim for a scriptural sanction for sati. In Orissa, Gandhians organized a rally of 10,000 women to gherao the head priest of the Puri temple, challenging him to prove his claim, which he could not. Opposition also came from the anti-caste movement in Maharashtra and rural women in Rajasthan.

Among the 'autonomous' women's groups, by the 1980s there was a clear shift away from mass campaigns to less dramatic work such as setting up of women's centres for legal aid, counselling, documentation, research, publication and the like, at least partly because it was felt that the mass campaigns with their focus on legal reform had not really succeeded in solving the problems they had set out to address. Many women's groups such as Saheli in Delhi felt it was important not only to focus on women's problems but also on their joys, and encouraged women to express themselves through music, dance and art. Others brought out magazines, acted as media watchdogs scanning advertisements and films derogatory to women, raised issues related to women's health, or campaigned against foeticide, for the rights of the girl child, or for water and housing for women in the slums. Many groups that worked with communities and not exclusively with women also brought a greater focus on women's issues into their work.

In Hyderabad, Anveshi was set up as a platform for theoretical studies of women's issues and in Delhi the Centre for Women's Development Studies promoted research and documentation, including in later years the launching of the *Journal for Gender Studies*. Many more university-based centres also came up in the 1990s, and enough research and writing was available for courses on Women's Studies to begin to appear in university curricula.

Clearly, the movement had entered another phase of institutionalization and consolidation as it had in the early 1950s, and what appeared to some activists as a watering down of the movement was more likely diffusion of its ideas into the wider society which was bound to be accompanied by some dilution of its sharp ideological content. It is also true that the movement suffered from a lack of unity about goals, strategies and methods, from sectarianism which was probably the contribution of the left, and a tendency for reacting to immediate crises rather than building a consensus on an agenda for action. It has also been alleged that some sections were swayed by the money received from foreign organizations into taking up issues that concerned the donors but had little relevance to the movement in India, and at least some of the more convoluted debates on theoretical issues that absorbed the energies of some feminists suggest that the charge is not without substance. The gap between urban educated women's groups and rural or poor urban women's concerns also remained, though it narrowed in some instances. The sense of achievement that was so palpable in the 1930s and 1940s, when the leaps in empowerment and consciousness were huge, was missing as one looked at the women's movement since the 1970s.

This is not to say that the efforts were in vain. Government policy was certainly affected, and it came up with a National Perspective Plan for Women in 1988, which detailed plans for women's health, education and political participation. In 1989, the Panchayati Raj bill was introduced (though it was passed only in 1993) which instituted one-third of the seats in the panchayats to be reserved for women. The scheme for Development of Women and Children in Rural Areas (DWACRA) was introduced which sponsored mahila mandals or sanghams in rural areas and it enabled many poor women who had no other access to organize and express themselves, often helped by local-level voluntary groups and political activists. Another innovative scheme called the Mahila Kosh was also started which extended credit to mahila mandals to enable their members to improve their skills and standards of living. The effectiveness of these depended on the capacity of their utilization at the local level, and this varied with the level of politicization and awareness of women's issues. But large numbers of groups were able to use the legitimacy or protective cover of a government scheme as a stepping stone to reach poor rural women who they would otherwise find difficult to touch.

Attempts to increase women's role in local and national politics are still being made. Since one-third of the seats in the panchayats are now reserved for women, women panchayat members and village pradhans are now being given special training to perform their new roles. A serious move to reserve one-third of the seats in parliament for women has been going on for some time and has received considerable support from women politicians and women's groups and some political parties, and generated a great deal of debate.

Health and Education: A Record

The flip side of the coin is that female literacy in Barmer, the worst district in the most backward state (Rajasthan), is 8 per cent, lower than Burkina Faso, the worst country in sub-Saharan Africa, where it is 10 per cent. The infant mortality rate in Ganjam, the worst district of India in this respect, is 164 per 1,000 live births, which is worse than Mali, the worst country in sub-Saharan Africa, where it is 161. The fertility rate in Uttar Pradesh is 5.1, which is higher than the average for all low-income countries and much higher than even Myanmar and Bangladesh. The female–male ratio, that is, number of women per 1,000 males, in Haryana is 865, a level lower than that of any country in the world. Among elderly widows, the mortality figures are generally 86 per cent higher than for married women of the same age.[6]

The population of rural females in the 12–14 age group who have never been enrolled in any school is one-half in India as a whole, above two-thirds in Uttar Pradesh, Madhya Pradesh and Bihar, and as high as 82 per cent in Rajasthan. Only 42 per cent of rural females in the 10–14 age group, and 40 per cent in the 5–9 age group are reported to be attending school. The dropout rate is also very high. Average number of years of schooling for persons aged 25 and above is 2.4 in India as a whole, while it is only 1.2 for females and 3.5 for males. In India, half of all females in the 15–19 age group are illiterate, in China less than 10 per cent.

The all-India averages and the focus on dark areas, however, hides the bright spots that hold out a candle of hope. The state of Kerala has a record that would be the envy of any developing country and in some respects is even equal to that of the developed countries. The adult literacy rate for women in 1990–91 was 86 per cent (and 94 per cent for men). This was far higher than China's which was 68 per cent for women and 86 per cent for men. It was even higher than any individual Chinese province. By

1987–88, Kerala had a female rural literacy rate of 98 per cent in the 10–14 age group. By 1992–93, 60 per cent of females aged 6 and above had completed primary education, the all-India average being only 28.1. The total fertility rate in 1992 was 1.8, which is below the replacement level of 2.1, which is the rate in the US and Sweden. The all-India average for fertility rate is 3.7. The infant mortality rate, which is closely tied, as is well known, to the position of women, was only 17 per 1,000 live births in Kerala in 1992, compared with 31 in China and 79 in India as a whole. The female–male ratio improved from 1,004 to 1,036 between 1901 and 1991, whereas at the all-India level it declined from 972 to 927 over the same period.

Fortunately, Kerala is not the only glowing example. Else it would appear that it is unique because of the historical advantage of having a very early start in the field of education, and because of the matrilineal customs of a significant part of its population. While both these advantages are a fact—the erstwhile princely states of Travancore and Cochin which constitute the bulk of modern Kerala, did give a very strong emphasis to education from the first quarter of the nineteenth century and the matrilineal system, which includes matrilocal residence, inheritance through females, etc. is a strong positive factor—other factors such as an activist and participatory political culture, itself helped by high literacy levels, positive public policies in the areas of health, public distribution system, and primary education, have been extremely important. And these are replicable, as shown by other success stories, notably Himachal Pradesh and Tamil Nadu.

As recently as 1961, the crude literacy rates in Himachal were 9 per cent for females (and 21 per cent for males), which were below the all-India averages. By 1987–88, literacy rates in the 10–14 age group were as high as 81 for females in rural areas and even higher at 97 per cent in the urban areas (the corresponding figures for males being 95 and 96 per cent). Thus, in urban areas women had outstripped men. Himachal Pradesh in this respect was second only to Kerala. In terms of number of girls in urban areas attending school, Himachal did even better than Kerala: 95 per cent versus 94 per cent. In rural areas, Kerala had the lead with 91 per cent versus Himachal's 73 per cent, but Himachal's figures were still higher than those of any other state. Other indicators followed suit. The female–male ratio in Himachal increased from 884 to 976 between 1901 and 1991, the biggest increase (plus 92) in the whole of India. Kerala had increased only from 1,004 to 1,036, though in absolute numbers it was way ahead. The ratio of female death rate to male death rate in the 0–4 age group was only 88.2 per cent in 1991, even lower than Kerala's figure of 91.1 per cent and way below the all-India average of 107.4 per cent. However, the infant mortality rate was still quite high at 70 per 1,000 live births in 1990–92, as was the fertility rate at 3.1 in 1991, though both were below the all-India average.

In Tamil Nadu as well, there have been dramatic improvements in various gender-related indicators. It stands second only to Kerala in its fertility rate, which was 2.2 in 1991. The infant mortality *rate was 58 per 1,000 live births in 1990–92, which was the third* lowest in the country, only Kerala and Punjab having lower rates. The female literacy rate in the 10–14 age group in 1987–88 was 85.6 per cent in urban and 70.8 per cent in rural areas. The ratio of female death rate to male death rate in 0–4 age group was 90.5 per cent in 1991, the all-India average being 107.4. About 97 per cent of children between the ages of 12 and 23 months had received some vaccination by 1992–93, 'the highest percentage in the country.

The extreme diversity that we have encountered enables us to analyse the factors that facilitate and inhibit positive trends in gender justice. While history and tradition are important and the south of the country, historically, has a better record than the north, a strong commitment in public policy can bring about rapid change, as shown by Himachal Pradesh. The diversity also shows that economic prosperity or growth does not automatically lead to greater gender justice; Punjab, and even more Haryana, two prosperous states, perform pretty poorly on the gender front. The factors which facilitate improvement in women's position also emerge quite clearly. Female literacy and education are unambiguous winners, with the links with improvement in all other indicators coming out very sharply. Conversely, low literacy and education levels lead to negative trends in other indicators.

Women, therefore, have been the main victims of India's failures on the elementary education and literacy fronts. When primary schools in villages do not function, boys are sent to neighbouring villages or towns or even to private schools, but girls are usually just kept at home. Social conservatism, combined with the notion that investing money in a girl's education is like watering a plant in another man's house, since the benefits will accrue to the girl's in-laws' family, lead to this decision. But if schools are available, and teachers are regular, and classes are held, a large proportion of girls do get sent to school in most parts of the country. The consciousness of the value of education has spread to this extent even among the poorest sections. In fact, the poor are more aware that education is their one route to upward social mobility. But in a situation when single-teacher schools accounted for one-third of all schools (in 1986) and where, as recent surveys have shown, two-thirds of teachers were found to be absent during inspections, where there are fifty-eight children for each teacher at the 6–10 age group level, where India ranks 82nd in terms of the proportion of public expenditure on education to GNP among 116 countries for which data is available, it is small wonder that the rate of female literacy is as low as 39 per cent (1990–91).

Another factor that is very important in improving gender justice is the provision of free primary health facilities at the grassroots level. As in the case of education, if health facilities are not easily accessible or are expensive, the loss is unequally that of women and female children. In fact, unequal access to improved facilities as well as to improved living standards is the major cause of the sharp decline in the female–male ratio in India from 972 to 927 between 1901 and 1991. It is not that the survival chances of women have decreased in absolute terms—on the contrary. But relative to men, women have gained less from the improved access to health facilities and better living standards and therefore their proportion has declined. To correct this imbalance, health facilities have to be brought within the reach of women. Where this has been done, as in Kerala, where over 90 per cent of women deliver their babies in medical institutions, the results are dramatic.

Thus, if the legal and political rights granted to women in the constitution, which are theirs by virtue of their own efforts as well as by all norms of social justice, are to be realized and democratized, millions of women have to become capable of understanding and exercising them. Kerala, and Himachal, at two poles of the country, have shown the way: the heartland has to follow. The women's movement also needs to incorporate education and health as priorities into its strategy for women's empowerment.

The Post-colonial Indian State and the Political Economy of Development: An Overview[1]

The national liberation struggle that gave birth to an independent India in 1947 left a deep imprint on the nature of the post-colonial Indian state. Its legacy has seen the nation through for more than sixty years, though now some of the forces against which the movement had stood so steadfastly have surfaced and threaten the nation's delicate fabric. The national movement or the liberation struggle was a multi-class popular movement of the Indian people. This century-long struggle led to a 'national revolution'; a revolution that was national in the sense that it cut across class, caste, religious community, gender, age, representing them all, even if differentially. Seldom has a revolution in any country attracted the finest of its people from such diverse spheres. Social and religious reformers, poets, writers, musicians, philosophers, traders, industrialists, political thinkers, statesmen, all joined hands with the common people, gave direction to and learnt from their initiative to bring about one of the biggest mass movements in human history. It is this character of the movement that lent the Indian nation state, which was 'new' in comparison to many others, a deep legitimacy and resilience.

Apart from the all-embracing, mass character of the national movement, there were certain other basic features of this remarkable occurrence which not only explain the survival of the nation state but its distinct character. These were its deep anti-imperialism, total commitment to secular democracy and an egalitarian, pro-poor orientation. Being a mass movement, as distinct from a cadre-based revolutionary movement, meant that these ideas were carried to the deepest layers of Indian society, making any reversal from these basic features an extremely difficult process. The kind of strong resistance governments in India faced in any move to distance themselves from these principles (witness the response to the temporary restriction on democratic rights during the Emergency, 1975–77) makes an interesting comparison with the ease with which the Soviet Union and China were able to do a virtual about-turn from the legacy of their socialist revolutions.

The extent to which the basic ideas of the Indian liberation struggle or national movement permeated into or impacted upon the governments or regimes that came to power after independence and on other state apparatuses such as the bureaucracy, police, judiciary, legislature, education system, media, political parties, etc., as well as on civil society, or among the people in general, was to play a critical role in determining the nature of the post-colonial Indian state. It is important to clarify at this stage that 'government' is not to be confused for the state, as is done often in common, day-to-day usage, though 'government' is an important, even critical, apparatus or organ of the state. Sole emphasis on the government may lead to hasty and inaccurate characterizations. For example, a government may be headed by a staunch socialist like Jawaharlal Nehru, it may get parliament and even the constitution to declare socialism as an objective, it may have the most radical laws for the protection of the poor, the landless, oppressed castes, tribals, bonded labour and other such sections, and yet the state may closer fit the definition of a bourgeois rather than, say, a socialist one, because the power balance in the other state apparatuses and in society as a whole may be very different from that reflected in the leadership of the government. It may determine how the laws, the constitution and other institutions are interpreted, implemented or used.

Building or transforming a state structure involves much more than just the government. Gandhiji understood the complex nature of the state. In his successful attempt to overthrow the colonial state he did not focus only on critiquing and changing the colonial government but on gradually corroding the power of the colonial state. This he sought to do by countering the colonial influence in the education system, media, bureaucracy, police and most importantly among the people. It is such an understanding, we shall see, which was missing among many who wanted to give an alternative direction to the post-colonial Indian state, if not to transform or overthrow it.

The Nationalist Legacy and the Post-colonial State

The legacy of the national movement resulted in the formation of a popular democratic, sovereign, multi-class 'national state' after 1947. The precise class balance in the state or its class character was to be moulded by the strategies of political mobilization and garnering of social support evolved by the constituent classes. Just as the open-ended nature of the national movement made it possible for its class orientation to be altered in favour of or against any class or group of classes, so was this the case in the popular democratic national state that it gave birth to. More on this later.

Second, a fundamental legacy of the national movement was anti-imperialism and maintenance of national sovereignty. The founding fathers of the Indian national movement had already by the last quarter of the nineteenth century developed a comprehensive and sophisticated critique of imperialism and the colonial structure. They were perhaps among the first, worldwide, to do so. They made an important shift in the understanding of how modern imperialism was keeping the colonies underdeveloped rather than deepening or creating the conditions for the development of capitalism, roughly at the same time as did Marx; even before Hobson and Lenin they worked out a detailed economic critique of colonialism. The long struggle against imperialism, the continuous updating and refining of its critique and the carrying of these ideas to the masses has had a lasting impact and it is perhaps in this sphere that the post-colonial state has stood most firm.

The model of a ruling coalition consisting of a 'triple alliance' between international capital, state (i.e., the indigenous government) and local capital, which was seen as central to dependent capitalist development in Latin America and even to parts of East Asia, though the role of international capital there was seen to be relatively less, did not apply to India.[2] In India, a foreign bourgeoisie or international capital did not constitute a part of the ruling class coalition or the Indian state after independence. The bargaining with international capital did not occur within the state or the ruling coalition of which international capital was a part, as is argued to be the case in many other post-colonial countries, but between an independent state, with an entirely indigenous ruling class coalition, and international capital—an important difference in terms of autonomy.

An Indian variant of the 'triple alliance' model, that is, that the Indian state after independence is dominated by the bourgeoisie/ big bourgeoisie and landlords who are increasingly collaborating with foreign finance capital/imperialism/TNCs as subordinate partners, has been supported for a long time by a section of the orthodox left. It is also argued that the Indian bourgeoisie or the capitalist class 'which came to power' at independence was comprador or compromising with imperialism and consequently the post-independence Indian state was neocolonial or dependent. In fact, having assumed the dependent nature of the colonial bourgeoisie, it has been argued that post-colonial countries like India cannot develop independently unless they overthrow their bourgeoisie and the capitalist system in favour of socialism. These views have been challenged and the overwhelming evidence to the contrary has by and large pushed such views to the fringes though there are a few loyal adherents surviving even in mainstream left scholarship.[3]

We have demonstrated at length elsewhere the political and economic independence of the Indian capitalist class and how it not only imbibed the anti-imperialist ethos of the national movement but was at the forefront of evolving an economic critique of imperialism since the 1920s.[4] The capitalists were very much part of the Nehruvian consensus at independence which was to put India on the path of planned, self-reliant economic development without succumbing to imperialist or foreign capital domination. In fact, one of the central objectives of the Nehru–Mahalanobis strategy was to free the Indian economy of foreign domination and dependence—an objective which was realized to a much greater degree under the leadership of Indira Gandhi when, *inter alia*, the role of foreign capital in India was brought down to negligible levels. Also, it may be noted that though the working class unionized on a large scale it increasingly moved in a corporatist direction. The left as a political alternative suffered a decline even among the working class. In other words, it never came close to posing a serious enough threat to the system, leading to the creation of the often-predicted classic situation where the bourgeoisie would go over to imperialism or seek external help for its survival. As for the feudal landlords, their power had been much weakened during the national movement itself and the land reforms after independence marginalized them completely except in a few pockets.

Critics belonging to the orthodox left, with some influence in Indian academia, have only grudgingly accepted that 1947 did not mean a transfer of power from a colonial to a neocolonial state with Nehru as 'the running dog of imperialism' (a view held by a section of Communists at independence). They periodically see in any move towards liberalization or opening up to the outside world the 'inherent' pro-imperialist, dependent nature of the Indian state 'finally' and 'inevitably' coming to the surface. This was the argument used, for example, during the mid-1960s when, faced with a major economic crisis, the rupee was devalued and some trade liberalization was briefly attempted. This criticism remained buried for some years with Indira Gandhi's sharp turn towards economic nationalism in the late 1960s and 1970s, only to resurface (for example, in a statement signed by a number of left economists) with the attempts at liberalization and the large IMF loan taken by India in the early 1980s (a loan which was eventually not even fully drawn and went a long way in helping India reduce her critical dependence on oil imports by massive increases in indigenous oil production). Again the recent, post-1991, efforts at reforms involving liberalization and a more active participation in the globalization process have been seen as 'a reversal in the direction of policy since decolonisation', a policy which had 'pointed toward relative autonomy from metropolitan capital'. It has been seen as virtually an imperialist project where 'the policies of the nation-state, instead of having the autonomy that decolonisation promised—are *dictated by the caprices of a bunch of international rentiers*'.[5]

The broad consensus that has emerged in India in recent years, however, does not take such a dim view of the reforms. The commonly perceived need for a shift away from the excessively dirigiste, inward-looking and protectionist strategy, which was leading to a dangerous fall in efficiency and productivity levels and the urge to participate in the globalization process in the altered circumstances of world capitalism in recent decades, where major possibilities have emerged of utilizing global capital and global markets for indigenous development, has led to the emergence of a broad consensus in favour of reform. This was a consensus reminiscent of the Nehruvian phase, both in terms of the objectives and width of support. The desire to achieve the goals set out at independence—of self-reliance, rapid growth and removal of poverty—and not their abandonment, now drew support for reform and the adoption of the new strategy.

In this context, it is interesting to see the major shift made by the former Left Dependency thinker F.H. Cordoso (as President of Brazil he guided the country through economic reforms and participation in the globalization process) from his earlier position. He pointed out how the nature of foreign capital had changed and could be used for indigenous development of underdeveloped countries. He argued that globalization was a fact that could not be ignored, and thus the issue is not whether to globalize, but how to globalize so that a better bargain is achieved for the backward countries and a proper cushion provided to the poor so that they are not made to bear the cost of the initial transition—a view which the supporters of reform from the left in India as well as the more sagacious business leaders have generally accepted. Very significantly, Cordoso had added that popular mobilization and community work would be necessary to ensure that the poor will be fully protected. He felt that the traditions created by Mahatma Gandhi in this respect give India a clear advantage over many other underdeveloped countries.[6]

The third major legacy of the national movement has been the adoption of democracy as a fundamental value by the Indian state. By any international standards, India has a fully thriving democracy, and not merely a 'formal' or 'partial' one, as argued by some. It is not a 'top-down' democracy which is a 'gift of its elite to the masses', nor is it a gift of the British. It is a product of a long-drawn struggle of the Indian people during the national movement and hence has firm roots in Indian society. The democratic base has been enlarged with a relatively high percentage of popular participation in elections and newer groups and classes getting actively involved in democratic institutions. In fact, the struggle for expanding the democratic space continues—witness the current vigorous campaign for greater transparency in government and other institutions and the people's right to information.

It is creditable that India has attempted its industrial transformation within a democratic framework, a unique experiment for which there is no precedent. The initial phase of 'primitive accumulation' (i.e., raising of surplus for investment and releasing of labour for industry), which was critical for the industrial transformation of all the industrialized countries, whether the advanced capitalist countries of the West, the socialist countries or the newly industrialized countries of East Asia, occurred in circumstances bereft of full democratic rights. The paths, for example, of enclosure movements (Britain), forced collectivization (Soviet Union), high land tax (Japan), slavery (US), total suppression of trade union rights (East Asia and others), and colonial surplus extraction (several countries; Britain, for example, received as *unilateral transfers from colonies in Asia and* West Indies a stupendous 85 per cent of its Gross Domestic Capital Formation in 1801), etc., were not open to democratic India.

Democracy ensured that in India the transition to industrialism was not to be on the back of the working class and the peasantry, drawing surplus for investment from them. The working class made major advances through collective bargaining and there was by and large a net transfer of resources to agriculture after independence rather than vice versa. Democracy and a free Press made inconceivable, what happened in China, where the world came to know many years later of an estimated 16 to 23 million famine deaths between 1959 and 1961. In India a free Press (with 8,600 daily newspapers and 33,000 periodicals today) has kept governments on their toes to help avert any scarcity situation and major famines, a regular feature in colonial times.

Democracy has given a voice to the poor in the process of development. Their interest cannot be bypassed. Democracy has, for example, made it unviable for any government since independence to pursue an inflationary strategy which hits the poor the hardest. The early 1950s saw falling prices and the trend rate of inflation did not exceed 8 per cent per year between 1956 and 1990 despite two oil shocks and several droughts. Even when necessary stabilization and structural adjustments were undertaken during the post-1991 reforms, these being measures which make the poor particularly vulnerable through contraction of public expenditure, democracy ensured that they were not left high and dry. Anti-poverty measures were expanded and a quick reversal of the rise in poverty that occurred during the first two years of reforms was achieved. In the dilemma between fiscal prudence and egalitarian commitment (a dilemma which, as Amartya Sen points out, is not a choice between good and bad but a genuine dilemma between two goods), democracy ensures (that it does not get resolved without adequate weight to the latter.[7]

The fourth major legacy of the national movement has been its equity and pro-poor orientation. The Indian state was certainly influenced by this legacy, though its full potential was far from realized. The impact of this legacy can be seen in the fact that each of the nine Five-Year Plans since independence treated removal of poverty as a key objective though the extent of focus on poverty removal varied between Plans. It is not accidental that even the right-wing political formations have repeatedly found it necessary to swear by the poor. Witness the BJP, in one of its incarnations in the early 1980s, wishing to bring about Gandhian socialism.

The Indian state was committed to wide-ranging land reforms at independence. The peasantry was essentially freed (except in some pockets) from the power and domination of the feudal-type landlords. Though it was indeed very creditable that India achieved land reforms within the framework of democracy, nevertheless the reforms occurred in a manner that initially the relatively better-off sections of the peasantry got unequal advantage from it compared to the poorer sections. This happened partially because the class balance at the ground level and in the perspectives of many state apparatuses such as the judiciary, the police and bureaucracy, particularly at the lower levels, was not in tune with that of the government. It was far less favourable to the poor, and the government in a democracy could not force its way. Over time, various governments, however, persisted with these measures and from the early 1970s there was a second wave of land reforms accompanied by several targeted efforts to reach the benefits of the Green Revolution strategy to the poor. The results were commendable though much still remained to be done. There is no comparison between the abject poverty faced by the rural poor all over the country where even two meals a day were not guaranteed and what prevails today in most parts of the country. Radical scholars like Daniel Thorner and other observers reported, on the basis of field surveys, a qualitative change in the lives of the rural poor. The land reforms, the spread of the Green Revolution to most parts of the country, and targeted anti-poverty programmes, particularly since the late 1960s, have provided succour to vast masses of the rural poor in India.

Even using the rather inadequate indices available for measuring poverty, it is seen that the proportion of the rural population below the poverty line declined from 58.75 per cent in 1970–71 (estimates for the 1950s when it would be much higher are not available to us) to 37.3 per cent in 1993–94. The corresponding figures for the total population, including both urban and rural, were 56.25 and 36. The total population below the poverty line fell further to 27.8 per cent by 2004–05. The average life expectancy, which was a miserable 32 years in 1950–51, nearly doubled, to over 63 years by the 1990s. The per capita income in 1996–97 was two and a half times higher than what it was in 1950–51 even though the population too had multiplied rapidly, showing an increase of more than 158 per cent over the same period. The literacy rate had risen from an abysmal 18.3 per cent in 1951 to 62 per cent in 1997. Infant mortality had come down from 146 to 71 per 1,000 between 1951 and 1997. Food self-sufficiency and public action have made famines a thing of the past.

Poverty, Democracy and the Indian State

Considerable achievements these—yet despite all this progress India still faces the intolerable situation where more than 300 million of its people continue to remain below the poverty line and nearly half the population is illiterate. The continuation of poverty despite considerable advances is partly a result of relatively slower growth (East Asia, particularly Indonesia and China, are good examples of high growth enabling dramatic reduction in poverty) and is partly reflective of the nature of the Indian state and the failure to sufficiently alter its class balance in favour of the poor through popular mobilization. However, increasingly it appears that the latter is the more important cause for the continuing poverty. It is significant that despite rapid growth for over twenty years, especially in the new millennium, India's ranking in the global Human Development Index actually fell between 2000 and 2004.

The sovereign, democratic national state that came into existence at independence was multi-class in nature and was open-ended in the sense that the class balance among the constituent classes could be altered. The Indian national state in other words constituted the arena in which several classes contended for influence, the capitalists in trade, industry and finance, the upper sections of the peasantry, a broad middle class consisting of professionals, clerical and managerial staff or 'knowledge workers', the organized working class and the rural and urban poor consisting of agricultural workers, poor peasants, petty artisans, unorganized urban workers and so on. (As argued above, the feudal landlords and the metropolitan bourgeoisie or international capital were not contenders in this internal struggle for hegemony over the state.) The manner in which this competition for influence would get resolved was to depend on how the various classes were politically mobilized and which class perspective was able to exercise a greater ideological hegemony or influence over society as a whole.

From the very beginning the Nehru–Mahalanobis strategy of growth with equity had assumed that popular mobilization from below would be necessary to effectively implement radical measures in favour of the poor (such as land reforms, cooperativization, universal education, and so on) initiated by the government led by Nehru. The problem, however, was in locating an 'agency' which was going to perform this task. With independence, the Congress party with Nehru at its head got transformed from a party of struggle and movement to a party of governance. Efforts to make Congress workers perform the former role, rather than try to learn the ropes of the latter, proved essentially unsuccessful. (Gandhiji anticipating this denouement had unsuccessfully called for the disbanding of Congress at independence and forming of a separate organization to struggle for people's causes, to be distinct from the one which governed.) Nehru tried to fill the void by creating a developmental bureaucracy from the local village worker to the highest level, and unwittingly created a byzantine institution whose main purpose increasingly appeared to be that of multiplying and feeding itself.

The task was essentially political and the bureaucracy could not be expected to act as a substitute. In fact, Nehru had expected the left would perform this task and he tried repeatedly, though unsuccessfully, to garner its support so that radical government programmes could be implemented and a gradual social transformation and an altering of the nature of the state could take place. The left had, however, initially characterized Nehru as 'the running dog of imperialism' and hence naturally to be opposed and overthrown. Later, after the left gave up this position, it still refused to cooperate as it saw such a task as 'reformist', which would only strengthen the 'bourgeois' state, while their role was to sharpen the contradictions and prepare for its overthrow. The left thus abandoned the space provided by the open-ended democratic structure of the Indian state (dismissing it as 'bourgeois' democracy), and did little to either try and alter the class balance in various state apparatuses such as in the bureaucracy, media (dismissed as the bourgeois Press), judiciary, education system etc., or to mobilize the poor so that they had a greater say within the existing state structure. Not recognizing the transformative possibilities of the Indian multi-class national state, it waited, and still waits, at least in theory, endlessly for the maturing of the contradictions so that an insurrectionary overthrow of the state can occur. This failure of the left, and a superior understanding of the nature of the democratic state by other forces such as the Indian business leaders, has led to a capitalist developmental perspective with an inadequate pro-poor, welfare orientation prevailing over the state apparatuses and society as a whole. It has also led to the democratic space increasingly getting occupied by casteist and communal tendencies which hurt the poor, even though the poor are often mobilized by communal forces.

The political space for mobilization in favour of the poor has thus largely remained untapped—though simple democratic arithmetic has secured the poor several concessions as all political formations have to seek their votes. Sporadic and scattered non-governmental organizations have often provided idealistic youth fora for such activity but these efforts, in the absence of their generalization through wider political intervention, can have only limited results. The recent efforts to empower the local self-governing institutions with the Panchayati Raj amendments to the constitution offer much promise. Recent popular mobilizations leading to progressive legislations like the National Rural Employment Guarantee Act and the Right to Information Act created the conditions for further deepening democracy and held out much promise of reaching out to and empowering the poor and underprivileged. How far that promise gets realized will depend on what extent the progressive political forces try to occupy this democratic space available at the grassroots level.

While persisting poverty has been the most important failure in India's post-independence development, the survival of the democratic structure has been its grandest success. The further deepening and maturing of this democratic structure is an important step in the direction of meeting the needs of the underprivileged.

However, a major political development that threatens the pursuance of a viable developmental path may be highlighted. The very success of India's democracy has led to growing demands on the state by various classes and groups including the poor. To accommodate these demands all political formations, since the late 1970s, began to indulge in competitive populism using state resources to distribute largesse to the various constituent classes of the Indian state including the poor. Subsidies (often reducing costs to the consumer to zero) for food, fertilizers, diesel, exports, electricity, to name just a few, proliferated to unsustainable levels pushing the country to the brink of default and economic chaos.

The survival and growth of the sovereign, democratic Indian state, requires a 'strong' state. Strong not 'as counterpoised to democracy, decentralization and empowerment of the people' but strong in the sense that it can, while accommodating moderate deviations, suppress forces that threaten democracy by operating outside its limits—viz., terrorists, separatist insurgencies, fanatical, fundamentalist and violent casteist or religious communal forces and so on.[8] A strong state can discipline capital which does not perform competitively (as Japan and other East Asian states have successfully done) as well as discipline sections of labour which do not perform at all or perform below societally accepted standards of productivity. A strong state, without resort to populism but keeping social justice as one of its central objectives, can guide the economy on to a path of rapid development and modernization, based on the advanced scientific breakthroughs of the contemporary world. A strong state can participate in the globalization process in a manner which not only does not diminish its sovereignty but increases it. A tall order but certainly not beyond the genius of the Indian people who have crossed some of the most difficult milestones creditably over the past sixty years.

Disarray in Institutions of Governance

Among the most significant features of India's political development has been the commitment of its leaders to democracy, national unity and economic development, accompanied by their ability to establish the necessary political institutions, both of the state and civil society, and to root them in Indian society—in other words, to create and maintain the structure of a democratic state. These institutions have been sustained despite rapid social change, with new social groups regularly entering the political arena and asserting their rights. The repeated successions of governments at the Centre, that have been brought about peacefully and constitutionally, have been a sign of the basic inner strength of this democratic structure.

However, the political system has been under strain, facing an increasing loss of vitality. There has been a certain disarray, a deterioration in political institutions. These are not able to respond adequately to the challenges posed by economic development and social change, the growing political awakening among the people and their aroused and rising expectations, the refusal of the oppressed and the disadvantaged to accept their social condition, and the growing class and caste conflict among contending social groups, especially in the countryside, for a larger share of political power and gains of economic development.

Most of the political institutions, as a consequence, have been losing their moral authority and the country has been difficult to govern—at least, difficult to govern well. This 'crisis of governability' takes multiple forms: unstable governments, frequent elections and changes of electoral moods, inability to accommodate and reconcile contending demands and needs of different social groups and classes, weakening of law and order, growing civil discord and disturbance, sometimes reaching the proportions of insurgency, communal violence, increasing recourse of people to violent and extra-constitutional agitations, growing corruption, and, above all, the failure of the governments at the Centre and the states to implement their policies or to provide effective governance.

At the same time, it would be wrong to suggest that the political system or its institutions have been crumbling or that India has been undergoing a crisis of the state. In spite of all their weaknesses, the political system and its institutions have proved to be quite resilient and have managed to function, even though inadequately; they have also retained their legitimacy, in part because of their very longevity, but much more because of the greater participation by the people in the political process, especially in elections.

Undoubtedly, apart from the skewed socio-economic structure, the major culprit for the weakening of the political institutions has been the quality of political leadership. It is the quality of political leadership which plays a critical role in nation-building and the development of political institutions. More than a crisis of the state or the political system, there has certainly been a crisis of leadership as the calibre of leaders both at the Centre and in the states has been going down over the years.

For several decades now, the political leadership has functioned without any strategic design or perspective, ideology or well-thought-out tactics for managing the political system. It has relied instead on ad hocism and gimmickry for meeting the challenges in the polity and on populism, personal appeal, and use of big and black money to maintain itself in power. At best, it has taken recourse to such tactical measures as opportunistic coalitions of ideologically and programmatically disparate political parties and groups, or putting together of caste and communal coalitions or the centralization of the party and government processes through coteries. Consequently, even major parties and political leaders have been living a sort of hand-to-mouth existence; they are able to win elections but thereafter are neither able to govern nor maintain their authority. Even such a tall leader as Indira Gandhi was not able to check the erosion in institutions like the party, parliament and the bureaucracy.

The Downslide of Parliament

Next to elections and civil liberties, parliament occupies a pivotal position in a parliamentary democracy. In India, parliament and the state legislatures not only legitimize a government, but they are also the supreme organs for formulation of policies, overseeing their implementation, and in general acting as 'watchdogs' over the functioning of the government. Unfortunately, over the years, there has been a general downslide in its performance, and signs of decay in the institution have set in.

Jawaharlal Nehru worked incessantly to install respect for parliament and ensured that it functioned with decorum and responsibility. He attended its settings regularly, however busy he was otherwise. He paid full attention to the views of the Opposition parties, treated them with respect as an integral part of the democratic process, and often let them influence and even change government policies. The Opposition parties, in turn, acted responsibly, abiding by the parliamentary rules of the game. The system continued to function quite well in the Nehru and immediate post-Nehru years. However, gradually, over the years, parliament started becoming ineffective. Its role began to diminish and its policy-making powers to atrophy. Its proceedings began to degenerate in the late 1960s. From then on, parliamentary procedures have been routinely ignored and parliament's and state legislatures' sessions have been marked by shouting and abuse and rowdy behaviour, even towards the prime minister. Also, frequent walk-outs, unruly scenes, disgraceful disorderliness, demonstrations by the members inside parliament and legislatures and other disruptive tactics, including the staging of dharnas (sit-ins), have progressively taken the place of reasoned arguments and parliamentary give and take. In recent years, quite often parliament has not been able to transact any business for days because of the disruption of its sittings by one party or the other.

Unlike in the Nehru period, in recent years, in general it is observed that once a government gets a majority in the legislature it formulates and tries to implement its policies, irrespective of the views of the Opposition, and the latter, in turn, opposes government policies and actions irrespective of their merit. Parliament and state legislatures seldom witness a confrontation of well-worked-out alternatives. There occurs a great deal of denunciation but little meaningful debate takes place. Often, the worth and efficacy of a government decision is tested not in parliament or a state legislature but in the streets and in the media. The Question Hour, once a pride of parliament, has degenerated into a shouting slug-fest and is often suspended.

Defectors, who crossed floors, changed parties, and toppled governments, not for political or ideological reasons but for personal gain, leading to rapid changes of governments, became common in the states after 1967. At the Centre, the malady was reflected in the toppling of the Janata government in 1977. It appeared at one stage that the entire parliamentary system would be turned into a mockery when a few defecting MLAs or MPs could make or unmake governments. The situation was, however, saved and the governments given greater stability and longevity by the anti-defection law of 1985. But in recent years defections and break up of alliances and coalitions have again become common with defectors smartly remaining within the ambit, though not the spirit, of the anti-defection law.

Overall, as a result of the inefficient functioning of state legislatures and parliament since the late 1960s, parliamentary institutions have been brought into disrepute, have declined in authority among the people and have been playing a diminishing role in policy formulation and governance. Even so, they have not become totally ineffectual. They continue to perform, though inadequately, the role assigned to them under the constitution: they still give some voice to public opinion and reflect the popular mood. The government still dreads the opening of a parliamentary or assembly session. Above all a government can continue to hold power only if it retains the confidence of the house—since 1977, seven governments at the Centre have fallen because of their losing majority in the Lok Sabha.

The Cabinet

The cabinet, chosen and headed by the prime minister and constituted by the senior ministers, forms the effective executive branch of the Indian political system and functions on the principle of collective responsibility. The strength of a government is measured by the strength of its cabinet. Unfortunately, the role and significance of the cabinet as a policy and decision-making institution has also been declining since 1969, that is, with the beginning of Indira Gandhi's government. Since then the cabinet has most often been bypassed and ignored by the prime minister, especially in policy-making. The cabinet ministers, owing their office to the prime minister's pleasure, have often accepted this position, expressing their dissent at the most on some minor issues. Moreover, there has hardly been a reversal of prime ministerial dominance over the cabinet under the much weaker political personalities that have occupied the prime minister's chair subsequent to Indira Gandhi. Individual cabinet ministers have continued to have some degree of influence depending on their personal calibre, the extent of their own political support base and the extent of popular support they bring to the party in power.

This decline in the role of the cabinet is because of the increasing centralization of power in both the government and party in the hands of prime ministers, which is in turn due to the reliance of the ruling parties on them for winning elections.

A second factor contributing to the erosion in the authority of the cabinet has been the emergence of the Prime Minister's Secretariat, known popularly as the PMO, as an independent and virtually parallel executive that encroaches on and usurps the powers and functions of individual ministries and the cabinet. The PMO gathers information, gives advice, initiates policies—even economic and foreign policies—oversees their implementation, and takes a hand in deciding appointments and promotions of high administrative officials. The domineering role of the PMO, starting with Shastri and Indira Gandhi, has continued through the Janata period, the BJP-led government, headed by Atal Bihari Vajpayee, and to some extent even to the UPA government headed by Manmohan Singh.

This concentration of power in the hands of the prime minister has been rather unhealthy and has had a deleterious effect on policy-making as well as governance in general. While it is necessary that the country and the government is provided with a strong leadership, such strong leadership is not to be equated with the concentration of power in the hands of one individual. A strong cabinet also enables a multiplicity of interests and regions and cultural zones to share power and take an effective part in decision-making.

The Judiciary

One political institution that has held its ground in all essentials is the judiciary. The high judiciary, especially the Supreme Court, has fully utilized its right and obligation to enforce and interpret the constitution. It has set high standards of independence from the executive and legislative arms of the government. It has also been in the forefront of the defence of Fundamental Rights. For these reasons, it enjoys high legitimacy and respect among the people.

An important criticism of the Indian judiciary has been with regard to its socially conservative and status quoist character. This, it is argued, has made it insensitive to social issues and movements and resulted in its standing in the way of radical socio-economic legislation in the name of the defence of individual rights. For example, for years the Supreme Court interpreted the right of property to negate land reforms, nationalization of banks, etc. It also tended to ignore the Directive Principles of State Policy laid down in the constitution. But these conservative rulings of the Supreme Court were largely rectified because of the easy procedure provided in the constitution for amendment of its provisions. As we have seen in the earlier chapters, this procedure was repeatedly used by Nehru and Indira Gandhi to bend the stick the other way.

Moreover, in recent years, the Supreme Court itself has become more sensitive to social issues, from the rights of women, workers and minorities, to ecology, human rights, social justice and equity and social discrimination. An example of its social activism has been the introduction of public interest litigation under which even a postcard dropped by a victimized citizen to the Chief Justice is treated as a writ petition. This does not mean that the poor and the disadvantaged have actually acquired easy access to the higher courts. But it has opened a window that was completely shut earlier.

Perhaps the two most negative features of the Indian judicial system today are (i) the inordinate delays in the dispensation of justice as a case can drag on for years and even decades—the backlog of the cases in the High Courts alone amounting to several lakhs, and (ii) the high costs of getting justice, thus limiting access to the courts only to the well-off.

In recent years, the Supreme Court has also been accused of 'judicial despotism' by arrogating to itself powers which are vested in the executive or the legislature by the constitution. Judicial 'activism', some have suggested, can go too far.

Two other constitutional institutions, namely, the President and the Election Commission, have also performed quite well in independent India. The Presidents have functioned with dignity and in a non-controversial manner and within the widely accepted interpretation of presidential powers as provided in the constitution. Similarly, the Election Commissions have on the whole fulfilled with credit their constitutional obligation to hold free and fair elections involving millions of voters, nearly a million polling booths, and thousands of candidates in state and central elections.

Public Administration and the Bureaucracy

Perhaps the most important institutional crisis India faces is that of the quality of public administration and the bureaucracy. The deterioration of administration, even while its role in the life of the citizen has grown manifold, lies at the core of the 'crisis of governability' in India, including the breakdown of law and order and growth of crime in several states and large cities. Even the best of social and developmental legislation and policy measures are nullified in the course of their implementation.

The Indian bureaucracy is, moreover, rigid, basically conservative, pro-status quo, and resistant to social change, especially in regard to empowerment of the poor or redistributive measures. It favours the dominant social groups and influential persons, especially in rural areas. With its non-performance character and 'file-pushing' procedures, it is also not geared to take on the new task of economic development and involving the people in its processes. Moreover, even for routine work the administrative system has hardly any mechanism for enforcing discipline and punishing inefficiency and poor performance or checking corruption and rewarding meritorious work and honesty.

Perhaps the worst feature of Indian administration is revealed in its dealings with common people. Government servants, especially policemen, are generally discourteous, domineering, unhelpful, corrupt, inefficient and arbitrary in their approach towards the ordinary citizen. And, of course, the question of their accountability to the citizen cannot even be raised. This relationship of the government servant with the citizens goes some way in explaining the anti-incumbency voting in recent years. Using democracy and their voting power, the people, in their desperate quest for a friendly, honest, cooperative and minimally efficient administration, have been changing governments at every election.

Even at the middle and higher levels of bureaucracy, because of complex rules, regulations and procedures, and the increased personal and discretionary powers, there prevail inefficiency, undue delays, low standards of integrity, and corruption. The number of capable efficient and honest officials may, however, be larger than popularly believed.

At the same time, there has been an inordinate expansion of the bureaucracy, which is completely out of proportion to its usefulness or productivity. Consequently, the central, state and local government bureaucracies have come to claim too large a share of public expenditure and government resources, leading to the neglect of developmental and welfare activities.

One positive feature of the Indian bureaucracy that still holds is its tradition of political neutrality, with bureaucrats implementing policies of the government in power irrespective of their own opinions. It is noteworthy that the Communist governments in West Bengal and Kerala have not complained of the higher bureaucracy obstructing or sabotaging their policies on political, ideological or class grounds.

The partisanship that has been increasingly betrayed by the bureaucracy in recent years has not been on ideological or political grounds but has been 'functional' in character. Because of their dependence on ministers, MLAs and MPs for their appointment to plum postings, promotions, transfers, extensions in service, post-retirement employment, protection from disciplinary action against misuse of authority and corruption, and, in the case of lower levels of bureaucracy, for recruitment in the first place, many in the bureaucracy and the police have been increasingly enmeshed in political intrigue and in implementing the personal or political agenda of their political masters. Political interference with the bureaucracy and the police has led to the undermining of their discipline and effectiveness and the promotion of corruption among them. A result of this is that 'the vaunted "steel frame" has come to resemble porous foam rubber'. The bureaucracy no longer possesses that old pride in its service and an *esprit de corps* or a sense of solidarity, derived from common interests and responsibilities.

It is true that the overthrow of the existing inflexible bureaucratic administrative system is not possible; to be rid of bureaucracy is Utopian. Nevertheless, the need for its radical reform, regeneration and restructuring, so as to make it a suitable instrument for good government and development and change has now acquired an urgency which can no longer be ignored. Interestingly, the ills of the administrative structure, as well as the required remedial measures, have been repeatedly studied by several administrative reform commissions and a galaxy of public administration experts and experienced and knowledgeable bureaucrats. Only the political will to undertake these measures has been lacking so far. Two other aspects of the role and impact of bureaucracy may be referred to here. The bureaucratic values, mentality and structures have spread to nearly all spheres. They pervade India's academic and scientific institutions and are largely responsible for the incapacity of our scientists and academics to realize a large part of their potential. Similarly, bureaucratization and bureaucratic control of the public sector undertakings, combined with political interference, has come in the way of their healthy development and functioning.

The Police

The Indian police, showing all the weaknesses of the bureaucracy, suffers from certain additional maladies. By any criterion, it is in a bad shape. Its degeneration is largely responsible for the marked deterioration in the law and order situation. This is despite a more than hundred-fold increase in expenditure on the police and its sister paramilitary forces over the last sixty years. As a result the state has routinely to rely on the latter or sometimes even call in the army for maintaining civil order. The Indian police does not adequately perform its conventional role of crime prevention and investigation and the punishment of criminals, who readily assume that they will not be apprehended and if apprehended will not be successfully prosecuted and punished; in many cases even complaints against them will not be registered. All this happens partly because of police inefficiency, poor training of policemen and their ostensible connivance with the criminals and partly because of the slow-moving courts and the reluctance of the ordinary citizen to give evidence against criminals because of the fear of unchecked reprisals.

One of the worst features of the Indian police is the negative attitude towards the common people which it has inherited from the colonial period. The poor not only get little help from the police when they need or seek it, but are often met with a certain inhumanity, ruthlessness, violence and brutality. People encountering the law and order machinery in the course of their struggles for social justice and enforcement of laws and policies existing for redressal of their grievances are frequently subjected to lathi-charges, tear-gas attacks and at times unprovoked firing. Moreover, because of the spread of communalism in its ranks, the police bias against the minorities gets reflected in partisanship during communal riots. The Indian police has also gained notoriety for brutality against undertrials leading sometimes even to deaths— the number of reported custodial deaths in 1997 was over 800. The overall result is that people view the police with fear, resentment and hostility.

Political interference and manipulation and use of the police by politicians has made matters worse and has led to its corruption and demoralization and the spread of indiscipline in its ranks.

On their part, ordinary policemen and policewomen are quite discontented because their pay and service conditions, promotional chances and social status are quite poor. The necessity to rescue the police as a crucial institution of the state from utter degeneration, and to restrain, reform and restructure it, besides altering its attitude towards the common people, has perhaps been perceived by successive governments as the most urgent administrative task for the last several decades. Yet, till now, no government has made even an attempt in that direction. One example of this neglect has been the failure of all the central and state governments to implement or even pay serious consideration to the National Police Commission Report of 1979.

The Armed Forces

The Indian military has continued to be a highly disciplined and professional non-political force and has maintained the tradition of respecting democratic institutions and functioning under civilian supremacy and control. While the military advises on defence policy and has full operational authority during an armed conflict, the basic contours of defence policy are determined by the civil authority.

This development of the military–civil authority relationship was not fortuitous; it was carefully thought out by the national leadership of independent India from the beginning, worried as it was that India might also go the way of most of the Third World countries in falling prey to some form of military domination. This, along with not wanting to divert resources from the urgent task of economic development, was a major reason why Nehru and other leaders kept the numbers as also the profile of the armed forces quite low till 1962. After the India–China war, the size of *the military was increased though in terms of the country's* population it continues to be smaller than that of China and Pakistan or even South Korea, Indonesia, the US and most of the European countries. India has also kept its defence budget low in terms of its ratio to the national income. The aim has been to ensure that India's defence forces are adequate to meet threats to its security while not letting them become an intolerable drag on economic development.

Indian political parties have also kept up the tradition of not letting defence affairs and the military become a matter of partisan political debate or inter-party struggle. The apolitical role of the military has also been strengthened by the stability of India's democratic institutions and the high level of legitimacy they enjoy among the people, including the armed forces.

Moreover, immediately after independence, the class and regional bias from colonial times in the recruitment of both the ranks and officers of the armed forces was given up. They are now recruited from diverse social strata and castes, religions and regions. This has given the Indian military a heterogeneous, all-India character, and along with its training has imparted it a pan-Indian, national perspective, and made it a force for national unity and integrity. This has also made it difficult for any section of the military or its officer corps to think of staging a coup by mobilizing and consolidating the armed forces behind a single unconstitutional political centre.

While there is little danger of military intervention in political affairs, a disquieting feature that has emerged recently is that of

678 India Since Independence

the glorification of the military and the military ethos by certain political forces and in the media.

Centre–State Relations

In the long view, Indian federalism with its fine balance between the powers of the Centre and the states, as envisaged in the constitution, has stood up well despite occasional hiccups. It has succeeded in conforming to, as well as protecting, the diversity of the Indian people.

It is, of course, true that from the beginning India's federal system has been based on a strong Centre as carefully provided for in the constitution. In the actual working of the system, the central government gradually acquired greater influence over the states because of the pattern of economic development adopted, which was based on planning, public sector, central funding of anti-poverty programmes, and central financial disbursement to the states from its greater tax resources. Besides, in the first decades after independence, the same party controlled the central and the state governments, which gave the prime minister and the central Congress leadership a certain leverage over the state governments. This leverage was, however, not used sufficiently by Nehru, especially to push through land reforms, and was used often, but not wisely, by Indira Gandhi and Rajiv Gandhi. On the other hand, as over the years the states increasingly came to be ruled by parties other than Congress, central influence over state governments has declined. The dismantling of the licence quota system and the lesser role of central planning have also had a similar effect.

Over the years, the need for a strong central government with greater authority to influence state administrations has been felt in certain crucial areas. In a multi-religious, multilingual and multi-ethnic country like India, the Centre has the critical role of protecting minorities of all kinds as also the disadvantaged groups such as the Scheduled Castes and Scheduled Tribes, women and the landless. A strong Centre is also required to mitigate or at least prevent the growth of acute regional disparities by use of different means. A strong Centre has also been found necessary to deal with divisive caste, communal and regional forces and inter-regional conflicts.

At the same time, it would be wrong to say that the federal character of the Indian political system has suffered erosion over time. The states have continued to enjoy the autonomy provided by the constitution, as is evident from the functioning of the states ruled by parties other than the one ruling at the Centre. The state governments have continued to enjoy full autonomy in the fields of culture, education, land reforms, agricultural development, irrigation, health care and water supply and other areas of public welfare, local government and industrial development, except in the case of big industries and foreign investment for which central licences were needed till recently. Moreover, nearly all the central government plans and schemes of economic and social development and welfare have been implemented—well or badly—through the states' administrative machinery.

Unfortunately, certain states are or have been misruled and are lagging behind in economic development and welfare activities, including maintenance of a peaceful environment for their citizens. But this is so not because of central intervention or lack of state autonomy but because of maladministration by the state governments concerned. For example, land reforms were stymied or did not benefit the landless in some of the states because of the obduracy of their state administrations and despite pressure from the central government. On the other hand, the Kerala and West Bengal governments did not have much difficulty in introducing pro-peasant land reforms despite their ruling parties having little say in the central government.

The only real encroachment by the Centre on the states' constitutionally guaranteed autonomy has been the frequent use of the constitutional provision under Article 356 to impose central rule in the form of President's Rule in a state. This power was designed to be exercised rarely and in extraordinary circumstances such as the breakdown of administration or constitutional government in a state. It was, however, frequently used during the 1970s to dismiss inconvenient Opposition-ruled state governments or to discipline the state units of the ruling party. Fortunately, this misuse was largely checked later. It would, however, be wrong to say that the misuse of Article 356 reduced the autonomy of the states 'to a farce'.

We may point out in the end that a federation is not a weaker form of a Union; it is a form of a strong Union suitable to a diverse society. Similarly, a strong Centre and strong states are not antithetical to each other in a federation. This was also the conclusion of the Sarkaria Commission, appointed in 1980 to examine Centre–state relations. The federal principle requires that both the Centre and the states should be strong enough to perform their functions and to deliver on their programmes and promises. Nor is there any contradiction between a strong nation state and decentralization of power. Democracy, national cohesion and development in a diverse society like India's require not greater centralization but greater devolution of power and decentralization of decision-making and decision implementation.

In fact, greater decentralization and devolution of power to the third tier of government, that is, local self-government, was a basic part of the national movement's political–administrative agenda as also of the constitutional design of independent India. Consequently, an attempt was made in the late 1950s to transfer a great deal of local administrative power to elected zilla (district) parishads and village panchayats, with a view to develop grassroots democracy and enable effective political participation by the people and involve them in the planning and implementation of various developmental schemes. The results of this attempt were, however, utterly disappointing because these three-tier institutions were soon downgraded and stifled by the bureaucracy and used by the landed elite to enhance the power they already exercised through control over land and greater access to state administration and local bureaucracy. Furthermore, the state governments were adverse to parting with any of their powers to institutions of local self-government. The only states where the Panchayati Raj experiment bore fruit in the 1980s were Karnataka and West Bengal. The panchayats have, however, been restructured on a sounder footing all over the country in recent years and are beginning to show better results. One million of their 3 million members are women. On the other hand, the municipal government in most of India's cities and towns continues to be inefficient and corrupt and lacking in effective administrative power; and there has been a continuous decline in urban facilities such as roads, parks, street lighting, water and electric supply, sewage, health care and sanitation, schooling and control of crime and pollution.

Political Parties

Political parties, which are the kingpins of a democratic political structure, have gradually become the weakest link in India's political system. Political parties and the party system have been decaying and suffer from several maladies. Among these are: inter- and intra-party instability; intense infighting and factionalism within parties; weak and inefficient organization in many of them, resulting in their fragmentation; the continuous proliferation of parties, leading to the formation of unstable coalitions; continuous shifting of loyalties of political leaders and workers from one party to another; lack of democracy and debate within most parties; failure to mobilize and provide support to developmental, welfare and social justice policies, with non-participation and lack of mobilization of large segments of disadvantaged groups except during elections. Most political parties function without any long-term political programme or developmental design and increasingly live from election to election, diverting political debate from programmes and policies to peripheral or personalized issues. Many of them rely upon appeal to caste, religion or regional chauvinism. For example, since 1989, all-India elections have been fought over such non-issues as the Bofors and hawala scandals, the reconstruction of a non-existing temple, reservations of a few thousand jobs in government service, the merits of a Vajpayee over a foreign-born Sonia Gandhi, or victory over a few hundred intruders in Kargil.

To retain or acquire power, political parties have been indulging in unlimited populism, placating the voters with proliferating grants and subsidies, promises of free electricity, cheap rice and so on. Many parties and political leaders have been weakening political institutions by emphasizing their personal role and rule. One symptom of India's political malaise is the refusal of political leaders to retire, however old or discredited they might be. They firmly believe in the old Sanskrit proverb: *'Trishna najeerna vayemesh jeenam.'* (It is we who have become old and not our desires.)

An important consequence is that the political leadership has been losing authority among the people and is, therefore, unable to make the necessary institutional improvements and changes in society even if it wants to and even when it is backed by the required electoral majority. The more dangerous result is that the entire realm of politics has been getting devalued. There is among the people a growing distrust of and a cynicism towards politicians and political parties. Most people tend to associate politics and public life with hypocrisy and corruption. Because public life has thus become so discredited, idealistic young people have not been entering politics; those who do so regard politics primarily as an avenue for their social and economic mobility.

Yet, political workers, leaders and parties are critical to the functioning of political democracy and good governance. To sneer at them or to denigrate politics is a sure recipe for political disaster and an invitation to authoritarianism, fascism and militarism.

The decay of Congress organization has been serious since the democratic polity has developed so far under its broad umbrella or dominance. For years now, the flabby Congress party organization has done little systematic political work at the grassroots and has been little more than an electoral machine, though it has become increasingly ineffective even as such.

As we have seen earlier, though Indira Gandhi succeeded in replenishing the party's social support base, she weakened its organizational structure further by centralizing its functioning and increasing its dependence on a single leader. Unfortunately, no alternative political formation has emerged to perform the political functions Congress has performed as 'the central integrative institution of the system'. Congress is still the only national party which has a presence in all parts of the country and which is committed to secular democracy with a left-of-centre political character.

When in the Opposition, non-Congress parties have failed to provide responsible, rational and effective criticism. When in power, as in 1977, 1989 or 1998, they have not been able to put forward an alternative national developmental programme or agenda. Moreover, most often from 1967 till this day, with rare exceptions as in Kerala and West Bengal, they have formed unprincipled, opportunistic alliances to get into power, ignoring all ideological, programmatic or policy differences.

Among the Opposition parties, only the CPM and the BJP have been partial exceptions to the process of the decay and in some cases disintegration and disappearance of political parties. The CPM, too, has been stagnating for some time. It has been rigid and dogmatic both in its organizational structure and political programme and policies. Even though it has accepted the logic of the parliamentary democratic system, its programme fails to reflect this recognition fully. While its political practice follows Euro-Communism or is social democratic, its guiding theoretical framework continues to be Stalinist, based on the notion of the violent overthrow of the capitalist system. Moreover, it too has no national developmental perspective within a parliamentary democratic framework. The only choice it offers the people is that of an alternative social system.

The BJP is the only political party which has grown continuously in recent years. The growth of the BJP is, however, ominous not only because of its appeal to religious and communal sentiments but even more so because of the RSS domination over it. Its basic cadre, leadership and ideological framework is provided by the RSS which seeks to establish Hindu Rashtra based on the exclusion of the minorities. Organizationally and ideologically undemocratic, the RSS ideology represents the Indian version of fascism. Without the RSS, the BJP would become, despite its communal outlook, just another right-wing party—a right-wing version of Congress—which emphasizes Hinduness or has a particular appeal to some sections of Hindus in the manner of the Christian Democratic parties of Italy and Germany or the US Republican Party.

The party has grown in recent years because of the gradual disappearance of all other right-wing parties, decline of Congress, and the support of the burgeoning middle classes, which have, however, hardly any commitment to equity and social justice. But the BJP, too, is beginning to suffer from many of the ailments of Congress as it grows electorally as an alternative to it on an all-India scale.

In recent years, a large number of regional or one-state, one-leader parties have come into existence as a result of specific local factors, the decline of Congress, and the immense possibilities of making economic gains through politics.

Corruption

The prevalence of large-scale corruption, growth of crime and criminalization of politics and police have become major threats to India's development, democracy and moral health.

The colonial administration was from the beginning inaccessible to the common people and ridden with corruption except at the top where salaries were very high. But because of the underdeveloped character of the economy and the limited character of the colonial state's functioning, corruption affected only a small segment of the people. However, with the introduction of the permit-licence-quota regime, shortages of consumer goods, and high taxation during the Second World War, blackmarketing, and tax evasion became widespread. But corruption had not yet pervaded the administration or touched the political system.

Economic development, a rapid and large increase in the development and regulatory functions of the state opened up vast areas of the economy and administration to corruption. Political patronage could also now be used to gain access to the economic resources of the state and to acquire permits, licences and quotas.

There were major signals in the Nehru era that political and administrative corruption, including large-scale tax evasion, was beginning to burgeon. Strong and timely steps could, however, have checked further erosion of the system as also reversed the trend. In the 1950s, the tentacles of corruption were not yet far-reaching and major barriers to it existed in the form of a political leadership and cadre with their roots in the freedom struggle and Gandhian ethos, a largely honest bureaucracy, especially in its middle and higher reaches, and a judiciary with high integrity. But little was done in the matter. Nehru did take up individual cases of corruption but no strategy was evolved to deal with the roots of the problem and to act expeditiously.

As a result, the scale of corruption went on increasing as the government began to assume a larger role in the life of the people. Over time, the political system too began to fall prey to corruption. Not tackled at the lower levels, corruption gradually reached the higher levels of administration and politics. With added fillip provided by political patronage, rampant and all-pervading corruption began to engulf and corrode the administration. Corruption is, however, no longer the preserve of bureaucrats and politicians. No section of society is free from it; the media, academia, the professions and the judiciary have also got tainted by it. Today, so far as the common citizens are concerned, corruption, along with administrative delays and inefficiency, has become the bane of their lives.

The saving grace, however, is that there are still a large number of honest officials and political workers and leaders, but they are neither rewarded nor given recognition for being honest and are overshadowed by the constant denunciation, and even exaggeration of corruption in administration and public life.

A major source of corruption in the Indian political system since the late 1960s is the funding of elections. Elections have been becoming costlier by the day giving unfair advantage to those backed by moneybags and black money.

For years, communal and caste riots have been initiating hooligans into politics. As a result of communalism and casteism, laxity in enforcement of law and order, corruption, and the use of money and muscle power in elections there has been criminalization of politics in some parts of the country, with a nexus developing between politicians, businessmen, bureaucracy, police and criminals. The two naked expressions of this unhealthy phenomenon are the large scale on which money, criminal gangs and civil servants are used for 'booth-capturing' and to rig elections in some states and the criminal records of some of those elected to parliament and the state legislatures. One positive development in this respect, however, is the growing debate in the country on the ways and means—ideological, political and institutional—needed to deal with the twin evils of corruption and the role of criminal elements and money power in politics.

Conclusion

Despite a certain disarray and deterioration in some of India's political institutions, they have continued to function and shown a resilience that has surprised many political scientists and dismayed the prophets of doom. Despite ineffective government, unstable central governments in recent years, greater violence in society, corruption in administration and political life, decay in political parties and party system, the prevalence of widespread cynicism regarding politics and political institutions, India's democracy has shown remarkable vitality and continues to flourish, and its institutions have taken deep root. The authority of the electoral system has gone unchallenged so far. Elections, conducted under the watchful eyes of an independent Election Commission, still validate leaders and parties. The weapon of the vote is cherished and freely used by the people, especially the poor and the intelligentsia, to express their desires, to show their preference for particular policies and to punish at the ballot box those who promise but do not deliver.

The only unfortunate part is that, as in other democracies, the Indian political system lacks a mechanism through which the direction and implementation of the policies preferred by the electorate can be enforced. There is, therefore, a strong need to reform and reinvigorate both political and administrative institutions to meet the changed needs of the time, especially the demands of the poor and the disadvantaged for a greater share in the fruits of development and for the lessening of their oppression. The institutions as they have functioned so far have been geared to the maintenance of the social status quo and stability; and they have not performed that task badly. But they have to be reshaped further to undertake the new twin tasks of economic development and social transformation, mandated by the immense politicization of the people brought about by the national movement and the functioning of democracy. Simultaneously, there was and is also the need to create fresh structures and institutions through which the people's energies are harnessed for these twin tasks. Clearly, the role of political parties and political leaders is critical in this respect. While political leaders of the type and calibre thrown up by the freedom struggle can perhaps no longer be expected, the future of the Indian people depends a great deal on their capacity to produce and reproduce leaders with a basic social and political commitment to the ideals cherished by the freedom struggle and embodied in the constitution.

The Dawn of the New Millennium: Achievements, Problems and Prospects

As we proceed further into the new millennium, fundamental questions confront us. What has India achieved so far? What problems does it face? And what are the tasks and prospects for the future?

Today, our newspapers, weeklies and books on current affairs, besides many intellectuals, tend to see India since independence as an area of darkness. In 1993, a writer, C. Thomas, pithily summarized, the 'torrent of wretchedness', though not sharing it, as follows:

> . . . language riots, caste riots, communal bloodshed, the assassination of Indira Gandhi and Rajiv Gandhi, wars with Pakistan and China, secessionism in Punjab, an uprising in Kashmir, bloodshed in Assam, anti-Hindi movements in the South, starvation, corruption, pollution, environmental catastrophe, disparities of wealth and poverty, caste prejudice, burning brides, *sati*, killing girl babies, bonded labour, child labour, criminalization of politics, discrimination against women, human rights abuses.[1]

This ran contrary to the optimism which many intellectuals maintained till Nehru was alive. But, as S. Gopal, one of our tallest historians, put it in 1984, with the passage of time, the Nehru era began to

> . . . appear more and more of a faded golden age . . . It is as if, when he died, he took a whole epoch with him. The

Nehru age, of confident assumptions, high aspirations and considerable achievements, seems today a vanished world. There is a sickening sense of lost ideals and missed opportunities. Public service is no longer a selfless pursuit, politics in India has become dispirited and the objectives which he gave his people, then so challenging, now seem tired and muddled . . . The collective self-confidence of India has received severe jolts, making the people less optimistic and economically self-assured and more fragmented socially and politically.[2]

There is, of course, much in India of yesterday and today which gives rise to despair and despondency among many, for who can deny the existence of mass poverty, gross inequality, intolerable illiteracy, social injustice, gender discrimination, social oppression, corruption, casteism and communalism and poor quality of life in general. But these and many other weaknesses should not cloud our vision. There is not enough reason for us to allow ourselves to be stifled in a pall of gloom, to be drowned in a sea of depression.

Certainly, we have by no means solved all our problems—some quite serious—even after sixty years of independence. Not all that the Indian people had hoped to achieve during the heady days of the freedom struggle or set out to accomplish on the eve of independence has been achieved. Undoubtedly, serious deficiencies have remained; fresh weaknesses have emerged; new dangers have arisen.

Still, it would be wrong not to acknowledge that India has made substantial all-round progress; its achievements in the last sixty years have been considerable by any historical standards, especially if we keep in view the level from which it started and 'how difficult was the terrain along which we had to tread'.[3] Vast political, economic and social changes have taken place. In the process, a lot of scum, gathered over the centuries, has also come to the top. But the legacy of the freedom struggle has held—and not got diluted significantly. The qualitative advance made by India in many areas has been ignored by many because it has occurred gradually and without any ostentation or drama. India is now making a breakthrough in many areas. The advance already made in the political, economic and social spheres, when taken in its entirety, should give the Indian people faith in their capacity to find solutions to the many remaining problems and ills of their society.

National Unity

A major Indian success has been scored in the strengthening of Indian unity politically, economically and emotionally and the pushing forward of the complex process of nation-in-the-making. India's immense diversity has not hampered the process, even while this diversity has been sustained and has, in fact, flowered. Also, tensions generated by immense social churning have not come in the way of further developing the sense and sentiment of Indianness, of Indians being one people.

There have, of course, been several challenges to Indian unity but they have mostly been overcome. The solution of the divisive official language issue, reorganization of linguistic states, refusal to counterpoise regional and cultural identities to an Indian identity, sympathetic handling of the problems of the tribals and their integration into the national mainstream, firm treatment of separatist movements even when showing an understanding of the feelings underlying them, genuine efforts, even when not very successful, to reduce regional inequality, have gone a long way in ensuring that Indian unity is no longer fragile and that the existence of India as a viable and assured political entity is under little threat.

Disparities between states still remain, but they do not threaten Indian unity, for they are often caused by infirmities internal to a state and are not the result of internal colonialism or sub-colonialism where a backward region is subjected to economic subordination and exploitation by another more advanced region or by the rest of the country.

A large number of regional or one-state parties have come into existence over the years. They have freely assumed power in the states and have even shared power at the Centre by allying with one or the other national party or becoming part of an alliance on an all-India basis. These parties fight for greater access to central resources and not for their own separate and fuller control over the region's resources for they already enjoy that.

Moreover, Indian politics, both electoral and non-electoral, has increasingly become national in nature. As a result of regular countrywide general elections, the dominant presence of all-India political parties, especially Congress, nationwide campaigns on economic and political issues, and the operation of all-India transport and communication networks, including radio, TV, newspapers and films, a single political culture—a unitary 'language of politics'—pervades all parts of the country. It has, therefore, not been accidental that even after the end of the Nehru era the electoral waves affecting the 1971, 1977, 1980 and 1984 general elections were national in character, as was the victory of the BJP-led NDA in the general election of 1999.

However, regional economic and developmental disparities still pose serious problems along with the communal and caste divide. Communalism, in particular, continues to stalk the land. For decades, communal forces were being contained electorally, and their ideological spread was also restricted. But in the last three decades or so, there has been a weakening of the anti-communal consensus among secular forces. Quite often, as in 1989, and more recently in 1998 and 1999, they have directly or indirectly allied with communal forces, thus giving the latter credibility and respectability. Communalism is today the chief threat to Indian unity for India cannot remain a strong and united nation except on the basis of secularism. We have seen in the chapter on Punjab, what can happen if communalism is not dealt with firmly and squarely in time, if religion is not completely separated from politics and if, instead, an effort is made to compromise with and conciliate communal forces. In this respect, an area needing particular attention and innovation is that of culture and tradition. Indigenous cultures and traditions and popular religions play an important part in the life of a people. If the communal and obscurantist forces are not to be permitted to appropriate India's cultural heritage, it is necessary for modern and secular forces to establish creative and critical links with the country's cultural heritage and tradition. They have, unfortunately, not fully explored this area of public life. In particular, secular, democratic elements must distinguish between religion as philosophy, spiritual experience, guide to morality and psychological solace and religion as dogma, bigotry and a vehicle for communalism.

In any case, it is very necessary to carefully nurture the process of nation-in-the-making as it is not a unilinear process and can therefore suffer setbacks and interruptions as it faces new challenges.

Democratic Political Systems

The great success story of independent India has been its secular, federal and multi-party political system. The nation has had to face tasks of immense magnitude and confront numerous problems, for example having to function in a backward economy with an impoverished citizenry, being torn by violent social conflicts, having to wage three major wars and face high costs of national defence since 1947, gradual weakening of many of its institutions and being constantly under international pressure. Despite all this, the political system has, however, shown remarkable resilience and flexibility and has stood the test of time and exhibited an ability to overcome several crises, for example those of 1967–69 and of 1974–77. Indira Gandhi was to put it pithily in August 1972 when asked to list India's achievements since 1947: 'I would say our greatest achievement is to have survived as a free and democratic nation.'[4]

Political stability has been an important characteristic of independent India's political system. There have been, since 1967, rapid changes of governments in the states and, since 1989, at the Centre, but political stability has persisted. Different political forces and formations have waged their political battles in the political arena prescribed by the constitution. Changes in governments have taken place according to constitutional and democratic rules and have invariably been quietly and often gracefully accepted by those voted out of power by parliament or the electorate. People have taken it for granted that elections, largely free and fair and held regularly, would decide who would rule the country, a state or a panchayat. Greater political participation by the people, including in its agitational forms, has not led to political instability.

The political system has also acquired more or less unquestioned legitimacy; the few who have questioned its basic tenets having fallen in line in the end. Thus, the Communists for several decades challenged, though only in theory, the basic constitutional structure as being geared to domination by the ruling, exploiting classes. But today they are among the more vocal defenders of the constitution. The communalists have been trying from the outset to undermine the secular character of Indian society and polity but even they pay verbal obeisance to secularism though they try to distort its character through redefinition. Similarly, though

Jayaprakash Narayan questioned the multi-party parliamentary system during the 1960s and the early 1970s, in the end he too accepted it after the lifting of the Emergency in 1977. It is also significant that new aspiring groups have been increasingly functioning within the broad parameters of the political system to advance their interests. In fact, the very longevity of the system, its continued functioning for over six decades has given it strength and enabled it to strike deep roots. What W.H. Morris-Jones wrote in 1966 is equally valid today: 'The combination of political stability with establishment of a free, and freely moving, political system is what we entitled to call India's political miracle.'[5]

Entrenchment of Democracy

Perhaps the most significant of India's achievements since 1947 is the firm entrenchment of political democracy and civil liberties which have become a basic feature of Indian life. Indians enjoy today a free Press, the freedom to speak, travel and form associations, the right to freely criticize the government; they have competitive elections, unrestricted working of political parties, an independent judiciary, the right to participate in political life and to change the government through the ballot box, and freedom from fear of arbitrary arrest.

India alone among the post-colonial countries has sustained a democratic and civil libertarian polity since its inception. Commitment to democratic values has deepened over the years among most Indians. Paradoxically, even the experience of the Emergency underlined this attachment. The belief has also taken root that social transformation through a democratic political framework is possible. Nationalization of banks and several industries, land reforms—even quite radical as in Kerala and West Bengal—and effective functioning of Panchayati Raj, with its provision for 30 per cent reservation of seats for women, and successful and unopposed working of the system of reservations for the SCs and STs in several states, has shown that political democracy as such is not an obstacle to social transformation and socio-economic reforms in the direction of equity and equality.

A prominent and positive feature of Indian political development in the post-independence period has been the steadily growing political awareness among the people and their greater direct and indirect participation in the political process.

The freedom struggle had already politicized large sections of the people. Popular agitational and electoral politics have pushed this process further. India has certainly become over time a politically more active society with an ever larger number of people and social groups being politically mobilized and 'incorporated into the body politic'.

The disadvantaged—women, agricultural labourers, small peasants, the urban poor—have increasingly come to believe that their social condition is unjust and is capable of being changed and that the desired change can be brought about through politics and by the assertion of their political rights. The people in general want a share in political power and a greater share of the wealth they produce. They are also no longer willing to tolerate certain naked forms of oppression, discrimination, deprivation and neglect. For example, a government which would let a large number of people die in a famine, as happened during the droughts in the colonial period, would not last even a few weeks.

People have also become aware of the power and value of their right to vote at various levels from the panchayats to parliament and of the benefits to be derived from its exercise. The politics of booth-capturing, sale and purchase of votes, vote banks and patronage have been gradually receding and the voter's choice becoming more autonomous. One example is the increasing refusal of women to vote according to the wishes of the male members of the family. Moreover, the poor and the oppressed no longer accept dictates in regard to their choice of parties and candidates. Though they are still open to populist appeals or appeals on grounds of caste, region or religious community, they can no longer be easily bullied or bought. People now tend to vote according to issues, policies, ideologies or group interests so as to garner greater advantage from the government's development and welfare schemes.

It is true that the role of caste in electoral politics has increased in recent years, but quite often caste as a political factor has come in primarily when other social, economic and political issues have been absent in the electoral arena or when such issues have got grouped around caste as in the case of jobs and educational opportunities. However, caste as a factor in politics has invariably receded when broader national issues have come to occupy centre-stage as in the *garibi hatao* election of 1971, the JP Movement of

1974–75, the anti-Emergency election of 1977 and the 1984 election, after the assassination of Indira Gandhi, when the country was seen to be in danger.

The voters have not only become more sensitive to the larger social, economic and political issues but are also more assertive and demanding—the people they vote for have to respond more actively to their needs and demands. A major reason for the volatility of the voters' behaviour in recent times, resulting in wide swings in electoral mandates, is the heightened voter expectation from the electoral process and the pressing demand by the voters for performance and fulfilment of the promises made during elections. Interestingly, elections at all levels have repeatedly shown that people have little hesitation in voting against those in power because they are no longer in awe or fear of people in authority.

Politicization and mobilization of the hitherto unpoliticized, which has been a continuous and ongoing process, has sometimes taken the form of popular agitations, which have involved many of the urban and some of the rural sections of society. They have, however, so far left the rural poor untouched in large parts of the country. The politics of protest has fed on demands for social justice, a share in the gains of development and participation in decision-making. It has grown as the more disadvantaged and oppressed classes and groups have come on the political stage. Power struggle and popular mobilization in rural areas has, however, often taken a casteist form in the absence of mobilization around class and of struggle against the caste system and caste oppression and discrimination.

A major step towards further democratization of the political system and greater people's participation as also greater control over their own lives has been taken with the inauguration of the freshly designed Panchayati Raj.

Popular Participation in the Political Process

Perhaps the most important political task today is to deepen democracy and make it more meaningful for the mass of the people by enabling their greater participation in the political process. Voting in periodic elections should not be regarded as the only form of such participation.

So far there has been a general failure to politically mobilize the poor and the disadvantaged and to shift the balance of social and political power in their favour. The capitalists, who are major beneficiaries of economic development, the landed peasants, who have gained most from land reforms and the Green Revolution, the intelligentsia, the professionals, and the middle classes, for whom immense opportunities have opened up after 1947, the government and public sector employees, the organized working class and the upper layers of the SCs and STs, all have been able to find various means of protecting and promoting their interests. They have thus been able to tilt democracy in their favour. But the poor have been unable to do so to any great extent. They have been left out of the larger decision-making process and have had little voice in the day-to-day decisions affecting their lives. Their access to resources being generated in the economy and the social system has remained limited. They have been unable to turn the strength of numbers into effective power because the level of their mobilization has been low. Their political self-activity has lain dormant. Even the radical parties, groups and organizations have tended to neglect their organization and mobilization. The poor do, of course, at times rise up in protest and sometimes even revolt, and at elections exercise, often enthusiastically, their voting right in the hope that the persons elected would help improve their social and economic condition. But much more accountability to the agenda of the poor is needed.

The widest mobilization of the bottom millions is also necessary because neither development nor social change and not even national unity can be fully promoted without their active involvement. That this should have been forgotten by the heirs to the freedom struggle is ironical, for was not a hallmark of that struggle the active role of the masses in it? And did not Gandhi's greatness lie precisely in promoting the non-violent mobilization of the common people, thus making India's freedom struggle perhaps the greatest mass movement in world history. Jawaharlal Nehru's design for development and social transformation too depended on active pressure from below; that he failed to implement his own design is another matter.

Forms of Political Protest

Political protest, along with the right to vote, is one of the basic ingredients and a normal part of democratic politics. For the oppressed sections of society, it is a critical part of their effective participation in politics and is essential for the expression of their demands and grievances. India is, therefore, going to have more, not less, protest as different sections of society awaken to political life and work for faster changes in their social condition. Protest movements are also very important means for the people to force those in authority, particularly those wielding political power, to respond to their demands. For the poor, perhaps this is the only means of doing so. All this should be taken for granted. The important question, therefore, is what are to be the forms of protest in a civil libertarian representative democracy? As of now, Indians have, however, failed to evolve appropriate forms of protest or a consensus on what they can or cannot do.

Popular protest movements by political parties, students, workers, farmers, government employees and common citizens have most often taken the form of demonstrations, hunger strikes, hartals, strikes in the workplace or educational institutions, dharnas, bandhs, gheraos, blockages of roads (rasta roko), satyagraha, civil disobedience or disobedience of laws, leading to mass arrests, and rioting. While some of these forms of protest are inherently coercive, others more often than not culminate in violence and breakdown of law and order and wanton violation of laws duly enacted by elected legislatures or rules laid down by those authorized to do so. In many cases the protesters coerce into joining their actions the very people they are supposed to represent. The protest, especially in the form of demonstrations, quite often ends up in attacks on cars, buses, trains, government and private property, college buildings and so on. The situation is quite often worsened by an overreaction and an equally and sometimes greater violent response by the authorities and the police, leading often to a vicious circle.

The purpose of such protest movements is, however, not to convince the concerned authority of the justness of their demands, or to win it over by 'changing his heart', to use a Gandhian phrase, but to erode its authority and to coerce it to accept their demands. The blame is, of course, not to be put only on one side, viz., the protesters. One reason why many take to violent protest is because those in power turn a deaf ear to peaceful protest and respond only to violent agitations. In this respect, what Myron Weiner wrote in 1962 continues to have relevance:

> Only when public order is endangered by a mass movement is the government willing to make a concession, not because they consider the demand legitimate, but because they then recognise the strength of the group making the demand and its capacity for destructiveness. Thus, the government often alternates between unresponsiveness to the demands of large but peaceful groups and total concession to groups that press their demands violently.[6]

In other words not only must the organizers of popular agitations not coerce the authorities but try to change their hearts, the latter too must be willing to undergo a change of heart whenever the protesters' demands are justified.

We believe that just as the effort to prevent or suppress peaceful protest is undemocratic, violent protest too poses a threat to the functioning of democracy.

We may raise another question in this context. Is even satyagraha or non-violent disobeying of laws legitimate in a democratic system, and, if so, under what conditions or circumstances? For some insights on this, we may turn for guidance to Gandhiji, the originator of satyagraha and in whose name protest movements have often been launched after independence. On the eve of independence Gandhiji warned the people that satyagraha and civil disobedience would no longer be the appropriate technique in free India against a government elected by the people themselves. Even against the British, he insisted on satyagraha and civil disobedience being completely non-violent in word and deed. In any case, they were to be 'the weapon of last resort' where gross injustice or immoral action by the government or other authorities was involved and all other methods of redressal had been tried and failed. The forms of protest tried out in independent India in imitation of Gandhiji's methods are, in fact, more akin to what he described as duragraha. We may give a long quotation from the *Conquest of Violence* by the Gandhian scholar Joan V. Bondurant to make the clear difference between satyagraha and duragraha as Gandhiji perceived it:

In the refinement of language for describing techniques of social action, duragraha serves to distinguish those techniques in which the use of harassment obscures or precludes supportive acts aimed at winning over the opponent . . . In those instances where democratic procedures have been damaged through default or design, and where the legal machinery has been turned towards a travesty of justice, civil disobedience may be called into play . . . But if civil disobedience is carried out in the style of duragraha, and not within the framework of satyagraha, it may well lead to widespread indifference to legality and lend itself to those who would use illegal tactics to undermine faith in democratic processes.[7]

Gandhiji would never have advised giving up of protest which was to him the breath of the life of a citizen. But he would also not have followed the route which some of the Gandhians and most of the non-Gandhians have followed since his death.

Smaller men could only imitate him. He would, however, have, as he did promise, innovated and evolved new forms of protest as also political activism suited to a self-governing, democratic and civil libertarian polity. That is also the task which leaders and organizers of popular protest should undertake today. That this can be done is shown by the civil rights movement in the US and the anti-nuclear peace movement in Britain.

Economic Performance

Independent India's economy has been quite vibrant and its performance on the whole satisfactory, as the chapters on the Indian economy bring out. It has made long strides in almost all its different aspects though the extent of achievement is not what was possible and what was needed.

India has overcome economic stagnation and broken the vicious circle of poverty–underdevelopment–poverty. It has also broken from the colonial economic structure and has been successful in laying the foundations of a self-reliant, independent economy. It has thus fulfilled the design of the founders of the Republic, to go from political independence to economic independence.

India has not been autarchic or self-sufficient or based on national seclusion, living within its own cocoon. That was in any case not possible. It could only develop as an integral part of the world economy. But independent India's integration with the world economy has been different from that of the colonial period; it is based on the needs of India's autonomous development and free of subordination to the economies of the advanced capitalist countries of Western Europe and North America. Nor has foreign capital any longer a stranglehold on Indian economy. In fact, dependence of independent India on foreign capital and foreign aid has been quite low. Today, neither finance nor any major or economically strategic industry is under the control of foreign capital. Multinational corporations have also played a relatively minor role in the Indian economy. However, for advanced technology India still continues to be dependent on some industrialized countries.

Immediately after independence, India successfully developed an economic pattern of its own, namely, a mixed economy, which placed equal emphasis on the active economic role of the state and the market and developed a complementary relationship between the public and the private sectors. Since 1991, India has also been able to carry through economic reforms; dismantling bureaucratic controls and the licence quota raj and developing a closer integration with the world economy, through a gradual process, without hurting the economy or the people's living standards.

India has also been able to transform its landlord-ridden, semi-feudal agrarian structure, though with many weaknesses and not to the benefit of the landless.

India has had consistent growth over the years in agriculture and industry and in national income. Indian economy has been remarkably stable and little susceptible to world cyclical swings. It was able to withstand without serious damage three major adversities in the world economy: the oil shock of the 1970s, the collapse of the socialist countries of Europe with which India had close and significant economic ties, and the East and South-east Asian economic crisis of 1997. It was also able to recover from the 1991 fiscal and foreign exchange crisis without serious cost or dislocation.

Stagnation of the colonial period in agricultural production and productivity has come to an end with agriculture growing more than three and a half times since 1950. India has achieved self-sufficiency in food with foodgrain production having grown at

3 per cent per year. Famines have become a distant memory, despite periodic droughts. The effect of the monsoons on agricultural production, though still there, lessens with the passage of time.

Industry has grown more than twenty-two times since 1950. It has, moreover, undergone structural transformation and considerable diversification. The weakness in the basic and capital goods sector has been overcome to a considerable, though not to the desirable, extent. The share of this sector in total industrial production has gone up sharply, and India's dependence on the advanced countries for basic goods and capital equipment has been greatly reduced.

There has also been a massive expansion of the power, transport and banking sectors. India has also become more or less self-sufficient in defence production with capacity to produce long-range missiles and atomic weapons, though it still has to purchase some highly sophisticated defence equipment from abroad. It has also acquired a large trained scientific and technical force.

India's national income has grown more than tenfold from 1950 to 2004–05 and its per capita income by 3.3 times despite a very high rate of population growth.

Referring to the Indian economy, a sympathetic scholar, Francine R. Frankel, had written in 1978: 'During much of the later 1960s and into the 1970s, there were chronic food shortages, sharp inflationary price spirals, low availability of domestic raw materials, shortfalls in industrial output, underutilised capacity in consumer goods industries, stagnant or declining rates of public investment, and diversion of scarce foreign exchange for imports of foodgrains and raw materials.'[8] Such a situation is not easy to conceive today. And her prediction that India was likely to 'return to a low-level equilibrium in which growth rates did not significantly exceed the rate of population increase' was proved false in the 1980s itself.[9]

India has during the last few years entered a period of high economic growth and is on the way to becoming an important global economic power. As such it is bound to play a major role in the world economy of the twenty-first century.

Economic Problems and Dangers

All the same the economic problems that India is yet to solve are enormous. It is likely to face major new challenges in the next few years. India is still a poor and backward country by world standards, and the economic gap vis-à-vis the advanced capitalist countries has widened instead of narrowing. This is especially true of the technological gap between the two. Despite the long strides Indian economy has taken, it still does not manage to fully satisfy the basic needs of all of its people, what to speak of their aspirations, in part because of the skewed income distribution.

Nor is India's economic independence irreversible. We are living in a world capitalist system which is utterly unequal and still divided into core and peripheral countries. The world system even now consists of competing sovereign states and national economies; and the core, developed countries do everything to maintain their privileged position in the world economy, while trying to weaken still further the relative position of the states and economies of the periphery. India's economic development, though independent so far, has not reached that stage where its economy, because of being incorporated into and integrated with the world capitalist system, no longer faces the danger of re-peripheralization, that is, subordination and subservience to the core economies.

Under Nehru and Indira Gandhi it was attempted to bridge the gap between India and the advanced countries by concentration on heavy industry and electricity generation. This was a necessary task for India had to compress in a few decades what Europe had achieved in more than 150 years. But while we were running to catch up with the past, the present was moving into the future in the advanced parts of the world. While the vision and the objectives of the Nehru era—that of catching up with the Western world while being self-reliant and retaining economic independence and on that basis building a more egalitarian and just society—have to continue to inspire the Indian people, the means and goals of technological transformation have to undergo a change. The world economy has entered a new, momentous phase. Application of science to industry, agriculture, trade and communication has taken another leap forward.

Today, economic development or the fourth industrial revolution is based on microchip, biotechnology, information technology, new sources of energy and advanced managerial techniques. All these rely overwhelmingly on the development of intellect or what may be described as 'brain-power' or the developed scientific, technical, managerial and other intellectual capacities of the citizens. There is every danger that there may be a new international division of labour where advanced technology, research and development and other 'brain' activities would get concentrated in currently advanced or core countries while India and other underdeveloped and developing countries would be confined to production of traditional consumer and producers' goods and to 'muscle and nerves' activities.

The danger of peripheralization also takes the form of domination through the investment of financial or industrial capital. But, obviously, not all foreign capital investment poses this danger. Indian economy, the Indian capitalist class and the Indian state have reached a stage where they can definitely take in a certain quantum of foreign capital, especially to serve the dual purposes of absorption of technology and organizational structures and skills and provide a degree of competition to indigenous entrepreneurs, private or state. What India has to avoid is the pattern of Latin American-style dependent development where the multinational corporations control key economic sectors and positions and determine the predominant patterns of internal production and international exchange. There is the great danger that though foreign capital investment would result in industrial development it would simultaneously perpetuate technological backwardness relative to the advanced capitalist countries. While some industries of the earlier phases or even of the latest phase of industrial revolution would be transferred to India, the advanced 'brain' activities would largely continue to be kept out of it and would remain the monopoly of the core, that is, advanced countries. While there is a need to moderate our former hostility to foreign capital, the policy of controlling its direction and role has to be continued.

Because the latest phase of the Industrial Revolution is based on brain activity, education, especially higher education, acquires great significance. However, its quality and not merely its spread is important. The fact that the education imparted to the overwhelming majority of students in rural as well as urban areas is of extremely low quality means that the country is deprived of the vast potential of its brain-power. In fact, this weakness may be described as internal brain drain. The task of renovating the utterly insufficient and defective educational system, therefore, acquires added urgency. Any populist effort, in its many guises, to neglect the quality of education has to be opposed, for the cost of neglect in this sphere is as great as the neglect of machine-making and other capital goods industries in the earlier periods.

For various reasons, India has been subjected to large-scale brain drain to the US and Europe. Ways and means have to be found to prevent and reverse this trend. More than NRI (non-resident Indian) capital we need the NRIs physically back in India; and we have to find ways to somehow check the continuing outflow.

Planning and an active role of the state in economic development, including the role of the public sector in production, still retain their great significance for without them India cannot hope to compete in the new technology sector. However, the public sector has to be made more productive through the more efficient use of resources and competition with the private sector. It also needs to be freed from the stranglehold of political patronage and the ill-fitting and incompetent bureaucracy.

The Areas of Darkness

Wide prevalence of poverty, inequality and social injustice and the poor quality of life of the vast majority of the people are the major areas of darkness in India's social and economic development. The Indian people enter the twenty-first century with a low per capita income, an intolerable level of illiteracy and a lowly position on the world index of human resource development, despite commendable achievements in terms of economic growth and political democracy. A change in the social and economic condition of the people has occurred since independence but at too slow a rate.

Putting forward the social objectives of planning before parliament in 1954, Jawaharlal Nehru had said:

> We are starting planning for the 360 million human beings in India . . . What do the 360 million people want? . . . it is obvious enough that they want food; it is obvious enough that they want clothing, that they want shelter, that they want health . . . I suggest that the only policy that we should have in mind is that we have to work for the 360 million people; not for a few, not for a group but the whole lot, and to bring them up on an equal basis.[10]

When placing the Second Five Year Plan before parliament, Nehru defined socialist society as a 'society in which there is equality of opportunity and the possibility for everyone to live a good life'.[11]

These objectives have been only partially fulfilled. A humane, egalitarian and just social order has still to come into existence. For too many, 'a good life' is still a pie in the sky.

We have dealt with social injustice and the efforts to overcome it in the chapters on caste and communalism. In the next two sections we will deal with the problems of poverty and the quality of life.

Poverty

Independent India has failed to eradicate poverty despite consistent economic growth in the years since 1947. This is a major blot on its record. Yet, it is also true that though poverty remains, it has been lessened.

In the early 1960s, the Planning Commission formulated the concept of the poverty line. Below this line were people whose consumption, especially of foodgrains, did not come up to a minimum level in terms of calories. While no figures were available for the colonial period or the early years after independence, it was calculated that in 1970–71 nearly 59 per cent of the population was living below the poverty line. Since then, this figure has been steadily going down. It had declined to 51.3 per cent in 1977–78, 44.5 per cent in 1983, 36 per cent in 1993–94, 26.1 per cent in 1999–2000, and 22.1 per cent in 2004–05. The obverse side of these figures is that over 244 million people are still below the poverty line. Moreover, poverty varies across different states, being as high as 42 per cent in Bihar and 9 per cent in Punjab in 2004–05. The main brunt of poverty is borne by landless agricultural labourers, small and marginal farmers and the urban poor.

The reduction in poverty levels was largely the result of various anti-poverty, mostly employment generating, programmes initiated in the mid-1970s by the Indira Gandhi government under the guidance of one of India's finest and socially committed economists, Sukhamoy Chakravarty. These programmes have been pursued more vigorously, though still inadequately financed, since 1984–85. As the figures show, they have had a significant impact despite corruption and the failure to always reach the targeted groups. Particularly effective has been the Employment Guarantee Scheme in Maharashtra which has been replicated by an act of parliament all over India from 2006. In this context, it may be pertinent to point out that what made possible the taking up and implementation of the anti-poverty programmes was the radical restructuring of the Indian economy brought about by the Nehruvian planning strategy during the 1950s and 1960s.

Even apart from the proof of the poverty line statistics, it is observed that Indians no longer live in abysmal poverty as they did under colonialism. The mass starvation of that period has been conquered. India has not had a major famine since the Bengal famine of 1943. In the worst drought of the century in 1987–88 very few died of hunger or disease. The same was the experience of the serious droughts of 1965–67 and 1972–73.

Similarly, in the colonial period and the immediate post-independence years a vast number of Indians went without two meals a day, several months in a year, and sometimes without even one meal. A recent study has shown that the number of people who could not obtain two square meals a day had dropped to 19 per cent of the households in 1983 and to less than 5 per cent in 1994.[12]

The reduction in the incidence of poverty is also indicated by the greater availability of foodgrains and other food items over the years. For example, per capita foodgrain consumption had fallen by over 24 per cent between 1901 and 1941; it increased from 394.9 grams per day in 1951 to 462.7 grams per day in 2002—an overall increase of 28 per cent. This growth in availability is also evident in the case of several other items of consumption. The annual availability of cloth per head was 9 metres in 1950, 15 metres in 1960 and 31.4 metres in 2002–03. The table presents the picture of annual per head availability of certain other important articles of consumption.

Year	Edible oils (kg)	Vanaspati (kg)	Sugar (kg)	Tea (gm)	Coffee (gm)	Electricity Domestic (kWh)
1955	2.5	0.7	5.0	362.0	67.0	2.4
1975	3.5	0.8	6.1	446.0	62.0	9.7
2002	7.2	1.4	16.3	670.0	55.0	79.0

Similarly, from 1950 to 2005 production of milk increased by nearly six times, from 17 million tonnes to 97.1 million tonnes, and milk availability per capita increased from 124 grams per day to 241 grams. Production of eggs increased in the same period by more than twenty-four times from 1,832 million to 46,231 million, and fish more than nine times from 0.7 million tonnes to 6.7 million tonnes.

Still, the incidence of poverty and especially endemic undernourishment, particularly among children, is very much there, though not stark hunger or utter destitution, except among the very old and the handicapped. A dent in poverty has been made, though it is not deep enough.

The problem of poverty has been further compounded by the existence of glaring inequality, social and economic. While the poor have not become poorer and have derived some benefit from economic growth, the gap between them and the rich has grown before our very eyes. The fruits of this growth and the resulting significant rise in national income have been disproportionately gathered by a few belonging to the upper and to a certain extent middle layers of society. Maldistribution of income, opportunities and power has been, moreover, built into the very social and class structure of the country. With the onset of liberalization of the economy and economic development on the basis of 'the animal spirits of the capitalists', inequality is likely to grow unless counter-steps are taken, even if economic development is somewhat hurt.

Quality of Life

Even apart from the problem of poverty, the quality of life of the masses in India is another major area of neglect as their physical and social needs have not been met even to a minimally desired level. Some progress has been made in this respect but it has been tardy and inadequate. India has been quite weak in the all-round transformation of human conditions. Its record is quite dismal when compared even with that of the other developing countries. In the latest index of human development, another name for the measurable parts of the quality of life, compiled by the United Nations Development Program (UNDP) in 2004, India occupies the 126th position among the 177 nations covered.

Quality of life encompasses certain immeasurable components, such as love, human relationships, appreciation of arts, music, literature. But progress or lack of it in some of its other components can be measured. We will first take up three of these pertaining to health and education—life expectancy at birth, infant mortality rate (IMR) and literacy—which are most commonly used in discussions on the subject.

A comparison of the post-independence record in these fields with that of the colonial period shows that India's performance has been quite creditable during the last five decades. This despite the fact that health and education are two areas which have received low priority from successive central and state governments in India. However, a very brief comparison of the statistical progress made by some other countries such as China and Sri Lanka reveals how far we are lagging behind in regard to these important areas and what we still have to achieve.

An Indian's life expectancy at birth which was 32 years in 1950 rose to 45.6 years in 1970 and to 63.6 years in 2004—very creditable indeed. But it was already 71.9 and 74.3 years in 2004 in China and Sri Lanka respectively. The rise in life expectancy in India was basically the result of the steep fall in death rate per 1,000 from 27.4 in 1940 to 14.9 in 1970 and 7.6 in 2005.

IMR rate per 1,000 live births which was 227 in 1941 had fallen to 130 in 1970 and to 58 in 2005. However, it was much lower for China (36) and Sri Lanka (12) in 2004. Another sad fact observed is that too many women still die in India during childbirth. The current maternity mortality rate per 100,000 live births in India is as high as 407 compared to 58 in China and 92 in Sri Lanka. One reason for this is that 60 per cent of all childbirths in rural India are still attended to only by untrained persons.

Perhaps India's biggest failure is the continuation of high illiteracy rates among its people. In 1950, nearly 82 per cent Indians were illiterate; this figure was still as high as 35.1 per cent in 2004. The comparative figures for China and Sri Lanka were already as low as 17.1 and 9.3 per cent respectively in 1997. Moreover, the gender gap in the case of literacy was astonishingly high in India, nearly twice as many women being illiterate as men.

As has been shown in earlier chapters, India's record in higher and technical education is far better. Also, there has been rapid expansion of school education in the last fifteen years with an increase in the percentage of school-age children going to school. The flip side is the deterioration in the quality of education in the case of both schools and institutions of higher education in recent years. With rare exceptions the system of public education has become virtually dysfunctional with the 'cooperation' of all concerned—the government, political parties, educational administrators, teachers, parents and students. The standard of rural schools has fallen so low that quite often a child who has spent five years in school is not able to read or write at all and is, at the most, able to write only his or her name, if even that.

Health care, especially in rural areas, is another area of human development that has been grossly neglected in the last fifty years. Large number of Indians do not have access to safe water supply, health services or sanitation. Forty-seven per cent of Indian children under five are underweight, though this ratio has been declining in the last few years. The bright spot in this respect is the great success of the programmes for the immunization of children against polio, tuberculosis, diphtheria, tetanus and whooping cough and eradication of smallpox.

As in the case of education, in the field of public health too, the quality of services provided is quite poor in most states, especially in the Hindi belt.

The housing situation shows improvement in rural areas of India where the number of pucca houses has increased dramatically, but it has been deteriorating in urban areas, with millions being homeless and living on pavements or in jhuggis (shanties), unprotected from sun, rain or cold and with hardly any provision for water, electricity or sanitation. Even otherwise, Indian cities have been declining in regard to many aspects of the quality of life—sanitation, housing, transport, electric supply, schooling.

Also, there is very low consumption, especially in rural areas, of goods which make life easier and more joyful: scooters and motorcycles, radios, electric fans, room coolers, telephones, televisions, electric or gas or even coal chullahs, refrigerators, washing machines, though their use is way above that at the time of independence.

On the other hand, the number of towns and villages electrified has expanded rapidly since 1950. In 2006, 86.2 per cent of the rural and almost all the urban households, except jhuggis, had acquired electric connections. Electricity generation went up from 5.1 billion kilowatt hours (kWh) in 1950 to 617 billion kWh in 2006. Indians, both rural and urban, have also acquired greater access to media and entertainment: newspapers, magazines, films, music and television.

The prevalence of large-scale under- and unemployment in India also has a highly adverse impact on the quality of life and not only at the level of physical existence. Economic development has failed to create enough jobs in industry and services to make a serious impact on the unemployment of the landless and the rural and urban educated, thus introducing serious psychological, social and economic disequilibrium in their lives.

We may make a few other observations. Both in terms of development and poverty and the quality of life, there exists a great deal of disparity between different states and among their sub-regions which has to be rectified. An improvement in the quality of life or in the indices of human development would invariably require the state to play a more active role in the social *sector than before.*

Agricultural labourers and marginal and small peasants, with no or small patches of land and increasingly unable to get employment, are the most deprived section of Indian society in all aspects of the quality of life and standard of living. They suffer more than others from poverty and disease and lack of education, housing, health facilities, protected water supply, sanitation, electricity, and cultural and entertainment facilities. They are also likely to be the victims of the most vicious caste discrimination and caste oppression. They are also least organized in class organizations and least involved in political processes.

Promises to Keep

No doubt we still have 'promises to keep and miles to go . . .' We still face the challenges of poverty, disease, illiteracy, inequality, social backwardness, and gender and caste discrimination and oppression. But there is no ground for pessimism or resignation, for frustration or lack of pride. Many of our current problems are the outcome of the tremendous changes we have undergone and not because of regression or stagnation. Despite many maladies and shortfalls, India has impressive achievements to its credit in the economic and political arenas. It has made significant progress towards social justice. As a result of economic development and transformation of the agricultural and industrial production base of society during the last half century, India has now the resources to further its social agenda. The earlier debate whether a poor society could pursue social justice is no longer relevant. There is no longer any need to counterpoise increase in production and productivity to the removal of poverty and better distribution of wealth and opportunities. Nehru's dilemma about how to combine development with equity has also disappeared, for we can now achieve this. It would, therefore, not be wrong to expect and to predict that in the next decade or so India is likely to make immense progress, to almost take a leap forward, in transforming the lives of the mass of the people and give them a decent standard of living.

The major reason for our optimism lies in our belief that a vibrant democracy can find a solution for these problems. Women, the rural poor and the oppressed have increasingly come to believe that a better, more humane life is possible. They have woken up to the political power that inheres in them. India's democratic political system, despite many weaknesses, provides them the framework in which to exercise that power. The power of the people in a democracy is the 'liberating deluge' that can, and we are sure will, sweep away the accumulated dirt of the ages. This is, of course, all the more reason for the preservation and deepening of democracy in India.

Notes

1. Introduction

1. Selig S. Harrison, *India—The Most Dangerous Decades*, Madras, 1960, p. 338.
2. Quoted in Norman D. Palmer, 'India's Fourth General Election', *Asian Survey*, Vol. 7, No. 5, May 1967, p. 277.
3. W.H. Morris-Jones, *Politics Mainly Indian*, Bombay, 1978, pp. 131–32.
4. *Collected Works of Mahatma Gandhi*, New Delhi, 1958–84, (hereafter Gandhi, *CW*), Vol. 88, p. 2.
5. Jawaharlal Nehru, *Letters to Chief Ministers, 1947–64*, 5 Volumes, New Delhi, (hereafter *LCM*), Vol. 4, p. 124.
6. *Ibid.*, p. 188.
7. S. Gopal, *Jawaharlal Nehru—A Biography*, 3 Volumes, Vol. 2, London, 1979, p. 317.
8. Verrier Elwin, *The Tribal World of Verrier Elwin*, Bombay, 1964, p. 327.
9. G.K. Gokhale, *Speeches*, Madras, 1916, p. 1113.

3. The National Movement and its Legacy

1. *Kesari*, 16 June 1908, quoted in Ashis Kumar Dhuliya, 'Aspects of Tilak's Strategy and His Struggle for Civil Liberties', M.Phil. dissertation, Centre for Historical Studies, Jawaharlal Nehru University, New Delhi, 1984, p. 269.
2. Gandhi, *CW*, Vol. 22, p. 142, and Vol. 69, p. 356.
3. *Selected Works of Jawaharlal Nehru*, general editor S. Gopal, 15 volumes, New Delhi, 1972–82; Gandhi, *CW*, Vol. 76, Vol. 7, p. 414 (hereafter Nehru, *SW*).
4. *National Planning Committee Report* (NPC), edited by K.T. Shah, Bombay, 1949, p. 47.
5. Pattabhi Sitaramayya, *The History of the Indian National Congress (1885–1935)*, no place, 1935, p. 782.

6. *NPC*, p. 40.
7. Pattabhi Sitaramayya, *The History of the Indian National Congress (1885–1935)*, p. 779.
8. Gandhi, *CW*, Vol. 76, p. 367.
9. Pattabhi Sitaramayya, *The History of the Indian National Congress (1885–1935)*, p. 780.
10. Gandhi, *SW*, Vol. 76.
11. Gandhi, *The Way to Communal Harmony*, compiled and edited by U.R. Rao, Ahmedabad, 1963, p. 398.
12. Gandhi, *CW*, Vol. 68, p. 138.
13. Nehru, *SW*, Vol. 7, p. 173.

4. The Evolution of the Constitution and Main Provisions

1. Mahatma Gandhi, in an article titled 'Independence' published in *Young India*, 5 January 1922, in Gandhi, *CW*, Vol. 22, pp. 140–42.
2. Editor's Note to 'The Constitution of India Bill, 1925', in B. Shiva Rao, ed., *The Framing of India's Constitution: Select Documents*, Vol. 1, New Delhi, 1966, p. 5.
3. Text of Congress–League Scheme, in *ibid.*, p. 26.
4. Text of Resolution, in *ibid.*, p. 31.
5. Text of authentic summary of the bill issued by the National Convention in 1925, in *ibid.*, p. 44.
6. Text of Indian Leaders' Memorandum to the Government of Britain on the Commonwealth of India Bill, in *ibid.*, p. 50.
7. Text of Resolution, in *ibid.*, p. 35.
8. *Indian Quarterly Register, 1925*, Vol. 1, p. 344, cited in B. Shiva Rao, ed., *The Framing of India's Constitution: A Study*, New Delhi, 1968, p. 12.
9. Cited in Editor's Introduction to the Nehru Report, in B. Shiva Rao, ed., *The Framing of India's Constitution: Select Documents*, Vol. 1, p. 58.
10. For the text of the Nehru Report and the quotes in this para, see *ibid.*, pp. 59–75.
11. Text of Resolution, in *ibid.*, p. 77.
12. All quotes in this paragraph are from Nehru's Presidential Address to the National Convention of Congress Legislators, March 1937, in *ibid.*, pp. 86–91.
13. Text of Resolution in *ibid.*, p. 93.
14. Text of Speech, in *ibid.*, p. 101.
15. The article, written on 19 November at Allahabad, was published in the *Harijan* weekly of 25 November 1939. See Gandhi, *CW*, Vol. 70, pp. 362–65.
16. For a full report on the discussions, see Gandhi, *CW*, Vol. 72, pp. 4–7.

17. For the text of Viceroy Linlithgow's statement making the 'August Offer', see Sir Maurice Gwyer and A. Appadurai, eds, *Speeches and Documents on the Indian Constitution: 1921–47*, London, 1957, Vol. 11, pp. 504–05.
18. Cripps Mission, Draft Declaration, published on 30 March 1942, in *ibid.*, pp. 520–21.
19. Statement of the Cabinet Mission and the Viceroy, 16 May 1946, in V.P. Menon, *The Transfer of Power in India*, Princeton, 1957, Appendix IV, p. 471.
20. Jawaharlal Nehru, in Constituent Assembly Debates (CAD), 11, p. 3, p. 326, cited in Granville Austin, *The Indian Constitution: Cornerstone of a Nation*, Oxford, 1966, p. 26.
21. Austin, *The Indian Constitution*, p. 13.
22. *Ibid.*, p. 22.
23. *Ibid.*, pp. 8–9.
24. *Ibid.*, p. 43.
25. CAD, XI, p. 9, p. 835, cited in *ibid.*, p. 46.
26. *Ibid.*,
27. K.M. Panikkar, *Hindu Society at Cross Roads*, Bombay, 3rd edition, 1961, p. 96.
28. Austin, *The Indian Constitution*, p. 144.
29. Subhash C. Kashyap, 'The Framing of the Constitution and the Process of Institution Building', in B.N. Pande, general editor, *A Centenary History of the Indian National Congress: Vol. IV 1947–1964*, editor, Iqbal Narain, New Delhi, 1990, p. 85.
30. Austin, *The Indian Constitution*, p. 50.
31. W.H. Morris-Jones, *The Government and Politics of India*, New York, 1967, first published in 1964, p. 72.
32. Vallabhbhai Patel's speech at the first meeting of the Advisory Committee on Fundamental Rights, 27 February 1947, in B. Shiva Rao, ed., *The Framing of India's Constitution: Select Documents*, Vol. 11, p. 66.
33. Jawaharlal Nehru, while moving for reference of Constitution (First) Amendment Bill, 1951, to Select Committee, Parliamentary Debates (16 May 1951), Vol. XII, cols. 8820–22, cited in Kashyap, 'Framing of the Constitution,' in Pande, *A Centenary History*, p. 94.
34. Austin, *The Indian Constitution*, p. 50.
35. Jawaharlal Nehru, cited in Mahajan, *Select Modern Governments*, p. 61.
36. S. Radhakrishnan, cited in *ibid*.

5. The Architecture of the Constitution: Basic Features and Institutions

1. All India Reporter (AIR) 1973 Supreme Court (SC) 1461.

2. D.D. Basu, *Introduction to the Constitution of India*, p. 151.
3. In the case of Indira Nehru Gandhi vs. Raj Narain, AIR 1975 SC 2299.
4. D.D. Basu, *Introduction to the Constitution of India*, p. 153.
5. AIR 1980 SC 1789.
6. D.D. Basu, *Introduction to The Constitution, of India*, p. 152.
7. Austin, *The Indian Constitution*, p. 186.
8. *Ibid.*, p. 187.
9. Ambedkar, cited in S.C. Kashyap, *Our Constitution*, New Delhi, 1994, p. 44.
10. Basu, *Introduction to the Constitution of India*, p. 62.
11. Ambedkar, in CAD, VII, p. 32, cited in M.V. Pylee, *Constitutional Government in India*, New Delhi, 4th edition, 1984, p. 265.
12. Rajendra Prasad, in CAD, X, p. 956, cited in Pylee, *Constitutional Government in India*, p. 265.
13. Cited in Robert L. Hardgrave and Stanley A. Kochanek, *India: Government and Politics in a Developing Nation*, San Diego, 1993, p. 84.
14. Jawaharlal Nehru, in CAD, cited in Mahajan, *Select Modern Governments*, Part 1, p. 383.
15. Cited in Mahajan, *Select Modern Governments*, p. 327.
16. Austin, *The Indian Constitution*, p. 49.
17. AIR 1986 SC 180.

6. *The Initial Years*

1. Nehru, *Speeches*, 5 volumes, New Delhi (hereafter referred to as *Speeches*), Vol. 1, p. 25.
2. *Ibid.*, pp. 25–26.
3. Nehru, *Selected Works of Jawaharlal Nehru*, Second Series, general editor S. Gopal, New Delhi, 1984 (hereafter Nehru, *SW*, S.S.), Vol. 4, p. 530.
4. W.H. Morris-Jones, *The Government and Politics of India*, Wistow (England), 1987 reprint, first published in 1964, p. 72.
5. Nehru, *LCM*, Vol. 4, p. 366.
6. *Ibid.*, p. 383.
7. Quoted in V.P. Menon, *Integration of the Indian States*, Madras, 1985 reprint, first published in 1956, p. 73.
8. *Ibid.*, p. 91.
9. Quoted in Norman D. Palmer, *The Indian Political System*, London, 1961, p. 88.
10. V.P. Menon, *op. cit.*, p. 94.
11. Quoted in S. Gopal, *Jawaharlal Nehru—A Biography*, Vol. 2, London, 1979, pp. 27–28.

12. Quoted in V.P. Menon, *op. cit.*, p. 354.
13. *Sardar Patel's Correspondence*, 10 volumes, edited by Durga Das, Ahmedabad, Vol. 7, pp. 211–12.
14. *Ibid.*, p. 254.
15. Nehru, *LCM*, Vol. 2, p. 508.
16. Nehru, *SW*, S.S., Vol. 4, p. 118.
17. *Nehru on Communalism*, edited by N.L. Gupta, New Delhi, 1965, p. 217.
18. Quoted in S. Gopal, *Jawaharlal Nehru: A Biography*, Vol. 2, p. 155.
19. Quoted in Rajmohan Gandhi, *Patel: A Life*, Ahmedabad, 1990, pp. 493, 497.
20. *Sardar Patel in Tune with the Millions*, Birth Centenary Vol. 3, G.M. Nandurkar, editor, Ahmedabad, 1976, pp. 166, 169.
21. Gandhi, *SW*, Vol. 89, p. 286.
22. Nehru, *Speeches*, Vol. 1, p. 42.
23. Nehru, *LCM*, Vol. 1, p. 33.
24. *Nehru, SW*, S.S., Vol. 12, New Delhi, 1991, p. 453.
25. Gyanesh Kudaisya, 'The Demographic Upheaval of Partition: Refugees and Agricultural Resettlement in India, 1947–67,' *South Asia*, Vol. XVIII, Special Issue, Armidale (Australia), 1995, p. 94.
26. Nehru, *SW*, S.S., Vol. 14, Part II, p. 95.
27. R.K. Karanjia, *The Philosophy of Mr Nehru*, London, 1966, pp. 159–60.

7. *Consolidation of India as a Nation (I)*

1. Nehru, *Speeches*, Vol. 3, p. 193.
2. Quoted in S. Gopal, *Jawaharlal Nehru—A Biography*, Vol. 3, p. 22.
3. Nehru, *LCM*, Vol. 2, p. 352.
4. *Ibid.*, p. 598.
5. Nehru, *SW*, Vol. 8, p. 831.
6. Gandhi, *CW*, Vol. 19, pp. 314–15.
7. *Ibid.*, Vol. 37, p. 22.
8. *Ibid.*, Vol. 85, p. 88.
9. Quoted in S. Mohan Kumaramangalam, *India's Language Crisis*, Madras, 1965, pp. 11–12.
10. Nehru, *Speeches*, Vol. 4, p. 60.
11. Jyotirindra Das Gupta, *Language Conflict and National Development*, Bombay, 1970, p. 162.
12. Quoted in *ibid.*, p. 192.
13. Quoted in *ibid.*, p. 232.
14. Nehru, *Speeches*, Vol. 4, pp. 54, 55, 60.
15. *Ibid.*, p. 64.

8. Consolidation of India as a Nation (II): The Linguistic Reorganization of the States

1. Quoted in S. Mohan Kumaramangalam, *India's Language Crisis*, Madras, 1965, p. 21.
2. Jawaharlal Nehru, *SW*, S.S., Vol. 4, p. 530.
3. S. Gopal, *Jawaharlal Nehru—A Biography*, Vol. 2, pp. 259–60.
4. Quoted in Geoffrey Tyson, *Nehru—The Years of Power*, London, 1966, p. 149.
5. W.H. Morris-Jones, *The Government and Politics of India*, London, 1987 edition, p. 100.
6. *Ibid.*, p. 100.
7. Rajni Kothari, *Politics in India*, New Delhi, 1986 reprint, pp. 114–15.
8. *Seminar*, July 1960.
9. Nehru, *Speeches*, Vol. 4, p. 63.
10. Nehru, *LCM*, Vol. 3, p. 342.

9. Consolidation of India as a Nation (III): Integration of the Tribals

1. Verrier Elwin, *The Tribal World of Verrier Elwin*, Bombay, 1964, p. 103.
2. Verrier Elwin, *A Philosophy for NEFA*, Shillong, 1959, p. 46.
3. Nehru, *LCM*, Vol. 3, p. 151.
4. Nehru, *Speeches*, Vol. 5, p. 582.
5. Nehru, Foreword to the 1st edition of Verrier Elwin's *A Philosophy for NEFA*.
6. *Ibid.*
7. Nehru, *Speeches*, Vol. 2, p. 582.
8. Nehru, Foreword to the 1st edition of Verrier Elwin's *A Philosophy for NEFA*.
9. Nehru, *Speeches*, Vol. 3, pp. 460, 461.
10. Nehru, Foreword to the 1st edition of Verrier Elwin's *A Philosophy for NEFA*.
11. Nehru, *Speeches*, Vol. 2, p. 581.
12. *Ibid.*, p. 579.
13. Nehru, *LCM*, Vol. 111, p. 150.
14. *Ibid.*, p. 163.
15. Christoph von Furer-Haimendorf, 'The Position of the Tribal Population in Modern India', in Philip Mason, ed., *India and Ceylon: Unity and Diversity*, London, 1967, p. 208.
16. Quoted in S. Gopal, *Jawaharlal Nehru—A Biography*, Vol. 2, p. 212.

10. Consolidation of India as a Nation (IV): Regionalism and Regional Inequality

1. Gandhi, *CW*, New Delhi, 1958–1984, Vol. 9, p. 458.
2. Quoted in Jolly Mohan Kaul, *Problems of National Integration*, New Delhi, 1963, p. 76.
3. Government of India, Planning Commission, *Third Five Year Plan*, New Delhi, 1961, p. 142.
4. Ajit Mozoomdar, 'The Political Economy of Modern Federalism', in Balveer Arora and Douglas V. Verney, eds., *Multiple Identities in a Single State*, Delhi, 1995, pp. 230-31.

11. The Years of Hope and Achievement, 1951–1964

1. Nehru, *SW*, S.S., Vol. 22, pp. 122–23.
2. Nehru, *LCM*, Vol. 4, p. 188.
3. S. Gopal, *Jawaharlal Nehru—A Biography*, Vol. 2, p. 162.
4. Quoted in *ibid.*, pp. 164–65.
5. Nehru, *LCM*, Vol. 2, p. 508.
6. *Nehru on Communalism*, edited by N.L. Gupta, New Delhi, 1965, p. 216.
7. C.D. Deshmukh, *The Course of My Life*, Delhi, 1974, p. 205.
8. Quoted in S. Gopal., *op. cit.*, Vol. 3, p. 65.
9. Nehru, *Speeches*, Vol. 1, p. 2.
10. Quoted in W.H. Morris-Jones, *The Government and Politics in India*, Wistow, 1987, p. 26, and in Rajmohan Gandhi, *Patel*, p. 501.
11. Quoted in S. Gopal, *op. cit.*, Vol. 2, pp. 158–59.
12. Tibor Mende, *Conversations with Mr Nehru*, London, 1956, pp. 54–55.
13. Nehru, *LCM*, Vol. 1, p. 123.
14. *Ibid.*, Vol. 5, p. 601.
15. Nehru, *SW*, Old Series, Vol. 8, p. 807.
16. Nehru, *LCM*, Vol. 4, p. 369.
17. Nehru, *SW*, Old Series, Vol. 3, p. 361.
18. Quoted in S. Gopal, *op. cit.*, Vol. 2, p. 169.
19. Nehru, *LCM*, Vol. 5, pp. 601 and 590 respectively.
20. Nehru, *Speeches*, Vol. 2, pp. 50–52, 54, 56.
21. *Ibid.*, Vol. 3, pp. 22, 25.
22. *Ibid.*, Vol. 5, p. 83.

12. Foreign Policy: The Nehru Era

1. Jawaharlal Nehru, cited in V.P. Dutt, *India and the World*, New Delhi, 1990, pp. 28–29.
2. K. Subrahmanyam, 'Evolution of Indian Defence Policy (1947–1964)', in B.N. Pande, ed., *A Centenary History of the Indian National Congress*, Vol. IV, New Delhi, 1990, pp. 512–13.

718 *Notes*

3. K.P.S. Menon, 'India and the Soviet Union', in B.R. Nanda, ed., *Indian Foreign Policy: The Nehru Years*, Delhi, 1976, p. 136.
4. *Hindustan Times*, 21 July 1954, cited in D.R. Sardesai, 'India and Southeast Asia', in *ibid.*, p. 87.
5. Cited in Rikhi Jaipal, 'Ideas and Issues in Indian Foreign Policy', in Pande, ed., *A Centenary History*, p. 434.
6. K. Subrahmanyam, 'Evolution of Indian Defence Policy (1947–1964)', in Pande, ed., *A Centenary History*, pp. 546–47.
7. K.P.S. Menon, *op. cit.*, in B.R. Nanda, ed., *Indian Foreign Policy*, p. 135.
8. *Ibid.*, p. 142.
9. K. Subrahmanyam, *op. cit.*, in Pande, ed., *A Centenary History*, p. 550.
10. *Op. cit.*, in Nanda, ed., *Indian Foreign Policy*, p. 148.
11. Speech in Lok Sabha, 27 November 1959, cited in V.P. Dutt, *India and the World*, pp. 42–44.
12. K. Subrahmanyam, *op. cit.*, in Pande, ed., *A Centenary History*, p. 516.
13. *India and the World*, pp. 53–54.
14. For his views, see *China and the World*, New York, 1966, *India's Foreign Policy*, New Delhi, 1984, *India and the World*, New Delhi, 1990, and *India's Foreign Policy in a Changing World*, New Delhi, 1999.
15. K. Subrahmanyam, *op. cit.*, in Pande, ed., *A Centenary History*, p. 567.
16. Cited in A.K. Damodaran, 'Foreign Policy in Action', in Pande, ed., *A Centenary History*, p. 469.

13. *Jawaharlal Nehru in Historical Perspective*

1. Nehru, *LCM*, Vol. 3, pp. 380–81.
2. Hugh Tinker, 'Is There an Indian Nation', in Philip Mason, ed., *India and Ceylon: Unity and Diversity*, London, 1967, p. 287.
3. Nehru, *LCM*, Vol. 4, p. 256.
4. *Ibid.*, Vol. 2, p. 598.
5. *Ibid.*, Vol. 3, p. 368.
6. R.K. Karanjia, *The Philosophy of Mr Nehru*, London, 1966, p. 123.
7. Quoted in S. Gopal, *Jawaharlal Nehru—A Biography*, Vol. 3, London, 1984, p. 170.
8. Nehru, *LCM*, Vol. 2, p. 368.
9. Quoted in S. Gopal, *Jawaharlal Nehru—A Biography*, Vol. 3, p. 278.
10. R.K. Karanjia, *The Mind of Mr Nehru*, London, 1960, p. 48.
11. Tibor Mende, *Conversations with Mr Nehru*, pp. 37, 108, 105.
12. Quoted in S. Gopal, *Jawaharlal Nehru—A Biography*, Vol. 2, London, 1979, pp. 192–93.

13. Nehru *SW*, S.S., general editor S. Gopal, Vol. 7, New Delhi, 1988, p. 384.
14. R.K. Karanjia, *The Philosophy of Mr Nehru*, p. 139.
15. Government of India, Planning Commission, *Third Five Year Plan*, New Delhi, 1961, p. 9.
16. Nehru, *Speeches*, Vol. 3, New Delhi, 1970 reprint, pp. 17–18.
17. Bimal Jalan, 'Introduction', *The Indian Economy, Problems and Prospects*, ed. Bimal Jalan, New Delhi, 1992, p. xiii.
18. Nehru, *LCM*, Vol. 2, p. 84.
19. Nehru, *Speeches*, Vol. 3, p. 37.
20. Geoffrey Tyson, *Nehru: The Years of Power*, London, 1966, p. 173.

14. Political Parties, 1947–1964: The Congress

1. Quoted in Myron Weiner, *Party Politics in India*, Princeton, 1957, p. 69.
2. Sardar Patel, *Sardar Patel in Tune With the Millions*, Vol. 3, edited by G.M. Nandurkar, Ahmedabad, 1976, pp. 164–169.
3. Quoted in Rajmohan Gandhi, *Patel: A Life*, Ahmedabad, 1990, p. 490.
4. Nehru, *SW*, S.S., Vol. 8, p. 438.
5. Quoted in S. Gopal, *Jawaharlal Nehru—A Biography*, Vol. 2, pp. 154–55.
6. Stanley A. Kochanek, *The Congress Party of India*, Princeton, 1968, p. 51.
7. Krishan Bhatia, *The Ordeal of Nationhood*, New York, 1971, p. 120.
8. Myron Weiner, *op. cit.*, p. 17.
9. Nehru, *SW*, S.S., Vol. 6, p. 438.
10. Quoted in S. Gopal, *op. cit.*, Vol. 2, pp. 74, 81, 92 respectively.
11. Quoted in Norman D. Palmer, *The Indian Political System*, London, 1961, p. 193.
12. Nehru, *SW*, S.S., Vol. 7, p. 382.
13. Quoted in Allan and Wendy Scarfe, *J.P: His Biography*, New Delhi, 1975, p. 237.
14. Quoted in S. Gopal, *op. cit.*, Vol. 2, p. 67.
15. Nehru, *SW*, S.S., Vol. 12, p. 455.
16. Quoted in Allan and Wendy Scarfe, *op. cit.*, pp. 245, 246.
17. Quoted in S. Gopal, *op. cit.*, Vol. 2, p. 205.
18. Quoted in *ibid.*, Vol. 3, pp. 21–22.
19. *Ibid.*, p. 22.
20. All India Congress Committee, *Resolutions on Economic Policy and Programme 1955–56*, New Delhi, 1956, p. l.
21. Nehru, *Speeches*, Vol. 3, p. 96.
22. Government of India, Planning Commission, *Third Five Year Plan*, p. 5.

15. Political Parties, 1947–1965: The Opposition

1. Quoted in Myron Weiner, *Party Politics in India*, Princeton, 1957, p. 61.
2. Quoted in *ibid.*, p. 106.
3. Lewis P. Fickett, Jr., 'The Praja Socialist Party of India—1952–1972: A Final Assessment', *Asian Survey*, Vol. 13, No. 9, September 1973, p. 829.
4. *CPU Programme*, 1964, p. 25.
5. M.S. Golwalkar, *We or Our Nationhood Defined*, Nagpur, 1947 edition, first published in 1939, p. 6.
6. *Ibid.*, pp. 52–56, 62 f.n.
7. *Ibid.*, p. 19.
8. *Organiser*, 17 November 1991, p. 9.
9. Krishan Bhatia, *The Ordeal of Nationhood*, New York, 1971, p. 103.
10. Quoted in Myron Weiner, *op. cit.*, p. 193.
11. Quoted in Donald E. Smith, *India as a Secular State*, Princeton, 1963, p. 471.
12. Resolution passed by Bharatiya Jan Sangh at its session held at Lucknow from 30 December 1960 to 1 January 1961, quoted in Motilal A. Jhangiani, *Jana Sangh and Swatantra: A Profile of the Rightist Parties in India*, Bombay, 1967, p. 48.
13. Bharatiya Jan Sangh Election Manifesto, 1962, p. 18, quoted in Jhangiani, *op. cit.*, p. 77.
14. Quoted in Norman D. Palmer, *The Indian Political System*, London, 1961, p. 200.

16. From Shastri to Indira Gandhi, 1964–1969

1. Krishan Bhatia, *The Ordeal of Nationhood*, New York, 1971, p. 150.
2. Quoted in Geoffrey Tyson, *Nehru: The Years of Power*, London, 1966, p. 191.
3. Indira Gandhi, *My Truth*, New Delhi, 1982, p. 116.
4. President Johnson, quoted in Lloyd I. Rudolph and Susanne Hoeber Rudolph, *The Regional Imperative*, Delhi, 1980, p. 38.
5. Quoted in Zareer Masani, *Indira Gandhi—A Biography*, London, 1975, p. 168.
6. *Ibid.*, pp. 179–80.
7. W.H. Morris-Jones, *Politics Mainly Indian*, Madras, 1978, p. xii.
8. Rajni Kothari, *Politics in India*, New Delhi, 1986 reprint, p. 183.

17. The Indira Gandhi Years, 1969–1973

1. Kuldip Nayar, *India: The Critical Years*, revised and enlarged edition, Delhi, 1971, pp. 31–32.

2. Zareer Masani, *Indira Gandhi—A Biography*, London, 1975, p. 181.
3. Quoted in *ibid.*, p. 209.
4. Quoted in *ibid.*, p. 241.
5. Quoted in Lloyd I. Rudolph, Susanne Hoeber Rudolph, et al., *The Regional Imperative*, Delhi, 1980, p. 46.
6. Indira Gandhi, *The Years of Endeavour*, New Delhi, 1975, p. 654–56.

18. The JP Movement and the Emergency: Indian Democracy Tested

1. Quoted in *Statesman*, 10 April 1974, cited in Francine R. Frankel, *India's Political Economy, 1947–1977*, Delhi, 1978, p. 528.
2. Quoted in Inder Malhotra, *Indira Gandhi*, London, 1989, p. 165.
3. Morarji Desai to Oriana Fallaci, *New Republic*, quoted in Francine R. Frankel, *op. cit.*, p. 544.
4. Inder Malhotra, *op. cit.*, pp. 173, 182.
5. Mary C. Carras, *Indira Gandhi: In the Crucible of Leadership*, Bombay, 1980, p. 100.
6. Tariq Ali, *The Nehrus and the Gandhis: An Indian Dynasty*, London, 1985 p. 194.
7. Quoted in Francine R. Frankel, *op. cit.*, p. 576.

19. The Janata Interregnum and Indira Gandhi's Second Coming, 1977–1984

1. Quoted in Pupul Jayakar, *Indira Gandhi—A Biography*, New Delhi, 1992, p. 474.

20. The Rajiv Years

1. Quoted in Nicholas Nugent, *Rajiv Gandhi: Son of a Dynasty*, New Delhi, 1991, p. 54.
2. The official figure is 2,733, but unofficial figures are as high as 3,870.
3. Quoted in S.S. Gill, *The Dynasty: A Political Biography of the Premier Ruling Family of India*, New Delhi, 1996, p. 401.
4. S.S. Gill, who served as Secretary, Information and Broadcasting, in Rajiv Gandhi's government, testifies to this. See *ibid.*, pp. 406–07.

21. Run-up to the New Millennium and After

1. Seema Mustafa, *The Lonely Prophet: V.P. Singh, A Political Biography*, New Delhi, 1995, p. 120.
2. *Ibid.*, p. 129.
3. See Chapter 37 on Caste and Dalit Politics in this volume.
4. A very useful recent collection of studies on caste in which a number of scholars address the issue is M.N. Srinivas, ed., *Caste: Its Twentieth*

Century Avatar, New Delhi, 1996. See particularly the essay by A.M. Shah.

5. Dreze and Sen, for example, show the strong link between disparities in education and social inequality and argue that a policy of universal and compulsory education is likely to lead to elimination of social inequalities. They stress that leaders of the freedom struggle were well aware of this and Dr Ambedkar himself saw education as the cornerstone of his strategy for liberation of oppressed castes, as he was conscious how in his own case his scholarship enabled him to overcome the stigma of untouchability. They also point to a common finding of village studies and household surveys that education is widely perceived by members of socially or economically disadvantaged groups as the most promising chance of upward mobility for their children. Jean Dreze and Amartya Sen, *India: Economic Development and Social Opportunity,* Delhi, 1996, especially pp. 96–97, 109–10.

6. In South India, there was no strong reaction because state governments had been implementing different levels of reservations for Backward Castes for many years. The caste structure in South India, with far more extreme forms of Brahmin domination, was quite different. Also, there was a long history of caste-based reservations which were introduced by the British in the 1920s and also by the princely states, as well as a long tradition of the non-Brahmin movement since the 1910s.

7. In 1993 the Congress government implemented the Mandal report, without much furore taking place, as by then people had got more used to the idea, thus proving the point that in a democracy you cannot ram decisions down people's throats but have to work through consensus.

8. V.P. Dutt, *India's Foreign Policy in a Changing World,* New Delhi, 1999, p. 15

9. *Times of India,* 23 June 1999.

10. Quoted in V.P. Dutt, *op. cit.,* pp. 368–69.

11. V.P. Dutt, *India's Foreign Policy Since Independence,* New Delhi, 2007, pp. 97–98.

12. *The Indian Express,* 28 July 2007.

13. *The Hindustan Times,* 28 July 2007.

23. Politics in the States (II): West Bengal and Jammu and Kashmir

1. Quoted in Atul Kohli, *Democracy and Discontent: India's Growing Crisis of Governability,* New Delhi, 1992, p. 289.

2. *Ibid.,* p. 288; Atul Kohli, 'Parliamentary Communism and Agrarian Reform—The Evidence from India's Bengal', *Asian Survey,* Vol. 23, No. 7, July 1983, pp. 780, 800.

3. Quoted in Geoffrey Tyson, *Nehru—The Years of Power*, London, 1966, p. 79.

24. The Punjab Crisis

1. Quoted in K.P.S. Gill, *The Knights of Falsehood*, New Delhi, 1997, p. 35.
2. Baldev Raj Nayar, 'Sikh Separatism in the Punjab', in Donald E. Smith, ed. *South Asian Politics and Religion*, Princeton, 1966, p. 168.
3. Quoted in K.P.S. Gill, p. 81.
4. *Ibid.*, p. 12.

25. Indian Economy, 1947–1965: The Nehruvian Legacy

1. See for details Bipan Chandra, et al., *India's Struggle for Independence*, New Delhi, 1989, chapter 29.
2. Aditya Mukherjee, *Imperialism, Nationalism and the Development of Indian Capitalism: The Making of the Indian Capitalist Class 1920–47* (forthcoming) and Aditya Mukherjee and Mridula Mukherjee, 'Imperialism and the Growth of Indian Capitalism in the Twentieth Century', *EPW*, 12 March 1988.
3. N.R. Sarkar, Presidential speech, FICCI, *Annual Report*, 1934, New Delhi, pp. 3–67. M. Visveswarayya was among the first to give a call for planned development in the 1920s.
4. Indian National Congress (INC), Economic Resolutions, p. 8.
5. *A Plan of Economic Development for India*, Parts 1 & 2, London, 1945, pp. 9–10. The authors of this plan were Purshottamdas Thakurdas, J.R.D. Tata, G.D. Birla, Ardeshir Dalai, Sri Ram, Kasturbhai Lalbhai, A.D Shroff and John Mathai.
6. *INC Economic. Resolutions*, p. 29. Emphasis added.
7. *Second Five Year Plan*, 1956, p. 44.
8. K.N. Raj, *Indian Economic Growth: Performance and Prospects*, New Delhi, 1965, p. 2.
9. A. Vaidyanathan, 'The Indian Economy Since Independence (1947–70)', in Dharma Kumar, ed., *The Cambridge Economic History of India*, Delhi, 1983, p. 961. Emphasis added.
10. J. Bhagwati and P. Desai, *India: Planning for Industrialisation*, London, 1970, table 10.6, pp. 185–87.
11. *Business Standard*, 9 January 1998.
12. Sukhamoy Chakravarty, *Development Planning: The Indian Experience*, Oxford, 1987, pp. 4, 81.

26. Indian Economy, 1965–1991

1. C. Rangarajan, 'Development, Inflation and Monetary Policy', in Isher J. Ahluwalia and I.M.D. Little, eds, *India's Economic Reforms*

and Development: Essays for Manmohan Singh, Delhi, 1998, p. 59.
2. See E.J. Hobsbawm, *Age of Extremes: The Short Twentieth Century,* Harmondsworth, 1994, for a brilliant analysis of the changes in world capitalism since the Second World War and pp. 261, 277 and 280 for the statistics in this paragraph.
3. *The East Asian Miracle: Economic Growth and Public Policy,* World Bank, New York, 1993, p. 38.
4. Vijay Joshi and I.M.D. Little, *India: Macroeconomics and Political Economy 1964–1991,* Washington, 1994, p. 58.

27. Economic Reforms Since 1991

1. For example, in his D. Phil. dissertation at Oxford in 1961 and his book *India's Export Trends,* London, 1964.
2. Ajit Singh, 'Liberalisation, the Stock Market, and the Market for Capital Control', in Isher Ahluwalia and I.M.D. Little, eds, *India's Economic Reforms and Development,* Delhi, 1998.
3. See *Economic Survey 1998–99,* Government of India, tables 10.6 and 10.7, p. 146,
4. Vijay Joshi and I.M.D. Little, *India's Economic Reforms, 1991–2001,* Oxford, 1996, pp. 222, 225.
5. Suresh D. Tendulkar, 'Indian Economic Policy Reforms and Poverty: An Assessment', in Ahluwalia and Little, eds, *India's Economic Reforms,* 1998, tables 12.1, 12.2, 12.3, pp. 290–294.
6. C.H. Hanumantha Rao, 'Agriculture: Policy and Performance', in Bimal Jalan, ed., *The Indian Economy,* New Delhi, 1992, p. 132.
7. *Economic Survey,* pp. 11, 18. Emphasis added.

28. The Indian Economy in the New Millennium

1. *Economic Survey* (hereafter *ES*), Government of India, 2002–03, pp. 155 ff., 2003–04, table 8.5, pp. 153–55 and 2006–07, table 1.2, p. 3.
2. Dani Rodrik and Arvind Subramanian, 'Why India Can Grow at 7 Per Cent a Year or More: Projections and Reflections', *Economic and Political Weekly* (hereafter *EPW*), 17 April 2004.
3. Jeffrey D. Sachs, *The End of Poverty: Economic Possibilities of Our Time,* New York, 2005. Emphasis added.
4. See, for example, Bibek Debroy, *Indian Express,* 2 June 2007.
5. Angus Maddison, *The World Economy: Vol. I A Millennial Perspective, Vol. II Historical Staistics,* OECD, 2006, Indian edition, New Delhi, 2007, table 8b, pp. 639–43.
6. *ES,* 2006–07. p. 106, table 6.1.
7. Bimal Jalan, *India 's Economy in the New Millennium,* New Delhi, 2002, pp. 25–26.
8. Calculated from table 1.5, S-8, *ES,* 2006–07.

9. Dani Rodrik and Arvind Subramanian, *EPW*, 17 April 2004, p. 1592.
10. Note that figures used here for the 1990s are different from those used in the previous chapter as different base years have been used by the CSO over time. See *ES* 1996–97, p. 19, 1998–99, p. 21 and 2006–07 p. 19 The previous chapter used the older figures.
11. *ES*, 2006–07, table 2.1, p. 19, table 2.11, p. 44, table 2.12, p. 48.
12. *ES*, 2006–07, table 2.3, p. 23.
13. Dani Rodrik and Arvind Subramanian, *EPW*, 17 April 2004.
14. *ES*, 2006–07, table 2.2, p. 21, p. 28.
15. *Ibid.*
16. *ES*, 2006–07, p. 3, table 1.2 and S-10, table 1.6.
17. See *ES*, 2006–07, p. 1, S-10, table 1.6.
18. Figures for 1951 are not strictly comparable as the figures include mining and quarrying in the primary sector while in 1971 mining and quarrying are included in the secondary sector. Yet the trend is clear enough. See Ruddar Dutt and K.P.M. Sundharam, *Indian Economy*, New Delhi, 2007, p. 84, table 5.
19. The figures are from a persuasive argumentative work on India's reform process by Baldev Raj Nayar, *India's Globalisation: Evaluating the Economic Consequences*, New Delhi, 2007, pp. 15–17, first published, Washington, 2006.
20. See *ES*, 2006–07, pp. 113–14, table 7.1a, S-78 and Baldev Nayar, 2007, p. 18.
21. *ES*, 2006–07, p. 108, table 6.2, p. 119, table 6.9.
22. *Ibid.*, p. 21
23. *ES*, 2004–05, p. 112 and *ES*, 2005–06, pp. 116-117
24. Jeffrey Sachs, *The End of Poverty*, 2005, p. 186.
25. *ES*, 2004–05, p. 111, 2005–06, p. 206, 2006–07, p. 108 and Baldev Nayar, 2007, p. 21.
26. *ES*, 2005–06, p. 105.
27. *ES*, 2007, pp. 6, 131, 135 and table 6.1b, S-69.
28. *The Hindustan Times* and *The Times of India*, 18 June 2007.
29. Report of Ernst and Young and Federation of Indian Chamber of Commerce and Industry cited in *The Times of India* and *The Hindustan Times*, 18 June 2007,
30. Quoted in Baldev Nayar, 2007, p. 45.
31. *ES*, 2006–07 p. 228 and p. 7.
32. *ES*, 2006–07, pp. 131–32, 2005–06, p. 130, 2003–04, p. 128.
33. See the chapter The Post Colonial Indian State, pp. 465–66, for a discussion of this aspect and Prabhat Patnaik, 'Political Strategies of Economic Development', in Partha Chatterjee, ed., *Wages of Freedom: Fifty Years of the Indian Nation-State*, Delhi, 1998 and Prabhat Patnaik, *The Retreat to Unfreedom: Essays on the Emerging World Order*, New Delhi, 2003.

34. This argument is made effectively by Baldev Nayar, 2007, pp. 39–41. The figures are cited by Nayar from a study by Nagesh Kumar, 'Liberalization, Foreign Direct Investment Flows, and Economic Development: The Indian Experience in the 1990s', RIS discussion paper 65/2003, Research and Information System for the Non-Aligned and Other Developing Countries, New Delhi, 2003.
35. *ES*, 2006–07, p. 139.
36. R. Nagaraj, 'Industrial Growth in China and India : A Preliminary Comparison', *EPW*, 21 May 2005, quoted in Baldev Nayar, 2007, pp. 85–86, f.n. 4.
37. Baldev Nayar, 2007, p. 41. The figures are from UNCTAD cited by Nayar in table 10, p. 42.
38. *ES*, 2006–07, p. 207 and *ES*, 2002–03, table 10.6, p. 213.
39. 'Prices and Poverty in India, 1987–2000', *EPW*, 25 January 2003.
40. K Sundaram and Suresh D. Tendulkar, 'Poverty Has Declined in the 1990s', *EPW*, 25 January 2003.
41. Himangshu, 'Recent Trends in Poverty and Inequality: Some Preliminary Results', *EPW*, 10 February 2007, and S. Mahendra Dev and C. Ravi, 'Poverty and Inequality: All-India and States, 1983–2005', *EPW*, 10 February 2007.
42. Himangshu, 2007, p. 499.
43. Dev and Ravi estimate it as 1.02 per cent per annum, 2007, p. 111.
44. Himangshu, 2007, p. 501.
45. Dev and Ravi, 2007, p. 511.
46. *Ibid.*, p. 510.
47. *Ibid.* pp. 510–11.
48. *Focus on Children Under Six*, Abridged Report, Right to Food Campaign, New Delhi, 2006.
49. See *National Family Health Survey (NFHS3) 2005–06, National Factsheet (Provisional Data)*, Ministry of Health and Family Welfare, Government of India.
50. *UNDP Human Development Report*, 2002 and 2006 cited in *ES*, 2006–07, table 10.1, p. 205.
51. See G.S. Bhalla, *Indian Agriculture Since Independence*, New Delhi, 2007, p. 295.
52. See, for example *Times of India*, 14 June 2007 and also *Report to the People: UPA Government 2004–07*.
53. *The Hindu*, 29 September 2007.
54. *ES*, 2005–06, p. 204.
55. Bimal Jalan, 2002, p. 25.

29. Land Reforms (I): Colonial Impact and the Legacy of the National and Peasant Movements

1. See Louis J. Walinsky, ed., *Agrarian Reform as Unfinished Business,*

The Selected Papers of Wolf Ladejinsky, OUP, 1977, p. 371 (hereafter Ladejinsky Papers).

2. See Bipan Chandra et al., *India's Struggle for Independence,* Penguin, New Delhi, 1988, 40th impression, 2006, Chapters 11 and 27 (hereafter Bipan Chandra, et al., *India's Struggle*).

3. See S.J. Patel, *Essays on Economic Transition,* Bombay, 1965, p. 76,
 ⸱ and Bipan Chandra, 'Peasantry and National Integration in Contemporary India', in *Nationalism and Colonialism in Modern India,* Orient Longman, New Delhi, 1979, p. 333.

4. See, for example, Resolution of Economic Planning Conference attended by Chief Ministers and Congress Presidents from the States, April 1950, and Indian National Congress, Economic Programme, Delhi Congress, October 1951, in *Indian National Congress, Resolutions on Economic Policy Programme and Allied Matters 1924–1969,* AICC, New Delhi, 1969, pp. 50, 66 (hereafter *INC Econ. Resolutions*)

5. See Bipan Chandra, 'Colonial India: British versus Indian Views of Development', *Review* (Fernand Braudel Center), vol. xiv, No. 1, Winter 1991, p. 85. For this section, see also Bipan Chandra, *Rise and Growth of Economic Nationalism in India, 1880–1905,* New Delhi, 1966, and Bipan Chandra, 1979.

6. See, for example Resolutions of Indian National Congress, 1888, 1889 and 1893 in A.M. Zaidi and S.G. Zaidi, *The Foundations of Indian Economic Planning,* New Delhi, 1979.

7. See Daniel Thorner, *The Shaping of Modern India,* New Delhi, 1980, p. 241 and Bipan Chandra, 1979, p. 337.

8. Bipan Chandra, 1979, p. 337.

9. Bipan Chandra, et al., *India's Struggle,* ch. 3.

10. For details, see, *ibid.* ch. 16.

11. For details, see, *ibid.* ch. 27.

12. The provisions listed above are from the slightly modified version of the Karachi resolutions which was issued by the AICC in Bombay in August 1931, *INC Econ. Resolutions,* pp. 3–9.

13. See *INC Econ. Resolutions;* pp.12–14

14. See Agrarian Programme, Lucknow Congress, 1936, and Election Manifesto, AICC, 1936, *INC Econ. Resolutions,* pp. 10–12, emphasis added.

15. This paragraph is based on Bipan Chandra, et al., *India's Struggle,* ch. 26.

16. See Bipan Chandra, 1979, p. 350, and Bipan Chandra, et al., *India's Struggle,* p. 528.

17. Mridula Mukherjee, in Bipan Chandra, et al., *India's Struggle,* ch. 27, p. 354.

18. A.M. Khusro, 'Land Reforms since Independence', in V. B. Singh, ed., *The Economic History of India, 1857–1956,* Delhi, 1965, pp. 185–86, emphasis added.

19. See *National Planning Committee Report*, Bombay, 1949, Purshottamdas Thakurdas, et al., *A plan for Economic Development for India* (Bombay Plan), Harmondsworth, 1945, and *INC Econ. Resolutions*, pp. 15–18.
20. *INC Econ. Resolutions*, p. 16, emphasis added.
21. 'Objectives and Economic Programme,' AICC, Delhi, November 1947, *INC Econ. Resolutions*, p. 19.
22. *INC Econ. Resolutions*, pp. 20–22.
23. See, example, Francine Frankel, *India's Political Economy 1947–77*, Delhi, 1978, p. 68.
24. *INC Econ. Resolutions*, p. 22, emphasis added. Frankel (see note 23), however, maintains that compulsory membership of service cooperatives was visualized.
25. *INC Econ. Resolutions*, p. 23.

30. Land Reforms (II): Zamindari Abolition and Tenancy Reforms

1. A.M. Khusro, in V.B. Singh, ed., *Economic History of India 1857–1956*, Delhi, 1965, p. 189.
2. *INC Econ. Resolutions*, p. 38.
3. Planning Commission, *Second Five Year Plan*, 1956, p. 188.
4. See P.S. Appu, 'Tenancy Reform in India', *EPW*, Special Number, August 1975, p. 1345.
5. See *ibid.*, p. 1347.
6. D. Bandyopadhyay, 'Land Reform in India: An Analysis', *EPW*, Review of Agriculture, June 1986.
7. L.I. Rudolph and S.H. Rudolph, *In Pursuit of Lakshmi: The Political Economy of the Indian State*, Chicago, 1987, p. 363.
8. P.S. Appu, pp. 1354–55, 1375.
9. Daniel Thorner, *The Shaping of Modern India*, New Delhi, 1980, p. 245.

31. Land Reforms (III): Ceiling and the Bhoodan Movement

1. *INC Econ. Resolutions*, p. 23.
2. Planning Commission, *First Five Year Plan*, New Delhi, 1953, pp. 188–191.
3. Indian National Congress, *Resolution on Economic Policy and Programme, 1924–54*, New Delhi, 1954, p. 75.
4. *Ibid.*, p. 121. Emphasis added.
5. Planning Commission, *Second Five Year Plan*, New Delhi 1956, pp. 196–97.
6. Quoted in Ladejinsky Papers, p. 483
7. C.H. Hanumantha Rao, 'Agriculture: Policy and Performance', in Bimal Jalan, ed., *The Indian Economy: Problems and Prospects*, New Delhi, p. 118.

8. D. Bandyopadhyay, 'Land Reforms in India: An Analysis', *EPW*, Review of Agriculture, June 1986.
9. Wolf Ladejinsky, otherwise an avid supporter of ceilings and land distribution, came to a similar conclusion in May 1972. Ladejinsky Papers, p. 513.
10. *Indian Express*, 16 June 1999.
11. G. Kotovsky, *Agrarian Reforms in India*, New Delhi, 1964, p. 119. See, for similar views, D. Bandyopadhyay, 'Reflections on Land Reforms in India Since Independence', in T.V. Sathyamurthy, ed., *Industry and Agriculture in India Since Independence*, Delhi, 1995.
12. *The Hindustan Times*, 4 and 9 January 1961, cited in Kotovsky, 1964, p. 125.
13. Kotovsky, 1964, p. 126, he cites E.M.S. Namboodiripad, 'Sarvodaya and Communism', *New Age*, Vol. vii, No. 1, January 1958, pp. 46–55.

32. Cooperatives and an Overview of Land Reforms

1. Recommendations of the Economic Programme Committee of the AICC, November 1947, *INC Econ. Resolutions*, p. 22. Emphasis added.
2. *INC Econ. Resolutions*, pp. 41–42. Emphasis added.
3. *Ibid.*
4. *Second Five Year Plan*, p. 201. Emphasis added.
5. *INC Econ. Resolutions*, pp. 120ff. Emphasis added.
6. *Third Five-Year Plan*, p. 209. (Quoted in Ladejinsky Papers, p. 388).
7. The figures in this paragraph are from Rudolph and Rudolph, *In Pursuit of Lakshmi*, table 42, p. 373.
8. Ladejinsky Papers, pp. 505–06.
9. The description below of the Kaira experiment is based on interviews with Verghese Kurien, Tribhuvandas Patel and others and a study of the experiment made by the authors in Anand and its neighbouring villages in July 1985. Materials provided by the NDDB, courtesy its present Managing Director, Dr Amrita Patel (whose own contribution to the movement is considerable), and Ruth Heredia, *The Amul India Story*, Tata McGraw-Hill, New Delhi, 1997, have also been used freely.
10. Wilfred Candler and Nalini Kumar, *India: The Dairy Revolution*, World Bank, Washington, 1998,
11. *Ibid.*, p. 48
12. *Ibid.*, pp. xxi, 6, 60. Emphasis added.
13. *Ibid.*, pp. xxi, 6. Emphasis added.
14. *Ibid.*, p. xv.
15. Daniel Thorner, *The Shaping of Modern India*, New Delhi, 1980, p. 245. Addition in parenthesis added.

16. The above figures are calculated from D. Bandyopadhyay, 'Land Reforms in India: An Analysis,' *EPW*, Review of Agriculture, June 1986.
17. *Ibid.*, p. 253.

33. Agricultural Growth and the Green Revolution

1. G.S. Bhalla, 'Nehru and Planning—Choices in Agriculture', *Working Paper Series*, School of Social Sciences, Jawaharlal Nehru University, New Delhi, 1990, p. 29.
2. Ladejinsky Papers, p. 494.
3. See, for example, G.S. Bhalla and Gurmail Singh, 'Recent Developments in Indian Agriculture: A State Level Analysis', *EPW*, 29 March 1997. The statistics in the rest of the paragraph are taken from this source.
4. Raj Krishna, 'Small Farmers Development', *EPW*, 26 May 1979, p. 913.
5. G.S. Bhalla and G.K. Chadha, 'Green Revolution and the Small Peasant—A Study of Income Distribution in Punjab Agriculture', *EPW*, 5 and 22 May 1982.
6. Ladejinsky Papers, pp. 436–440
7. See C.H. Hanumantha Rao, 'Agriculture: Policy and Performance/', in Bimal Jalan, ed., *The Indian Economy: Problems and Prospects*, New Delhi, 1992, pp. 128–29.
8. See Daniel Thorner, *The Shaping of Modern India*, 202 ff., 224ff.
9. C.H. Hanumantha Rao, *op. cit.*, pp. 129–30. Emphasis added.
10. M.S. Swaminathan, 'Growth and Sustainability', *Frontline*, 9–22 August 1997.

34. Agrarian Struggles Since Independence

1. The best collection of essays on the subject remains A.R. Desai, ed., *Agrarian Struggles in India After Independence*, Delhi, 1986.
2. P. Sundarayya, *Telangana People's Struggle and Its Lessons*, Communist Party of India (Marxist), Calcutta, 1972, pp. 115–16, 239–40, 424.
3. Interview with Baba Bachhitar Singh, cited in Mridula Mukherjee, 'Communists and Peasants in Punjab: A Focus on the Muzara Movement in Patiala, 1937–53', in Bipan Chandra, ed., *The Indian Left: Critical Appraisals*, New Delhi, 1983.
4. See Mridula Mukherjee, 'Peasant Resistance and Peasant Consciousness in Colonial India: "Subalterns" and Beyond', *EPW*, 1988, October 8 and 15.
5. See Staffan Lindberg, 'New Farmers' Movements in India as Structural Response and Collective Identity Formation: The Cases of the Shetkari Sangathana and the BKU', in Tom Brass, ed., *New Farmers' Movements in India*, Ilford, 1995, pp. 95–125, and other articles in this volume for a consideration of this issue.

35. Revival and Growth of Communalism

1. Gandhi, *CW*, Vol. 76, p. 402.

36. Communalism and the Use of State Power

1. See chapter on Revival and Growth of Communalism for a detailed discussion of this aspect.
2. Savarkar was tried for the assassination of the Mahatma but was let off on technical grounds. Sardar Patel, being a fine criminal lawyer, was personally convinced of Savarkar's guilt, otherwise he would not have agreed to put him up for trial. He told Jawaharlal Nehru in unambiguous terms: 'It was a fanatical wing of the Hindu Mahasabha directly under Savarkar that [hatched] the conspiracy and saw it through.' *Sardar Patel Correspondence, 1945–50*, (hereafter *SPC*) ed by Durga Das, Navajivan Publishing House, Ahmedabad, Vol. VI, p. 56. However, when the Commission of Inquiry set up in 1965 under Justice Jiwan Lal Kapoor, a former judge of the Supreme Court of India, gave its report, it came to the following conclusion: 'All these facts taken together were destructive of any theory other than the conspiracy to murder by Savarkar and his group.' *Report of Commission of Inquiry into Conspiracy to Murder Mahatma Gandhi* (Kapur Commission Report), New Delhi, 1970, p. 303, para 25.106.
3. A book edited by Dina Nath Batra of the RSS, called *The Enemies of Indianisation: The Children of Marx, Macaulay and Madarsa* was published on 15 August 2001. The book, which was an attack on scientific secular history and historians, contained an article listing 41 distortions in the existing NCERT books. The NCERT director J.S. Rajput himself had contributed an article in the volume listing a few more distortions.
4. See *The Times of India*, 5 October 2001. Emphasis added
5. See *The Hindustan Times*, 4 December 2001.
6. See the RSS mouthpiece, *Organiser*, 4 November 2001.
7. *The Hindustan Times*, 8 December 2001.
8. *The Indian Express*, 20 December 2001.
9. 'History and the Enterprise of Knowledge', address delivered to the Indian History Congress by Amartya Sen, January 2001, Calcutta. See also Amartya Sen, *The Argumentative Indian: Writings on Indian History, Culture and Identity*, Allen Lane, Penguin, London, 2005, for a brilliant critique of the communal interpretation of Indian history.
10. *Harijan*, 5 December 1936, quoted in Bipan Chandra, 'Gandhiji, Secularism and Communalism', *Social Scientist*. Also reprinted in Irfan Habib, Bipan Chandra, et al., *Gandhi Reconsidered: Towards a Secular and Modern India*, Sahmat, New Delhi, 2004.

11. Irfan Habib, Suvira Jaiswal and Aditya Mukherjee, *History in the New NCERT Textbooks: A Report and an Index of Errors*, Approved and Published by the Executive Committee, Indian History Congress, Kolkata, 2003.
12. *The Hindu*, 3 March 2002.
13. *The Hindu*, 30 April 2002.
14. *The Hindu*, 1 May 2002.
15. *Ibid.*,
16. *Ibid.*,
17. *Ibid.*, 2 May 2002.
18. *Ibid.*, 30 April 2002.
19. *Ibid.*, 3 May 2002.
20. *Ibid.*
21. *Ibid.*, 17 August 2002.
22. *Ibid.*, 3 September and 29 October 2002.
23. *Ibid.*, 16 December 2002.

37. Caste, Untouchability, and Anti-caste Politics and Strategies

1. For these, see Bipan Chandra, et al, *India's Struggle for Independence. 1857–1947*, chapter 18.
2. For a useful overview of Dalit politics, especially from 1957 onwards, see V. Suresh, 'The Dalit Movement in India', in T.V. Sathyamurthy, *Social Change and Political Discourse in India*, Vol. 3, *Region, Religion, Caste, Gender, and Culture in Contemporary India*, 1996, pp. 355–87.
3. See Jean Dreze and Amartya Sen, *India: Economic Development and Social Opportunity*, Delhi, 1995, p. 97.
4. *Ibid.*, table 6.1, p. 112.
5. For an interesting attempt to argue for Dalit–Backward Caste unity, especially in the context of the attempt to forge links with the Shetkari Sangathana in Maharashtra, see Gail Omvedt, 'The Anti-Caste Movement and the Discourse of Power,' in T.V. Sathyamurthy, *op. cit.*, pp. 334–54, and Gail Omvedt, 'We Want the Return of Our Sweat: The New Peasant Movement in India and the Formation of a New Agricultural Policy', in Tom Brass, ed., *New Farmers' Movements in India*, Ilford, 1995, pp. 126–64.

38. Indian Women Since Independence

1. Based on Mridula Mukherjee's interview with Professor Usha Mehta.
2. The most comprehensive account of women's movements is to be found in Radha Kumar, *The History of Doing*, New Delhi, 1993, and I have used it extensively.
3. See, for example, Mridula Mukherjee, 'Interview with Sushila Chain', in *Manushi*.

4. For a detailed account of this very interesting movement, see Ramachandra Guha, *The Unquiet Woods: Ecological Change and Peasant Resistance in the Himalaya,* Delhi, 1989.
5. For a detailed study of the agitations against dowry, the Muslim Women's Bill and sati, see Rajni Palriwala and Indu Agnihotri, 'Tradition, the Family and the State: Politics of the Contemporary Women's Movement', in T.V. Sathyamurthy, ed., *Social Change and Political Discourse in India,* Vol. 3, *Region, Religon, Caste, Gender and Culture in Contemporary India,* Delhi, 1996, pp. 503–32.
6. For the data and much of the conclusions in this and the following paragraphs, I have relied greatly on the path-breaking work of Jean Dreze and Amartya K. Sen. See, for example, their *India: Economic Development and Social Opportunity,* Delhi, 1995.

39. The Post-colonial Indian State and the Political Economy

1. For the broad theoretical framework adopted in this chapter some of the works I have been most influenced by are listed below. Bipan Chandra, *Indian National Movement, The Long Term Dynamic,* New Delhi, 1988, first delivered as the Presidential Address, Indian History Congress, 1985, Amritsar; Ralph Miliband, *Marxism and Politics,* 1977; Ernesto Laclau, *Politics and Ideology in Marxist Theory,* London, 1977; Nicos Poulantzas, *Classes in Contemporary Capitalism,* London, 1975, and the recent writings of Mohit Sen; the leading left intellectual who has been closely associated with left politics for nearly half a century.
2. See, for example, Peter Evans, *Dependent Development: The Alliance of Multinational, State and Local Capital in Brazil,* Princeton, 1979, pp. 31–34, 52 and Gary Gereffi and Donald Wyman, 'Development Strategies in Latin America and East Asia', 1985, mimeo.
3. See, for example, Bipan Chandra, *Nationalism and Colonialism in Modern India,* New Delhi, 1979, and 'The Colonial Legacy', in Bimal Jalan, ed., *The Indian Economy: Problems and Prospects,* New Delhi, 1992; K.N. Raj, 'The Politics and Economics of Intermediate Regimes', *EPW,* 1 July 1973; Sudipto Mundle, 'State Character and Economic Policy', *Social Scientist,* May 1974; Pranab Bardhan, *The Political Economy of Development in India,* Delhi, 1998 (expanded edition); and Aditya Mukherjee and Mridula Mukherjee, 'Imperialism and the Growth of Indian Capitalism in the Twentieth Century', *EPW,* 12 March 1988.
4. See, for example, Aditya Mukherjee, 'The Indian Capitalist Class: Aspects of its Economic, Political and Ideological Development in the Colonial Period', in S. Bhattacharya and Romila Thapar, eds, *Situating Indian History,* Delhi, 1986 and *Imperialism, Nationalism and the Development of Indian Capitalism: The Making of the Indian Capitalist Class,* New Delhi (forthcoming).

5. Prabhat Patnaik, 'Political Strategies of Economic Development', in Partha Chatterjee, ed., *Wages of Freedom: Fifty Years of the Indian Nation-State,* Delhi, 1998, pp. 58–59. Emphasis added.

6. F.H. Cordoso, 'Social Consequences of Globalisation', Lecture at India International Centre, New Delhi, 27 January 1996.

7. Amartya Sen, 'Social Commitment and Democracy', *New Thinking Communist,* 1 November 1998.

8. Bipan Chandra, 'The Real Danger of Foreign Domination: Peripheralization', in his *Essays on Contemporary India,* revised edition, New Delhi, 1999.

41. The Dawn of the New Millennium: Achievements, Problems and Prospects

1. C. Thomas in Geeti Sen, ed., *Receiving India,* New Delhi, 1993, p. 266.

2. S. Gopal, *Jawaharlal Nehru—A Biography,* Vol. 3, London, 1984, p. 301.

3. Mohit Sen, 'Entering the Fiftieth Year', *New Thinking Communist,* 15 August 1996, p. 2.

4. Quoted in Zareer Masani, *Indira Gandhi—A Biography,* London, 1975, p. 299.

5. W.H. Morris-Jones, *Politics Mainly Indian,* Bombay, 1978, p. 131.

6. Myron Weiner, *The Politics of Scarcity,* Bombay, 1963, p. 216.

7. Joan V. Bondurant, *Conquest of Violence: The Gandhian Philosophy of Conflict,* revised edition, Berkeley, 1971, pp. viii–ix.

8. Francine R. Frankel, *India's Political Economy,* 1947–1977, Delhi, 1978, p. 4.

9. *Ibid.*

10. *Ibid.,* pp. 4–6.

11. Nehru, *Speeches,* Vol. 3, p. 96.

12. India Development Report 1999–2000, ed., Kirit S. Parikh, New Delhi, 1999, p. 5. Most of the statistics in this and the next section are taken from this work. Economic Survey, 1998–99, UNDP's *Human Development Report, 1999,* and National Council of Applied Economic Research's *India Human Development Report, 1999.*

Select Bibliography

General

1. Krishan Bhatia, *The Ordeal of Nationhood*, New York, 1971.
2. Rajni Kothari, *Politics in India*, New Delhi, 1970.
3. Achin Vanaik, *The Painful Transition: Bourgeois Democracy in India*, London, 1990.
4. Francine R. Frankel, *India's Political Economy, 1947–1977*, Delhi, 1978.
5. L.I. Rudolph and S.H. Rudolph, *In Pursuit of Lakshmi: The Political Economy of the Indian State*, Bombay, 1987.
6. Atul Kohli, ed., *India's Democracy*, Princeton, 1988.
7. Shashi Tharoor, *India From Midnight to the Millennium*, New Delhi, 1997.
8. Sunil Khilnani, *The Idea of India*, London, 1997.
9. Paul R. Brass, *The Politics of India Since Independence*, Indian edition, New Delhi, 1992.
10. W.H. Morris-Jones, *Politics Mainly Indian*, New Delhi, 1978.
11. W.H. Morris-Jones, *The Government and Politics of India*, Wistow, Huntingdon, 1987 edition.
12. Robert L. Hardgrave, Jr. and Stanley A. Kochanek, *India: Government and Politics in a Developing Nation*, fifth edition, San Diego, 1993.
13. Daniel Thorner, *The Shaping of Modern India*, Delhi, 1980.
14. Yogendra Singh, *Social Change in India*, New Delhi, 1993.
15. Bipan Chandra, *Essays on Contemporary India*, revised edition, New Delhi, 1999.
16. Aditya Mukherjee, *Imperialism, Nationalism and the Marketing of the Indian Capitalist Class 1927–1947*, New Delhi, 2002.
17. Mridula Mukherjee, *Colonialising Agriculture: The Myth of Punjab Exceptionalism*, New Delhi, 2006.
18. Mridula Mukherjee, *Peasants in India's Non-violent Revolution, Practice and Theory*, New Delhi, 2004.

19. Upendra Baxi and Bhikhu Parekh, eds, *Crisis and Change in Contemporary India*, New Delhi, 1995.
20. Myron Weiner, *The Indian Paradox: Essays in Indian Politics*, New Delhi, 1989.
21. Partha Chatterjee, ed., *Wages of Freedom: Fifty Years of the Indian Nation-State*, Delhi, 1998.
22. Jean Dreze and Amartya Sen, *India: Economic Development and Social Opportunity*, Delhi, 1996.
23. Vijay Joshi and I.M.D. Little, eds *India: Macroeconomics and Political Economy 1964–1991*, Washington, 1994.
24. Bimal Jalan, ed.. *The Indian Economy: Problems and Prospects*, New Delhi, 1992.
25. E.J. Hobsbawm, *Age of Extremes: The Short Twentieth Century*, Harmondsworth, 1994.
26. Hiranmay Karlekar, *Independent India: The First Fifty Years*, Delhi, 1998.
27. Amartya Sen, *The Argumentative Indian: Writings on Indian History, Culture and Identity*, Allen Lane, Penguin London, 2005.

Chapter 2

1. Bipan Chandra, (i) *Essays on Colonialism*, New Delhi, 1999. (ii) *Nationalism and Colonialism in Modern India*, New Delhi, 1979. (iii) The Colonial Legacy', in Bimal Jalan, ed., *The Indian Economy: Problems and Prospects*, New Delhi, 1992. (iv) *Modern India*, New Delhi, 1990.
2. Aditya Mukherjee and Mridula Mukherjee, 'Imperialism and the Growth of Indian Capitalism in Twentieth Century', *Economic and Political Weekly* (hereafter *EPW*), 12 March 1988, reprinted in *Capitalist Development: Critical Essays*, Ghanshyam Shah ed., Bombay, 1990.
3. Irfan Habib, 'Colonialization of Indian Economy', *Social Scientist*, March 1975.
4. Angus Maddison, *Class Structure and Economic Growth: India and Pakistan Since the Moghuls*, London, 1971.
5. V.B. Singh, *Economic History of India, 1857–1956*, Bombay, 1965.
6. R. Palme Dutt, *India Today*, Bombay, 1949.
7. A.R. Desai, *Social Background of Indian Nationalism*, Bombay, 1959.

Chapter 3

1. Bipan Chandra, et al., *India's Struggle for Independence 1857–1947*, New Delhi, 1988.
2. Bipan Chandra, (i) *Epic Struggle*, New Delhi. (ii) *Indian National Movement: The Long-term Dynamics*, New Delhi, 1988. (iii) *Essays in Indian Nationalism*, New Delhi, 1993.

3. W.H. Morris-Jones, *The Government and Politics of India*, Wistow, England, 1987 edition.

Chapters 4–5

1. B. Shiva Rao, ed., *The Framing of India's Constitution: A Study*, New Delhi, 1968.
2. Vidya Dhar Mahajan, *Select Modern Governments*, New Delhi, 17th edition, 1995.
3. V.P. Menon, *The Transfer of Power in India*, Princeton, 1957.
4. Granville Austin, *The Indian Constitution: Cornerstone of a Nation*, Oxford 1966.
5. Subhash C. Kashyap, 'The Framing of the Constitution and the Process of Institution Building', in *A Centenary History of The Indian National Congress*, in B.N. Pande, general editor, vol. IV, New Delhi, 1990.
6. W.H. Morris-Jones, *The Government and Politics of India*, New York, 1967, first published, London, 1964.
7. S.C. Kashyap, *Our Constitution*, New Delhi, 1994.
8. S.K. Chaube, *Constituent Assembly of India: Springboard of Revolution*, New Delhi, 1973.
9. D.D. Basu, *Introduction to the Constitution of India*, New Delhi, 8th edition, 1984.
10. M.V. Pylee, *Constitutional Government in India*, New Delhi, 4th edition, 1984.
11. David Potter, *India's Political Administrators* 1918–83, Oxford, 1986.

Chapter 6

1. S. Gopal, *Jawaharlal Nehru—A Biography*, vol. 2 (1947–1956), London and Delhi, 1979.
2. Rajmohan Gandhi, *Patel: A Life*, Ahmedabad, 1990.
3. V.P. Menon, *Integration of the Indian States*, Madras, 1985, reprint 1985.
4. Sisir K. Gupta, *Kashmir: A Study in Indian Pakistan Relations*, London, 1967.
5. P. Mishra, 'Consolidation of Independence: Challenge and Response', *A Centenary History of the Indian National Congress*, general editor, B.N. Pande, vol. IV, ed., Iqbal Narain, New Delhi, 1990.

Chapter 7

1. Bipan Chandra, 'Indian Nationalism—Redefined', and 'Will the Indian Nation Hold', in Bipan Chandra, *Essays on Contemporary India*, New Delhi, 1993.
2. Boris I. Kluev, *India: National and Language Problem*, New Delhi, 1981.

3. S. Mohan Kumaramangalam, *India's Language Crisis*, Madras, 1965.
4. Hugh Tinker, 'Is There an Indian Nation', in Philip Mason, ed., *India and Ceylon: Unity and Diversity*, London, 1967.
5. Jyotirindra Das Gupta, *Language Conflict and National Development: Group Politics and National Language Policy in India*, Berkeley and Bombay, 1970.
6. Nirmal Kumar Bose, 'Problems of National Integration', *Science and Culture*, vol. 30, No.4, April 1964.
7. Zoya Hasan, 'Introduction: State and Identity in Modern India', in Zoya Hasan, S.N. Jha and Rasheeduddin Khan, eds, *The State, Political Processes and Identity*, New Delhi, 1989.
8. Rajni Kothari, *Politics in India*, Chapter VIII, New Delhi, 1970.

Chapter 8

1. Jolly Mohan Kaul, *Problems of National Integration*, New Delhi, 1963.
2. Boris I. Kluev, *India: National and Language Problem*, New Delhi, 1981.
3. Joseph E. Schwartzberg, 'Factors in the Linguistic Reorganization of India', in Paul Wallace, ed., *Region and Nation in India*, New Delhi, 1985.
4. Ather Farouqi, 'The Emerging Dilemma of the Urdu Press in India', *South Asia*, Vol. XVIII, No. 2, 1995.
5. Ralph Russell, 'Urdu in India Since Independence', *EPW*, 9 January 1999.

Chapter 9

1. Verrier Elwin, (i) *A Philosophy for NEFA*, Shillong, 1959. (ii) *The Tribal World of Verrier Elwin*, Bombay, 1964.
2. Christoph von Furer-Haimendorf (i) 'The Position of the Tribal Populations in Modern India', in Philip Mason, ed., *India and Ceylon: Unity and Diversity*, London, 1967. (ii) 'The Changing Position of Tribal Population in India,' in D. Taylor and M. Yapp, *Political Identity in South Asia*, London, 1979.
3. K.S. Singh, ed., *Tribal Movements in India*, 2 Volumes, New Delhi, 1982.
4. Stuart Corbridge, 'The Ideology of Tribal Economy and Society: Politics in the Jharkhand, 1950–1980', *Modern Asian Studies*, Vol. 22, No. l, 1988.
5. Nirmal Kumar Bose, (i) 'Change in Tribal Culture Before and After Independence', *Man in India*, Vol. 44, No. l, January–March 1964. (ii) 'Integration of Tribes in Andhra Pradesh', *Man in India*, Vol. 44, No. 2, April–June 1964.
6. Jolly M. Kaul, *Problems of National Integration*, New Delhi, 1963.

7. Urmila Phadnis, *Ethnicity and Nation-Building in South Asia,* New Delhi, 1989.
8. B.K. Roy-Burman, *Indigenous and Tribal Peoples,* New Delhi, 1994.

Chapter 10

1. Balveer Arora and Douglas V. Verney, *Multiple Identities in a Single State,* Delhi, 1993.
2. N. Mukerji and Balveer Arora, *Federalism in India,* New Delhi, 1991.
3. C.N. Vakil, 'National Integration', in J.C. Daruvala, ed., *Tensions in Economic Development in South East Asia,* Bombay, 1961.
4. Ashok Mathur, 'The Character of Industrialization in the Indian Economy', unpublished paper, Jawaharlal Nehru University, New Delhi, May 1998.
5. Jolly M. Kaul, *Problems of National Integration,* New Delhi, 1963.
6. Myron Weiner, *Sons of the Soil: Migration and Ethnic Conflict in India,* Princeton, 1978.
7. Dipankar Gupta, *Nationalism in a Metropolis: The Shiv Sena in Bombay,* New Delhi, 1982.

Chapters 11 and 13

1. S. Gopal, *Jawaharlal Nehru—A Biography,* Vols. 2 and 3, London and Delhi, 1979 and 1984.
2. Bipan Chandra, 'Jawaharlal Nehru in Historical Perspective', and 'Nehru and Communalism', in Bipan Chandra, *Ideology and Politics in Modern India,* New Delhi, 1994.
3. B.R. Nanda, *Jawaharlal Nehru: Rebel and Statesman,* Delhi, 1995.
4. B.R. Nanda, P.C. Joshi and Raj Krishna, *Gandhi and Nehru,* Delhi, 1979.
5. Sudipto Kaviraj, 'Apparent Paradoxes of Jawaharlal Nehru', *Mainstream,* 15 November–13 December 1980.
6. Geoffrey Tyson, *Nehru: The Years of Power,* London, 1966.
7. Bagendu Ganguli and Mira Ganguly, 'Electoral Politics and Partisan Choice', *A Centenary History of the Indian National Congress,* general editor B.N. Pande, Vol. IV, ed. Iqbal Narain, New Delhi, 1990.
8. Bimal Prasad, *Gandhi, Nehru and J.P.: Studies in Leadership,* Delhi, 1985.
9. E.M.S. Namboodiripad, *Economics and Politics of India's Socialist Pattern,* New Delhi, 1966.
10. W.H. Morris-Jones, *Parliament in India,* London, 1957.
11. B.N. Pande, general editor, *A Centenary History of the Indian National Congress,* Vol.IV, ed. Iqbal Narain, New Delhi, 1990.

Chapter 12

1. V.P. Dutt, *India and the World,* New Delhi, 1990.
2. K. Subrahmanyam, 'Evolution of Indian Defence Policy (1947–1964)', in B.N. Pande, general editor, *A Centenary History of the Indian National Congress,* Vol. IV, New Delhi, 1990.
3. B.R. Nanda, ed., *Indian Foreign Policy: The Nehru Years,* Delhi, 1976.
4. Rikhi Jaipal, 'Ideas and Issues in Indian Foreign Policy', in B.N. Pande, ed., *A Centenary History.*
5. V.P. Dutt, *India's Foreign Policy,* New Delhi, 1984.
6. A.K. Damodaran, 'Foreign Policy in Action', in B.N. Pande, ed., *A Centenary History.*
7. S. Gopal, *Jawaharlal Nehru—A Biography,* Vols 2 and 3, London, 1979 and 1984.
8. Neville George Anthony Maxwell, *India's China War,* London, 1970.
9. M.S. Rajan, *India in World Affairs,* New York, 1964.
10. W. Norman Brown, *The United States and India, Pakistan, Bangladesh,* Cambridge, Massachusetts, 1972.
11. Sisir K. Gupta, *Kashmir: A Study in Indo-Pak Relations,* Bombay, 1966.

Chapter 14

1. Rajni Kothari, (i) 'The Congress "System" in India', *Asian Survey,* Vol. IV, No. 12, December 1964. (ii) *Politics in India,* Chapter V, New Delhi, 1970.
2. S. Gopal, *Jawaharlal Nehru—A Biography,* Vols. 2 and 3, London and Delhi, 1979 and 1984.
3. Stanley A. Kochanek, *The Congress Party of India,* Princeton, 1968.
4. V.M. Siriskar and L. Fernandes, *Indian Political Parties,* Meerut, 1984.
5. All India Congress Committee, *A Contemporary History of the Indian National Congress,* general editor B.N. Pande, Vol. IV, ed. Iqbal Narain, New Delhi, 1990.
6. W.H. Morris-Jones, (i) 'Congress, Dead or Alive', *Pacific Affairs,* Vol. 42, No. 2, 1969. (ii) 'The Indian Congress Party: A Dilemma of Dominance', in *Politics Mainly Indian,* Bombay, 1978. Also in *Modern Asian Studies,* Vol. 1, No. 2, April 1967. (iii) *The Government and Politics of India,* Chapter 5, Wistow, 1987 edition.

Chapter 15

1. Myron Weiner, *Party Politics in India,* Princeton, 1957, Delhi, 1990.
2. Lewis P. Fickett, Jr., (i) *The Major Socialist Parties of India,* Syracuse, New York, 1976. (ii) 'The Praja Socialist Party of India—1952–1972: A Final Assessment', *Asian Survey,* Vol. 13, No. 9, September 1973.

3. Howard L. Erdman, (i) *The Swatantra Party and Indian Conservatism*, Cambridge, 1967. (ii) 'India's Swatantra Party', *Pacific Affairs*, Vol. 36, No. 4, Winter 1963–64.
4. Bhabani Sengupta, *Communism in Indian Politics*, New York, 1971.
5. Mohit Sen, *Glimpses of the History of the Indian Communist Movement*, Madras, 1997.
6. B.D. Graham, *Hindu Nationalism and Indian Politics: The Origins and Development of the Bharatiya Jan Sangh*, Cambridge, 1990.
7. Hari Kishore Singh, *A History of the Praja Socialist Party*, Lucknow, 1959.
8. Mohan Ram, *Indian Communism*, Delhi, 1969.
9. D.R. Goyal, *Rashtriya Swayam Sewak Sangh*, New Delhi, 1979.
10. Craig Baxter, *The Jan Sangh*, Philadelphia, 1969.
11. Achin Vanaik, 'The Indian Left', *New Left Review*, No. 159.
12. Madhu Dandavate, *Evolution of Socialist Policies and Perspective 1934–1984*, Bombay, 1986.
13. E.M.S. Namboodiripad, *Conflicts and Crisis: Political India—1974*, Bombay, 1974.
14. Haridev Sharma, et al., *Fifty Years of Socialist Movement in India*, New Delhi, 1984.

Chapters 16 to 19

1. Inder Malhotra, *Indira Gandhi: A Personal and Political Biography*, London, 1989.
2. Zareer Masani, *Indira Gandhi—A Biography*, London, 1975.
3. Pupul Jayakar, *Indira Gandhi—A Biography*, New Delhi, 1992.
4. Mary C. Carras, *Indira Gandhi: In the Crucible of Leadership*, Bombay, 1979.
5. Morarji Desai, *The Story of My life*, Vol. 2, Delhi, 1974.
6. C.P. Srivastava, *Lal Bahadur Shastri*, Delhi, 1995.
7. Tariq Ali, *The Nehrus and the Gandhis*, London, 1985.
8. S.S. Gill, *The Dynasty: A Political Biography of the Premier Ruling Family of Modern India*, New Delhi, 1996.
9. Sudipto Kaviraj, 'Indira Gandhi and Indian Politics', *EPW*, 20–27 September 1986.
10. Rajni Kothari, *Politics in India*, Chapter V, New Delhi, 1970.
11. Rabindra Ray, *The Naxalites and Their Ideology*, Delhi, 1988.
12. Mahendra Prasad Singh, *Split in a Predominant Party: The Indian National Congress in 1969*, New Delhi, 1981.
13. Krishan Bhatia, *Indira: A Biography of Prime Minister Gandhi*, London, 1974.
14. W.H. Morris-Jones, 'India Elects for Change—and Stability', *Asian Survey*, Vol. XI, No. 8, August 1971, Berkeley. Also in his *Politics Mainly Indian*, Bombay, 1978.

15. Norman D. Palmer, 'India's Fourth General Elections', *Asian Survey*, Vol. VII, no. 5, May 1967.
16. Ashis Nandy, 'Indira Gandhi and the Culture of Indian Politics', in his *At the Edge of Psychology: Essays in Politics and Culture*, Delhi, 1980.
17. Harry W. Blair, 'Mrs. Gandhi's Emergency, The Indian Elections of 1977, Pluralism and Marxism: Problems with Paradigms', *Modern Asian Studies*, Vol. 14, No. 2, 1980.

Chapter 18

A. The JP Movement

1. Ghanshyam Shah, *Protest Movements in Two Indian States: A Study of the Gujarat and Bihar Movements*, Delhi, 1977.
2. Bimal Prasad, *Gandhi, Nehru and J.P.: Studies in Leadership*, Delhi, 1985.
3. Minoo Masani, *Is J.P. the Answer?*, Delhi, 1975.
4. John R. Wood, 'Extra-Parliamentary Opposition in India: An Analysis of Populist Agitations in Gujarat and Bihar', *Pacific Affairs*, Vol. XLVIII, No. 3, Fall 1975.
5. Ajit Bhattacharjea, *Jayaprakash Narayan: A Political Biography*, Delhi, 1975.

B. The Emergency

1. Henry C. Hart, ed., *Indira Gandhi's India*, Boulder (Colorado), 1976.
2. Max Zins, *Strains on Indian Democracy*, New Delhi, 1988. Also in Zoya Hasan, S.N. Jha and Rasheeduddin Khan, *The State, Political Processes and Identity*, New Delhi, 1989.
3. V.P. Dutt, 'The Emergency in India: Background and Rationale', *Asian Survey*, Vol. XVI, No. 12, December 1976.
4. *Seminar*, March 1977, New Delhi.
5. Balraj Puri, 'Fuller Views of Emergency', *EPW*, 15 July 1995.
6. Kuldip Nayar, *The Judgement: Inside Story of the Emergency in India*, New Delhi, 1977.
7. W.H. Morris-Jones, 'Creeping but Uneasy Authoritarianism: India 1975–76,' *Government and Opposition*, Vol. 12, No. 1, Winter 1977.
8. David Selbourne, *An Eye to India: The Unmasking of a Tyranny*, London, 1977.

C. The Janata Government

1. C.P. Bhambri, *The Janata Party: A Profile*, New Delhi, 1980.
2. Janardan Thakur, *All the Janata Men*, New Delhi, 1978.

3. J. Das Gupta, 'The Janata Phase: Reorganisation and Redirection in Indian Politics', *Asian Survey*, Vol. XIX, No. 4, April 1979.
4. Iqbal Narain, 'India 1977: From Promise to Disenchantment', *Asian Survey*, Vol. XVIII, No. 2, February 1978.
5. Robert L. Hardgrave, Jr. and Stanley A. Kochanek, *India: Government and Politics in a Developing Nation*, 5th edition, pp. 276–82.
6. L.I. Rudolph and S.H. Rudolph, *In Pursuit of Lakshmi: The Political Economy of the Indian State*, Chapter 5, Bombay, 1987.

Chapter 20

1. Bhabani Sen Gupta, *Rajiv Gandhi: A Political Study*, New Delhi, 1989.
2. Mohan Ram, *Sri Lanka: The Fractured Island*, New Delhi, 1989.
3. Minhaz Merchant, *Rajiv Gandhi: The End of a Dream*, New Delhi, 1991.
4. Nicholas Nugent, *Rajiv Gandhi: Son of a Dynasty*, New Delhi, 1991.
5. Ved Mehta, *Rajiv Gandhi and Rama's Kingdom*, New Haven and London, 1994.
6. S.S. Gill, *The Dynasty: A Political Biography of the Premier Ruling Family of India*, New Delhi, 1996.
7. Raju G.C. Thomas, *Indian Security Policy*, Princeton, 1986.
8. R. Venkataraman, *My Presidential Years*, New Delhi, 1994.
9. Ramesh Thakur, *The Politics and Economics of India's Foreign Policy*, London, 1994.

Chapter 21

1. Seema Mustafa, *The Lonely Prophet: V.P. Singh, A Political Biography*, New Delhi, 1995.
2. David Butler, Ashok Lahiri and Prannoy Roy, *India Decides: Elections 1952–1995*. New Delhi, 3rd edition, 1995.
3. Paul R. Brass, *The New Cambridge History of India*, IV.; *The Politics of India Since Independence*, Cambridge, 2nd edition, 1994.
4. R. Venkataraman, *My Presidential Years*, New Delhi, 1994.
5. M.N. Srinivas, ed., *Caste: Its Twentieth Century Avatar*, New Delhi, 1996.
6. Yogendra Yadav, et al., 'The Maturing of a Democracy', in *India Today*, Vol. xxi, No. 16, 1996.
7. Yogendra Yadav, 'Reconfiguration in Indian Politics: State Assembly Elections, 1993–96', *EPW*, Vol. 32, Nos. 2–3, 1996.
8. Thomas Blom Hansen and Christophe Jaffrelot, *The BJP and the Compulsions of Politics in India*, Delhi, 1998.
9. V.P. Dutt, *India's Foreign Policy in a Changing World*, New Delhi, 1999.

10. Lalit Mansingh, et al., *Indian Foreign Policy: Agenda for the 21st Century,* New Delhi, 1997.
11. Air Commodore Jasjit Singh, ed., *Nuclear India,* New Delhi, 1998.
12. Amitabh Mattoo, ed., *India's Nuclear Deterrent: Pokhran II and Beyond,* New Delhi, 1999.
13. V.P. Dutt, *India's Foreign Policy Since Independence,* New Delhi, 2007.
14. J.N. Dixit, *India–Pakistan in War and Peace,* Routledge, 2003.
15. Air Commodore Jasjit Singh, *Kargil 1999: Pakistan's Fourth War for Kashmir,* Knowledge World, New Delhi, 1999.
16. C. Raja Mohan, *Impossible Allies: Nuclear India, United States and the Global Order,* New Delhi, 2006.

Chapter 22

A. Tamil Nadu

1. S.N. Balasundaram, 'The Dravidian (Non-Brahmin) Movements in Madras', and C. Annadurai, 'D.M.K. As I See It', in Iqbal Narain, ed., *State Politics in India,* Meerut, 1967.
2. Pandav Nayak, 'Politics of Pragmatism', in Iqbal Narain, ed., *State Politics in India,* Meerut, 1976.
3. Marguerite Ross Barnett, *The Politics of Cultural Nationalism in South India,* Princeton, 1976.
4. David Washbrook, 'Caste, Class and Dominance in Modern Tamil Nadu: Non-Brahmanism, Dravidianism and Tamil Nationalism', in Francine R. Frankel and M.S.A. Rao, eds, *Dominance and State Power in Modern India: Decline of a Social Order,* Vol. 1, Delhi, 1989.
5. Urmila Phadnis, 'The Dravidian Movement and Tamil Ethnicity in India', in her *Ethnicity and Nation-Building in South Asia,* New Delhi, 1989.

B. Andhra Pradesh

1. Hugh Gray, (i) 'The Demand for a Separate Telengana State in India', *Asian Survey,* Vol. XI, No. 5, May 1971. (ii) 'The Failure of the Demand for a Separate Andhra State', *Asian Survey,* Vol. XIV, No. 4 April 1974.
2. G. Ram Reddy, 'Andhra Pradesh: The Citadel of the Congress', in Iqbal Narain, ed., *State Politics in India,* Meerut, 1976.
3. Mohit Sen, 'Showdown in Andhra', *EPW,* 23 December 1972.
4. Dagmar Bernstorff, 'Region and Nation: The Telengana Movement's Dual Identity', in Taylor and Yapp, *Political Identity in South Asia,* London, 1979.

D. Assam

1. Sanjib Baruah, (i) 'Immigration, Ethnic Conflict, and Political Turmoil—Assam, 1979–1985,' *Asian Survey*, Vol. XXVI, No. 11, November 1986. (ii) 'Ethnic Conflict or State-Society Struggle', *Modern Asian Studies*, Vol. 28, No. 3, 1994.
2. Myron Weiner, *Sons of the Soil: Migration and Ethnic Conflict in India*, Princeton, 1978.
3. Hiren Gohain, 'Ethnic Unrest in the North-East', *EPW*, 22 February 1997.
4. J. Das Gupta, 'Ethnicity, Democracy and Development in India: Assam in a General Perspective', in Atul Kohli, ed., *India's Democracy*, Princeton, 1988.

Chapter 23

A. West Bengal

1. Atul Kohli, (i) 'West Bengal: Parliamentary Communism and Reform from Above', in Atul Kohli, *The State and Poverty in India*, Cambridge, 1987. (ii) *Democracy and Discontent*, Chapters 6, 10, 13, Cambridge, 1991. (iii) 'Parliamentary Communism and Agrarian Reform: The Evidence from India's Bengal', *Asian Survey*, Vol. 23, No. 7, July 1983. (iv) 'From Elite Activism to Democratic Consolidation: The Rise of Reform Communism in West Bengal', in Francine R. Frankel and M.S.A. Rao, eds, *Dominance and State Power in Modern India: Decline of a Social Order*, Vols. I and II, Delhi, 1989, 1990.

B. Jammu and Kashmir

1. S. Gopal, *Jawaharlal Nehru—A Biography*, Vols 2 and 3, London and New Delhi, 1979 and 1984.
2. Balraj Puri, 'Jammu and Kashmir', in Myron Weiner, *State Politics in India*, Princeton, 1968.
3. Ajit Bhattacharjea, *Kashmir—The Wounded Valley*, New Delhi, 1994.
4. B.C. Verghese, 'Fourth Option: Towards a Settlement in Jammu and Kashmir', in Upendra Baxi, Alice Jacob and Tarlok Singh, *Reconstructing the Republic*, New Delhi, 1999.
5. Roop Krishen Bhatt, 'Politics of Integration', in Iqbal Narain, ed., *State Politics in India*, Meerut, 1976.

Chapter 24

1. Baldev Raj Nayar, (i) *Minority Politics in the Punjab*, Princeton, 1966. (ii) 'Sikh Separatism in the Punjab', in Donald E. Smith, ed., *South Asian Politics and Religion*, Princeton, 1966.

2. Rajni A. Kapur, *Sikh Separatism: The Politics of Faith*, London, 1986.
3. K.P.S. Gill, *The Knights of Falsehood*, New Delhi, 1997.
4. Amarjit Kaur, et al., *The Punjab Story*, New Delhi, 1984.
5. Satyapal Dang, *Genesis of Terrorism: An Analytical Study of Punjab Terrorists*, New Delhi, 1988.
6. Amrik Singh, ed., *Punjab in Indian Politics*, Delhi, 1985.
7. *Seminar*, February 1984.
8. Pramod Kumar, et al., *Punjab Crisis: Context and Trends*, Chandigarh, 1984.
9. Sucha Singh Gill and K.C. Singhal, 'The Punjab Problem: Its Historical Roots', *EPW*, April 1984.
10. Bikash Chandra, *Punjab Crisis—Perceptions and Perspectives of the Indian Intelligentsia*, New Delhi, 1993.

Chapters 25–33

1. A.M. Khusro, 'Land Reforms Since Independence', in V.B. Singh, ed. *The Economic History of India, 1857–1956*, Delhi, 1965.
2. A. Vaidyanathan, 'The Indian Economy Since Independence (1947–70)', in Dharma Kumar, ed., *The Cambridge Economic History of India*, Delhi, 1984 reprint.
3. Aditya Mukherjee, *Imperialism, Nationalism and the Marketing of the Indian Capitalist Class 1920–1947*, New Delhi, 2002.
4. Aditya Mukherjee and Mridula Mukherjee. 'Imperialism and the Growth of Indian Capitalism in the Twentieth Century', *EPW*, 12 March 1988.
5. Amartya Sen, 'How is India Doing?,' *New York Review of Books*, 1982, reprinted in *Mainstream*, 26 January 1983.
6. Amartya Sen, 'Social Commitment and Democracy', *New Thinking Communist*, 1 November 1998.
7. Angus Maddison, *The Word Economy: Vol. I A Millennial Perspective, Vol. II Historical Statistics*, OECD, 2006, Indian edition, New Delhi, 2007.
8. Atul Kohli, 'Politics of Economic Liberalization in India', *World Development*, Vol. 17, No. 3, 1989.
9. Atul Kohli, *Democracy and Discontent*, Cambridge, 1990.
10. B.R. Tomlinson, *The Economy of Modern India, 1860–1970*, Cambridge, 1993.
11. Baldev Raj Nayar, *India's Globalisation: Evaluating the Economic Consequences*, New Delhi, 2007.
12. Bimal Jalan, ed., *The Indian Economy: Problems and Prospects*, New Delhi, 1992.
13. Bimal Jalan, *India's Economy in the New Millennium*, New Delhi, 2002.

14. Bipan Chandra, *Essays on Colonialism*, New Delhi, 1999.
15. Amit Bhaduri and Deepak Nayyar, *The Intelligent Person's Guide to Liberalization*, New Delhi, 1996.
16. Dani Rodrik and Arvind Subramanian, 'Why India Can Grow at 7 Per Cent a Year or More: Projections and Reflections', *EPW*, 17 April 2004.
17. G.S. Bhalla, *Indian Agriculture Since Independence*, New Delhi, 2007.
18. Himangshu, 'Recent Trends in Poverty and Inequality: Some Preliminary Results', *EPW*, 10 February 2007.
19. Jeffrey D. Sachs, *The End of Poverty: Economic Possibilities of Our Time*, New York, 2005.
20. Jeffrey D. Sachs, Ashutosh Varshney and Nirupam Bajpai, eds,. *India in the Era of Economic Reforms*, New Delhi, 1999.
21. Kyoko Inoue, *Industrial Development Policy of India*, Tokyo, 1992.
22. K.N. Raj, *Indian Economic Growth: Performance and Prospects*, New Delhi, 1965.
23. K. Sundaram and Suresh D. Tendulkar, 'Poverty *Has* Declined in the 1990s', *EPW*, 25 January 2003.
24. L.I. Rudolph and S.H. Rudolph, *In Pursuit of Lakshmi: The Political Economy of the Indian State*, Chicago, 1987.
25. Louis J. Walinsky, ed., *Agrarian Reform as Unfinished Business, The Selected Papers of Wolf Ladejinsky*, New York, 1977.
26. Mridula Mukherjee, *Colonialising Agriculture: The Myth of Punjab Exceptionalism*, New Delhi, 2006.
27. Nariaki Nakazato, 'The Origins of Development Planning in India', in Fumiko Oshikawa, ed., *South Asia under the Economic Reforms*, Osaka, 1999.
28. *National Planning Committee Report*, Bombay, 1949.
29. Nitin Desai, 'Development Planning in India: A Review', in *India Since Independence*, Vol. I, Proceedings of National Seminar, Indian Council of Social Science Research, New Delhi, 1988.
30. Prabhat Patnaik, *The Retreat to Unfreedom: Essays on the Emerging World Order*, New Delhi, 2003.
31. P.C. Joshi, 'Land Reform in India and Pakistan,' *EPW*, 26 December 1970.
32. P.S. Appu, 'Tenancy Reform in India', *EPW*, Special Number, August 1975.
33. Prabhat Patnaik, 'Political Strategies of Economic Development', in Partha Chatterjee, ed., *Wages of Freedom: Fifty Years of the Indian Nation-State*, Delhi, 1998.
34. Pranab Bardhan, *The Political Economy of Development in India*, Delhi, 1998 (expanded edition).
35. Purshottamdas Thakurdas, et al., *A Plan of Economic Development for India*, Parts 1 & 2, Harmondsworth, 1945.

36. R. Nagraj, 'Industrial Growth in China and India: A Preliminary Comparison' *EPW*, 21 May 2005.
37. Ruth Heredia, *The Amul India Story*, New Delhi, 1997.
38. S.J. Patel, *Essays on Economic Transition*, Bombay, 1965.
39. Sukhamoy Chakravarty, *Development Planning: The Indian Experience*, Oxford, 1987.
40. T.V. Sathyamurthy, ed., *Industry and Agriculture in India Since Independence*, Delhi, 1995.
41. C.H. Hanumantha Rao, 'Agriculture: Policy and Performance', in Bimal Jalan, ed., *The Indian Economy: Problems and Prospects*, New Delhi, 1992.
42. D. Bandyopadhyay, 'Land Reform in India: An Analysis', *EPW*, Review of Agriculture, June 1986.
43. Daniel Thorner, *The Shaping of Modern India*, New Delhi, 1980.
44. Economic Survey, Government of India, various years.
45. Five Year Plans, I to IX, Planning Commission, Government of India, various dates.
46. Francine R. Frankel, *India's Political Economy 1947–77*, Delhi.
47. G. Kotovsky, *Agrarian Reforms in India*, New Delhi, 1964.
48. G.S. Bhalla, 'Nehru and Planning—Choices in Agriculture', *Working Paper Series*, School of Social Sciences, Jawaharlal Nehru University, New Delhi, 1990.
49. G.S. Bhalla and G.K. Chadha, 'Green Revolution and the Small Peasant—A Study of Income Distribution in Punjab Agriculture', *EPW*, 15 and 22 May 1982.
50. G.S. Bhalla and Gurmail Singh, 'Recent Developments in Indian Agriculture: A State Level Analysis', *EPW*, 29 March 1997.
51. Ghanshyam Shah, ed., *Capitalist Development: Critical Essays*, Bombay, 1990.
52. Indian National Congress, *Resolutions on Economic Policy Programme and Allied Matters 1924–1969*, New Delhi, 1969.
53. Isher J. Ahluwalia, *Industrial Growth in India*, Delhi, 1985.
54. Isher J. Ahluwalia and I.M.D. Little, eds, *India's Economic Reforms and Development: Essays for Manmohan Singh*, Delhi, 1998.
55. J.C. Sandesara, 'Indian Industrialisation: Tendencies, Interpretations and Issues', in *India Since Independence*, Volume 1, Proceedings of National Seminar, Indian Council of Social Science Research, New Delhi, 1988.
56. Jagdish Bhagwati, *India in Transition: Freeing the Economy*, Delhi, 1994.
57. Jagdish Bhagwati and T.N. Srinivasan, *India's Economic Reforms*, 1993, A Report prepared at the request of Manmohan Singh, Finance Minster of India, reprinted by the Associated Chamber of Commerce and Industry of India, New Delhi.

58. Jagdish N. Bhagwati and Padma Desai, *India: Planning for Industrialisation, Industrialisation and Trade Policies Since 1951*, London, 1970.
59. Jean Dreze and Amartya Sen, *India: Economic Development and Social Opportunity*, Delhi, 1996.
60. S. Mahendra Dev and C. Ravi, 'Poverty and Inequality: All-India and States, 1983–2005', *EPW*, 10 February 2007.
61. *The East Asian Miracle: Economic Growth and Public Policy*, World Bank, New York, 1993.
62. V.B. Singh, ed., *Economic History of India: 1857–1956*, Bombay, 1965.
63. Vijay Joshi and I.M.D. Little, *India: Macroeconomics and Political Economy 1964–1991*, Washington, 1994
64. Vijay Joshi and I.M.D. Little, *India's Economic Reforms 1991–2001*, Oxford, 1996.
65. Wilfred Candler and Nalini Kumar, *India: The Dairy Revolution*, Washington, 1998.
66. Arjun Sengupta, 'Fifty Years of Development Policy in India', in Hiranmay Karlekar, ed., *Independent India: The First Fifty Years*, Delhi, 1988.

Chapter 34

1. A.R. Desai, ed., *Agrarian Struggles in India After Independence*, Delhi, 1986.
2. P. Sundarayya, *Telangana People's Struggle and Its Lessons*, Calcutta, 1972.
3. Ravi Narayan Reddy, *Heroic Telangana: Reminiscences and Experiences*, New Delhi, 1973.
4. Barry Pavier, *The Telangana Movement: 1944–51*, New Delhi, 1981.
5. Mridula Mukherjee, 'Communists and Peasants in Punjab: A Focus on the Muzara Movement in Patiala, 1937–53', in Bipan Chandra, ed., *The Indian Left: Critical Appraisals*, New Delhi, 1983.
6. Mridula Mukherjee, 'Peasant Resistance and Peasant Consciousness in Colonial India: Subalterns and Beyond', *EPW*, 1988, 8 and 15 October.
7. Mridula Mukherjee, *Peasants in India's Non-violent Revolution, Practice and Theory*, New Delhi, 2004.
8. Marcus F. Franda, *Radical Politics in West Bengal*, Cambridge, Massachusetts, 1971.
9. Sumanta Banerjee, *In the Wake of Naxalbari: A History of the Naxalite Movement in India*, Calcutta, 1980.
10. Shantha Sinha, *Maoists in Andhra Pradesh*, Delhi, 1989.
11. Sunil Sahasrabudhey, *Peasant Movement in Modern India*, Allahabad, 1989.

12. Tom Brass, ed., *New Farmers' Movements in India*, Ilford, 1995.
13. Gail Omvedt, *Reinventing Revolution: New Social Movements and the Socialist Tradition in India*, London, 1993.
14. Manoranjan Mohanty and Parma Nath Mukherji, eds, *People's Rights and the State in the Third World*, New Delhi, 1998.

Chapter 35

1. Bipan Chandra, (i) *Communalism in Modern India* (ii) *Ideology and Politics in Modern India*, Chapters 4, 5, 6, 7, New Delhi, 1994. (iii) *Essays in Contemporary India*, Part II, New Delhi, 1993.
2. Pramod Kumar, ed., (i) *Towards Understanding Communalism*, Chandigarh, 1992. (ii) *Polluting Sacred Faith: A Study on Communalism and Violence*, Delhi, 1992.
3. Asghar Ali Engineer, (i) *Communalism in India: A Historical Empirical Study.* (ii) *Communalism and Communal Violence in India*, Delhi, 1989.
4. Achin Vanaik, *Communalism Contested: Religion, Modernity and Secularization*, New Delhi, 1997.
5. P.N. Rajagopal, *Communal Violence in India*, New Delhi, 1987.
6. S.K. Ghosh, *Communal Riots in India*, New Delhi, 1987.
7. Christophe Jaffrelot, *The Hindu Nationalist Movement and Indian Politics, 1925 to the 1990s*, London, 1996.
8. S. Gopal, ed., *Anatomy of a Confrontation: The Babri Masjid–Ramjanambhoomi Issue*, New Delhi, 1991.
9. Randhir Singh, 'Theorising Communalism', *EPW*, 23 July 1988.
10. Parveen Patel, 'Communal Riots in Contemporary India: Towards a Sociological Explanation', in Upendra Baxi and Bhikhu Parekh, eds, *Crisis and Change in Contemporary India*, New Delhi, 1995.
11. Gyanendra Pandey, *Hindus and Others: The Question of Identity in India Today*, New Delhi, 1993.
12. D.R. Goyal, *Rashtriya Swayamsevak Sangh*, New Delhi, 1979.
13. Subrata Kumar Mitra, 'Desecularising the State: Religion and Politics in India After Independence', *Comparative Study of Society and History*, Vol. 33, 1991.

Chapter 36

1. Aditya Mukherjee and Mridula Mukherjee, eds., *Communalisation of Education, The History Textbook Controversy*, Delhi Historians' Group, 2002, also in *Mainstream*, Annual Number, 22 December 2001.
2. Aditya Mukherjee, Mridula Mukherjee and Sucheta Mahajan, *RSS, School Texts and the Murder of Mahatma Gandhi: The Hindu Communal Project*, New Delhi 2008.
3. Amartya Sen, *The Argumentative Indian: Writings on Indian History, Culture and Identity*, London, 2005.

4. Bipan Chandra, *Communalism: A Primer*, Anamika, New Delhi, 2004.
5. Christophe Jaffrelot, *The Hindu Nationalist Movement and Indian Politics, 1925 to the 1990s: Strategy of Identity Building, Implantation and Mobilisation with special reference to Central India*, London, 1996 (first published as *Les nationalists hindoues*, Paris, 1993).
6. Christophe Jaffrelot, ed. *The Sangh Parivar: A Reader*, New Delhi, 2005.
7. *Communalisation of Education: The Assault on History Press Reportage, Editorials, and Articles*, Sahmat, 2002.
8. Desh Raj Goyal, *Rastriya Swayamsevak Sangh*, New Delhi, 2000.
9. Irfan Habib, Suvira Jaiswal and Aditya Mukherjee, *History in the New NCERT Textbooks: A Report and Index of Errors*, Approved and Published by the Executive Committee, Indian History Congress, Kolkata, 2003.
10. Pralay Kanungo, *RSS's Tryst with Politics: From Hedgewar to Sudarshan*, New Delhi, 2002.
11. *Report of Commission of Inquiry into Conspiracy to Murder Mahatma Gandhi* (Kapur Commission Report), New Delhi, 1970.
12. Romila Thapar, H. Mukhia and B. Chandra, *Communalism and the Writing of Indian History*, Delhi, 1969.
13. *Saffronised and Substantiated: A Critique of the New NCERT Textbooks*, Sahmat, 2002.
14. Sucheta Mahajan, *Independence and Partition: The Erosion of Colonial Power in India*, New Delhi, 2000.
15. *The Communal Problem: Report of the Kanpur Riots Enquiry Committee*, New Delhi, 2005. First published by Sunderlal, Secretary, Kanpur Riots Enquiry Committee in 1933. This was a Report of the committee appointed by the Indian National Congress (Karachi Session 1931) to enquire into the Kanpur riots of March 1931.
16. Achin, Vanaik, *Situating the Threat of Hindu Nationalism: Problem with the Fascist Paradigm*, New Delhi, 1994.

Chapter 37

1. Eleanor Zelliot, *From Untouchable to Dalit: Essays on the Ambedkar Movement*, New Delhi, 1992.
2. M.N. Srinivas, *The Cohesive Role of Sanskritisation and Other Essays*, Delhi, 1989.
3. Bipan Chandra, et al, *India's Struggle for Independence, 1857–1947*, Chapter 18.
4. Jean Dreze and Amartya Sen, *India: Economic Development and Social Opportunity*, Delhi, 1995.
5. V. Suresh, 'The Dalit Movement in India', in T.V. Sathyamurthy, *Social Change and Political Discourse in India*, Vol. 3, *Region, Religion, Caste, Gender and Culture in Contemporary India*, 1996.

6. Gail Omvedt, 'The Anti-Caste Movement and the Discourse of Power', in *ibid*.
7. Gail Omvedt, '"We Want the Return of Our Sweat": The New Peasant Movement in India and the Formation of a New Agricultural Policy', in Tom Brass, ed., *New Farmers' Movements in India*, Ilford, 1995.
8. Gail Omvedt, *Dalits and the Democratic Revolution: Dr Ambedkar and the Dalit Movement in Colonial India*, New Delhi, 1994.
9. M.S. Gore, *The Social Content of an Ideology: Ambedkar's Political and Social Thought*, Bombay, 1993.
10. Francine R. Frankel and M.S.A. Rao, eds, *Dominance and State Power in Modern India: Decline of a Social Order*, Delhi, 1989, 1990.

Chapter 38

1. Committee on the Status of Women in India, *Towards Equality*, New Delhi, 1974.
2. M. Chaudhuri, *Indian Women's Movement*, New Delhi, 1993.
3. Karuna Chanana, ed., *Socialisation, Education and Women: Explorations in Gender Identity*, New Delhi, 1988.
4. Radha Kumar, *The History of Doing: An Illustrated Account of Movements for Women's Rights and Feminism in India, 1800–1990*, New Delhi, 1993.
5. Joanna Liddle and Rama Joshi, *Daughters of Independence*, Delhi, 1986.
6. Kumkum Sangari and Sudesh Vaid, eds, *Recasting Women*, Delhi, 1989.
7. Madhu Kishwar and Ruth Vanita, eds, *In Search of Answers: Indian Women's Voices from* Manushi, London, 1984.
8. *Manushi*, various issues.
9. Ramachandra Guha, *The Unquiet Woods: Ecological Change and Peasant Resistance in the Himalaya*, Delhi, 1989.
10. Rajni Palriwala and Indu Agnihotri, 'Tradition, the Family and the State: Politics of the Contemporary Women's Movement', in T.V. Sathyamurthy, ed., *Social Change and Political Discourse in India*, Vol. 3. *Region, Religion, Caste, Gender and Culture in Contemporary India*, Delhi, 1996.
11. Ilina Sen, 'Women's Politics in India', in *ibid*.
12. Jean Dreze and Amartya Sen, *India: Economic Development and Social Opportunity*, Delhi, 1995.

Chapter 39

1. Achin Vanaik, *The Painful Transition: Bourgeois Democracy in India*, London, 1990.

2. Aditya Mukherjee, *Imperialism, Nationalism and the Making of the Indian Capitalist Class 1920–47*, New Delhi, 2002.

3. Aditya Mukherjee and Mridula Mukherjee, 'Imperialism and the Growth of Indian Capitalism in the Twentieth Century', *EPW*, 12 March 1988.

4. Atul Kohli, *Democracy and Discontent: India's Crisis of Governability*, Cambridge, 1991.

5. Ernesto Laclau, *Politics and Ideology in Marxist Theory*, London, 1977.

6. Francine R. Frankel, *India's Political Economy 1947–77*, Delhi.

7. K.N. Raj, 'The Politics and Economics of Intermediate Regimes', *EPW*, 7 July 1973.

8. L.I. Rudolph and S.H. Rudolph, *In Pursuit of Lakshmi: The Political Economy of the Indian State*, Chicago, 1987.

9. Myron Weiner, *Indian Paradox: Essays in Indian Politics*, ed., Ashutosh Varshney, New Delhi, 1989.

10. Nicos Poulantzas, *Classes in Contemporary Capitalism*, London, 1975.

11. Peter Evans, *Dependent Development: The Alliance of Local Capital in Brazil*, Princeton, 1979.

12. Prabhat Patnaik, 'Political Strategies of Economic Development', in Partha Chatterjee, ed., *Wages of Freedom: Fifty Years of the Indian Nation-State*, Delhi, 1998.

13. Pranab Bardhan, (i) *The Political Economy of Development in India*, Delhi, 1998 (expanded edition). (ii) 'Dominant Proprietary Classes and India's Democracy' in Atul Kohli, ed., *India's Democracy*, Princeton, 1988.

14. Ralph Miliband, *Marxism and Politics*, Oxford, 1977.

15. Sudipto Mundle, 'State Characters and Economic Policy', *Social Scientist*, May 1974.

16. Ajit Ray, *Political Power in India*, Calcutta, 1981 edition.

17. B. Berberoghi, *Class, State and Development in India*, New Delhi, 1992.

Chapter 40 (*In addition to books in the General List*)

1. Sudipto Kaviraj, 'On the Crisis of Political Institutions in India,' *Contributions to Indian Sociology*, N.S., Vol.18, No.2, 1984.

2. Rajni Kothari, (i) 'The Crisis of the Moderate State and the Decline of Democracy', in Peter Lyon and James Manor, eds, *Transfer and Transformation*, Leicester, 1983. (ii) *State Against Democracy: In Search of Humane Governance*, Delhi, 1988.

3. C.P. Bhambri, *The Indian State: Fifty Years*, Delhi, 1997.

4. Atul Kohli, *Democracy and Discontent: India's Crisis of Governability*, Cambridge, 1991.

5. Myron Weiner, (i) *The Indian Paradox: Essays in Indian Politics*, Chapter 3, New Delhi, 1988. (ii) 'The Wounded Tiger: Maintaining India's Democratic Institutions', in Peter Lyon and James Manor, eds, *Transfer and Transformation*, Leicester, 1983.
6. Henry C. Hart, 'The Indian Constitution: Political Development and Decay', *Asian Survey*, Vol. XX, No. 4, April 1980.
7. A. Surya Prakash, *What Ails Indian Parliament*, New Delhi, 1995.
8. S.C. Kashyap, 'Parliament: A Mixed Balance Sheet', in Hiranmay Karlekar, *Independent India: The First Fifty Years*, Delhi, 1998.
9. N.S. Saxena, *Law and Order in India*, New Delhi, 1987.
10. P.C. Alexander, 'Civil Service: Continuity and Change', in Hiranmay Karlekar, ed., *Independent India: The First Fifty Years*, Delhi, 1998.
11. David H. Bayley, 'The Police and Political Order in India', *Asian Survey*, Vol. XXIII, No. 4, April 1983.
12. *Indian Police Journal*, Special Issue on Police Reforms, Vol. XLVI, No. 1, January–March 1999.
13. Stephen P. Cohen, 'The Military and Indian Democracy', in Atul Kohli, ed., *India's Democracy: An Analysis of Changing State–Society Relations*, Princeton, 1988.
14. Lt. General S.L. Menezes, *Fidelity and Honour: The Indian Army from the 17th to 21st Century*, New Delhi, 1993.

Chapter 41

1. Rajni Kothari, (i) *Politics in India*, Chapter IX, New Delhi, 1970. (ii) *Democratic Polity and Social Change in India*, Bombay, 1976.
2. Arend Lipjhart, 'The Puzzle of Indian Democracy: A Consociational Interpretation,' *American Political Science Review*, Vol. 90, No. 2, June 1996.
3. Daniel Thorner, *The Shaping of Modern India*, pp. 138–47.
4. Tarlok Singh, 'Paths of Social Change in a Period of Transition', in Upendra Baxi, Alice Jacob and Tarlok Singh, eds, *Reconstructing the Republic*, New Delhi, 1999.
5. Atul Kohli, *The State and Poverty in India: The Politics of Reform*, Cambridge and Bombay, 1987.
6. Myron Weiner, *The Indian Paradox: Essays in Indian Politics*, Chapter 12, New Delhi, 1989.
7. Ghanshyam Shah, 'Grass-Roots Mobilization in Indian Politics', in Atul Kohli, ed., *India's Democracy*, Princeton, 1988.
8. Bipan Chandra, (i) 'Transformation from a Colonial to an Independent Economy: A Case Study of India', in his *Essays on Colonialism*, New Delhi, 1999. (ii) 'India from 1947 to the 1990s and the Real Danger of Foreign Domination: Peripheralization', in his *Essays on Contemporary India*, revised edition, New Delhi, 1999.

9. Aditya Mukherjee and Mridula Mukherjee, 'Imperialism and the Growth of Indian Capitalism in the Twentieth Century', *EPW*, Vol. XXIII, No. 11, 12 March 1988.
10. V.M. Dandekar and N. Rath, 'Poverty in India: Dimensions and Trends', *EPW*, 2 and 9 January 1971.
11. S.D. Tendulkar, 'Economic Inequality in an Indian Perspective', in A. Beteille, ed., *Equality and Inequality*, Delhi, 1983.
12. Amartya Sen, (i) 'Indian Development: Lessons and Non-Lessons', *Daedalus*, Vol.118, 1989. (ii) 'How is India Doing', *New York Review of Books*, reprinted in *Mainstream*, 26 January 1983.
13. Amartya Sen, 'The Doing and Undoing of India', *EPW*, 12 February 1983.
14. Jean Dreze and Amartya Sen, *India: Economic Development and Social Opportunity*, Delhi, 1995.
15. Kirit S. Parekh, ed., *India Development Report 1999–2000*, New Delhi, 1999.
16. United Nations Development Program, *Human Development Report 1999*, New Delhi, 1999.
17. Abusaleh Shariff, National Council of Applied Economic Research, *India Human Development Report*, New Delhi, 1999.
18. Government of India, Ministry of Finance, *Economic Survey 1998–99*, New Delhi, 1999.
19. Ashutosh Varshney, 'The Self-Correcting Mechanisms of Indian Democracy', *Seminar*, 425, January 1995.
20. Tapas Majumdar, 'Education: Uneven Progress, Difficult Choices', in Hiranmay Karlekar, *Independent India: The First Fifty Years*, Delhi, 1998.

A Note on Style

In order to ensure the continuity of the book's narrative, the authors of the various chapters are mentioned here and nowhere else in the volume. Chapters 1–3, 6–11, 13–19, 22–24, 35, 40 and 41 have been written by Bipan Chandra, Chapters 4, 5, 12, 20, 21, 34, 36–38 by Mridula Mukherjee, and Chapters 25–33 and 39 by Aditya Mukherjee.

Index

Abdullah, Farooq, 74, 364–65, 420
Abdullah, Sheikh Muhammad, 93, 205, 277, 415, 418
Advani, L.K., 362, 385; rath yatra, 365, 368, 611
Agra Summit, 2001, 384–85
agrarian, agricultural, agriculture, 2, 11, 12, 13, 14–15, 29, 333–34, 441, 452–53, 456, 477, 486, 492, 512–13, 544–45, 566–67; capitalist, 511–13; classes, 567; commercialization, 15, 148, 507, 631; cooperatives, 240, 268, 444, 520, 537; development, 492; extension, 450; government investment, 574; growth, 503, 552, 574–75, 579, 636; indebtedness, 516–19; labourers, 15, 271, 411, 557, 578, 580, 594, 639, 646, 704, 709; mechanization, 577, 579–80; radicalism, 396; reforms, 4, 175, 309; relations, 29, 522, 603; structure, 293, 699
Akali Dal, Akalis, 129, 273, 286–87, 298, 300, 331, 423ff, 423–28, 430–34, 588, 590, 591, 598, 606
All-India Congress Committee (AICC), 39, 44, 47, 51, 237, 239, 243, 299, 350, 445–46, 519, 528, 537–38, 546, 552, 554. See also Congress
All India Anna Dravida Munnetra Kazhagam (AIADMK), 64, 67, 331, 332, 370, 372, 395
Ambedkar, Dr. B.R., 8, 51, 63, 65, 89, 90, 632–34, 642
Anand pattern of milk cooperatives (pattern), 561–563, 565
Andhra Pradesh, 128; Bhoodan Movement, 547; caste, untouch-ability and anti-caste politics, 637; communal violence/communalism, 601; CPI in, 259–60; Congress decline, 287; formation on linguistic basis, 127; grassroots popular movements, 505; Green Revolution, 577, 580, 581; land ceilings legislation, 534, 539, 540, 541, 542; Naxalites, 292; peasant movements, 136, 593; political parties, 335, 338; sons of the soil movements, 162, 164; tenancy reforms, 534; supportive of Urdu 133–34; Urdu speaking population, 133; women's movements, 644
Anti-Untouchability Law, 1955, 182
Arunachal Pradesh, 143, 212, 404
Assam, 47, 143, 157, 369; demographic transformation, 404; economic backwardness, 401; immigration, 161; land ceilings legislation, 539, 542; linguistic minorities, 131; Official Language Act, 144; political turmoil, 401–406; sons of the soil movements, 161, 162, 164; tribal resentment against, 144
Assam Gana Parishad (AGP), 405
Assamese: identity, 401; language, 402, 404; Muslims and Bengalis, 406
Atomic Energy Commission (AEC), 181, 310, 454
Ayodhya, Ram mandir dispute, 365, 368, 371, 598, 607

Babri Masjid-Ram Janmabhoomi issue, 369, 411, 476, 609–13
backward castes, 365–366, 506, 635, 639, 640; movement, 597